120652

D1601628

DATE DUE			
DEC 1 2 1988			
FEB 1 5 1996			
DEC 0 3 1999			
NOV 2 0 2000			
GAYLORD 234			PRINTED IN U. S. A.

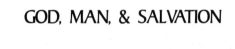

GOD, MAN, & SALVATION

GOD, MAN, & SALVATION

A BIBLICAL THEOLOGY

by

W. T. PURKISER, Ph.D.
RICHARD S. TAYLOR, Th.D.
WILLARD H. TAYLOR, Ph.D.

BEACON HILL PRESS OF KANSAS CITY
KANSAS CITY, MISSOURI

Contents

Foreword

For those who recognize the final authority of holy Scripture, biblical theology is an essential discipline.

Biblical theology draws upon the tested results of both textual and historical criticism and employs the principles of scientific biblical exegesis. In addition, evangelical biblical theology frankly reflects certain supranaturalistic presuppositions: the reality and purpose of the living God, the deity and saviorhood of Jesus Christ, the deity and personal ministry of the Holy Spirit, as well as the full inspiration and unity of holy Scripture as the Word of God written.

This is not a work of systematic theology. It is systematic in its plan of organization, and any future systematic theology will necessarily stand in its debt; but it does not attempt to construct a system of thought which addresses twentieth-century culture as such. It confines itself rather to the preliminary task of essaying to answer the question, "What do the Scriptures say?"

Since biblical theology is the work of human writers, this volume naturally reflects its authors' theological biases. Such is inevitable in any work of this nature; every theologian has his stance. Drs. Westlake T. Purkiser, Richard S. Taylor, and Willard H. Taylor write from the general perspective of Wesleyan faith. They are seasoned teachers with a combined history of more than 75 years in the classroom, mostly on the graduate level. They are recognized scholars whose authority must be reckoned with by any minister or teacher in the Wesleyan tradition.

Here is a scholarly presentation of the progressive disclosure of God and His redemptive purpose as this is found in its preparatory form in the Old Testament and in its perfect expression in the New. As you work through these pages, "prove all things; hold fast that which is good" (1 Thess. 5:21).

The authors of this treatment of biblical thought subscribe to John Wesley's doctrine of Christian perfection and find in the Scriptures an unfolding disclosure of this truth. For them, Christ's work of redemption issues in the sanctifying activity of the Spirit who cleanses the heart from its sinful bias, fills it with God's pure love, and restores one to the image of God. This holiness is both gradual and instantaneous, personal and social: it is mediated to the believer through personal trust in Christ and is experienced in the fellowship of His body. Christian perfection, moreover, is teleological: its final expression awaits the return of Christ in glory with the attendant victory of the kingdom of God. Such is the vision of the writers of this study.

I am happy to commend this volume to ministers, teachers, and serious students of Scripture. It is a veritable mine of biblical truth, and to it Wesleyan scholarship will long be indebted. It not only deserves a place on your library shelves; it also merits your careful and persistent study as you seek to "rightly divide the word of truth."

—WILLIAM M. GREATHOUSE
General Superintendent
Church of the Nazarene

Preface

A major portion of our century has witnessed a remarkably sustained interest in recovering and understanding the message of the Bible in its wholeness. While biblical studies in the nineteenth century were highly critical and in many respects unproductive of faith, biblical studies in the twentieth century have been more trusting and wholesome in their expectations and results. Unquestionably, this healthy change was brought about by a profound reassertion of the truth of special revelation with its primal focus upon Christ, the Living Word, during the early decades of this century. A high view of Christ always evokes fresh desire to explore the written Word with the hope of seeing more clearly its message of God's mighty saving act in Christ within the broad sweep of biblical history and thought. It is therefore not unexpected that several excellent biblical theologies have been published in recent years, each one obviously an attempt to capture the full-orbed message of the Bible.

The present volume is a product of this movement. If it has a right to publication, the reason is to be found in the commitment of its authors to the Arminian-Wesleyan way of looking at the Scriptures. Thus the reader will discover an honest effort throughout to give expression to this historic position. This approach, however, has not precluded drawing upon the rich resources of scholarship from across the spectrum of viewpoints.

This is a biblical theology, not a systematic theology. While systematic theology develops its own rubrics for arriving at a structured view of the faith, biblical theology seeks to find its guidelines in the Word itself. It attempts to state the faith affirmations of the Bible according to whatever "system" is discernible in the Scriptures themselves. Biblical theology is a bringing together of those proclamatory truths which give the Bible unity and which constitute it a Gospel.

The theme of salvation, which is evident throughout this study, is the central theme of the Bible. God working in history, and more particularly and marvelously in Christ, has provided all mankind with a way of salvation.

All of this is preliminary work for the systematic theologians. There are numerous questions to be asked this biblical material, and able systematic scholars will confront those questions. They will use every resource of human thought to provide answers which will expand the church's understanding of the gospel and of her own life in the world.

Moreover, we hope that many students of the precious Word —collegians, seminarians, preachers, laypersons, and, yes, trained theologians—will discover some new insights here which will lead to renewed exploration of the Word.

One of the writing team, Dr. W. T. Purkiser, is owed a special word of thanks for serving so capably as our editorial coordinator. He has spent countless hours corresponding with us, proofreading the manuscript, and preparing the bibliography and subject index. Our heartfelt thanks is expressed also to Dr. J. Fred Parker, book editor, for his knowledgeable handling of all the details of a volume of this size and nature and for his hours of tedious labor in preparing the manuscript for printing. Besides these two men, we remember with thanks the students and secretaries who have assisted in checking references and in typing rough drafts of the many chapters.

May the God of all grace, who lovingly provided salvation for us in Christ His Son, place His blessings upon our effort to express the meaning of this glorious salvation.

—WILLARD H. TAYLOR

NOTE CONCERNING WRITERS' ASSIGNMENTS—
The specific chapters contributed by the various members of the writing team are as follows:

W. T. Purkiser: General Introduction and all of Part I (Old Testament)

Richard S. Taylor: Chapters 15—17; 24—29; 33—35

Willard H. Taylor: Introduction to Part II and chapters 12—14; 18—23; 30—32

Abbreviations

AB—*The Anchor Bible*
ATB—*Ashland Theological Bulletin*
BAR—*Biblical Archaeology Reader*
BBC—*Beacon Bible Commentary*
BDCE—*Baker's Dictionary of Christian Ethics*
BDT—*Baker's Dictionary of Theology*
BNTC—*Black's New Testament Commentary*
BS—*Bibliotheca Sacra*
CT—*Christianity Today*
EB—*Expositor's Bible*
EDNTW—W. E. Vine, *Expository Dictionary of New Testament Words*
EGT—*Expositor's Greek Testament*
ET—*Expository Times*
HQ—*Hartford Quarterly*
ICC—*International Critical Commentary*
IDB—*Interpreter's Dictionary of the Bible*
JBL—*Journal of Biblical Literature*
MQ—*McCormick Quarterly*
NBC—*New Bible Commentary*
NBD—*New Bible Dictionary*
NICNT—*New International Commentary on the New Testament*
NTS—*New Testament Studies*
PC—*Pulpit Commentary*
RE—*Review and Expositor*
SJT—*Scottish Journal of Theology*
ST—*Studia Theologica*
TDNT—*Theological Dictionary of the New Testament,* Kittel
TWBB—*A Theological Word Book of the Bible,* Richardson
WesBC—*Wesleyan Bible Commentary*
WTJ—*Wesleyan Theological Journal*
WyBC—*Wycliffe Bible Commentary*

Introduction

The Nature and Scope of Biblical Theology

Theology, in the simplest terms, is our human attempt to think clearly and correctly about God. It is the study of ways to organize and communicate thought about God and the created order. The mind can have no greater challenge than to reflect on the meaning of religion and the Scriptures.

That theology has often seemed abstract and unimportant is more the fault of theologians than of the subject itself. The most meaningful questions in life are basically theological questions. No person, religious or otherwise, can escape the need to grapple with problems of the source and nature of reality and the meaning and destiny of life.

The importance of Christian theology can hardly be overstated. Theology is not optional with the Church. It is every Christian's business. William Hordern writes, "The Christian who claims to have no theology is, in fact, hiding from himself the theological premises by which he lives and as a result he fails to bring them under any creative criticism."[1] The result is a "folk theology" in which contradictory ideas are held with no recognition of their actual incompatibility. We need a rediscovery of "the theologianhood of all believers."[2] The cure for poor theology is not no theology but better theology. If theology is to fulfill its proper function, it must no longer be thought of as the monopoly of experts.

---

1. *New Directions in Theology Today* (Philadelphia: The Westminster Press, 1966), 1:138.
2. *Ibid.*

"The effort to be practicing Christians without knowing what Christianity is about must always fail," says A. W. Tozer. "The true Christian should be, indeed must be, a theologian. He must know at least something of the wealth of truth revealed in the Holy Scriptures. And he must know it with sufficient clarity to state it and defend his statement. And what can be stated and defended is a creed."[3]

The never-ending task of the Church is to interpret its faith to the contemporary world. To do this requires an understanding of what is essential to the faith and what is incidental. Failure at this point not only cripples personal piety; it garbles the proclamation of the gospel to the world.

I. THE LOGICAL STRUCTURE OF THEOLOGY

But what, exactly, is theology? The term itself points to its meaning. It is derived from two Greek words—*Theos,* "God"; and *logos,* "word" or "reasoned discourse." *Logos* is the root from which we get the English words *logic* and *logical.* We find it in the suffix, "-logy," in the names of most of the various branches of human learning. In each case, "-logy" means the application of principles of logical thought to some particular subject matter.

For example, geology is the application of principles of logical thought to observed facts about the *geos,* or earth. Anthropology is the application of principles of logical thought to observed facts about *anthropos,* man. Psychology is the application of principles of logical thought to observations about the *psyche,* literally the soul or "soulish" self. Sociology is the application of principles of logical thought to observations about the *socius,* society. The list is almost endless as the various sciences become more and more specialized.

A long tradition speaks of theology as "the Queen of the Sciences."[4] Using the term *science* in relation to theology can be helpful if not pressed too far. Just as each of the sciences is the result of applying principles of correct thinking to a defined subject matter, so theology is the application of principles of logical thought to truth about *Theos,* God.

---

3. *That Incredible Christian* (Harrisburg, Pa.: Christian Publications, Inc., 1964), pp. 22-23.

4. See H. Orton Wiley, *Christian Theology* (Kansas City: Beacon Hill Press, 1940), 1:14-15.

A. Fact and Interpretation

Besides its name, there is another point of resemblance between theology and the various sciences. Any science is the result of two processes of the mind: observation and interpretation. Learning begins with observation. It moves on to interpretation, grasping relationships and meanings. Then it returns to more observation to verify or establish the relationships and meanings it has formulated.

The work of any science is to seek those principles, laws, theories, or hypotheses which unify, integrate, and interpret the separate facts and phenomena of its particular subject matter. Each area of investigation includes a large array of separate or discrete phenomena, facts, events, and objects. Many "facts" appear contradictory. Paradox abounds. The task of the scientist is to unify, interpret, and describe this often bewildering array of facts in terms of coherent patterns of explanation. Professor C. A. Coulson, a theoretical physicist, writes that "scientific truth means coherence in a pattern which is recognized as meaningful and sensible."[5]

We have mentioned that thinking involves both observation and interpretation. But these are not rigidly separated processes. As thought moves from observation to interpretation, logicians speak of "induction." As thought moves from interpretation or generalization back to further observation, logicians speak of "deduction." But any process of truth-seeking involves both movements, both induction and deduction. Facts are observed, a generalization is made by induction; that generalization is used as a theory or hypothesis, and its consequences are predicted by deduction. Only so can it be tested and either verified or revised.

As observation begins, patterns of relationship and meaning emerge. These patterns influence further study, both in the selection and interpretation of data. Where the data are complex, divergent theories may be held by different observers. Often these theories succeed each other, as first one and then another is tested and set aside. The history of science is largely the story of discarded and revised hypotheses. In some cases—as, for example, in theories of the nature of light—competing hypotheses may endure side by side as each in turn serves to explain a portion of the data.

---

5. C. A. Coulson, *Science and Christian Belief* (Chapel Hill, N.C.: The University of North Carolina Press, 1955), p. 49. Cf. William G. Pollard, *Science and Faith: Twin Mysteries* (New York: Thomas Nelson, Inc., 1970) for a scientist's description of the way hypotheses develop.

In a comparable way, the facts of religion (in which the Scriptures provide a major source of data) are unified and interpreted in theology. "Theology is the exhibition of the facts of Scripture in their proper order and relation with the principles or general truths involved in the facts themselves, and which pervade and harmonize the whole."[6] Christian theology is "the Church's reflection under the guidance of the Holy Spirit upon the Word given to it by God."[7] "Theology is the science of Christianity; much that is wrongly called theology is mere psychological guesswork, verifiable only from experience. Christian theology is the ordered exposition of revelation certainties."[8]

As is true to a lesser degree in other sciences dealing with complex data, the data of religion have yielded divergent patterns of interpretation. These become the "schools" or "systems" of theology as in Catholicism, Lutheranism, Calvinism, Arminianism, neoorthodoxy, process theology, etc. Each such pattern to some degree controls the selection and interpretation of data for those who hold it.

B. Objectivity in Theology

Harold O. J. Brown, for one, has argued that theology cannot properly be considered a "science." Science, Brown points out, demands objectivity or impartiality on the part of those who pursue it. Theology, on the other hand, must be done either by those committed to the God about whom they think and write or by those in rebellion against Him.[9]

A measure of truth in this contention may be conceded. Objectivity, however, does not necessarily mean lack of commitment or disinterest. It means amenability to the data, the subjection of theory to fact. In this respect the theologian may be as objective as the chemist or the biologist. Here the caution of Mildred Bangs Wynkoop is apropos:

> Nature will remain hidden from the scientist who refuses to
> be taught by nature. Nature is first, and always, the master to be

---

6. Charles Hodge; quoted by H. Orton Wiley, *Christian Theology,* 1:15.

7. John Huxtable, *The Bible Says* (Naperville, Ill.: SCM Book Club, 1962), p. 112.

8. Oswald Chambers, *He Shall Glorify Me: Talks on the Holy Spirit and Other Themes* (London: Simpkin Marshall, Ltd., 1949 reprint), p. 146.

9. Harold O. J. Brown, *The Protest of a Troubled Protestant* (New Rochelle, N.Y.: Arlington House, 1969), pp. 15-28. Cf. also Stephen Neill, *The Interpretation of the New Testament, 1861-1961* (New York: Oxford University Press, 1964), p. 337.

served before it will submit itself to the scientist's will. The same principle holds for theology and the Scriptures. All of us, Calvinist and Wesleyan, must distinguish carefully and honestly between the Word of God and the opinions and interpretations with which we approach it.[10]

While no theory is as certain as the data upon which it rests, it is both logically and psychologically impossible to operate apart from some general ordering principles of interpretation. Herein lies the need for theology and the importance of finding the very best possible framework or pattern of doctrine within which to approach the facts of the religious life and the statements of the Scriptures.

II. THE SOURCES OF THEOLOGY

It is possible to describe types of theology in different ways. H. Orton Wiley divides "theology in general" into Christian theology and ethnic theology. He subdivides Christian theology into Exegetical, Historical, Systematic, and Practical.[11]

One useful classification distinguishes types of theology according to the sources of their data and the principle of arrangement of their materials, as in the following divisions.

A. Natural Theology

"Natural theology" looks for its data in the observation of nature, the religious tendencies in humanity, and the history, psychology, and sociology of religion. It depends upon the philosophy of theism and the use of metaphysical reasoning to arrive at the knowledge of God. It is usually the type of theology found in apologetics as an important first step in Christian evidences. The preambles in the *Summa Theologica* of Thomas Aquinas, Bishop Joseph Butler's *The Analogy of Religion, Natural and Revealed, to the Constitution and Course of Nature,* and William Temple's monumental *Nature, Man, and God* are classical examples of natural theology.

No natural theology written by those nurtured in the Christian tradition can be "pure." The influence of tradition and the Scriptures are inescapable. Nevertheless, to the extent to which reasoning starts from and works with the data supplied by nature—physical

---

10. Mildred Bangs Wynkoop, *Foundations of Wesleyan-Arminian Theology* (Kansas City: Beacon Hill Press of Kansas City, 1967), p. 85.
    11. *Christian Theology,* 1:24.

and psychological—without conscious appeal to the Bible or the historic creeds, the result may fairly be described as "natural" theology.

The neoorthodox rejection of natural theology is well known. Natural theology easily drifts into humanism. Its God, except for His power, may too nearly be created in the image of man. Its function is one of preparation. At best, it may serve as a "schoolmaster" to lead the mind to Christ. At worst, it may be a stumbling block in the way of the acceptance of a sound revelational theology.

B. Systematic Theology

A second major type of theology is systematic or dogmatic theology. It is the type most commonly known by the generic term *theology*. Its sources of data include the Scriptures, the great creeds of the church, observations of religious life and institutions within the framework of the church, and the psychology of Christian experience and worship.

The overarching systems of theology in Christendom have been systematic or dogmatic. Catholicism, Lutheranism, Calvinism, and Arminianism are historic systems drawing from a variety of available sources. Each of these systems appeals to the Scriptures as its primary Source of data. But each system also accepts data in varying ways and amounts from the creeds, the traditions, and the life and experience of the church.

C. Biblical Theology

Biblical theology is the third major type of theological formulation. In a broad sense, any theology that sincerely attempts to be faithful to the content of the Scriptures may be called "biblical."

However, a more specialized use of the term *biblical theology* has developed recently. It is the serious effort to discover at first hand what biblical writers meant by what they said—as contrasted with what it has easily been assumed that they meant. Biblical theology in this sense focuses more exclusively on the data set forth in the Scriptures—the events, statements, and teachings reported in the Bible.

The Bible itself is not theology, although it provides materials from which theology may be constructed. Theology is the church's response to the revelation given in the Scriptures. That revelation is given by historical record, by prophetic and apostolic comment, by recorded devotion and prayer in poetry and psalm, by reflection on life as in the Wisdom Writings, by oracle (the direct, quoted words of God), and supremely in the life, teachings, and atoning death and resurrection of Jesus Christ.

Many statements in the Bible do, in fact, represent first order theological affirmations. The reflection of the psalmists and prophets on Israel's history, the teachings of Jesus, and the didactic writings of both Old and New Testaments are true theology; they are examples of the first essential stages in generalization. Biblical theology takes these as its data—the "facts" with which it works—as well as information from the historical framework in which they are embedded.

The task of biblical theology, as Geoffrey W. Bromiley has summarized it, is to "interpret the detailed sayings and books of the Bible in terms of their own background and presuppositions rather than those drawn from other sources."[12] The execution of this task calls for careful word studies as basic to the theological exegesis of the Scriptures. It also calls for a sense of historical context and the significance of history for theology. One of the very real and practical gains of biblical theology has been a new recognition of the unity of the Scriptures within admitted diversity. The indispensable context of every scripture narrative and assertion is the entire Bible itself.

Biblical theology, then, is the attempt to state systematically the faith-affirmations of the Bible. It represents a systematization of the biblical faith. Its system is not that of "systematic" theology but that which grows out of developing revelation in the Bible. It seeks to trace patterns of meaning inherent in the Scriptures themselves.

Myron S. Augsburger reminds us that "biblical theology as a discipline is set between systematics and exegetics."[13] It is not a substitute for systematic theology but a preparation for it. "It aims to gather the content of revelation in the biblical form."[14] Exegesis is concerned to discover the truth of the biblical revelation in its parts. Systematic theology attempts to gather the content of revelation together and to present it in logical form. "Biblical theology stands between these two seeking to relate the biblical parts in such a way as to be consistent with the total content of the biblical disclosure."[15]

---

12. "Biblical Theology," *Baker's Dictionary of Theology*, Everett F. Harrison, ed. (Grand Rapids, Mich.: Baker Book House, 1960), p. 95.

13. Chester K. Lehman, "Introduction," *Biblical Theology* (Scottdale, Pa.: Herald Press, 1971), p. 11. (Introduction written by Augsburger.)

14. *Ibid.*

15. *Ibid.*

Chester Lehman also compares biblical theology with systematic: "Biblical theology examines the process of the unfolding of God's Word to man. It is concerned with the mode, the process, the progress, and content of divine revelation. Systematic theology, on the other hand, looks at the total revelation of God, seeks to systematize these teachings, and to give a logical presentation of them in doctrinal form."[16]

D. Biblical Theology as Basic

There is admitted interaction between the major types of theology. Yet biblical theology has a rightful claim to primacy in Christian circles. Virtually all Protestant communions affirm that the Bible is their only Rule of faith and practice. Biblical theology is an attempt to take that affirmation seriously—to get behind creeds, institutions, and systems of interpretation to the ground and source of truth in the Scriptures.

Robert C. Dentan has identified two values of biblical theology in relation to systematic theology:

1. Biblical theology "provides the basic materials for systematic theology." While systematic theology adds to its data materials drawn from natural theology, from the Christian creeds and the history of Christian experience, it still must find its primary source in the Bible if it is to be truly Christian theology. The best way to secure the biblical data is by the comprehensive study of the religious ideas of the Old and New Testament, rather than seeking to support ideas drawn from other sources by the citation of specific biblical proof texts.

2. Biblical theology "provides a norm for systematic theology . . . by which later theological developments may be judged." Biblical theology may serve as a touchstone by which the formulations of systematic theology may be evaluated. Theology cut off from its biblical roots tends always to become subjective and the creature rather than the critic of its times.[17]

Edmond Jacob wrote: "If [dogmatics] wishes to remain 'Christian' it will always have to make fresh assessments of its declarations by comparing them with the essential biblical data, the elucidation of which is precisely the task of biblical theology, itself based on

---

16. *Ibid.,* p. 37.
17. Robert C. Dentan, *Preface to Old Testament Theology* (New York: The Seabury Press, 1963 rev. ed.), pp. 102-3.

well-founded exegesis."[18] Supplying its raw materials and defining the limits of systematic theology, biblical theology helps preserve dogmatics from "falling in a subjectivism where the essential might be sacrificed to the accessory."[19]

This need has long been recognized. Before the development of the "biblical theology movement" of our day, Olin A. Curtis called for "a genuine biblical theology" as a basis for systematic theology. He said, "I mean here something far beyond the fragmentary works which are often published in the name of biblical theology. The whole Bible must be philosophically grasped as a Christian unity which is manifested in variety. The moment this is done there will be a center to the Bible; and without doubt this center is the death of our Lord."[20]

III. VARIETIES AND TRENDS IN BIBLICAL THEOLOGY

The term *biblical theology* has been used in a broad sense to describe any theological formulation that emphasizes the Scriptures as its major Source of data. Such a use first occurs in the middle of the seventeenth century in Calovius' *Systematic Theology*.[21] In the seventeenth and eighteenth centuries the term *biblical theology* was used chiefly in Germany to describe works both supporting and criticizing traditional orthodoxy. The nineteenth century, again particularly in Germany, witnessed the development of the *Religionsgeschichte* school in which biblical theology, particularly of the Old Testament, became a study of the history of the religion of Israel.

A. The Theological Emphasis

The tension between historical and theological interests continued into the twentieth century and has not as yet been completely resolved. As stress is placed upon the *theology* in *biblical theology*, the discipline tends to conform to Dentan's definition of Old Testament theology: "That Christian theological discipline which treats of the religious ideas of the Old Testament *systematically*, i.e., not from the point of view of historical development, but from that of the structural unity of Old Testament religion, and which gives due regard to

---

18. Edmond Jacob, *Theology of the Old Testament* (New York: Harper and Brothers, 1958), p. 31.
19. *Ibid.*
20. *The Christian Faith* (New York: Methodist Book Concern, 1903), p. 185.
21. Dentan, *Preface to OT Theology*, p. 15.

the historical and ideological relationship of that religion to the religion of the New Testament."[22]

The result is a structuring of the material patterned after the traditional divisions of systematic theology: God, man, sin, and salvation. In addition to Dentan, such an arrangement of materials or a modification thereof is favored by Otto J. Baab, Millar Burrows, A.B. Davidson, Albert Gelin, Gustav Oehler, J. Barton Payne, Hermann Schultz, C. Ryder Smith, and Norman Snaith.

B. The Biblical Emphasis

On the other hand, as stress is placed upon the *biblical* in *biblical theology*, the result is an ordering of materials seeking to expound truth about God, man, and redemption in a series of historical events, or "moments," prophetically interpreted. Strong emphasis is placed on historical development. Representative of this trend in Old Testament theology are Walther Eichrodt, Edmond Jacob, Ludwig Kohler, Edmund Clowney, H. H. Rowley, J. N. Schofield, George Ernest Wright, Gerhard von Rad; and in the New Testament, Archibald Hunter.

Writers in both groups have attempted to resolve the tension between the biblical and the theological approaches but without conspicuous success. Either some sacrifice must be made of logical unity, or the basically historical ordering of materials in the Scriptures themselves must be set aside. Any attempt at resolution of the tension will result in a compromise that must remain unsatisfactory to some. Biblical theology must always struggle to be both biblical and theological.

C. Characteristics of Biblical Theology

Biblical theology is obviously not easily defined. It is the application of principles of logical thought, both inductive and deductive, to the statements, facts, data, and events of the Scriptures considered in their historical context with a view to developing comprehensive patterns of interpretation.

Brevard S. Childs, who is sharply critical of achievements to date in modern biblical theology, lists five major characteristics of the discipline:

1. It is marked by the rediscovery of the theological dimension in the Bible. In this, it is a reaction against an excessively analytical

---

22. *Ibid.*, pp. 94-95.

maceration of the Scriptures. Biblical studies had tended to become more and more technical, and more and more concerned with abstractions and spiritually barren minutiae. The forest had been lost in the trees, the message lost in the mechanics of its transmission. Biblical theology seeks to grasp the message of the whole Bible while gratefully acknowledging the illumination which may be derived from grammatical exegesis or the mechanics of textual scholarship.

2. There is an emphasis on the "unity within diversity" to be found in the entire Bible. This applies both to the unity of each of the major Testaments and the common truth that binds the two Testaments together into one Book.

3. The revelation of God is set in its historical context. In its earliest stages, the revelation is true but incomplete. The later stages presuppose the earlier.

4. There is a growing recognition of the characteristically biblical or Hebraic world view of the Scriptures, as distinguished from a Hellenistic or Greek world view.

5. There is a recognition of the distinctiveness of the Bible—its contrast with its environment.[23]

Commenting on the present scene in biblical studies, Childs says: "The danger is acute that the Biblical disciplines will again be fragmented. There is need for a discipline that will attempt to retain and develop a picture of the whole, and that will have a responsibility to synthesize as well as analyze."[24]

IV. History in Biblical Theology

Two distinctives of biblical theology mentioned by Childs deserve additional consideration. One is the strong sense of the historical context of revelation in the Scriptures. G. Ernest Wright makes this point:

> The Bible, unlike other religious literature of the world, is not centered in a series of moral, spiritual, and liturgical teachings, but in the story of a people who lived at a certain time and place. Biblical man learned to confess his faith by telling the story of what had happened to his people and by seeing within it the hand of God. Biblical faith is the knowledge of life's meaning in

---

23. *Biblical Theology in Crisis* (Philadelphia: The Westminster Press, 1970), pp. 32-50.

24. *Ibid.*, p. 92. Cf. also Gerhard F. Hasel, *Old Testament Theology: Basic Issues in the Current Debate* (Grand Rapids, Mich.: William B. Eerdmans Publishing Co., 1972).

the light of what God did in a particular history. Thus the Bible cannot be understood unless the history it relates is taken seriously. Knowledge of biblical history is essential to the understanding of biblical faith.[25]

The biblical theologian is impressed by the fact that in the Hebrew Scriptures those books known as "the former prophets" (Joshua—Esther) are actually historical in content. There are also important historical sections in the Law (our Pentateuch) and in "the latter prophets" (which we call the major and minor prophets). God speaks through the history of His people. In the Bible, history is "His story" in a very literal sense. What became real in the Incarnation—"the Word . . . made flesh"—is symbolized in the "enfleshment" of the Word of God in the concrete historical events of the Old Testament.

Edmund Clowney argues that the divisions of biblical theology must be the historical periods of redemption—Creation, the Fall, the Flood, the call of Abraham, the Exodus, and the coming of Christ. He states: "The most fruitful understanding of biblical theology is that which recognizes both the historical and progressive character of revelation and the unity of the divine counsel which it declares. Its interest is not exclusively theological, because then the history of the revelatory process would be comparatively incidental. Neither is its interest exclusively historical."[26]

Biblical theology is the interpretation of God's mighty acts of judgment and salvation, preparing for and climaxing in the death, resurrection, and exaltation of the Lord Jesus Christ—as understood in the historical context of the redemptive or covenant community.

It is important to note that history alone is not revelation. It is history as interpreted by prophets and apostles whose words are "God breathed" (2 Tim. 3:16) that makes God known to man. God, as Kenneth Kantzer incisively wrote, is not a "deaf mute" acting out a role but unable to speak.[27] He both acts and speaks, and part of His speaking is through the interpretation of sacred history by inspired men. "The historical happening and its interpretation, the deed and the word of God as its commentary, these constitute the Biblical event."[28]

---

25. *Biblical Archaeology*, abr. ed. (Philadelphia: The Westminster Press, 1960), p. ix.
26. *Preaching and Biblical Theology* (Grand Rapids, Mich.: William B. Eerdmans Publishing Co., 1961), pp. 16-17.
27. *Bibliotheca Sacra*, vol. 115, no. 459 (July, 1958), p. 225.
28. G. Ernest Wright, *The Old Testament and Theology* (New York: Harper and Row, Publishers, 1969), p. 44.

V. The Unity of the Bible

A second distinctive that needs additional comment is the growing conviction that the Bible is one Book—that it displays unity within its diversity. The Bible is genuinely the Word, not just many words.[29] C. Ryder Smith writes:

> In the latter part of the last century and the earlier part of this, students of Biblical Theology tended to concentrate upon the doctrine of each new writer or class of writers within the Bible. At that time this was both desirable and valuable. It readily led, however, to an emphasis on the differences within the Bible rather than upon the unity of Bible teaching. More recently it has been recognized that Biblical Theology is an organic unity, beginning, however imperfectly, in the Old Testament, and reaching its completion in the New.[30]

Robert Dentan adds: "For Christian faith the connection of the Old Testament with the New is integral and organic so that the two together form an indissoluble unity, the one being the necessary completion and fulfillment of the other."[31]

It goes without saying that both a continuity and discontinuity exists between the Old and the New Testaments. The study of this problem of the relationship between the Testaments has been intense, especially, as we have noted, since the resurgence of biblical theology.

The rubrics of promise and fulfillment of salvation seem to offer the best solution to the issue of continuity: the Old is promise; the New is fulfillment. Never can we divorce the New from the Old. The tragedy of such action is clearly seen in the attempt of Marcion of the second century (ca. A.D. 140) who rejected the Old Testament totally and even asserted that only 10 Epistles of Paul (Pastorals rejected) and a mutilated Gospel of Luke were acceptable for instruction in the Christian way.

The incompleteness of the earlier revelation in the Old Testament does not constitute error. Preparation and fulfillment are different but not contrary. To "fulfill" is not to contradict. When Jesus used the formula, "Ye have heard that it hath been said . . . but I say

---

29. Truman B. Douglass, *Preaching and the New Reformation* (New York: Harper and Brothers, 1956), p. 32.

30. C. Ryder Smith, *The Bible Doctrine of Man* (London: The Epworth Press, 1951), p. ix.

31. *Preface to OT Theology,* p. 99.

unto you," He was speaking in terms of enlargement and deepening, not revocation or denial. "For the child, two times two equals four is the beginning and end of arithmetic. The mathematician sees far beyond that, but two times two is four for him also with the same unconditional validity as for the child."[32]

There are two possible errors in regard to the relationship of the Old and New Testaments. One is the heresy of Marcion we have just mentioned: so completely to separate the two as to set them in opposition to each other. The other is to read the New Testament back into the Old Testament so completely as to obscure progression in revelation throughout the Bible and the final authority of Christ. Hermann Schultz early caught the essential relationship of Old and New Testament thought when he wrote:

> It is perfectly clear that no one can expound New Testament theology without a thorough knowledge of Old Testament theology. But it is no less true that one who does not thoroughly understand New Testament theology cannot have anything but a one-sided view of Old Testament theology. He who does not know the destination will fail to understand many a bend in the road. For him who has not seen the fruit, much, both in bud and blossom, will always remain a riddle.[33]

"The Old Testament," wrote A. B. Davidson, "should be read by us always in the light of the end, and . . . in framing an Old Testament theology we should have the New Testament completion of it in view."[34]

Emil Brunner twice uses a sparkling analogy to illustrate the unity of the Scriptures: "The Old Testament is related to the New Testament as is the beginning of a sentence to the end. Only the whole sentence with beginning and end, gives the sense."[35] "Just as a sentence has many words, but one meaning, so the revelation of God in the Scripture, in the Old and New Testament, in the law and the Gospel, has one meaning: Jesus Christ . . . stammeringly or clearly, all the books of the Bible spell this one name; they instruct

32. Ludwig Kohler, *Old Testament Theology*. Translated by A. S. Todd (Philadelphia: The Westminster Press, 1957), p. 64.

33. Hermann Schultz, *Old Testament Theology*. Translated by J. A. Paterson (Edinburgh: T. and T. Clark, 1909), 1:59. Cf. Dentan, *Preface to OT Theology*, pp. 55-56.

34. *The Theology of the Old Testament* (Edinburgh: T. and T. Clark, 1904), p. 10.

35. *Die Unentbehrlichkeit des Alten Testamentes fuer die missionierende Kirche*, quoted by G. Ernest Wright in Gerald H. Anderson, ed., *The Theology of the Christian Mission* (New York: McGraw-Hill Book Co., Inc., 1961), p. 26.

us, on the one hand, prospectively, on the other hand, retrospectively, of this meaningful fact of the incarnation."[36]

It has grown increasingly clear in recent biblical studies that the New Testament is not to be read as a Hellenistic book growing out of classical Greek philosophy and culture. Its language is Greek, but its world view is Hebraic. Norman Snaith wrote: "The Old Testament is the foundation of the New. The message of the New Testament is in the Hebrew tradition as against the Greek tradition. Our tutors to Christ are Moses and the Prophets, and not Plato and the Academies."[37]

An important document entitled "Guiding Principles for the Interpretation of the Bible" was formulated by an ecumenical study conference held at Oxford in 1949. Two items relate to the unity of the Bible:

It is agreed that the centre and goal of the whole Bible is Jesus Christ. This gives the two Testaments a perspective in which Jesus Christ is seen both as the fulfilment and the end of the Law. . . .

It is agreed that the unity of the Old and the New Testaments is not to be found in any naturalistic development, or in any static identity, but in the ongoing redemptive activity of God in the history of one people, reaching its fulfilment in Christ.

Accordingly it is of decisive importance for the hermeneutical method to interpret the Old Testament in the light of the total revelation in the person of Jesus Christ, the Incarnate Word of God, from which arises the full Trinitarian faith of the Church.[38]

In similar vein, Ryder Smith noted that

the New Testament writers assume that their readers will take their words in their contemporary sense, and only the study of the Old Testament reveals this. None the less, the Old Testament chapters . . . only prepare the way for the discussion of New Testament teaching. For Christians this is final.[39]

The unity of the Bible may be seen in a variety of ways. The concept of God—Yahweh of the Old Testament as the God and Father of our Lord Jesus Christ in the New—is one basis of unity. The

36. *Philosophy of Religion*, p. 76; quoted by Paul King Jewett, "Emil Brunner's Doctrine of Scripture," *Inspiration and Interpretation*, ed. John F. Walvoord (Grand Rapids, Mich.: William B. Eerdmans Publishing Co., 1957), p. 16.
37. *The Distinctive Ideas of the Old Testament* (Philadelphia: The Westminster Press, 1946), p. 204.
38. *Biblical Authority for Today*, ed. Alan Richardson and W. Schweitzer (Philadelphia: The Westminster Press, 1951), p. 241.
39. *The Bible Doctrine of Sin* (London: The Epworth Press, 1953), p. 7.

relationship of preparation to fulfillment is another. "Covenant"—old and new—is a unifying concept. The whole Bible is the context within which each part must be understood. There is a unity of theme throughout the Bible: God and man in salvation. The Old Testament must be viewed "in terms of that to which it led as well as that out of which it arose."[40] The meaning of the Magna Charta is not exhausted in a study of the reign of King John, "any more than the full significance of the invention of the wheel is to be found in the first primitive vehicle in which it was used."[41] Just as ideas and inventions have significance beyond the immediate intention of their creators, so "the spiritual ideas which were given to men through the leaders of Israel, and which were enshrined in the Old Testament, had a life which extended into the New Testament, as well as into post-Biblical Judaism."[42]

---

40. H. H. Rowley, *The Unity of the Bible* (Philadelphia: The Westminster Press, 1953), p. 7.
41. *Ibid.*
42. *Ibid.*

PART 1

OLD TESTAMENT FOUNDATIONS

1

Old Testament Theology
and Divine Revelation

In part, at least, the role of Old Testament theology in Christian thought has already begun to appear. It is necessary to review and restate it, and to look at the whole idea of the revelation of God as it appears in the Old Testament. Old Testament theology is an essential foundation for biblical theology as a whole.

I. THE SCOPE OF OLD TESTAMENT THEOLOGY

Old Testament theology is an effort to expound systematically the major truths about God and man in redemption as these are unfolded in the 39 books from Genesis to Malachi. "Old Testament theology, if we are to be guided by the Bible in our definition, is nothing more nor less than the study of God in His self-revelation in the history of redemption."[1]

The task of Old Testament theology is "to define the characteristic features of *the message of the Old Testament*."[2] Because it is theology, many things may be left out that are the proper sphere of a study of the religion of Israel. Th. C. Vriezen writes:

> The theology of the Old Testament seeks *particularly the element of revelation in the message of the Old Testament;* it must work, therefore, with *theological standards,* and must give *its own evaluation*

---

1. Edward J. Young, *The Study of Old Testament Theology Today* (New York: Fleming H. Revell Co., 1959), p. 3.

2. Th. C. Vriezen, *An Outline of Old Testament Theology* (Boston: Charles T. Branford Co., 1958), p. 132.

of the Old Testament message on the ground of its Christian theological starting-point. . . . So, as a part of Christian theology, Old Testament theology in the full sense of the word gives an insight into the Old Testament message and a judgement of this message from the point of view of the Christian faith.[3]

Robert Dentan details what he calls "The Scope of Old Testament Theology."[4] Two major limitations are established:

1. Old Testament theology should deal only with the canonical books of the Old Testament. The intertestamental literature, both apocryphal and pseudepigraphical, are more properly part of New Testament theology if not relegated to a special study.

2. Old Testament theology should deal only with the distinctive and characteristic *religious* ideas of the Old Testament. This limitation would exclude archaeological information as such, and primary concern with history or institutions. The concern of Old Testament theology should be with the *normative* religion of the Old Testament, not the "folk theology" or popular religious ideas of the times. It should include all of the major elements of normative Hebrew religion, including priestly and wisdom elements as well as prophetic elements. It must give consideration to ethical principles, since ethics and religion are indissolubly connected in the Old Testament. It should also include the discussion of Hebrew piety—the practical expression of theology in life.

Dentan concludes:

> While the religious ideas of the Old Testament do not, for the most part, appear in theological form, there is a *theology* in the Old Testament in the sense of a structural complex of ideas which are logically dependent upon the central idea of God, and it has been the historic task of Old Testament theology to explore that structure of thought and expound it.[5]

A. The Unity of Old Testament Thought

Because the prevailing trends in Old Testament scholarship in the late nineteenth and early twentieth centuries emphasized the differences to be found in successive strata of the biblical documents, it is the more important to recognize the underlying unity of this portion of the Scriptures.

---

3. *Ibid.,* italics in original.
4. *Preface to OT Theology,* p. 105.
5. *Ibid.,* p. 108.

There is an obvious unity in historical continuity. The Old Testament, from Genesis to Malachi, relates the history of one people. Law, wisdom, poetry, and prophecy all find their place within one historical framework. Amos N. Wilder notes: "The characteristic theme of this biblical theology is that God has revealed himself in a series of related historical episodes, all pointing toward his final purpose for mankind though at first involving a particular people."[6]

More important than historical continuity is the unity of world view and understanding of God and man that pervades the Old Testament. Walther Eichrodt, for example, contends that the religion of the Old Testament, in spite of all changes through the 16 centuries of history it covers in some detail, was yet a self-contained unity of constant basic tendency and type. He writes:

> The verdict against a systematic presentation of the totality of Israel's faith will likewise lose its stringent character, if the variety of the OT testimonies, which must of course be carefully taken into account in its place, is interpreted not as a discontinuity of the revelatory process, but as the result of observing a complex reality from various angles in ways which are in principle concordant one with another. There is in fact no legitimate reason why we should be forbidden to look for an inner agreement in these testimonies of faith which we have so carefully analyzed; and in this agreement, despite their great differentiations and internal tensions, certain common basic features emerge which in combination constitute a system of belief which is both unitary in its essential structure and fundamental orientation and also unique in the history of religions.[7]

There is, it has been claimed, a "theology" of J, and of E, and of P, and of D—referring to the alleged literary sources upon which the Old Testament and particularly the Pentateuch is based. But as Norman Snaith has shown, what is important now is the "theology of J-E-P-D," the end result of the processes involved in the formation of the Old Testament canon.[8] The "sources" were brought together because they belong together.

Old Testament theology presupposes the Old Testament as it is. How it has come to be that way is the legitimate inquiry of historical criticism. Distinguishing between the Torah, the poetic and wisdom literature, and the Prophets does not imply different theologies. At

---

6. *Otherworldliness and the New Testament* (New York: Harper and Brothers, 1954), p. 53.

7. *Theology of the Old Testament*, trans. J. A. Baker (Philadelphia: The Westminster Press, 1961), 1:517.

8. Snaith, *Distinctive Ideas*, p. 112 fn.

most we have differing emphases and stages of development of the one theology which is the theology of the whole. Old Testament theology starts with a "given"—the Scriptures of the Hebrew people. The writings as we have them are writings in a context, not unrelated productions. That context must always be taken into consideration.

B. The Central Theme

A number of different unifying principles have been suggested as the key to Old Testament faith. Eichrodt has argued for the concept of the covenant as the unifying principle. Hermann Schultz, and more recently John Bright,[9] have chosen the kingdom of God as the unifying theme. Ludwig Kohler finds the unity of the Old Testament in the concept of God as "Lord" *(Adon).* Others have suggested election, the Exodus, or salvation history as unifying themes. None of these have been conspicuously successful when the attempt has been made to work them through the entire literature.[10]

The central idea of the Old Testament is indeed the idea of God, in all its richness and depth. But the object of God's concern, man, comes immediately into view—with salvation, or redemption, as the purpose both of the covenant and the kingdom of God. God and man in redemptive relationship is the theme of the Old Testament that extends into and throughout the New.

II. THE VALUES OF OLD TESTAMENT THEOLOGY

Since the Old Testament is admittedly preparatory and forward-looking toward the New Testament, why is special concern with Old Testament theology a necessary interest? In what sense is the Old Testament foundational for biblical theology?

Many of the considerations given in the discussion of the unity of the Bible in Chapter 1 apply here:

1. Old Testament theology is a necessary foundation upon which New Testament theology builds. Each Testament has its characteristic emphasis. The emphasis of the Old Testament is upon the holiness of God. The emphasis of the New Testament is upon the love

---

9. *The Kingdom of God: The Biblical Concept and Its Meaning for the Church* (New York: Abingdon Press, 1953).

10. Cf. the survey by Dentan, *Preface to OT Theology,* pp. 117-20; Gerhard F. Hasel, *OT Theology: Basic Issues,* pp. 49-63.

of God. But the God of the Bible is, in the happy phrase first used by Peter Forsyth and later by William Temple and H. Orton Wiley, the God of holy love. This is in no sense to subscribe to the thesis of Marcion that the God of the New Testament is a God of love and grace, and the God of the Old Testament merely a God of wrath and justice. But as Dentan remarked, "The New Testament, it is true, gives special emphasis to the gentler attributes of God, but these by themselves do not constitute a doctrine of God and, taken out of their Old Testament framework, can easily lead to theological sentimentalism."[11]

2. The Old Testament adds some distinctive ideas to the whole scope of Christian theology. Included are descriptions of God's work in creation, His sovereignty in providence and history, the sources of man's inclination to evil and self-destruction, the kingdom of God, and the main outlines of piety. "Where the New Testament is silent on certain matters, it assumes that the teaching of the Old Testament is still valid. Jesus did not come to destroy, but to fulfill, the law and the prophets, and it seems self-evident that one cannot hope to understand Jesus or His first interpreters unless one first of all understands the law and the prophets."[12]

3. Old Testament theology makes clear the experiential character of all true thinking about God. It helps theology keep its feet on the ground. It is a theology of experience arising out of God's dealings with His people—a theology that can be fully understood only as it is heard in faith and obedience. Truth is expressed in concrete examples much more than in abstractions. Peter Forsyth wrote, "The bane of so much theology, old and new, is that it has been denuded of prayer and prepared in a vacuum."[13]

4. A helpful summary and conclusion is offered by Dentan under the section title "Present Value of the Discipline." He makes four points:

a. Old Testament theology can assist in "combating the unfortunate effects of *undue fragmentation of biblical studies* and will help to restore that sense of the unity of the Old Testament and of the whole of Scripture which has been lost by an exaggerated emphasis

---

11. *Preface to OT Theology,* pp. 99-100.
12. *Ibid.,* p. 99.
13. *The Cure of Souls: An Anthology of P. T. Forsyth's Practical Writings,* ed. Harry Escott (Grand Rapids, Mich.: William B. Eerdmans Publishing Co., 1971), p. 25.

upon the minutiae of exegesis and upon source and form criticism."[14]
The message and meaning of the Bible as a whole is lost when only
a few favorite passages are studied.

   b. Old Testament theology can help "to restore the balance
which has been lost by *the increasing secularization of biblical studies.*"
This has "tended to put the major emphasis upon the linguistic,
archaeological, and cultural-historical aspects of Old Testament
science." Contra, a sound theology of the Old Testament "will tend
to recall the attention of the scholarly world to that which is central
in the Old Testament and which alone justifies the amount of time
and energy spent in studying it, viz., its religious world-view."[15]

   c. The study of Old Testament theology can help "to restore a
sense for *the values which have been lost in modern liberal Christian theology,*
particularly in regard to its tendency to denature and sentimentalize
the character of God and to place too high a valuation upon the
goodness and perfectibility of man."[16]

   d. Old Testament theology can help "to correct *the excesses of
certain contemporary 'biblicist' theologies.*" Such systems "seize upon particular aspects of Old Testament religion, such as the Wrath of God,
the Idea of Judgment, and the Fallen Nature of Man and, by isolating
them from their larger context, actually give a false impression of
the character of the God of the Old Testament and of the characteristic moods of Hebrew piety."[17] Old Testament theology can be true
to all the valid elements of Israel's faith "and thus help to maintain
a proper balance in modern theological thought as the latter quite
rightly seeks to renew its vitality by drawing more deeply from the
springs of biblical religion."[18]

III. God's Self-revelation in the Old Testament

It is an axiom in the Old Testament that God makes himself known
to chosen men in the context of their history. This is a truth never
argued. It is assumed as a fundamental fact.

   The self-disclosure of God through the Scriptures is described
by the general term *revelation*. "*Revelation* implies for the Old Testa-

---

14. *Preface to OT Theology,* p. 123; italics original.
15. *Ibid.,* pp. 123-24; italics original.
16. *Ibid.,* p. 124; italics original.
17. *Ibid.;* italics original.
18. *Ibid.,* p. 125.

ment *the means God uses to make possible a knowledge of God for men.* In and by himself man does not have a knowledge of God: all knowledge of the kind must be granted to him by God, must be made known to him. This communication or notification where God is its author we call revelation."[19]

The self-disclosure of God in the Old Testament is not first of all in abstract statements about Him. It is first of all the direct encounter of Person with person. As James G. S. S. Thomson has written, "Revelation is personal encounter with the living God. Indeed, revelation in the Old Testament should be understood in terms of communion; communion between God who is making Himself known existentially, and man to whom the divine self-disclosure is being granted."[20]

Further, it is always God who takes the initiative in such encounter. He does not wait for man to seek Him. The first divine-human encounter after sin entered the Garden in Eden was God's call to Adam, "Where are you?" (Gen. 3:9). The Lord appeared to Abraham in ways and times quite unexpected (Gen. 12:1, 7). He made known His name and nature to Moses (Exod. 6:3). "The fact that God has fellowship with man is due to His free groundless will and is His first and fundamental deed."[21] In an eloquent paragraph, Edward J. Young writes:

> We are not dealing with the gropings of ignorant and superstitious Hebrews after God, if haply they might find Him. We are dealing with what God Himself spoke to these Hebrews. They were ignorant; they were in darkness; they were in bondage. But they were the recipients of light. To them the Word of God came, dispelling the darkness, and banishing the ignorance. No longer need they be like the nations round about them, for they were a peculiar people. They could know the truth about God and about their relation to Him, for unto them the very oracles of God had been entrusted.[22]

This truth is summarized in the title of Abraham Heschel's book, *God in Search of Man.* "All human history as described in the Bible may be summarized in one phrase, God in Search of Man," he writes.[23] What Jesus said of himself is true of God from the beginning: "The Son of man came to seek and to save the lost" (Luke 19:10).

---

19. Kohler, *OT Theology,* p. 99, italics in original.
20. James G. S. S. Thomson, *The Old Testament View of Revelation* (Grand Rapids, Mich.: William B. Eerdmans Publishing Co., 1960), p. 9.
21. Kohler, *OT Theology,* p. 59.
22. *OT Theology Today,* p. 85.
23. Abraham Heschel, *God in Search of Man* (New York: Farrar, Straus, 1955), p. 136.

IV. Modes of Revelation

God revealed himself in many ways. "In many and various ways God spoke of old to our fathers by the prophets" (Heb. 1:1). The record of that revelation is found in the writings that together have come to be known as the Scriptures. The books of the Bible are themselves the inspired and authoritative Source of truth about God and His purposes for men.

A. In Creation

God reveals himself in creation (Ps. 19:1; 102:25; Amos 5:8).

> *Lift up your eyes on high and see:*
> *who created these?*
> *He who brings out their host by number,*
> *calling them all by name;*
> *by the greatness of his might*
> *and because he is strong in power*
> *not one is missing.*
> *Why do you say, O Jacob,*
> *and speak, O Israel*
> *"My way is hid from the Lord,*
> *and my right is disregarded by my God"?*
> *Have you not known? Have you not heard?*
> *The Lord is the everlasting God,*
> *the Creator of the ends of the earth.*
> *He does not faint or grow weary,*
> *his understanding is unsearchable* (Isa. 40:26-28).

That the heavens declare the glory of God is not to be understood as a form of the "cosmological argument"—reasoning from the existence of the world to the existence of the Creator. It is rather that in nature we see the wonder and majestic might of the God we have otherwise come to know. Not *that* God is, but *how great* God is constitutes the testimony of nature. As Thomson notes:

> Not that the Old Testament teaches that through nature man discovers an unknown God, but rather that man sees more clearly the God whom he already knows. In the Old Testament it is the God of revelation who is seen in nature. The Psalmist already knows God through His redemptive acts in history, but in nature he sees something more of the glory of God, until he is compelled to exclaim, "O Lord our Lord, how excellent is thy name in all the earth!"[24]

---

24. *OT View of Revelation*, pp. 25-26.

B. In His Mighty Acts in History

God reveals himself in His works, particularly in the history of His people: "And the Egyptians shall know that I am the Lord, when I stretch forth my hand upon Egypt and bring out the people of Israel from among them" (Exod. 7:5; cf. 16:6; 18:11; 1 Kings 18:27-39; Isa. 45:3; Jer. 16:21; Mic. 6:5). It is not accidental that 14 of the 39 books of the Old Testament are books of history—and to this number Jonah and Ruth may be added. In the prophetic books, in Lamentations, and in a number of the Psalms, history is a significant theme. In the Hebrew canon, books we describe as historical are known as "The Former Prophets." "The Old Testament knows only of a God who is active in history."[25] Eric Sauer writes:

> *World history is the scaffolding for the history of salvation.* Not only has revelation a history but history is a revelation. It is not only a 'work' but a stimulating 'word' of God. It is a veiled self-unveiling of God, Who while revealing Himself, at the same time remains the 'concealed God,' the *'deus absconditus'* (the hidden God of Luther). It is a sphere of the power, grace, and judgment of the Lord of the worlds as ruler of the nations.[26]

C. In Visions

God reveals himself in visions and visual appearances to men and women. The Old Testament, like the New, knows that "no one has ever seen God" (John 1:18; 5:37; Exod. 33:20). Yet there are occasions when, as to Moses in the desert of Sinai, God permits a visual experience of His presence: "And the angel of the Lord appeared to him in a flame of fire out of the midst of a bush; and he looked, and lo, the bush was burning, yet it was not consumed. And Moses said, 'I will turn aside and see this great sight, why the bush is not burnt.' When the Lord saw that he turned aside to see, God called to him out of the bush, 'Moses, Moses!' And he said, 'Here am I'" (Exod. 3:2-4; cf. also Gen. 16:7-14; 18:1-22; Josh. 5:13-16; Judg. 2:1-5; Isa. 6:1-8; Ezek. 44:1-2). The angel who appears is identified with the God who speaks.

Such divine appearances are known as "theophanies," accommodating the nature of the invisible God to the limitations and

---

25. Kohler, *OT Theology,* p. 92.
26. *The Dawn of World Redemption,* trans. G. H. Lang, foreword by F. F. Bruce (Grand Rapids, Mich.: William B. Eerdmans Publishing Co., 1952), p. 94; italics in original.

necessities of human experience. There is no one single type of appearance. Characteristically, we are told how the vision begins but not how it ends. But when the vision departs, the word remains—as when Isaiah heard the word of the Lord saying, "Whom shall I send, and who will go for us?" (6:8).

D. Through Prophets and Their Word

A major mode of divine revelation in the Old Testament is through prophets and the word they speak in God's name. This is specifically recognized in Heb. 1:1-2, "Long ago God spoke to our ancestors by means of the prophets, but the revelation which was given through them was fragmentary and varied. But now, as time as we know it is coming to an end, he has spoken in one whose relation to himself is that of Son, that Son into whose possession he gave all things, and by whose agency he created the present world and the world to come."[27]

The characteristic introduction to the prophet's message is "Thus says the Lord." Most of the "oracles" in the prophetic literature—that is, those first-person passages in which God speaks verbatim through the prophet's lips—close with the formula "says the Lord" (e.g., Amos 1:3-5, 6-8, 13-15; 2:1-3, etc.).

What the prophets spoke is always called *the* word of the Lord. It is never *a* word of God or *words* of God. The expression "The word of the Lord" (or "of God") occurs nearly 400 times in the Old Testament.[28] That God thus speaks to man is added witness to the direct personal relationship between God and man. It is by words that the deepest feelings of one's heart can find echo in another. To biblical man, far more than to the typical modern, words were laden with power.[29] *Dabar* ("word") means God's act as well as His word.

Revelation therefore is "propositional" (by means of words) as well as historical (by means of deeds). It consists of affirmations as well as acts. To say, "Revelation is not communication but communion" is to express a false disjunction. Communion between persons always involves communication, and the content of the communication is expressed in words.[30]

---

27. William Barclay, *The New Testament: a New Translation*, 2 vols., "The Letters and the Revelation" (London: Collins, 1969), 2:173.

28. *Ibid.*, p. 245, n.; Thomson, *OT View of Revelation*, p. 57.

29. Vriezen, *Outline of OT Theology*, p. 253.

30. Clowney, *Preaching and Biblical Theology*, pp. 26-27.

E. Through the Law

Akin to the word of God through the Prophets is His revelation through the Law. The "laws" of the Old Testament are variously classified, but the major grouping consists of laws with moral content (of which the Decalogue is the prime example), and laws for the regulation of the cult and its worship. *"In the law God reveals Himself decisively. Man's hearing or not hearing of this revelation is a matter of life and death."*[31]

It was of the Law that Moses said, "I call heaven and earth to witness against you this day, that I have set before you life and death, blessing and curse; therefore choose life, that you and your descendants may live, loving the Lord your God, obeying his voice, and cleaving to him; for that means life to you and length of days, that you may dwell in the land which the Lord swore to your fathers, to Abraham, to Isaac, and to Jacob, to give them" (Deut. 30:19-20).

F. Through Appointed Symbols

In addition to other ways, God makes himself known through specially appointed symbols of His presence and power with His people—the Tabernacle and later the Temple, with its altars, the ark of the covenant, and the structure of the sanctuary. Although indirect, these representations were important sources of knowledge about the divine.[32]

G. In the Scriptures as a Whole

All major religions have their scriptures, their collections of holy writings. But no faith is as deeply rooted in a canon of inspired writings as is the faith of Israel. While the full biblical doctrine of the inspiration of the Scriptures is expressed in the New Testament, it has its foundations in the Old Testament writings themselves.

The Old Testament speaks of "this book of the law" (Deut. 29:21; 30:10; 31:26; Josh. 1:8); "the book of this law" (Deut. 28:61); "the book of the law of Moses" (Josh. 8:31; 23:6; 2 Kings 14:6); "the book of the law" (Josh. 8:34); and "the book of Moses" (2 Chron. 25:4) in terms that recognize its complete authority.

"The book of the law of the Lord" (2 Chron. 17:9) was used in Jehoshaphat's time to teach the people. The scroll discovered in the

---

31. Kohler, *OT Theology*, p. 110; italics in the original.
32. *Ibid.,* p. 120 ff.

Temple by Hilkiah the priest is described as "the book of the law" (2 Kings 22:8, 11), "the book of the covenant" (2 Kings 23:2, 21; 2 Chron. 34:30), "the book of the law of the Lord given through Moses" (2 Chron. 34:14), and "the book of Moses" (2 Chron. 35:12). Its authority was unquestioned when its identity was recognized.

Ezra speaks of "the book of Moses" (6:18). "The book of the law of Moses" and "the book of the law of God" are used in parallel passages in Neh. 8:1, 3, 8, 18; 9:3. Neh. 13:1 identifies Deut. 23:3-5 as coming from "the book of Moses." "The law of Moses" is mentioned in 1 Kings 2:3 and Dan. 9:13. In each instance, the amenability of human conduct to the expressed will of God is assumed.

God's word was not only spoken by prophets but written (Exod. 34:27; Deut. 31:19; Isa. 8:1-2; Jer. 30:2; 36:2, 17, 28; Hab. 2:2) to be preserved as a permanent record in a "book." It was an historical event—the defeat of the Amalekites—that occasioned the first mention of writing as "a memorial" for the future (Exod. 17:14; cf. Deut. 17:18; 31:24; 1 Sam. 10:25; 1 Chron. 29:29; Neh. 8:5). Frequent references throughout the Old Testament to the commandments, the covenant, the law, the judgments or precepts of the Lord make it clear that these were known in relatively permanent form (Ps. 19: 7-11; 119).

V. Revelation as Progressive

The revelation of God in Old Testament times was not given all at once. It was progressive in character. This does not mean that the early stages of the revelation were untrue. It means that they were incomplete. God added to the sum of knowledge about himself as the mind and maturity of man was able to comprehend it.

An example of the progressive nature of revelation is found in Exod. 6:3—"I appeared to Abraham, to Isaac, and to Jacob, as God Almighty, but by my name [or in the *meaning* of My name] the Lord I did not make myself known to them." The same God who led the patriarchs later added important truth about himself in His appearance to Moses. The apex of the divine self-disclosure lies beyond the scope of the Old Testament. It is found in Christ (Heb. 1:1-4—a passage which both validates and moves beyond the Old Testament).

While the early stages of revelation were incomplete, they were not unimportant. The multiplication table is not the whole of mathematics, but mathematics never gets beyond its need for the multiplication table. The beginning of a sentence is not the whole sentence; but it is still essential to the meaning of the whole.

Although the divine self-communication as recorded in the Scriptures was historically conditioned, it serves in the present as the means whereby God still confronts men in judgment and redemption. John Marsh struck an authentic note when he said:

> What needs to be made clear is that the Bible, as a record of events that are past, functions now, under the illumination of the Spirit, as the events once did, as the appointed means by which men meet with the ever-living God. He imparts himself to us now by means of what he has done in the past, and that lifts both past and present out of the confines of mere temporality and succession, and sets them in a vital relationship to God who dwells in eternity.[33]

VI. REVELATION AS ENCOUNTER

The opening chapters of Genesis assume that the knowledge of God comes through an encounter with God.

A. The Meaning of Knowledge

The Hebrew term *yada,* "to know," does not mean knowledge through reasoning. It is rather knowledge through direct experience. *Yada* is the word used to describe the most intimate relationship in human life (Gen. 4:1, 17, 25, *passim*). In relation to the knowledge of God, it is encountering His love or His wrath in the concrete events of life. To know God in the true sense is to have fellowship with Him. It is to know Him by "acquaintance with" rather than "knowledge about."[34]

"The God of the Bible," as Pascal noted, "is not the God of the philosophers, but the God of Abraham, Isaac and Jacob, the God who reveals himself in history as the Saviour, whose presence is experienced by a whole line of privileged persons and mystics."[35]

There is therefore a sharp contrast between what "knowledge" means for the Westerner in the Greek tradition, and what it meant for biblical man. For the Occidental mind, knowledge results from analysis, explanation of causes and conditions, and relating the ob-

---

33. *The Fulness of Time,* p. 9; quoted by Theodore R. Clark, *Saved by His Life: A Study of the New Testament Doctrine of Reconciliation and Salvation* (New York: The Macmillan Co., 1959), pp. 129-30.

34. Schultz, *OT Theology,* 2:100-102; A. B. Davidson, *Theology of the OT,* pp. 30-36, 73-82; and Jacob, *Theology of the OT,* pp. 37-38.

35. Quoted by Albert Gelin, *The Key Concepts of the Old Testament,* trans. George Lamb (New York: Sheed and Ward, 1955), p. 16.

ject of cognition with the whole range of accepted ideas. For biblical man, knowledge is "living in a close relationship with Something or somebody, such a relationship as to cause what may be called communion. . . . When Peter denies Christ and says 'I do not know the man,' he denies that there has been relationship between himself and Christ."[36]

Knowledge of God in a biblical framework is not concerned with theories about the nature of God. It is not ontological but existential—"life in the true relationship to God."[37] It is knowledge that comes from doing God's will. An oft-quoted passage from William Temple expresses this truth:

> In the Hebrew-Christian tradition, God is revealed as holy love and righteousness, demanding righteousness of life. *The real acceptance of such revelation is not only intellectual assent: it is submission of will. And this must be submission to the revelation as personally received, not only to the record of it as received by some one else. Every revelation of God is a demand, and the way to knowledge of God is by obedience. It is impossible to have knowledge of God as we have knowledge of things, because God is not a thing. We can only know a person by the direct communion of sympathetic intercourse; and God is personal. But besides this he is Creator, so that the communion of man with God is communion of creature with Creator: it is worship and obedience, or else it does not exist.*[38]

Yet the knowledge of God for Old Testament man is claimed only with a measure of humility. Alan Richardson has noted that "the Hebrew mind did not share the optimism of the Greeks of the classical period concerning the possibility of man's knowledge of ultimate reality."[39] The Greek philosophers, who asserted that man's highest achievement was to know, believed that it was possible for man to comprehend cognitively what constitutes ultimate reality or ultimate being. The Hebrews, on the other hand, rejected intellectual contemplation as a way of "knowing" the ultimate being. They consistently declared that obedience to the revealed commandments of God makes possible the knowledge of God. The stress therefore falls upon obedient action rather than upon mystic vision or philosophical speculation, upon response rather than upon reflection, upon "hearing" rather than upon "seeing."[40]

---

36. *Ibid.*, p. 129.
37. *Nature, Man, and God* (London: Macmillan, Ltd., first ed., 1934), p. 354.
38. *Ibid.*; italics in the original.
39. *An Introduction to the Theology of the New Testament* (New York: Harper and Brothers, Publishers, 1958), p. 39.
40. *Ibid.*

Of all men of their times, the prophets were the most concerned with the knowledge of God. Their interests were not academic but moral and religious. In their given life-situations, they discerned that their people possessed no real knowledge of God. So Isaiah declares in unparalleled descriptive words, "The ox knows its owner, and the ass its master's crib; but Israel does not know, my people does not understand" (Isa. 1:3).

Using the struggles of his own marriage to symbolize Israel's tragic spiritual condition, Hosea concludes that "there is . . . no knowledge of God in the land" (4:1). Speaking for Yahweh, the same prophet writes, "For I desire steadfast love and not sacrifice, the knowledge of God, rather than burnt offerings" (6:6).

In looking forward to the new age and the establishment of a new covenant, Jeremiah prophesies: "And no longer shall each man teach his neighbor and each his brother, saying 'Know the Lord,' for they shall all know me, from the least of them to the greatest, says the Lord" (Jer. 31:34; cf. Isa. 11:9; 33:6).

Quite obviously, as we learn from the contexts from which these scriptures are taken, a relationship exists between obedience and knowledge. If the people will obey the commandments of Yahweh, they will "know" Him. This connection is made abundantly clear in the words of Jeremiah: "Did not your father eat and drink and do justice and righteousness? Then it was well with him. He judged the cause of the poor and needy; then it was well. Is not this to know me? says the Lord" (22:15*b*-16). Richardson concludes: "The knowledge of God is a fourfold strand binding together obedience to God's will, worship of his name, social righteousness and national prosperity; ignorance of God *per contra* spells disobedience, idolatry, social injustice and national disaster."[41]

Etymological studies must be employed with caution in authenticating views on biblical themes.[42] But even after the most cautious analysis and evaluation, a study of the Hebrew word *yada* ("to know") supports the view that knowledge of God for the Hebrew writer is not contemplative or speculative knowledge. *Yada* signifies the knowledge of relationship between persons rather than the knowledge of logical analysis or reasoning.

---

41. *Ibid.*
42. Cf. James Barr, *The Semantics of Biblical Language* (Oxford: University Press, 1961), pp. 158-59.

As we have seen, this verb is employed to denote the sexual act between husband and wife, as in the case of Gen. 4:1: "Now Adam *knew [yada]* Eve his wife, and she conceived and bore Cain."[43] The intimacy of the sexual act permits "the most active and satisfying knowing that exists" in the marital relationship.

When the Hebrew writer therefore refers to "the knowledge of God," he is referring to knowledge in a special sense. He is not speaking of a knowledge of God's eternal essence. Rather, it is "a knowledge of His claim, whether present in direct commands or contained in His rule. It is thus respectful and obedient acknowledgement of the power and grace and demand of God. This means that knowledge is not thought of in terms of the possession of information. It is possessed only in its exercise or actualization."[44]

The Hebrew writer is speaking of the knowing which comes when God enters into personal relationships with Israel in such a way as to disclose His love and mercy. In such an encounter, trust in God as sovereign Lord is born and nurtured, and worship of Him as the one true God results. Richardson comments: "To disobey God is to refuse to enter into the relation which he has so graciously made possible and hence is to remain ignorant of him."[45] Essentially, the knowledge of God for the Hebrew constitutes his personal redemption, a point to which we will return later.

B. The Limitations of Knowledge

It is not claimed or assumed that the knowledge of God in the Old Testament was complete or perfect. A fine balance is maintained between assurance and reticence. Even in the most intimate self-disclosure of God, there is a sense of mystery about the Divine. Worship combines knowledge of God with awe in the presence of indescribable holiness and light (Exod. 33:13-23).

The limitations in man's knowledge of God are due both to the necessary limits to all human knowledge and the greatness of God. God is too big to be contained in the minds of finite human beings. Zophar's rhetorical question summarizes the Old Testament view at this point: "Can you find out the deep things of God? Can you find out the limit of the Almighty?" (Job 11:7). And Job himself says that

---

43. Cf. Gen. 4:17, 25; Num. 31:18, 35; Judg. 21:12; *et al.*

44. Rudolf Bultmann, "ginosko, *et al.," Theological Dictionary of the New Testament,* ed. Gerhard Kittel (Grand Rapids, Mich.: William B. Eerdmans Publishing Co., 1964), 1:698; hereafter referred to as TDNT.

45. *Theology of the NT,* pp. 40-41.

all nature reveals "but the outskirts of his ways; and how small a whisper do we hear of him! But the thunder of his power who can understand?" (Job 26:8-14). His understanding is unsearchable and God himself says, "As the heavens are higher than the earth, so are my ways higher than your ways and my thoughts than your thoughts" (Isa. 55:9; cf. 45:15, 28; Ps. 139:6; 145:3).

Yet the Old Testament never surrenders to the kind of agnosticism which argues that because we cannot know all there is to know about God and because the finite cannot encompass the infinite, therefore we can know nothing truly. The Infinite has ways of making himself known to His creatures in such a manner and measure as they have need to know Him. Otherwise He would not be infinite.

Section One

Creation and Covenant

---·•·---

2

God as Creator and Redeemer

Theology in the Old Testament unfolds through three stages in the life of the chosen people. These are represented by the three great divisions of the Hebrew Scriptures: the Law, the Prophets, and the Writings (sometimes called "the Psalms"—as in Luke 24:44—since this book came first).

The English Bible follows the Greek translation of the Old Testament known as the Septuagint and arranges the books in slightly different order. Each division adds to the truth of the whole:

1. The Law (the *Torah* or Pentateuch) deals with Creation and the Covenant.

2. The Psalms and Wisdom Literature are concerned with Devotion and Duty—the piety and ethics of the Old Testament.

3. The Major and Minor Prophets place a fitting capstone on the whole in the Prophetic Vision.

The 12 historical books which appear in our English Bibles between Deuteronomy and Job provide a chronological framework and a wealth of illustrative material for the major religious ideas of the Old Testament. In form, the Old Testament includes narrative, poetry, history, chronicle, and drama. But in intent and message, it is data for the highest and truest theology.

The written revelation of God in the Old Testament therefore begins with a group of five books known in the Hebrew Bible as the *Torah* or "law." Both in the Hebrew Scriptures and in the Christian Bible the Torah or Pentateuch ("fivefold book") stands first. While firmly fixed in usage, *law* is actually too narrow a term to convey the full meaning of *torah*. It is a term that also includes ideas of instruction, guidance, or teaching. It is in fact almost synonymous with *revelation* itself.

I. The Key Concept of the Old Testament

The first 11 chapters of Genesis provide theological data of unequalled importance. They are a prologue to the specific history which began with Abraham. Even on the most conservative chronology, they span a greater length of time than all the rest of the Bible put together. As G. Ernest Wright has said, these chapters

> enunciate the unifying theme of the Bible. By means of this prologue the Church has learned and taught that God is the Creator, that man is made in God's image, and that man also is a sinner who has fallen away from God and whose civilization is in a sense a product, not of obedient service given to God, but of self-worship in defiance of God. These chapters reveal God's relation to us and to our world; he is our Maker and, therefore, our Lord. They also make clear the human problem because of which God's saving acts took place.[1]

Gen. 1:1 introduces us to the central Figure of the Old Testament: "In the beginning God . . ." The Hebrew term *reshith*, "beginning" (from *rosh*, "the head," "first") not only means first in point of time but "first, chief, principal thing" in importance. In a real and exact sense, the concept of God is the key to both the Scriptures and theology.

Theology by definition implies the logical priority of the doctrine of God. Religion may be approached psychologically—beginning with the human predicament and the needs of man. But the biblical approach is theological with first consideration given to the nature and claims of God.

---

1. G. Ernest Wright and Reginald H. Fuller, *The Book of the Acts of God* (New York: Doubleday and Co., Inc., 1957), p. 54.

H. Orton Wiley wrote in his definitive, three-volume *Christian Theology:* "The first task of theology is to establish and unfold the doctrine of God. The existence of God is a fundamental concept in religion and therefore a determinative factor in theological thought. The nature ascribed to God gives color to the entire system. To fail here is to fail in the whole compass of truth."[2]

For all the acknowledged progression in divine revelation throughout the Old Testament, the concept of God remains essentially the same. A. B. Davidson wrote, "My impression is that even in the most ancient passages of the Old Testament essentially the same thought of Jehovah is to be found as appears in the Prophets and the later literature."[3]

Some scholars have seen Israel's belief in one God as the result of a long, evolutionary process. The facts of the history of religions tend to show that the direction is just the opposite. Gods become more numerous as others are added to the pantheon rather than fewer in number by consolidation until only one is left. Where there are many, there always seems to be room for one more.

The evidence points to an original monotheism in Israel rather than a mere particularism or "henotheism"—worship of one God while recognizing the existence of others. Biblical writers do indeed refer to the gods of pagan mythology. They use the common religious terminology in reference to "other gods" without thereby affirming belief in their reality—much as we today might allude to Venus or Mars without giving credence to the Greek and Roman pantheons.[4]

There is no effort to "prove" the existence of God in the Old Testament. Such an idea would never have occurred to a Hebrew.[5] The Bible, in Alan Richardson's words, "is a book of witness, not of argument. . . . A God whose existence could be proved, or rendered more probable by argument, would not be the God of the Bible. The God of Israel is not an Ultimate Being who appears at the end of a chain of reasoning."[6]

---

2. *Christian Theology* (Kansas City: Beacon Hill Press, 1940), 1:217.
3. *Theology of the OT.* p. 180.
4. *Ibid.,* pp. 63-67; Gelin, *Key Concepts of the OT,* pp. 22-24.
5. Jacob, *Theology of the OT,* pp. 37-38.
6. *Preface to Bible Study,* p. 40; quoted by J. K. S. Reid, *The Authority of Scripture: A Study of the Reformation and Post-Reformation Understanding of the Bible* (London: Metheun and Co., Ltd., 1957), p. 269.

The unbelief reflected at times in the Old Testament when men are said to "know not God" is better translated "had no regard for the Lord." To think or say in one's heart, "There is no God" (1 Sam. 2:12; Ps. 10:4; 14:1; 53:1; Jer. 2:8; 4:22), is not philosophical atheism but moral rejection. "To know not God" is to care nothing for Him.

For this reason, there are no "theistic proofs" (arguments for the existence of God) in the Old Testament. Nature texts such as Ps. 19:1-2 emphasize the wonders of nature as adding to the knowledge of God—broadening and deepening a conception of Deity already known. The movement of thought is from God to nature rather than from nature to God.

II. The Importance of the Divine Names

The names of God in the Old Testament are important in understanding who He is and what He is like. The divine names are intended to express important facts about God's nature.

For the Hebrew, names were descriptive and expressed meanings. They were never used simply to distinguish one person from another. A person's name was a kind of *alter ego*.[7] It embodied his distinctive essence, his character, an essential element in his personality.[8] A man's name was almost the equivalent of his being and individuality.[9] "The inner nature of a person or object is expressed in the name. 'The name of a thing is the imprint of its nature and the expression of the impression its nature makes.'"[10] The name of a man might represent an ideal he did not approximate; it might be more than he was. Contra, the name of God cannot fully measure what He is. Yet in spite of their limitations, the names applied to Deity are important theological data.

Even the term *shem* (name) when used of God carries special meaning. God's name is in effect the sum of all His revelation of himself. It is so used in Ps. 8:1, "O Lord, our Lord, how majestic is thy name in all the earth!" (cf. also v. 9; and 89:12). The Levitical blessing of Num. 6:22-27 is putting or "laying" the Lord's name upon the people, assuring them of His presence:[11] "Say to Aaron and his sons,

---

7. Eichrodt, *Theology of the OT*, 1:207.
8. Thomson, *OT View of Revelation*, p. 187.
9. J. Barton Payne, *The Theology of the Older Testament* (Grand Rapids, Mich.: Zondervan Publishing House, 1962), p. 144.
10. Sauer, *Dawn of World Redemption*, p. 187.
11. Eichrodt, *Theology of the OT*, p. 207.

Thus you shall bless the people of Israel: you shall say to them, The Lord bless you and keep you: the Lord make his face to shine upon you, and be gracious to you: the Lord lift up his countenance upon you, and give you peace. So shall they *put my name* upon the people of Israel, and I will bless them" (vv. 23-27). The name of the Lord is also used as an expression for the fact of God's presence. The tribes were to go to worship at "the place which the Lord your God will choose out of all your tribes to put his name and make his habitation there; thither you shall go, and thither you shall bring your burnt offerings and your sacrifices, your tithes and the offering you present" (Deut. 12:5-6, *passim;* cf. also 1 Kings 8:29; Isa. 18:7; Jer. 7:12).[12]

To "call upon the name of the Lord" is to call upon God himself and expresses the essence of worship. In the days of Enos, son of Seth, "men began to call upon the name of the Lord" (Gen. 4:26). Abraham built an altar near Bethel on his first arrival in Palestine "and called on the name of the Lord" (12:8; cf. also 13:4; 21:33; 26:25; 1 Kings 18:24; *passim*).

That name is holy (Lev. 20:3; 22:2, 32; 1 Chron. 16:10; and often in the Psalms). It is not to be taken in vain (Exod. 20:7; Deut. 5:11). To "proclaim the name of the Lord" is to tell what God is like (Exod. 33:19; 34:6-7). To speak (Deut. 18:22; 1 Chron. 21:19), bless (Deut. 21:5; 2 Sam. 6:18), or act (1 Sam. 17:45; Ps. 118:10-12) in the name of the Lord is to speak, bless, or act with His authority and power.

There are several specific divine names to be considered, but the two most important are given in the first three chapters of Genesis. A. B. Davidson wrote: "It will be found, I think, that all other designations of God, and all other assertions respecting Him, and all other attributes assigned to Him, may be embraced under one or other of the two names given to God in the opening chapters of Genesis."[13] These names are *Elohim* (God; Gen. 1:1-23) and *Yahweh* (the Lord; 2:5 ff.).

III. The Creator God

Old Testament theology begins where the Bible begins, with the Creator God of Gen. 1:1—"In the beginning God . . ." The Bible first

12. Payne, *loc. cit.*
13. *Theology of the OT,* p. 83; cf. Sauer, *Dawn of World Redemption,* p. 187.

answers the question "Who is God?" with the affirmation "God is the Creator of the heavens and the earth, and of all that is in them."

"The beginning" refers specifically to the origin of the finite universe. The Bible speaks of realities "before the foundation of the world" and the "glory . . . before the world was made" (John 17:24; 17:5; cf. Eph. 1:4; Titus 1:2; 1 Pet. 1:20). As Francis Schaeffer summarizes the data: "Something existed before creation and that something was personal and not static; the Father loved the Son; there was a plan; there was communication; and promises were made prior to the creation of the heavens and the earth."[14]

A. Elohim and El

The term here translated "God" (and throughout the Old Testament in virtually every English version) is *Elohim. Elohim* occurs 2,550 times in the Hebrew Old Testament. It is used as the designation for the true and living God more than 2,200 times. It is used some 245 times to describe the gods of the heathen, or for angels or men of superior rank.[15]

Elohim is plural in form, the so-called "plural of majesty." Davidson says, "Semitic languages use the plural as a means of heightening the idea of the singular."[16]

The derivation and original meaning of *Elohim* are uncertain. The root *El* is common to other Semitic languages such as Assyrian, Phoenician, and Aramaic. It is thought to mean "to be strong," "the strong one," "to be in the forefront, the Leader." When used as a common noun, as in Gen. 31:29, it is translated "power."[17]

When the singular *El* is used of God, it is nearly always modified by some other term: for example, "God Most High" (*El Elyon*—Gen. 14:18-20, 22; Num. 24:16; Dan. 3:26—usually from the lips of non-Hebrews); "God Almighty" (*El Shaddai*—Gen. 17:1 and frequently in the patriarchal literature); "the eternal God" (*El olam*—Gen. 21:33); "the living God" (*El chay*—Deut. 5:26); "the God of mercy" (*El rahum* —Exod. 34:6); and "the God who sees" (*El ro'i*—Gen. 16:13).

---

14. Francis A. Schaeffer, *Genesis in Space and Time* (Downers Grove, Ill.: Intervarsity Press, 1972), p. 18.

15. Robert Baker Girdlestone, *Synonyms of the Old Testament* (Grand Rapids, Mich.: William B. Eerdmans Publishing Co., 1956 reprint of 1897 second ed.), p. 19.

16. *Theology of the OT*, p. 99. Some have seen here, as in the plural pronouns of Gen. 1:26; 3:22; and Isa. 6:8, an intimation of the Trinity.

17. C. F. Burney, *Outlines of Old Testament Theology* (New York: Edwin S. Gorham, 1902), pp. 11-18.

El also occurs many times in names of persons and places—Israel ("God strives"), Bethel ("house of God"), Immanuel ("God with us"), Joel ("Jehovah is God"), etc. The singular form *Eloah* is used 41 times in Job but rarely elsewhere.

B. El Shaddai

Two of the defining terms used with *El* are important enough for further notice. One of these, *El Shaddai,* "God Almighty," occurs first in Gen. 17:1 in God's call to Abraham to walk before Him and be perfect. The phrase occurs four other times in Genesis (28:3; 35:11; 43:14; 48:3), once in Exodus (6:3) as the name by which God had chiefly been known to the patriarchs, and once in Ezekiel (10:5). *Ha-Shaddai* ("the Almighty"), however, occurs 42 times: three times each in the Pentateuch and in the Prophets, and the remainder of the times in the poetic literature—most frequently in Job. It is always used of the true God.

As is the case with many other Old Testament Hebrew terms, the exact derivation of *Shaddai* is not known. All suggested explanations have one idea in common—"that of power: power that protects and blesses (Gen. 17:1, Job 8:5, Ps. 91:1), or power that punishes (Job 5:17, 6:4, 21:20, Isa. 13:6)."[18] When used of protection and blessing, the thought of God as the bountiful Giver is particularly in mind.[19]

C. El Chay

"The living God" *(El chay)* occurs some 14 times in the Old Testament (Deut. 5:26; Josh. 3:10; 1 Sam. 17:26, 36; 2 Kings 19:4, 16, *passim*). In addition, such expressions as "the Lord lives" and "'as I live,' says the Lord" are comparatively frequent (Num. 14:21, 28; Deut. 32:40; and often in the historical books).

In many ways, *El chay* is the most characteristic designation of the true God in the Old Testament as well as in the New. "God who is the living God is never static, never simply the highest mode of being, but He is always active, and active in the whole life of man. Life is the essential characteristic of the living God. He is the Creator and Sustainer of all, Sovereign over all, blessed for ever."[20]

---

18. Thomson, *OT View of Revelation,* pp. 52-53.
19. Girdlestone, *Synonyms of the OT,* p. 32.
20. Thompson, *OT View of Revelation,* pp. 81-82.

D. God the Creator

Elohim therefore generally carries with it the meaning of strength, power, and might. It is the term fittingly employed throughout Gen. 1:1—2:3 when the work of creation is described. *Elohim* is the Creator God who brings all things into being by the word of His power. He is the Source and Ground of all reality.

On its very first pages, the Bible rejects both philosophical pantheism (the teaching that God and the total universe are identical) and deism (the theory that God started the universe operating and left it to its own impersonal laws thereafter). God is not identified with His universe. It is His handiwork. On the other hand, the universe could not exist apart from God's creative and sustaining power. "The heaven and the earth" (Gen. 1:1) corresponds with what we would call "the universe"—the finite, materially based realm of physical and psychic beings.

Just as the existence of God was never questioned by the Hebrew mind, His creative activity was never questioned. Each major division of the Old Testament contains this emphasis. Genesis, Psalms, and Isaiah particularly stress the fact of divine creation—not as defending a doctrine, but as explaining the beginnings of human history and expressing praise for and faith in God's continuing control of His world. "The order of nature is simply the expression of the divine wisdom."[21]

The creation account is not properly described as mythological. It contains no trace of what scholars have increasingly held to be the essence of myth, namely, ritual repetition. As Jacob wrote:

A myth only lives in the measure in which it is repeated and actualized in ritual, thus the Babylonian myth of creation was recited and represented in the New Year festival, because each year it was necessary to celebrate the cosmic power of Marduk if one wished to assure the prosperity of men and things and above all that of Babylon, of which Marduk was the national god. To Babylon—and the case holds for other civilizations—creation, remaining limited to the domain of myth and ritual, was not able to become the point of departure for a movement in history, so the world of the gods and historical reality remained closed to each other. For Israel creation marks a commencement. The word *reshit* ("in the beginning"—Gen. 1:1) is a whole plan of action, because it shows us that God's plan in history has creation as its starting point.[22]

---

21. Schultz, *OT Theology*, 2:180-82.
22. *Theology of the OT*, pp. 138-39.

E. The Creation Account

While the account of creation in the Bible is not mythological, neither is it intended to be cosmological or scientific. It is not designed to answer the question "Where did the world come from?" It is designed to answer the question "What is the meaning of the unfolding history of God's people?" "In other words, *the Creation* in the Old Testament does not belong to the sphere of natural science but to the history of man."[23]

Reason finds no better answer to the question of origins than Gen. 1:1, "In the beginning God created the heavens and the earth." If anything now is, something always was—self-existent, underived, the ontological ground of all reality. Time, space, matter, force, motion, and law have all been suggested for this role—singly and in various combinations. But any or all of these would force the conclusion that the higher has risen from the lower, that the nonrational has given rise to rational, self-conscious beings. Such a conclusion takes more credulity for most minds than the simple affirmation of the first words of Genesis.

There are four summary points to note in what H. Orton Wiley called "The Hymn of Creation" or "The Poem of the Dawn."[24]

---

23. Kohler, *OT Theology*, p. 89; italics in the original. It is a fallacy to throw the Bible and science into opposition. The points of view are entirely different. Science is concerned with the physical man under physical law—an idea quite unknown to the Old Testament where moral principles are the guidelines of interpretation. Cf. Davidson, *Theology of the OT*, p. 496.
Augustine wrote in the fourth century of the Christian era:

"It is both improper and mischievous for any Christian man to speak on such matters as if authorized by Scripture and yet talk so foolishly that the unbeliever, observing the extravagance of his mistakes, is scarcely able to keep from laughing. And the real trouble is not so much that the man is laughed at for his blunders, but the writers of Scripture are believed to have taught such things and are so condemned and rejected as ignorant by people outside the Church, to the great loss of those whose salvation we so desire.

"They find one belonging to the Christian body so far wrong on a subject they themselves know so well; and, on top of it, find him enforcing his groundless opinions by the authority of our Holy Bible. So they come to regard the Scriptures as unsound on subjects they have learned by observation or unquestioned evidence. Are they likely therefore to put their trust in these Scriptures about the resurrection of the dead, the hope of eternal life, and the kingdom of heaven?" Quoted by J. Edwin Orr in *One Hundred Questions About God* (Glendale, Calif.: Regal Books, 1966), p. 82.
24. *Christian Theology*, 1:449-54.

1. The existence of the universe is due to the creative act of an intelligent, omnipotent, personal God. The physical order is not eternal and self-existent. Neither did its orderly and systematic processes come by chance.

2. Two kinds of divine activity are mentioned. The first is immediate creation (Gen. 1:1, 21, 27). The Hebrew verb *bara* is used exclusively of God's work.[25] It means to bring into existence what had previously had no being. Driver says that the Hebrew verb here "in the simple conjugation . . . is used exclusively of God, to denote . . . the production of something fundamentally new, by the exercise of a sovereign originative power, altogether transcending that possessed by man."[26] Jacob wrote: "The specific term for the creative act of God was not borrowed from anthropomorphic speech: the verb *bara'*, both in the Qal and Niphal forms (active and passive), is used only of God and designates an activity peculiar to God and to him alone."[27]

Jarislov Pelikan called attention to the New Testament parallel:

> The verb used for "create" in the first verse of the Bible is *bara*. The same verb is used to designate the sovereign action of God in other passages of the Pentateuch (e.g., Ex. 34:10, Num. 16:30). . . . All instances of the verb support this generalization: *bara* always has God as its subject, never creatures. The same is true of *ktizein*, the verb used by the New Testament to translate *bara*. Sometimes *ktizein* refers to the original constitution of the world; sometimes it refers to an action of God in history, especially to the coming of Christ as the "new creation." But always it refers to an action whose ultimate actor is God, though the action may take place through created agents.[28]

The second kind of divine activity described in Genesis 1 is formation. This is described by such verbs as "make" and "made" *(asah)* or simply "let there be" *(ichi)*. These terms imply the shaping or forming of material already existing. An intermediate sort of

---

25. George A. F. Knight, *A Christian Theology of the Old Testament* (Richmond, Va.: John Knox Press, 1959), p. 110.

26. Quoted by John Wick Bowman, *Prophetic Realism and the Gospel* (Philadelphia: The Westminster Press, 1955), p. 85.

27. *Theology of the OT,* pp. 142-43.

28. "The Christian Intellectual," *Religious Perspectives,* vol. 14 (New York: Harper and Row, 1965), p. 40.

formation is implied in the commands of Gen. 1:11, 20, and 24, "Let the waters bring forth" and "Let the earth bring forth."[29]

In addition to the creative acts mentioned in Gen. 1:1, 21, 27, there are seven formative acts listed:

a. The origin of cosmic light (1:3)

b. The making of the expanse (firmament) of the sky. At the same time the waters were gathered into oceans and lakes and the dry land appeared (1:6-10).

c. The beginning of vegetation (1:11-13)

d. The appearance of solar bodies—by the clearing away of encircling mists around the earth? (1:14-19)

e. Life in the waters and sky (1:20-23)

f. Life on the land (1:24-25)

g. The human body—which in connection with the creative act of 1:27 and the infused life of 2:7 brought the whole creative epoch to its apex and fulfilled its purpose (1:26).

3. The creative and formative acts of God (cf. "created and made," 2:3) occurred under a temporal form. The Hebrew term *yom,* here translated "day" in the English versions, is used 1,480 times in the Old Testament. It is translated by more than 50 different English words in different contexts including "time," "life," "today," "age," "forever," "continually," and "perpetually."

Wiley wrote: "The best Hebrew exegesis has never regarded the days of Genesis as solar days, but as day-periods of indefinite duration. . . . Nor is this a metaphorical meaning of the word but the original, which signifies 'to put period to' or to denote a self-completed time."[30] That *yom* in the context of the creation account is not necessarily to be considered a 24-hour period of time is seen by its use in 2:4 to cover the entire six-period span. There is little reason to quarrel with the judgment of Bernard Ramm at this point: "The

---

29. In addition to *bara* and *asah,* two other terms are used to describe the origination of earthly existences: *yatsar* (to form, Amos 4:13; Isa. 43:1; 45:18); and *kun* (to establish, Isa. 45:18; Ezek. 28:13). All four terms are found in Isa. 45:18:

> For thus says the Lord,
> who created [*bara*] the heavens
>   (he is God!),
> who formed [*yatsar*] the earth and made [*asah*] it
>   (he established [*kun*] it;
> he did not create [*bara*] it a chaos,
>   he formed [*yatsar*] it to be inhabited!).

Cf. Lehman, *Biblical Theology,* 1:48-49.

30. *Christian Theology,* 1:456. Cf. Lehman, *Biblical Theology,* 1:48-49.

world made in two billion years is no less a miracle than a world made in twenty-four hours."[31] It may, in fact, be a greater wonder.

Some have attempted to reconcile belief in literal 24-hour days in Genesis 1 with the persistent evidence in science concerning the age of the earth by postulating a gap between verses 1 and 2. They argue that verse 2 means "the earth became without form and void."

The difficulty, as Lehman points out, is that "there is no sound exegetical basis for translating the verb *hayithah* (was) as *become* (Gen. 1:2)."[32] In Hebrew as well as in Greek and English, "to be" and "to become" represent distinct ideas. The forms of the verb "to be" point to persistence in being. The verb "to become" suggests change from one thing or form to another. There is no justification for translating the verb "to be" as if it meant "to become." "The 'gap' theory has no foundation either in this passage or anywhere else in the Scriptures."[33]

4. The Spirit of God is named as the divine Agent in bringing order out of the primeval chaos. "And the Spirit of God moved [or, was brooding] upon the face of the deep" (1:2). In Ps. 104:30 we are told that the Lord sends out His Spirit in the origination of individual creatures. Job 26:7-13 describes the creation of the physical order in highly poetic words. The writer notes that it is by the Spirit ("wind," RSV) of God that created objects are "garnished" or "made fair." While the biblical doctrine of the Spirit finds its definition only in the New Testament, the truth to be later revealed was safeguarded by the way Old Testament writers spoke of the Spirit of God or Spirit of the Lord.

Parallels have been noted between the Genesis account of creation and the cosmogonies of some other ancient cultures. But W. F. Albright was no doubt correct when he wrote:

> The account of Creation is unique in ancient literature. It undoubtedly reflects an advanced monotheistic point of view, with a sequence of creative phases so rational that modern science cannot improve on it, given the same language and the same range of ideas in which to state its conclusions. In fact, modern

---

31. *The Christian View of Science and Scripture* (Grand Rapids, Mich.: William B. Eerdmans Publishing Co., 1954), p. 225.

32. Lehman, *Biblical Theology,* 1:51.

33. *Ibid.* Francis A. Schaeffer quotes Benjamin B. Warfield, "It is to theology, as such, a matter of entire indifference how long man has existed on earth" (*Genesis in Space and Time,* pp. 161-62).

scientific cosmogonies show a disconcerting tendency to be short lived and it may be seriously doubted whether science has yet caught up with the Biblical story.[34]

Debate between "science" and "the Bible" often loses sight of the fact that the interest in the Scriptures is theological, not cosmological. The doctrine of creation is not an effort to explain the universe. Its purpose is to lay the basis for the history of salvation that follows. Stephen Neill wrote: "There can be no sound theology of redemption, indeed there can be no sound theology at all, unless it is based on a valid doctrine of creation."[35]

IV. THE COVENANT GOD

In addition to *Elohim* in the creation account of Gen. 1:1—2:3, another name is added in 2:4—3:24. It is the sacred name *Yahweh,* known also as the "Tetragrammaton" from its four Hebrew consonants JHVH. *Yahweh* is used extensively from 4:1 throughout the Old Testament both alone and in conjunction with *Elohim.* It occurs some 6,800 times in the Hebrew Scriptures.

A. The Meaning of Yahweh

Yahweh is a proper name, not a class term. The KJV, the RSV, the ERV, the Berkeley, the NEB, and most modern versions follow the lead of Jewish tradition in the Septuagint and the practice of the New Testament and translate it with the words "the LORD." Since Hebrew has another word for "lord" *(adon, adonai),* the occurrence of *Yahweh* in the original is shown by the use of an initial capital and smaller capitals in the English versions (the LORD). *Adonai* is translated with an initial capital and lower case "ord" (the Lord) when used, as it usually is, of God. Since the personal name of the true God was deemed too sacred to be spoken, Jewish custom from time immemorial has been to read *Adonai* whenever *Yahweh* is found in the Scriptures.

The ASV translated *Yahweh* as "Jehovah." The term "Jehovah" is used seven times in the KJV, of which three are in compound place names (Gen. 22:14; Exod. 6:3; 17:15; Judg. 6:24; Ps. 83:18; Isa. 12:2;

34. "The Old Testament and Archaeology," *Old Testament Commentary,* ed. Herbert C. Alleman and Elmer E. Flack (Philadelphia: Muhlenberg Press, 1948), p. 135.

35. *Christian Holiness* (New York: Harper and Brothers, Publishers, 1960), p. 16.

26:4).[36] Moffatt uses "the Eternal" as his English rendering of *Yahweh.*

As in the case of *Elohim,* the exact derivation and meaning of *Yahweh* has long been discussed by biblical scholars. The word itself is derived from a form of the verb "to be" (cf. Exod. 3:14; 6:2-3). It has variously been taken to mean:

1. The eternally self-existent One, hence changeless—self-originating, self-dependent, "exposed to no alteration by the power of the world and of time."[37]

2. He who causes to be or to come into being.[38]

3. He who is present, who will be with His people.[39]

These suggested meanings are not necessarily mutually exclusive. Each adds to the rich insight given in the name.

Exod. 3:13-14 and 6:2-3 have been understood by some to imply that the name *Yahweh* was first made known to Moses. Gen. 4:26, however, states that in the days of Enos, son of Seth, "began men to call upon the name of the LORD *[Yahweh].*" What the Exodus passages rather mean is that for the first time the name was explained to Moses. The Hebrew usage shows that the point of Moses' inquiry was not "Who are You?" or "What is Your name?" but "What finds expression in or lies concealed behind the name?"[40]

A. B. Davidson pointed out that *Yahweh* is not an ontological but a redemptive name. It expresses God's faithfulness, His constancy, the whole idea of the divine-human covenant of salvation. It is concerned not so much with God's essential nature as with His relation to Israel as the God of the covenant.[41] *Yahweh* is the "name of His covenant, and of His redeeming love."[42] J. Barton Payne wrote:

---

36. "Jehovah" is no true rendering of *Yahweh.* "Jehovah" is not a biblical name at all. It was coined by Galatinus in the sixteenth century by combining the vowels of *Adonai* with the consonants of the Tetragrammaton. Cf. Knight, *Christian Theology of the OT,* p. 50.

37. Schultz, *OT Theology,* 2:144; Burney, *OT Theology,* pp. 19-26; Kohler, *OT Theology,* p. 43.

38. W. F. Albright, "Recent Discoveries in Bible Lands," *Young's Analytical Concordance to the Bible* (New York: Funk and Wagnalls Co., 1955), p. 35.

39. Martin Buber, *Moses: The Revelation and the Covenant* (New York: Harper and Brothers, 1958), p. 53; Vriezen, *Outline of OT Theology,* pp. 235-6; Jacob, *Theology of the OT,* p. 52; Knight, *Christian Theology of the OT,* pp. 44-5; Payne, *Theology of the Older Testament,* pp. 148 ff.; Eichrodt, *Theology of the OT,* 1:189; Gerhard von Rad, *Old Testament Theology.* Trans. by D. M. G. Stalker (New York: Harper and Brothers Publishers, 1962), 1:180.

40. Exod. 3:13; cf. Buber, *Moses,* p. 48.

41. *Theology of the OT,* pp. 45-58.

42. Sauer, *Dawn of World Redemption,* p. 187.

It *(Yahweh)* carries the connotation of God's nearness, of His concern for man, of His redemptive, testamentary revelation. So Moses selected *Elohim* as the appropriate term for Genesis 1:1— 2:3, God transcendent in creation; but *Yahweh* for Genesis 2:4-25, God immanent in Eden's revelations. Similar shifts in names, corresponding to God's shift in activity from general sovereignty to personal redemption, appear in the Genesis passages that follow.[43]

Yahweh is also found in combinations with other names and in compound names. Some compounds are used to describe places where significant events took place in which God revealed himself: *Jehovah (Yahweh) Jireh,* "The Lord will provide" (Gen. 22:14); *Jehovah (Yahweh) Nissi,* "The Lord is my banner" (Exod. 17:15); *Jehovah (Yahweh) Shalom,* "The Lord is peace" (Judg. 6:24).

B. Compound Names

Two compound names not related to places serve to enlarge and enrich the connotation of *Yahweh.* One is *Yahweh Mekaddishkem,* translated in the KJV as "the LORD that doth sanctify you" (Exod. 31:13) or, as in the RSV, "the LORD who sanctify you" (Lev. 20:8). The name occurs 10 times, each in the form "I am *Yahweh Mekaddishkem*" as spoken directly by God. Moses was instructed to "say to the people of Israel, 'You shall keep my sabbaths, for this is a sign between me and you throughout your generations, that you may know that I, the Lord, sanctify you *[Yahweh Mekaddishkem]*'" (Exod. 31:13). Israel was commanded: "Consecrate yourselves therefore, and be holy: for I am the Lord your God. Keep my statutes, and do them; I am the Lord who sanctify you *[Yahweh Mekaddishkem]*" (Lev. 20:7-8; cf. Lev. 20:9-21; 21:9; Ezek. 20:12-13; 37:23).

A second compound name found first in 1 Sam. 1:3 and 278 times thereafter is *Yahweh Sabaoth,* "the Lord of hosts." Occasionally in the Psalms but rarely elsewhere it is given as *Yahweh Elohim Sabaoth,* "Lord God of hosts." While the phrase itself first appears in Samuel, the idea is much older. It is found in passages where God is

---

43. *Theology of the Older Testament,* p. 148. This is an explanation of the shift from *Elohim* to *Yahweh* at least as worthy of consideration as the widely published but now critically questioned documentary hypothesis with its J, E, D, P apparatus. Cf. Cyrus H. Gordon, "Higher Critics and Forbidden Fruit," in Frank E. Gaebelein, ed., *Christianity Today Reader* (New York: Meredith Press, 1966), pp. 67-73. Dr. Gordon, a Jewish scholar, professor of Near Eastern Studies and chairman of the Department of Mediterranean Studies at Brandeis University, is highly critical of the documentary hypothesis.

described as Israel's General, the invisible Leader fighting for and with His people (e.g., Exod. 14:1-3; Josh. 5:14; Num. 21:14).

The Lord of hosts is "The Lord strong and mighty, the Lord mighty in battle" (Ps. 24:8, 10). Angels, the "sons of God," even the stars, are included among the hosts of God along with the armies of Israel. The hosts include "all earthly and heavenly forces—nature (Gen. 2:1), military might (1 Sam. 4:4 f., cf. Ps. 44:9), the stars (Deut. 4:19; cf. Ps. 33:6), and the angels (Josh. 5:14; 1 Kings 22:19; cf. Ps. 103:21)."[44] *Yahweh Sabaoth* is therefore a name supremely expressive of the sovereignty of God.

The Old Testament abounds with human names in which the root *Yah* is employed. Random examples include *Jehoida*, "the Lord knows"; *Jehoiakim*, "the Lord will set up"; *Jehu*, "the Lord is He"; *Jotham*, "the Lord is upright"; and most significant of all, *Joshua*, "the Lord is salvation" or "the Lord the Saviour"—the name that becomes "Jesus" in the Greek New Testament.

C. Adonai (Lord)

Closely related to *Yahweh* is the third most common name for God, *Adonai*. Translated "Lord," it is used of Deity some 340 times. The root, *Adon*, means "master," "lord," "owner," and "sir." *Adon* itself is usually used of men of rank or dignity but is applied to God a number of times. *Adonai* is a later form used generally of God (vocalized distinctively as "Adonoy") but occasionally as plural for men.

The special meaning of *Adonai* is to indicate man's dependence upon God and God's right to be the Master of men. Its frequent use with *Yahweh* (Exod. 23:17; 34:23; Isa. 1:24; 3:15; 10:16; Amos 8:1; and often in Ezekiel) shows that it indicates the divine lordship as *Yahweh* alone could not do. Because of the awkwardness of translating "Lord LORD," the common English versions use the phrase "Lord God" for *Adonai Yahweh*. The ASV uses "Lord Jehovah."

V. ANTHROPOMORPHISMS

In addition to the names for God, the divine personality is further stressed by the use of what have come to be called "anthropomorphisms" (from *morphos*, form; and *anthropos*, man). From its earliest chapters, the Scriptures abound in statements about God drawn from concrete human experience and human nature.

---

44. Thomson, *OT View of Revelation*, p. 56.

God is said to talk (Gen. 1:3; 8:15), to rest and sit (Gen. 2:2; Ps. 47:8), to see and hear (Gen. 6:12; Exod. 16:12), to smell (Gen. 8:21; 1 Sam. 26:19—RSV, "accept"), to walk down from heaven (Gen. 11:5), and to have a face and back (Exod. 33:20, 23; Num. 6:25; Ps. 104:29). God grieves (Gen. 6:6), is angry (Exod. 15:7), is jealous (Exod. 20:5; 34:14—or zealous for His glory),[45] hates sin (Deut. 12:31), and rejoices (Deut. 28:63).

We are given graphic pictures of God's activity. He fashions man out of the dust of the earth and breathes into him the breath of life (Gen. 2:7). He plants a garden (Gen. 2:8). He walks in the garden in the cool of the day (Gen. 3:8). He locks the door of the ark (Gen. 7:16). There are many more.

A. Metaphor in Anthropomorphism

Many anthropomorphic expressions are clearly metaphorical. The arms of God represent the security His covenant gives (Deut. 33:27). His hands describe both bountiful giving and acts of judgment (Ezra 7:9; 1 Sam. 5:11). To behold the face of the Lord is to worship Him truly (Ps. 17:15). To have His face "shine upon" one is to receive His favor and blessing (Num. 6:25; Ps. 31:16). The list could be extended to cover virtually all anthropomorphisms. Poetry may speak of God as having wings, feathers, as being a rock, a fortress, without in any sense intending a literal understanding of such language (Ps. 91:2, 4).

Anthropomorphism has been criticized as a crude effort to "make God in man's own image." That such anthropomorphic expressions were not understood literally, however, is clearly indicated by other passages that liken God to animals: an eagle (Hos. 8:1), a lion (Hos. 11:10; Amos 1:2), a leopard or a bear (Hos. 13:7-8), a bird (Ps. 17:8; 91:4), etc. Other passages definitely state that God does not have human form, sense perceptions, or human emotions: "God is not man, that he should lie, or a son of man, that he should repent. Has he said, and will he not do it? Or has he spoken, and will he not fulfil it?" (Num. 23:19). "But will God dwell indeed with man on the earth? Behold, heaven and the highest heaven cannot contain thee; how much less this house which I have built!" (2 Chron. 6:18; cf. 1 Sam. 15:29; Job 10:4; Ps. 121:4; Isa. 40:28; Hos. 11:9, etc.).

---

45. Vriezen, *Outline of OT Theology*, pp. 153-54.

B. The Religious Value of Anthropomorphism

Anthropomorphisms were not an early mode of expression outgrown in the later prophetic period. In fact, the very reverse is true: The prophets abound in warm, intimate expressions of God's nearness and availability.[46] "Anthropomorphism does not aim at humanizing God, but . . . to bring God close to man as a warm, living person, and thus to preserve and strengthen religious life."[47]

As G. Ernest Wright described it: "The language of the faith was inevitably anthropomorphic, that is, filled with human words to describe the deity. . . . Yet this language is not a luxury or a primitivism which later stages of the faith outgrew. It was and is a necessity of the faith. The relationship of God to people and of people to God can be depicted in no other way, when the covenant as the framework of understanding is central in the faith."[48] Jacob reminds us that "a line not always straight, but none the less continuous, leads from the anthropomorphism of the earliest pages of the Bible to the incarnation of God in Jesus Christ."[49]

The Old Testament concept of God is always religious, not philosophical or metaphysical. Old Testament writers knew nothing of the modern impersonal "God" of religious or philosophical pantheism on the one hand or secular scientism on the other. God to them was a divine Person with rational intelligence, capable of purpose and choice, and with capacity for valuation.

Both creation and the covenant point to a personal God. In creation, God is contrasted with the created order as self-conscious reason, and as free, wise, and moral will. In the covenant, likewise, there is a Person-to-people relationship established. Hermann Schultz wrote: "In contrast with the material, that is, the needy dependent being, eager for enjoyment and outward satisfaction, and tied down to a definite outward form, God is spiritual, *Elohim;* that is, perfect, independent, and in need of nothing. He is the living God, the God of life, in whom life is present as a property, and that, too, an inalienable property (Deut. 5:26; 32:40; Jer. 10:10)."[50]

The Hebrew language is rich in concrete expressions but lacking in abstractions. Men of Old Testament times spoke and thought con-

---

46. Eichrodt, *Theology of the OT,* 1:211-12.
47. Paul Heinisch, *Theology of the Old Testament* (Collegeville, Minn.: The Liturgical Press, 1950), p. 67.
48. *The Book of the Acts of God* (New York: Doubleday and Co., Inc., 1957), p. 93.
49. *Theology of the OT,* p. 32.
50. *OT Theology,* 2:112. Cf. also pp. 103 ff.

cretely rather than abstractly. But they recognized the limits of anthropomorphism. The prohibition contained in the second commandment shows this (Exod. 20:4). The fashioning of any representation of the Divine is forbidden. Where anthropomorphisms were used, they were understood symbolically, as a host of other references reveals.[51] Old Testament man was always aware of the truth Isaiah stated: "For my thoughts are not your thoughts, neither are your ways my ways, says the Lord. For as the heavens are higher than the earth, so are my ways higher than your ways and my thoughts than your thoughts" (Isa. 55:8-9).

---

51. Jacob, *Theology of the OT*, pp. 41-42; Thomson, *OT View of Revelation*, p. 84.

3

The Nature of Man

The Bible turns immediately from its consideration of God and creation to the nature and significance of man. Scripture is the Word *of* God and the Word *about* man. Genesis devotes 2 chapters to creation and 12 to Abraham.

The importance of a right understanding of human nature can scarcely be overstated. The truth about the nature and destiny of man is crucial in the great struggles of the last third of the twentieth century. The "ideologies" we hear so much about are in fact anthropologies—answers to the biblical question "What is man?" (Job 7:17; Ps. 8:4; 144:3).[1]

Modern secular views of man err in that they are either overly optimistic or unduly pessimistic in their estimates of human nature. The biblical view of man is thoroughly realistic. It holds in balance both the dignity and the degradation of that creature who is, in Francis Thompson's phrase, akin both to clod and cherubim. An older popular psychologist has written: "The greatest and most authentic textbook on personality is still the Bible, and the discoveries which psychologists have made tend to confirm rather than to contradict the codification of personality found there."[2]

I. General Terms for Man

The Old Testament uses four major terms to designate the human species and its members. These are not technical terms, used with

---

1. J. S. Whale, *Christian Doctrine* (New York: The Macmillan Co., 1942), p. 35.
2. Henry C. Link, *The Return to Religion* (New York: The Macmillan Co., 1937), p. 103.

rigid consistency, but they do reflect shades of meaning clearly distinguishable.

1. The most important term relating to man is *adam* (Gen. 1:26-27; 2:5, 7-8; a total of 15 times in Gen. 1:26—3:24). *Adam* is derived from *adamah*, "earth," and stresses the origin of the body as well as its destiny at the end of this life: "Then the Lord God formed man [Heb., *ha-adam*, "the man"] of dust from the ground, and breathed into his nostrils the breath of life; and man [*ha-adam*, "the man"] became a living being" (Gen. 2:7). "In the sweat of your face you shall eat bread till you return to the ground [*ha-adamah*], for out of it you were taken; you are dust, and to dust you shall return" (3:19).

In the Hebrew Bible, *adam* appears as a personal name from Gen. 3:17 on. The KJV translates *ha-adam* ("the man") as Adam from 2:19 on.

2. *Ish* (Gen. 2:23-24; 4:1) expresses the idea of man in the exercise of his power of will and choice. It is the term used in marriage: a man is the *ish* or husband of the one he has chosen. *Ish* occurs in compound names: Ishbosheth, man of shame; Ishhod, man of renown; Ishtob, man from Tob.

3. *Enosh* (Gen. 6:4; 12:20) represents the converse of *ish* and stands for man in his weakness and mortality. It is a term often found in parallel with *adam* in the poetic writings: "What is man [*enosh*] that thou art mindful of him, and the son of man [*bene adam*] that thou dost care for him?" (Ps. 8:4). "Thou turnest man [*enosh*] back to the dust, and sayest, 'Turn back, O children of men [*bene adam*]!'" (Ps. 90:3; cf. Job 10:4-5, etc.).

4. *Geber*, like *ish*, stresses strength and is often used to distinguish a man from a woman or child.[3] Vowing to hold the women and children, Pharaoh made the offer to Moses, "Go, the men [*geberim*] among you, and serve the Lord, for that is what you desire" (Exod. 10:11). The people of Israel numbered "about six hundred thousand men [*geberim*] on foot, besides women and children" (Exod. 12:37).

The very terms used to describe man show the Old Testament tension between the humility and the honor of the human estate. Man in his humility is *adam*, *enosh*. In his dignity and honor, he is *ish* and *geber*. Jacob comments: "Alongside the statement of man's ephemeral and limited nature the Old Testament proclaims unceasingly the eminent dignity conferred upon him by his peculiar

---

3. Jacob, *Theology of the OT*, pp. 156-57.

association with God." This connection, Jacob says, "is not a relation of kinship; man is no fallen god; he is not as in the Babylonian myth partly composed of divine substance; he is placed by God as an independent and autonomous creature to whom as God's image dominion over the rest of creation is entrusted."[4]

II. OLD TESTAMENT "PSYCHOLOGY"

Several specific terms are used of the constituents of human personality in the Old Testament.

1. The material element is called dust (*aphar*—also translated "earth," "powder," "ashes," and "ground"). Gen. 2:7 is a key verse in Old Testament anthropology: "Then the Lord God formed man of dust from the ground, and breathed into his nostrils the breath of life; and man became a living being."

Taken from the dust, the body is destined to return to the dust (Gen. 3:19; Job 34:15; Ps. 30:9; Eccles. 3:20; 12:7). In addition to its use in relation to the body, *aphar* is used in the Old Testament to describe a large number ("as the dust of the earth for multitude") and to speak of humiliation, weakness, and distress ("dust and ashes"). Along with *adamah, aphar* is also used of the physical earth (Gen. 26:15; Job 8:19; 19:25; 28:2; *passim*).

2. Dust infused with breath *(neshamah)* becomes flesh *(basar)*. *Neshamah,* with the term "spirit" *(ruach)* often used in connection with it, stands for the nonphysical aspect of life. Man is not *neshamah* but *has* it.[5] Breath is something God gives to man (Gen. 2:7; Job 12:10) and takes away: "When thou hidest thy face, they are dismayed; when thou takest away their breath, they die and return to their dust" (Ps. 104:29).

Both man and beast have breath. It was recorded of the Flood that "all flesh died that moved upon the earth, birds, cattle, beasts, all swarming creatures that swarm upon the earth, and every man; everything on the dry land in whose nostrils was the breath of life died" (Gen. 7:21-22; cf. Eccles. 3:19). *Neshamah* comes very close to being what we should call the physical phenomenon of life. In Ezekiel's vision of the valley of dry bones, even after the flesh was restored to the skeletons, "There was no breath in them. Then he said to me, 'Prophesy to the breath, prophesy, son of man, and say to

---

4. *Ibid.,* p. 152.
5. Smith, *Bible Doctrine of Man,* p. 6 ff.

the breath, Thus says the Lord God: Come from the four winds, O breath, and breathe upon these slain, that they may live.' So I prophesied as he commanded me, and the breath came into them, and they lived, and stood upon their feet, an exceedingly great host" (Ezek. 37:8-10).

3. Flesh (*basar*—Gen. 2:21, 23-24; 6:3, 12-13) is the Hebrew term closest to our English word *body* (it is so translated in the KJV of Isa. 10:18 and Ezek. 10:12). Flesh is "living, ensouled matter."[6] It is never merely material substance. It is organic, animal structure—living usually—but still described as "flesh" between the time of death and dissolution.

While flesh and spirit are often viewed as in antithesis, it is not a moral antithesis. The Old Testament contains no suggestion that flesh is ethically evil. Spirit is often used for power and flesh for weakness: "The Egyptians are men, and not God; and their horses are flesh, and not spirit" (Isa. 31:3). Flesh may be weak but it is not inherently sinful. Its use in sacrifices indicates that it is not unholy or unclean. It is God's creation, and the Eternal Son was later to be made "flesh" (John 1:14). Paul's technical use of "flesh" in Romans and Galatians in contrast to Spirit finds no counterpart in the Old Testament.[7]

Flesh is used (1) of the individual physical body: Adam said of Eve, "This at last is bone of my bones and flesh of my flesh" (Gen. 2:23; cf. v. 21); (2) of generic humankind: "And God saw the earth, and behold, it was corrupt; for all flesh had corrupted their way upon the earth" (Gen. 6:12); (3) of man's limited probation: "Then the Lord said, 'My spirit shall not abide in man for ever, for he is flesh" (Gen. 6:3); (4) of the solidarity of the family relationship: Judah urged his brothers to spare the life of Joseph, "for he is our brother, our own flesh" (Gen. 37:27); and (5) even of a dead body, as when Joseph said to the doomed baker in Pharaoh's prison, "Within three days Pharaoh will lift up your head—from you!—and hang you on a tree; and the birds will eat the flesh from you" (Gen. 40:19).

4. Spirit *(ruach)* united with flesh *(basar)* results in soul *(nephesh;* see below). As Otto Baab notes, spirit is

---

6. Davidson, *Theology of the OT*, p. 203.

7. Smith, *Bible Doctrine of Man*, pp. 24-25; Otto J. Baab, *Theology of the Old Testament* (New York: Abingdon-Cokesbury, 1949), p. 68.

that element in human nature which is most closely connected
with the nature of God. It is the endowment of man with the
energy and the capacity for religious activity. Through its possession man may lift his face from the clod and turn to the eternal
verities of truth, beauty, and goodness. The spirit in man enables
him to hold communion with the spirit of God. This term suggests more than any other the content and meaning of the phrase
"in the image of God."[8]

Only God possesses spirit in its fullness. For man, spirit comes
from above.[9] Although not as comprehensive a term, *spirit* is often
used as a synonym for soul.[10] *Ruach* is used on occasion as the equivalent of the self, as in Job 19:17 where the sufferer complains,
"My *ruach* is strange to my wife" (the KJV translates *ruach* here as
"breath"—cf. also Gen. 45:27; Judg. 15:19). In general usage, man
shares "soul" with the animals or lower forms of life; he shares
"spirit" with God, from whom he receives it (Zech. 12:1) and to
whom it goes when he dies: "And the dust returns to the earth as it
was, and the spirit returns to God who gave it" (Eccles. 12:7).

The variety of the human spirit's manifestations is seen in that
it may be troubled (Gen. 41:8), be revived (45:27), suffer anguish
(Exod. 6:9), express wisdom (31:3), be made willing (35:21), be jealous (Num. 5:14), sorrow (1 Sam. 1:15), be stirred (Ezra 1:1), understand (Job 20:3), and be without guile (Ps. 32:2).

5. Soul *(nephesh)* is defined as the "self-conscious life with feelings and desires . . . the individual conscious life."[11] "The *nephesh* is the
self, and all that this self embraces."[12] "Then the Lord God formed
man of dust from the ground, and breathed into his nostrils the
breath of life; and man became a living being *[nephesh]*" (Gen. 2:7).

Nephesh is used 756 times in the Old Testament, and the KJV
uses 42 different English terms to translate it—of which the most
common are "soul" (428) and "life" (117). Brown, Driver, and Briggs
list nine meanings: soul, living being, life, self, person, desire, appetite, emotion, and passion.

"Soul is the nature of man, not his possession."[13]

8. *Theology of the OT,* p. 65.
9. Jacob, *Theology of the OT,* pp. 161-62.
10. Knight, *Christian Theology of the OT,* p. 36.
11. Schultz, *OT Theology,* 2:246.
12. Jacob, *Theology of the OT,* p. 161.
13. Kohler, *OT Theology,* p. 142.

Soul [is] a convenient symbol for the identification of the whole life of a man, more particularly in its affective and non-bodily form. This life is the self, distinguished not so much by having memory, reflection, or moral integrity as by having the principle of vitality, which disappears at death. The term means both biological and psychic life.[14]

Dust plus breath equals flesh; flesh plus spirit equals soul.

Nephesh is both the biological and psychic life principle. Its major applications are to indicate life as opposed to death; to designate what we would call *a man* or *people* (Gen. 2:7; 12:5); and to describe the core of personal experience whether it belongs in the realm of knowing, willing, or feeling—with the emphasis on feeling.[15]

The soul blesses others (Gen. 27:4), sins (Lev. 4:2), is afflicted (23:27), loves (Deut. 6:5), may be converted (Ps. 19:7), experiences physical hunger and thirst (Ps. 107:9; Prov. 25:25)—and so on and on, experiencing every emotion and determining every action possible to man. While there is an inescapable sense of dualism in biblical psychology, the soul is much more intimately bound up with the body in Hebrew usage than it would be, for example, in the sharp body-soul dichotomy of Greek thought. It is the whole of the inner life (Ps. 103:1).

6. One other term is used for the inner personal life of man. It is the term "heart" *(leb, lebab)*, defined in Brown, Driver, and Briggs's *Lexicon* as "inner man, mind, will, heart." Like soul, heart may be used of any mental experience. "The heart seems to them (the Hebrews) a concentration of all the vital powers, as Johs. Pedersen is impelled to write: '*Nephesh* is the soul in the sum of its totality, such as it appears; the heart is the soul in its inner value.'"[16]

Of the more than 850 times *leb* and *lebab* appear in the Old Testament, the KJV translates them "heart" 718 times, "understanding" 23, "mind" 15, "wisdom" 6, and a dozen other English terms to account for the balance. The heart "not only includes the motives, feelings, affections, and desires, but also the will, the aims, the principles, the thoughts, and the intellect of man. In fact, it embraces the whole inner man."[17]

---

14. Baab, *Theology of the OT*, p. 66.
15. Smith, *Bible Doctrine of Man*, c. 13.
16. Jacob, *Theology of the OT*, p. 163.
17. Girdlestone, *Synonyms of the OT*, pp. 65-66.

In a reversal of our popular way of speaking, soul is used more commonly of the affective or feeling side of the inner life, and heart is used more commonly of the thinking or intellectual aspect of the inner man.

The heart is the seat of knowledge. It devises plans: "And Nathan said to the king, 'Go, do all that is in your heart; for the Lord is with you'" (2 Sam. 7:3); "David said to Solomon, 'My son, I had it in my heart to build a house to the name of the Lord my God'" (1 Chron. 22:7).

The heart may be spoken of as—

wise: "Behold, I now do according to your word. Behold, I give you a wise and discerning mind *[leb],* so that none like you has been before you and none like you shall arise after you" (1 Kings 3:12);

pure: "Create in me a clean heart, O God, and put a new and right spirit within me" (Ps. 51:10);

honest and righteous: God said to Abimelech in reference to Abraham's deception regarding Sarah, "Yes, I know that you have done this in the integrity of your heart, and it was I who kept you from sinning against me" (Gen. 20:6);

circumcised: "And the Lord your God will circumcise your heart and the heart of your offspring, so that you will love the Lord your God with all your heart and with all your soul, that you may live" (Deut. 30:6). This phrase occurs in the New Testament in Rom. 2:29 in connection with the spiritual descendents of Abraham by faith, "a circumcision made without hands, by putting off the body of flesh in the circumcision of Christ" (Col. 2:11);

perverse: "Perverseness of heart shall be far from me; I will know nothing of evil" (Ps. 101:4);

wicked and stubborn: "They shall no more stubbornly follow their own evil heart" (Jer. 3:17);

haughty and proud: Of the prince of Tyre, the Lord said, "Because your heart is proud, and you have said, 'I am a god, I sit in the seat of the gods, in the heart of the seas,' yet you are but a man, and no god, though you consider yourself as wise as a god" (Ezek. 28:2);

depraved: "The Lord saw that the wickedness of man was great in the earth, and that every imagination of the thoughts of his heart was only evil continually" (Gen. 6:5; cf. 8:21);

deceitful: "The heart is deceitful above all things, and desperately corrupt; who can understand it?" (Jer. 17:9);

may be hardened: "Then the Lord said to Moses, 'Pharaoh's heart is hardened, he refuses to let the people go'" (Exod. 7:14; cf. 8:15; *passim*).

Every action, thought, feeling, or purpose of man may be attributed to the heart.

In a special sense, the heart is the center of the moral life. Only as a man guards his heart will he experience life in the fullest sense: "Keep [guard] your heart with all vigilance; for from it flow the springs of life" (Prov. 4:23).[18]

7. A minor term *(kelayoth)* used 13 times of man's inner life in the Old Testament is translated "reins" in the KJV. Recent translations use "heart," "soul," or "emotions" and "attitude" (Berk.).

As is true of "heart," "reins" had an anatomical meaning. It was the Hebrew term for kidneys—a connection still found in modern medicine, where *renal* describes functions related to the kidneys. When the Old Testament uses *kelayoth* in relation to man's inner life, it is almost always in relation to "trying" or "searching" (Ps. 7:9; 26:2; Jer. 11:20). Ryder Smith concludes that "probably there is always a direct or indirect reference to God's searching of what *we* call the conscience."[19] "My reins also instruct me" (Ps. 16:7, KJV) implies at least an inner impulse toward what is morally right.

III. Tensions in Old Testament Views of Man

It must be recognized that the biblical concern with man is not analytical or scientific, but spiritual and moral. An absence of technical terms has already been noted. Words are used with no effort at mechanical precision in meaning. Paradox and tension between opposing concepts are accepted. Biblical psychology and biblical anthropology are expressed in terms drawn from popular speech and with the religious interest uppermost.

A. Individualism and Collectivism

One of the major tensions in the Old Testament's view of man is the tension between a collective view on the one hand and a feeling for individual responsibility on the other. It has sometimes been

---

18. Cf. Gustave F. Oehler, *Theology of the Old Testament,* trans. George E. Day (Grand Rapids, Mich.: Zondervan Publishing House, reprint of 1889 edition), pp. 152-54.

19. *Bible Doctrine of Man,* p. 23.

assumed that the earliest concepts in the Old Testament were collectivistic, and that individualism developed only with the breakdown of Israel's political and social life during the period of the Babylonian exile. Such a generalization is only partially correct.

There was indeed a strong sense of the solidarity of the family, the clan, and later the nation among Old Testament men. It was early seen that often the whole group would suffer for the sins of the few. We may also read, "But the people of Israel broke faith in regard to the devoted things; for Achan . . . took some of the devoted things" (Josh. 7:1), in which the sin of Achan is regarded as the sin of the nation. The covenant was not per se made with individuals severally but with the nation (goy, am) collectively (Exod. 19:5-6).

Yet from the earliest times, there was alongside such collectivism an individualistic way of thinking. While a man might indeed implicate others by his acts, each man was viewed as standing for himself before God. The very form of the covenant commandments (Exod. 20:1-17) indicates this. None of the commandments of the Decalogue have to do with social issues. All relate to individual conduct.[20]

Deut. 24:16 explicitly forbids punishment of others in the immediate family because of the sins of fathers or their sons, a prohibition echoed in 2 Kings 14:6; 2 Chron. 25:4; Jer. 31:29-30; and Ezek. 18:20: "The fathers shall not be put to death for the children, nor shall the children be put to death for the fathers; but every man shall be put to death for his own sin." Men may indeed act alike and may influence each other by their actions and thus be subject to the same judgments. But the fact that the motive is considered in the law itself (Exod. 21:29, 36) and knowledge and intention determine guilt shows that each individual is judged before God on the basis of his own purposes.

B. Monism and Dualism

While there is also a sense in which the dualism of matter and spirit, body and soul, so familiar to students of Greek thought, is absent from the thinking of biblical man, it is still the case that an almost inevitable dualism does appear. The Old Testament has indeed a strong sense of the psychophysical unity of the human being. The sense of

---

20. Walther Eichrodt, *Man in the Old Testament* (Chicago: Henry Regnery Co., 1951), pp. 7-16; Jacob, *Theology of the OT*, pp. 154-55.

need for the resurrection of the body in a full experience of the after-life is found even in Old Testament times (see Chapter 8). Still the fact that a person survives death in *Sheol* while the body is laid in the earth with no special care for its preservation argues for some sort of dualism.

It is instructive that there was no "cult of the dead" in Israel such as flourished in Egypt and other ancient Oriental cultures in which the greatest possible care was given to the preservation of the body. The pyramids were not originally erected as marvels of en-gineering skill. They were the tombs of Egyptian kings and their families. There were no pyramids in Israel.

IV. The Image of God

A basic concept in the biblical view of man is found in the phrase "the image of God." It first occurs in Gen. 1:26-27 and again in 9:6, with the synonym "likeness" in Gen. 1:26 and 5:1. "Then God said, 'Let us make man in our image, after our likeness; and let them have dominion over the fish of the sea, and over the birds of the air, and over the cattle, and over all the earth, and over every creeping thing that creeps upon the earth.' So God created man in his own image, in the image of God he created him; male and female he created them" (1:26-27). "When God created man, he made him in the likeness of God" (5:1). "For God made man in his own image" (9:6).

A. The Nature of the Divine Image

A distinction is often made between the "natural" and "moral" image of God in man. In the "natural" image are located such capacities as reason, memory, self-direction or will, and immortality. In the "moral" image, holiness, a right relationship with God, and freedom from sinful tendencies and dispositions are identified. It is often held that after the Fall, the "natural" image remained more or less intact while the "moral" image was shattered—to be restored in full redemption through Christ.

It is probably more biblical to say that the image of God in its wholeness is perverted and corrupted in fallen man, but that man is still in an important sense a creature who bears the image of his Creator. Even after the Fall and the Flood, murder was forbidden because "God made man in his own image" (Gen. 9:6). "This image is sullied by sin and . . . is restored by divine salvation."[21] It is the *imago dei* that is our manness. What it means to be a man and not just a more complex kind of animal is comprehended in the image of God.

There is still room for distinguishing between the "creation-image" and the "redemption-image" which is Christological and eschatological. Carl F. H. Henry's distinctions at this point are helpful:

> (1) The creation-image was once-for-all wholly given at the creation of the first Adam; the redemption-image is gradually fashioned. (2) The creation-image is conferred in some respect upon the whole human race; the redemption-image only upon the redeemed. (3) The creation-image distinguishes man from the animals; the redemption-image distinguishes the regenerate family of faith from unregenerate mankind.[22]

The term "image" *(tselem)* is consistently used elsewhere in the Old Testament in the sense of "visible representation of." An image represents the reality behind it.[23] It is a common term for the idols of the heathen (Num. 33:52; 1 Sam. 6:5, 11; 2 Kings 11:18), and is used repeatedly in Daniel 2—3 both for the figure Nebuchadnezzar saw in his vision and the one he erected to be worshipped by the people. The Hebrew term for "likeness" *(demuth)* is virtually a synonym for "image" but carries with it more of the suggestion of resemblance, whereas *tselem* more nearly connotes representation.

"Man is 'theomorphic,' like God, rather than God 'anthropomorphic,' like man. Mankind was made like God to exercise his authority over all created beings."[24] This involves human awareness of God as One demanding the complete surrender of life—a special relatedness to God that consists in a capacity to respond to the divine.[25]

B. Implications of the Divine Image

Two additional if paradoxical ideas follow from the biblical understanding of the image of God.

---

21. Carl F. H. Henry, "Man," *Baker's Dictionary of Theology*, p. 338.

22. *Ibid.*, p. 340.

23. Jacob, *Theology of the OT*, pp. 169-71.

24. J. N. Schofield, *Introducing Old Testament Theology* (Naperville, Ill.: SCM Book Club, 1964), p. 29.

25. Cf. Emil Brunner, "The Christian Understanding of Man," *The Christian Understanding of Man*, vol. 2 of the Report of the Oxford Conference on Church, Community, and State (London: George Allen and Unwin, Ltd., 1938), pp. 141-78.

1. God and man are not identical; nor, on the other hand, are God and man wholly other. C. Ryder Smith points out:

> There can be no fellowship between two persons who are altogether alike—nor between two who are altogether unlike. Indeed, both concepts are artificial, for every man is in some ways like every other and in some unlike all others. It is from this human analogy that we may best begin to understand the fellowship of God with man. Between them there is the difference between the infinite and the finite—in power, wisdom, holiness, love, and so on—and therefore there is between them a gulf beside which the difference between the sun and a grain of sand is small. The sentence, 'Ye shall be holy, for I the Lord your God am holy' (Lv. 19:2), is very far from meaning 'Ye shall be *as holy* as the Lord your God.' On the other hand, God is no 'wholly other', in the sense of 'wholly different', or man could not know Him at all. There are likenesses between man and God, even as there are likenesses between the sun and a sand-grain. There is an example in the text: 'With the merciful thou wilt show thyself merciful; with the perfect man thou wilt show thyself perfect; with the pure thou wilt show thyself pure' (Ps. 18:25 f).[26]

On the same point, Archbishop William Temple earlier wrote:

> In so far as God and man are spiritual they are of one kind; in so far as God and man are rational, they are of one kind. But in so far as God creates, redeems and sanctifies while man is created, redeemed and sanctified, they are of two kinds. God is not creature; man is not creator. God is not redeemed sinner; man is not redeemer from sin. At this point the Otherness is complete.[27]

2. Man therefore can never be submerged in nature. The image of God forever distinguishes him from lower orders of life. He stands uniquely before God, addressed as "thou" (Gen. 3:9, KJV). While the Old Testament does not weigh problems of freedom and determinism as such, it everywhere assumes that man can choose even to the extent of choosing between God and the gods (Josh. 24:15).[28]

Along with the question "What is man?" the Old Testament is concerned with the question "What is good?" (Mic. 6:8). The psychological interest is overshadowed by the more comprehensive ethical concern. To the question, "What ought a man to be?" the biblical writers answer, "A man is what he ought to be when he does what the Lord commands him to do."[29]

---

26. *Bible Doctrine of Man*, pp. 36-37.

27. *Nature, Man, and God*, p. 396; cf. H. H. Rowley, *The Faith of Israel: Aspects of Old Testament Thought* (Philadelphia: The Westminster Press, 1956), pp. 83-84; Vriezen, *Outline of OT Theology*, p. 147; and Eichrodt, *Man in the OT*, pp. 29-30.

28. Eichrodt, *Man in the OT*, pp. 29-30.

29. Smith, *Bible Doctrine of Man*, p. 31.

4

The Origin of Sin

The great drama of the Fall is played out in Genesis 3. It is beyond all question one of the key passages in the entire Bible. Genesis 3 is "one of the most profound understandings of the human predicament ever penned."[1] After God and man, sin becomes the third major theme of the Scriptures.

Theologically, the doctrine of sin holds a crucial place. As Richard S. Taylor has shown in *A Right Conception of Sin*, the whole tenor of a theological system is revealed in its understanding of the nature of sin. Ryder Smith writes:

> Historically, there have been two chief definitions of (sin) . . . and, though there may not seem at first to be much difference between them, it is in fact so great as almost to demand two different theologies. One school of theologians has defined sin as "anything contrary to the will of God," while another has preferred to say, "anything contrary to the *known* will of God." The second school has gone on to emphasize the element of choice or will.[2]

Although the Old Testament does not formally define sin, the weight of its evidence is rather decisively toward the concept that sin is "anything contrary to the *known* will of God."

---

1. Arnold B. Rhodes, "The Message of the Bible," introduction to *The Layman's Bible Commentary*, Balmer H. Kelly, ed. (Richmond, Va.: John Knox Press, 1959), 1:76-77.

2. *The Bible Doctrine of Salvation* (London: The Epworth Press, 1941), pp. 2-3. It is one of the values of Smith's complete study in the companion volume, *The Bible Doctrine of Sin*, p. 2 and throughout, that he so conclusively shows the latter, or ethical, concept of sin to be the definitive Bible concept in both the Old and New Testaments.

I. Sin as Intrusion

Genesis 1—3 makes it clear that sin was not inherent in human nature as it issued from the hand of God. Sin in both deed and disposition is an intrusion in the life of man. Adam and Eve were part of the creation on which God placed His seal of approval: "And God saw everything that he had made, and, behold, it was very good" (Gen. 1:31). "The Old Testament speaks of man as a sinner, not because he is of human kind, but because he has rebelled against his God."[3] Sinfulness is a fact of man's condition, not of his nature as man.

This truth is dramatized both by Adam's gesture in hiding from the Lord after his act of sin in eating forbidden fruit (Gen. 3:8) and by his expulsion from the Garden (3:23-24). "Sin is the violation of covenant and rebellion against God's personal Lordship. It is more than an aberration or a failure which added knowledge can correct. It is a violation of relationship, a betrayal of trust."[4]

Nor may sin be equated with finiteness. The proposition "All sinners are finite beings" cannot be turned into the proposition "All finite beings are sinful." As Jacob notes: "What may be termed the finitude of man is distinct from his guilt, even though it prepared ground favourable for guilt. Finitude is based on the difference between God and man in the order of creation, while guilt consists in the antithesis between holiness and sin."[5]

Created in righteousness, conformed to God's purpose, holy and good, Adam and Eve lived in harmony with both God and nature in the Garden of Eden. This was a condition which might have extended to the entire realm of nature had sin not entered the earthly scene. Nature itself became subject to a curse at the time of the Fall. An environment favorable to the moral development of man in rebellion against God was obviously quite different from the kind of environment possible for man in harmony with God. Later Old Testament passages (Isa. 11:1-9; 35:1-2, etc.) and the New Testament (Acts 3:20-21; Rom. 8:19-23; 2 Pet. 3:13) speak of the restoration of nature as part of God's final redemption.

Immortality in the sense of deathless existence is implied as a possibility in the unfallen state of Adam and Eve. Sin and human

---

3. Jacob, *Theology of the OT*, p. 283.
4. Wright, *Book of the Acts of God*, p. 94.
5. *Theology of the OT*, p. 283 fn.

death are related as cause and consequence. The presence of "the tree of life" in the Garden and man's exclusion from access to it after his sin (Gen. 3:22-24) appear to relate to some provision in Eden for life without end. As Arnold Rhodes wrote: "Genesis 3 makes it clear that there is a connection between sin and death (compare Ezek. 18; Pss. 41, 107). Death, as man experiences it, is what it is because man has sinned. 'The sting of death is sin' (1 Cor. 15:56). Death in its deepest dimension is not the opposite of biological life but of eternal life (Eph. 2:1, 5; Col. 2:13; Rev. 3:1)."[6]

Nor was sin necessary for man's moral selfhood. To be created in the image of God was to have the capacity for self-direction or choice. Such freedom of choice was essential to the development of moral character, whether good or evil. The capacity to love God implies the capacity to resist or reject love. Sin is in no sense necessary for moral character, but choice is; and choice always implies the possibility of sin.[7] Jacob wrote:

> In the Garden of Eden, man could normally have listened and should have listened to the voice of Yahweh, whose prohibition against the eating of one tree was a very little thing in comparison with the pleasures that were granted, and the serpent's temptation, despite its seductive power, was not unavoidable. Sin is presented as a rebellion: finding it unbearable to be content with much when he thought it possible for him to grasp everything, man rebelled against his divine partner in order to seize, as his booty, the gift that had been withheld.[8]

II. THE FALL

Two elements appear in the first sin.

A. An Objective Law

One was the prior establishment and knowledge of an objective law involving a specific commandment. The form of the commandment was negative. Rather than being a limitation, this had the effect of releasing action and initiative in every area except the one forbidden. The placing of one tree "off limits" made all the rest of the trees of the Garden legitimate objects for human action. "You may freely eat of every tree of the garden; but of the tree of the knowledge of good

---

6. "Message of the Bible," pp. 76-77.
7. Cf. Schultz, *OT Theology,* 2:303; Rowley, *Faith of Israel,* pp. 88-89.
8. *Theology of the OT,* pp. 282-83.

and evil you shall not eat, for in the day that you eat of it you shall die" (Gen. 2:16-17).

Obedience to the commandment was both reasonable and possible. The Old Testament knows nothing of sin as man's failure to conform to a perfect standard of righteousness beyond his capacity. Acts of sin arise in the freedom of the human will. "God forbids sin. Hence it can never be explained as due to His will. God punishes it. Hence it can never claim to have been decreed by Him."[9] H. H. Rowley wrote:

> When man listens to the seductive voices that call him away from God, his act is essentially his own. But the fundamental character of sin is seen in that it comes between a man and God, and isolates him from his Maker. In the profoundly penetrating story of the Garden of Eden this is well brought out. After his act of disobedience Adam hid himself from the face of God. Before God drove him forth from the garden he had thus withdrawn himself from God and was conscious of a barrier which was not of God's creation, but his own.[10]

B. The Nature of Temptation

The second element in man's first sin was the presence in the Garden of the serpent *(nahash)* who was no mere animal but an incarnation of Satan. The Apostle Paul wrote: "But I am afraid that as the serpent deceived Eve by his cunning, your thoughts will be led astray from a sincere and pure devotion to Christ. . . . And no wonder, for even Satan disguises himself as an angel of light" (2 Cor. 11:3, 14). There is a clear reference to the deception of Adam and Eve in the Garden in Rev. 12:9, "And the great dragon was thrown down, that ancient serpent, who is called the Devil and Satan, the deceiver of the whole world" (cf. also John 8:44).[11] The Bible is silent at the point of the origin of Satan ("the adversary") and of moral evil in the universe. But the sin in the Garden was obviously not the first act of rebellion against God by a finite creature.

The method of the adversary with Eve was to insinuate doubt into her mind. When Eve reported the Lord's direction, "You shall not eat of the fruit of the tree which is in the midst of the garden, neither shall you touch it, lest you die," the serpent said, "You will not die" (Gen. 3:2-4). There was also an appeal to the curiosity that is

---

9. Schultz, *ibid.*
10. *Faith of Israel,* pp. 88-89.
11. Cf. Gelin, *Key Concepts of the OT,* p. 88.

a legitimate part of human nature, the thirst for knowledge. Finally, the woman was told that if she would eat, she and her husband would be "as gods"—or, as the Hebrew may properly be translated, "as God" (Gen. 3:5)—equal to and therefore independent of God.

The record of the Fall makes it clear that a sinless heart may be tempted and may yield to that temptation. The possibility of heart purity in the Christian life is sometimes rejected on the argument that if there were no evil within, temptation would have nothing to take hold of. Since all are liable to temptation and capable of transgression, it is argued that therefore no person in this life can be free from inner sin despite New Testament affirmations of such redemptive cleansing (Matt. 5:8; Acts 15:8-9; 1 John 1:7).

But Adam and Eve were without inner sin before their transgression. Temptation came through the presentation of an object that was "good for food, and . . . a delight to the eyes, and . . . to be desired to make one wise" (Gen. 3:6). Eve and later Adam gave the consent of their wills to a desire not in itself sinful but the satisfaction of which involved disobedience to a specific command. Sin can and does originate in the assent of the will to satisfaction of a natural desire in a way or under conditions contrary to God's commandment (Jas. 1:14-16).

III. Sin as Action

Biblical references to sin are in general of two sorts. Sin is a matter of man's condition, his moral state. It is also a matter of his action, what he does. Although the Old Testament does not formally define sin as deed or action, its varied terminology and its descriptions of moral evil make the nature of such sin apparent. Acts of sin are in essence violations of the law of God.[12] "The main root of sin is unbelief, which sees in the gift of God's love an unfriendly limitation,"[13] and therefore the sinner acts in rebellion against the recognized will of God.

Sin puts at the center of life a man's own self-seeking will in place of God's self-giving will. As Ryder Smith notes, "The ultimate definition of 'sin' in the Old Testament is *ethical*, and . . . this definition obtains throughout the New. This definition of 'sin', however, is a *resultant* of the definition of 'righteousness'. If 'righteousness' is

---

12. Cf. Schultz, *OT Theology*, 2:292-304.
13. *Ibid.*, p. 305.

wholly ethical, then, *ipso facto,* so is 'sin'. The two definitions go as inevitably together as the concave and convex of a curve."[14] We shall take up this matter more extensively in Chapter 7, "Deepening Concepts of Sin."

Reference to "sins of ignorance" in Lev. 4:2; 5:14-17; 22:14; and Num. 15:27-29 do not void the general conclusion that sin for the Old Testament as well as the New involves an ethical element of knowledge and volition. The context of the phrase "sin of ignorance" chiefly concerns the ritual law. Where it does not, as Eichrodt points out, such offences as disclaiming knowledge of trust money, perjury, and extortion "can hardly be regarded as unintentional sins or sins of inadvertence."[15]

For this reason, Eichrodt argues,

> It may be that the meaning customarily ascribed to the term *bisgaga,* 'unwittingly', ought to be abandoned for the more general sense 'in human frailty', reserving the opposite phrase *beyad rama,* 'with a high hand', not so much for deliberate offences as for open apostasy and impenitent contempt for the Law. The difference between the two kinds could be tested by the person's willingness to confess his sin and his effort to make reparation.[16]

IV. Sinfulness as Racial

The fact of sinfulness as a state or condition, as well as the fact of sinning as an act or deed, finds expression in the early chapters of Genesis. "Racial sinfulness," "inbred or original sin," and "depravity" are all names given to the same reality in human experience. It is traced to what is subtly but effectively described as the fact that while Adam was created in the image of God (5:1), Adam himself "became the father of a son in his own likeness, after his image" (5:3). The image in which Adam begat his children was still the image of God but that image "deprived" of its created harmony with the Divine and therefore "depraved"—marred, defaced, broken, sullied, soiled, or tarnished.

---

14. Smith, *Bible Doctrine of Sin,* p. 2.
15. *Theology of the OT,* 1:161 fn.
16. *Ibid.*

"Sin is seeking to be one's own God, and at the same time it is a family affair; through sin all of life is cursed."[17] Although it is a debated question among Old Testament theologians,[18] A. B. Davidson stated the case clearly:

> The further conclusions to which the passages of the Old Testament lead us are these: first, that what is specifically called *original sin* is taught there very distinctly, i.e., "That corruption of man's whole nature which is commonly called original sin," and that it is also taught that this sin is inherited; *second,* that no explanation is given in the Old Testament of the rationale of this inherited corruption beyond the assumption that the race is a unity, and each member of the race is sinful because the race is sinful.[19]

The effect of such racial sin is vividly described in two key passages: "The Lord saw that the wickedness of man was great in the earth, and that every imagination of the thoughts of his heart was only evil continually" (Gen. 6:5); and "For the imagination of man's heart is evil from his youth" (Gen. 8:21). The term translated "youth" is *nourah*—from *na'ar,* used of children from infancy to adolescence and variously translated "babe, boy, child, damsel, lad, servant, young man." It is used in Exod. 2:6 of the infant Moses and of Samuel before he was presented to Eli in the Tabernacle (1 Sam. 1:22).

Men are not only individually sinners; they are collectively sinful in the light of their corporate sharing in the human race. Of Gen. 6:5, Vriezen says, "We see how sin poisons the human heart. . . . A more emphatic statement of the wickedness of the human heart is hardly conceivable. This is emphasized once more because in 8:21 the same judgment is pronounced on humanity after the Flood."[20]

The term "imagination" as here used means more than "fancy, dream, idea" or even "thought." The Hebrew term *yetser* is derived from a verb that means "to press, squeeze, mould, determine." It is

---

17. Rhodes, "Message of the Bible," p. 77.
18. Cf. Smith, *Bible Doctrine of Sin,* pp. 37 ff.; and Vriezen, *Outline of OT Theology,* p. 211.
19. *Theology of the OT,* p. 225. The sharp contradiction between Smith and Vriezen on the one hand and Davidson on the other may be explained to some extent. Smith and Vriezen look for a doctrine of original sin in the Old Testament and do not find it. Davidson looks for the evidence on which such a doctrine may legitimately be based, and finds it in abundance. It comes close to the matter to say that a doctrine of original sin is assumed by Old Testament writers although not explicitly stated.
20. *Outline of OT Theology,* p. 210.

used in the sense of purpose, propensity, tendency, direction, movement, motivation (observe the usage in Deut. 31:21; 1 Chron. 28:9;
Isa. 29:16 [KJV, "framed"], and in Ps. 103:14, "frame," or Hab. 2:18
"maker"). *Ha ra-yetser* ("the evil tendency") became the rabbinical
expression for original sin.

V. Racial Sin as Privative

Girdlestone points out that even where specific terms for original or
racial sin are not used, the writers of the Old Testament recognize

> that human nature, in its personal and social aspects, is distorted
> and out of course; that the chain of love which ought to bind the
> great family in one has been snapped asunder; that isolation and
> desolation have taken the place of unity and happiness; that the
> relationship between man and his Maker has become obscured,
> and that even when man knows the will of God, there is some-
> thing in his nature which prompts him to rebel against it; . . . and
> that this state of things is not original, but is opposed to men's
> best instincts, and frustrates the original design of their creation.[21]

While the Old Testament is by no means explicit as to the
exact nature of this "distortion," its evidence inclines in the direction
of privative, relational, and dynamic categories. Original sin is the
human self corrupted, diseased, fevered, or warped—a condition
brought about by alienation from God. "Deprivity" in respect to the
initial conditioning of man's nature toward fellowship with and
obedience to God becomes depravity in which the human psyche is
conditioned toward self-regarding and God-denying action. The fact
is clearly stated. The how and why are not. The Bible is always less
concerned with the disease than with the remedy.

It is the estrangement of our humanity from its spiritual life
that is both the cause and the essential constituent of man's moral
disorder. Not until divine grace cleanses the corruption, heals the
disease, reduces the fever, and straightens the crookedness is death
replaced by life, darkness by light, spiritual poverty by plenty, and
sickness of the soul by moral health.

The Old Testament regards man's sinfulness as a positive evil.
But it is a positive evil that befalls him by reason of what has been
lost. In the metaphor of the Vine and the branches, the corruption
and death of the severed branch is a real and positive evil (John

21. *Synonyms of the OT,* p. 76.

15:1-6). But the real and positive evil comes by being cut off from the Vine and its life.

Depravity, original sin, inbred sin, or carnality—by whatever name the fact may be described—is best defined not as a thing, an entity or quantity having ontic status, but as the moral condition of a personal being. It is caused by estrangement, severance, alienation, "deprivity," or loss. It is manifested in attitudes, dispositions, tendencies, or propensities—in psychological terminology, a state of readiness or conditioning. Speaking, like Paul, after the manner of men (Rom. 6:19; 1 Cor. 15:32; Gal. 3:15), one may say that original sin is more like disease, poverty, blindness, darkness, or the corruption of a severed branch than it is like a root, a cancer, or a decayed tooth.

There is no speculation in the Old Testament as to the "mode" by which the universal infection of sinfulness is passed from one generation to another. The fact was observed; its explanation was not attempted. The comment that the image Adam passed on to his descendents was in some sense "his image" (Gen. 5:3) as well as the image of God (Gen. 9:6) would suggest a "genetic" view. In this, as in much else in biblical theology, the facts are more explicit than their explanations.

5

Covenant and Cult

Just as the ideas of God, man, and sin appear early in the Sacred Record, so the idea of salvation makes its appearance early. The record of the Fall itself is not without a note of redemption. In what has come to be called the *protevangelium,* there is a glimpse of redemption and its cost. The language is both restrained and precise: "I will put enmity between you [the serpent] and the woman, and between your seed and her seed; he shall bruise [trample, crush—Rom. 16:20] your head, and you shall bruise his heel" (Gen. 3:15).

The prediction is not about the seed of Adam but "the seed of the woman"—a hint of the virgin birth of Jesus, an idea picked up again in Gal. 4:4. He will crush the serpent's head and do it at the cost of injury to himself (Isa. 53:4). E. F. Kevan wrote:

> There is a natural suggestiveness in the figure used here. The serpent kills by striking the heel of man, but man destroys the serpent by crushing its head. . . . Note the transition from the serpent's 'seed' to the serpent himself, and also the fact that the 'seed' of the woman is in the singular. Only in Christ, 'the seed of the woman', could this victory be accomplished (see 1 John iii.8), and from this it was to become true for mankind in Him (Rom. 16:20; I Cor. 15:57).[1]

As we have seen, a unifying theme in the Bible has been sought in different directions. The covenant, the doctrine of God, the Kingdom, Christology, and other themes have had their advocates. All these themes are basic and important. Overshadowing all others, however, is the concept of salvation. The Bible is the Book about

---

1. "Genesis," *The New Bible Commentary,* ed. F. Davidson, A. M. Stibbs, and E. F. Kevan (Grand Rapids, Mich.: William B. Eerdmans Publishing Co., 1956), p. 80.

salvation. God is the "God of salvation." Christ was given the human name *Jesus* from *Yeshua* or *Yehoshuah,* "salvation" or "The Lord our salvation."

Bible history is the history of salvation. The sacrificial altar of the Old Testament with its fulfillment in the New Testament on a cross outside the city wall is the means of salvation. The Spirit of God, the Holy Spirit, is the Agent of salvation. Heaven is the final end of salvation as hell is the rejection of salvation. Without denying or obscuring the variety of themes and emphases throughout the Scriptures, we should keep in mind the overarching and all-pervasive idea of salvation.

I. PREPARATION FOR THE COVENANT

The note of redemption or salvation becomes most prominent in the idea of covenant. All God's covenants are covenants of salvation.

A. The Covenant with Noah

The term "covenant" *(berith)* first occurs in God's dealings with Noah on the eve of the Flood: "But I will establish my covenant with you; and you shall come into the ark, you, your sons, your wife, and your sons' wives with you" (Gen. 6:18). It is repeated again as the waters recede from the earth: "Behold, I establish my covenant with you and your descendants after you, and with every living creature that is with you, the birds, the cattle, and every beast of the earth with you, as many as came out of the ark" (Gen. 9:9-10). This is to be "the everlasting covenant between God and every living creature of all flesh that is upon the earth" (v. 16).

The covenant with Noah is sometimes identified as a "covenant with the human race." Its terms were simple but comprehensive. To man was given the duty to replenish and govern the earth. All animals were to be available for food with the exception that the blood should not be eaten with the flesh. Murder was forbidden on the basis of the "image" of God in man (Gen. 9:2-7). On His part, God promised never again to destroy the earth with a flood. In token of this He set the rainbow in the sky (cf. also Gen. 8:22). "The last word does not lie with the waters of the Flood, but with the Rainbow of promise."[2]

---

2. Knight, *Christian Theology of the OT,* p. 142. Cf. Lehman, *Biblical Theology,* 1:77-79.

B. The Covenant with Abraham

A second milestone in the developing concept of covenant came in the call of and covenant with Abram of Ur. Here the covenant begins to take on specific form and the idea of election comes to the fore.

Genesis 12 marks a transition from an account of the general history of mankind to the story of a single tribe and nation. The sons of Shem, known as the Semitic people, migrated to the plains of Babylonia and settled near the mouth of the Euphrates at Ur. Extensive archaeological diggings have uncovered an ancient and advanced civilization there.

Another migration is described. Its reason is not explained in the Scriptures, but tradition relates it to the worship of one true God as opposed to the prevailing polytheism of Ur. The Semite Terah, his son Abram, his grandson Lot, and Abram's wife Sarai travelled west to Aram (later Assyria and modern Turkey) on the way to the land of Canaan (Gen. 11:31). For some reason not explained, they settled in Haran (named after a deceased son of Terah), where Terah later died. Here the Lord said to Abram, "Go from your country and your kindred and your father's house to the land that I will show you" (Gen. 12:1).

The covenant made at that time with Abram was conditioned on his obedient response to the call to "go out under the stars." It included the promise of numerous posterity, a great name, blessing to those who would bless him, and a curse upon those who would curse him. Most important of all was the promise, "I will bless you . . . that you will be a blessing . . . and by you all the families of the earth shall bless themselves" (Gen. 12:2-3). L. R. Ringenberg notes: "The covenant was as simple but as comprehensive as the redemptive purpose of God for the nations. It consisted of a command and a promise. The command was twofold. He must leave home. He must go where God led. The promise was threefold. God would make of him a nation; he would give him a land; and he would bless him and make him a blessing to all families of the earth."[3]

C. Melchizedek

A raid of marauding sheiks on Sodom and Gomorrah and the cities of the lower Jordan plain (Genesis 14) brought Abram into contact with an otherwise unknown priest-king by the name of Melchizedek. He is described as "the priest of God Most High" (v. 18)—a designa-

---

3. *The Word of God in History* (Butler, Ind.: The Higley Press, 1953), p. 48.

tion for the true God used most frequently by those outside the covenant line that began with Abram (cf. Num. 24:16; Dan. 3:26). This is the first time the term "priest" occurs in the Scriptures, and as E. F. Kevan notes, "The biblical conception of the priesthood cannot be properly grasped if this singular fact is ignored."[4]

D. Election and the Covenant

The importance of the covenant with Abram is further explained in Genesis 15. G. Ernest Wright commented that this covenant becomes the central meaning of the Abraham story, and all that follows is understood as the fulfillment of this promise.[5]

The concept of election is included in the covenant. A particular line of Abram's descendents became a chosen people. They were chosen not to privilege alone but to responsibility as well. Election did come to be understood in a very exclusive sense in later Judaism. But its purpose was inclusive, not exclusive. It was through the descendents of Abraham, and particularly One, that blessing was to come to all men. In order for divine love to be shown to all, it must be revealed first to some. An idea must take root somewhere in particular before it can be reproduced everywhere. Rather than God's elective love for Israel (Deut. 7:6-8) meaning that He did not love all, it meant the very opposite. God showed His love to Israel that Israel in turn might make it known to all men. It was God's plan that "all families of the earth be blessed" (Gen. 12:3, mg.).[6]

Wright noted further that the covenant with Abram was one of promise and looked forward to its fulfillment. This fulfillment came partly in and through the nation Israel. "Yet at the end of the Old Testament the chosen nation was still looking forward to the completion of the promise. The Christian Church understood that only in Christ was the covenant fulfilled. He is the fullness of Israel and the fulfillment of God's promises to his people."[7]

E. The Angel of the Lord

In God's dealings with Abraham (to which Abram's name was changed—Gen. 17:5) and his family, the "angel of the Lord" first appears (Gen. 16:7; Gen. 18). E. F. Kevan writes:

4. *NBC*, p. 89.
5. *Book of the Acts of God*, p. 72.
6. Donald G. Miller, *The People of God* (Naperville, Ill.: SCM Book Club, 1959), p. 46.
7. *Book of the Acts of God*, p. 75.

As in several places He is apparently identified with Jehovah, a number of questions arise. Is He just one of the created angels? But the angel speaks in the first person interchangeably with Jehovah. Is He a direct theophany? But this does not do justice to the distinction which is made between Jehovah and the angel. Is He a self-distinction of Jehovah? This is to regard the revelation through the angel as pointing to a real distinction in the nature of God such as is found in the New Testament 'Logos' or 'Son'. So long as we avoid reading back the New Testament into the conceptions of the Old, we are justified in the light of the New Testament in seeing some hint and recognition of a richness within the unity of the Godhead. With the revelation of God in Christ before us, we may regard the angel as the Second Person of the Holy Trinity.[8]

F. Circumcision

At least passing reference should be made to circumcision, appearing first as a sign of God's covenant with Abraham (Gen. 17:11). The rite was commanded for all the males of Abraham's progeny (vv. 12-14; Exod. 4:24 ff.; Josh. 5:2 ff.). Even in the Old Testament, circumcision begins to take on deeper meaning than the physical fact itself. It is to be the symbol of an internal change (Deut. 10:16; 30:6). Its larger meaning in the Bible is summarized by Eric Sauer:

> Circumcision is indeed no *means* to justification (Rom. 4:9-12) or sanctification (Gal. 5:2-12), but it is nevertheless a *symbol* or more exactly a *type,* of sanctification, and more especially of the principle of the surrender of the sinful self-nature unto death, the "cutting off" of the God-estranged life and all its impulses. Therefore the "circumcision not made with hands" is "the putting off of the body of the flesh," that is, being crucified and dead together with Christ (Col. 2:11, comp. Rom. 6:2-4).[9]

G. Abraham's Descendents

While it is in the Exodus and the giving of the Law on Mount Sinai that the covenant finds its definitive statement, some of the implications of election are worked out in concrete historical situations in the lives of Isaac, Jacob, and Joseph. The nature of election finds illustration in the choice of Isaac over Ishmael and Abraham's other sons, and in the selection of Jacob instead of Esau (Genesis 25).

8. *NBC,* p. 90; cf. also Oehler, *Theology of the OT,* pp. 129-34; and Everett F. Harrison, *A Short Life of Christ* (Grand Rapids, Mich.: William B. Eerdmans Publishing Co., 1968), pp. 34-35.

9. *Dawn of World Redemption,* p. 105.

Something of the duality in man's experience of God seen in conversion and entire sanctification in the New Testament finds illustration in the life of Jacob (Gen. 28:10-22 in comparison with 32:24-30)—as it had in the life of his grandfather before him (Gen. 12:1-5 in connection with 17:1-8). The nature and scope of divine providence is illustrated in the stirring events of the life of Joseph (Genesis 37; 39—47). The meaning of it all begins to take shape in God's mighty acts in Egypt, at the Red Sea, and on Sinai.

II. THE EXODUS

Genesis, the book of beginnings, is followed by what may properly be called "the book of redemption." Exodus tells how God not only brought His people out of bondage in Egypt, but also how He brought them into a special covenant relationship with himself in which they became His purchased possession, His "peculiar people," His "own possession among all peoples" (Exod. 19:5).

A. The Key Importance of the Exodus

The Exodus (Greek, "going out") from Egypt was more than just a momentous event in history. It became the living center of Israel's faith. Over and over, the Lord is identified as "your God, who brought you out of the land of Egypt, out of the house of bondage" (Exod. 20:2; 29:46; Lev. 11:45, etc.). G. Ernest Wright says:

> At the center of Israel's faith was this supreme act of divine love and grace. The very existence of the nation was due solely to this miraculous happening. In confessions of faith it is the central affirmation. (Note such confessions in Deuteronomy 6:20-25; 26:5-10.) Who is God? For Israel it was unnecessary to elaborate abstract terms and phrases as we do in our confessions. It was only necessary to say that he is the "God, who brought thee out of the land of Egypt, out of the house of bondage" (Exodus 20:2). What more was needed to identify or to describe God than that? His complete control over nature and man is adequately implied in the statement; his purposive action in history in fighting the injustice of the strong and making even their sin to serve and praise him is also directly implied; so also is his redemptive love, which saves and uses the weak of the world to accomplish his purpose even among the strong.[10]

---

10. *Book of the Acts of God,* p. 77.

It is with good reason that H. H. Rowley sees in the story of the Exodus an Old Testament prefiguring of the death and resurrection of Christ and regards it as the central point in the unity of the Bible.[11]

B. The Book of Redemption

The Book of Exodus is therefore the book of redemption (6:6; 15:13). "To redeem" (Heb., *gaal,* translated "to deliver," "to ransom," "to redeem") is literally "to serve as a kinsman for," as a relative would redeem the property or person of one who could not help himself. It includes in its scope the basic ideas of redemption developed elsewhere in the Scriptures: deliverance from bondage by the personal intervention of the Redeemer, and bringing the redeemed into a special relationship with their Redeemer. The first idea in redemption reaches its culmination in the Passover (Exodus 12). The second underlies the inauguration of the Sinai covenant (Exodus 19).

The New Testament uses "Exodus language" throughout to describe the saving work of Christ. In Luke 9:31, Jesus is pictured as talking with Moses and Elijah about "his departure [Greek, *exodus*], which He was to accomplish at Jerusalem." Both Jesus and Paul spoke of the atonement as Christ's passover (Luke 22:15, "passover" from *pascha,* "suffer" from *paschō;* 1 Cor. 5:7). John 19:36 applies a Passover requirement to the death of Christ: "You shall not break a bone of it" (Exod. 12:46). The Christian life is viewed in the light of the deliverance at the Red Sea (1 Cor. 10:1-13). Jesus was the "prophet . . . like" Moses (Deut. 18:15-19). He was the "new Moses" who gave His people a new law from a new mount, and who used the very term "ransom" (Mark 10:45; cf. Exod. 6:6; 15:13) to describe His mission.

Gabriel Hebert wrote:

> The Second Exodus as it was fulfilled in Jesus Christ was not at all a political deliverance, but rather the deliverance of a redeemed People of the Lord from the true enemy of man, the Evil One and all his hosts, into the liberty of the children of God: a liberty which is to be enjoyed already in the Church of the New Covenant, but which is to be fully perfected only in the Life of the World to Come.[12]

---

11. *Unity of the Bible, passim.*
12. *When Israel Came out of Egypt* (Naperville, Ill.: SCM Book Club, 1961), pp. 116-17.

III. THE MEANING OF THE SINAI COVENANT

The scope of the redemption accomplished at the Exodus is spelled out in the covenant given at Sinai. The term for "covenant" *(berith)* is of uncertain derivation. It comes either from an Assyrian root *baru* which means "to bind" and therefore stands for a bond or obligation,[13] or from the verb "to cut," since it was common to speak of "cutting" a covenant.[14] In any case, it means "a solemn agreement made between two parties who stand previously unrelated; in which certain mutual obligations are undertaken, for the sake of certain benefits, generally mutual, which are to ensue from the connection."[15] It was an agreement entered with solemn ceremonies of sacrifice.

Old Testament scholars have noted striking resemblances between the Sinai covenant and the treaties of the ancient world between an emperor and the lesser kings who were bound to him. The form of these "suzerain" treaties identified the "great king"; detailed the historical background in the relations between the great king and his vassals, emphasizing the benevolent disposition of the great king; set forth the obligations of the vassal, always including exclusive loyalty to the emperor; stipulated that the document be deposited in the sanctuary of the vassal and that it be publicly read at regular intervals; and set forth the rewards or punishment which would attend the keeping or violation of the covenant. All of these elements may be seen in the covenant God made with His people (cf. Exod. 20:1-2; Josh. 24:2-13; Exod. 34:13; Deut. 31:9-13; Josh. 24: 26; Exod. 23:20-33; Leviticus 26; Deuteronomy 27—28; Josh. 8:34 —read in this order).[16]

The importance of the covenant is seen in the fact that it is made the basis of salvation in both the Old Testament and the New. Ryder Smith wrote: "The ruling idea of the Old Testament is the idea of Covenant. The term is found in the documents of all periods, but even where the term is absent the idea is present. Apart from one or two such small books as the Song of Songs, it is the presupposition of every book in the Old Testament. Without this idea, no Hebrew

---

13. Burney, *Outlines of OT Theology,* p. 49.
14. Davidson, *Theology of the OT,* pp. 238-42.
15. Burney, *Outlines of OT Theology, loc. cit.*
16. Cf. George Mendenhall, *Law and Covenant in Israel and the Ancient Near East;* quoted by Wright, *Biblical Archaeology,* pp. 56-57; and *Book of the Acts of God,* pp. 89-91.

story would have a *motif,* no Hebrew prophet a message, no Hebrew psalmist a plea."[17]

The covenant, however, was not merely a legal contract or a commercial transaction with profit as its motive. It was more analogous to marriage in two important particulars: it was the result of God's choice, His initiative; and it was based upon love, trust, service, and fellowship.[18]

The initiative for the covenant rests with God. "The one responsible for this agreement is always God alone. It is always said that God makes a covenant with somebody, never that God and somebody made a covenant."[19] Yet the response of the people is their own choice. This is declared emphatically (e.g., Josh. 24:14, 21-22).[20] Vriezen noted:

> The Covenant is, therefore, "unilateral", not bilateral in origin; it is a relationship originating with one of the partners, though that does not mean that Israel was not regarded as a partner and that Israel's will could not be appealed to. Israel is expected to obey the rules of the Covenant drawn up by God and by *Him* alone.[21]

IV. THE LAW

The giving of the law was an essential part of the establishment of the covenant. The law was the charter of the covenant. So close is the relationship that "covenant" and "commandments" became interchangeable terms. Moses said to the people of Israel, "And he declared to you his covenant, which he commanded you to perform, that is, the ten commandments; and he wrote them upon two tablets of stone" (Deut. 4:13; cf. 5:1-2). The stone tablets bearing the Ten Commandments were placed in the sacred chest covered with the "mercy seat" and known as "the ark of the covenant" (Num. 10:33; Deut. 31:26; Josh. 4:7; Judg. 20:27, *passim*). 1 Kings 8:9 refers to the commandments as the "covenant [made] with the children of Israel, when they came out of the land of Egypt." To break the commandments was to violate the covenant. To keep the commandments was to maintain the covenant relationship.

---

17. *Bible Doctrine of Salvation,* p. 16.
18. Smith, *loc. cit.*
19. Kohler, *OT Theology,* p. 62.
20. *Ibid.,* p. 68.
21. *Outline of OT Theology,* p. 141; italics in the original.

A. The Nature of "Law"

The making of the covenant and the giving of the law which sealed it was an act of God's loving grace manifest toward His people. The law was never a means of earning the favor of God. It was the means whereby men could show their gratitude for God's favor.

The Hebrew word for law *(torah)* itself meant more than legislation. It meant "instruction, teaching, guidance, counsel," the "word of revelation."[22] The law was God's way of showing His people what was involved in living in a covenant relationship with the Lord. As Donald Miller expressed it, "The commandments were not so much prohibitions as they were statements of what is not done in covenant relations. They give a picture of the way a man would want to live who was in right relation with God."[23]

The law given on Sinai differs in significant ways from other oriental codes, of which several have been discovered and deciphered. The entire law is referred to God as its Author—in contrast, for example, to the Code of Hammurabi in which the entire set of laws from start to finish is said to have been the work of the king. A higher value is placed on human life than on material values. There is no death penalty for offences against property, whereas in the Babylonian law capital punishment was used frequently for crimes involving property.

Gross brutality in punishment was excluded from the Hebrew law. Even the so-called "lex talionis"—"an eye for an eye, and a tooth for a tooth" (cf. Exod. 21:23-25)—was a limitation in the punishment that might be meted out for offences against the persons of others. The punishment could be no more than the damage actually inflicted. There was a heightening of the moral sense in relations between the sexes in the Sinai law.

B. Morality and Religion

The most fundamental difference between Israel's law and the codes of neighboring nations was the direct relation between morality and religion in the biblical law. Moral precepts are given as the commands of God. Walther Eichrodt writes:

> The really remarkable feature of the Decalogue is rather *the definite connection of the moral precepts with the basic religious commands.* It is the expression of a conviction that moral action is inseparably

---

22. *Ibid.*, p. 256.
23. *People of God*, p. 44.

bound up with the worship of God. This means, however, that God whose help man craves regards obedience to the moral standards as equally important with the exclusive worship of himself; and consequently his whole will and purpose is directed to that which is morally good.[24]

The law is the expression of God's claim to lordship. It replaced, for Israel, the many ways of determining the will of the gods that prevailed among Israel's pagan neighbors—astrology, omens, inspection of the livers of sacrificed animals, to mention the more common.[25] Yet the law was not in itself intended or sufficient to cover all the details of life. Legally, biblical commandments would be classed as case laws rather than code laws. Theologically, they were for the most part sets of examples embodying principles rather than narrow specifics. Further, the will of God for His people could be known even when it was not expressed in words. The "heart" is spoken of on occasion as almost equivalent to conscience in the sense of moral intuition. It would "smite" a man for or approve him in specific actions (e.g., 1 Sam. 24:5; 2 Sam. 24:10).[26]

V. The Ceremonial Law

Closely connected with the covenant and the moral law upon which it was based is what has come to be called the "ceremonial law." In the technical use of the term, this is known as the "cult," a prescribed mode of worship.

The underlying ground-plan of the Book of Exodus illustrates the relationship of covenant, law, and worship. Redemption came first in the deliverance from bondage in Egypt (Exodus 1—18). The law followed (cc. 19—23), setting forth the kind of conduct and character befitting those redeemed and brought into a covenant relationship with God. "Then worship was instituted, not only to remind them of redemption, but to aid in securing and maintaining a character worthy of God's saving act (Ex. 24-40). Worship meant the offering of the redeemed soul to God for his service, and the dedication of one's self to the ethical behaviour which the covenant demanded."[27]

---

24. *Theology of the OT,* 1:76-77; italics in the original. Cf. Eichrodt's entire treatment, pp. 74-82.

25. Vriezen, *Outline of OT Theology,* p. 254.

26. Kohler, *OT Theology,* p. 202.

27. Miller, *People of God,* p. 49.

A. Ritual as Symbolism

The ritual and the sacrifices were not in themselves of sacramental value. They were not channels through which grace might be conveyed to individuals or to the nation. They were not designed to gain God's favor. They were an open recognition of the fact that God had already, by His own initiative, extended His mercy and His grace to the people. The sacrifices and offerings themselves were not something man gave to God. They were the return to God of what He had first given to man. They were, in purpose and intent, the response of obedient faith to divine grace.[28]

Many in Israel undoubtedly considered the sacrifices themselves to have a sort of magical efficacy. Outside Israel such a concept was virtually universal. But the law itself, as well as the prophets later, continually challenged the idea that formal acts of sacrifice had intrinsic merit.

Along with sacrifice, the law demanded the confession of sin and humble penitence of spirit. Where the sin was against another and was of such sort that restitution could be made, payment was required. In the ritual of the Day of Atonement, confession as well as sacrifice was to be made (Lev. 16:21). In a summary statement, Ryder Smith said, "The intelligent Jew, therefore, thought that, whenever in any sacrifice (cf. Leviticus 1:4), the blood was offered, it symbolized both the fact of the Covenant, the truth that he had broken it, and the further truth that, as he now came to God with a penitent heart and in His appointed way, the covenant was renewed and was valid for him."[29]

B. The Purpose of Sacrifice

Schultz finds a threefold basis for the ritual and sacrifices established in connection with the covenant. A fourth may be added.[30]

1. The first purpose was to teach the holiness of God. The priesthood and the laws of sacrifice were a perpetual reminder that the service of God requires holiness in the sense of freedom from defilement.[31] Similarly, W. H. Griffith Thomas wrote, "The keynote of the

---

28. *Ibid.*, pp. 84-85.
29. *Bible Doctrine of Salvation*, pp. 78-79; cf. Rowley, *Faith of Israel*, p. 95.
30. *OT Theology*, 2:65-68.
31. Cf. Davidson, *Theology of the OT*, pp. 306-11.

book (of Leviticus) is 'holiness,' in its primary meaning of Separation, which includes separation *from* evil and separation *to* God."[32]

This positive spiritual value was stressed by Vriezen:

> In Israel the cult exists in order to *maintain and purify the communion between God and man* (for fundamentally the relation between God and man is good): *the cult exists as a means to integrate the communion between God and man which God has instituted in His Covenant, in other words, the cult exists for the sake of the atonement* (this word taken in the general sense of "reconciliation"). . . . *Israel's God does not demand a cult from which He could reap benefit, but on the contrary He gives His people a cult that enables them to maintain communion with Him by means of the atonement* (Lev. xvii.11). In Israel the cult preserves the communion with God, helps to establish the intercourse between God and man; it ensures, as it were, that this intercourse should continue. The cult is, as it were, a road for two-way traffic: in the cult God comes to man, but man also comes to God. Thus God comes to man as a forgiving God and affords him an opportunity to cleanse himself regularly of his sins; and in the cult man comes to God with his confession of guilt, with his tokens of thankfulness and adoration.[33]

2. A second purpose for the ritual was to enforce principles of health. This was the rationale behind many of the food taboos that were part of the ceremonial law.[34]

3. A third reason was to preserve Israel's separation from paganism. In this connection, Knight remarks that "the sacrificial laws kept Israel in touch with Yahweh at those points in her life where she was tempted to follow her Canaanite neighbours in their worship of the fertility gods."[35]

4. The prominence of blood sacrifices indicates a fourth reason for the Old Testament cult. It was a forward look to "the Lamb of God, who takes away the sin of the world" (John 1:29). This point looms large in New Testament statements about the crucifixion of Jesus.

The Old Testament contains no reasoned explanation of the meaning of the shedding of blood in ritual sacrifice, but it clearly states the necessity. "For the life of the flesh is in the blood; and I have given it for you upon the altar to make atonement for your

---

32. *Through the Pentateuch Chapter by Chapter* (Grand Rapids, Mich.: William B. Eerdmans Publishing Co., 1957), p. 108.

33. *Outline of OT Theology*, pp. 380-81; italics in the original.

34. See a modern statement of this in S. I. McMillen, *None of These Diseases* (Westwood, N.J.: Fleming H. Revell Co., 1963).

35. *Christian Theology of the OT*, p. 231.

souls; for it is the blood that makes atonement, by reason of the life" (Lev. 17:11).

In terms of the Old Testament itself, it has been conjectured that the prominence of blood in the sacrificial ritual was that blood was thought of as the bond uniting members of group or family. Blood rites were used to induct individuals as members of family or clan. The sprinkling of blood indicated that all enmity or barriers to fellowship were removed and the individual concerned then had all the privileges and responsibilities as a member of the group. When an animal that was devoted to God was killed, its blood could be thought of as the blood of God (cf. Acts 20:28, KJV). The sprinkling of that blood removed the barriers and cleansed away the sins, and by the blood men became one with God. J. N. Schofield writes, "Deuteronomy 12:23 says the blood is the life; sharing the blood means sharing the life; in Hebrew thought there was no fiction or pretense about it, it actually happened. This thought was used in the New Testament to express some of the meaning of the death of Jesus."[36]

Many of the laws set forth in the Book of Leviticus are purely cultic or ceremonial. Yet even ceremonial laws have symbolic meaning. Oswald T. Allis wrote:

> This is the New Testament gospel for sinners stated in Old Testament terms and enshrined in the ritual of sacrifice; and it finds its fullest expression in the ritual of the day of atonement. "For the like of the great day of atonement we look in vain in any other people. If every sacrifice pointed to Christ, this most luminously of all. What the fifty-third of Isaiah is to Messianic prophecy, that, we may truly say, is the sixteenth of Leviticus to the whole system of Mosaic types, the most consummate flower of the Messianic symbolism" (S. H. Kellog). To understand Calvary, and to see it in its tragic glory, we must view it with all the light of sacred story centered upon it.[37]

C. The Sacrifices and Atonement

It is God himself who atones or covers the sin of man. "For the life of the flesh is in the blood; and I have given it for you upon the altar to make atonement for your souls" (Lev. 17:11). The animal belongs

---

36. *Introduction to OT Theology*, p. 13. It may be noted, however, that in the case of the very poor, an offering of meal was acceptable in place of blood (Lev. 5:11).

37. "Leviticus," *NBC*, p. 135. Cf. John L. McKenzie, *Theology of the Old Testament* (New York: Doubleday and Co., Inc., 1974), pp. 37-57.

to God; its blood is His gift, shed at His command. A. B. Davidson
saw two lines in the Old Testament concept of atonement:

1. For sins outside the covenant relation—the so-called "sins
with a high hand"—voluntary, and fully culpable, God himself provides the "covering." Here atonement has the meaning of invalidat-
ing the penalty of the sin thus covered. It is used always in relation
to the sin, not in relation to God. It has the effect of purging or
putting away the iniquity.

2. For sins of frailty and infirmity within the covenant, the
blood of sacrifice is also required. The atonement (in the literal sense
of "at-one-ment" or reconciliation) is for the persons or souls of the
worshipers rather than for the sins as such.

Davidson further suggests that in the New Testament all sin is
viewed as voluntary, culpable, and incurring the judgment of God,
and that all atonement requires a blood sacrifice.[38]

VI. The Priesthood

The basic law governing the priesthood is given in Leviticus 8—10.
The record of its inauguration is found in Numbers. The nature of
this office cannot be seen in its full light, however, until we are in a
position to compare it with the prophetic order. It is sufficient here
to note that the priest, who exemplifies the "institutional" aspect of
Israel's religion, served in a vital role.

It was the priest who represented the people before the altar of
the holy God. It was the priest who interpreted the meaning of
ceremony and sacrifice to the people. Instruction in the moral and
religious laws was an important part of the priestly function. The
priests were keepers of the written record as it came into being. They
applied the law to the everyday life of the people. Because the priesthood was a hereditary order, it easily became corrupted. But in its
purpose and in much of its practice, it was essential to the stability
of Israel's religious life.[39]

VII. The Covenant in Israel's History

A. In Numbers and Deuteronomy

The history of Israel under the covenant actually begins in Numbers.

38. *Theology of the OT,* pp. 324-27.
39. Cf. Vriezen, *Outline of OT Theology,* pp. 265-66; Eichrodt, *Theology of the OT,*
1:435-36.

The story is one of alternating defeat and victory. But here the truth finds expression that the underlying causes in history are not geographical, economic, sociological, or military; they are spiritual and moral.

The Book of Deuteronomy (literally, "second law") is a profound application of the covenant principle to both the past and future of the people of Israel. The covenant also is presupposed in the books of Joshua, Judges, Samuel, and Kings; and it underlies the emphasis of the prophets later in the history of the nation.

Deuteronomy is composed chiefly of three addresses of Moses: concerning the past, a retrospect (1:1—4:40); present duties and exhortations (4:44—26:19); and a prospectus or forward look—actually the purpose of the whole (27:1—30:20). The past is reviewed and the present surveyed as part of preparation for the invasion and conquest of the Promised Land. The emphasis upon the covenant is seen in 27 references in the book to this important theme.

B. The Period of the Judges

The lesson taught in Numbers and expounded in Deuteronomy is reinforced over and over throughout the period of Israel's history as a loose confederation of tribes. The record is given in Joshua, Judges, Ruth, and the early chapters of 1 Samuel. This is history in the sense of "His story." It is a highly selective account illustrating the working out of the implications of the covenant.

An example of the structured nature of the biblical history is seen in the cyclical form of Judges. There, through six different cycles, the pattern of loyalty to God, disobedience, bondage to foreign powers, repentance and prayer, and deliverance is repeatedly worked out. The "judges" (Hebrew, *shophetim*—governors to lead the people and execute divine judgment on their behalf) could well be called "champions."[40]

G. Ernest Wright stated that to the author of the Book of Judges "the security of Israel lay solely in the covenant and in entire loyalty to her Lord."[41] The attraction of paganism was "subtle and alluring." Canaanite gods made few demands, were conveniently followed, and promised much. Yet when Israel turned to the baals (as the local divinities were known), she not only lost the favor of God

---

40. Kohler, *OT Theology*, p. 164.
41. *Book of the Acts of God*, p. 110.

but also the bond that held the tribes together. Under such circumstances, the people became easy prey to any maurauder.[42]

The Book of Ruth is a quiet little pastoral showing a different side to the turbulent period of the Judges. It is considered part of the third division of the Jewish canon, the Writings, and is used in connection with observance of the Feast of Pentecost because of the harvest scene that is so important a part of the story. Since the namesake of the book is a Moabitess, Ruth (along with Job and Jonah) bears a clear testimony to the fact that the exclusiveness developed later in Judaism was not an essential part of the Old Testament message.

C. The Kingdom

The events of the early kingdom period clearly illustrate the truth that Israel's security depended upon loyalty to the covenant. The initial success of Saul and the career of David were credited to obedience to the God of the covenant. The disaster that marked the end of Saul's life and occasional defeats in the life of David are traced to rebellion or disobedience. As F. F. Bruce wrote:

> The historians from Joshua to 2 Kings are frequently said to display the Deuteronomic philosophy of history, so called because it finds clearest expression in Deuteronomy. The cause of prosperity is found in obedience to the will of God, and especially in the avoidance of the native Baalism of Canaan, with its demoralizing fertility cults; adversity is the sure sequel to departure from this strait path.[43]

Through years of success and failure, victory and defeat, dominance and subjection, it became increasingly clear that Israel's election was not unconditional or indestructible. The converse of election was rejection. Election was to service more than to privilege. "Israel is not elected for privilege, i.e. to be served by other nations, but in order to serve them (cf. Mark 10:45); she was redeemed from Egypt and made *laos hagios Kurio* (Deut. 7:6) in order that she might serve God (7:11) and his purpose for the nations (e.g. Isa. 45:4-6)."[44]

42. *Ibid.*
43. "Judges," *NBC*, p. 237.
44. Alan Richardson, *An Introduction to the Theology of the New Testament* (New York: Harper and Brothers, 1959), p. 272.

D. Prophetic and Priestly Views of History

Deuteronomy, Joshua, Judges, 1 and 2 Samuel, and 1 and 2 Kings form a continuous history of the covenant people from Sinai to the Exile. They represent what may properly be called the "prophetic" view of the history. 1 and 2 Chronicles, Ezra, and Nehemiah likewise present a continuous history of the covenant people from David (with an introduction composed of extensive genealogies going back to Adam, 1 Chron. 1—9) to the return from Exile. They represent the priestly point of view.

Chronicles—Nehemiah is concerned more with what God had ordained—the ideal. Its emphasis is upon two divine institutions, the Temple and the throne of David. The life of Israel as a religious community is portrayed. While Chronicles does not minimize the failures of rulers and people, its prevailing emphasis is on the religious side of the national life in contrast with the civil aspects of the history.

E. Wars of Annihilation

The Christian conscience, informed as it is by the careful concern of the New Testament for individual human life, is sometimes troubled by Old Testament accounts of wars of extermination and the "ban" or curse placed on entire populations by what was clearly understood to be the immediate will of God. Conservative Old Testament scholarship does not have the escape from this dilemma open to liberal thinkers—that the Hebrews in their conquests attributed to God what was actually their own drive for security and a place in the sun.

The problem is not an easy one, and no simple answers readily appear. Hugh J. Blair makes two suggestions worthy of note:

1. The destruction of the Canaanites was a divine judgment on the moral abandon and almost indescribable vice of a pagan society.

> [The Israelites] were the instruments by which God exercised judgment on the wickedness of the people of the land. Just as He had destroyed Sodom and Gomorrah for the same kind of unspeakable corruption, without the instrumentality of human hands, so He used the Israelites to punish and root out the cancerous depravity of the Canaanites. And if there be a moral government of the world at all, such a dread possibility of judgment and divine surgery, however executed, cannot be excluded.[45]

In this connection, one should note that the "ban" (*cherem,* usually translated "curse") was regarded as placing a religious duty

---

45. "Joshua," *NBC,* p. 224.

on the conquerors and restrained looting and the more terrible aspects of the warfare of the times. "This was no lust for booty or for blood; it was a divine duty which must be performed."[46]

2. The ban was "prophylactic" in the sense that it protected the religion of the Israelites from infection by the abominations of the heathen. For the sake of Israel's high mission as a vehicle of true revelation to the world, drastic action was necessary. It was the excision of a cancerous growth in order that the host body might live.[47]

It should not be necessary to add that definite commands by God to engage in such religious warfare can never be used to justify modern aggressive warfare under any consideration. Here the New Testament must be our guide, not generalizations based on specific instances in the Old Testament.

---

46. *Ibid.*
47. *Ibid.* Cf. Lehman, *Biblical Theology,* 1:176.

Section Two

Devotion and Duty: The Human Side of Salvation

6

Old Testament Ethics

Following the Pentateuch and historical writings in our Old Testament is a body of material known as the poetical and wisdom literature: Job, Psalms, Proverbs, the Song of Solomon, and Ecclesiastes. There are significant differences among these books. But all represent what might be called the personal aspect of Israel's faith as compared with its historical and institutional aspects. The emphasis is devotional and ethical. It is concerned with some of the most enduring principles of biblical religion and some of the perennial problems of the human mind. Here is the human side of salvation.

I. The Nature of Wisdom

The wisdom literature of the Old Testament consists of the Books of Job, Proverbs, and Ecclesiastes. To these should be added a number of psalms generally classified as "wisdom psalms" (1; 19; 37; 49; 73; 112; 119; 127—128; 133). Hebrew wisdom is recognized in the Bible as part of a larger whole: "Solomon's wisdom surpassed the wisdom of all the people of the east, and all the wisdom of Egypt. For he was wiser than all other men, wiser than Ethan the Ezrahite, and Heman, Calcol, and Darda, the sons of Mahol" (1 Kings 4:30; cf. Obad. 8 and Jer. 49:7).

J. C. Rylaarsdam summarizes the essential points of agreement among the wisdom teachers of the ancient Near East: (1) The conviction that existence is fundamentally rational and moral; (2) the keen awareness that man is a creature in a world that is moral and rational; (3) as a result, overconcern and pessimism sometimes resulted; but (4) despair and moral irresponsibility never prevailed.[1] In Israel distinctively, however, wisdom was centered in the one living and true God, and was regarded as derived from Him and thus His direct revelation.[2]

A. "The Wise"

The Old Testament recognized a distinct class or guild of teachers known as "the wise" *(chakhamim),* who transmitted their wisdom from generation to generation (Prov. 1:6; 22:17; 24:23; Eccles. 9:17; 12:11; Isa. 29:14; Jer. 8:8 f.; 18:18; Ezek. 27:8-9). Thus along with the functions of priest and prophet, the Old Testament speaks of the work of the wise man or wisdom teacher. All three groups existed together and with different emphases conveyed the will and purpose of God to His people.[3]

The wise men or sages of the Old Testament were in fundamental agreement with the priests and prophets. "They could sit where common folk sat and for such they 'broke down small' the lofty message of the prophets that truth might enter in at lowly doors. They were religious middlemen and mediated the prophetic word to the man in the street."[4] Likewise, although the sages said little about ritual, their wisdom assumed the validity of divine worship as carried on in the Temple and synagogue.

The theme of the wisdom literature is spelled out in Proverbs, its most typical book: "The fear of the Lord is the beginning of wis-

---

1. *Revelation in Jewish Wisdom Literature* (Chicago: The University of Chicago Press, 1946), pp. 14-15.
2. F. F. Bruce and Francis Davidson, "The Wisdom Literature of the Old Testament," *NBC,* p. 43.
3. Cf. Edgar Jones, *Proverbs and Ecclesiastes,* "Torch Bible Commentary" (New York: The Macmillan Co., 1961), p. 31.
4. John Paterson, *The Wisdom of Israel: Job and Proverbs* (Nashville: Abingdon Press, 1961), pp. 57-58.

dom" (Prov. 9:10; cf. 1:7; 15:33). "Beginning" *(reshith)* here means "foundation" or "prime element." "The purpose of the Sages was to demonstrate that religion was concerned with a man's whole life and that it involved total commitment. . . . All life was to be integrated in His service and all the unredeemed aspects of life were to be brought within the religious sphere."[5]

B. Distinctives in Hebrew Wisdom

What the Bible contains of philosophy is to be found chiefly in the wisdom books. It is not the analytical philosophy of Greek rationalism; it is the synthetic insight that comes from intuition and enlightened reflection on the meaning of life. Hebrew philosophy was intuitive rather than speculative. As such, it was concerned to transmit the traditional sayings and popular maxims that crystallized the lore of ancient times. It was reflection on "the mysteries of human experience" carried on by men "who were most sensitive to the impact of the ultimate facts of sin, sorrow and death."[6]

Also distinctive in Hebrew wisdom is the conviction that man does not discover wisdom; God gives it. The chief Source of wisdom is divine. Wisdom is spoken of in such a way as to indicate that it is almost an independent being, intermediary between God and His creation, preexistent and sharing with God in the work of creation (Proverbs 8—9; cf. 8:27-31). Edgar Jones goes so far as to suggest that Wisdom in Proverbs 8 plays the same role as the Logos in John 1: 1-18 and contains the germ of the development of trinitarian concepts within Jewish monotheism.[7]

II. The Ethical Ideal

The Old Testament holds in careful balance the contrasting truths that man lives in community and that he is individually responsible for his choices and acts. Both insights must be given proper emphasis if the ethic of the Old Testament is to be understood. While there was a tendency in the tribal and early kingdom period to emphasize the "corporate personality" of the people, the idea of personal responsibility was never totally lacking. Nor do the later prophets—particularly Jeremiah and Ezekiel, with their strong emphasis on the

---

5. *Ibid.*, pp. 56-57.
6. Jones, *Proverbs and Ecclesiastes*, p. 28.
7. *Ibid.*, p. 44.

individual—ever forget that each man is implicated in the life of the community in ways he can never escape.

For modern thought, the problem is to understand how individuals create a true community. For biblical man, the situation was just the reverse. His question was not that of creating community. The community was the "given" with which he started. The problem was "the emergence within the community of individuals with personal value and personal responsibility."[8]

The law itself was addressed to individuals as well as to the nation (e.g., the Ten Commandments).[9] Yet individual piety and ethical responsibility becomes focal in the wisdom and prophetical books.[10]

Biblical ethics finds its basic expression in the moral content of the law. In the Bible, ethical theory is never viewed humanistically. The source of man's good lies in the nature of God, not ultimately in the nature of man. Righteousness, justice, mercy, and goodness are not abstractions apart from the will of God. Nor are they the result of impulses from within. They are responses to commands from above. This is expressed in the dictum already cited as the foundation of wisdom for life: "The fear of the Lord is the beginning of knowledge" (Prov. 1:7; cf. Job 28:28; Prov. 9:10).

Edmond Jacob wrote:

> If man's nature can be defined by the theme of the image of God, his function can be qualified as an imitation of God. This involves a double obligation for man, we might say a double outlook: one eye turned towards God and the other towards the world. The Old Testament re-echoes both a piety in which communion with God reaches the highest intensity (Psalm 73) and a realism which underlies much social legislation.[11]

This blending of religion and ethics in the Bible is unique in ancient times. The "Wisdom of Amen-em-ope," an author believed to have lived in Egypt sometime between 1500 and 1300 B.C., contains many of the same ethical teachings as are to be found in the Book of Proverbs and the wisdom literature of the Old Testament. But the motivations are worlds apart.

It could not be said that the maxims of Amen-em-ope are completely lacking in religious feeling. Yet the sanctions to which they appeal are limited to the pragmatic and prudential. They are human-

---

8. Kohler, *OT Theology*, p. 161.
9. See Chap. 6, III, A, "Individualism and Collectivism"
10. CF. Vriezen, *Outline of OT Theology*, p. 324; Baab, *Theology of the OT*, p. 72.
11. *Theology of the OT*, p. 173.

istic rather than theistic. One of Amen-em-ope's injunctions to honesty is "Do not lean on the scales, nor falsify the weights, nor damage the fractions of the measure" (ch. 16). A parallel in Proverbs reads, "Diverse weights and diverse measures are both alike an abomination to the Lord" (20:10). W. A. Rees Jones and Andrew F. Walls comment, "And that makes all the difference."[12]

A. Personal Conduct

Job and the Book of Proverbs summarize Old Testament teaching about norms for personal ethics.

1. Job 31 has been called "the high-water mark of the OT ethic."[13] It is in the form of an "oath of purgation" or "oath of clearance" in which an accused man would appeal to God, under direst penalties to himself if he be found a liar, to vindicate his innocence. H. Wheeler Robinson wrote that this chapter "should be carefully studied by anyone who desires to know what were the ethical ideals of the Hebrews. . . . It has been rightly said that 'if we want a summary of moral duties from the Old Testament, it might better be found in Job's soliloquy as he turns away from his friends and reviews his past life, than in the Ten Commandments.'"[14] The passage "has been called 'The Sermon on the Mount of the Old Testament,' for it reminds us of the teachings of Jesus. Nowhere in the Old Testament do we have a statement of higher ethical views."[15]

The ideals expressed in Job 31 include sexual purity (vv. 1-4, 9-12), truthfulness (vv. 5-6), integrity (vv. 7-8), fairness to subordinates (vv. 13-15), compassion and charity toward the poor and defenceless (vv. 16-23, 31-32), independence of mind with regard to material possessions (vv. 24-25), magnanimity toward personal enemies (vv. 29-30), candor in the confession of wrongdoing (vv. 33-34), and honesty in business (vv. 38-40).

2. The Book of Proverbs also has a great deal of say about personal conduct. While there are social and community ethics in Proverbs, as we shall see in the next section, the emphasis is on the individual rather than on the community. Evidence for this conten-

---

12. *NBC*, p. 516.
13. *Ibid.*, p. 403.
14. *The Cross in the Old Testament* (Philadelphia: The Westminster Press, 1955), p. 30.
15. William B. Ward, *Out of the Whirlwind* (Richmond, Va.: John Knox Press, 1958), p. 76.

tion is seen in the fact that the term "Israel" occurs not at all, while "mankind" *(adam)* is used 33 times.[16]

Personal conduct, not religious experience, is the chief subject matter of the Proverbs. "The wisdom and knowledge of which 'the wise' are about to speak are not mainly occupied with what we call the 'inner life'; they have chiefly to do with conduct. The wise man professes to teach the most difficult of all lessons, how rightly to master the secrets, fulfil the duties, and overcome the temptations which meet all men in actual life."[17]

The characteristics of the good man are very similar to the listing found in Job 31:

a. Honesty—"A false balance is an abomination to the Lord, but a just weight is his delight" (11:1); "Different weights, and different measures, the Eternal loathes them alike" (20:10, Moffatt; cf. also 1:10-19; 15:27; 16:11; 20:14, 23).

b. Integrity—"The integrity of the upright guides them, but the crookedness of the treacherous destroys them" (11:3); "Better is a poor man who walks in his integrity than a man who is perverse in speech, and is a fool" (19:1; cf. also 11:3; 20:7). *Integrity* is the English term used to translate a Hebrew root, *tam,* meaning "whole, perfect, complete."

c. Truthfulness—one of the major themes of Proverbs—"Put away from you crooked speech, and put devious talk far from you" (4:24); "He who speaks the truth gives honest evidence, but a false witness utters deceit. There is one whose rash words are like sword thrusts, but the tongue of the wise brings healing. Truthful lips endure for ever, but a lying tongue is but for a moment" (12:17-19; cf. 6:19; 10:13, 18-21, 31-32; 11:9, 13; 12:6, 13-14; 13:5; 14:5, 25; 15:2, 4, 28, *passim.*).

d. Humility—"The fear of the Lord is hatred of evil. Pride and arrogance and the way of evil and perverted speech I hate" (8:13); "The fear of the Lord is instruction in wisdom, and humility goes before honor" (15:33); and, of course, the familiar "Pride goes before destruction, and a haughty spirit before a fall" (16:18; cf. also 11:2; 13:10; 15:25; 16:5, 19; 18:12; 21:4, 24; 26:12).

e. Sobriety—"Wine is a mocker, strong drink a brawler; and whoever is led astray by it is not wise" (20:1).

---

16. Jones, *Proverbs and Ecclesiastes,* pp. 44-45.
17. W. T. Davison, *The Wisdom Literature of the Old Testament* (London: Charles H. Kelly, 1894), p. 133.

> *Who has woe? Who has sorrow?*
> *Who has strife? Who has complaining?*
> *Who has wounds without cause?*
> *Who has redness of eyes?*
> *Those who tarry long over wine,*
> *those who go to try mixed wine.*
> *Do not look at wine when it is red,*
> *when it sparkles in the cup*
> *and goes down smoothly.*
> *At the last it bites like a serpent,*
> *and stings like an adder* (23:29-32).

Cf. also 23:20-21, 33-35.

f. Prudence—the virtue of sagacity, common sense, and sound judgment—is highly prized in Proverbs—"No cautious man blurts out all that he knows, but a fool comes out with his folly" (12:23, Moffatt); "The wisdom of a prudent man is to discern his way, but the folly of fools is deceiving" (14:8; cf. also 6:1-5; 11:15; 13:16; 15:5; 16:20; 18:13, 15; 20:16; 21:20; 22:3).

g. Sexual purity is praised in some of the most eloquent passages in Proverbs.

> *For the lips of a loose woman drip honey,*
> *and her speech is smoother than oil;*
> *but in the end she is bitter as wormwood,*
> *sharp as a two-edged sword* (5:3-4).

"This is the way of an adulteress: she eats, and wipes her mouth, and says, 'I have done no wrong'" (30:20; cf. 2:16-19; 5:5-20; 6:23-35; 7:4-27; 9:13-18; 12:4; 23:27-28).

h. Liberality—"One man gives freely, yet grows all the richer; another withholds what he should give, and only suffers want. A liberal man will be enriched, and one who waters will himself be watered" (11:24-25; cf. 21:26; 22:9).

i. Self-control—particularly the control of speech and spirit—"He who guards his mouth preserves his life; he who opens wide his lips comes to ruin" (13:3); "He who is slow to anger is better than the mighty, and he who rules his spirit than he who takes a city" (16:32; cf. 14:17, 29; 17:28; 19:19; 21:17, 23; 25:28; 29:11).

j. Industry, like truthfulness, is a major theme—"The soul of the sluggard [Moffatt, lazy man] craves, and gets nothing, while the soul of the diligent is richly supplied" (13:4); "I passed by the field of a lazy man, by the vineyard of a man who lacked understanding; and, see, it was completely overgrown with thorns; the ground was covered with nettles, and its stone wall was broken down. So I looked and took it to heart; I observed and received instruction. 'Yet a little sleep, a little slumber, a little folding of the hands to rest'—and your poverty will come upon you as a bandit, and your want like an unyielding warrior" (24:30-34, Berk.; cf. 6:6-11; 10:4-5, 26; 12:11, 24, 27; 14:23; 15:19; 16:26; 18:9; 19:15, 24; 20:4, 13; 21:5, 25; 26:13-15).

k. Compassion for those in need, and even towards one's enemies —"Do not withhold good from those to whom it is due, when it is in your power to do it" (3:27); "He who is kind to the poor lends to the Lord, and he will repay him for his deed" (19:17); "If your enemy is hungry, give him bread to eat; and if he is thirsty, give him water to drink; for you will heap coals of fire on his head, and the Lord will reward you" (25:21-22; cf. 3:31; 11:17; 12:10; 14:31; 16:6; 17:5; 21:13; 28:27).

l. Justice, fairness—"To do righteousness and justice is more acceptable to the Lord than sacrifice" (21:3; cf. 3:29; 17:26; 18:5; 21:7).

m. Peaceableness—to live in harmony with one's fellows—is another prime virtue of the good man in Proverbs—"Do not contend with a man for no reason, when he has done you no harm" (3:30); "As charcoal to hot embers and wood to fire, so is a quarrelsome man for kindling strife" (26:21; cf. 11:29; 12:16; 15:1, 18; 16:14, 24, 28; 17:1, 14, 19; 18:19; 20:3; 21:14).

While practical duties are detailed by the wise men, it remained for one of the prophets to give the great Old Testament summary of individual religious ethics: "He has declared to you, O man, what is good, and what does the Lord require of you but to do justice, to love mercy and to walk humbly with your God?" (Mic. 6:8, Berk.).

More will be said later about man's freedom of ethical choice. Here it is sufficient to observe that the Old Testament takes it for granted that a man may live in such a way as to fulfill the requirements of God's law both within his own character and conduct and in the community. "The very fact that Israel's ethical leaders—the prophets, the wise men, and the lawgivers—urge upon the people the doing of good shows their belief in its possibility."[18]

B. Social Ethics

The Old Testament emphasis on community or social ethics revolves around two foci: the institution of family and home; and justice in the exercise of civil authority.

---

18. Baab, *Theology of the OT,* p. 69.

1. The wisdom writers, notably in Proverbs, extol marriage and homelife. "He who finds a wife finds a good thing, and obtains favor from the Lord" (Prov. 18:22). Homelife may be less than ideal, to be sure: "A senseless son is a calamity to his father, and the nagging of a wife is an endless dripping. House and riches a man inherits from his father, but a sensible wife comes from the Eternal" (19:13-14, Moffatt; cf. 21:9, 19). No better tribute to women as homemakers has ever been penned than the alphabetical poem that makes up the closing section of Proverbs (31:10-31).

Fundamental to homelife is the training of children. This has been written into the very nature of the covenant and its undergirding law: "And these words which I command you this day shall be upon your heart; and you shall teach them diligently to your children, and shall talk of them when you sit in your house, and when you walk by the way, and when you lie down, and when you rise" (Deut. 6:6-7; cf. 4:9-10; 11:18-21; 32:46-47; *passim*).

The training of children is therefore a major theme in Proverbs: "Train up a child in the way he should go, and when he is old he will not depart from it" (22:6); "The rod and reproof give wisdom, but a child left to himself brings shame to his mother" (29:15; cf. 13:24; 19:18; 23:13-14, 24-25).

Children, on their part, are to have regard for their parents: "If one curses his father or his mother, his lamp will be put out in utter darkness" (20:20); "Hearken to your father who begot you, and do not despise your mother when she is old" (23:22; cf. 19:26).

Allowance had been made in the "second law" for divorce under certain conditions (Deut. 24:1-4). Yet the Old Testament intimates, as Jesus stated later (Matt. 19:3-9), that such an allowance was a departure from God's purpose for marriage: "The Lord was witness to the covenant between you and the wife of your youth, to whom you have been faithless, though she is your companion and your wife by covenant. . . . So take heed to yourselves, and let none be faithless to the wife of his youth. 'For I hate divorce,' says the Lord God of Israel, 'and covering one's garment with violence,' says the Lord of hosts. So take heed to yourselves and do not be faithless" (Mal. 2:14-16).

2. Justice for the poor and oppressed was a major demand upon rulers—kings, princes, judges, and the wealthy. Amos among the prophets was unceasing in his denunciation of those who enslaved the poor and exploited the helpless (2:6-7; 4:1; 5:11-12; 8:5).

Those to whom the needy might look for help were corrupted by bribery (Mic. 3:11). Otto Baab comments:

> In all of these poignant prophetic cries is a glimpse of a magnificent social vision. In them is foreshadowed the coming of justice for the innocent and the helpless poor, of personal decency and social responsibility for the wealthy, of honor and good faith among the judges, of honesty among merchants, and of a sense of integrity among realtors. When justice comes, men who have the power given by wealth and position will use it with a high feeling of obligation to the common good. Religious leaders, be they prophets or priests or teachers, will use their ecclesiastical office in an unselfish desire to advance God's good purposes in the world and will avoid maneuvering for personal advantage or gain. And laymen will not use the formulas and formal observances of religion as a substitute for ethical obedience to the moral law.[19]

III. DIVINE SOVEREIGNTY AND HUMAN FREEDOM

The Old Testament assumes that right conduct is within the power of man. He may repent, wash his hands of the blood of violence, help the widow and the orphan, substitute justice for bloodshed, and shape his life to please his divine Lord.

Just as the Bible balances the collective and individual aspects of human life, it balances the sovereignty of God and the freedom of man. The sovereign will of God establishes the limits and consequences of human choice. But within those limits and in the light of those consequences, that same sovereignty guarantees the responsibility of human choice.[20]

The sovereignty of God is not arbitrary. God does what He pleases, but what He pleases is right and morally good.[21] Both the sovereignty of God and the responsibility of man are recognized clearly by Old Testament writers. Schultz writes:

---

19. *Ibid.*, pp. 71-72.

20. Cf. E. L. Cherbonnier: "The argument most commonly urged in support of predestination is that, if man were free, this would detract from the majesty of God. Any defense of freedom automatically convicts itself of a presumptuous attempt to usurp divine prerogatives. But what if [God] willed to create individuals independent of himself and capable of responding freely to him? Within the terms of the argument under consideration, he would have to apply to the theologian for a permit. And his application would be rejected!"—*Hardness of Heart*, A Contemporary Interpretation of the Doctrine of Sin. Christian Faith Series, Reinhold Niebuhr, consulting ed. (Garden City, N.Y.: Doubleday and Co., Inc., 1955), p. 37.

21. Davidson, *Theology of the OT*, pp. 130-32.

The most difficult side of this question is to understand the relation of the divine activity to personal beings conscious of their own actions. Piety demands such an emphasizing of God's action as would logically take away man's freedom. Moral consciousness, on the other hand, demands a freedom which, looked at by itself, would exclude all divine co-operation and order. It may be impossible for philosophy to solve this contradiction, based, as it is, on the inability of finite thought to comprehend a divine activity that works in a way unlike anything in the present world. But the Old Testament knows nothing of this dividing gulf—or, indeed, of this whole difficulty—as invariably is the case with simple faith. It holds fast to the moral claim. The emphasis it lays upon moral duty, and the prominence it gives to the responsibility which every one has for his own destiny, are clear enough proofs of this.[22]

What is not stated in so many words is everywhere assumed throughout the Old Testament. Men are commanded to choose. They are treated as morally responsible. While their freedom is a freedom within limits, and the limits are drawn by the divine will, the freedom within those limits is real. As Albert C. Knudson wrote, "Had the Hebrew felt it necessary to choose between human freedom, on the one hand, and the divine sovereignty on the other, it is possible that his choice might have fallen on the latter. But no such necessity presented itself to his mind."[23]

A. The Symbolism of Sovereign and Subjects

While there was no attempt at reconciling the terms of the paradox, the Hebrew concept of God as King is helpful. That God is King even when His rule is not recognized (2 Chron. 20:6; Ps. 22:28) is a fact asserted some 50 times in the Old Testament, most frequently in the Psalms (5:2; 44:4; 68:24; 74:12; 84:3; 98:6; 145:1; cf. 1 Sam. 12:12; Isa. 33:22; 43:15; Ezek. 20:33). Although God is particularly Israel's King, in truth His kingdom is worldwide: "Thine, O Lord, is the greatness, and the power, and the glory, and the victory, and the majesty; for all that is in the heavens and in the earth is thine; thine is the kingdom, O Lord, and thou art exalted as head above all. Both riches and honor come from thee, and thou rulest over all" (1 Chron. 29:11-12; cf. Dan. 2:44; 4:31, 34).[24]

---

22. *OT Theology,* 2:196.
23. *The Religious Teaching of the Old Testament* (New York: Abingdon-Cokesbury Press, 1918), pp. 237-38.
24. Cf. Kohler, *OT Theology,* p. 31; and Eichrodt, *Theology of the OT,* 1:199.

The Oriental monarch was an absolute sovereign. Yet often he had to deal with rebellious subjects. Sovereignty was not conceived in the fashion of a puppeteer with his puppets or a mechanic with a robot but in terms of a king and his people. The ruler who can overcome rebellion and win the love and loyalty of his people is more truly sovereign than one who could control puppets.[25]

B. Freedom and Responsibility

God's sovereignty is such that He uses the free and responsible choices of men to work His purposes in human life. An early example of this is found in the story of Joseph. When Joseph was made known to his brothers, he said to them concerning their betrayal of him: "As for you, you meant evil against me; but God meant it for good, to bring it about that many people should be kept alive, as they are today" (Gen. 50:20).

Pharaoh in his confrontation with Moses acted on his own in hardening his heart (Exod. 8:15, 32; 9:34). As a result, it was said that Pharaoh's heart "was hardened" (7:14, 22; 8:19; 9:7, 35) and "God hardened" Pharaoh's heart (7:3; 9:12; 10:1, 20, 27; 14:4, 8). These are three ways of describing the same fact. But God said He would use Pharaoh's decision "to show . . . my power, so that my name may be declared throughout all the earth" (Exod. 9:16).

The Assyrians were driven by their own lust for plunder and power, and their choices were consciously their own (Isa. 10:7). Yet they were the rod of God's anger, the axe and the saw in His hand, working out His moral purposes in the history of Israel (vv. 5-6, 12, 15).

"The wrath of man" is man's own wrath, and for its results he is fully responsible. Yet the sovereign God causes that wrath to "praise" (derived from a Hebrew root which also means "confess" or "serve") Him (Ps. 76:10).

Such passages as these have been interpreted in favor of an arbitrary sovereignty on the part of God exercised without respect to human choice. These, together with similar expressions in the New Testament, rather describe "the law of habit—the law that a good man grows better and a bad man worse through his right or wrong choice—and this is a law God *has imposed* on man."[26] Likewise, the

---

25. Cf. Smith, *Bible Doctrine of Man,* pp. 25-27.
26. *Ibid.,* p. 27.

acted parable of the potter and the clay (Jer. 18:1-6) simply shows that God can remake a disobedient people—otherwise the potter would have made the marred vessel as marred.[27]

C. God Is Lord of All

That God is the ruling Lord *"is the one fundamental statement in the theology of the Old Testament. . . .* Everything else derives from it."[28] It is for this reason that the relationship between God and man in the Bible is *"the relation between command and obedience. It is a relation of wills: the subjection of the ruled to the will of the ruler."*[29]

Leon Roth noted that it has become fashionable to speak of the relationship between God and man as that of a dialogue. At least it should be recognized that the "dialogue" is not the idle conversation of a social occasion. "It is rather a call, even a calling to account; and it is curious to observe from the record how some of those called upon found it in terror and suffering and how some, for varying reasons, tried to evade it."[30]

In the exercise of His sovereignty, it is to be noted that God permits what He does not necessarily purpose. He allows what He does not intend. But even the evil God permits is not "running loose." It is under control. The conviction expressed by Paul in Rom. 8:28 is true of the writers of the Old Testament: "We know that in everything God works for good with those who love him, who are called according to his purpose."

---

27. *Ibid.,* p. 26.
28. Kohler, *OT Theology,* p. 30; emphasis original.
29. *Ibid.;* emphasis original.
30. *God and Man in the Old Testament* (New York: The Macmillan Co., 1955), p. 19.

7

Deepening Concepts of Sin and Human Suffering

The long shadow of sin darkened human life after the Fall. It is often noted in the earliest books of the Old Testament. The concept of sin, however, is immeasurably deepened in the later writings. The earlier references were in terms of specific acts and their consequences. Later, an extensive vocabulary develops.

There are many biblical terms for moral evil. But all run back to one concept: "To disobey God is to sin."[1] Ryder Smith wrote: "Terms denoting 'evil' are numerous in Hebrew,—more numerous than terms denoting 'good', for, while there is only one way of doing right, there are many of doing wrong."[2]

It should be remembered that good and evil are personal terms. They are qualities and acts of persons, not abstractions having independent existence. H. H. Rowley wrote: "Goodness alone is eternal, for God is good, and He alone exists from eternity. Its logical correlate, evil, came into existence in the first evil being who opposed the will of God, and it continues in evil persons so long as evil persons continue to be. There is here nothing to threaten monotheism, or our philosophic desire for ultimate unity."[3]

---

1. C. Ryder Smith, *The Bible Doctrine of Sin*, p. 1.
2. *Ibid.*, p. 15; cf. von Rad, *OT Theology*, 1:263.
3. *The Relevance of Apocalyptic*, second ed. (London: Lutterworth Press, 1947), pp. 159-60.

I. Sin in Conduct

Ryder Smith makes a helpful classification of Old Testament terms for sin. He divides them into three categories: generic terms, metaphors, and terms of moral contrast.[4]

A. Generic Terms

There are three major generic terms for moral evil in the Old Testament.

1. The first is *ra* with its derivatives, used some 800 times. *Ra* is as broad in meaning as "bad" is in English. The KJV uses a total of 33 different English words to translate *ra*, including adversity, affliction, bad, calamity, evil (444 times), grief, harm, hurt (20 times), mischief (22 times), trouble, wicked (31 times), wickedness (54 times), and wrong.

Ra may be used of anything that is harmful, whether in a moral or nonmoral sense. In the nonmoral sense, the Scriptures speak of a "bad beast" (Gen. 37:20), "bad herbs" (2 Kings 4:41); and "bad figs" (Jer. 24:8). In a moral sense, it is first used of Er who was "wicked in the sight of the Lord" (Gen. 38:7), and is particularly prominent in the poetic and wisdom literature (e.g., Job 1:1; 42:11; Ps. 23:4; 34:13-14; 51:4; Prov. 8:13).

2. *Rasha* is another term whose generic meaning is evil. *Rasha* and its derivatives occur approximately 350 times. They are translated "wicked" or "wickedness" over 300 times. While *ra* frequently occurs in a nonmoral sense, *rasha* always had the meaning of moral evil. When used of a person, its literal meaning was "one proved guilty of a charge."[5]

Rasha is used both of those who wrong man and of those who wrong God (Exod. 2:13; Ps. 9:16). It is used both of individual deeds, and in a collective sense for people of sinful character. The enemies of God are the *rasha*, "the wicked." The wicked man is the opposite of the righteous man (e.g., Psalm 1)—the one who refuses to live by the law of the Lord.[6]

3. A third generic term, *asham*, occurs some 100 times. Of these occurrences, 35 refer to some sort of sacrifice and are translated "trespass offering" or "guilt offering"—texts which in general are

---

4. *Bible Doctrine of Sin.* Smith's classification is followed but not necessarily his analysis.
5. Kohler, *OT Theology,* p. 171.
6. Cf. Schultz, *OT Theology,* 2:281-91.

found in references to the ritual in Leviticus, Numbers, and Ezekiel.

Asham itself ordinarily means "guilt, guilty," and it is also translated "trespass," "faulty," "desolate," and "offend." The essential idea is theological—that of guilt before God (Ps. 68:21; 34:22).

B. Metaphors

A second class of Old Testament terms for evil includes words used as metaphors. For convenience, the metaphors also may be divided into three groups.

1. The first group of metaphors are words whose literal meaning is "to err, to deviate, or to miss the way or the mark." They may be used negatively, in the sense of mistake; or positively, in the sense of a voluntary and culpable act.

a. The most common of the metaphors for "missing the way" is *chata.* It is almost an exact equivalent of the New Testament *hamartanō*—"to miss the mark." It means "missing the right way, (following) the opposite of a straight course."[7]

Chata is found occasionally in a literal sense, as in Judg. 20:16 where we are told of slingers who "could sling a stone at a hair, and not miss"; and Prov. 19:2, "He who makes haste with his feet misses his way."

Chata is used only 30 times in the Old Testament to refer to sins against man. It is used more than 500 times of sin against God. Especially numerous are references to *chata* in Job, the Psalms, and Proverbs.

While *chata* might occasionally be used of "unwitting sin" in the ritual code, the most typical use of the term has clear reference to conscious and voluntary sins. Thus Ryder Smith is fully justified in the remark, "The hundreds of examples of the word's *moral* use require that the wicked man 'misses the right path' *because he deliberately follows a wrong one.*"[8] That is, there is no idea of innocent mistake or the negative thought of involuntary failure in *chata.*

b. Avon is another metaphor for evil derived from the idea of deviation from the norm. It comes from a root that means "to curve, to be bent, to bend or make crooked." It is translated "iniquity" 220 times in the KJV, and less frequently "fault," "mischief," and "sin." Schultz sees in *avon* a description of sin as a condition, a state

---

7. *Ibid.,* p. 281 f.
8. *Bible Doctrine of Sin,* p. 17.

contrary to the divine righteousness or "straightness."⁹ This is the term used by the seraph in Isaiah's Temple vision, translated more accurately in the KJV than in the RSV, "Thine *iniquity* is taken away, and thy sin purged" (Isa. 6:7, KJV).

c. Avlah occurs 29 times in the Old Testament. It comes from a root meaning "to turn away" and carries the sense of turning away from the right way. The KJV translates *avlah* "iniquity" 18 times, "wickedness" 6 times, and also occasionally uses "perverseness" and "unrighteousness." Baab suggests "injustice" or "unrighteousness" as the best translation, and cites Deut. 25:16; Job 36:23; Ps. 58:2-3; Isa. 59:3 ("untruth," KJV); and Mal. 2:6 as typical uses.¹⁰

d. Abar is literally "to pass over." When used in a moral sense, it is rendered "transgress" in the KJV—an English word derived from a Latin source that also means "to step across." It is almost always used in connection with the law, the covenant, or God's commandments (e.g., Isa. 24:5; Hos. 8:1).

e. Shagah, shagag mean "straying, wandering." These terms and their derivatives may be used for unwitting transgression and are usually translated "to err." In the sense of unconscious error, the terms are found most frequently in the ritual literature. But Ryder Smith cites numerous instances where they are used of moral action or conscious sin (e.g., 1 Sam. 26:21; Job 6:24; 19:4; Ps. 119:21, 118; Prov. 5:23; 19:2).¹¹

f. Taah, "to wander away," concludes the survey of metaphors derived from missing the mark or missing the way. It is translated "go astray," "err," "wander," and "be out of the way." Ryder Smith claims that when used of men's actions, *taah* always indicates a wandering that is deliberate and not accidental—sin that is conscious and willful. While one *may* wander without meaning to, he also may choose to wander. The entire idea is that a man sins because he does something for which, either by choice or culpable neglect, he is responsible. "There is no sin in altogether innocent error."¹²

2. A second group of metaphors for moral evil are words denoting enmity, rebellion, or treachery in one form or another. The underlying thought is that disobeying the king makes a citizen his enemy.

9. *OT Theology,* 2:306.
10. *Theology of the OT,* p. 89.
11. *Bible Doctrine of Sin,* pp. 19-20.
12. *Ibid.,* p. 20.

a. The most common and hence most important term of this sort is *pesha* (a noun used 130 times) and *pasha* (the verb used 41 times). The noun is usually translated "transgression," but the root meaning is "rebellion." The term occurs a few times in connection with rebellion against a human king, but usually it speaks of rebellion against God.

Ludwig Kohler calls *pesha* "the Old Testament's most profound word for sin." He states that it shows clearly that

> essentially and in the last resort in the Old Testament revelation sin is not the violation of objective commandments and prohibitions and not the iniquities of men which demonstrate their weakness and folly (I Chron. 21:8!) and perversity. *Sin is revolt of the human will against the divine will:* men are *theostugeis* (haters of God), Rom. 1:30.[13]

Oehler likewise claims that *"design* and *set purpose* are always implied in" the use of *pesha.*[14]

b. Other terms in this class are *marah* and *marad* (rebellion, but more exactly stubbornness—derived from verbs meaning "to be contentious, refractory"—Job 24:13; Ps. 5:10; 78:8; 105:28); *sarar* (revolting, stubborn, backsliding, "turning aside, defection, apostasy"—Ps. 78:8; Isa. 1:4-5; 31:6-7); *maal* (treachery, usually against God) and *bagad* (treachery, usually against man but with the implication that to deal treacherously with men was to be guilty of treachery against God); and *chamas* ("breach of fair and honorable conduct on the part of a citizen"[15]—translated variously "violence," "wrong," "injustice," or "cruel, false, unrighteous").

3. A third, if minor, group of metaphors for evil includes:

a. Aven, literally "trouble," but used almost always in a moral sense and most frequently translated "iniquity." Its underlying idea is that man's sin inevitably brings trouble upon him (Ps. 5:5; 6:8; typical of many uses of "workers of *aven*").

b. Beli-ya'al, a compound noun meaning "worthlessness" or "disorder." It was later used as a proper name, transliterated as Belial (cf. "sons of *beli-ya'al*," Judg. 19:22, "base fellows").

13. *OT Theology*, p. 170.
14. *Theology of the OT*, p. 160. Cf. Davidson: "This is the Old Testament view in general: sin has reference to God the Person, not to His will or His law as formulated externally. And in this view the term *pasha* is a more accurate definition of it than *chata*, although the latter term is also used quite commonly of sinning against a person" (*Theology of the OT*, p. 213).
15. Schultz, *OT Theology*, 2:281.

c. Shiqqutz and *to'ebah,* synonyms meaning "that which nauseates," and thus "abomination." These words are generally used to describe idolatry and the practices that went with it as "abomination" to God.

C. Moral Opposites

There is a final grouping of Old Testament words that express the moral opposites of what a man ought to be.[16]

1. *Chalel,* from the root "to loose, let loose," the opposite of holiness. It is best translated "profane," although the KJV often uses "defile" or "pollute." *Chalel,* especially frequent in the priestly literature, stands on the borderline between the ritual and the ethical. "God's name can be defiled by both cultic and ethical corruption."[17]

2. *Tame',* "filthiness," is the opposite of purity and is also common in ritual passages. The usual KJV translation is "unclean." Again there is an easy transition from ritual to ethical offences. A shrine may be unclean because the worshippers are both morally and ritually filthy (Lev. 16:16). God will purify Israel from her filthiness and idols (Ezek. 36:25-29).

3. Hebrew terms rendered "folly" and "fool" include *kesil, 'evil, nabal,* and *sakal.* Together they stand for the opposite of wisdom. Together with *pethi,* and all translated "fool" and "folly," they occur more than 100 times in Proverbs alone. The *pethi* is the "teachable" fool. The term means "simple" and is derived from "open." The *pethi* has not yet closed his mind against wisdom.[18] *Kesil* and *'evil* come from roots with similar meaning, "to be thick or fat" in the negative sense of thickheaded and hardened. It is the *nabal* who says in his heart, "There is no God" (Ps. 14:1).[19] "For the Hebrew 'wisdom' and 'folly' are not mere knowledge and ignorance. They describe two ways of choosing to live."[20] The same truth carries through into the New Testament, as, for example, in Matt. 25:1-13.

4. Another group of synonyms is summarized by the term *bosheth,* "shame," the opposite of glory. Shame is the feeling a man ought to have when he sins, but which he may not have (Jer. 6:15). *Bosheth* may be used for the contempt that sound public opinion

---

16. Smith, *Bible Doctrine of Sin,* p. 22.
17. Baab, *Theology of the OT,* p. 90.
18. Paterson, *Wisdom of Israel,* p. 64.
19. *Ibid.,* p. 65; cf. also Knight, *Christian Theology of the OT,* p. 260.
20. Smith, *Bible Doctrine of Sin,* p. 25.

shows toward those who sin shamelessly. Thus, "let the wicked be ashamed" or "let them be put to shame" are phrases frequently used (Ps. 6:10; 25:3; 31:17; 35:26; *passim;* and Ps. 44:7; 53:5; 119:21; Prov. 25:10).

Ryder Smith states by way of general summary: "Three general conclusions may be drawn from this long discussion,—that fundamentally 'to sin' is to disobey God; that, while 'disobedience' involves both positive and negative ideas, the emphasis is on positive refusal and not on negative omission; and that this refusal may take multitudinous forms."[21]

II. SIN IN CHARACTER

Characteristic of the Hebrew mind, the Old Testament usually speaks of sin in terms of acts or deeds, with the use of active verbs. Coming out of this discussion, however, is the recognition that the problem of man's estrangement from God is more than a matter of what he does. It is also a matter of what he *is*—the sinfulness of his character. As early as the record of the Fall, the sinfulness or depravity of the race is clearly recognized. Schultz states that the term "sin" is not limited to individual acts, but is regarded as a bias inherited as part of fallen human nature.[22]

A. In the Psalms

The inwardness of sin is described in the Psalms (particularly 32; 51; 130; and 143) "with such penetration that they have justly been described as 'Pauline'."[23]

In Psalm 51 particularly we hear the plea for a change of heart. "In this psalm the Old Testament tells at last the whole truth about sin."[24] Prayer for forgiveness is blended with the cry for a deeper cleansing. "Wash me thoroughly from my iniquity, and cleanse me from my sin. . . . Behold, I was brought forth in iniquity, and in sin did my mother conceive me. Behold, thou desirest truth in the inward being; therefore teach me wisdom in my secret heart. Purge me with hyssop, and I shall be clean; wash me, and I shall be whiter than snow. . . . Create in me a clean heart, O God, and put a new

---

21. *Ibid.,* p. 28.
22. *OT Theology,* 2:292 ff.
23. Gelin, *Key Concepts of the OT,* p. 85.
24. Ryder Smith, *Bible Doctrine of Salvation,* p. 62.

and right spirit within me. Cast me not away from thy presence, and take not thy holy Spirit from me" (vv. 2, 5-7, 10-11).

The locus of man's sinfulness is not the physical body. It is not weakness of the flesh in contrast with spirit. It is not sexual reproduction, although Ps. 51:5 finds it present from the moment of conception. It is, as Otto Baab has noted, in "the mind and will of man, which is corrupted by human pride and arrogance. This will is the spirit of apostasy and defiance abhorred by the prophets; it is the unresigned rebellion of men who have had a taste of power, and to whom the recognition of a higher power is utterly repugnant."[25]

B. Specific Terms

Most of the concern of the Old Testament with the problem of sin has to do with outward acts. There are, however, a number of concepts dealing specifically with the underlying nature that governs or at least conditions man's conduct.

The first indications of "original sin," or the sinfulness of man's character, were in simple terms. The image of God was modified to become in some sense also the image of Adam (Gen. 5:1, 3). *Ha rayetser,* the evil tendency from man's earliest years, is noted in Gen. 6:5 and 8:21.[26]

Just as a more extensive vocabulary developed to describe sinful acts, so some significant terms were used later to define sinfulness as an abiding disposition in the human condition. The most important of these are:

1. *Avah,* "perversity," the crookedness or distortion of nature lamented in such texts as 1 Sam. 20:30; 2 Sam. 19:19; Isa. 19:14; Lam. 3:9. "A man is commended according to his good sense, but one of perverse mind is despised" (Prov. 12:8). "A voice on the bare heights is heard, the weeping and pleading of Israel's sons, because they have perverted their way, they have forgotten the Lord their God" (Jer. 3:21). While the source of such perversion is not stated, von Rad notes that it "has its roots in an evil disposition."[27]

2. *Sheriruth,* "stubbornness" (KJV, "imagination"), is a particular concern of the prophets. Jeremiah especially emphasizes this as the source of his nation's delinquency: "At that time Jerusalem

25. *Theology of the OT,* p. 110.
26. Cf. George Allen Turner, *The Vision Which Transforms* (Kansas City: Beacon Hill Press of Kansas City, 1964), pp. 29-31.
27. *OT Theology,* 1:263.

shall be called the throne of the Lord, and all nations shall gather
to it, to the presence of the Lord in Jerusalem, and they shall no
more stubbornly follow their own evil heart" (3:17); "But they did
not obey or incline their ear, but walked in their own counsels and
the stubbornness of their evil hearts, and went backward and not
forward" (7:24; cf. also 9:14; 11:8; 13:10; 16:12; *passim. Sarar,* a term
with much the same meaning, is used in Deut. 21:18, 20; Ps. 78:8;
Prov. 7:11).

3. *Machashebeth* in the sense of "evil purpose" also implies the
sinful condition of the heart. One of the six things the Lord hates is
"a heart that devises wicked plans" (Prov. 6:18). "Thou hast seen all
their vengeance, all their devices against me" (Lam. 3:60). The same
term is translated "thought" (Gen. 6:5; Job 21:27; Ps. 56:5; 94:11;
Prov. 15:26) and "device" (Esther 9:25; Ps. 33:10; Jer. 18:12, 18) in
the KJV—usually with the clear indication of evil disposition.

4. *Iqqesh,* "perverse," "warped or crooked," is usually translated "froward" in the KJV. It means habitually disposed to opposition and disobedience. "Perverseness of heart shall be far from me;
I will know nothing of evil" (Ps. 101:4); "Men of perverse mind are
an abomination to the Lord, but those of blameless ways are his
delight" (Prov. 11:20; cf. also Deut. 32:5; Ps. 18:26; Prov. 8:8; 17:20;
19:1; 22:5).

As George Allen Turner summarizes, "The many synonyms for
a sinful disposition attest the concern for the source as well as the
acts of sin. These ideas are the basis for the Christian doctrine of
'original sin' or innate depravity."[28]

C. The Problem of Suffering

In the wisdom literature of the Old Testament the problem of what
is known as "natural evil" comes into sharp focus. The Old Testament, as well as philosophers of a later age, distinguishes between
the evils men do ("moral evil") and the evils they suffer ("natural
evil"). The issue of individual suffering becomes critical in the tension
that was felt between the doctrine of rewards found in Deuteronomy,
Proverbs, and many of the Psalms—and the undeniable fact that
good men suffer (as in the Book of Job and in some of the wisdom
psalms).

---

28. *Vision Which Transforms,* p. 31.

The Old Testament recognizes that natural evil comes about because of the existence of moral evil. This is at least one meaning of the "curse" on nature alluded to in Gen. 3:17-19 and Rom. 8:19-23.

The Old Testament also recognizes that one man's natural evil (what he suffers) may be caused by another man's moral evil (what he does). This is reflected in the psalms of persecution and conflict in such a case as when the bloodthirsty conquests of Assyria became the occasion of suffering and judgment for Israel (Isa. 10:5-7).[29]

1. *The Suffering of the Righteous.* The general position of much of the Psalms, Proverbs, and the rest of the Old Testament has come to be called "the doctrine of rewards." It is the conviction that the normal result of goodness and piety is health, happiness, and prosperity. The sinful and rebellious, on the other hand, find sickness and suffering to be their lot.

The "psalms of moral contrast," such as 1; 15; 34; 37; 52; etc., claim without qualification that the man whose delight is in the law of the Lord "is like a tree planted by streams of water, that yields its fruit in its season, and its leaf does not wither. In all that he does, he prospers" (1:2-3). The pious man "shall never be moved" (15:5). "Goodness and mercy shall follow . . . [him] all the days of . . . [his] life" (23:6). "The angel of the Lord encamps around those who fear him, and delivers them. . . . Those who fear him have no want! The young lions suffer want and hunger; but those who seek the Lord lack no good thing" (34:9-10). "A thousand may fall at your side, ten thousand at your right hand; but it will not come near you" (91:7).

In similar fashion the prudential values of Proverbs are reinforced over and over with the promise of prosperity, wealth, and all that passes for human happiness (3:13-18; 4:18; 10:2—22:16).

Conversely, the wicked are "like chaff which the wind drives away." They shall not stand; their way shall perish (Ps. 1:4-6). God will send snares, fire and brimstone, and a horrible tempest upon the wicked: "this shall be the portion of their cup" (Ps. 11:6).

"The way of the wicked is like deep darkness; they do not know over what they stumble" (Prov. 4:19). The characteristic form of the 374 proverbs entitled "The Proverbs of Solomon" (10:1—22:16) is to affirm the happiness and prosperity of the righteous *but* the misery and suffering of the wicked. "The way of transgressors is hard" (13:15, KJV) is a summary statement that characterizes the whole.

---

29. Cf. Baab, *Theology of the OT,* p. 246.

It was against a shortsighted and unthinking application of this orthodoxy that the Book of Job was composed and Psalms 37, 49, 73, and 94 were written. What tends to be true "in the long run" and in general terms may fail tragically in individual cases.

The Book of Ecclesiastes is likewise an examination of the "doctrine of rewards" but from an opposite point of view. Job and the Psalms listed above test the doctrine of rewards from the point of view of a righteous man who suffers while evil men around him prosper. Ecclesiastes, at least in part, examines the doctrine from the point of view of a man who during his early years was cynical and abandoned to pleasure and the ways of the world—and yet was wealthy and able to live as he chose.

2. *Attempted Solutions.* If it must be said that the Old Testament does not "solve" the problem of suffering, it must also be said that it offers practically every major solution later contrived for this purpose by the mind of man.

a. In the Psalms. Psalm 37 notes that the prosperity of the wicked is such that the righteous are tempted to envy it. Yet such prosperity is temporary and will soon give way to misery. The righteous, on the other hand, will ultimately come into their own.

Psalm 49 resolves the problem of the disparity in outward circumstances and inward character by noting that death ends the dream of the wicked. Wise man, fool, and "brutish person" (KJV) all alike die "and leave their wealth to others" (v. 10). The righteous, on the contrary, have hope that God will redeem their souls from the power of *Sheol,* the place of the dead: "For he will receive me" (v. 15).

Psalms 73 and 94 epitomize the answer of Job. In Psalm 73, the poet confesses his perplexity at the prosperity, health, and apparent happiness of the wicked (vv. 2-13). His own suffering and privation are in sharp contrast (vv. 14-15). Understanding came to him in "the sanctuary of God." The wicked will be brought to desolation. But the righteous will have the assurance of God's presence, guidance, and future glory (vv. 16-28). A similar note is sounded in Psalm 94.

b. In the Book of Job. The Book of Job is the Old Testament classic dealing with the problem posed by the suffering of the godly. Three times Job was said to be "blameless and upright" (1:1, 8; 2:3), one who feared God and avoided evil. The religious background of the Book of Job is that of the patriarchal age before the giving of the Law and the establishment of the priesthood. Job as the head of the clan offered sacrifices and acted as priest in a simple form of worship that was acceptable to God.

The contest between the Lord and Satan (or "the satan," the adversary) was over the issue of loyalty to God without prosperity as its reward. Job had been faithful in his worship, but he was very wealthy and by every human measure a happy man. The question was whether he would serve the Lord if he was not thus rewarded for his piety. Successively stripped of his property (1:13-17), his children (1:18-19), his health (2:7-8), and the sympathy and support of his wife (2:9), Job still maintained his integrity and "did not sin with his lips" (2:10).

The dramatic power of the Book of Job is heightened by the nature of Job's illness. The disease is generally conceded to be some form of leprosy, perhaps elephantiasis—but certainly humanly incurable and finally fatal. Job's trial was increased by the visit of his three friends with their insistent advocacy of the orthodox doctrine of rewards that Job himself had held.

Neither Job nor his friends knew the causes for his suffering. The friends drew the conclusions obvious to them but not to Job—that Job's sufferings must be due to some secret sin in his life. Eliphaz represented the best in Jewish mysticism (4:12-21). Bildad presented the case for tradition (8:8-10), while Zophar spoke with the dogmatism of "common sense" (11:1-20). Elihu, described as an "angry young man," spoke when his elders had concluded. He added the thought that suffering has value as discipline. When its purpose is accomplished, the suffering will end (32:6—37:24). None of the "comforters" were helpful, and their smug complacency irritated more than it consoled (16:1-5).

The theophany (appearance of God) in cc. 38—41 did not really answer the questions Job had repeatedly raised. It rather assured the sufferer of the all-embracing wisdom and sovereignty of the Lord God, compared with the ignorance and weakness of the best of men. Job's reaction was to affirm his faith in and subjection to God—satisfied that having before heard by the hearing of the ear, now his eye had seen the Lord (42:1-6). Job did not find the answer; he came to trust more fully the Answerer. T. H. Robinson wrote:

> But what of Job's problem? God has not said a word about it, and Job himself is satisfied to leave the matter without further mention. Once again, the overwhelming experience of direct contact with God has left no room for a problem. God being what Job has seen Him to be, there must be a solution, and that is

enough. It does not matter that Job should get an answer to his question; it does not matter that he should be able to grasp the answer if he had it. He has been in the direct presence of God, and that experience leaves no room for anything else. The problem may remain as an intellectual exercise, but it can no longer touch the sufferer's heart or repeat the torture through which Job has gone. He has seen God, and his soul needs no more.[30]

In the epilogue (42:7-16), Job prayed for his friends. He was restored to twice the prosperity of his earlier life. He was given other children equal in number to those he had lost. Some have questioned the propriety of the epilogue. But it serves to vindicate the righteousness of Job in the only terms that would have been meaningful to his contemporaries. For Job himself, as Walther Eichrodt said, inner integrity and the experience of hope in a final divine vindication (19:23-27) were of greater value than outward prosperity and happiness ever could have been.[31]

---

30. *Job and His Friends* (London: SCM Press, Ltd., 1954), pp. 123-24.
31. Cf. the extended discussion in *Man in the OT*, pp. 40-63.

8

Angels, Satan, and the Life After Death

The drama of Job, as considered in the preceding chapter, serves to bring into focus Old Testament teaching on two additional themes: (1) the nature of angels, and (2) the life after death.

I. ANGELS

Angelic beings are present in the Old Testament record from the Garden of Eden (Gen. 3:24) on. Some scholars have maintained that the idea of angels as intermediaries between God and men was introduced in the postexilic period. But Knight is entirely correct in his statement that there is no evidence in the Old Testament that the conception of angels is a late one. While the apocryphal literature did indeed multiply the numbers and hierarchical ranks of angels, "the conception that God could be represented on earth by an angel is as old as some of the oldest extant literature of the OT that we possess."[1]

A. The Meaning of the Term

The Hebrew term for "angel" is *malak*. The word means "messenger" as does the Greek *angelos* (translated "angel") in the New Testament. *Malak* is used 209 times in the Old Testament. In the KJV it is translated "angel" 111 times and "messenger" 98 times. There is sometimes a question whether a supernatural being or a human messenger is in mind. But there is no doubt that the visitors to

---

1. *Christian Theology of the OT*, pp. 74-75.

Abraham's tent (Gen. 18:2; 19:1), the figures on Jacob's ladder (Gen. 28:12), the "man" who met Joshua on the plain outside Jericho (Josh. 5:13), and the "man" who appeared to Gideon (Judg. 6:11-12) and to Samson's parents (13:3) were angels in the true sense. Kohler wrote: "They look like ordinary men (there are no female angels in the Old Testament) and they have no wings or they would not have required a ladder."[2]

Angels are created personal beings (Exod. 20:11; Ps. 148:2-5) brought into being before the creation of the earth (Job 38:7). They are said to be a vast host (1 Kings 22:19; Ps. 68:17; 148:2; Dan. 7:9-10). They are known also as *elohim* ("gods," "mighty ones," "supernatural beings") and *bene elohim* ("sons of God"). Mighty in strength (Ps. 103:19-21), they are ordinarily invisible to men (2 Kings 6:17).

In general, angels represent in a personal manner God's care of His people. Whenever they appear, it is to execute some divine commission. They are also God's agents of judgment and destruction (Gen. 19:1-22; 2 Kings 19:35 and the parallel in Isa. 37:36; Ps. 78:49). Special manifestations of the divine and communications of God's will come by means of angels.

There is particular emphasis in the Old Testament on "*the* angel of the Lord" as compared with "*an* angel of the Lord." He first appears in God's dealings with Abraham (see Chap. 5). Many Old Testament scholars—including Davidson, Schultz, Oehler, and Payne—regard "the angel of the Lord" as a preincarnate appearance of the Second Person of the Trinity, the *Logos* of John 1:1-14. Davidson speaks of "the angel of the Lord" as "Jehovah fully manifest."[3] Schultz says that the angel of the Lord is so closely identified with His revelation as rightly to be thought of as the preincarnate Word.[4] In Mal. 3:1, the "angel of the covenant" (KJV) is clearly the Messiah who was to come. The angel of the Lord is both distinguished from God and yet speaks as God (cf. Gen. 18:1-33; Exod. 3:2-6; Judg. 6:12-16).

B. Cherubim and Seraphim

Cherubim (plural of *cherub*) are agents of God's personal manifestation in the affairs of earth. They are not angels but symbolic figures combining "the noblest qualities of the created world,—a man being the symbol of intelligence, a lion of sovereignty, an ox of strength, and an

2. *OT Theology*, p. 158.
3. *Theology of the OT*, pp. 291-300.
4. *OT Theology*, 2:214-37.

eagle of swiftness."⁵ The *seraphim* (plural of *seraph*) of Isa. 6:2, 6 would appear to be a variation of *cherubim*. Wings are an essential part of the symbolism of *cherubim* and *seraphim* (Exod. 25:18-20; 37:7-9; 1 Kings 6:23-27; etc.).

II. SATAN

Satan is a supernatural figure who appears occasionally in the Old Testament, although with less clear indication of origin and nature than in the New Testament. The name "satan" comes from a root that "expresses the act of putting oneself crosswise."⁶ It is used in the verb form six times in the Old Testament and is translated "to be an adversary to" or "to resist." "Those who render me evil for good are my adversaries [lit., "satan me"] because I follow after good" (Ps. 38:20). "Then he showed me Joshua the high priest standing before the angel of the Lord, and Satan standing at his right hand to accuse [lit., "to satan"] him" (Zech. 3:1).

A. Old Testament Usage

The noun form *s-t-n* appears in the Hebrew Old Testament 26 times. Seven times in the KJV and RSV it is translated "adversary." Human beings are called "satans": "But now the Lord my God has given me rest on every side; there is neither adversary [Heb., *satan*] nor misfortune" (1 Kings 5:4); "May my accusers be put to shame and consumed; with scorn and disgrace may they be covered who seek my hurt" (Ps. 71:13). Once "the angel of the Lord" is said to be a *satan* to errant Balaam: "But God's anger was kindled because he went; and the angel of the Lord took his stand in the way as his adversary [*satan*]. . . . And the angel of the Lord said to him, "Why have you struck your ass these three times? Behold, I have come forth to withstand [lit., "to satan"] you, because your way is perverse before me" (Num. 22:22, 32).

B. As a Proper Name

The Hebrew *s-t-n* is translated "Satan" as a proper name 19 times in the KJV. The first such use is in 1 Chron. 21:1, where "Satan stood up against Israel, and incited David to number Israel." Satan appeared "also" among the "sons of God" in Job 1:6-12 and 2:1-7.

---

5. *Ibid.*, p. 236; cf. Exod. 25:20; Ezek. 10:1-22.
6. Jacob, *Theology of the OT*, p. 70.

Since the Hebrew *s-t-n* characteristically appears in the original with the definite article as "the satan"; since "the satan" was seen in heaven among the "sons of God"; and since 1 Chron. 21:1 attributes an act to "the satan" which 2 Sam. 24:1 attributes to the Lord, some conservative scholars have concluded that the Satan of the Old Testament is still "an angel of God, a minister of God, a being who has only as much power as God entrusts to him."[7] It is probably better, however, to accept the evidence of the New Testament to clarify the ambiguity of the Old, and to hold that Satan throughout the Scriptures is the cosmic enemy of God and His people—although originally one of the created angels. Little can be said, however, for any literal identification of Satan with Lucifer in Isa. 14:4-23 where the context clearly shows that Nebuchadnezzar is intended, or with the king of Tyre as described in Ezek. 28:11-19.

The New Testament provides warrant for identifying the serpent of Gen. 3:1 with Satan (John 8:44; 2 Cor. 11:3, 14; Rev. 12:9; 20:2). The Greek *diabolos*—from which by contraction we derive the English word *devil*—is used in the Septuagint and in the New Testament as the equivalent of the Hebrew *s-t-n* in the Old Testament. "Belial" in the Old Testament and "Abaddon," "Apollyon," and "Beelzebub" in the New are other names used to identify this malignant personification of evil in the cosmos.

The Bible says little about the origin of Satan; but it leaves no doubt about his end. He, with those who follow him, will be cast into "the lake of fire and brimstone" (Rev. 20:10; cf. Matt. 25:41).

III. THE LIFE AFTER DEATH

The Old Testament attitude toward death reveals two elements. The first is the recognition that death is natural in that it comes to all men. The second is the conviction that human death is in the world as a consequence of sin.

Death is natural. It comes to all men. The Bible is a book of life; it is also a book of death. The presence of the "grim reaper" is everywhere seen from the Garden of Eden on.

There is some hint that human death might not have occurred had not the virus of sin entered the moral bloodstream of the race. The end of man's earthly existence might have been like that of Enoch (Gen. 5:24). Or virtually endless life might have been possible

---

7. H. L. Ellison, "I and II Chronicles," *NBC*, p. 349.

in a setting like that of the Garden of Eden with its access to the "tree of life" (Gen. 2:9; 3:22). But as things are, the human body is destined to return to the dust from whence it came. All earthly life ends in death.

Otto Baab points out the general indifference to death on the part of Old Testament writers. It is reported almost casually. There is seldom any reflection on its meaning, at least in the earlier writings. Opposition to death takes the form of action to avoid the death of particular persons, and legal prohibitions against taking human life by murder. There is never any tendency to condone suicide, and it is rare in the Old Testament. In general, biblical man held a "common sense" attitude toward the end of the earthly life.[8] Jacob wrote: "Along with the Semitic people as a whole, Israel shares belief in the fatal and inevitable character of death."[9]

There is a good death when one is "old and full of years." To "die the death of the righteous" is to be desired (Num. 23:10). It is the early and untimely death that is to be feared.[10]

A. Death as Related to Sin

Along with the recognition that man is mortal because he is earthly, there is the conviction that death is "something at variance with the innermost essence of human personality, a judgment; and whenever this personality has reached its pure and perfect ideal, it must at the same time be conceived of as raised above death."[11]

Human death is the consequence of sin. "In the day that you eat of it you shall die" was God's warning to Adam and Eve in the Garden (Gen. 2:17). Death laid its heavy hand on the entire race as a consequence of the first sin. As Vriezen wrote:

> Man would not live with God as His child, but wanted to face God as an equal, and this original sin brought death on him. But man himself, made from the dust of the earth, is already mortal; the fact that he *must* die is due to the punishment of sin inflicted by God, because that is the reason why he must leave the garden of Eden with the tree of life. Hence St. Paul is quite right in saying that the wages of sin is death.[12]

8. *Theology of the OT*, pp. 198-204.
9. *Theology of the OT*, p. 299.
10. Vriezen, *Outline of OT Theology*, p. 203.
11. Schultz, *OT Theology*, 2:313.
12. *Outline of OT Theology*, p. 204.

Something of this aspect of death as judgment is seen in the fact that the Old Testament never presents death as liberation from bondage to the body. It is never viewed as the gateway to a better existence. Both these ideas, however, were current among the Greeks and other ancient peoples.[13]

The relationship between sin and death is also seen in the fact that ritual defilement resulted from contact with anything dead (Num. 5:2; 6:6, 9). Throughout the Old Testament, godliness is equated with life—"the path of life," the fullness of life. Sin and folly, on the other hand, led to death.

B. Intimations of Life After Death

While there is little conscious reflection on the meaning of death in the Old Testament, there are some clear intimations of life beyond the grave.

It must be recognized that there was no record of an Easter morning in the Old Testament. There is nothing comparable to 1 Corinthians 15. It was Christ who "brought life and immortality to light through the gospel" (2 Tim. 1:10).

1. *A Partial Revelation.* On the other hand, there was no "cult of the dead" in Israel such as flourished in Egypt and led to the practices of embalming the body to preserve it from destruction and building pyramids as tombs for the kings. Yet there was the universal conviction that death does not mean the end of existence. A. B. Davidson wrote:

> The life and immortality brought to light in the gospel are being reached from many sides, in fragments, and many times only by the arm of faith reached out and striving to grasp them as brilliant rainbow forms. In the Old Testament, truth has not yet attained its unity. But everywhere in it the ground of hope or assurance is the spiritual fellowship already enjoyed with God. Our Lord's argument, "God is not the God of the dead, but of the living," is the expression of the whole spirit of the Old Testament on this great subject. The temple of truth is not yet reared, perhaps the idea of it hardly conceived in its full proportion. Yet everywhere workmen are employed preparing for it, and all around there lie the exquisite products of their labour; and here we may see one laying a foundation, and there one carving a chapiter, and there another wreathing a pillar or polishing a corner-stone, working singly most of them, able only to take in the idea of the one piece on which he is engaged, till the master-builder comes in whose mind the full idea of the temple bodies

---

13. Jacob, *Theology of the OT,* p. 299.

itself forth, and at whose command each single piece of workmanship arises and stands in its fit place.[14]

Such gleams as were given do not arise from a philosophy that sees in man a being too great to die, or a life too rich to come to its final end in the grave. What we have is the conviction that a righteous life centers in God. In some way not clearly seen but cherished in faith, it is believed that God will enable the man who walks with Him to transcend or "overleap" *Sheol* and so escape its gloom and shadow. "It is God who offers life that is worthy to be called life, both here and in the beyond, and he offers life because he offers himself. It is because the abiding God is the source of that life that the life itself is abiding. Such a thought is closely akin to what we find in some passages in the New Testament."[15] Devout men in Old Testament times "had life with God, and they felt that immortality was involved in their communion with Him."[16]

2. *Developing Concepts.* Faith in life for the individual beyond death becomes stronger as the growing light of revelation becomes clearer. Early ideas of immortality were related to the continued existence of the community or the family. This is one reason why to die without progeny was regarded as such a calamity. Much of the life of the Old Testament was intimately wrapped up in the life of the clan or the nation. As the sense of individual responsibility developed more and more clearly, the hope of individual survival beyond death became more clear and important.[17]

Not all scholars are willing to concede as much as here claimed.[18] Yet for all the hesitancies and uncertainties we find, there is still strong evidence for faith in individual survival. It is particularly clear in the Psalms and in Job.

David's conduct at the death of his son shows awareness of a community of existence beyond death. As long as the child lived, his father fasted and prayed. When the child died, David rallied. Questioned by his servants, he said, "While the child was still alive, I fasted and wept; for I said, 'Who knows whether the Lord will be gracious to me, that the child may live?' But now he is dead; why should I fast? Can I bring him back again? *I shall go to him,* but he will not return to me" (2 Sam. 12:22-23).

---

14. *Theology of the OT,* p. 532.
15. Rowley, *Faith of Israel,* p. 175.
16. Davidson, *Theology of the OT,* p. 417.
17. *Ibid.,* p. 244.
18. Cf. Snaith, *Distinctive Ideas of the OT,* pp. 9 and 112-13 fn. where Old Testament belief in an afterlife is denied.

3. *In the Psalms.* Ps. 17:15, from a psalm titled "a prayer of David," reads: "As for me, I shall behold thy face in righteousness; when I awake, I shall be satisfied with beholding thy form." Answering the claim that the psalmist had in mind only awaking to a new day from the sleep of night, W. O. E. Oesterley wrote:

> It is difficult to understand these words in the sense of awakening from natural sleep; the psalmist shows that he is in constant communion with God, and experiences the unceasing nearness of God; he never contemplates separation from God; why, then, should he be satisfied with the divine appearance only on awakening from natural sleep? . . . It can scarcely be doubted, therefore, that the psalmist is here thinking of awaking from the sleep of death, and thus expresses belief in the life hereafter.[19]

In Psalm 49 the poet touches what has always been one of the chief reasons for belief in life beyond the grave. This is one of several wisdom psalms wrestling with the problem of the disparity between righteousness and rewards. The Psalmist writes of the wicked who prosper in this life: "Like sheep they are appointed for Sheol; Death shall be their shepherd; straight to the grave they descend, and their form shall waste away; Sheol shall be their home" (v. 14).

In contrast is the hope of the righteous: "But God will ransom my soul from the power of Sheol, for he will receive me" (v. 15). The justice of God will be vindicated in the hereafter. It was this very sort of reasoning that led Immanuel Kant in *The Critique of Practical Reason* to postulate the existence of God, the freedom of man, and the immortality of the soul. A moral universe demands at least that much. H. H. Rowley wrote: "The wicked may have good fortune here, but the miseries of Sheol are all that he can look forward to; whereas the righteous may have suffering here, but hereafter he will have bliss, for God will take him to himself."[20]

Rowley added: "C. F. Burney says 'The more I examine this psalm the more does the conviction force itself upon me that the writer has in view something more than the mere temporary recompense of the righteous during this earthly life.' With this view I find myself in fullest agreement."[21]

---

19. *The Psalms* (London: S.P.C.K., 1953), p. 90.
20. *Faith of Israel*, p. 171.
21. *Ibid.*

Psalm 73 is cited by Jacob as one of the two "most advanced expressions of" faith in an afterlife in the Old Testament.[22] Its hope is based on the reality of the present communion with God enjoyed by the Psalmist:

> *Thou dost guide me with thy counsel,*
> *and afterward thou wilt receive me to glory.*
> *Whom have I in heaven but thee?*
> *And there is nothing upon earth that I desire besides thee.*
> *My flesh and my heart may fail,*
> *but God is the strength of my heart and my portion for*
> *ever* (vv. 24-26).

This means, Oesterley says, that "union with the eternal, unchanging God cannot be interrupted by death. As in life on this earth God is with his servant, so in the world to come God will be with him. In the presence of God there is life."[23]

4. *In Job.* As in Psalms 49 and 73, the disparity of rewards and righteousness in this life also led Job to expressions of faith in his vindication in a life after death. Although poetry is admittedly difficult to translate and there are textual problems in Job. 19:25-27, Edmond Jacob is certainly correct in pointing to this passage as the other of the two "most advanced expressions" of belief in life after death.[24]

> *For I know that my Redeemer lives,*
> *and at last he will stand upon the earth;*
> *and after my skin has been thus destroyed,*
> *then without* [marg., *from*] *my flesh I shall see God,*
> *whom I shall see on my side,*
> *and my eyes shall behold, and not another.*

"And not another" is expressively translated in the RV margin, "and not as a stranger."

This is Job's greatest affirmation of faith. In it, he reaches a pinnacle. As T. H. Robinson has written: "There can be no doubt as to the real meaning of v. 27. The last clause contains the most conclusive and final word in the Hebrew language. 'Consumed' implies that a thing has absolutely and irrevocably ceased to be. There can be only one interpretation which satisfies this term: Job is contemplating some experience which will come to him after his physical frame has disintegrated altogether."[25]

---

22. *Theology of the OT,* p. 308.
23. *Psalms,* p. 91.
24. *Theology of the OT,* p. 308.
25. *Job and His Friends,* p. 103.

The experience of Job is almost an epitome of the experience of Old Testament man. Robert Dentan wrote:

> Israel had first of all to learn the full meaning of life with God in the present world. Then, when the time came, the idea of eternal life arose as a natural, and almost inevitable consequence. But even then the essential content of eternal life never became merely the survival of personal identity; for biblical man eternal life means a life lived in such firm fellowship with God that even death cannot destroy it.[26]

C. The Nature of Sheol

The characteristic Hebrew term for the place of the dead, both righteous and wicked, is *sheol*. It is perhaps derived from *shaal*, "to be hollow" (as the German *Hohle*, "a cavern," is the probable source of the English *hell*); or from *shul*, "a ravine or abyss."

1. *Old Testament Usage.* Sheol is used 65 times in the Old Testament. The KJV translates *sheol* "grave" 31 times, "hell" 31 times, and "pit" three times. The tendency of more recent translations (e.g., ASV, Goodspeed, RSV, Berk., NEB) is to transliterate the term and print it as "Sheol." Moffatt uses "death" or "Death-land."

It is reasonably clear that *sheol* does not mean "grave" in the sense of a tomb. The phrase "gathered to the fathers" is frequently used in such a way as clearly to indicate a community of existence after death that no individual grave or tomb could provide.[27]

The concept of *sheol* is yet another way the Old Testament expresses the conviction that death does not end personal existence.

Sheol is in the depths. One always goes "down" to *sheol* (Num. 16:30; Deut. 32:22; Ps. 63:9; Isa. 14:15; Ezek. 31:14; 32:18). It is a place of darkness and forgetfulness (Job 10:21-22; Ps. 88:12). It is a realm of silence (Ps. 94:17), although on occasion there may be communication among its people (Isa. 14:4-12). It is like a hideous, insatiable monster (Prov. 30:15-16; Isa. 5:14). It is the "land of no return" (Job 7:9-10), a prison house with gates (Job 17:16; 38:16-17; Ps. 107:18), to be feared and avoided as long as possible (Ps. 28:1; 88:11; Eccles. 9:10)—although in certain instances it might be preferable to extreme misery in this life (Job 3:17-19).[28]

2. *Moral Distinctions in Sheol.* In most of the Old Testament, there are no sharp moral distinctions in *sheol*. The apparition of Samuel can

26. *Design of the Scriptures,* p. 174.
27. Cf. Schultz, *OT Theology,* 2:322-32.
28. Cf. Gelin, *Key Concepts of the OT,* pp. 71-72.

say to King Saul, on the verge of suicide, "Tomorrow you and your sons shall be with me" in *sheol* (1 Sam. 28:19). *Sheol* is a place neither of blessedness nor of punitive misery. It is a state of bare existence.[29] It is the condition of the dead in contrast to what they knew in the realm of light and life (Prov. 15:24; Ezek. 26:20).

Yet at the lowest point in *sheol* lay a pit (Job 33:18; Ps. 28:1; 30:9; 40:2; Isa. 14:15) which may suggest an early concept of different states in *sheol* analogous to the distinction between *hades* and "Abraham's bosom" in the New Testament (Luke 16:19-31). The concept of the *gehenna*-hell of final punishment for the unrepentant is a New Testament truth rather than one drawn from the Old Testament.

A. B. Davidson has argued that the tenor of the Old Testament is consistent with the view clearly presented in the New Testament that the eternal state is an extension of the moral dichotomy of the present. Admittedly, however, the chief interest of the Old Testament is with the just rather than the wicked. There is little indication of an aggravation of the misery of the lost beyond that which is part of being in *sheol*.[30] In the Old Testament, punishment for sin is mainly in this life. Punishment for sin in the future life is more by privation than by positive judgment—although an exception to this general position may well be indicated in the "everlasting contempt" (Heb., "an object of aversion, abhorrence") to which some shall awake (Dan. 12:2).

D. Resurrection in the Old Testament

While the body is observed to return to the dust from whence it came (Gen. 3:19; Eccles. 12:7), such dissolution is not its final destiny. "Thy dead shall live, their bodies shall rise. O dwellers in the dust, awake and sing for joy! For thy dew is a dew of light, and on the land of the shades thou wilt let it fall" (Isa. 26:19; cf. 25:8). God's word to His people is "Shall I ransom them from the power of Sheol? Shall I redeem them from Death? O Death, where are your plagues? O Sheol, where is your destruction? Compassion is hid from my eyes" (Hos. 13:14). The Apostle Paul understood this suggestion of God's power over death to be related to the resurrection (1 Cor. 15:51-57). There is an undoubted element of poetic and metaphorical expres-

---

29. Cf. Davidson, *Theology of the OT,* pp. 425-32.
30. *Theology of the OT,* pp. 530-31.

sion in these passages. Yet intimations of resurrection in a literal sense are also present.

The resurrection in Ezekiel's "valley of dry bones" (Ezek. 37:1-14) is admittedly a national and spiritual resurrection. But the passage would be meaningless if there were no concept at all of a resurrection of the body. Dan. 12:2-3 anticipates the teaching of the New Testament: "And many of those who sleep in the dust of the earth shall awake, some to everlasting life, and some to shame and everlasting contempt. And those who are wise shall shine like the brightness of the firmament; and those who turn many to righteousness, like the stars for ever and ever."

Section Three

The Prophetic Vision

—————— · ◆ · ——————

9

The God of the Prophets

As the books are arranged in our English Bibles, the third major division of the Old Testament is devoted to the Prophets. These are "the latter prophets" of the Jewish canon with the addition of Lamentations and Daniel. The arrangement in the Jewish Bible places the Prophets, "Former" and "Latter," next to the Torah. It puts the Writings—the poetical and wisdom books plus Ruth, Lamentations, Esther, Daniel, Ezra-Nehemiah, and 1 and 2 Chronicles—in last place. Yet in the broad sweep of the Bible as a whole, there is reason to consider the prophets an important keystone in the arch reaching across the centuries to the New Testament.

I. The Nature of the Prophetic Office

At the risk of some oversimplification, it may be said that three great stages in Old Testament history are characterized by the preeminence respectively of patriarchs, priests, and prophets. The patriarchs were not only tribal rulers; in the line of election that extends from Seth to Jacob they were also the religious heads of their clans. They performed the function of sacrifice later delegated to the priests.

They represented their families before God and transmitted the "blessing" which normally went to the oldest male—although in conspicuous instances this rule of "primogeniture" might be set aside (Gen. 25:23; 48:13-20). Divine visitations in the pre-Mosaic era were almost always to the patriarch.

With the giving of the Law at Sinai, the priestly functions of the patriarch passed to the tribe of Levi—and in particular to the family of Aaron in the line of Kohath. The priestly line, as the patriarchal, was hereditary. Like any hereditary order, it tended to become corrupt. Although the priests retained their institutional and conservative function on into New Testament times, the real moral and spiritual leadership of the nation in the kingdom period passed to the prophets.

A. The Importance of the Prophets

The importance of the prophets in biblical history is apparent on the surface. What the apostles are in the New Testament, the prophets are in the Old. It was the prophets who were responsible for the creation and preservation of many of the books of the Old Testament. While Abraham was the first man to be identified by the term "prophet" (Gen. 20:7), Moses, the lawgiver, was regarded as the prototype of all the prophets who should follow and the antetype of the Prophet-Messiah who was to come (Deut. 18:15-18; 34:10). Samuel, the last of the judges, is also the first of a prophetic order recognized as a distinct element in Hebrew religious life.

The importance of the prophets as recorders of sacred history is seen in the title applied in the Jewish canon to what we would describe as typically historical books, namely, "The Former Prophets" (Joshua, Judges, 1 and 2 Samuel, and 1 and 2 Kings). Eric Sauer summarized the scope of the prophet's work in outline form:

> In three chief spheres prophecy completes in detail the discharge of its calling.
>
> i. Illumination of the past, especially as historical writing;
>
> ii. Judgment of the present, especially as admonition and call to repentance;
>
> iii. Foretelling of the future, especially as warning and comfort, namely:
>
> > (1) judgment upon Israel;
> > (2) judgment upon the nations of the world;
> > (3) the conversion of Israel;

(4) the conversion of the nations of the world;
(5) the Messiah and His kingdom.[1]

B. Descriptive Terms

Two basic Hebrew concepts are used to describe the nature of the prophetic office. The first, expressed in the synonyms *roeh* and *chozeh*, had to do with the prophet's vision. Both *roeh* and *chozeh* are derived from terms that mean "to see, behold, gaze upon, view, perceive, contemplate, or have visions of." The statement "He who is now called a prophet was formerly called a seer" (1 Sam. 9:9) indicates that the term *roeh* (seer) was an early term that later went out of common use and therefore needed to be explained. The prophet was one who saw, and the prophet's message was often called his "vision" (1 Sam. 3:1; Prov. 29:18, KJV; Isa. 1:1; Lam. 2:9; Obad. 1; Nah. 1:1; Hab. 2:2-3).

The second concept is by far the most common. The later and more usual word for prophet was *nabi*. The *roeh* or *chozeh* was one who sees. The *nabi* was one who speaks. A *nabi* is "one who announces," or more exactly, "one who speaks for another." Because Moses was "slow of speech," Aaron, his brother, was sent to be Moses' spokesman or *nabi*, his "prophet": Aaron "shall speak for you to the people; and he shall be a mouth for you, and you shall be to him as God. . . . And the Lord said to Moses, 'See, I make you as God to Pharaoh; and Aaron your brother shall be your prophet" (Exod. 4:16; 7:1).

The distinction between the true and the false prophet was that the true prophet spoke what God gave him to speak; the false prophet spoke from his own imagination: "'The prophet who presumes to speak a word in my name which I have not commanded him to speak, or who speaks in the name of other gods, that same prophet shall die.' And if you say in your heart, 'How may we know the word which the Lord has not spoken?'—when a prophet speaks in the name of the Lord, if the word does not come to pass or come true, that is a word which the Lord has not spoken; the prophet has spoken it presumptuously, you need not be afraid of him" (Deut. 18: 20-22; cf. 1 Kings 22:6-28; Isa. 9:15; Jer. 6:13; 8:10; 28:15-17; *passim*).

Speaking the word of the Lord frequently involved prediction, foretelling the future. More often it meant proclamation, "forthtelling" a message from God.

---

1. *Dawn of World Redemption,* p. 148.

Jeremiah was assured that God would put His words in the prophet's mouth (Jer. 1:9). The prophet was privileged to stand in the council of God (Jer. 23:18, 22; Amos 3:7). His function was to mediate the word of the Lord to the people, to speak to them in the name of their God. His typical preface was "Thus saith the Lord."

C. The Prophet's Inspiration

The prophet received the word by divine inspiration but communicated it through his own personality. The communication therefore bears the mark of the prophet's personality as well as the credentials of its divine authorship.[2] The prophets were "men who knew the intimacy of fellowship with God to whom something of his spirit was given, men who looked on the world in the light of what they had seen in the heart of God, men who spoke because they had to and not because they wanted to, upon whom the constraint of God had been laid, and men who delivered a word not alone relevant to the needs of the hour, but of enduring importance to men."[3] Eric Sauer wrote:

> Old Testament prophecy is no mere aerial line which does not touch the ground. Much rather, at many points, there is allusion to events and persons of the then present or the near future. From a definite situation the prophets speak to men in a definite situation. They often draw from their surroundings the shapes and colours for the presentation of their message. Everything is historically conditioned and yet at the same time interpenetrated with eternity. All is at once human and divine, temporal and super-temporal.[4]

Kohler uses the term "charismatic" to describe the prophet office. The prophet, unlike the priest, was not born to his office. He was called to it and especially endued with the Spirit of the Lord to accomplish its purposes. His experience of the divine was never for the sake of his own mystical enjoyment. It was always in the interests of the service of God for the salvation of His people.[5]

As the messenger of the Lord, the prophet conveyed the message in the form in which he received it. When God spoke in the first person, the prophet conveyed His message in the first person. As Vriezen has noted, this does not mean that the prophet identified himself with God, a view some have advocated. The "oracle"—the

2. Cf. Rowley, *Faith of Israel,* pp. 38-39.
3. *Ibid.*
4. *Dawn of World Redemption,* p. 145.
5. *OT Theology,* pp. 165-66.

first-person message spoken directly as from the Lord—is given thus because the prophet "is a faithful servant and messenger of God."[6]

The mission of the prophets was to bring an understanding of the will of God as it applies to all of life. The prophets were undying foes of cloistered piety, religion confined to the Temple ritual. Politics, commerce, justice, and the daily dealings of man with man were all brought under the judgment of God.

The prophets usually preached in opposition to the popular mood. When all went well and in times of universal optimism, the prophets were heralds of judgment and doom. But when judgment came and the mood of the nation was one of utter despair, the prophets spoke of a glorious future. "Their message became one of evangelical hope and encouragement."[7]

The prophets were the proponents of personal religion. "What raised the individual divine-human relationship to a new plane, making it a full and living reality, was the way in which the prophets carried to its logical conclusion the belief that *man's relations with God were explicitly personal in character.*"[8]

II. The Prophetic Vision of God

In no sense did the prophets think of themselves as innovators. They were men inspired with a vision of the God of Abraham, Isaac, and Jacob. They saw their task to be that of calling their people back to a faith they were all too apt to leave. Yet the prophets immeasurably enlarged the self-revelation of God that had earlier been given. Building on the foundation of God's mighty acts in Israel's history and on the insights of poets and wise men, the prophets enriched and deepened Old Testament man's understanding of his divine Lord.

The prophets do not speak of the "attributes" of God as a systematic theologian would. Abstract nouns are almost nonexistent in biblical Hebrew. Rather, the Old Testament abounds in verbs and active participles when it speaks of God. Not only are terms such as "omnipresence," "omniscience," and "immutability" lacking in the language of the Old Testament, the ideas themselves are largely

---

6. *Outline of OT Theology*, p. 258.
7. Dentan, *Design of Scripture*, p. 47.
8. Eichrodt, *Theology of the OT*, 1:356-57.

foreign to Hebrew thought. In their place are rich and meaningful descriptions of God in action.[9]

A. "No God Besides"

Confronted with the idolatry of their own people and the paganism of their neighbors, the prophets tirelessly insisted as those before them that "the Lord . . . is one Lord" (Deut. 4:35; 6:4; 32:39; Ps. 86: 10) and besides the Lord "there is no God" (2 Sam. 7:22; 2 Kings 19:15).

> *Thus says the Lord, the King of Israel*
> *and his Redeemer, the Lord of hosts:*
> *"I am the first and the last;*
> *besides me there is no god.*
> *Who is like me? Let him proclaim it,*
> *let him declare and set it forth before me.*
> *Who has announced from of old the things to come?*
> *Let them tell us what is yet to be.*
> *Fear not, nor be afraid;*
> *have I not told you from of old and declared it?*
> *And you are my witnesses!*
> *Is there a God besides me?*
> *There is no Rock; I know not any"*
> (Isa. 44:6-8; cf. 45:5, 21-22; Jer. 2:5,
> 11; *passim*).

Here, as at other points, the prophets were not innovators. To suppose that they were the creators of the monotheism of Israel is a total misreading of the Old Testament. Nowhere do they introduce the idea of one true God as something new. Everywhere they de-

---

9. Cf. Knight, *Christian Theology of the OT*, p. 88, 101 ff.; Stephen Neill, ed., *Twentieth Century Christianity* (Garden City, N.Y.: Doubleday and Co., Inc., 1963), p. 273; and the following:

"The classical Hebrew language, and the mind that produced it, worked almost exclusively with nouns and verbs, that is, with pictures of things and descriptions of actions. The Bible writers have a camera's eye, but this does not mean that they have a camera's brain. Their thoughts are as profound as ours. Only their way of expressing them is not the same as our own.

"They use the data of the senses—the sounds, sights, and smells of the world—to carry their message. They cannot take refuge in that bane of all theological writing, the vague abstraction and the convenient label. We might speak of 'premature self-congratulation in the absence of the requisite physical and mental capabilities to effectualize it in the concrete exigencies of vital experience.' Hebrew is innocent of this welter of adjectives and abstractions and prefers to say, 'Let not him that girds on his armor boast himself as he that puts it off' (1 Kings 20:11)."—Lawrence Toombs, *The Old Testament in Christian Preaching* (Philadelphia: The Westminster Press, 1961), pp. 37-38.

manded simply "that the people should adhere to Yahweh, whose will was already known to them."[10]

The assertion that "there is no God besides" the Lord God of Israel (Isa. 45:21) contradicts polytheism, belief in the multiplicity of gods. It also rules out the dualism of Persian Zoroastrianism: belief in two eternally antagonistic deities, the "god of light" and the "god of darkness." The Satan of the Old Testament, though he be a real and malignant personal spirit of great power, was still a creature of the one God and subject to the limits of His will. Nor is there any trace in the Old Testament of the disintegration of the Godhead into male and female principles such as marked other Semitic religions. The Lord God needed not in any way to be complemented. The Hebrew language has no word for "goddess."[11]

B. "The Everlasting God"

As positively as language could say it, the Old Testament affirms that God is the eternal One, without beginning or end, transcending the limitations of time. The evidence for this is unmistakable. There is no sort of "theogony" in the Old Testament—no account of the "birth" or origin of the gods—such as is found in other ancient religions. God has no beginning and can have no ending. He is "the first and the last" (Isa. 44:6), "The high and lofty One who inhabits eternity" (57:15).[12]

That God is eternal is a necessary corollary of the idea of creation. The existence of the world in time is a clue to the eternity of God. As Henry Ralston succinctly expressed it, "If anything now exists, something must have been eternal."[13] All thought about origins must necessarily start with the self-existent and underived. It is inconceivable that something should have come from nothing.

The Old Testament does not stand against materialism simply on the basis that matter cannot be eternal. The problem is not whether there is something or someone eternal. The issue concerns how adequate the concept of the eternal is in explaining the temporal. "Before the mountains were brought forth, or ever thou hadst formed the earth and the world, from everlasting to everlasting thou

---

10. Vriezen, *Outline of OT Theology*, pp. 178-79.

11. Cf. Eichrodt, *Theology of the OT*, 1:223.

12. Cf. Vriezen, *Outline of OT Theology*, pp. 181-82.

13. *Elements of Divinity* (Nashville: Publishing House of the M. E. Church, South, 1919), p. 22.

art God" (Ps. 90:2; cf. 93:2; 102:24, 27; 106:48; Deut. 33:27; Isa. 26:4; 33:14; Jer. 10:10). He is "the everlasting God" (Isa. 40:28).

C. Perfect in Knowledge and Infinite in Wisdom

1. *God's Knowledge.* God knows all things, the deep recesses of the human soul as well as events upon the earth. "For the Lord searches all hearts, and understands every plan and thought" (1 Chron. 28:9); "And the Spirit of the Lord fell upon me, and he said to me, 'Say, Thus says the Lord: So you think, O house of Israel; for I know the things that come into your mind" (Ezek. 11:5; cf. also 2 Chron. 16:9; Job 34:21-22; Prov. 15:3, 11; 24:11-12).

God is "perfect in knowledge" (Job 37:16). Darkness and light are alike to Him (Ps. 139:1-6, 12; Dan. 2:22). His understanding is infinite (Ps. 147:5). It was God's knowledge of men's thoughts and intentions that seemed most important to men of the Bible. "It seemed wonderful that the Lord knows all the secrets of the universe; but it was even more wonderful that He could look into the human heart and know all man's hidden thoughts and impulses."[14]

Old Testament writers do not speculate about the foreknowledge of events not determined in God's purpose. But they do affirm that the Lord knows the future. "Behold, the former things have come to pass, and new things I now declare; before they spring forth I tell you of them" (Isa. 42:9); "Remember the former things of old; for I am God, and there is no other; I am God, and there is none like me, declaring the end from the beginning and from ancient times things not yet done, saying, 'My counsel shall stand, and I will accomplish all my purpose'" (46:9-10).

2. *God's Wisdom.* The wisdom of God is also extolled. "It is he who made the earth by his power, who established the world by his wisdom, and by his understanding stretched out the heavens" (Jer. 10:12). "Daniel said: 'Blessed be the name of God for ever and ever, to whom belong wisdom and might. . . . he gives wisdom to the wise and knowledge to those who have understanding; he reveals deep and mysterious things; he knows what is in the darkness, and the light dwells with him" (Dan. 2:20-22). Wisdom is defined as the combination of knowledge and benevolence. It is the capacity to choose means appropriate for its ends. It is the disposition to use knowledge rightly.

---

14. Dentan, *Design of Scripture,* p. 99.

God's wisdom is manifested in His power to use the forces of nature to serve His will without making them any less natural. It is seen in His ability to use the thoughts and actions of men without making them any less human. The Assyrian serves as the rod of God's anger (Isa. 10:5) although unaware of that fact (10:7) and while following the evil bent of his own nature. "In his patience and long-suffering God uses the conflicting desires and purposes of men to achieve his will, without destroying human freedom or converting man into a mere puppet in his hands."[15] God is the Source of all wisdom (Job 28), and man cannot fully understand His ways (Isa. 55:8-9).

D. The Lord Is "God Almighty"

The irresistible power of God is affirmed through the whole of the Scriptures. To Abraham, the Lord said, "I am God Almighty *(El Shaddai);* walk before me, and be blameless" (Gen. 17:1; 35:11). Whatever He wills, He can do. "I am God, and also henceforth I am He; there is none who can deliver from my hand; I work and who can hinder it?" (Isa. 43:13). "All the inhabitants of the earth are accounted as nothing; and he does according to his will in the host of heaven and among the inhabitants of the earth; and none can stay his hand or say to him, 'What doest thou?'" (Dan. 4:35; cf. Job 9:10; Hab. 3:3-6).

Creation itself is the prime evidence of God's power. "It is he who made the earth by his power, who established the world by his wisdom, and by his understanding stretched out the heavens. When he utters his voice there is a tumult of waters in the heavens, and he makes the mist rise from the ends of the earth. He makes lightnings for the rain, and he brings forth the wind from his storehouses" (Jer. 10:12-13). "Ah Lord God! It is thou who hast made the heavens and the earth by thy great power and by thy outstretched arm! Nothing is too hard for thee" (32:17; cf. Job 26:14).

Correcting the myth that biblical man was overawed by the greatness of the earth, Eric Sauer wrote:

> Far from seeing in this small earth *"the* world," constituting the mathematical centre and chief point of the entire creation, to the Bible the nations are but as a "drop in a bucket," as a "grain of sand" which remains in the scales (Isa. 40:15); and to it the islands are as "small dust," and the whole of mankind as "grass-hoppers" (Isa. 40:22). Indeed, the whole globe is to the Bible only

---

15. Rowley, *Faith of Israel,* p. 61.

a "footstool" to the heavenly throne (Matt. 5:35; Acts 7:49). "The heaven is my throne, and the earth the footstool of my feet" (Isa. 66:1).[16]

God's power implies His sovereignty over men and nations. All manifestations of His power are directed to moral ends (Ps. 50: 21-22).[17] It is the sovereign power of God that makes providence and miracles completely at home in the biblical world. God can never be excluded from His creation. "In the faith of Israel he was too real and personal to be reduced to impotence in his own world, or regarded as one who idly watched while men worked out their own destiny, and this faith is integral to any worthwhile faith in God."[18]

E. The Lord Is Everywhere

God is present everywhere, not by being diffused or spread out through space but by His essential nature. "Heaven and the highest heaven cannot contain" Him (1 Kings 8:27; 2 Chron. 6:18). It is impossible to escape His presence. The Psalmist wrote:

> *Where can I escape Thy Spirit,*
> *or where can I flee from Thy presence?*
> *If I ascend to heaven, Thou art there;*
> *If I made the underworld my couch, then Thou art there!*
> *If I were to take the wings of the dawn*
> *and dwell in the remotest part of the sea,*
> *even there Thy hand would lead me*
> *and Thy right hand would take hold of me.*
> *If I should say, "Surely the darkness will cover me,"*
> *then the night (would become) light around me;*
> *(for) even darkness does not hide from Thee,*
> *but night is as bright as day;*
> *darkness is the same as light (to Thee)* (Ps. 139:7-12,
> Berk.; cf. Amos 9:2-3).

God's eyes are in every place (Prov. 15:3). "Heaven is my throne and the earth is my footstool" (Isa. 66:1). "Can a man hide himself in secret places so that I cannot see him? says the Lord. Do not I fill heaven and earth? says the Lord" (Jer. 23:24). This language does not rule out references to "localization"—e.g., God's presence in His house or in heaven. But God is where He acts, and since all things are upheld by the word of His power (Heb. 1:3), He is everywhere.

---

16. *Dawn of World Redemption*, p. 25.
17. Cf. Davidson, *Theology of the OT*, pp. 160-69.
18. Rowley, *Faith of Israel*, p. 58; cf. Schultz, *OT Theology*, 2:194-95.

Implied in God's universal presence is "incorporeality" or "spirituality." God is not in physical form and does not have a "body." While it remained for Jesus to assert without qualification that "God is Spirit" (John 4:24), the Old Testament presents substantial evidence in this direction. This includes (1) the "delocalization" of the worship of the Lord (Deut. 26:15; Jer. 7:12-14); (2) the prohibition of any kind of representation of the Lord (Deut. 4:15-19); (3) the recognition of "anthropomorphisms" as being symbolic and not literal (Num. 23:19); (4) the transcendence (Ps. 99:5) and nearness (Ps. 69:13; 73:23) of God; (5) the contrast of flesh and spirit (Isa. 31:3); and (6) God's invisibility (Job 9:11). All of these require us to understand references to the divine face, hands, voice, walking, and "image" for what they are—accommodations to the limitations of our human understanding.[19]

F. The Lord Is Trustworthy

That the Lord does not change (Job 23:13; Ps. 102:27; Mal. 3:6) means that He is dependable and a worthy Object of abiding trust. In relation to His creatures, living under the forms of space and time, the Lord is the living God. His action in the world is conditioned by historical events. Hezekiah sent to Isaiah for prayer on behalf of Judah's deliverance from the Assyrians—"It may be that the Lord your God heard the words of the Rabshakeh, whom his master the king of Assyria has sent to mock the living God, and will rebuke the words which the Lord your God has heard; therefore lift up your prayer for the remnant that is left" (Isa. 37:4).

Jeremiah contrasts the God of Israel with the gods of the heathen: "But the Lord is the true God; he is the living God and the everlasting King. At his wrath the earth quakes, and the nations cannot endure his indignation" (Jer. 10:10; cf. vv. 1-16; Deut. 5:26; Josh. 3:10; 1 Sam. 17:26, 36; 2 Kings 19:4, 16; Ps. 42:2; 84:2; Jer. 23:36; Dan. 6:26; Hos. 1:10).

God's being is not static changelessness. But His character and His purposes are dependable. Thus Isaiah can say, "Trust in the Lord forever, for the Lord God is the Rock of Ages" (26:4, Berk.).

This is also the point of frequent references to God as the God of "truth." The usual Hebrew terms translated "truth" *(emunah, emeth)* mean "steadfastness, stability, faithfulness." When the Psalmist says, "All the paths of the Lord are steadfast love and faithfulness, for

---

19. Cf. Gelin, *Key Concepts of the OT,* pp. 24-35.

those who keep his covenant and his testimonies" (Ps. 25:10); when Isaiah states that the throne shall be established in mercy and that God shall "sit in faithfulness in the tent of David [as] one who judges and seeks justice and is swift to do righteousness" (16:5); when Jeremiah affirms that "the Lord lives, in truth, in justice, and in uprightness" (4:2)—they are all declaring the dependability and faithfulness of God (cf. Ps. 96:13; 100:5). He is worthy of the confidence and trust of His people.

G. Righteousness and Justice

The righteousness and justice of God are consistently taught throughout the Old Testament. "Declare and present your case; let them take counsel together! Who told this long ago? Who declared it of old? Was it not I, the Lord? And there is no other god besides me, a righteous God and a Savior; there is none besides me" (Isa. 45:21). "The Lord within her is righteous, he does no wrong; every morning he shows forth his justice, each dawn he does not fail; but the unjust knows no shame" (Zeph. 3:5; cf. also Gen. 18:25; Deut. 32:4; Job 8:3; 34:12; Ps. 89:14).

Justice is essential to the divine government of the world. It is both legislative in prescribing what is right, and judicial in applying the law to human conduct, rewarding and punishing. In the latter sense, the justice of God is impartial—without "respect of persons": "Now then, let the fear of the Lord be upon you; take heed what you do, for there is no perversion of justice with the Lord our God, or partiality, or taking bribes" (2 Chron. 19:7; cf. Prov. 24:23; 28:21).

The righteousness and justice of God are more concerned with the vindication of the oppressed than with retribution for the oppressor. The note of punishment for evil is by no means absent. But, as Jacob points out,

> Never in the Old Testament does justice appear as distributive in the strict meaning of the term. The justice of Yahweh is not of the type of the blindfolded maiden holding a balance in her hand, the justice of Yahweh extends one arm to the wretch stretched out on the ground whilst the other pushes away the one who causes the misfortunes, and so its saving aspect does not exclude every distributive element.[20]

---

20. Jacob, *Theology of the OT*, pp. 99-100.

H. God of Mercy and Love

The lovingkindness and tender mercies of the Lord are a constant theme throughout the Old Testament. "I will recount the loving-kindnesses of the Lord, the praises of the Lord, according to all that the Lord has done for us and the great goodness to the house of Israel which He showed them, according to His mercy and according to the abundance of His loving-kindness" (Isa. 63:7, Berk.). "Let him who glories glory in this, that he understands and knows me, that I am the Lord who practice steadfast love, justice, and righteousness in the earth; for in these things I delight, says the Lord" (Jer. 9:24; cf. Deut. 4:37; 7:7-8; 10:15; 23:5; *passim*).

It has been claimed that the God of the Old Testament is a God of wrath while the Lord of the New Testament is a Lord of love. Such a contrast is biblically false. As Ryder Smith wrote, "It is clear that it was not left for the New Testament to declare that God *loves sinners*. Its distinction is that it shows *how much* He loves them."[21]

The modern sense of contradiction between the love and the wrath of God nowhere appears in the Bible. As we shall see, the love of God is the love of the holy God. Conversely, as Emil Brunner has commented, "The Holiness which the Bible teaches is the Holiness of the God who is Love, therefore, the truth of the Holiness of God is completed in the knowledge of His Love."[22]

Noting a certain reticence in the early parts of the Old Testament to speak directly of the love of God, Walther Eichrodt states that it was the prophets who first spoke freely of God's love "under the impact of direct divine self-revelation."[23] Hosea, in particular, developed the metaphor of marriage in relation to God's love for Israel, a metaphor frequently used later in the Bible and most fully in the New Testament.

Two Hebrew words chiefly convey the truth of God's love. One is *chesed*, covenant love. The other is *ahabah*, a noun used approximately 30 times in the Old Testament; and the verb form, *aheb*, used a total of 163 times and expressing the idea of unconditioned love.

1. *Unconditioned Love*. *Aheb* and *ahabah* are approximately as broad in their usage as the English word *love*. They mean "affection, desire, inclination." They describe the love of brothers (2 Sam.

---

21. *Bible Doctrine of Sin*, p. 56; italics in original.
22. *The Christian Doctrine of God*, trans. Olive Wyon; *Dogmatics* (Philadelphia: The Westminster Press, 1950), 1:183.
23. *Theology of the OT*, 1:251.

1:26); sexual love both good and evil (Gen. 29:20; 2 Sam. 13:15; Song of Sol. 2:4; *passim*); married love (Prov. 5:19; Eccles. 9:9); as well as inclination for such things as food and places (Gen. 27:14; Jer. 22:20, 22). They are used both of God's love for man (Isa. 63:9; Hos. 3:1; 11:4) and of man's love for God (Ps. 109:4-5; 116:1; Dan. 9:4).

In contrast to *chesed, ahabah* is unconditioned love. Norman Snaith wrote: "It is not limited to the conditions of any covenant, but it is the only cause of the existence of the Covenant between God and Israel. *Ahabah* is the cause of the Covenant; *chesed* is the means of its continuance. Thus *ahabah* is God's Election-love, while *chesed* is His Covenant-love."[24]

God's love for Israel is a sovereign love that depends upon no prior conditions. Israel's love for God is in response to the love that God has already shown in His offer of the covenant.[25] For the Old Testament as for the New, "We love because He first loved us" (1 John 4:19, Berk.).

It is the nature of God's love to choose. It chooses not in order to exclude others but in order to provide a bridgehead from which God's love for all mankind might be made known. God's love was especially manifested to Israel in order that it might be demonstrated to all. "It was not because you were more in number than any other people that the Lord set his love upon you and chose you, for you were the fewest of all peoples; but it is because the Lord loves you, and is keeping the oath which he swore to your fathers, that the Lord has brought you out with a mighty hand, and redeemed you from the house of bondage, from the hand of Pharaoh king of Egypt" (Deut. 7:7-8; cf. also 1 Kings 10:9; 2 Chron. 2:11; 9:8).

2. *Covenant Love. Chesed* expresses the idea of faithful love within an established relationship. It is love based on a prior covenant. When used of man, it carries the meaning of piety. When used of God, it carries the meaning of grace. Oesterley notes that *chesed*

> is not merely a mode of action or an emotion. It is an essential quality of soul, a spiritual endowment which goes deep down into the very nature of him who has it. It implies a full recognition of the value of personality, and adds to that recognition a consecration of one to another. No other word means so much to the Hebrew ear, and its cultivation in the human heart is the highest

---

24. *Distinctive Ideas of the OT*, p. 119.
25. *Ibid.*, p. 172.

demand of the prophetic morality. In all its completeness it can be seen only in Yahweh.[26]

Because no single English word quite covers the breadth of the meaning of this kind of love, translators of the Old Testament have employed different terms. The Septuagint usually renders it with the Greek *eleos,* "mercy." Modern English translations have employed "love," "kindness," "loving-kindness," "grace," "fidelity," and "steadfast love." Thomson calls it "the great Old Testament word for the grace of God," and says that it "means loving-kindness that is by nature steadfast, unalterable, faithful."[27]

One of the root meanings of *chesed* is "strength," and it is frequently coupled with *'emeth,* "truth," in the sense of stability, faithfulness, and reliability. "Stability" and "loyalty" are other attempts to convey its meaning. Vriezen wrote: "The words *chesed* (union) and *'emeth* (faithfulness, steadfastness) are found together again and again and often constitute one single idea: a firm, faithful union which is indissoluble."[28]

The essential connection between *chesed* and covenant has been noted. *Chesed* is love in relationship. The connection with the covenant is not lost in the prophetic literature, but it is surpassed. It is not the covenant that results in *chesed,* but the *chesed Yahweh* that leads to the restoration of the covenant after the people had broken it by their sins (Jer. 31:3). It is, in fact, the everlasting love of God that issues in the promise of the "new covenant" (Jer. 31:31-34).

We have noted that in Hosea the transition takes place from the image of love in a covenant relationship to that of love in the marriage relationship. More accurately, the nature of the covenant is redefined from a political contract to a marriage bond whose essence is loyal love. The marriage bond becomes the supreme demonstration of the Lord's love for Israel. This was a metaphor which Hosea "acquired the right to use only at the price of his own heart's blood."[29] God gives His word to His people: "And in that day, says the Lord, you will call me, 'My husband,' and no longer will you call me, 'My Ba'al.' . . . And I will betroth you to me for ever; I will betroth you to me in righteousness and in justice, in steadfast love *[chesed],* and in mercy. I will betroth you to me in faithfulness; and you shall know the Lord" (Hos. 2:16, 19-20).

---

26. W. O. E. Oesterley, *The Psalms* (London: SPCK, 1953), p. 80.

27. *OT View of Revelation,* p. 103; cf. also Jacob, *Theology of the OT,* p. 103.

28. *Outline of OT Theology,* p. 164.

29. Eichrodt, *Theology of the OT,* 1:251.

Isaiah and Jeremiah also use this metaphor, and also in the same way—in relation to the steadfast love of God. "For your Maker is your husband, the Lord of hosts is his name; and the Holy One of Israel is your Redeemer, the God of the whole earth he is called" (Isa. 54:5; cf. 62:5). "Return, O faithless children, says the Lord; for I am your master ["I am married unto you," KJV]; I will take you, one from a city and two from a family, and I will bring you to Zion" (Jer. 3:14; cf. 2:2; 31:32).

3. *God as Father.* Just as the love of God is affirmed, so the idea of the divine fatherhood also finds expression in the Old Testament (Isa. 63:16; Jer. 3:4; Hos. 11:1-7). Usually the truth emphasized is the authority and worthiness of the father—the obligation of the son to be obedient to his father (Mal. 1:6; 3:17). "Is this the way to treat the Lord, you foolish and senseless people? Is he not your father who created you, who made you and fashioned you?" (Deut. 32:6, Smith-Goodspeed).

The fatherhood of God is most frequently spoken of in connection with the nation as a whole. It is not usually Israel who calls God his Father, but God who calls Israel His son.[30]

"For I am a father to Israel
 and Ephraim is my first-born" (Jer. 31:9).
"Yet, O Lord, thou art our Father;
 we are the clay, and thou art our potter;
 we are all the work of thy hand" (Isa. 64:8).

Yet within the nation as a whole, God's care of individuals may be described as fatherhood. "Father of the fatherless and protector of widows is God in his holy habitation" (Ps. 68:5; cf. 89:26). Best loved of all is "As a father pities his children, so the Lord pities those who fear him" (Ps. 103:13).

It is probable that use of the Father-son relationship in the Old Testament is as rare as it is because of the quite literal and grossly physical ideas of a divine fatherhood current among Israel's pagan neighbors. "The concept of the fatherhood of God is clearly at home in the Old Testament, although it is not as pronounced as it might have been had the baalism of the day made no similar designation for its male deity (Jer. 2:27)."[31]

4. *God as Saviour.* The term most commonly used to describe Jesus in the New Testament is freely used of God in the Old Testa-

---

30. Cf. Jacob, *Theology of the OT*, p. 62. Jacob's unqualified statement must be modified by "usually."

31. Baab, *Theology of the OT*, p. 123.

ment. He is *Yeshua*, the Saviour, who is the Light and Salvation of His people (Ps. 27:1) and whose salvation is near those who fear Him (Ps. 85:9). God is the "everlasting God of justice, creative power, and holiness *as he seeks to save men* from their sins and to help them live a new life."[32]

That God is the Saviour of His people is a concept found often in the prophetic literature. "For I am the Lord your God, the Holy One of Israel, your Savior. I give Egypt as your ransom, Ethiopia and Seba in exchange for you . . . I, I am the Lord, and besides me there is no savior" (Isa. 43:3, 11; cf. 35:4; 45:15, 21; *passim*). "I will save my flock, they shall no longer be a prey" (Ezek. 34:22). "I am the Lord your God from the land of Egypt; you know no God but me, and besides me there is no savior" (Hos. 13:4).

5. *God as Redeemer.* The most typical word describing God as the Redeemer of His people is *ga'al*. It is a term for which there is no exact English equivalent. It means "to do the part of a kinsman" as in Ruth 3:13. As Kohler has noted: "The original meaning of *ga'al*, to do one's duty as a kinsman where blood has been shed, or where a name will die out, or where the land has fallen into strange hands, is no longer present where God is called *ga'al*. In this case the word always means that God frees the redeemed person from the power and authority of another."[33]

The term *ga'al* is often used in connection with deliverance from death and *sheol*. "Shall I ransom them from the power of Sheol? Shall I redeem them from Death? O Death, where are your plagues? O Sheol, where is your destruction? Compassion is hid from my eyes" (Hos. 13:14; cf. Ps. 103:4). Isaiah made most frequent use of the idea of redemption in his predictions of the exile in and deliverance from Babylon, usually in relation to the "Holy One of Israel." "Fear not, you worm Jacob, you men of Israel! I will help you, says the Lord; your redeemer is the Holy One of Israel. . . . Thus says the Lord, your Redeemer, the Holy One of Israel" (Isa. 41:14; 43:14; cf. 44:6, 24; 48:17; 49:7, 26; *passim*).

I. The Wrath of God

Closely connected with the love of God is its converse, the concept of His wrath. God who loves is also angry with all that (or who) would destroy the objects of His love.

32. *Ibid.*, p. 17.
33. *OT Theology*, p. 234.

The wrath of God is the converse of His love, not its contradictory. The contradictory of love is hate. Hate is described as God's attitude toward a man only as a Semitic expression for a lesser estimate or secondary place in the affections (Mal. 1:2-3 in relation to Luke 14:26).

It is exactly those prophets who emphasize God's love most strongly—that is, Hosea and Jeremiah—who also stress the divine wrath.[34] "The Bible knows nothing of a universe that includes heaven and not hell; nor of a theology of a loving God who does not destroy evil."[35] In Schofield's words:

> The wrath of God is the necessary corollary to the love of God. His gracious mercy is part of the permanent character of God, but his wrath flashes out for a moment against all that would send a streak of evil through his creation or destroy it, or against anyone who persistently identifies himself with that evil. His constant cry is 'Turn ye, turn ye, why will ye die?'; the way is always open out of the circle of his wrath into the love of the God who is plenteous in mercy and long-suffering if the sinner will turn to him.[36]

The purpose of God's wrath is to destroy evil from the world He loves. If we identify ourselves with that evil, His love must become His wrath and destroy us.[37]

The wrath of God, however, is not a permanent element of His character such as is His holiness, righteousness, and love. It is God's "holy intolerance of that which is not merely antithetical to his own character, but also hostile to man's deepest interest."[38] God's wrath will have accomplished its end when evil is banished and those He loves are reconciled to himself. The wrath of God "can only be understood as, so to speak, a footnote to the will to fellowship of the covenant God."[39]

The wrath of God is always personal. It is never, as C. H. Dodd has speculated concerning "the wrath" in the New Testament, an abstract principle of action in an impersonal order of justice—an objectively necessary universal law. Nor, on the other hand, is it capricious or impulsive. As Rowley wrote: "The wrath of God and his love are not to be set over against one another. His wrath was the expres-

34. Vriezen, *Outline of OT Theology*, p. 157.
35. Schofield, *Intro. OT Theology*, p. 157.
36. *Ibid.*, p. 44.
37. *Ibid.*, p. 54.
38. Rowley, *Faith of Israel*, p. 65.
39. Eichrodt, *Theology of the OT*, 1:262.

sion of his love, no less than his justice was. For love is not soft indulgence; nor is the wrath of God a display of temper."[40] "There is nothing capricious about his destructive wrath. It is so terrible because it is the other side of his love, and is as great as his love."[41]

However great the wrath of God, a repentant people can always find mercy. The last word is not anger but forgiveness. Hermann Schultz wrote:

> This belief that God's covenant love for Israel will outlive all His wrath is the keynote of the prophetic method of writing history. . . . It is the expression of the belief that God is the life of His people, and His love the immovable foundationstone both of their present and their future; that the people may have deserved nothing but wrath and punishment, but that God's mercy is greater than Israel's sin.[42]

J. The Holiness of God

A major feature of the Old Testament vision of God is its emphasis on the divine holiness. The holiness of God is implicit in the Bible from the beginning. It finds explicit statement in connection with the Exodus and the institution of the covenant. In the Song of Moses at the deliverance of Israel from Egypt, we find the first use of the term so often repeated throughout the balance of the Old Testament: "Who is like thee, O Lord, among the gods? Who is like thee, majestic in holiness, terrible in glorious deeds, doing wonders?" (Exod. 15:11).

The theme is continued through the provisions for worship and sacrifice in the remainder of Exodus and in Leviticus. It runs through the recapitulation of the law and covenant in Deuteronomy. It underlies the philosophy of history in Joshua, Judges, Samuel, Kings, and Chronicles. It is a persistent note in the poetic literature. With the prophets, however, the holiness of God is seen in its true light as infused with righteousness and thoroughly ethical in its implications for human worship and conduct.

1. *The Nature of God.* Biblical theology does not concern itself with the debate over whether the holiness of God is one divine attribute among others, or is the sum total of the attributes. The Old Testament speaks of holiness as so completely connected with the concept of deity that it constitutes God's very nature, "the godness of

---

40. *Faith of Israel*, p. 65.
41. Schofield, *Intro. OT Theology*, p. 54.
42. Schultz, *OT Theology*, 2:30.

God." Holiness is the glory and majesty of the Lord's revealed being, the perfect fullness of His Godhead.[43]

No descriptive term is used of God in the Old Testament in the same way as "holy" and "holiness." He is "the holy [one] of Israel," the *qadosh* (2 Kings 19:22; Ps. 71:22; 78:41; 89:18; Isa. 1:4; 5:19—and a total of 30 times in Isaiah; Jer. 50:29; 51:1; Ezek. 39:7; Hos. 11:9; Hab. 1:12; 3:3). *Qadosh* (holy) is used both in "oracle"—"I am the Lord your God, the Holy One of Israel, your Savior" (Isa. 43:3)—and in attribution—"They have forsaken the Lord, they have despised the Holy One of Israel" (Isa. 1:4). While English usage makes it necessary to translate as a phrase, "Holy One," the Hebrew simply says "the Holy" of Israel with no other substantive included.

Much as the New Testament affirms that "God is love" rather than "loving" (1 John 4:8, 16), so the Old Testament states that God is holiness rather than simply "holy" as a quality or attribute. Davidson says, "It seems clear, therefore, that *Kadosh* (holy) is not a word that expresses any attribute of deity, but deity itself."[44] It is a term describing the essential nature of God, that which is most intimately divine, rather than one of His attributes or qualities. The God of the Bible is thus in Peter Forsyth's phrase "The God of holy love."[45]

2. *The Meaning of Holiness.* "Holiness" *(qodesh)* and "holy" *(qadosh)* and their cognates occur 605 times in the Old Testament. Approximately 450 times, the terms are used in relation to things, usually associated with the cult or ritual. When attributed to God, holiness is His nature. When ascribed to men and things, holiness is a relation, not chiefly a property or quality. Gerhard von Rad says, "If an object or a place or a day or a man is 'sanctified,' this means to begin with only that it is separated, assigned to God, for God is the source of all that is holy. . . . Considering that in the last analysis the holiness of all that is sanctified derives solely from its having been brought into contact with Jahweh, it has been rightly observed that the term indicates a relationship more than a quality."[46]

43. *Ibid.,* pp. 167-77; Snaith, *Distinctive Ideas of the OT,* pp. 100 ff.
44. *Theology of the OT,* p. 151.
45. Cf. Vriezen, *Outline of OT Theology,* p. 151: "The holiness of God is not only the central idea of the Old Testament faith in God, but also the continuous background to the message of love in the New Testament. In this respect the two are in complete agreement, and here the Christian faith is based on the revelation of God in the Old Testament." Cf. also Thompson, *OT View of Revelation,* p. 90.
46. *OT Theology,* 1:205.

This is not to deny that holiness in the Old Testament has a strong ethical element when applied to men. But the earliest and even the predominant meaning in the Old Testament is "positional" rather than "ethical." It is always positional, of course, when applied to impersonal objects such as days, mountains, garments, altars, and the Tabernacle or the Temple (Exod. 3:5; 16:23; 28:2; Lev. 6:30; 8:9; Ps. 11:4; Isa. 11:9; Ezek. 20:40; *passim*).[47] G. Ernest Wright notes that

holiness simply refers to that mystery in the Divine being which distinguishes him as God. It is possessed by creatures and objects only in a derived sense, when these are separated by God himself to a specialized function. Of all the divine "attributes" holiness comes nearest to describing God's being rather than his activity. Yet it is no static, definable "quality" like the Greek truth, beauty and goodness, for it is that indefinable mystery in God which distinguishes him from all that he has created; and its presence in the world is the sign of his active direction of its affairs.[48]

3. *Constituents of God's Holiness.* Three elements are to be identified in the holiness of God:

a. The first is God's transcendent majesty. He is Lord over all, "God and not man, the Holy One in your midst" (Hos. 11:9). When the vision of the holiness of God came to Isaiah, "the Lord [was] high and lifted up," "sitting upon a throne," with a "train[49] [that] filled the temple" (6:1).

Holiness appears as power, channelled even through inanimate objects in which it was invested (e.g., the untouchable mountain, Exod. 19:12-13; and more clearly, the death of Uzzah, 2 Sam. 6:6-7). When the men of Bethshemesh died because they desecrated the ark of the Lord, their survivors asked, "Who is able to stand before the Lord, this holy God?" (1 Sam. 6:19-20).

b. The second element in the holiness of God is the unapproachable radiance of His being—the *shekinah,* the glory that was the "radiating power of His being,"[50] "the splendor of impenetrable light by which God is at once revealed and concealed."[51] He is a "devouring fire" (Exod. 24:17), and His splendor such that it had to be concealed under the cloud (Exod. 40:34-38).

---

47. Traces of the "positional" concept of holiness or sanctification are found in the New Testament: e.g., the Temple that sanctifies the gold (Matt. 23:17, 19) and the believing wife who sanctifies an unbelieving family (1 Cor. 7:14).

48. "God Who Acts; Biblical Theology as Recital," *Studies in Biblical Theology* (London: SCM Press, 1952), pp. 84-85.

49. Robe, skirt—from a root meaning "to hang down."

50. Buber's phrase, quoted by Vriezen, *Outline of OT Theology,* p. 246.

51. G. F. Moore, quoted by Thomson, *OT View of Revelation,* pp. 32-33.

c. The third element in God's holiness is the absolute purity of His nature. He is "of purer eyes than to behold evil" (Hab. 1:13). It is this last element that becomes uppermost as holiness is related to human beings. God's command "You shall be holy, for I the Lord your God am holy" (Lev. 19:2) does not refer to the majesty or glory of the Divine, but to separation and freedom from all that would defile.

That holiness and righteousness are to us words of such similar meaning is a tribute to the prophets from Amos onward. These men make it clear that the moral and spiritual demands of service to God far outweigh the cultic and ritual meanings of holiness.

This prophetic concept of holiness as ethical righteousness carries forward into the New Testament and becomes the background for the understanding of the Greek root *hagios* and its derivatives ("holy," "sanctified"; "make holy," "sanctify"). Because *qodesh* had become a term with moral significance as well as the more primitive cultic meaning, the translators of the Old Testament into Greek (the Septuagint) chose *hagios* as a term with ethical overtones instead of the more common Greek term *hieros. Hagios* has a moral significance which *hieros* does not.[52]

III. Spirit of God and Spirit of the Lord

A large and important body of teaching concerning the Spirit of God and the Spirit of the Lord is found in the Old Testament. A total of 86 references occur, of which more than one-third are found in Isaiah and Ezekiel.

The Hebrew term *ruach* is used for both the human spirit and the divine Spirit—as well as in its primary meaning of "breath," "air," and "wind." In this, *ruach* is almost an exact counterpart of the Greek term *pneuma* in the New Testament—also translated "spirit" or "Spirit," and more rarely "breath" or "wind."

The underlying idea in *ruach* is that of strength, power, and even violence.[53] Isaiah contrasts the power of God with the strength of men: "The Egyptians are men, and not God; and their horses are flesh, and not spirit. When the Lord stretches out his hand, the helper will stumble, and he who is helped will fall, and they will all perish together" (Isa. 31:3).

52. Cf. Snaith, *Distinctive Ideas of the OT,* pp. 56-57.
53. *Ibid.,* p. 196.

In considering Old Testament teaching concerning the Spirit of the Lord, we are immediately faced with the relationship of these ideas to the full Trinitarian concept of God as implied in the data of the New Testament. So great was the peril of polytheism in Old Testament times that the major emphasis there is on the unity of the Godhead. While Old Testament references may be interpreted in places as expressing the idea of the Spirit as a distinct hypostasis or Person, such an idea would probably not have occurred to a Hebrew student of the Scriptures. It is only in the Last Supper Discourses of Jesus (John 14—16) that the full light of the personality and deity of the Spirit of God shines forth.

Davidson, however, is undoubtedly correct when he says that the Old Testament concept paves the way for the New Testament doctrine.[54] Examples of Old Testament passages that lean toward the Trinitarian understanding of the Spirit are: "But they rebelled and grieved his holy spirit; therefore he turned to be their enemy, and himself fought against them. Then he remembered the days of old, of Moses his servant. Where is he who brought up out of the sea the shepherds of his flock? Where is he who put in the midst of them his holy Spirit?" (Isa. 63:10-11). That the Spirit could be "grieved" suggests a personal dimension at least latent in the idea. "My Spirit abides among you; fear not" (Hag. 2:5). "This is the word of the Lord to Zerubbabel: Not by might, nor by power, but by my Spirit, says the Lord of hosts" (Zech. 4:6).

The Old Testament refers to the Spirit as "holy" three times, twice in the passage from Isaiah 63 quoted above, and once in Ps. 51:11.

In terms of Old Testament usage, the Spirit is God active in His world. The Spirit is the "life-giving, energy-creating power of God."[55] While no hard and fast rule can be laid down, references to the Spirit of God *(Ruach Elohim)* and the Spirit of the Lord *(Ruach Yahweh)* tend to preserve the distinction noted earlier between Elohim, God as Creator, and Yahweh, the Lord as Redeemer. "The Spirit of God" refers to the power, might, and majesty of the Creator God. "The Spirit of the Lord" relates to the love, favor, and help of the Redeemer God.[56] Of the two, "the Spirit of the Lord" is the more frequently used phrase. In the historical and prophetical books, it is used almost exclusively.

54. *Theology of the OT,* p. 125.
55. Snaith, *Distinctive Ideas of the OT,* p. 196.
56. Davidson, *Theology of the OT,* p. 125.

William M. Greathouse divides the Old Testament references to the Spirit into three groups in a useful classification. First are those that relate to the Spirit's activity in the world in general. Second are those which speak of God acting redemptively by His Spirit in and through His people. Third are references to the coming of the Messiah and the age of the Spirit which He would introduce.[57]

A. The Spirit and the Cosmos

The Spirit of God "was moving upon the face of the deep" in creation (Gen. 1:2). The heavens and all the host that is in them were made by the word of the Lord and the breath (*ruach* or spirit) of His mouth (Job 26:7-13; Ps. 33:6). The Spirit is the Source of both animal (Gen. 6:17; 7:15, 22) and human life (Gen. 6:3; Ps. 104:29-30).

The Spirit of God bestows supernatural knowledge and wisdom (Gen. 41:38); gives special artistic ability (Exod. 35:31-32) and wisdom to govern (Judg. 3:10). The Spirit is omnipresent in the created order (Ps. 139:7-10). Dr. Greathouse writes: "He is personal Spirit, permeating yet distinct from His creation. He is present, moreover, not only as the sustaining power of the world, but also as a disturbing moral influence in the lives of sinful men."[58]

B. The Spirit of the Lord in Redemption

There are frequent references to the Spirit in relation to God's redemptive activity among His people. These occur often in the context of deliverance from oppression and danger. In Judges and in 1 Samuel in particular, there is frequent mention of the Spirit as "coming upon" or "coming mightily upon" specific judges and leaders as a supernatural power taking hold of them and enabling them to do exploits beyond the ordinary. Othniel (Judg. 3:10), Gideon (Judg. 6:34), Jephthah (Judg. 11:29), Samson (Judg. 13:25; 14:6, 19; 15:14), Saul (1 Sam. 10:6), and David (1 Sam. 16:13) are mentioned in connection with such exploits. Here the common thought is that the Spirit is "the giver of strength."[59]

Prophecy in the Old Testament is credited to the Spirit. Moses said, "Would that all the Lord's people were prophets, that the Lord would put his spirit upon them!" (Num. 11:29; cf. vv. 25-28; also 1 Sam. 19:20; Ezek. 2:1-3; 3:13-14; 8:3; 11:1).

---

57. *The Fullness of the Spirit* (Kansas City: Beacon Hill Press of Kansas City, 1958), pp. 41-46.

58. *Ibid.,* p. 42.

59. Dentan, *Design of Scripture,* p. 155.

The two passages that speak of the "holy Spirit" are found within the framework of moral and spiritual redemption (Ps. 51:11; Isa. 63:10-11). It is not to be claimed that these passages teach a regenerating or sanctifying work of the Holy Spirit in Old Testament times that was exactly equivalent to what we find in the New Testament. The age of the Spirit was yet to come. John comments concerning Jesus' promise of the Spirit that "the Spirit had not been given, because Jesus was not yet glorified" (John 7:39). These Old Testament passages rather testify to the fact that the redemptive workings of God in behalf of His own and the impulses and responses of the soul in worship are the province of the Spirit's ministry in all ages, before Pentecost as well as afterward.

C. The Spirit and the Messianic Prophecies

A third class of Old Testament references to the Spirit relate to the coming Deliverer and to an age of the Spirit that would characterize His coming. Isaiah, in particular, spoke of the Spirit anointing the Branch (11:2) and anointing the Servant of the Lord (42:1). He repeats the commission which Jesus accepted as His own (Luke 4:18): "The Spirit of the Lord God is upon me, because the Lord has anointed me to bring good tidings to the afflicted; he has sent me to bind up the brokenhearted, to proclaim liberty to the captives, and the opening of the prison to those who are bound; to proclaim the year of the Lord's favor, and the day of vengeance of our God" (61:1-2).

The Messianic age is to be peculiarly the age of the Spirit.

> For the palace will be forsaken,
>   the populous city deserted;
> the hill and the watchtower
>   will become dens for ever,
> a joy of wild asses,
>   a pasture of flocks;
> until the Spirit is poured upon us from on high,
>   and the wilderness becomes a fruitful field,
>   and the fruitful field is deemed a forest (Isa. 32:14-15).
> For I will pour water on the thirsty land,
>   and streams on the dry ground;
> I will pour my Spirit upon your descendants,
>   and my blessing on your offspring (Isa. 44:3; cf. also 59:19;
>   Ezek. 36:25-27; Joel 2:28-29; and Zech. 12:10).

The ministry of the Spirit is to be universal and inward.

Long after the close of the Old Testament canon, the Jewish rabbis held that because of the sins of the nation, the Spirit had been withdrawn. But He would return at the time of the Messiah to be diffused upon all, both Jew and Gentile. An interesting paraphrase of Ezek. 36:24 is given by Rabbi Simeon b. Johai, "And God said, 'In this age, because the evil impulse exists in you, ye have sinned against me; but in the age to come, I will eradicate it from you."[60]

---

60. Quoted, Greathouse, *Fullness of the Spirit*, pp. 45-46; cf. also Turner, *Vision Which Transforms*, pp. 68-72.

10

Personal Piety
in the Old Testament

Personal piety was very real in the Old Testmaent times. It is unfortunate that many have formed their views of Old Testament religion from what the New Testament says about the sterile formalism of later Judaism. Personal religion in the Old Testament was a vital, alive, and joyful expression of devotion to God. The later legalism was but the husk from which the kernel was lost.

The personal warmth of faith in the Old Testament is mirrored in the Psalms whose expression of devotion makes them the favorite hymnbook of the church as well as of the synagogue. The Psalms reflect a level of spirituality which many in the Christian era fail to reach, or rise to only rarely. "The Psalms show clearly . . . that religion gave the pious Israelite comfort and security, because it filled him with a deep and fervent faith in God, a faith that was given a classical expression in hymns such as Pss. xvi and xxiii, to mention only two."[1]

No less personal was the faith of the prophets. Active participants themselves in the events they described, men like Isaiah, Jeremiah, Ezekiel, Daniel, and the 12 minor prophets exemplified in life what the Psalmists had extolled in prayer and praise. Three main topics should be considered in relation to the normative faith of the Old Testament.

---

1. Cf. Vriezen, *Outline of OT Theology*, p. 303.

I. SALVATION

Salvation is the all-embracing word of the Old Testament as of the New. Holiness, righteousness, and salvation in the sense of a personal relationship with God—His nearness and involvement in life and immanence in experience—are clearly implied in the Old Testament concept of God and His dealings with men.[2] The *protevangelium,* election, the covenant, and the Law are all concerned with salvation. But it is in the Psalms and the prophets that the personal dimensions of salvation become increasingly clear.

A. General Meaning of the Term

God's saving acts are appropriate to the need. There is nothing in the term "salvation" *(yasha')* itself to indicate the mode or limit the extent of salvation. Every kind of spiritual and temporal evil to which man may be subjected is included within the scope of its deliverance.[3] God's intervention at the Red Sea was an act of salvation (Exod. 14:13), the first specific use of the term in the Bible (cf. a general use in Gen. 49:18). Salvation is frequently mentioned in relation to deliverance from military enemies: "Hear, O Israel, you draw near this day to battle against your enemies: let not your heart faint; do not fear, or tremble, or be in dread of them; for the Lord your God is he that goes with you, to fight for you against your enemies, to give you the victory" (Deut. 20:3-4; cf. 1 Sam. 14:45; 19:5). The term is also used in relation to long life and prosperity: "With long life I will satisfy him, and show him my salvation" (Ps. 91:16).

B. Salvation from Sin

More important are the frequent references to salvation in connection with deliverance from the corruption of sin. "With the perception that His compassion reached down beyond man's physical estate to his spiritual condition it was seen that His salvation reached as far as His compassion. Nowhere is He a helpless God. His resources are ever equal to His purposes."[4]

Salvation is used in relation to righteousness (Ps. 24:5), to truth (25:5), to faithfulness (40:10), to joy (51:12), to spiritual gifts (68:19-20), to the hearing of prayer (69:13), and to the forgiveness of sins (79:9).

---

2. Cf. Snaith, *Distinctive Ideas of the OT,* pp. 100 ff.
3. Girdlestone, *Synonyms of the OT,* p. 125.
4. Rowley, *Unity of the Bible,* p. 68.

Ryder Smith points out that "in the vast majority of texts the words 'save' and 'salvation' are related in some way to Israel's sin or righteousness."[5] One of the goals of salvation is communion with God and the personal renunciation of self-will, pride, and sin—with the transformation of character that these imply.[6]

Salvation from sin is an essential idea in the covenant itself. The covenant obligated Israel to obedience to her transcendent Lord. In the face of failure, assurance is given of forgiveness, atonement, and reconciliation. Sin is essentially a revolt against God's lordship. It can only be absolved by humble repentance and divine forgiveness. "The pagan . . . may feel guilt, regret and despair at having fallen short of what was demanded of him, but he knows nothing of the Biblical sense of sin, contrition, repentance and forgiveness, of the joy that comes from doing God's will, or in any way being undeserving of the Divine blessing heaped upon him."[7]

H. H. Rowley writes:

> There are many levels in the Old Testament, but certain constants are found at all levels. Salvation from the Egyptian bondage or from neighboring foes is not on the same level as salvation from sin, and salvation from unwitting sin is not on the same level as salvation from sins of the spirit. Yet at all levels salvation was perceived to be God's act. Its condition is always presented as humble surrender and faith, with repentance where there had been sin. . . . Throughout the Old Testament the love of God is presented. For though human sin is an offence to him, his eager yearning for the restoration of fellowship is seen in his discipline and his warning, and in his ready response to man's desire for the restoration of fellowship by the exercise of his divine power to remove the barrier which man had erected.[8]

C. The Call to Repentance and Faith

The prophets were constant in their call for the people to "return" to the Lord. To return to Him implied forsaking idols and coming back to the historic covenant with God as well as the renunciation of personal sin. Hosea spoke of Israel's idols as her lovers: "She shall pursue her lovers, but not overtake them; and she shall seek them, but shall not find them. Then she shall say, 'I will go and return to my first husband, for it was better with me then than now'" (2:7). Isaiah's call was, "Seek the Lord while he may be found, call upon him

5. *The Bible Doctrine of Grace* (London: The Epworth Press, 1956), p. 17.
6. Cf. Baab, *Theology of the OT*, p. 20.
7. Wright, *God Who Acts*, p. 22.
8. *Faith of Israel*, p. 98.

while he is near; let the wicked forsake his way, and the unrighteous man his thoughts; let him return to the Lord, that he may have mercy on him, and to our God, for he will abundantly pardon" (55:6-7).

The term translated "return" *(shub),* Baab notes, "is really extremely complex, for it marks a deep recognition of the demands of God, and admission of sin, an act of repentance, and a reorganization of life."[9]

Jeremiah was to say to his people, "Return, faithless Israel, says the Lord. I will not look on you in anger, for I am merciful, says the Lord; I will not be angry for ever. Only acknowledge your guilt, that you rebelled against the Lord your God and scattered your favors among strangers under every green tree [in the worship of idols], and that you have not obeyed my voice, says the Lord" (Jer. 3:12-13).

Hosea's hope for the future was that "afterward the children of Israel shall return and seek the Lord their God, and David their king; and they shall come in fear to the Lord and to his goodness in the latter days" (3:5).

The act of turning from idolatry and sin implied both repentance (in the narrow sense of renunciation of sin) and faith. To turn from idols was by that very act to turn "to God . . . to serve a living and true God" (1 Thess. 1:9). True repentance and saving faith are two sides to the single act of turning. Otto Baab writes:

> Salvation obviously must include the arrival of a sense of humility and dependence upon God as a consequence of the breakdown of pride and arrogance. It requires an honest admission of man's creatureliness and an acknowledgement of the weakness and limitations which this condition imposes upon man. It presupposes the surrender of the will to God and the full acceptance of the divine will as determinative for all of life. It demands complete submission to God as the arbiter of man's destiny and the reorganization of life in harmony with this surrender. All of this involves adjustments of a difficult and complicated personal nature, calling for psychological changes, radically revolutionary ethical commitments of a new self seeing values in a new light, and a transformation of man's volitional nature in a response to goals and influences originating in the being of God. Such a change is incredibly fantastic when man's moral and psychological resources and limitations are considered. Salvation from sin appears to be impossible in view of these enormous difficulties. . . . Only through the action of a higher Power outside of himself

---

9. *Theology of the OT,* p. 146.

can man come to that final humility which is the basis and the starting point of salvation.[10]

D. God's Forgiveness

God's response to man's return is forgiveness. "Let him return to the Lord, that he may have mercy on him, and to our God, for he will abundantly pardon" (Isa. 55:7). Four leading Old Testament words express the idea of forgiveness.

1. The first is *salach*, "to pardon, forgive, pass over." It was the word used in the prayer of Moses after the idolatry of the people (Exod. 34:9). It is used frequently in the Psalms, with their deepening sense of the "exceeding sinfulness" of sin (e.g., Ps. 25:11; 103:3). The prophets used it often in promise and petition (Isa. 55:7; Jer. 33:8). Forgiveness removes the onus of guilt. It delivers from some of the consequences of sin—although not necessarily from all (2 Sam. 12:13-14).

Some have inferred from Num. 15:30 that deliberate sin as contrasted with ritual sin or sins of weakness could not be forgiven. But the "presumptuous sin," or "sin with a high hand" as the Hebrew phrase puts it, almost certainly had to do with sin as the expression of a settled and permanent disposition of the soul in which the God of the covenant himself was spurned (as in Num. 15:31). It was unrepented sin, arising from despising the word of the Lord. To cut oneself off from the word of the Lord was to sever oneself from the only Source of obedient faith. Other passages in the Old Testament promise forgiveness for the most serious offences: "Come now, let us reason together, says the Lord: though your sins are like scarlet, they shall be as white as snow; though they are red like crimson, they shall become like wool" (Isa. 1:18; cf. 55:6-7). "Sin with a high hand" was almost akin to the "blasphemy against the Holy Spirit" (Matt. 12:31-32) which turned away from the only Source of pardon by identifying Him with Beelzebul (Matt. 12:27). "Correspondingly, any man who is honestly concerned about the unforgivable sin, Old Testament or New Testament, cannot have committed it!"[11]

On the positive side, *salach* represents the whole process whereby the offender is restored to favor. Girdlestone recognizes the close connection of forgiveness with atonement: "Though not identical with atonement, the two are nearly related. In fact, the covering of

10. *Ibid.,* p. 20.
11. Payne, *Theology of the Older Testament,* p. 353.

the sin and the forgiveness of the sinner can only be understood as two aspects of one truth; for both found their fulness in God's provision of mercy through Christ."[12]

2. The second term describing divine forgiveness is *padhah*, "to buy off, to deliver, to redeem, to ransom." This is a term that means "to take a thing or a man out of the possession and ownership of another into one's own possession and ownership by giving an equivalent for it . . . [although] in all 33 Old Testament passages where God is the one who ransoms . . . no equivalent is mentioned."[13]

While *padhah*, the parallel Hebrew term *ga'al* ("to be a kinsman to"), and the New Testament Greek equivalent *lutroo* were the basis for the patristic "ransom" theory of the atonement, the idea of "paying a price to" someone does not appear prominently in the Scriptures. The term implies deliverance from an old state of bondage into a new relationship of freedom by the personal effort or intervention of the redeemer.[14]

3. The third term for forgiveness is *nasa*, "to take away guilt; to accept, bear, carry, lift up, forgive." It is found all through the Old Testament. Some typical references are Exod. 10:17; 32:32; 1 Sam. 25:28; Job 7:21; Ps. 25:18; 32:1, 5; 85:2; 99:8; Isa. 2:9.

4. *Kipper*, the fourth word in this group, means "covering"; from *kaphar*, "to cover over." It is usually translated "atonement" and "to make atonement." The related Akkadian term means "to wash away." It is found extensively in the liturgical sections (Exodus 29 ff.; Leviticus; and Numbers) and in such passages as Deut. 32:43; Ps. 32:1; 65:3; Isa. 6:7; 22:14; 27:9; Jer. 18:23 (translated "forgive"); Ezek. 43: 20, 26; 45:15, 17 ("make atonement"); Dan. 9:24 ("to atone").

E. The Life of Piety

The life to which God calls His people is defined in the "Golden Text of the Old Testament," Mic. 6:8: "He has showed you, O man, what is good; and what does the Lord require of you but to do justice, and to love kindness, and to walk humbly with your God?"

Returning to God leads to the knowledge of God in the sense of agreement with and conformity to His will. Hosea is preeminently the prophet of the "knowledge of the Lord." "I will betroth you to me in faithfulness; and you shall know the Lord" (2:20). "Let us

12. *Synonyms of the OT*, p. 136.
13. Kohler, *OT Theology*, p. 233.
14. Cf. Vriezen, *Outline of the OT Theology*, p. 273.

know, let us press on to know the Lord; his going forth is sure as the dawn; he will come to us as the showers, as the spring rains that water the earth" (6:3; cf. also 4:1, 6; 5:4; 6:6).

Knowledge of God such as this issues in trust and confidence: "In returning and rest you shall be saved; in quietness and in trust shall be your strength" ("Isa. 30:15). It brings peace: "Thou dost keep him in perfect peace, whose mind is stayed on thee, because he trusts in thee" (Isa. 26:3). It imparts joy: "And the ransomed of the Lord shall return, and come to Zion with singing; everlasting joy shall be upon their heads; they shall obtain joy and gladness, and sorrow and sighing shall flee away" (Isa. 35:10; cf. 12:3; 29:19; 51:11).

F. Piety as Personal

The changed conditions during the Exile made profound changes in the nature of Old Testament religion. The rites of the Temple were no longer possible. While worship and instruction centering in the synagogue was still largely limited to the people of Israel, participation became more and more a matter of individual choice. "In place of membership by birth and residential qualification comes membership by free and responsible resolve."[15] As Kohler wrote: "The one community of those exiles faithful to Jahweh consists of many small local communities: and each local community has its own synagogue: each synagogue has its meetings, its rolls of Scripture, its expositions, its instructors and its pupils. The Temple is replaced by the School, sacrifice by Scripture, priest by Rabbi, pilgrimage by Sabbath and Sabbath walk to the Synagogue."[16]

These changes had their beginnings earlier in the teachings of the wise and the preaching of the prophets. Prophetic religion was not only personal and voluntary, it was profoundly moral. What the prophets emphasized was not something new. It was rather a growing emphasis. "In Israel it was perceived in germ in the beginning, and with increasing clearness as time passed, that what God is they who worship him should become. Thus the religion of Israel is ethical in its essence, and not merely in its demands."[17]

A proper relationship to the Lord God depended on moral integrity and devotion to justice, goodness, and truth. When the very existence of the Temple was threatened, Jeremiah preached the first of his great "Temple Sermons":

15. Kohler, *OT Theology*, p. 83.
16. *Ibid.*
17. Rowley, *Unity of the Bible*, p. 59.

> Hear the word of the Lord, all you men of Judah who enter these gates to worship the Lord. Thus says the Lord of hosts, the God of Israel, Amend your ways and your doings, and I will let you dwell in this place. Do not trust in these deceptive words: 'This is the temple of the Lord, the temple of the Lord, the temple of the Lord.' For if you truly amend your ways and your doings, if you truly execute justice one with another, if you do not oppress the alien, the fatherless or the widow, or shed innocent blood in this place, and if you do not go after other gods to your own hurt, then I will let you dwell in this place, in the land that I gave of old to your fathers for ever *(7:2-7).*

Ezekiel voiced a similar standard:

> If a man is righteous and does what is lawful and right—if he does not eat upon the mountains or lift up his eyes to the idols of the house of Israel, does not defile his neighbor's wife or approach a woman in her time of impurity, does not oppress any one, but restores to the debtor his pledge, commits no robbery, gives his bread to the hungry and covers the naked with a garment, does not lend at interest or take any increase, withholds his hand from iniquity, executes true justice between man and man, walks in my statutes, and is careful to observe my ordinances—he is righteous, he shall surely live, says the Lord God *(18:5-9).*

Summarizing these and other passages, Hermann Schultz wrote: "In the eyes of God, sacred forms have absolutely no value, except as expressions of faith, humility, and obedience. Such is the burden of the prophetic messages from Amos and Hosea down to the Exile."[18]

Jeremiah's prophecy of the new covenant clearly shows a deep concept of sin together with a sense of the need for individual conversion and a radical inner change: "This is the covenant that I will make with the house of Israel after those days, says the Lord: I will put my law in their inward parts, and upon their hearts will I write it; I will be their God and they shall be My people. And no longer shall each man teach his neighbor and each his brother, saying, 'Know the Lord,' for they shall all know Me, from the least of them to the greatest, says the Lord; for I will forgive their iniquity, and their sin will I remember no more" (31:33-34, Berk.). "Jeremiah says that no mere attempt to alter outward behaviour will serve, for a man can only give up sinning if his heart is changed."[19]

---

18. *OT Theology,* 2:53-54.
19. Smith, *Bible Doctrine of Salvation,* p. 47.

II. HOLINESS IN THE OLD TESTAMENT

Personal piety in the Old Testament is frequently described in terms of holiness. Israel had early been called to be a "holy nation" (Exod. 19:6; Lev. 19:2; 20:26). This involved both cultic or ritual holiness, and moral conduct or ethical holiness.[20]

A. The Moral Element in Holiness

The command "Be ye holy" applies both to morals and to ritual—and often to both at once as in the holiness code of Leviticus 17—26 (cf. especially Lev. 19:1-37). Here respect for parents, Sabbath observance, idolatry, offerings, compassion on the poor, honesty and truthfulness, talebearing, hatred and grudge-holding, vengeance, sex morality, and the atonement ritual are all dealt with in the span of 19 verses (19:2-20).

The cultic or ritual elements tended to overshadow the ethical in the earliest Old Testament emphasis. But never was the ethical entirely absent. In the prophets, the emphasis was on the moral or ethical aspects of holiness, but never was the ritual completely lost. The prophets came to define the life to which God calls His people in terms of likeness to Him and partaking of His nature.[21] "While the doctrine of the holiness of Israel described at first a distinctive way-of-life in which ritual and ethics were blent indistinguishably, at the last it denoted a way-of-life where the two were still blent but in which ethics were the essential and paramount element."[22]

An older statement of the moral content of holiness was made by Alfred Edersheim:

> The Hebrew term for "Holy" is generally supposed to mean "separated, set apart." But this is only its secondary signification, derived from the purpose of that which is holy. Its primary meaning is to be splendid, beautiful, pure, and uncontaminated. God is holy—as the Absolutely Pure, Resplendent, and Glorious One. Hence this is symbolized by the light. God dwelleth in light that is unapproachable; He is "the Father of lights, with whom is no variableness, neither shadow of turning"—light which can never grow dimmer, nor give place to darkness. Christ is the light that shineth in the darkness of our world, "The true light which lighteth every man." And Israel was to be a holy people as dwelling in the light, through its covenant-relationship to God.

20. Cf. Payne, *Theology of the Older Testament*, p. 101.
21. Cf. Davidson, *Theology of the OT*, pp. 152 ff.
22. Smith, *The Bible Doctrine of Man*, p. 46.

It was not the selection of Israel from all other nations that made them holy, but the relationship to God into which it brought the people. The call of Israel, their election and selection, were only the means. Holiness itself was to be attained through the covenant, which provided forgiveness and sanctification, and in which by the discipline of His law and the guidance of His Holy Arm, Israel was to be led onward and upward. Thus, if God showed the excellence of His name or His glory in creation, the way of His holiness was among Israel.[23]

John Wick Bowman distinguishes between what he calls the priestly and the prophetic meanings of holiness. The priestly meaning of holiness was ceremonial in the sense of being set apart, dedicated, separated. The prophetic meaning of holiness is that in which the ethical element is paramount, as in the vision of Isaiah 6. Both meanings, as we have seen, combine in the "holiness code" of Leviticus 19. "The New Testament, finally, takes up only the prophetic side of the term and perpetuates it. All Christians are to be 'saints' (holy ones— Rom. 1:7), that is, ethically holy, separated, consecrated to God's service (Mark 6:20; John 17:17; Rev. 3:7), that they may have fellowship with a holy God (Acts 9:13; Rom. 1:7; Heb. 6:10; Rev. 5:8)."[24]

Walther Eichrodt stresses much the same point:

> The decisive element in the concept of holiness is shown to be that of belonging to God—not that of separation, which is secondary—but holiness itself, from being a relational concept, becomes a condition, a personal quality. The man who belongs to God must possess a particular kind of nature, which by comprising at once outward and inward, ritual and moral purity will correspond to the nature of the holy God.[25]

B. Isaiah's Temple Vision

The vision of Isaiah in the Temple described in 6:1-8 clearly reveals the ethical nature of holiness as it relates to human experience. Isaiah was not stricken chiefly with a sense of his weakness and humanity in contrast to the power and sovereignty of God. He was stricken with the sense of his inner sinfulness. He cried out, "Woe is me, for I am undone"—literally, "I am shattered."

---

23. *Bible History: Old Testament* (Grand Rapids, Mich.: William B. Eerdmans Publishing Co., 1949 reprint), 2:110.

24. *Prophetic Realism and the Gospel* (Philadelphia: Westminster Press, 1955), pp. 161-63.

25. *Theology of the OT,* 1:137.

Nor was Isaiah's conviction related to what he had been doing. The problem of early rebellion against the Lord had been settled before he assumed the prophet's mantle (cf. 1:1 as indicating that Isaiah's prophetic ministry had begun during the last years of Uzziah's life). His conviction related to what he was: "I am a man . . . unclean." His lips mirrored the state of his inner nature: "Out of the abundance of the heart the mouth speaks" (Matt. 12:34; 15:18). Ludwig Kohler says of this confession: "Here holiness is the opposite of sinfulness. God is holy because He does not tolerate sin, He uncovers it, He rebukes it, refuses to connive at it, punishes it or atoning for it forgives it. Sin separates a person from the holy God."[26]

The result of Isaiah's confession was immediate. The seraph flew with a live coal, touched the prophet's lips, and said, "Behold, this has touched your lips; your guilt [*avon*, "perversity," "sin as a state or principle"] is taken away, and your sin forgiven [*kaphar, pual,* "cleansed, purged"]" (v. 7). Ryder Smith writes:

> The whole man is cleansed from sin, not his lips only. The word rendered "purged" is kipper. At this point there is no need to discuss the vexed question of its origin and meaning, for the whole Vision shows that, whatever else the word means, there is cleansing from sin. Among the Hebrews, of course, the arts of smelting and refining were both practiced, and in both fire purifies and cleanses. Malachi uses the word "refine" *(zaqaq)* to denote the "purifying" and saving of the Sons of Levi (Ma. 3:3). In Isaiah the rendering of *kipper* by "purge" best expresses the meaning of the passage.[27]

It was after this purging that the prophet heard the Lord speak, and his prophetic mission was affirmed and enlarged.

C. Summary

Davidson gives a valuable summary of holiness in the Old Testament both in relation to God and in relation to man:

> (1) We see *Holy* as a designation of Jehovah; having reference to His Godhead, or to anything which was a manifestation of His Godhead.
> (2) We have it as used of men and things. These it describes as belonging to Jehovah, dedicated to Him, devoted or set apart to Him. Primarily, therefore, it expressed merely the relation.
> (3) But naturally the conception of dedication to Jehovah brought into view Jehovah's character, which reacted on the

26. *OT Theology,* p. 53; cf. Vriezen, *Outline of OT Theology,* p. 159.
27. *Bible Doctrine of Grace,* pp. 18-19.

things or persons devoted to Him. Hence a two-fold filling up on the circumference of the word "holy" took place.

(a) As to men devoted to Him, they must share His character, and thus the term "holy" took on a moral complexion.

(b) As to things, they must be fit to be Jehovah's. Even when "clean" is used here by the prophets, it denotes moral purity.[28]

III. The Call for Social Justice

Tied in with the prophetic emphasis on personal religion is the persistent call for social justice. Both the "first" and "second" commandments of the New Testament (Mark 12:28-33), love of God and love for neighbor, are based upon Old Testament injunctions: "You shall love the Lord your God with all your heart, and with all your soul, and with all your might" (Deut. 6:5); and "You shall love your neighbor as yourself" (Lev. 19:18). Neither the New Testament nor the Old knows anything of the modern disjunction between a "personal gospel" and a "social gospel."

While most of the prophets show their concern for right dealings between man and man, Amos is particularly emphatic in this regard. "Amos' demand for justice is grounded in the fundamental principle of Hebrew ethics—as God acts toward Israel so the Israelites should act toward one another."[29] Heartless oppression of the poor (2:6-8; 5:11), the selfish luxury of the wealthy (6:1-6), and shameless economic exploitation of the masses (8:4-6) are among the sins that led the prophet to speak in God's name: "I hate, I despise your feasts. . . . Even though you offer me your burnt offerings and cereal offerings, I will not accept them, and the peace offerings of your fatted beasts I will not look upon" (5:21-22).

28. *Theology of the OT,* p. 248.
29. Lawrence E. Toombs, *The Old Testament in Christian Preaching* (Philadelphia: The Westminster Press, 1961), p. 139.

11

The Messianic Hope
and Eschatology

The meaning and even the existence in the Old Testament of what has traditionally been known as "the Messianic hope" has been vigorously debated. Liberal Jewish thought and Christian rationalism have both denied that there is any genuine messianism in the Old Testament. Yet it is all but undeniable that the Old Testament is a forward-looking Book whose fulfillment lies beyond the scope of its own record. As H. H. Rowley has argued throughout his volume *The Unity of the Bible,* if the Old Testament is not fulfilled in Christ, it has not been fulfilled at all.

I. THE MEANING OF "MESSIAH"

While the term *Messiah* occurs but once in the KJV Old Testament (Dan. 9:25-27), the Hebrew *meschiach,* of which "Messiah" is an English transliteration, is freely used in the Hebrew Bible. *Meshiach* means "the anointed." The anointing may refer to the induction of priests, of prophets, or of kings to their respective offices. The term has great meaning for Christians. *Christos,* from which "Christ" is derived, is the Greek equivalent of the Hebrew *meschiach* or "Messiah." On the early pages of the New Testament, *Christos* occurs with the definite article, "the Christ" (e.g., Matt. 16:16; 27:22; John 4:29; 1 John 2:22; 5:1). It was only later that "Christ" came to function as a name rather than as a title.

The Messianic references of the Old Testament are those statements that relate to a coming Deliverer, or One who would accomplish through His own sacrifice the redemption of the people of God.[1] Edmond Jacob claims that "a theology of the Old Testament which is founded not on certain isolated verses, but on the Old Testament as a whole, can only be a Christology, for what was revealed under the old covenant, through a long and varied history, in events, persons and institutions, is, in Christ, gathered together and brought to perfection."[2] Gerhard von Rad is equally emphatic:

> No special hermeneutic method is necessary to see the whole diversified movement of the Old Testament saving events, made up of God's promises and their temporary fulfilments, as pointing to their future fulfilment in Jesus Christ. This can be said quite categorically. The coming of Jesus Christ as a historical reality leaves the exegete no choice at all; he must interpret the Old Testament as pointing to Christ, whom he must understand in its light.[3]

There are early intimations of the Messiah in the Old Testament (e.g., Gen. 3:15; 49:10). But it is in the Psalms and the Prophets that the vision comes more and more into focus.[4] The Messianic emphasis becomes, in fact, a bridge over the chasm that would otherwise separate the Old Testament from the New. Eichrodt writes:

> The distinctive quality of the prophetic attitude resides therefore in this; that while it is certainly rooted in that history which is the product of God's operation, it yet feels itself pointed beyond this to a new perfection, in which alone the true sense and meaning of the present is to be fulfilled, and which therefore calls for steadfast endurance in the fierce tension between the present and the future.[5]

While there is admittedly some variation in the Messianic expectations of the Old Testament,[6] in general they revolved around two foci: (1) the Davidic King and the realization of the kingdom of God on earth; and (2) the "Suffering Servant" as in Isaiah and certain of the psalms. Both the crown and the Cross are represented.[7]

---

1. Vriezen, *Outline of OT Theology*, p. 353.
2. *Theology of the OT*, p. 12.
3. *OT Theology*, 2:374.
4. For a different interpretation see Young, *Study of OT Theology Today*, p. 78.
5. *Theology of the OT*, 1:389.
6. Vriezen, *Outline of OT Theology*, p. 353.
7. Cf. Davidson, *Theology of the OT*, pp. 365-67; Smith, *Bible Doctrine of Salvation*, pp. 34-43.

II. MESSIAH AS THE DAVIDIC KING

As early as Gen. 49:10, the tribe of Judah was identified as the tribe from which "the scepter shall not depart . . . until he comes to whom it belongs; and to him shall be the obedience of the peoples." Shiloh, the "rest-giver," describes an attribute of Christ stressed in the New Testament (Matt. 11:28-30; Heb. 4:1-11). Judah was the royal family in Israel from the time of David on, and the nature of God's promise to the house of David has unquestioned Messianic application: "And your house and your kingdom shall be made sure for ever before me; your throne shall be established for ever" (2 Sam. 7:16; cf. vv. 12-15 and 1 Chron. 22:10).

A. In the Psalms

The concept of the kingly Messiah is a common note in the Psalms (2; 45; 72; 89:19-37; 110; 132:11). Of these, Psalm 110 is the most important since this is the psalm most frequently quoted in the New Testament in reference to Christ: "The Lord says to my lord: 'Sit at my right hand, till I make your enemies your footstool.' The Lord sends forth from Zion your mighty scepter. Rule in the midst of your foes! . . . The Lord has sworn and will not change his mind, 'You are a priest for ever after the order of Melchizedek.'" The reference to Melchizedek, who combined in himself the kingly and priestly offices, provides a crucial link in the argument in Hebrews 5 and 7 in the New Testament.

These psalms were both "royal" and Messianic. H. H. Rowley wrote: "There is reason to believe that while they may have been royal psalms, used in the royal rites of the temple, they were also 'messianic'. They held before the king the ideal king, both as his inspiration and guide for the present, and as the hope of the future."[8]

Helmer Ringgren made the same point:

> From the very beginning the Christian church understood these (royal) psalms as prophecies of Christ, and to a certain extent modern research has justified this interpretation. It has been shown that the messianic hope in Israel grew out of the idea of the king as the God-sent ruler. The royal psalms prepare the way for the Christian belief in the Messiah, and thus form an important and essential part of the history of revelation. As a matter of fact, the Christian belief in Jesus as the messianic King and

8. *Faith of Israel*, p. 192.

Saviour would be unthinkable and unintelligible apart from the background of the Old Testament kingship ideology as expressed in the royal psalms.[9]

B. In the Prophets

The royal Messiah is most clearly depicted in the prophets. Isaiah speaks of "the branch of the Lord" and "a root of Jesse" in respect to the coming reign of righteousness over all the earth (4:2; 11:10). Both Jeremiah (23:5-6; 33:15-26) and Zechariah (3:8; 6:12) also write of the "Branch." "Behold, the days are coming, says the Lord, when I will raise up for David a righteous Branch, and he shall reign as king and deal wisely, and shall execute justice and righteousness in the land. In his days Judah will be saved, and Israel will dwell securely. And this is the name by which he will be called: 'The Lord is our righteousness'" (Jer. 23:5-6).

1. *The Early Prophets.* The "Immanuel" promise of Isa. 7:14 is explicitly applied to the virgin birth of Jesus in Matt. 1:23, where the chronological sign given to Ahab becomes an ontological sign testifying to the unique character of the Son of Mary. That there was only one true Virgin Birth in the history of mankind should make conservative scholars careful about contending for a translation of Isa. 7:14 that would imply a "virgin birth" in the historical fulfillment of the promise in Ahab's time (8:3-4; cf. 2 Kings 15:29-30).

The Hebrew "prophetic perfect" as used in Isa. 9:6-7 expressed the certainty in the prophet's mind that what God had spoken would come to pass: "For to us a child is [Heb., has been] born, to us a son is [has been] given. . . . Of the increase of his government and of peace there will be no end." Here the deity of the Messiah is affirmed, as well as His kingly lineage from the house of David. Isa. 24:23 and 25:9 also state that "the Lord of hosts will reign," and "It will be said on that day, 'Lo, this is our God; we have waited for him, that he might save us.'"

Isa. 28:16-17 predicts the laying "in Zion for a foundation a stone, a tested stone, a precious cornerstone, of a sure foundation"— words applied to Jesus three times in the New Testament (Rom. 9:33; Eph. 2:20; 1 Pet. 2:6-8). A king reigning in righteousness whose influence will be "like streams of water in a dry place, like the shade of a great rock in a weary land" is foreseen in 32:1-6—"the king in his beauty" (33:17).

---

9. *The Faith of the Psalmists* (Philadelphia: Fortress Press, 1963), p. 114.

A foreshadowing of the Trinity is seen in Isa. 48:16 by Ethelbert Stauffer:[10] "Draw near to me, hear this: from the beginning I have not spoken in secret, from the time it came to be I have been there. And now the Lord God has sent me and his Spirit." God's "everlasting covenant . . . [and] the sure mercies of David" are the basis of God's universal invitation to the spiritually thirsty and hungry (55: 1-4). Isa. 61:1-3 is the passage quoted by Jesus of himself in the synagogue at Nazareth (Luke 4:18-19).

Like Isaiah, his contemporary Micah envisions the reign of peace when "strong nations . . . shall beat their swords into plowshares, and their spears into pruning hooks" (4:1-4). Micah named Bethlehem as the town from which He should come forth who was "to be ruler in Israel, whose origin is from of old, from ancient days" (5:2).

2. *Prophets of the Exile.* In addition to Jeremiah's allusion to the righteous Branch and the King to be raised "unto David" (23:5-6; 33:15-26), the prophet also speaks of a "David *redevivis*" in 30:9—"But they shall serve the Lord their God and David their king, whom I will raise up for them."

Ezekiel speaks of "David" as the princely shepherd over God's people: "And I will set up over them one shepherd, my servant David, and he shall feed them: he shall feed them and be their shepherd. And I, the Lord, will be their God, and my servant David shall be prince among them; I, the Lord, have spoken" (34:23-24). Similar language is used in 37:24-25 and Hos. 3:5.

Daniel is the source of the "Son of man" concept of the Messiah. The point of Daniel's prophecy is not the humanity and humility sometimes associated with the phrase "Son of man." It is rather that "dominion, and glory, and a kingdom" are to be given to the Son of Man, "that all people, nations, and languages should serve him" (7:9-14). Daniel also speaks explicitly of "Messiah the Prince" (KJV) who is to be "cut off, but not for himself" (9:25-27).

3. *Postexilic Prophets.* As previously noted, Zechariah, along with Isaiah and Jeremiah, also refers to the Messiah as the "Branch" (Zech. 3:8; 6:12). He speaks of the King who will come riding on a donkey (9:9-16), the prediction of the Triumphal Entry into Jerusalem cited in Matt. 21:5. The Davidic ancestry of the coming One is mentioned in Zech. 12:8 (KJV). A prediction of Messiah's coming to the Mount

10. *New Testament Theology,* trans. from the German by John Marsh (New York: The Macmillan Co., 1955), p. 327.

of Olives is given in 14:3-4. David Baron wrote: "Perhaps in no other single book in the Old Testament is Messiah's Divinity so clearly taught as in Zechariah."[11]

Malachi completes the roster of Old Testament prophets who speak of Messiah's coming in kingly power and judgment. "Behold, I send my messenger to prepare the way before me, and the Lord whom you seek will suddenly come to his temple; the messenger of the covenant in whom you delight, behold, he is coming, says the Lord of hosts. But who can endure the day of his coming, and who can stand when he appears? For he is like a refiner's fire and like fullers' soap; he will sit as a refiner and purifier of silver, and he will purify the sons of Levi and refine them like gold and silver, till they present right offerings to the Lord. Then the offering of Judah and Jerusalem will be pleasing to the Lord as in the days of old and as in former years" (3:1-4). "But for you who fear my name the sun of righteousness shall rise, with healing in its wings. You shall go forth leaping like calves from the stall. And you shall tread down the wicked, for they will be ashes under the soles of your feet, on the day when I act, says the Lord of hosts" (4:2-3).

C. The New Testament Fulfillment

That the nature of the Kingdom was misunderstood and made a political realm is the consensus of the New Testament witness. The prophecies and promises of the Old Testament are not abrogated but transformed. That there is a "kingdom of glory" yet to come does not set aside the reality of the "kingdom of grace" that now exists wherever the King reigns in the hearts of men (Matt. 18:3; Mark 12:34; John 3:3; 18:36). As Gelin wrote:

> The Promise, which was apparently concerned with the possession of Canaan and the setting up of an earthly kingdom, was transformed into the promise of spiritual blessings (Matt. v.5; Rom. iv.18); the Covenant with Moses was transformed into the New Covenant (2 Cor. iii). The Kingdom of David was transformed into the Kingdom of Heaven (Matt. v. 3); and the salvation of the exiles became the justice inherent in the soul (Rom. i:16-17) —a wonderful development, guided by the hand of God, and a marvellous educative process, gradually leading the souls of men

11. *Rays of Messiah's Glory: Christ in the Old Testament* (Grand Rapids, Mich.: Zondervan Publishing House, reprint 1955), p. 77 fn.

to an understanding of the nature of the 'Messianic' goods, i.e., the whole complex of eternal values that were to come into the world with Jesus Christ.[12]

Just as the idea of the covenant in the Old Testament was transformed into a new covenant in the New Testament, so the idea of the kingly reign of Messiah becomes infinitely enriched and spiritualized in the context of the total canon.

III. MESSIAH AS THE "SUFFERING SERVANT"

Along with the concept of Messiah as King—and in most of the same Old Testament books—is the picture of Messiah as suffering with or on behalf of His people.

The *protevangelium* of Gen. 3:15 speaks of the "seed" of the woman who will trample the serpent's head, but do it at the cost of personal injury to himself. God said to the serpent, "He shall bruise your head, and you shall bruise his heel."

A. In the Psalms

Most noteworthy are the large number of references in the Psalms which the New Testament Gospels apply directly to the crucifixion of Jesus. Ps. 16:8-10 is the passage quoted by Peter as scriptural evidence for the resurrection of Christ (Acts 2:25-28): "For thou dost not give me up to Sheol [the realm of the dead], or let thy godly one see the Pit" (v. 10).

Psalm 22 is uniquely "The Psalm of the Cross." It opens with the cry of dereliction, "My God, my God, why hast thou forsaken me?" (v. 1; Matt. 27:46; Mark 15:34). It continues with reference to the scorn of the bystanders (vv. 7-8; Matt. 27:43), the horrible thirst associated with crucifixion (v. 15; John 19:28), the piercing of hands and feet (v. 16; John 20:25), and the triumph in which God's name is declared to the Church (v. 22; Heb. 2:12).

Ps. 31:5 is the source of the word of committal on the Cross, "Into thy hand I commit my spirit" (Luke 23:46). John 19:36 cites Ps. 34:20 as fulfilled by the Roman spear thrust into the side of Jesus instead of the customary breaking of the leg bones of the crucified. Ps. 40:6-8 is quoted in Heb. 10:5-7 as characterizing the submission of Christ to the Father's will. The betrayal is hinted in 41:9 (John 13:18). Ps. 68:18 is given by Paul as indicating the Messiah's ascent to the Father (Eph. 4:8).

---

12. *Key Concepts of the OT*, p. 47.

The gall and vinegar offered on the Cross (Matt. 27:34, 48) is mentioned in Ps. 69:21. Paul sees in 69:22-23 a prediction of the results of Messiah's rejection by His people: "Let their own table before them become a snare; let their sacrificial feasts be a trap. Let their eyes be darkened, so that they cannot see; and make their loins tremble continually" (cf. Rom. 11:9-10). Ps. 109:8 is seen by Peter in Acts 1:20 as a reference to the betrayer: "May his days be few; may another scize his goods!" Ps. 118:22 is cited by all the synoptic Gospels and by Peter as referring to Christ's rejection and subsequent exaltation: "The stone which the builders rejected has become the head of the corner" (cf. Matt. 21:43; Mark 12:10-11; Luke 20:17; Acts 4:11; 1 Pet. 2:7).

B. The "Servant Songs" of Isaiah

The great "Servant Songs" of Isaiah (42:1-7; 49:1-7; 50:4-11; 52:13—53:12) have occasioned much discussion among Old Testament scholars. The identity of the "Servant" has variously been given as the prophet himself, the nation collectively, the people of Israel as a corporate personality, the ideal nation, and the Messiah. H. Wheeler Robinson holds that the immediate reference is to Israel as a corporate personality. Then he adds: "It is no rhetorical exaggeration, but sober truth in the light of criticism, history and psychology, to describe the Songs of the Servant as the Old Testament portrait of Jesus Christ."[13]

Identified and named by B. Duhm in 1922, the "Songs" have been called "one of the most outstanding sections of all the divine revelation. . . . In thought and teaching they are linked more closely with the New Testament than any other Old Testament scriptures."[14]

The first passage (42:1-7 or 9) describes the office to which the Servant is called. The second song (49:1-7) records the Servant's task. In the third passage (50:4-9 or 11), the Servant voices His obedience and trust in the Lord God who had called Him.[15]

The "fourth Servant Song" (52:13—53:12) is deservedly the most famous. This is the clearest Old Testament statement of a substitutionary sacrifice. All of the major writers of the New Testament describe the death of Christ in language drawn from Isaiah

---

13. *The Cross in the Old Testament* (Philadelphia: The Westminster Press, 1955), p. 57.
14. W. Fitch, "Isaiah," *NBC*, p. 591.
15. *Ibid.*, pp. 591, 596, 598.

53. H. Wheeler Robinson again says, "The cardinal fact for the Christian student is that to those ideas Jesus of Nazareth has served Himself heir, and He has blended the details of its portrait with His own. This fact alone is sufficient to make 'the fifty-third of Isaiah' the most important page of the Old Testament for the student of the New."[16] Hermann Schultz wrote, "If it is true anywhere in the history of poetry and prophecy, it is true here that the writer, being full of the Spirit, has said more than he himself meant to say and more than he himself understood."[17]

The third stanza of the Song (53:4-6) is undoubtedly the greatest description of vicarious suffering in the literature of the world: "Surely he has borne our griefs and carried our sorrows; yet we esteemed him stricken, smitten by God, and afflicted. But he was wounded for our transgressions, he was bruised for our iniquities; upon him was the chastisement that made us whole, and with his stripes we are healed. All we like sheep have gone astray; we have turned every one to his own way; and the Lord has laid on him the iniquity of us all." It is suffering accepted without complaint (v. 7) as a result of which many are justified (v. 11).

The Servant (52:13) bears our griefs, carries our sorrows, is wounded for our transgressions, bruised for our iniquities. He was stricken for the transgression of the people (v. 8), and in His death He was laid with the rich (v. 9), having been numbered with the transgressors (v. 12; Mark 15:28; Luke 22:27). *"He is a Messiah who suffers vicariously,"* wrote Ludwig Kohler. "At this point the theology of the Old Testament comes to an end. In the New Testament the question is asked: 'Understandest thou what thou readest?' Acts 8:30."[18] The words of H. H. Rowley are worth quoting:

> Of no other than Christ can the terms of the fourth Servant Song be predicated with even remote relevance; it would be hard for even the most sceptical to declare them absurd in relation to Him. For whether we like it or not, and whether we can explain it or not, countless numbers of men and women, of many races and countries, and of every age from His day to ours, have experienced a major change of heart and life when they have stood before the Cross of Christ, and have felt that no words but those of Isa. liii.5 were adequate to express their thought. . . . If the hand of God is found in the promise, then fulfillment it ought to have, and here

---

16. *Cross in the OT,* p. 66.
17. *OT Theology,* 2:432-33.
18. *OT Theology,* p. 238, italics in original.

fulfillment is to be seen. If the hand of God is denied in the promise, then it is passing strange that it should find so remarkable a fulfillment.[19]

C. The Later Prophetic Teaching

The note of betrayal and suffering for the Messiah also occurs in the only passage in the KJV Old Testament in which the term itself is found in English: "Know therefore and understand, that from the going forth of the commandment to restore and to build Jerusalem unto the Messiah the Prince shall be seven weeks and threescore and two weeks: the street shall be built again, and the wall, even in troublous times. And after threescore and two weeks shall Messiah be cut off, but not for himself: and the people of the prince that shall come shall destroy the city and the sanctuary" (Dan. 9:25-26, KJV).

Zech. 13:6-7 describes the wounds in the hands of the One "wounded in the house of" His friends: "And if one asks him, 'What are these wounds on your back?' he will say, 'The wounds I received in the house of my friends.' Awake, O sword, against my shepherd, against the man who stands next to me, says the Lord of hosts. Strike the shepherd, that the sheep may be scattered; I will turn my hand against the little ones." Matthew connects the smiting of the Shepherd and the scattering of the sheep with the crucifixion of Jesus (Matt. 26:31).

D. The Cross and the Crown

The development of the two Messianic strands from the Old Testament in the later tradition is revealing. Both crown and Cross are foreshadowed. But the crown tends to crowd out the Cross. By New Testament times the idea of a suffering Messiah had almost entirely disappeared and had become all but incredible. It is natural for man to grasp the crown while avoiding the Cross. Such proved indeed to be the chief obstacle to recognition of the Messianic claims of the Early Church for its Founder and Head. The predominance of the political overtones of the crown in the minds of the people was also the probable basis for the "Messianic secret" Jesus consistently imposed on His disciples (e.g., Matt. 16:20; 17:9; Mark 3:12; 5:43).

While the Messianic hope was in no sense an afterthought in the Old Testament, the outlines did become clearer with the passing centuries. Both the kingdom and the sacrifice of the Messiah took on

---

19. *Unity of the Bible,* p. 107.

deeper meaning when the sovereignty of the nation was lost and the sacrificial offerings of the Temple were suspended. Schultz wrote:

> Now, just as the outward forms of sacrifice begin to fade away into shadows, the age is lighted up with the pregnant thought of a nobler sacrifice about to come. The Servant of God who represents Israel's calling, and who, uniting the sinful people with its God, becomes Himself an atonement for Israel, suffers and dies in His vocation in order to secure this reconciliation. His death, freely endured for the people, is a means of reconciliation of a new kind, an offering for sin unlike the victims slain of old. Thus, as the shadows disappear, prophecy grasps the substance.[20]

The Old Testament ends with a word of judgment. But the warning of judgment is itself the vehicle of hope. "But for you who fear my name the sun of righteousness shall rise, with healing in its wings. You shall go forth leaping like calves from the stall" (Mal. 4:2).

IV. THE ESCHATOLOGY OF THE OLD TESTAMENT

"Eschatology" is the technical term for the doctrine of the last days, the ending of human history, and the transition of time into eternity. While eschatology in the Old Testament takes a number of forms,[21] its chief ideas cluster around the very complex concept of "the day of the Lord."

A. The Day of the Lord

In contrast with others of the ancient East, Israel's writers looked forward as well as back. Time for them was not cyclical but linear. It had a beginning—when God created. It would have an end—and that end is to be more than the last moment in a long sequence of moments. It is then that man will find the meaning and purpose of the whole span of history. The "day of the Lord" is more than the last day in point of time. It is the goal and destination toward which all moves.[22]

1. *Salvation and Judgment*. When we take the books in their probable order of writing, the first reference to the day of the Lord in the Old Testament occurs in Amos 5:18, about 760 B.C.[23] Amos spoke of the day of the Lord as a matter of common and hopeful anticipation among the people. But he sounds one of the most characteristic notes

---

20. *OT Theology*, 2:96.
21. Knight, *Christian Theology of the OT*, pp. 294-333.
22. *Ibid.*, pp. 294-95.
23. Cf. Payne, *Theology of the Older Testament*, p. 464.

in the prophetic handling of this theme: "The day of the Lord is darkness, and not light" (5:18-20). The people thought of God only as the Source of blessing and His coming day as a time of their vindication. They forgot His justice and ignored their sins of idolatry and the oppression of the helpless and poor.[24]

Although the exact expression "The day of the Lord" is not used, Isa. 21:11-12 symbolizes its two sides: "One is calling to me from Seir, 'Watchman, what of the night? Watchman, what of the night?' The watchman says: 'Morning comes, and also the night.'" The righteous may hope for the day of the Lord as the time of their vindication and blessing. For them it is morning. But the wicked and the godless must be warned to fear the day of the Lord as the hour of their judgment. For them it is night.

The day of the Lord was always associated with the personal intervention of God in the affairs of men. It is connected with His coming, personally and objectively. Thus it unfolds along three general lines: the impending judgment on the nation; the Messianic Kingdom; and the consummation of history.

It is in regard to the day of the Lord as the consummation of history that its most common use is found. The double aspect of salvation and judgment is consistently stated. "The day of the Lord is great and very terrible; who can endure it? . . . The sun shall be turned to darkness, and the moon to blood, before the great and terrible day of the Lord comes. And it shall come to pass that all who call upon the name of the Lord shall be delivered; for in Mount Zion and in Jerusalem there shall be those who escape, as the Lord has said, and among the survivors shall be those whom the Lord calls" (Joel 2:11, 31-32).

2. The "Foreshortened Perspective." The prophets lived and wrote with a sense of the approaching day of judgment on their nation. They also tended to include both the impending catastrophe to Israel and the Messianic age with events to occur at the end of time. Thus "the day of the Lord" in the Old Testament, as in the New, includes much which we would now recognize as relating to the second coming of Christ.

Rowley describes what has been called the "foreshortened perspective" of the prophets: "To the Church, which stands between the First Advent and the Second Advent, there is a long time process between the one and the other, but to prophets who saw the future

---

24. Kohler, *OT Theology*, p. 220.

afar off the depth in time was lost, as depth in space is lost to the eye of one who looks at the stars, and the First Advent and the Second Advent are therefore fused in prophecy."[25] It is thus common to find side by side in the Old Testament what the fuller light of the New Testament shows to be events separated by at least 2,000 years (e.g., Joel 2:28-31).

Mention has been made of the prophetic sense of imminence in respect to the day of the Lord. It must be recognized that in both the Old Testament and the New, statements of imminence have a logical as well as chronological meaning. Biblical writers speak of what they know to be certain either as already having occurred (the prophetic present) or as being near at hand. The prophets of the Old Testament and the apostles of the New Testament were therefore not necessarily mistaken when they affirmed that the day of the Lord is at hand. They were expressing their certainty that it would come.

B. Apocalyptic and the Eschaton

Closely associated with the day of the Lord was a form of writing known as "apocalyptic." Apocalyptic literature forms a class by itself. The bulk of it falls in the Apocrypha—that group of books originating between the writing of Malachi and the coming of Jesus. But portions of Isaiah, Ezekiel, Daniel, Joel, and Zechariah—as well as the Book of Revelation in the New Testament—are examples of biblical apocalyptic.

The terms *apocalypse* and *apocalyptic* come from the Greek *apoka-lypto*—literally, to "uncover, bring to light what is hidden; reveal; set in a clear light." The noun *apokalypsis* means "a disclosure, a revelation"; and, metaphorically, "illumination, instruction, manifestation, or appearance."

Apocalyptic is prophecy couched in cryptic language, employing symbolic figures and events, dealing particularly with the *eschaton*, the last days. Its universal theme is how God will intervene to wind up the affairs of men, judge His enemies, and set up His kingdom.

Apocalyptic came into its own during the closing days of the Old Testament period. It is, as H. H. Rowley says, "the child of prophecy." Prophecy tends to merge into apocalyptic. Apocalyptic developed

---

25. *Faith of Israel,* p. 200.

from prophecy as life grew increasingly difficult for the people of Israel. Apocalyptic flourishes in times of national or community crisis.[26]

Yet prophecy becomes tinged with apocalyptic early in its history. There are apocalyptic aspects in the typically prophetic announcement of "the day of the Lord" as early as c. 760 B.C.[27] Isaiah dips his pen in apocalyptic symbolism in Isaiah 24—27, a passage sometimes known as the Isaiah-Apocalypse.[28] Joel may be as late as the time immediately following 586 B.C.; yet Joel 2:28—3:3 illustrates the ease with which prophecy merges into apocalyptic.

It was, however, during the Exile and on through the second century of the Christian era that apocalyptic attained full stature both in canonical and extracanonical writing.[29] Extracanonical apocalyptic, in contrast with biblical apocalyptic, tended to go to seed and run wild with few limits to the imagination.

There is a connection also between apocalyptic and the wisdom movement, as diverse as the two at first appear. Daniel, for example, represents wisdom both in his training and in his position (Dan. 1:3 ff.; 2:48; 5:11) and the same conjunction of wisdom and apocalyptic appears in some of the extracanonical writing such as 1 Enoch and the Apocalypse of Enoch.[30]

While apocalyptic is difficult to define, its main features may be readily noted. Some of these are *differentia* from prophecy while still showing the relationship between prophecy and apocalyptic.

Vision is characteristic of apocalyptic while audition is more characteristic of prophecy. The prophet reports the word of the Lord which he hears. The apocalyptic writer describes the visions he sees.[31] In this connection, apocalyptic is not as concerned with ethics as is prophecy. Its message is not for the masses, as was the prophet's word, but for the chosen remnant, the embattled elect. There is no "gospel" in apocalyptic—no call to repentance, no promise of forgiveness and reconciliation.

---

26. Cf. Leon Morris, *Apocalyptic* (Grand Rapids, Mich.: William B. Eerdmans Publishing Co., 1972), pp. 25 ff.

27. Cf. Stanley Brice Frost, *Old Testament Apocalyptic: Its Origins and Growth* (London: The Epworth Press, 1952), pp. 46-56.

28. *Ibid.*, pp. 143 ff.

29. H. H. Rowley, *The Relevance of Apocalyptic: A Study of Jewish and Christian Apocalypses from Daniel to the Revelation* (New York: Association Press, new and revised ed. 1963), p. 166.

30. Von Rad, *OT Theology*, 2:306; cf. also Morris, *Apocalyptic*, pp. 57-58.

31. Cf. Morris, *Apocalyptic*, pp. 32-34.

Symbols, we have already noted, are a prominent feature of apocalyptic. As is characteristic of symbolism, the meanings are not always clear to those outside the circle in which their use is current. The apocalyptists rarely explain their symbols. They assume that their readers will understand. It is possible, as Morris suggests, that the apocalyptic recourse to symbols was in part due to the fact that what they were trying to describe was too large for words.[32]

A despair of human adequacy that almost amounts to pessimism pervades the apocalyptic literature. Human remedies cannot avail. This is expressive of the crisis milieu in which apocalyptic flourished. Only God is sufficient for such times.

Yet there is no doubt about the ultimate outcome. The triumph of God is assured. The apocalyptists share the prophets' theocratic philosophy of history. One may despair of this world, but there is hope in the age to come. Death may overtake the individual in the present age, but the light of a future resurrection and life becomes all the more important (e.g., Ezek. 37:1-14; Dan. 12:1-4). History will end in certain victory for God and His faithful remnant.[33]

A sort of dualism pervades apocalyptic. There is constant contrast between the present age and the age to come. The age to come is not just an age next in succession to the present age. It is radically different. It is literally "a new heaven and a new earth" (phraseology actually found in the extracanonical 1 Enoch 45:4 ff. and 91:16). Instead of an age shot through with evil and the suffering of the righteous, the age to come will be one in which the will of God shall be done.[34]

The apocalyptists show their despair of history. For the prophets, history was still a continuous process out of which would emerge the triumph of righteousness, but the apocalyptists have given up on history. There must be a radical break somewhere in the historical process. Writers of apocalyptic have no faith in politics. "No future worth having, they think, can emerge from the normal processes of history. Something different has to happen. God can do no more with the present system or within the present system. He must shatter it and start again."[35]

32. *Ibid.*, pp. 34-37.
33. *Ibid.*, pp. 41-47.
34. *Ibid.*, pp. 47-50.
35. Henry McKeating, *God and the Future* (Naperville, Ill.: SCM Book Club, 1974), p. 37.

While apocalyptic is difficult to define and the limits of the movement are somewhat imprecise, there is no doubt of the purpose of this kind of writing. It is to put heart into the beleaguered people of God, to inspire faith and courage in the face of persecution and peril. For all its grim foreboding in respect to society as a whole, the purpose of apocalyptic is to comfort and cheer the righteous. There will always be need for writing such as this, particularly in times of persecution. Stanley Brice Frost concludes:

> But the last word must be of what was central in the apocalyptist's thought. In the midst of a world no more at peace or secure than theirs, with a future as difficult to penetrate as that they faced, with persecution breaking out against God's people in many lands and none knowing where it may establish itself next; at this time when what was laboriously built has been cast down overnight, and the foes we thought smitten have revived a thousandfold; in *this* world, the apocalyptist reminds us that there is righteousness, and that oppression and propaganda are never lasting; that truth is eternal, and that life can be without fear or sighing, without sin or death, and that he that endureth to the end, the same shall be saved.[36]

Apocalyptic *is* difficult for the modern mind. What we must seek is the faith of which it is expressive. Behind all the threatening visage of a future that seems worse the closer we come to it, we see the God who reigns over all and whose will ultimately shall be done. As John Bright summarizes the faith of the apocalyptists:

> Yet strange though this "apocalyptic mind" is to us, we must not forget that there lived in it a great faith which even those who sneer at it would do well to copy. For all its fundamental pessimism about the world, it was in the profoundest sense optimistic. At a time when the current scene yielded only despair, when the power of evil was unbroken beyond human power to break it, there lived here the faith that the victory of God was nonetheless sure: God holds the issues of history; he is a God *whose Kingdom comes.* Let those of us to whom the prayer "Thy kingdom come" has become a form to be rattled off without meaning, who find the Apocalyptic amusing, yet who tremble every time a Communist makes a speech—note it well. The Apocalyptic further insists that the world struggle is neither political nor economic, but essentially of the spirit and cosmic in scope. Behind all earthly striving it sees a continuing combat between good and evil, light and darkness, the Creator God and the destructive power of chaos, which summons men to take sides. There can be no neutrality. Whoever decides for the right, however humble he may be, has struck a blow for the kingdom of God in a combat of decisive

---

36. *OT Apocalyptic,* p. 258.

significance. In any case, there was in the Apocalyptic a faith that strengthened thousands of little men to an obedience unto the death, confident that their reward was with God (Dan. 12:1-4). Let all who scoff ask themselves if their more polite religion does as much.[37]

The interpretation of apocalyptic affords particular difficulty to literal-minded Westerners. The tendency is to allegorize the account —that is, to try to find specific meaning in each detail. In such allegorizing, imagination finds fertile field for uncontrolled speculation. The bewildering variety in theories of the tribulation, rapture, "revelation," millennium, Armageddon, and the battle of Gog and Magog is an eloquent testimony to the barrenness of such allegorical interpretation.

Apocalyptic is to be interpreted as parables are interpreted, with chief attention to the central truth conveyed. Of the total meaning of apocalyptic there is no doubt at all: The Lord God omnipotent reigns, and the final outcomes of human history will not be decided in Moscow, Peiping, Havana—or even in Washington or London. God's kingdom comes not as the achievement of man—even men of the Church—but as the fruit of the victory won at Calvary and in the empty tomb (Col. 2:13-15).

Old Testament theology ends as the Old Testament itself, with a forward look. Foundations were laid deep and strong. Their form can be seen in the superstructure erected upon them. Ahead were the silent centuries between Malachi and Matthew. Yet the silent centuries are bridged with the admonition and promise that close the last book in the Old Testament as arranged in our Christian Bibles: "Remember the law of my servant Moses, the statutes and ordinances that I commanded him at Horeb for all Israel. Behold, I will send you Elijah the prophet before the great and terrible day of the Lord comes. And he will turn the hearts of fathers to their children and the hearts of children to their fathers, lest I come and smite the land with a curse" (Mal. 4:4-6).

37. *Kingdom of God*, p. 169.

PART 2

THE NEW
TESTAMENT

Introduction

We turn now to the New Testament or the New Covenant. It goes without saying that both a continuity and discontinuity exists between the Old and the New Testaments. The study of this problem of the relationship between the Testaments has become particularly significant with the rising emphasis upon biblical theology. (See Introduction of this volume.)

The essential element in the discontinuity between the Old and the New rests in the person of Christ, the Divine Person, who offers through His teachings, death, resurrection, and intercession the assurance of salvation for all men. He is the *Nova Res* of the New Testament. What had been hoped for in the way of redemption in the Old Testament through sacrifices and in early Judaism through the keeping of the Torah and the "traditions of the elders" is now made possible only in faith-identification with Christ. Therefore, the teachings about Christ in the New Testament and the teachings about salvation are interlaced. New Testament theology is "Christo-normative," any way we look at it. And it is expected that every explanation of the New Testament will find its focus there.

SOME GENERAL HERMENEUTICAL GUIDELINES

The New Testament writings, like many of the Old Testament, are "occasional" compositions. Each was written to meet the need of some particular occasion. We cannot consider them systematic treatises.

This is not to say that the New Testament books are not theological. On the contrary, they contain profound affirmations relating to all the varied questions of theology. However, a certain amount of "reading between the lines" and positing of presuppositions is necessary in order to draw out what might be finally designated as "the theology of John," "the theology of Hebrews," or "the theology of Paul." Our task here, however, is an attempt to deal with these books as a unit to ascertain what assured declarations they make about salvation in Christ. We concede that the unity rests in Him and

His relationship to God's redemptive workings in history or what is known as *Die Heilsgeschichte* ("the salvation history").

In keeping with our commitment to Christ as the interpretative principle of the New Testament is our trust in the written Word, especially the Gospels and the Book of Acts. Some current New Testament thought labors the fallacious point that these writings are not factual, contrary to a truly conservative stance.[1] The Gospels, in particular, are said to record a tradition which represents the *Sitz im Leben* ("life situation") of the Early Community rather than the *Sitz im Leben* of Jesus of Nazareth. The speeches in the Book of Acts are thought to be inventions of the author of the Luke-Acts material.

Such skepticism finds no place in our study. We understand the New Testament to be Holy Scripture, a divinely inspired book of truth, given by plenary inspiration. By plenary inspiration we mean that the whole and every part has been brought into being under specific direction, and as a result of that inspiration these writings are "the final and authoritative Rule of Faith in the Church" (cf. 2 Tim. 3:16-17; 2 Pet. 1:20-21; 3:2, 16; see also John 3:31, 34; 10:35; Heb. 10:16-17).

Several further declarations are in order at this juncture. While acknowledging the *kerygmatic* and evangelistic nature of the Gospel and Acts writings, it is not necessary to assume that they are raw creations of those who composed them. Nevertheless, behind the record and in the record are reliable witnesses to Jesus' life, ministry, death, and resurrection. The same historical assurance prevails with regard to the life and ministry of the Church in her earliest days.

The Early Church did not create the tradition about Jesus; she simply and faithfully expounded it for her generation. She did this to meet the needs of those who paused long enough to listen to her message and to join her ranks. As T. W. Manson has so well stated, form criticism, which has raised this ugly issue, has unjustifiably gone beyond its literary domain in attempting to rule theologically on the validity of the biblical record. Its only right to existence is to analyze the literary forms.[2]

---

1. Cf. Edgar V. McKnight, *What Is Form Criticism?* (Philadelphia: Fortress Press, 1969); Norman Perrin, *What Is Redaction Criticism?* (Philadelphia: Fortress Press, 1969). This type of Gospel criticism has not remained static; numerous modifications and spin-offs have developed since the early works of Bultmann, Schmidt, and Dibelius. Nevertheless, the tendency has been to erode trust in the historicity of the biblical record.

2. Cf. T. W. Manson, *Studies in the Gospels and Epistles*, ed. by Matthew Black (Manchester: The University Press, 1962), pp. 3-12. Manson's attack on form criticism

It is readily acknowledged here that the New Testament possesses a supernaturalistic and eschatological character.[3] But this element does not detract from nor discredit the record. Supernaturalism is of the very essence of the biblical Word. In these "later days" God has acted savingly in Christ Jesus. The eternal Word, the Christ of promise, has come into our order to fulfill the redemptive purpose of God. The element of the miracle, and the humanly unaccountable character of the life of our Lord and of the winning ways of His early followers are the genius of the faith. No man therefore can hope to account for the existence of the faith by resorting alone to literary or historical analysis. The biblical disciplines must eventually confront the supernatural fact, and its demand for commitment. These disciplines, themselves, come under the judgment of the Word of God as revealed through Christ and written down by God-appointed authors.

It is acknowledged, nevertheless, that as the Church carried out her mission in the world, her understanding of her faith matured, both in experience and in oral and written expression. This maturation came at a remarkably rapid pace because of the richness of her heritage in the Hebrew faith. She possessed the old Scriptures to which she could and did readily turn for comprehension of Christ and herself. Essentially what she was enjoying was not a new religion but the reconstituted old faith, grounded now, however, in *the personalized and historicized Word of God.*

The Apostle Paul in particular could write with considerable depth of understanding as to what had transpired in Israel's history in the coming of Christ. He could also testify to what had transpired in his own history when he met the risen Lord on the road to Damascus and became "a man in Christ." Significantly, as Albert E. Barnett rightly pointed out, this man of Tarsus became "a literary influence."[4] He was also a theological force. Many of his concepts of the faith are paralleled in Hebrews and 1 Peter. It seems reasonable to conclude that Pauline thought is a primary source for a New Tes-

is without mercy. "In fact if form criticism had stuck to its proper business, it would not have made any real stir. We should have taken it as we take the forms of Hebrew poetry or the forms of musical composition."

3. Cf. Frederick C. Grant, *An Introduction to New Testament Thought* (New York: Abingdon Press, 1950), p. 51; George Eldon Ladd, *The Pattern of New Testament Truth* (Grand Rapids, Mich.: Wm. B. Eerdmans Publishing Co., 1968), pp. 108-11.
4. Albert E. Barnett, *Paul Becomes a Literary Influence* (Chicago: University of Chicago Press, 1941).

tament theology. If so, we must see it as part of the workings of the Spirit in drawing out the richest expression of the faith at the earliest time, through the informed and committed mind of the Apostle Paul.

Obviously, not every passage relating to a subject under consideration can be expounded or even mentioned. However, an attempt will be made to take the reader to those portions of the New Testament which are pivotal to a reasonably broad understanding of the faith.

Section One

The God
of Our Salvation

12

The Knowledge of God

New Testament thought, just as Old Testament thought, is theo-centric.[1] God is both the Subject and the Object of the written Record. He is the principal Actor in the story. He brings the cosmos with all of its inhabitants into existence, and He takes the initiative

---

1. Oscar Cullmann, *The Christology of the New Testament,* trans. Shirley C. Guthrie and Charles A. M. Hall (Philadelphia: Westminster Press, Rev. ed., 1963), pp. 1-3, 324-27. Cullmann argues on the basis of the earliest confessions and Trinitarian formulas in the New Testament that "early Christian theology is in reality almost exclusively Christology." In effect for him New Testament theology begins and ends in Christology. As we shall come to assert later, Christ is normative for all that is Christian, but it appears to the writer that Cullmann's position tends to diminish the relationship of the Old Testament faith to the New. Most certainly the focus of the Old faith is God himself. The commitment of the New Testament writers to God is precisely identical to that of the writers of the Old. Thus, a "theology" infuses the thought of the New Testament writers and must be treated as more than a presupposition. To do

in redeeming created man when the latter falls into sin through disobedience (Eph. 1:3-8). At the divinely specified time, He "spoke" *(elalēsen)* to us by His Son, "who reflects the glory" of the Father and "bears the very stamp of his nature" (Heb. 1:1-3; cf. Gal. 4:4-6).

In the ongoing life of the new community, brought into existence through the word and work of the Son, there arose special servants like the Apostle Paul; they were "called by the will of God" to function in redemptive ways for God (cf. 1 Cor. 1:1; Eph. 1:1; 1 Tim. 1:1; Jas. 1:1). Thus, the New Testament presents its Central Figure as actively at work in a variety of ways on behalf of mankind. What had been planned in the distant eternities and prophesied by the prophets is now being realized in God's mighty activity in Christ.

On the other hand, God is the Object of His own action. When He acted in Christ, He disclosed the character of His own nature as the One who is infinitely holy, righteous, merciful, forgiving, creative, and just. The primal result of the redemptive deed was the recovery of "the knowledge of God." Thus, men who respond to God's gracious work in Christ come to "know" God. Paul writes to the Galatians: "Formerly, when you did not know God, you were in bondage to beings that by nature are no gods; but now that you have come to know God *[gnontes theon]*, or rather to be known by God *[gnōsthentes hupo theou]*, how can you turn back again to the weak and beggarly elemental spirits, whose slaves you want to be once more?" (Gal. 4:8-9; cf. Titus 1:16).

Peter's salutation in his second letter reads: "May grace and peace be multiplied to you in the knowledge of God *[epignōsei tou theou]* and of Jesus our Lord" (2 Pet. 1:2).[2] If God himself is the Focus of the Bible and if the knowledge of Him constitutes the essence of redemption (John 17:3), it becomes necessary to examine closely what is meant by knowledge and how such knowledge relates to the redemption which is made available through Christ.

---

justice to the theology of the New Testament, it is imperative to elucidate what is said about God and at the same time demonstrate how God is related to Christ or vice versa.

2. Cf. 1:3; 2:20; 3:18. Note should be taken of the tendency to equate the knowledge of God with the knowledge of Christ. In the developed thought of the NT the distinctions between God and Christ grow dim, especially at the points where worship and growth in the Christian life are emphasized.

I. NEW TESTAMENT WORDS FOR KNOWLEDGE

We have already noted the Old Testament view of knowledge as it relates to God.[3] The New Testament view is essentially the same. In popular usage the Greek word "to know" *(ginōskein)* raises no problems theologically, for it refers to knowledge in the ordinary senses: "to detect" (Mark 5:29; Luke 8:46); "to note" (Mark 8:17; 12:12; 2 Cor. 2:4; John 5:42; 8:27); "to recognize" (Luke 7:39; Matt. 12:25; Gal. 3:7); "to learn" (Mark 5:43; 15:45; Luke 9:11; John 11:57; Acts 17:13, 19; Phil. 1:12; 2:19); "to confirm" (Mark 6:38; 13:28 ff.; Luke 1:18; John 4:42; 7:51; 1 Cor. 4:19; 2 Cor. 13:6); "to be aware" (Matt. 24:50; Luke 2:43; Heb. 10:34; Rev. 3:3); and "to understand" (Luke 18:34; John 3:10; Acts 8:30; 1 Cor. 14:7, 9).

The compound *epiginōskein* is often used to convey the same meaning as *ginōskein*. In many instances there is no general distinction between the simple and compound forms. This fact is shown by a comparison of Mark 2:8 with 8:17; Mark 5:30 with Luke 8:46; Mark 6:33, 54 with Luke 9:11; Col. 1:6 with 2 Cor. 8:9. "Even in 1 Cor. 13:12 the alternation is purely rhetorical; the compound is also an equivalent of the simple form at 1 Cor. 8:3; Gal. 4:9. Thus *epiginōskein to dikaiōma tou theou* at Rom. 1:32 corresponds to *ginōskein to thelēma* at 2:18."[4] The compound perhaps at times is used for "to confirm" (cf. Acts 22:24; 23:28).

Special meaning appears in the use of these words where the Old Testament concepts have influenced New Testament thought. In such cases the emphasis is not upon objective confirmation but "a knowledge which accepts the consequences of knowledge" (cf. Matt. 24:43; Luke 10:11; Eph. 5:5; Jas. 1:3; 5:20; 2 Tim. 3:1; 2 Pet. 1:20; 3:3). "To know" is to have insight into the will of God, to acknowledge it, and to become obedient to it (cf. Rom. 3:17; 10:19; Heb. 3:10). There are references to the knowledge of God's will (Rom. 2:18; Acts 22:14), to the knowledge of Christian salvation (2 Cor. 8:9), and to knowledge of a special grace of God (Gal. 2:9; Rev. 3:9). A certain theoretical element is suggested in some instances of *ginōskein* but it is not decisive.[5]

Gnōsis occurs in numerous places but it usually carries the Old

---

3. See chapter 2.
4. Cf. W. E. Vine, *Expository Dictionary of New Testament Words* (London: Oliphants, 1939), 2:297-99.
5. Cf. Rom. 1:18-23; 1 Cor. 1:21; 8:4-6; Gal. 4:8 ff.; see also John 1:10.

Testament sense of "obedient acknowledgement of the will of God" (cf. Rom. 2:20; 11:33). Luke 1:77 is explicit: "to give knowledge of salvation to his people in the forgiveness of their sins." The definition of salvation in this verse precludes any thought that theoretical speculation is intended. *Epignōsis* is employed almost in a technical sense to denote the decisive knowledge of God which comes in conversion to the Christian faith. The Pastoral Epistles contain several instances of *epignōsis* (cf. 1 Tim. 2:4; 2 Tim. 2:25, 3:7; Titus 1:1; cf. also Heb. 10:26). While in some cases theoretical knowledge is implied, usually "it is assumed that Christian knowledge carries with it a corresponding manner of life."[6]

In summary, the New Testament terminology for "knowledge" is heavily influenced by the Old Testament thinking. The major thrust of *ginōskein, gnōsis,* and their compounds is in the direction of obedient acknowledgment of God as He encounters man in His sovereignty, mercy, and redemptive love. This fact suggests that God is actively engaged in the disclosure of the knowledge of himself. The Christian's knowledge or *gnōsis* is to be regarded as "a gift of grace which marks the life of the Christian by determining its expression" (1 Cor. 1:5; 12:8; 2 Cor. 8:7).[7] Any reflective inquiry or theoretical elements in this knowledge is grounded in love which controls the patterns of behavior in life (Col. 1:9; 3:10; 1 Pet. 3:7). The Johannine writings relate "knowing" and "believing" and "loving" in the most complete expression of this special New Testament understanding of knowledge.[8]

II. The Redemptive Character of the Knowledge of God

Speaking of religious knowledge as opposed to other forms of knowledge, William L. Bradley points out that it is based neither upon first principles nor upon sense perception but yet can be said to yield information. Being personal in nature, it yields the type of information that one receives from another person through a glance or an

---

6. Rudolf Bultmann, "ginōskō, *et al.," Theological Dictionary of the New Testament,* ed. Gerhard Kittel (Grand Rapids, Mich.: Wm. B. Eerdmans Publishing Co., 1964), 1:707; hereafter referred to as TDNT.

7. *Ibid.,* p. 708.

8. For a full discussion of John's use of these terms, cf. C. H. Dodd, *The Interpretation of the Fourth Gospel* (Cambridge: University Press, 1953), pp. 151 ff.

unconscious movement. Thus one comes to know something about that person in a particular intersubjective relationship.[9]

Bradley goes on to assert that such knowledge is "neither rational nor irrational." Yet it carries with it a strong element of validity. It cannot be tested as one tests a scientific hypothesis or a fact of recent history. But it is not necessarily contrary to other forms of knowledge. Many times it coincides with logical analysis and scientific investigation. Nevertheless, its basic verification lies in the encounter itself.[10] This is existential knowledge. It comes in the unique effects of an encounter with another in the very throes of one's own existence.[11]

This is what the Old Testament as well as the New means by the knowledge of God.[12] God has brought about a saving encounter with His creatures. Acting out of the fullness of His personhood, He has visited man in Christ; visited us with love, mercy, and with readiness to forgive and to live with His creatures. Those who respond to His "coming in Person" know Him as the God of all grace and love—and this is the truth God wishes most of all to convey about himself.

Thus in this "knowing" there is salvation as well as a revelation of the nature of God. The response of faith to the visitation of God brings about renewal of the person because faith is a moral act involving obedience. The old life of alienation disappears and a joyful entrance into the greater life offered by God himself takes place. Moreover, this redeeming relationship with its increasing disclosure of the nature of the Redeemer and its richness of personal growth is maintained only by continued obedience to the One who called it into existence. This "knowledge" therefore is uniquely "a saving knowledge."

---

9. William L. Bradley, "Revelation," *The Hartford Quarterly*, 1962.

10. *Ibid.*, p. 45.

11. R. W. Dale observes: ". . . real existences must be known immediately—not by inferences from real existences belonging to another sphere . . ." (*Christian Doctrine* [London: Hodder & Stoughton, 1896], p. 279).

12. Cf. Addison H. Leitch, *Interpreting Basic Theology* (New York: Channel Press, 1961), p. 21. "Just as we come to know our friends by their clothes, by their walk, their appearance, the sound of their voices, and yet never really know them beyond their willingness to reveal to us their true natures, so with God. All our reasoning about Him gives us only broken lights of Him until He gives us His light."

III. CHRIST-MEDIATED KNOWLEDGE

As intimated earlier, the knowledge of God is mediated through Christ. The most expressive statement of this comes from the Lord himself. In an amazing Matthean verse, which has been described as "a Johannine thunderbolt in the synoptic sky," Jesus says, "All things have been delivered to me by the Father, and no one knows *[epiginōs-kei]* the Son except the Father, and no one knows the Father except the Son and any one to whom the Son chooses to reveal him" (Matt. 11:27). While the word "Father" has special significance in Jesus' message, it is not so much the fatherhood of God that is here revealed by the Son, but rather God's essential being. "Wise men" *(sophoi)*, because of their lack of submissiveness, do not know the Father, but "babes" *(nēpioi)* in their simple trust receive from the Son a revelation of God himself (11:25).

In both word and deed in the Synoptics, Jesus gives expression to divine attributes and prerogatives. When He says to the paralytic, "My son, your sins are forgiven," immediately the observing religionists accuse him of blasphemy. Rhetorically they ask, "Who can forgive sins but God alone?" (Mark 2:5-7). Jesus also assumes divine authority in the Sermon on the Mount where He repeatedly uses the awesome introductory clause, "But I say to you." Matthew's note on the effect of Jesus' teaching on the crowd offers further insight into the subtleties of the divine revelation through His ministry. "And when Jesus finished these sayings, the crowds were astonished at his teaching, for he taught them as one who had authority, and not as their scribes" (Matt. 7:28-29).

Writing near the end of the first century, John gave special attention to Christ's revelatory role. No more explicit word on this matter has been written than John 1:18: "No one has ever seen God; the only begotten Son, who is in the bosom of the Father, he has made him known" *(exēgēsato*, "exegeted" or "interpreted").

A mild surprise, to say the least, is registered by the Lord when Philip asks, "Lord, show us the Father, and we shall be satisfied."

Jesus said to him, "Have I been with you so long, and yet you do not know me, Philip? He who has seen me has seen the Father; how can you say, 'Show me the Father'? Do you not believe that I am in the Father and the Father in me?" (John 14:8-10a). Unqualifiedly, Jesus asserts that His word and His works are simultaneously the word and work of the Father (John 10:31-39). The glory, the very presence of the Father, is disclosed in the Son (1:14). When the

Son is glorified, that is to say, when His true nature is unfolded, the Father's being is revealed at the same time (11:4, 40).[13]

The Apostle Paul affirms this revelatory character of Christ's life. In fact, he is amazingly explicit. For example, to the Corinthians he declares "For it is the God who said, 'Let light shine out of darkness' who has shone in our hearts to give the light of the knowledge of the glory of God in the face of Christ" (2 Cor. 4:6). In response to gnosticizing interpreters, who sought to separate the Father and the Son, Paul asserts: "For in him [Christ] all the fullness of God was pleased to dwell" (Col. 1:19); "For in him the whole fullness of deity dwells bodily [sōmatikōs, "personally, substantively"], and you have come to fullness of life in him, who is the head of all rule and authority" (Col. 2:9-10). Thus, in Christ we have a full disclosure of the being of God. Richardson writes: "The Son is the divinely appointed means of bringing the knowledge of God to the world."[14]

In essence, there can be no knowledge of God in the New Testament sense apart from relationship to Christ. It is precisely at this limiting point that the gospel is a *skandalon*, a stumbling block (cf. Rom. 9:33; 1 Cor. 1:23; Gal. 5:11; 1 Pet. 2:6-8). Human questing for relatedness to the ultimate reality is fruitless unless it brings us finally to the Son, for He alone can give us a glimpse of the Father. God has determined that He is to be known through the person and work of His Son.

While there is a kind of vision of God mediated through nature and reason, it is not a saving knowledge. Therefore it receives little attention from biblical writers. The hints of God's existence which break through to man from his world fail to lay upon him the divine claim to moral and righteous obedience. Olin Curtis comments pointedly: "The fact is that the more men know about nature, and the more they rely upon nature, the more agnostic and hopeless they become. For one thing, men need to be told a few plain things about

---

13. Cf. G. Kittel, TDNT, 2:245 ff.: "When the translator of the OT first thought of giving *doxa* for *kavod*, he initiated a linguistic change of far-reaching significance, giving to the Greek term a distinctiveness of sense which could hardly be surpassed. Taking a word for opinion, which implies all the subjectivity and therefore all the vacillation of human views and conjectures, he made it something absolutely objective, i.e. the reality of God.... It is obvious that the NT usage of *doxa* follows the LXX rather than Greek usage. With the sense of 'reputation' and 'power' already mentioned, the word is also used strictly in the NT to express the 'divine mode of being'."

14. *Introduction to the Theology of the NT*, p. 44.

themselves, about their origin, about their spiritual condition, and about their destiny."[15]

Karl Barth's word is also instructive:

> Who God is and what it is to be divine is something we have to learn where God has revealed himself and His nature, the essence of the divine. And if He has revealed himself in Jesus Christ as the God who does this (His reconciling work), it is not for us to be wiser than He and to say that it is in contradiction with the divine essence. We have to be ready to be taught by Him that we have been too small and perverted in our thinking about Him within the framework of a false idea of God.[16]

Christian proclamation, when it is validly Christian, confronts men with the incarnate, dying, and risen Christ. Through that encounter comes a revelation of God as infinitely loving and merciful. Such a revelation places man under an imperative to respond in trust and obedience. The record of Paul's experience at Athens clearly supports this fact. All the philosophical ruminations of all the philosophers of that ancient center of learning produced only an altar dedicated "to an unknown god." When Paul began to speak of the need for repentance and "a man" whom God had appointed and raised from the dead and who gave men life, a new understanding of Deity was given. Negative reactions predominated; however, a few responded to the Word (Acts 17:16-34).

Cullmann's observation summarizes the point: "The New Testament neither is able nor intends to give information about how we are to conceive the being of God beyond the history of revelation, about whether it really is a being only in the philosophical sense. . . . The reticent allusions to something beyond revelation are made on the periphery of the New Testament witness."[17]

In conclusion, because their interests lie in the realm of redemption, biblical writers are concerned primarily with that knowledge of God which pertains to His moral and spiritual nature. This revelation is mediated through the Incarnate Son, and carries with it a moral demand; it requires a response from man, whether negative or affirmative. Because this revelation is initiated by God, it is self-validating and unimpeachable. God does not and cannot misrepresent himself. When man has such an encounter with God and

---

15. Olin F. Curtis, *The Christian Faith* (New York: Eaton and Mains, 1905), p. 107.

16. Karl Barth, *Church Dogmatics*, 4:1, ed. G. W. Bromiley and T. F. Torrance (Edinburgh: T. & T. Clark, 1958), p. 186.

17. *Christology*, p. 327.

"knows" Him as He really is, he cannot finally deny the fact of God's reality. A negative response is rebellion but a positive response is both obedience to the implicit moral demand and trust in the loving and merciful being of God.

IV. THE GENERAL KNOWLEDGE OF GOD

The previous discussion naturally raises the question of the possibility of knowing God through any diffused revelation in the whole of nature. The term *general* is a better word than *natural* to describe this aspect of the divine revelation. Natural theology has signified for many the possibilities of an inclusive and self-authenticating revelation of divine things in the world of nature and man.

In the judgment of the writers, there can be no such legitimate Christian discipline as "natural theology" because of the special revelatory deeds of God throughout the history of mankind which are recorded in the Bible. God has acted in special ways to make His character and will known. The Old Testament records the overwhelmingly convincing interventions of God in the affairs of the Israelites; sometimes to deliver them from their enemies, and sometimes to offer them a "covenant way of life" with Him, maintained by obedience to His specially given Torah.

With respect to the New Testament era, the song of Zechariah, the father of John the Baptist, expresses the identical truth. It declares: "Blessed be the Lord God of Israel, for he has visited *[episkepsato]*[18] and redeemed his people, and has raised up a horn of salvation for us in the house of his servant David" (Luke 1:68-69). The disclosure of God through mighty deeds in history—especially in the Exodus from Egypt and in the Incarnation—introduces a unique dimension in revelation. This dimension supersedes and limits the significance of whatever revelation is mediated through the cosmos and man. Christian theology is grounded in and controlled by this special dimension of God's disclosure.

In a number of New Testament statements of the faith, a concept of general revelation is given. At Caesarea, in the house of

18. Cf. Arndt & Gingrich, *A Greek-English Lexicon of the New Testament* (Chicago: University of Chicago Press, 1957): *episkeptomai,* "of God's gracious visitation in bringing salvation." See also Luke 1:78; Acts 15:14; Heb. 2:6; Ps. 8:4: "What is man that thou art mindful of him, and the son of man that thou dost care *[pagad,* 'visit'] for him?"

Cornelius, Peter preached: "Truly I perceive that God shows no partiality, but in every nation any one who fears him and does what is right is acceptable to him" (Acts 10:34-35). Paul announced in Lystra that God, who had created "the heaven and the earth and the sea and all that is in them, in past generations . . . allowed all the nations to walk in their own ways; yet he did not leave himself without a witness, for he did good and gave you from heaven rains and fruitful seasons, satisfying your hearts with food and gladness" (Acts 14:15-17).

In the prologue to his Gospel, John speaks of Christ as "the true light that enlightens every man" (1:9). While there is a sense in which the Word gives light (understanding) only to those who believe (John 3:19 ff.), all men have been morally enlightened in a general way. God has revealed something of himself to all men (Rom. 1:20).[19] The most significant New Testament passages are Acts 17:22-31 (Paul's speech on Mars' Hill); Rom. 1:18-32; 2:12-16; 2 Cor. 4:6; Gal. 4:8-10; and those passages in which the New Testament writers employ the word "conscience" (*suneidēsis*—Rom. 2:15; 13:5; 1 Cor. 8:7; 1 Tim. 1:5; Heb. 10:22; 1 Pet. 3:16).

A. Acts 17:22-34

F. F. Bruce comments: "If the address at Pisidian Antioch in 13:16ff. is intended to be a sample of Paul's proclamation of the Gospel to Jewish and God-fearing audiences, the present address may well be

---

19. The construction of John 1:9 presents a problem which has profound theological relevance. The issue lies in the participle "coming" *(erchomanon)*. It may be connected with "man"—"the true light that enlightens every *man* coming into the world." This has been a very common view. It may be combined with "was" *(en)*, making a periphrastic form—"The true light, which enlightens every man, *was coming* into the world." Another view relates it to the light, so that it reads, "There was the true light that enlightens every man *by coming into the world.*" Leon Morris is correct in saying that "this verse stands at the head of a section dealing with the incarnation, where a statement about the incarnation rather than one about men in general seems required. . . . The Evangelist is speaking about the Word as 'the true light', and leading on from that, about the illumination He gives to men." Morris does not deny a general illumination of mankind, but he finds John attributing it to the Word. "The Gospel According to John," *The New International Commentary on the New Testament* (Grand Rapids, Mich.: Wm. B. Eerdmans Publishing Co., 1971), pp. 93-95; cf. also George B. Stevens, *The Theology of the New Testament* (New York: Charles Scribner's Sons, 1947), pp. 582-83; John Wesley, following Calvin, comments: "And this light, if man did not hinder, would shine more and more to the perfect day" (*Explanatory Notes upon the New Testament* [Naperville, Ill.: Alec R. Allenson, Inc., 1950, reprint], p. 303); for a contrary view, see R. H. Strachan, *The Fourth Gospel* (London: SCM Press, Ltd., 3rd rev. ed., 1941), pp. 99-100.

intended as a sample of his approach to pagans."[20] As a point of contact, the apostle calls attention to an altar on which is an inscription "to an unknown god" (17:23). He then asserts that what they worship "as unknown" *(agnoountes)* or "without knowing" is the One about whom he will preach to them. His message essentially says that God is a Spirit who does not need images nor sacrifices; He is the Creator of the world, the Bestower of life and the good things of life. He is not far from His creatures and desires that men should seek to find Him. The Athenians, however, in Paul's judgment, have acted contrary to the divine purpose and have become idolatrous, making gold, silver, and stone representations of God.[21]

The conclusion Paul draws is that, while God was brought within range of the mind of the Athenians by His revelations, He was not really known by them. So B. Gartner writes: "The whole of their ignorance is manifested in their worship, particularly when they even erect an altar to a God Whom they do not know, but Whom they ought to have known."[22] Their ignorance is culpable, however, because God "commands all men everywhere to repent" (17:30). Paul announces as a reason for repentance that a day of judgment is coming in which the entire world will be judged in righteousness by Christ (17:31).

Two aspects of this message must be noted. First, the speech is concerned with "the true knowledge of God." Such knowledge is not that of "mere intellectual discipline; it involves moral and religious responsibilities, and for lack of this knowledge, in the measure in which it was available to them, men are called upon to repent."[23] Paul is not presenting arguments for the existence of God. Rather, he is describing what form the worship of men will take whenever they reject what they do know about God.

Second, Paul's teaching and preaching must always be viewed

20. "Commentary on the Book of Acts," *New International Commentary on the New Testament* (Grand Rapids, Mich.: Wm. B. Eerdmans Publishing Co., 1956), pp. 354-55.

21. The reference to one of their poets (17:28) and the seeming alignment of thought with similar theories of the Stoics need not be taken to suggest that Paul has taken over Stoic philosophy, as per J. Weiss, *Earliest Christianity,* trans. F. C. Grant (New York: Harper & Bros., 1959), p. 241; cf. C. S. Williams, "A Commentary on the Acts of the Apostles," *Black's New Testament Commentaries* (London: Adam and Charles Black, 1957), who suggests that the passage can be interpreted from the OT-Jewish tradition, and we do not read into it any philosophical meaning from Stoicism.

22. B. Gartner, *The Areopagus Speech and Natural Revelation* (Uppsala: C. W. K. Gleerup, 1955), p. 238.

23. Bruce, *Acts,* p. 362.

within the context of *Die Heilsgeschichte*. Paul is concerned about what time it is in the divine redemptive scheme. This fact is suggested by the statement that "the time of ignorance God overlooked" (17:30). Christ has come; God has disclosed himself fully in Christ. All men can now know with certainty concerning God's identity and will. Therefore, with that knowledge any thoughtful and serious person would repent of all his false worship and idolatry. The moral, rather than the philosophical, issue comes into focus whenever the message relates itself to the history of God's saving deeds.

B. Romans 1:18-32

The purpose of the Epistle to the Romans governs the interpretation of this difficult section. In vv. 16-17 Paul has stated in unforgettable words the nature of the gospel as "the power of God for salvation." He now goes on to show the necessity for such a gospel. Succinctly, "the world is lost without it." Indeed, as Sanday and Headlam comment, there has been a "complete breakdown of righteousness" among men (3:10, 19).[24] The way of redemption that Paul proposes, which is the way of the gospel, is deliverance from sin by faith and not by works (v. 17).

The Gentile world must submit to the way of faith, too, "for what can be known of God [*to gnōston tou theou*] is plain to them, because God has shown it to them" (v. 19).[25] *To gnōston tou theou* is defined in v. 20 as "his invisible nature, namely his eternal power and deity." What is clearly seen is that "God is God and not man."[26] The universe as created does present some raw materials of the knowledge of God. But Paul proceeds to assert that though the Gentiles "knew [*gnontes*] God they did not honor [*edoxasan*] him as God or give thanks to him" (v. 21). As Stauffer makes clear, "The revelation of the divine glory in creation contains a demand within

---

24. Wm. Sanday and A. C. Headlam, "A Critical and Exegetical Commentary on the Epistle to the Romans," *International Critical Commentary* (New York: Charles Scribner's Sons, 1923), p. 40.

25. "To them" is the translation of *en autois*. This phrase could be rendered "among them," which means substantially the same as "to them," emphasizing the manifestation of God in the world about them. It could be rendered "in them," suggesting "in their minds," as a personal possession. Subsequent references to creation militates against this latter translation.

26. C. K. Barrett, "The Epistle to the Romans," *Black's New Testament Commentaries* (London: Adam and Charles Black, 1957), p. 35.

itself. It is intended to quicken men's hearts to glorify God in thanksgiving and praise."[27]

The inexcusable condition of the Gentiles, which has brought them under the wrath of God, is the result of their rejection of the "rudimentary knowledge of God that was open to them."[28] The issue here is not the failure to acknowledge the existence or being of God but rather the failure to submit to His lordship and to live in grateful obedience to Him. The glory is not given to God but is showered upon man himself (v. 25).

One cannot explain away the Pauline declaration that some disclosure of God comes through the natural order (cf. v. 20). In fact, Paul's views here parallel the teachings of rabbinic Judaism, which had formulated a doctrine of the universal knowledge of God.[29] However, Paul's thrust in this passage is not so much upon the enunciation of a theory of natural religion as upon two elements, namely, (1) the moral basis of God's revealed wrath (v. 18), and (2) the demonstration that at this stage in man's history God's answer to sin through Christ is the only answer.

The moral tragedy of mankind, which evokes God's wrath, is expressed in the awesome fall of man from high possibilities of relationship to God to the abyss of idolatry, sensual living, and wrath. Man has passed through the stages: knowledge of God rejected, glory of self, ignorance of God, wickedness, culpability, and finally life under the wrath of God. Man as we find him lives under sin and death. Verse 32 bears out this fact: "Though they all knew God's righteous ordinances that those who do such things deserve to die, they not only do them but approve those who practice them" (personal translation). Three times Paul speaks of "a divine *permissio*"; God "gave them up" to their sinful ways (vv. 24, 26, 28).

The second element mentioned above (that Christ is the only Answer to man's need) is epitomized in Rom. 3:21-26 but is expressed fully in the entire Epistle. The presupposition exists that the nations might have responded to the limited revelation, obeyed God, and thus have come to enjoy His blessings. But in the moral history of mankind, such did not transpire. Therefore the special revelation of God himself in Christ with its provision of redemption from sin was foreordained and in God's time transpired (Gal. 4:4; Eph. 1:3-10).

---

27. E. Stauffer, *New Testament Theology*, trans. John March (London: SCM Press, 1955), p. 88.
28. Barrett, *Romans*, p. 36.
29. W. D. Davies, *Paul and Rabbinic Judaism* (London: SPCK, 1948), pp. 115-17.

C. Romans 2:12-16

In the preceding paragraph (2:1-11) Paul has concluded that Jews and Gentiles are equal before God with respect to moral matters. Tribulation, distress, and judgment await all who do evil, for "God shows no partiality *[prosōpolēmpsia]"* (2:11). The essential difference between the two groups does not relate to race but to revelation. The Jews have had the law, which has not been available to the Gentiles, or, at least, it has not been proclaimed to them. Thus, from the perspective of the revelation of the law, the Jews are "under the law" *(ennomo)* whereas the Gentiles are "without the law" *(anomos)*. Nevertheless, both are subject to judgment if they commit sin. Paul asserts in verse 13 that for the Jews the law is not "a talisman calculated to preserve those who possess it. It is an instrument of judgment, and sin is not less sin, but more, when it is wrought within the sphere of the law (cf. 7:13)."[30]

But Paul still has the issue of the Gentiles. On what basis can they be held accountable since they are "without the law?" The apostle's response is found in verse 14: "When Gentiles who have not the law do by nature what the law requires, they are a law to themselves, even though they do not have the law."

This definitive verse states several facts about the moral and religious ways of the Gentiles. First, they sometimes behave in accordance with the prescriptions of the Mosaic law.

Second, when they so conduct themselves, they do it "by nature" *(phusei).*[31] The phrase "by nature" is clarified in verse 15, which asserts that the Gentiles have the requirements (*to ergon ton nomou,* "what the law requires") written "on their hearts."[32] The argument of Paul here leads to the conclusion that "there is something in the very pattern of created existence which should, and sometimes does, lead the Gentiles to an attitude of humble, and grateful, dependent creatureliness. When this takes place they are a law for themselves."[33] The statement "They are a law to themselves" might better be translated, according to Richardson, "they are their own legislators."[34] Paul

---

30. Barrett, *Romans,* p. 49.

31. Hebrew does not have a word for *nature.* The Old Testament does not employ the idea of nature. It might well be that Paul found this concept from current thought helpful in explaining his views here. Cf. 1 Cor. 11:14.

32. The phrase *To ergon ton nomou* is literally "the work of the law" or "the effect of the law." Barrett decided that the phrase is subjective genitive and should be translated "the law's effects" (*Romans,* p. 53).

33. *Ibid.,* p. 52.

34. *Introduction to the Theology of the NT,* p. 50.

further refers to their consciences as bearing witness to their actions and their moral judgments either accusing or excusing them in the light of the reaction of conscience (2:15).

Third, if the Gentiles do not have "the law," what is this moral "something" which functions in their lives? Commentators readily respond by suggesting some form of universal moral law, going back to the time of creation and which was renewed in the covenant with Noah (Gen. 9:1-7).[35] This view rests upon the teachings of the rabbis who were well aware that the Gentiles maintained some ethical standards.

However, it must not be assumed that the rabbis would support any type of natural law, in the common usage of that term. As Richardson notes, "They instinctively perceived that such moral awareness could ultimately have come only from the God of righteousness, whose special revelation of himself had been given in the Torah of Moses."[36] As with Paul, so with the rabbis, Torah represented more than legalistic prescriptions. *Torah* in its essential character constituted the whole of the divine teaching, the divine will, and for that reason laid a moral claim upon every human being, both Jew and Gentile.[37]

The Mosaic law was the most complete revelation of the will of God. What had been disclosed through creation (Rom. 1:20) was not essentially different, but was a less precise and complete revelation of that eternal will of God. However, limited as it was, this disclosure carried a demand for submission to the sovereignty of God. Stauffer observes: "Every revelation of God contains a summons, an ethical demand."[38] Barrett's word at this point seems reasonable. He insists that Paul does not distinguish between ritual and moral law; indeed, he does not think in these terms. What the law requires ultimately is "neither ceremonial nor moral conformity . . . but believing obedience, or obedient faith (cf. 1:5). This is the only

35. Cf. Sanday and Headlam, *Romans,* p. 62; Grant, *An Introduction to New Testament Thought,* p. 71; Richardson, *Introduction to the Theology of the NT,* p. 49. Contra: Barrett, *Romans,* p. 51.

36. *Introduction to the Theology of the NT,* p. 49.

37. Cf. C. H. Dodd, *The Bible and the Greeks* (London: Hodder and Stoughton, 1935); W. A. Whithouse, "Law," *A Theological Word Book of the Bible,* ed. Alan Richardson (London: SCM Press, 1950), pp. 122-25: "Torah . . . is the whole content of God's revelation of his nature and purpose, which incidentally makes clear man's responsibility before God."

38. Stauffer, *NT Theology,* p. 173.

tolerable basis of relationship between man and his Creator."[39] When the Gentile conducts himself in obedience to what he knows to be right, it may be said that he does "by nature" what the law requires.

Both Rom. 1:18-32 and 2:12-16 clearly assert that some form of divine disclosure was made to mankind so that men possessed the possibility of knowing the Creator. This revelation may have come by means of the creation or by response to the *requirements* of the law "written on their hearts." What is important, however, is Paul's development in Romans of his theme of "justification by faith." His arresting conclusion is that "in actuality man does not grasp the possibility, given to him by God's creation, of existence in God's presence, and that therefore, in spite of these 'spiritual' capacities, 'all have sinned and come short of the glory of God' (Rom. 3:23)."[40]

D. Galatians 4:8-9

This passage has significance for the discussion because the recipients of the letter for the most part were converted pagans. Paul describes their pre-Christian state as one in which they "did not know God" *(ouk eidotes theon).* They were "ignorant of God," a phrase which Duncan takes as a description regularly applied in the New Testament to the life of paganism.[41] Ignorant of God, the pagans indulged in idolatry (cf. Rom. 1:18-32). But the apostle acknowledges emphatically, with the use of the adversative conjunctive phrase *nun de* ("but now"), that they currently "know God" *(gnontes theon).* One need not attempt to find a difference between *eidotes* and *gnontes,* as if the former refers to exterior knowledge of personal relationship rather than theoretical knowledge. Burton notes that *theon* is anarthrous (without the definite article) which suggests the qualities or attributes of Deity as against the mere being of Deity.[42]

The clause, "or rather to be known by God," is not intended to deny the former fact of the Galatians' knowledge of God; rather it amplifies the character of the relationship between the Galatians and God. Duncan observes that the word *gnōsthentes* ("to be known") has

---

39. *Romans,* p. 51.

40. Werner G. Kummel, *Theology of the New Testament* (New York: Abingdon Press, 1973), p. 176.

41. George S. Duncan, "The Epistle of Paul to the Galatians," *Moffatt New Testament Commentary* (London: Hodder and Stoughton, 1934), p. 133.

42. Cf. E. Dewitt Burton, "The Epistle to the Galatians," *International Critical Commentary* (Edinburgh: T. & T. Clark, 1921), p. 229.

the force of "acknowledge" (cf. 1 Cor. 8:3; 2 Tim. 2:19). Paul's point is that "the Galatians have not merely come to know God as Father, but have (by the gift of the Spirit) been brought into such filial relationship with Him that they are acknowledged by Him as sons."[43] Purely cognitive knowledge is not intended here, because Paul would not have thought that God did not always possess knowledge of the Galatians. "To be known by God" signifies that they have "become objects of his favorable attention."[44]

E. Conscience

This term, which appears with fair frequency in the New Testament outside the Gospels, also relates to the wider issue of the knowledge of God.[45] A cognate of the Latin *conscientia*, it literally means "co-knowledge," suggesting "a second reflective consciousness which a man has alongside his original consciousness of an act."[46]

A variety of statements are made about the conscience in the New Testament:

1. It bears witness to, or pronounces judgment upon actions already performed (Acts 24:16; Rom. 9:1; Heb. 9:14; 1 Pet. 3:16, 21).

2. It functions with regard to matters other than religious (Rom. 13:5; 1 Cor. 10:25-29).

3. One is said to have a "good conscience" if he follows its dictates (Acts 23:1; 1 Tim. 1:5, 19; Heb. 13:18; 1 Pet. 3:16, 21).

4. The conscience can be misinformed (1 Cor. 8:7-12) and it can become "seared" (1 Tim. 4:2; Titus 1:15).

5. The authority of the conscience rests upon its identification with the will of God (1 Pet. 2:19; cf. Greek text).

Is the conscience a universal human phenomenon? Paul con-

---

43. Galatians, p. 133. Cf. Richardson, *Introduction to the Theology of the NT*, p. 48: He emphasizes the initiative of God. "We love only because God 'knows' us (1 Cor. 8:3), that is, in biblical language, calls us, enters into personal relations with us, commissions us to his service, and so on. It is not our cleverness or merit which has led us to the knowledge of God. . . . It was by the preaching of the word of Christ that the converts from paganism have come to the knowledge of the true God, but this has taken place only because God in his outgoing love had first 'known' them."

44. Burton, *Galatians*, p. 229.

45. For extended discussion, cf. J. P. Thornton-Duesbery, "Conscience," *Theological Wordbook of the Bible*, ed. Alan Richardson (London: SCM Press, 1950), pp. 52-53; S. S. Smalley, "Conscience," *New Bible Dictionary* (Grand Rapids, Mich.: Wm. B. Eerdmans Publishing Co., 1962), pp. 248-50; C. A. Pierce, *Conscience in the NT* (London: SCM Press, 1955).

46. Thornton-Duesbery, *Theological Wordbook*, p. 52.

sidered it such, according to Rom. 2:15. Conscience judges the rightness or wrongness of one's behavior, thus indicating a degree of knowledge of what is right and wrong. Furthermore, Paul seems to understand conscience as functioning in such a way as to lay the demand of God upon the individual. The outcome of the future judgment rests on how a person responds to the directions of the conscience (Rom. 2:16).

The apostle assumes that the heathen have a conscience. Since there is a divine demand in the judgmental actions of the conscience, the heathen know the demands of the law, even though they do not know the law *per se.* The law's requirements are "written in their hearts," and it is by virtue of their "conscience" that they know them.

This analysis of conscience suggests a "transcendent source of authority" lying behind it, or, better, constituting its existence. Peter intimates that its authority rests upon the will of God (1 Pet. 2:19). This being the case, Paul's substitution of "faith" for "conscience" with respect to the Christian life is legitimate, for faith like conscience includes obedience to the demand of God.[47] In dealing with the relationship of the strong Christian to the weak Christian, Paul argues in 1 Corinthians 8 on the basis of conscience, but in Romans 14 he argues the same point on the basis of faith. "Thus, the verdict of 'conscience' coincides for the Christian (as a man of 'faith') with the verdict of 'faith.'"[48]

From this cursory survey, it can be deduced that the New Testament views conscience as a universal phenomenon related to the revelatory activity of God. Because of man's depraved condition, John Wesley, along with others, did not see conscience as an inherent element in human nature. Whatever good a man engages in results from prevenient grace. He writes:

> Allowing that all the souls of men are dead in sin by *nature,* this excuses none, seeing no man is in a mere state of nature. There is no man, unless he has quenched the Spirit, that is totally void of the grace of God. No man living is devoid of what is vulgarly called *natural conscience.* But this is not natural: it is more properly termed *preventing grace.* . . . So that no man sins because he has not grace, but because he doth not use the grace that he hath.[49]

---

47. *Ibid.,* p. 220.
48. *Ibid.*
49. John Wesley, *Works* (Kansas City, Mo.: Nazarene Publishing House, n.d.), 6:512; 7:187.

Nevertheless, conscience's moral demand can be rejected and its future effective functioning can be diminished. Paul's reference to the conscience in the pivotal passage in Rom. 2:12-16 must not be construed primarily as an attempt to establish a "law of the conscience" but rather to depict the tragically sinful condition of mankind because of the failure of man to respond to divine overtures.

F. The Failure of Natural Theology[50]

This phrase is Stauffer's way of stating the New Testament's approach to the problem of the general revelation of God. Because man refused both the possibility of a theology of creation (Rom. 1:18-32) and a theology of history (2 Cor. 1:12) through submission to the wisdom of God, he chose to be his own theologian. Working out of his own wisdom, he became a pseudo-theologian, seeking to create a natural theology. Subsequently when God removes himself from the situation, man goes from a "natural theology to a theology of nature" because he cannot distinguish between God and idols. His ethic becomes a natural ethic or "a morality of nature" (Rom. 1:24 ff.). "Mankind has closed its eye to God's light, so as to be led by its own light, and has thus fallen victim to the delusions of a demonic will-o'-the-wisp."[51] The condition of the world of men is that they do not know God. That, however, is not God's fault. Men are to blame because they have chosen to live out of their own wisdom and not to respond to the demand of God. Conscience will "appear in court against man as a witness for the prosecution in the last judgment" (cf. Rom. 2:12 ff.). Stauffer concludes: "For this reason natural theology and natural ethics are bound to be wrecked by the very effects they produce, and so produce that extremity for man which is God's opportunity (Acts 17:29ff.)."[52]

The word of the Cross is the possibility of a new theology of creation and history. But man must hear and respond to it. Floyd V. Filson concludes that the passages which speak of a universal knowledge are not used "to vindicate a natural theology which would lessen the need of the gospel. On the contrary the few passages . . . are used to show that the Gentiles have knowledge and are responsible for their sin, and should repent. . . . All men need Christ."[53]

---

50. Stauffer, *NT Theology*, pp. 86-90.
51. *Ibid.*, p. 89.
52. *Ibid.*
53. Floyd V. Filson, *Jesus Christ the Risen Lord* (New York: Abingdon Press, 1956), p. 61.

13

Creator and Father-King

I. GOD AS CREATOR

A. The Double Strand

The New Testament view of God's creatorship is identical to that which is found in the Old Testament. However, we cannot find in the New Testament a restatement of the primal events of God's creating activities as recorded in Genesis. One might reason that the absence of this material is the result of the Early Church's acceptance of the old Scriptures without qualification, thus making the retelling of the creation events unnecessary. Also, repetition was not called for because the Church's interest centered in the story of redemption. Occasionally, the New Testament writers mention the creation but do not give major attention to it.

The references to creatorship present a double strand, one asserting God as Creator and the other designating Christ's role in creation. The Synoptic materials speak indirectly about God's relationship to the cosmos. For example, believers are urged not to be anxious about their daily existence, for God surely will care for them since He brought everything into existence and He sustains it. He clothed the lilies with beauty and He unfailingly feeds the birds of the air. "But if God so clothes the grass of the field, which today is alive and tomorrow is thrown into the oven, will he not much more clothe you, O men of little faith?" (Matt. 6:25-34; cf. Luke 12:22-30). The lack of faith on the part of Christ's hearers was due to their failure to observe the total involvement of God in sustaining His created order. That custodial relationship was His obligation by virtue of His originating relationship to creation.

In Eph. 3:9, Paul explicitly declares that God "created all things," virtually repeating words from Genesis 1. He also alludes to creation when he writes, "For it is the God who said, 'Let light shine out of darkness'" (2 Cor. 4:6). In an instructive word to young Timothy, the apostle asserts that God created foods; and since everything created by God is good, it is not to be rejected if it is received with thanksgiving (1 Tim. 4:4). Other Pauline passages which clearly support a God-centered view of creation are Rom. 4:17 ("who gives life to the dead and calls into existence the things that do exist"); 11:36 ("For from him and through him and to him are all things"); 1 Cor. 11:12 ("and all things are from God"). The writer to the Hebrews includes in his catalog of "evidences of faith" his belief in the creation of the world "by the word of God" (11:3).

The Christological strand is likewise explicit in the New Testament. The Evangelist John writes: "All things were made through him *[panta di' autou egeneto],* and without him was not anything made that was made *[chōris autou egeneto oude en ho gegonen]*" (John 1:3). Paul affirms in Col. 1:16, "For in him all things were created *[en autō ektisthē ta panta]* . . . all things were created through him and for him *[ta panta di' autou kai eis auton ektistai].*" Paul further declares that Christ's role in the created order is also that of sustaining it: "In him all things hold together *[sunestēken,* 'stand together']." Through Christ's action we have "a cosmos instead of a chaos." Following the same line of thought, the writer to the Hebrews speaks of the Son as the One through whom *(di' hou)* God "created the world" *(epoisēsen tous aiōnas),* and who upholds "the universe by the word of his power" *(pherōn te ta panta,* 1:2-3). Thus, as Stauffer suggests, "Christ is creation's lifegiver."[1]

In Hebrews, the praise of the exalted Lord, who is superior to the angels, includes a reference to Ps. 102:25-27. "Thou, Lord, didst found the earth in the beginning, and the heavens are the work of thy hands" (1:10). Unlike the immutable character of Christ himself, the things of the material order perish, grow old, and are subject to the Christ's commands (1:11-12).

Filson insists that "the role of the Son in creating and upholding the created order plays no central role in the New Testament." He acknowledges, however, two important dimensions of the Church's

---

1. *NT Theology,* p. 57.

theologizing on this issue. First, as the Church matured in her under-standing of the event of Christ, she necessarily had to look behind the Incarnation to determine Christ's relationship to God in the total scheme of things. Thus, the fact of Christ's creatorship came to be asserted. Second, Christ's cosmic role, while not fully understood and affirmed in the earliest days of the Church, was later affirmed, and there was no objection to it. Filson thus concludes: "Only a quarter of a century after the death of Jesus, within the lifetime of eyewitnesses and personal disciples of the Galilean ministry, Paul could state this conviction as a settled conclusion of Christian thinking, and there is no evidence that other Christian leaders challenged his Christology."[2]

B. Cooperating Agent

In 1 Corinthians, where the Apostle Paul discusses meats offered to idols, an amazing declaration appears which places God and Christ on virtually equal terms with respect to creation. "Yet for us there is one God, the Father, from whom are all things and for whom we exist, and one Lord, Jesus Christ, through whom are all things and through whom we exist" (1 Cor. 8:6). Careful analysis of this passage and the others which speak of Christ in creation discloses that Christ's role is a mediatorial or cooperating one. Our biblical writers declare that it is "through" Christ (*di' hou,* 1 Cor. 8:6; Heb. 1:2) or "in" Christ (*en autō,* Col. 1:16) that the world came into being. Obviously, some distinction between the Father and the Son was attempted. God created the world by his Christ; everything comes from God but through Christ. Stauffer proposes that when, in John 1:3, the apostle identified the creative Christ with the creative Word, he unified the statements "God creates through his Word" and "God creates through his Christ." These two statements, he asserts, remained "pretty well unconnected" in Paul.[3]

Cullmann's interpretation, though following a different ap-proach, arrives at the same conclusion. He cites 1 Cor. 8:6 and recog-nizes that both God and Christ have to do with creation. However, he continues, "The variation lies only in the prepositions: *ex* and *eis* in

2. *Jesus Christ the Risen Lord,* pp. 59-60; cf. Bultmann, *Theology of the NT,* 1:132: "Whether Paul was the first to ascribe *to Christ this cosmic role as mediator of creation,* cannot be said; the way he speaks of it as if it were a matter of course rather inclines one to conclude that he was not alone in doing so."

3. *NT Theology,* p. 58; cf. H. E. Dana and Julius R. Mantey, *A Manual Grammar of the Greek New Testament* (New York: Macmillan Co., 1927), p. 102: Christ is not an "independent creator but rather the intermediate agent in creation."

connection with God; *dia* in connection with Christ, *'through* whom all things' *(di' hou ta panta)."*[4] The distinction found here is not between Creator and Redeemer, but between Source and Goal of creation on the one hand and the Mediator of that creation on the other hand. God as Source of creation expresses God as He exists independently of His redemptive revelation, whereas the reference to Christ as Mediator expresses God as He reveals himself to the world.

Cullmann's Christology leads him thus to affirm that "the Father and the Son can be meaningfully distinguished only in the time of revelatory history, that is, in the time which begins with the creation of the world and continues until the end."[5] Cullmann's thought here is controlled by his commitment to a functional Christology, which focuses on the work of Christ rather than upon the person of Christ. Jesus Christ is God in His self-revelation. This being the case, it is affirmed that all of God's revelation is centered in Christ, whether creation or redemption. There is thus no "distinction between God as the Creator and Christ as the Redeemer, since creation and redemption belong together as God's communication of himself to the world."[6]

One must finally settle this issue on a soteriological rather than an ontological-cosmological basis.[7] For the Church, Christ was her Saviour. To be such, He had to be genuinely related to God for all time. When the question of His role in the formation of the cosmos was raised, it was answered simply by identifying Him as "God's Agent." Athanasius pointed out in *De Incarnatione* that the Redeemer could be no other than the Creator, no secondary, alien, or substitute

---

4. *Christology,* p. 2.
5. *Ibid.,* pp. 326-27.
6. *Ibid.,* p. 326.
7. Cf. Wolfhart Pannenberg, *Jesus—God and Man,* trans. Lewis L. Wilkins and Duane A. Priebe (Philadelphia: The Westminster Press, 1968), pp. 168-69; 390-97: "The statement that all things and beings are created through Jesus Christ means that *eschaton* that has appeared beforehand in Jesus represents the time and point from which the creation took place. . . . Christ's mediation of creation is not to be thought of primarily in terms of the temporal beginning of the world. It is rather to be understood in terms of the whole of the world process that receives its unity and meaning in the light of its end that has appeared in advance in the history of Jesus, so that the essence of every individual occurrence, whose meaning is relative to the whole to which it belongs, is first decided in the light of this end. . . . God's eternal act of creation will be entirely unfolded in time first in the *eschaton.*" This view, in the judgment of the writer, fails to do justice to the normal tendency of the Early Church to attempt to take in the full sweep of Christ's meaning for them, which included His relationship to God before the Incarnation.

being. The New Testament writers had already come to that same conclusion.

It is in these soteriological terms that expressions of the divine creatorship in the New Testament, especially in Paul, must be understood. The Church accepted the Old Testament's concept of the creatorship of God and left the matter there. Her major concern was redemptional in nature; thus she mentioned only casually the creative activity of Christ. However, she could not totally ignore it, since to proclaim Christ as Redeemer, in the sense in which she understood that term, meant that Christ was to be proclaimed Creator too.

Redemption heightens the concept of creatorship rather than the reverse. Christ is Creator because He is Redeemer, as understood in the framework of the kerygmatic activity of the Early Community. Moreover, Paul makes it clear that the ultimate responsibility of man, as contemplated in the divine creativity, is to glorify God (Rom. 1:18-32). Christ as God's Agent in creation makes it possible for man to render this praise (cf. Col. 1:9-19; Eph. 1:12). It is through Christ that God is glorified. In keeping with this soteriological approach, everything that happens in the created order is at God's redeeming service, a point which John brings out clearly (cf. John 9; 11:4). Lastly, the created order, writhing now under the power of sin's rulers, is to be redeemed ultimately through the work of Christ (Rom. 8:18-23).

II. GOD AS FATHER-KING

The redemption of God, which is made available by His visitation to man in the person of His Son, involves also the characterization of himself as King. He is indeed the Redeemer-King and in a special sense the Father-King.[8]

A. The Kingship Concept in the Teachings of Jesus

The Hebrews from the earliest time conceived of God as King. By the time of the Lord's incarnation many devout Jews were looking for "the consolation of Israel" (Luke 2:25). The eager Zealots wanted to hasten the day by enforced political action, while the Pharisees were continuing to believe that perfect obedience to the Law by the elect

---

8. Cf. John Bright, *The Kingdom of God* (New York: Abingdon Press, Father-King, 1953), p. 7: "The concept of the Kingdom of God involves, in a real sense, the total message of the Bible." The phrase "the kingdom of God" might justifiably be translated "the kingship of God." Cf. also Grant, *Introduction to NT Thought*, p. 117.

people would bring it to pass. John the Baptist burst upon the first century proclaiming, "Repent, for the kingdom of heaven is at hand" (Matt. 3:2). John revived the old prophetic truth that the day of the Lord would be a day of reckoning both for the Jews and the Gentiles. Therefore, he called for repentance from everyone, even the religious leaders (Luke 3:7-9).

In keeping with the prophetic proclamation and especially as it was sounded anew in John the Baptist's message, Jesus took up the theme of God's kingship in His preaching. The Gospel of Mark summarizes His message: "Jesus came into Galilee, preaching the gospel of God, and saying, 'The time is fulfilled, and the kingdom of God is at hand; repent, and believe the gospel" (1:14-15; cf. Matt. 4:23). Jesus taught His disciples to pray:

> Thy Kingdom come.
> Thy will be done,
> On earth as it is in heaven (Matt. 6:10).

The more than 70 instances of the phrase "the kingdom of God" (*basileia tou theou*) or "the kingdom of heaven"[9] in the Gospels has led modern scholarship to conclude quite unanimously that the kingdom of God was the central message of Jesus.[10] The concept of kingship is essential to an understanding of the nature of God.

The word "kingdom" (*basileia*), as used in Jesus' teaching, has a dual meaning. On one hand it denotes a "realm," "territory," "domain," or "people over whom a king rules." Mark 3:24 reads: "If a kingdom is divided against itself, that kingdom cannot stand." Also, Matt. 24:7 states that "nation shall rise against nation, and kingdom against kingdom." But kingdom also denotes "sovereignty," "royal power," "dominion," or "rulership." For example, Luke 1:33: "And he will reign over the house of Jacob for ever." Or Luke 19:12: "A nobleman went into a far country to receive kingly power" ("a kingdom," KJV; cf. RSV, Luke 23:42; John 18:36; Rev. 17:12). Thus, whenever we encounter the word "kingdom" in the teaching of

9. The phrase "kingdom of heaven" is a circumlocution for the phrase "kingdom of God." It was employed by the Jews as "a reverential avoidance of the use of the word 'God'."

10. Cf. G. E. Ladd, *Jesus and the Kingdom* (New York: Harper and Row, 1964); G. Lundstom, *The Kingdom of God in the Teaching of Jesus* (Philadelphia: Westminster Press, 1963); H. N. Ridderbos, *The Coming of the Kingdom*, trans. H. de Jongste (Philadelphia: Presbyterian and Reformed Publishing Co., 1972); Willard H. Taylor, "The Kingdom of God," *Exploring Our Christian Faith*, ed. W. T. Purkiser, et al. (Kansas City: Beacon Hill Press, 1960), pp. 519 ff.

Jesus, we must determine whether the reference implies realm or rulership.[11]

"The kingdom of God" as used by Jesus designates not only the new order which He was establishing with all its blessings of salvation but also "the kingly rule of God" in the hearts of men made possible through relationship to himself. The kingdom of God refers to the kingship of the King of Kings as well as to His domain. The kingdom of God exists wherever hearts render obeisance to God as King. This latter concept is, for Jesus, the central meaning of *basileia*.

Jesus preached that the kingdom of God was being realized in a new and unique way in His time and in His own work. He did not emphasize primarily the long-established view that God's kingdom was an eternal kingdom; rather He spoke of a decisive manifestation of it in the *now* time. Two important verses speak of this sovereign power of God in Christ's time. In Matt. 12:28, Jesus is recorded as telling His opponents, "But if it is by the Spirit of God that I cast out demons, then the kingdom of God has come upon you."[12] The Greek word *ephthasen,* translated "has come," cannot be taken as simply meaning "proximity" but rather "actual presence." Unquestionably Jesus taught that the kingship of God was being exercised in that time in the attack on the forces of evil, and in particular, on the kingdom of Satan.

Another verse of importance is Luke 17:21. It is a response of Christ to an inquiry from the Pharisees as to when the kingdom of God was coming. "Nor will they say, 'Lo, here it is!' or 'There!' for behold the Kingdom of God is in the midst of you." This reply clearly speaks of a dimension of presentness of God's reign. The Pharisees' question probably arose out of the prevailing apocalyptic view of the Kingdom. But Jesus replied that the kingdom of God was already in the midst of them, unaccompanied by the expected signs.

Among scholars the debate over the phrase *entos humōn* continues. Is "within you" or "in the midst of you" intended by Jesus? The choice of the second translation leads naturally to the conclusion that in the person of Jesus the reign of God was being realized. Ladd concludes that "'in your midst,' in Jesus' person, best fits the total context of his teaching."[13]

---

11. G. E. Ladd, "The Kingdom of God—Reign or Realm?" JBL 31 (1962), pp. 230-38.

12. See Luke 11:20, which uses the phrase "the finger of God," reminiscent of the Exodus deliverance of the people of Israel, Exod. 8:19.

13. *Theology of the NT,* p. 68. For a fuller discussion on "The Kingdom of God," see

If the core of Jesus' teaching is the kingdom of God or "the kingly rule of God" in the hearts of men, it follows that, for Jesus, God in His essential nature is King of all. He is the eternal Sovereign and man must render complete loyalty to Him if he hopes to live abundantly. The Master's own constant obedience speaks of His immediate recognition of the Kingship of God. His Garden of Gethsemane prayer, "Nevertheless not my will, but thine, be done," is an eloquent example of the submission of an obedient subject to the eternal King (Luke 22:42).

What is most scandalous in the gospel is that Jesus shares that Kingship and sovereignty in His own person and mission. The Incarnation itself is therefore a revelation of the reign of God. All who "come to Christ" know the King.

B. The Kingship Concept in the Non-Gospel Writings

The radical scholar Alfred Loisy concluded after investigating the few references to the Kingdom in the rest of the New Testament that "Jesus announced the kingdom of God, but it was the Church which appeared."[14] While this skepticism is hardly justified, it is surprising that the focal theme of Christ's preaching receives so little attention in the non-Gospel material in the New Testament. Paul mentions "the kingdom of God" in some way in Rom. 14:17; 1 Cor. 4:20; 6:10; 15:24, 50; Gal. 5:21; Eph. 5:5; Col. 4:11; 1 Thess. 2:12; and 2 Thess. 1:5. James 2:5 reads: "Has not God chosen those who are poor in the world to be rich in faith and heirs of the kingdom which he has promised to those who love him?" Eight verses in the extra-Gospel material speak of "the kingdom of Christ" (1 Cor. 15:24; Eph. 5:5; Col. 1:13; 2 Tim. 4:1, 18; Heb. 1:8; 2 Pet. 1:11; Rev. 11:15).

What is to be concluded from this apparent lack of emphasis upon the Kingdom? First, while the references are not many, they do include the concept in the total message of the apostles, especially in that of Paul. In addition, the language of sovereignty in these writings must be laid alongside the Kingdom references. Paul teaches that those who have received grace and righteousness shall reign in the life of the age to come (Rom. 5:17). He further speaks of

Chap. 32. On the question of the "present" and "future" nature of the Kingdom, see C. H. Dodd, *The Parables of the Kingdom* (London: Nisbet and Co., Ltd., 1935), (London: SCM Press, Ltd., 1954), pp. 20-34.

14. Alfred Loisy, *The Gospel and the Church*, trans. Christopher Home (New York: Charles Scribner's Sons, 1904).

the saints as exercising judgment over the angels (1 Cor. 6:2 ff.). Reflecting on his long years of nerve-wracking yet effective missionary service and viewing the prospects ahead, Paul writes to Timothy: "If we have died with him, we shall also live with him; if we endure, we shall also reign with him" (2 Tim. 2:11-12). In Paul's doxological passages the sovereignty emphasis appears also (cf. 1 Tim. 1:17; 6:15). Peter sees the Church as a "kingdom of priests" (1 Pet. 2:9 f.; cf. Rev. 1:6; 5:10; 20:6). With regard to Christ, Paul writes that He will visibly take up His reign over the nations at the Parousia (Rom. 15:12).[15]

Second, a change in the focus and statement of the message occurred naturally in the Early Church. Filson sees this shift as expected in the light of the epochal events of the Cross and the Resurrection. These early followers "lived, worshiped, and witnessed in the light of the Resurrection. . . . Christ had to be the center of their message."[16] There was therefore no forgetting Jesus' message on the Kingdom. "It was to see God establishing his reign through the ministry and death and resurrection of Christ, through the gift of the Spirit, and through the continuing lordship of Christ over his widening church."[17]

Modern man might take offence at this idea of kingship because it conjures up notions of monarchal extravagance, autocratic power, and distance from people. The reading of ancient history, however, which describes the unforgiveable ways of the kings, generates a view of kingship entirely out of keeping with the biblical understanding. Grant reminds us that the Israelite thought of God under the model of the local prince or king—the city kings of the Semitic times and of Homer. While such a ruler lived on a large estate and in luxury, he genuinely cared about the welfare of his people. "Kingship of this kind, local, personal, familiar, was among the connotations of the term in religious application."[18]

While God was understood to hold power that could remove men from the divine presence instantly and irrevocably, the richest Old Testament teaching, as well as that of Christ, did not conceive God's kingship in such autocratic terms. Grant writes: "To know him was to love him, as you might love a good king whose palace lay up the hill above your village, or more probably in the center of your

15. Cf. Richardson, *Introduction to the Theology of the NT*, pp. 88-89.
16. *Jesus Christ the Risen Lord*, p. 109.
17. *Ibid.*, p. 110.
18. *Introduction to NT Thought*, pp. 102-3.

walled city, and whose sons and daughters came and went and were seen every day."[19] Essentially, the ancient writers and prophets, along with Jesus, depicted God's kingship as redeeming for men. As King, God lives to help, to deliver, to redeem His subjects from their sins and their enemies. Paul and the writers of the General Epistles share this view of God.

C. The Fatherhood of God

Standing alongside of, and intermingling with, the concept that God is King is the view that God is a Father. As a thesis, it is proposed here that this latter characterization of God represents for the New Testament a way of expressing the soteriological relationship of God to mankind. A father loves, cares, and releases his resources to assist his own. Bowman comments that "father . . . is a name for the redemptive side of God's nature."[20] After surveying the use of the idea of fatherhood in ancient oriental culture, Joachim Jeremias concludes that Israel's concept has a difference: "The certainty that God is Father and Israel his son is grounded not in mythology but in a unique act of salvation by God, which Israel had experienced in history."[21]

Jesus heightened the use of the word "Father," in speaking of God, beyond that previously employed by the Jews or used in His own time by Palestinian Judaism. He not only clarified the proffered redeeming relationship by reference to the fatherhood of God but, as Jeremias has brilliantly demonstrated, Jesus identified His own union with the Father by calling God "Abba." He used this endearing and intimate term to reveal the very basis of His communion with God. The Gethsemane prayer of Jesus begins with a double address in Mark 14:36: "Abba, Father" *(Abba ho patēr)*. When the disciples asked for a prayer of their own, Jesus gave them the familiar Lord's Prayer in which they, too, were permitted to share with Him this same intimacy suggested by the word *Abba* (Matt. 6:9-13). The Greek word *patēr* is equivalent to the Aramaic *Abba.*[22] Moreover, Jesus announced that only the person who reflects in spirit this childlike

---

19. *Ibid.,* p. 103.

20. *Prophetic Realism and the Gospel,* p. 172.

21. Joachim Jeremias, *The Central Message of the New Testament* (New York: Charles Scribner's Sons, 1965), p. 11; Joachim Jeremias, *New Testament Theology: The Proclamation of Jesus,* trans. John Bowman (New York: Charles Scribner's Sons, 1971), pp. 178 ff.; cf. T. W. Manson, *The Teaching of Jesus,* 2nd ed. (Cambridge: Cambridge University Press, 1935), pp. 90 ff.

22. *Ibid.,* p. 28.

Abba shall enter into the kingdom of God.[23] Thus Jesus himself intensified the redemptive significance of the concept of father as applied to God.

In the Pauline corpus and the General Epistles the term "father" appears frequently, Paul being the more frequent user. He quite consistently and with variations uses the title "God our Father" (1 Cor. 1:3; 2 Cor. 1:2; Eph. 1:2; Phil. 1:2; Col. 1:2; 2 Thess. 1:1; Philem. 3) and "God the Father" (1 Cor. 15:24; Gal. 1:1, 3; Eph. 6:23; Phil. 2:11; 1 Tim. 1:2; Titus 1:4; cf. 2 Pet. 1:17; Jude 1). In several instances, God is referred to as "the Father of the Lord Jesus Christ" or some modification of that idea (Rom. 15:6; 2 Cor. 1:3; 11:31; Eph. 1:3; Col. 1:3; Heb. 1:5 ["I will be to him a father"]; 1 Pet. 1:3).

Richardson contends that these phrases have special meaning in the sense that God is Father, not because we are sons, for in that case He would be Father only in a secondary sense. Rather, He is Father because Christ is truly His Son. The Father is dependent not on our sonship but on Christ's sonship. Christ is "the source of Fatherhood." Thus, by our being *en Christō,* "God is really and essentially our Father."[24]

Occasionally, a qualifying word concerning the nature of the Father appears, such as "the Father of glory" (Eph. 1:17; cf. Rom. 6:4); "the Father of mercies" (2 Cor. 1:3); "the Father of spirits" (Heb. 12:9); "the Father of lights" (James 1:17); *et al.*

Special note must be taken of certain passages, where it might be misconstrued that the writers are thinking of God as Father of mankind but where the emphasis falls rather upon the community of believers who have the right to call Him Father. For example, in 1 Cor. 8:6 Paul sets God the Father over against the heathen gods, which do not exist. He writes: "Yet *for us* there is one God, the Father, from whom are all things and for whom we exist." Pleading with the Corinthians not to be yoked to unbelievers, Paul quotes from several Old Testament scriptures for support. One of these declares, "I will be a father to you, and you shall be my sons and daughters, says the Lord Almighty" (2 Cor. 6:18).

Among the seven unities in Eph. 4:4-6, Paul includes the phrase "one God and Father of us all." Quite obviously, when he makes this reference, the apostle has in mind the believing community and not the whole of mankind. These verses, along with others, emphasize

---

23. *Ibid.,* p. 29.
24. *Introduction to the Theology of the NT,* p. 264.

that the Church is the New Israel. In the Old Testament it is to Israel
in a primary sense that God is Father. Manson says:

> In the Old Testament God is the Father of Israel in the sense
> that he is founder and creator of the nation (Deut. 32:6; Isa. 63:
> 16; Mal. 2:10). . . . Fatherhood in the Old Testament relates pecu-
> liarly to the historical event of the deliverance of the people of
> Israel from Egypt. This act by which Yahweh becomes the Father
> of Israel is adoption rather than creation.[25]

Manson thus concludes that God is "the creator of all the people; but Israel is in a special sense his son (Hos. 11:1), even his firstborn (Exod. 4:22; Jer. 31:9)."[26] Likewise in the New Testament the
fatherhood of God relates peculiarly to the Church (cf. Gal. 1:4;
Heb. 12:3-11; 1 Pet. 1:17), which is the true Israel (Gal. 6:16).

The most significant occurrences of the father concept are found
in Paul's explications of sonship in Rom. 8:15 and Gal. 4:6-7. Because
of our sinfulness, Paul writes, we are no longer sons through creation. One becomes a son only through adoption. The proof of his new
relationship to the Father is that he receives the Spirit of adoption,
whereby he is entitled to address God as "Abba, Father." Following
Jesus, then, the apostle applies fatherhood to soteriological matters.
God is Father only to believers as adopted sons. As "children of God"
we are "heirs of God" and "fellow heirs with Christ" (Rom. 8:17), and
no longer slaves (Gal. 4:7). Jeremias notes that "the ancient Christian
liturgies show their awareness of the greatness of this gift [sonship]
in that they preface the Lord's Prayer with the words: 'We *make bold*
to say: Our Father'."[27]

In summary, the dual concepts of kingship and fatherhood as
announced by the New Testament writers should not be considered
polarities. Since both are centrally redemptive in their thrust, they
should be brought together and hyphenated. It is proper to speak of
God as the Father-King. His sovereignty must not be conceived as
arbitrary or in any sense tyrannical; it is mixed with mercy and love.
While He exercises rulership over the whole of the created order,
that rulership is guided by His desire to enter into a saving relationship with His creatures.

The redeeming gifts of "God the Father and our Lord Jesus
Christ," says Paul, are "grace and peace" (Gal. 1:3). God the Father
wishes to be addressed as "Abba," and He further desires that His

---

25. *Teachings of Jesus,* p. 91.
26. *Ibid.*
27. *Central Message of the New Testament,* p. 29.

children accept His disciplinary actions when necessary. By so doing we "share his holiness" and enjoy "the peaceful fruit of righteousness" (Heb. 12:9-11). When we are adopted into His family, we at the same time become subjects in loving obedience to the King of Kings and Lord of Lords. To be a citizen of the kingdom of God is to be a member of the family of God.

Paul approaches a union of these ideas in two places in particular. In Eph. 2:11-19, he reminds the recipients that through Christ they "have access by one Spirit to the Father" (v. 18). As a result, they are no longer strangers and sojourners, but "fellow citizens *[sumpolitai]* with the saints *and* members of the household of God *[oikeioi tou theou]*" (v. 19). In the majestic resurrection chapter in 1 Corinthians, the apostle glimpses the future and declares: "Then comes the end, when he [Christ] delivers the kingdom to God the Father after destroying every rule and every authority and power" (15:24).

14

The Servant Spirit

When the Israelites of the Old Testament order met for worship, they recited together the *Shema*,[1] confessing that "the Lord our God is one Lord" (Deut. 6:4-5). This dominating and persistent Jewish confession that "God is One" was transmitted through the synagogue and Christ into the Christian community. The learned scribe asked the Master which commandment was the central one of all the commandments of God, and He responded by quoting the *Shema* (Mark 12:28 ff.). Paul employs monotheistic formulas frequently (Rom. 3:30; 16:27; 1 Cor. 8:4; Gal. 3:20; 1 Thess. 1:9; 1 Tim. 1:17). James 2:19 states in typically creedal form, "God is one." In a doxological exaltation, Jude speaks of "the only God, our Saviour through Jesus Christ our Lord" (v. 25). The Early Church, in keeping with her Hebrew heritage, especially as it was mediated through such strong leaders as Paul and James, did not surrender the great doctrine of the Oneness of God. Reflecting on these facts, Stauffer comments: "Such monotheistic formulae are not in any way compromised by the Church's christology."[2]

I. FORMULAS OF THREENESS

The Early Church developed, however, along with her commitment to the old faith, a trinitarian doctrine. The formulated dogma appeared later in the period of the ecclesiastical councils, but the

---

1. *Shema* is the first Hebrew word in the creed; it is translated "Hear."
2. *NT Theology*, p. 243.

embryonic elements come to expression in the New Testament trinitarian formulas.[3] Jesus commissioned His disciples to "go therefore and make disciples of all nations, baptizing them in the name of the Father and of the Son and of the Holy Spirit" (Matt. 28:19). This same triad, "Father-Son [or Christ, Lord]-Spirit," also appears in several other places in the Pauline and General Epistles (1 Cor. 12:3 ff.; 2 Cor. 1:21 ff.; 13:14; 2 Thess. 2:13; 1 Pet. 1:2).

The New Testament writers understand God in a threefold sense, that is, in terms of trinity—God the Father, God the Son, and God the Holy Spirit. While God is for the Early Church indisputably One, He is, at the same time, Three. Threeness must not be taken in the sense of tritheism, that is to say, that there are three different Gods, namely, one God who is Father, one God who is Son, and one God who is Holy Spirit. Rather, as Edwin Lewis states: "He is a unitary Being whose inner life has a threefoldness which we describe as respectively the Father, the Son, and the Holy Spirit."[4] For the New Testament writers, the accents in these triadic formulas fall equally upon the word "God" and upon the words "Father, Son, and Holy Spirit."

Careful examination of the relevant passages where creation, redemption, and sanctification are discussed will reveal that Christ and the Holy Spirit function in equality with God in determining the course of these activities. As Richardson concludes, "In every activity of each of the three 'persons' of the Godhead it is always the one-and-the-same-God who acts."[5] Yet subordinate roles are suggested for the Son and Holy Spirit. In relation to the Son, the Holy Spirit acts in a self-effacing manner, not calling attention to himself (John 16:14-15).

Having admitted this dependent element in the redemption process, the truth nevertheless persists that Christ and the Spirit are coequally God. Paul can write of the "Spirit of God," the "Spirit of Christ," and "Christ" with no change of subject:

> You are not in the flesh, you are in the Spirit, if the Spirit of God really dwells in you. Any one who does not have the Spirit of Christ does not belong to him. But if Christ is in you, although your bodies are dead because of sin, your spirits are alive because of righteousness. If the Spirit of him who raised Jesus from the dead dwells in you, he who raised Christ Jesus from the dead will give life to your mortal bodies also through his Spirit which dwells in you (Rom. 8:9-11; cf. also Gal. 4:6).

---

3. *Ibid.*, p. 252.
4. *The Ministry of the Holy Spirit* (Nashville, Tenn.: Tidings, 1944), p. 25.
5. *Introduction to the Theology of the NT*, p. 123.

But what is meant when we speak of God as Spirit? If we use a small *s* in the word *spirit*, we simply signify that God is not body. He exists without the normal bodily limitations of men. He is of the spirit world; He transcends the limits of man's observation and action. On the other hand, if the *S* is capitalized, we are suggesting the Holy Spirit. "Holy Spirit" describes one of the personal expressions of Deity. The New Testament writers distinguish between God functioning as Father, God functioning as Son, and God functioning as Holy Spirit. Thus, Holy Spirit represents one of God's ways of being God.

What about the personhood of the Spirit? John's Gospel identifies *to Pneuma* (a neuter noun) as *ho Paraklētos* (a masculine noun; 14:26; cf. also 14:15-16; 15:26-27; 16:7-11). Notice also the use of the masculine pronouns in 14:26; 15:26; 16:7-8, 13-14 (*ekeinos* and *autos*). These can in no way be interpreted as signifying a tendency or influence.[6] "But the Counselor *[Paraklētos]*, the Holy Spirit, whom *[ho]* the Father will send in my name, he *[ekeinos]* will teach you all things" (14:26). "But when the Counselor *[Paraklētos]* comes, whom *[ho]* I shall send to you from the Father, even the Spirit of truth, who proceeds *[ho]* from the Father, he *[ekeinos]* will bear witness to me" (15:26).

The Pauline corpus readily supports the view that the Holy Spirit is a person. The Spirit "wills" (1 Cor. 12:11), "leads" (Rom. 8:14), "teaches" (1 Cor. 2:13). All of these actions are functions properly associated with persons. Paul's doxology in 2 Cor. 13:14 gives distinctive place to the Spirit as a person along with the Father and the Son: "The grace of the Lord Jesus Christ and the love of God and the fellowship of the Holy Spirit be with you all." Likewise in the "seven unities" in Eph. 4:4-6, the Spirit is listed along with the Father and the Son, suggesting that He has divine status with the other two members of the Godhead—and surely implying personhood.

The sending of the Spirit is an activity of both the Father and the Son, but John 15:26 says that He "proceeds *[ekporeuetai]* from the Father." We should not, however, overload the verb theologically. The temporal mission of witnessing to Christ by the Holy Spirit seems to be the focus of the verse rather than "eternal procession." The work of the Spirit is that of continuing the ministry of Jesus in

6. Cf. Raymond E. Brown, "The Gospel According to John," *The Anchor Bible* (Garden City, N.Y.: Doubleday and Co., 1970), 2:639, 650, 1135-43; Leon Morris, *The Gospel According to John*, NICNT (1971), p. 683.

the world. The historic work of Christ was temporal. It commenced at a particular time in history and concluded at a specific time. The Spirit's work, however, goes on "perpetually accomplishing the fulfillment of the great saving process."

II. THE SPIRIT AS SERVANT

Edwin Lewis recommends that we think of the Holy Spirit as "God the Servant."[7] He writes:

> The words "Father" and "Son" convey a definite meaning to us, because they indicate a relation which our own experience enables us to understand. The case is different with "Holy Spirit." It suggests something vague, elusive, intangible. We *talk* about the Holy Spirit as One who does definite things, but the name he bears does not indicate his office.[8]

"Servant" is a valid description because He uniquely serves the Father and the Son, who have sent Him. "He will not speak on his own authority, but whatever he hears he will speak" (John 16:13). The Holy Spirit has the task of effecting the divine purposes in the world. Accordingly, in whatever way God acts in the world, He acts by and through this Third Person.

To speak of the Holy Spirit as Servant is to speak of the redeeming activity of God in the world in this post-Resurrection time. The Holy Spirit is essentially God in action, or God-at-work saving men. The New Testament writers preserved the teaching of the Old Testament, for there the Spirit of God is essentially "the power or presence of God at work in the world. He works . . . through his Spirit."[9] Without denying the concept of person as applied to the Spirit, it can be asserted that "the very idea of the divine Spirit is the sense of activity and power."[10] The Spirit is God's *dunamis* (power) in action, creating the Church and enabling the Church to witness to the world.[11]

In the history of salvation, Pentecost becomes an important event in the Spirit's function because it signalizes the *universalizing* of God's saving activity. The Spirit is "God-at-hand" in a way He has never been before in redemptive purposes. Peter preached: "For the

7. *Ministry of the Spirit,* p. 31.
8. *Ibid.*
9. Filson, *Jesus Christ the Risen Lord,* p. 156.
10. *Ibid.,* p. 157.
11. Notice the references to the Spirit as "the Spirit of power": Rom. 15:13; 1 Cor. 2:4; Eph. 3:15; 2 Tim. 1:7.

promise is to you and to your children and to all that are far off, every one whom the Lord our God calls to him" (Acts 2:39). The Church is brought into existence as "an extension of the incarnation" and provides the basic channel through which the Spirit can work. It remains, now, for us to explore with our New Testament writers how they conceive the ministry of the Holy Spirit.

This ministry in the history of mankind and in the life of the Church is manifold. There is some justification in concluding that the Spirit has assumed all the divine redemptive responsibilities. In the New Testament the Spirit is pictured as the Inspirer and Interpreter of the Scriptures, the Interceder for men, the Administrator of salvation, and the Life-giver of the Church. Once again, it must be emphasized that the concept of the Spirit in the Christian tradition signifies the redemptive activity of God in this post-Resurrection and post-Pentecostal period of the Church.

III. THE INSPIRER AND INTERPRETER OF THE SCRIPTURES

When referring to the Spirit as the Source of the Scriptures, we are restricted to Peter and Paul primarily. The Epistle to the Hebrews expressly states in three instances that the Holy Spirit speaks through the Scriptures, but beyond that has nothing to offer as to the Spirit's role in bringing the written Word into being (3:7; 9:8; 10:15; cf. 4:12). Paul's statement appears in his correspondence with Timothy. "All scripture is inspired by God [*pasa graphē theopneustos*] and profitable for teaching, for reproof, for correction, and for training in righteousness" (2 Tim. 3:16).[12] Quite obviously, since there were no canonized New Testament writings at the time, Paul is making reference to the Old Testament. However, the apostle has announced the *fact* of inspiration, which simply asserts that the Holy Scriptures came into existence through special acts of God. His central concern here is to show that the old writings are valuable for the instruction of the young Christian in fostering maturation and preparation for effective living and serving.

Peter's statement offers more explicit information. He is desirous of emphasizing care in the interpretation of the Scripture, but in so doing he gives expression to the truth that the Holy Spirit

---

12. The Greek text has no verb form in this sentence; it is necessary to supply one. A valid translation is "Every God-inspired [*theopneustos*] scripture is also profitable for teaching."

inspired men to write the Word. "First of all you must understand this, that no prophecy of scripture is a matter of one's own interpretation, because no prophecy ever came by the impulse of man, but men moved by the Holy Spirit spoke from God *[hupo pneumatos hagion pheromenoi elalēsan apo theou anthrōpoi]*" (2 Pet. 1:20-21). Inspiration by the Holy Spirit is indisputably affirmed in this passage.

In creating the Scriptures, the Holy Spirit chose "holy men" who were willing to be "carried along"[13] by Him into the unimpeachable truth of the gospel. As chosen men, their minds were "elevated" or granted an enlargement of understanding and conception beyond that of natural man. Wiley adds the factor of "suggestion" by which is meant "a direct and immediate suggestion from God to man by the Spirit as to the thoughts which he shall use or even the very words which he shall employ in order to make them agencies in conveying His will to others."[14] The biblical record does not systematize this process of inspiration, but it does strongly affirm that the work of the Holy Spirit in the process was for the purpose of creating an "infallible word of God, an authoritative rule of faith and practice for the church."

It follows necessarily that if the Holy Spirit inspires the writings, He also would be intimately involved in their interpretation. Our writers assert that He is *Spiritus Interpres Scripturae* ("Interpreter of the Scriptures"). Peter makes clear (2 Pet. 1:20-21) that the interpretation cannot be a private enterprise[15] because the Spirit must be taken into account as the One who inspired it. There must be dependence upon the ministry of the Spirit in the task of explicating Holy Writ.

Pursuing lines of thought similar to Peter's, the Lord is recorded in the Gospel of John as saying that the Spirit will "teach you all things" (14:26) and "guide you into all truth" (16:13). Also, the Apostle Paul writes to the Corinthians: "'What no eye has seen, nor ear heard, nor the heart of man conceived, what God has prepared for those who love him,' God has revealed to us through the Spirit.

---

13. *Pheromenoi* is a participial form from the verb *pherō*, which is translated "to bear" or "to carry along." The NIV of 2 Pet. 1:21 properly reads: "but men spoke from God as they were carried along by the Holy Spirit."

14. *Christian Theology*, 1:170.

15. The noun *epiluseōs* is used but once in the New Testament, although the verb form appears in Mark 4:34 and Acts 19:39. In both instances it means to unravel a problem. Literally, *epiluseos* means "untying." Cf. Michael Green, *The Second Epistle of Peter*, "The Tyndale New Testament Commentaries" (Grand Rapids, Mich.: Wm. B. Eerdmans Publishing Co., 1968), pp. 89-92.

... So also no one comprehends the thoughts of God except the Spirit of God. Now we have received not the spirit of the world, but the Spirit which is from God, that we might understand the gifts bestowed on us by God. And we impart this in words not taught by human wisdom but taught by the Spirit, interpreting the spiritual truths to those who possess the Spirit" (1 Cor. 2:9-13).

For Paul, the Spirit is the *Grand Interpreter* of things spiritual. But the apostle goes further and applies this thesis to the exposition of the Scriptures (2 Cor. 3:12-18). He declares that the Jews read the old Scriptures faithfully but they do not understand them. A veil, like that which they wear in synagogues when the Word is read, has covered the Old Covenant. Paul recalls that when Moses came down from Mount Sinai, he, too, wore a veil to hide the fading splendor on his face (Exodus 34). Similarly there is a veil over the Scriptures.

But now through Christ that hindrance has been removed, and those who have "the Spirit of Christ" can understand the Old Covenant.[16] Thus, "with unveiled face," that is, with the acceptance of Christ and the reception of His Spirit, Christians can penetrate the mysteries of God and thereby be changed into Christ's likeness. The veil is lifted from the Scriptures whenever men turn to Christ, and when His Spirit becomes the Interpreter of divine matters to them.[17]

IV. THE ADMINISTRATOR OF SALVATION

The author of Hebrews, in pleading with his readers to remain faithful to God in times of persecution, warns of the punishment that will come to those who have "spurned the Son of God, and profaned the blood of the covenant . . . and outraged the Spirit of grace" (10:29). The choice of the phrase "the Spirit of grace" is a delightful one. Unlike any other biblical terminology, it expresses the Servanthood of the Spirit in bringing to human life that which was intended by the divine will. If grace signifies God's gift of new life through the Spirit, then indeed it is proper to speak of the Spirit as "the Spirit of grace," for His primary ministry is that of administering God's salvation.

---

16. Peter's view of the OT prophets' understanding of the divine plan grants that they possessed "the Spirit of Christ" (1 Pet. 1:10-11).

17. Cf. John 5:39; Stauffer, *New Testament Theology,* p. 174: "The primitive Church gave the established understanding and exegesis of the OT a thoroughgoing reorientation."

At every point in the journey of spiritually needy mankind, from conviction through initial redemption to the possession of the ultimate spiritual home, the Spirit works with him.

The Spirit, acting as the Spirit of liberty, releases men from the bondage to the law (Gal. 5:13-18; cf. Rom. 8:2; 2 Cor. 3:6). The Holy Spirit enables men to confess Christ as Lord (1 Cor. 12:3; cf. 1 John 4:2). Regeneration *[poliggenesias]* and renewal *[anakaiōsis]* are effected by the ministry of the Spirit (Titus 3:5). He is the Spirit of life, who breathes life into believers (cf. 1 Cor. 15:45). Heb. 6:4 speaks of becoming "partakers of the Holy Spirit" in the same context in which reference is made to "tasting the heavenly gift"—obviously a reference to the divine life. The Spirit is also the Spirit of adoption, since He witnesses to the believer that he is accepted into the family of God and has the right of addressing God as "Abba" (Rom. 8:12-17; Gal. 4:6-7).[18]

Moreover, the Spirit strengthens the inner life (Eph. 3:17), indwells and fills (Rom. 8:9; Eph. 5:18; 2 Tim. 1:14), sanctifies (2 Thess. 2:13; 1 Pet. 1:2), leads (Gal. 5:18), and produces in the Christian the nine spiritual graces called "the fruit of the Spirit," namely, love, joy, peace, patience, kindness, goodness, faithfulness, gentleness, and self-control (Gal. 5:22-23; cf. Rom. 5:5; 14:17). The Spirit also seals the God-possessed until the day of redemption (Eph. 1:13-14; 4:30; cf. 2 Cor. 1:22). Of special importance is Paul's reference to the Spirit's ministry in prayer. Whenever the Christian is unable to articulate his petitions, the Holy Spirit prays *within* him, thus making intercession for him (Rom. 8:26-27). This intercessory role of the Spirit is based upon His knowledge of the will of God.

Redeemed men, at least for Paul, are Spirit-endowed men. Baptism is the sign of admission into the Christian life as well as the sign of the initial reception of the Holy Spirit. "For by one Spirit we were all baptized into one body—Jews or Greeks, slaves or free—and all were made to drink of one spirit" (1 Cor. 12:13; cf. Titus 3:5, "washing . . . by the Holy Spirit"). Christians are the *pneumatikoi,* the Spirit-indwelt ones; non-Christians are *sarkikoi,* flesh-controlled men (1 Cor.

---

18. After reviewing what is written in the New Testament as a whole, one can agree with Stauffer's conclusion that Paul's "most distinctive contribution [to the concept of the Spirit] concerns the realization of the Spirit in the personal life of the believer" (*NT Theology,* p. 166). Basil of Caesarea considered this the greatest witness for the inclusion of the Holy Spirit in the Trinity. Cf. W. Pannenberg, *Jesus—God and Man.* Trans. Lewis L. Wilkins and Duane A. Priebe (Philadelphia: The Westminster Press, 1968), pp. 172-73.

2:13—3:3; 14:37; Gal. 6:1). This distinction surfaces also in Paul's famous antithesis, *kata pneuma* and *kata sarka,* in Rom. 8:1-8. Christians live in conformity with the Spirit's mode of action.

V. THE LIFE OF THE CHURCH

The fellowship *(koinōnia)* into which Christians are born is the fellowship of the Holy Spirit (2 Cor. 13:14; Phil. 2:1). This communion is maintained only by the unity-creating Spirit. Paul exhorts the Ephesians to be "eager to maintain the unity of the Spirit in the bond of peace" (4:3). In combating the schism at Corinth, Paul appeals to their understanding of the nature of the Church as the temple of God's Spirit. He questions rhetorically: "Do you not know that you are God's temple and that God's Spirit dwells in you? If anyone destroys God's temple, God will destroy him. For God's temple is holy, and that temple you are" (1 Cor. 3:16-17).

True worship in the Church is Spirit-prompted according to Paul (1 Corinthians 12—14; Eph. 5:18-20). Also, a variety of gifts is given the members of this fellowship for the purpose of witnessing to the world and of edifying the believers (1 Cor. 12:8-10; Eph. 4:11-16). Though not explicitly stated in them, the pastoral letters of Paul recognize the ministry of the Spirit in preparing and selecting preachers, teachers, and evangelists for the Church. The ministry of the Spirit is so essential to creating and maintaining the Church that all members must keep open to the Spirit's leadership. To "quench the Spirit" is tantamount to destroying the Church and her ministry (1 Thess. 5:19).

H. Wheeler Robinson speaks about "the kenosis of the Spirit." He means "that God as Holy Spirit enters into a relation to human nature which is comparable with that of the Incarnation of the Son of God at a particular point of human history."[19] If this is true, then the Church is "the extension of the Incarnation" because her members possess the Spirit. The presence of the Spirit is indeed the presence of Christ.[20] The conclusion of this thought is simply that the concept of God as Spirit indicates the continuing redemptive activity of God in history. The incarnation of the Spirit creates the Church which is the servant of the now-ascended Christ.

---

19. *Redemption and Revelation* (New York: Harper and Bros., 1942), p. 290.

20. Cf. George S. Hendry, *The Gospel of the Incarnation* (Philadelphia: The Westminster Press, 1958), p. 159.

The eschatological character of the bestowal of the Spirit is also emphasized in the New Testament. The outpouring of the Spirit at Pentecost was the fulfillment of Joel's prophecy for the end of days (Acts 2:1 ff.). Paul speaks of the gift of the Spirit as "the first fruits" (Rom. 8:23) or the "guarantee" (2 Cor. 1:22; 5:5) of future glory. According to Heb. 6:4 ff., the baptized, who have become partakers of the Holy Spirit, have already "tasted . . . the powers of the age to come." 1 Peter speaks of those "sanctified by the Spirit" as "heirs-apparent of the eschatological salvation soon to appear."

The "futurity" of the Spirit's work cannot be gainsaid. Richardson concurs: "The Holy Spirit is the gift of God's presence and power within us in this life and the pledge of the fullness of the divine life that will be ours in the Age to Come."[21]

VI. Christ and the Spirit

It remains for us to consider the relationship of the Spirit to Christ. That the two are to be distinguished is indicated by the New Testament's record. Christ, along with the Father, gave the Spirit to the Church. Referring unquestionably to the Holy Spirit, Jesus tells the disciples, "And behold, I send the promise of my Father upon you; but stay in the city until you are clothed with power from on high" (Luke 24:49; Acts 1:4, 8). John 15:26 reads: "But when the Counselor comes, whom I shall send to you from the Father, even the Spirit of truth, who proceeds from the Father, he will bear witness to me." The note in John 7:39 also acknowledges the distinction. "Now this he said about the Spirit, which those who believed in him were to receive; for as yet the Spirit had not been given, because Jesus was not yet glorified." Moreover, the trinitarian formulas, to which we have already referred, offer further evidence that the New Testament writers did not conceive of the Holy Spirit and Christ as being essentially one. The doxology of Paul in 2 Cor. 13:14 also supports the separation.

On the other hand, several passages suggest identification. Paul employs the term *pneuma* in referring to Christ: "God has sent the Spirit of his Son into our hearts" (Gal. 4:6); "Now the Lord is the Spirit" and "where the Spirit of the Lord is, there is liberty" (2 Cor. 3:17); "from the Lord who is the Spirit" (2 Cor. 3:18); "the Spirit of

---

21. *Introduction to the Theology of the NT*, p. 116.

Jesus" (Phil. 1:19). The most important of the apostle's statements is found in Rom. 8:9-11, where he employs "Spirit of God," "Spirit of Christ," and "Spirit" interchangeably (cf. 1 Pet. 1:10-12).

This apparent looseness of terminology has brought a variety of reactions. George Barker Stevens concludes:

> The Spirit is at once distinguished from Christ and identified with Christ. This in itself is proof enough that Paul could not have had any such fixed, definite conception of the Spirit as theology afterwards undertook to define. . . . His point of view was religious, not theoretical.[22]

Filson simply acknowledges the fact that "the New Testament writers do not keep them clearly separate" but he does not offer any suggestions as to how this would be possible for the biblical writer.[23]

Richardson attempts to come to grips with the problem by suggesting that the three Members of the Trinity are simultaneously involved in redemption. The interchangeable terminology might simply represent difference of emphasis, as in the case of Paul distinguishing between the exalted Christ as Intercessor and the Spirit as Intercessor in Rom. 8:26 and 34. "The Spirit intercedes within us, even in our most inarticulate groanings, while Christ intercedes for us 'at the right hand of God.'"[24]

Pannenberg asserts that Paul does not make any "qualitative distinction between the present reality of the Spirit and that of the resurrected Lord just as elsewhere he can speak almost promiscuously of the dwelling of the Spirit and of Christ in the believers (Rom. 8:9f)." He then goes on to suggest that the primitive community lived "so close to the Easter event and so much in the expectation of Jesus' imminent Parousia that its own present was wholly saturated by this."[25] The difference between the Spirit's activity in the community in the absence of the Lord only begins to develop in Paul's debate with the Corinthians. Pannenberg thus concludes:

> The independence of the Spirit, which became increasingly clear with increasing distance from the Easter event and with the decreasing expectation of the nearness of the *eschaton*, can be taken as an indication that a third independent moment in God's essence is to be assumed only when a personal relation and thus also a difference of the Spirit from the Son can be demonstrated.[26]

22. *The Theology of the New Testament* (New York: Charles Scribner's Sons, 1899), pp. 443-45.

23. *Jesus Christ the Risen Lord*, p. 179.

24. *Introduction to the Theology of the NT*, pp. 123-24.

25. *Jesus, God and Man*, p. 178.

26. *Ibid.*, p. 179.

While this explanation does not offer us a fully satisfying solution to this knotty problem, it does emphasize the "unity of God in all the difference of his three modes of being which diverge in the revelatory event."[27]

In summary, to speak of God as Spirit is not only to declare the threefoldness of His nature but to acknowledge His servanthood in seeking to redeem His creatures. God as Spirit means God-in-action and God-at-hand in a way He has never been before. Intimately and powerfully God through His Spirit makes redeemingly effective in the lives of men that which He provided in His Son. Through the Spirit, the work of Christ is made continuous and universal. This occurs through the Church which bears the image of Christ and becomes the medium through which the Incarnation is extended into all history and to all men.

---

27. *Ibid.*

Section Two

The Creature of God's Saving Concern

15

The New Testament View of Man

Man, the subject of God's redemptive concern, is also the preoccupation of much current science and philosophy. Almost all the social sciences have a vital stake in this field of inquiry if they are to know the directions which education, science, and the state must take to resolve conflicts and control behavior. Is man a product of blind chance, unprogrammed but sociologically and genetically manipulable? Is he merely an "electrochemical machine"? Is he totally a product of his genes and environment, whose "freedom" is an illusion, as believed by Skinner?[1] Or, in a different vein, is man, as be-

---

1. See Francis A. Schaeffer, *Back to Freedom and Dignity* (Downers Grove, Ill.: Inter-Varsity Press, 1972), for a discussion of some of these views.

lieved by Teilhard de Chardin, "the spearhead of the evolutionary process, whose end is in God"?[2]

"Today, more than at any time," comments G. C. Berkouwer, "the question, 'What is man?' is at the center of theological and philosophical concern."[3] The problem is not just in acquiring facts about man as an object of study, but of attaining to a real and valid self-knowledge. How can we know man if we do not know ourselves? Berkouwer points out the inner hiddenness of individual man, and adds:

> He can indeed obtain all sorts of theoretical knowledge, and work up various views on the ontological "composition" of man's nature—but this does not answer the question, What is man?. The way to self-knowledge appears blocked, closed with impassable barricades. And hence we need not wonder that the question again arises whether it is possible either by way of science or of inner examination to acquire knowledge of man, or whether it is not religion alone which furnishes the most profound source of self-knowledge.[4]

The view of man found in the Bible is of a being in personal and moral relation to God. Karl Barth says that man's nature "must from the very beginning be understood as a nature standing *in some kind of relation to God.*"[5] Berkouwer insists that "man cannot be understood apart from this relation" since it is not something added to a nature otherwise complete and self-contained, but "is essential and constitutive for man's nature."[6]

I. CONTINUITY WITH THE OLD TESTAMENT

At no point is the overarching unity of the two Testaments seen more strikingly than in the fact that the New Testament advances no new or novel view of man. However, as we shall see, certain aspects of man's nature are clarified and brought into sharp focus. (For the Old Testament doctrine of man, see Chapter 3.)

That "all things" were created by God, as affirmed in Genesis, is

---

2. William Nicholls, ed., *Conflicting Images of Man* (New York: The Seabury Press, 1966), p. 5; see Pierre Teilhard de Chardin, *The Phenomenon of Man,* for exposition of his views.

3. *Man: The Image of God* (Grand Rapids, Mich.: Wm. B. Eerdmans Publishing Co., 1962), p. 9.

4. *Ibid.,* p. 20.

5. *Kirchliche Dogmatick,* 3:2; 83 ff. Quoted by Berkouwer, p. 23.

6. *Man: The Image of God,* p. 23; see pp. 29-35.

everywhere assumed in the New Testament (Eph. 3:9; Mark 13:19). The special creation of man as a unique and climactic being is also affirmed. In the creative week God made man "male and female," said Jesus (Mark 10:6). Paul informed the Athenians that God not only "made the world and everything in it" but also "He made from one every nation of men" (Acts 17:24, 26). All peoples have one common progenitor, Adam, who himself was created apart from all other creation by a special act of God.[7]

A. Dignity and Destiny

The Psalmist's insight into man's nobility is echoed in Hebrews, "Thou didst make him for a little while lower than the angels, thou hast crowned him with glory and honor" (2:7-8). Here is the biblical answer to the inescapable question, "What is man?" God's original design for man, lost through the Fall but to be recovered in Christ, was almost inconceivably lofty, far exceeding the temporary limitations of an earthly biological organism. This destiny is expressed as God "putting everything in subjection under his feet" (v. 8). The "obsolescent dispensation" of law may have been committed to angels (Heb. 2:2), but a greater glory is man's, in that even the "world to come" (v. 5) is to be "under human dominion and administration. The angels are left behind; there is no room for angelic government."[8] This ultimate destiny in its grandeur and majesty far surpasses the initiatory commission in the Garden to subdue the animal order (cf. Ps. 8:7).

Some Bible students associate God's purpose for man as being His means of effecting a final and eternal conquest of Satan's kingdom of darkness. Man was placed on earth "to counteract the devil," said Oswald Chambers.[9] The glory of God is not to be displayed by conquering fallen angels with unfallen angels, but by means of a very vulnerable being who, though physically and intellectually inferior, possesses moral potential sufficient to vindicate God and foil

---

7. Vine calls attention to the fact that the word *ktizo* and its variants, found throughout the New Testament for God's creative activity, was used consistently by the Greeks for man's creative activity, but never for God's. This Vine sees as a "significant confirmation" of Rom. 1:20-21. Since man would have deduced a human maker from human artifacts, he should equally have deduced a Divine Maker from the physical order; "so that they are without excuse." *Expository Dictionary of New Testament Words* (Westwood, N.J.: Fleming H. Revell Co., reprint, 1966), p. 255.

8. Marcus Dod, "The Epistle to the Hebrews," *The Expositor's Greek Testament* (Grand Rapids, Mich.: Wm. B. Eerdmans Publishing Co., 1967), 4:263.

9. *Biblical Psychology* (London: Simpkin Marshall, Ltd. [1941], reprint, 1948), p. 4.

Satan. Such a being, whose power is moral rather than physical, can retake this derelict globe for the eternal kingdom of God. Eric Sauer represents this view in the words: "Thus man's appointed vocation in Paradise consisted in the winning back of the earth for God, and this again was based on the sovereignty of God over man and the sovereignty of man over the earth."[10]

But greater by far than man's destiny to rule, or even being an instrument in the conquest of evil, is his appointment to fellowship eternally with God as a son. The redemptive recovery of our right to become "children of God" (John 1:12) reflects the original design, a plan never abandoned or modified (cf. 2 Pet. 1:4; Gal. 4:6-7).

B. The Divine Image

The Greek equivalent to the Hebrew word *tselem*, "image," is *eikon*, found 20 times in the New Testament. The teaching of the Old Testament that man was created in God's image governs the thinking of the New, not so much in numerous specific references as in total approach. Man's creation in God's likeness is seen by James as the basis of the sanctity of the person (3:9), reminiscent of Gen. 9:6. Peter had to learn that he should "not call any man common or unclean" (Acts 10:28). Paul would likely have explained this inherent value of every man by repeating his endorsement of the Greek poets, "For we are indeed his offspring" (Acts 17:28-29). The word here is *genos*, in this case meaning *posterity*, "family."[11] What the Greeks traced to their gods Paul ascribed to Yahweh; but he meant not a polytheistic procreation but a kinship based on creation.[12]

It is most important to see that these references to man's likeness to God are not dependent on redemption, but refer to man as he is, even in his sinful state. No matter how corrupt, man remains the one terrestrial being which in nature is essentially godlike. What is commonly called the *natural image* is not totally effaced by sin. There

---

10. *The King of the Earth* (Grand Rapids, Mich.: Wm. B. Eerdmans Publishing Co., 1962), p. 92.

11. Marvin R. Vincent says: "A line from Aratus, a poet of Paul's own province of Cilicia. The same words occur in the fine hymn of Cleanthes to Jove. Hence the words, 'Some of your own poets'." From *Word Studies in the New Testament* (Grand Rapids, Mich.: Wm. B. Eerdmans Publishing Co., 1965 [1887]), 1:545.

12. Paul here follows "Stoic belief in ascribing relationship with God to all men on the basis of their existence," believes Buchsel, in *Theological Dictionary of the New Testament*, ed. Gerhard Kittel; trans. and ed., Geoffrey W. Bromiley (Grand Rapids, Mich.: Wm. B. Eerdmans Publishing Co., 1969), 1:684.

is yet a common ground between God and man; otherwise a re-establishment of amicable relationship would be impossible. The Bible does not analyze this common ground, but frequent references to *conscience* (especially in Paul) and the constant assumption of man's freedom and responsibility as a moral agent give us some clues. Man and God are the same kind of being in that they are self-conscious, self-identifying persons capable of free action, possessing moral sense, and capable of entering into voluntary, meaningful, and communicating relationships with other persons, both divine and human. This is the metaphysical basis for fellowship, whether original or restored.[13]

C. The Image Marred

The New Testament equally supports the Old in witnessing to man's fallenness. While not effaced completely, the image of God in man is defaced, so that the real man seems to give the lie to ideal man (cf. Rom. 3:10-15, *et al.*; see Chapters 16—17). Without biblical data the social sciences are doomed to perpetual confusion in trying to determine normality and abnormality, naturalness and unnaturalness. Are men's self-destructive traits normal or abnormal? is their problem. If normalcy is determined by what is in fact universally observable, then self-destructiveness is normal; but if normalcy is determined by the criterion of orderly and harmonious functioning, man is abnormal. The biblical data solve the puzzle, for they indicate that through the dislocation of sin many human traits are now natural to man as fallen, which are not natural to human nature per se as created.

Clearly something has gone wrong with this noble masterpiece of God's creation who was intended to rule as king of the earth. Speaking of man's "deeply ingrained self-centeredness, generating exploitativeness and envy and mistrust," Nathan A. Scott, Jr., says:

> Man is created in the image of God, made for covenant-partnership with God and for fellowship with his human neighbors; but he is a good thing spoiled, a creature radically evil, who changes "the glory of the immortal God for images resembling mortal man" (Rom. 1:23).[14]

---

13. "The essence of the image of God in man," writes Eric Sauer, "lies in the spiritual and moral. It is based on the nature of his inner life on the real substance of his spiritual personality" (*King of the Earth,* p. 140).

14. Nicholls, *Conflicting Images,* p. 13.

II. The Nature of Humanness

What does it really mean to be human? Perhaps an epitomized answer is in Heb. 9:27: ". . . it is appointed for men to die once, and after that comes judgment." This declaration says that man is a biological being now subject to death; but also he is a being whose responsible, conscious identity does not terminate with death. His existence is therefore in two parts, pre-death and post-death.

For man to be "judgment bound" means that he is observed and held accountable by the Judge; hence he is a *moral being*. Stage One therefore must be preparatory for Stage Two; or, to use an old-fashioned word, *probationary*. Such an epitome of man is compressed in this verse; and it is equally clear that the verse itself is in many respects an epitome of the entire Bible. As the context shows (Heb. 9:23-28), the Christ-event finds its ultimate meaning in this fact about man. Man, then, is a being in religious relationship to a Creator who will treat him as a morally accountable free agent. As such he experiences both necessity and freedom. "Death" is symbolic of man viewed from the side of necessity; "judgment" symbolizes man viewed from the side of freedom and responsibility.

A. "Man" and His "Manness"

The Greek counterpart of the Hebrew *adam* is *anthrōpos*, "man," that is, a human being. This is the generic term, and as such is used without sex distinction; from this term is derived *anthropology*. The counterpart of the Hebrew *ish* is *anēr*, a "man," a "husband." Often this is simply a synonym for *anthrōpos*, but is also used when it is desired to specify males in distinction from women (Matt. 15:38; Luke 1:27, 34; Rom. 7:3; 1 Cor. 11:3-14). Jesus' favorite self-designation was "Son of man" (*anthrōpos*, never *anēr*).

A man may be either evil or good (2 Tim. 3:13-17). Therefore sin as such is no essential element of "manness." Implicit also in *anthrōpos* is acknowledgment of man's finiteness and creatureliness (Heb. 2:6; 1 Pet. 1:24; Rev. 13:18). Very significant, moreover, is Rev. 21:3, which describes a post-judgment, therefore Stage Two scene: "Behold, the dwelling of God is with men." Much that now seems necessary to humanness will have been laid aside, but essential manness will remain. Human nature would seem therefore to consist not *primarily* in its earthly, bodily form, but in those modes of being that are spiritual, relational, and eternal. This is supported by a rather frequent use of *anthrōpos* in reference to the real self encased in flesh, as "the hidden person of the heart" (1 Pet. 3:4; cf. Rom. 7:22; 2 Cor. 4:16; Eph. 3:16).

B. Flesh and Body

The Greek *sarx,* "flesh," is the counterpart to the Hebrew *basar* (see Chapter 3); however, it is further removed from the English word *body,* which is represented in the New Testament by *sōma.* The word *sōma,* "body," may be used for man's form of existence in either Stage One (2 Cor. 5:8) or Stage Two (1 Cor. 15:35, 44). *Sarx,* however, is used only in reference to man on earth.

Body in respect to Stage One is the material, biological house in which one lives (John 2:21; Rom. 4:19; 2 Cor. 12:2). When the spirit has departed, it is a corpse destined for decay and dissolution (Luke 23:52; Acts 9:40), but capable in cases of divine miracle of revivification (viz., Lazarus, John 11:44; Dorcas, Acts 9:40). The body is not evil because material; rather, it was divinely created to be the temple of the Holy Spirit (1 Cor. 6:19) and an instrument for glorifying God (v. 20).[15] Though in itself neutral, the body may be prostituted to the service of sin (Rom. 1:24, *et al.*) or presented for the service of God (Rom. 12:1);[16] and because it is a vigorous, dynamic organism, it must be disciplined (1 Cor. 9:27).

The term *sarx,* "flesh," however, is not so precise as *sōma.* In general it qualifies manness in this earthly setting, with the limitations of time, space, and matter. *Sarx* also has the added limitation of extreme feebleness and transitoriness—man's momentary liability to death (2 Cor. 4:11; 12:7; Mark 14:38; Jas. 4:14; Phil. 3:3; 1 Pet. 1:24; 3:18). At times Paul uses *sarx* also in a distinctively ethical sense, referring to fallen man; i.e., human nature as infected by sin and without the Spirit (Rom. 7:5, 18, 25; 8:3, 13; Gal. 5:13-24). A more detailed study of *flesh* in this connotation must await our study of the New Testament doctrine of sin (see Chapter 16).

C. Soul and Spirit

In 1 Cor. 15:45 Paul quotes Gen. 2:7, "the first MAN Adam BECAME A LIVING SOUL" (NASB). Here in the place of the Hebrew *nephesh,* "living being," he follows the Septuagint in using the Greek *psychē,* "soul"

---

15. Putting "to death the deeds of the body" (Rom. 8:13) is to be understood metaphorically, as a denial of their imperial authority, not as an ascetic rejection of their legitimate functions.

16. KJV is particularly unfortunate in its use of "vile" for *tapeinōsis* in Phil. 3:21. NASB: "the body of our humble state."

(from which comes *psychology*). Apparently both Paul and the Septuagint translators considered *psychē* an adequate translation of what is intended by *nephesh*. This is a toehold for wider understanding. Millar Burrows says that *psychē* may mean *(a)* simply "life" of "a particular person or animal" (Matt. 2:20; Mark 10:45; John 10:11; Rom. 11:3); or *(b)* it often stands for "person" (Acts 27:37; KJV, "souls"). Also *(c)* it could be translated by "self," as possibly in the case of the rich fool who said, "'And I will say to my soul'" (Luke 12:19). Though this idiom is not as common in the New Testament as in the Old, Burrows counsels: "The meaning 'self' should therefore be kept in mind as a possibility wherever the word 'soul' is encountered in the English New Testament; in fact 'self' comes as near as any English word can to a comprehensive rendering of the Greek and the Hebrew and Aramaic nouns."[17]

The matter becomes more complex when we seek to understand "soul" in relation to *pneuma*, "spirit" (cf. Hebrew *ruach*). The delineation between them is not always sharp or consistent. When Mary bursts out, "My soul magnifies the Lord, and my spirit rejoices in God my Savior" (Luke 1:46-47), she illustrates a quite typical interchangeability of the two terms in the New Testament (e.g., cf. Luke 23:46; Acts 2:27).[18] Both words may be used for "the immortal part of man" (Rev. 6:9; 20:4; cf. with 1 Cor. 5:5; also Acts 7:59).[19]

However, we must try to understand certain passages which seem to emphasize a real distinction between the two. Paul's contrast between Adam as a "living soul" and Christ as a "life-giving spirit" suggests *soul* as that which was peculiar to Adam as Stage One *man*, while *spirit* was that peculiar to the glorified Christ as the *God-man*.

---

17. *An Outline of Biblical Theology* (Philadelphia: The Westminster Press, 1946), p. 136. There are still other less common usages of *psychē*, "soul," such as "heart" (once, Eph. 6:6), and "mind" (Phil. 1:27, where unity of purpose is meant). A more significant usage relates to the emotional, appetitive, and affectional self. This is likely the sense of "soul" in the command to love God "with all your soul" (Mark 12:30). Hence it may be related to *splagchnon, bowels*, or *seat of the affections*, suggesting the very human blending of visceral and spiritual emotions (2 Cor. 6:12; 7:15; Phil. 1:8; 2:1; Col. 3:12; 1 John 3:17).

18. Commenting on Mary's song of praise, Charles L. Childers says: "These two verses form a typical couplet, which is the simplest stanza form of Hebrew poetry. It is composed of two parallel lines, the second of which restates the approximate meaning of the first with different words." From *Beacon Bible Commentary* (Kansas City: Beacon Hill Press, 1964), 6:439.

19. Burrows, *Outline of Biblical Theology*, p. 137. Also, both spirit and soul are said to be the subject of salvation, but more frequently the soul (cf. 1 Cor. 5:5 with Heb. 10:39; Jas. 1:21; 5:20; 1 Pet. 1:9, 22).

The one was oriented to human life in the flesh, the other to the heavenly order (1 Cor. 15:45).

A similar contrast is observed in Paul's use of *pneumatikos,* "spiritual," and *psychikos,* "soulish" or "natural." In 1 Corinthians 15 the contrast concerns the natural body, which dies, and the spiritual body which will be ours in Stage Two. But more significant for our immediate purpose is the contrast between the natural man and spiritual man in 1 Cor. 2:9-15. The man who is merely *soulish* cannot understand either spiritual truths or spiritual persons—"they are folly to him" (v. 14). Evidently a side of his nature is dormant. Yet, as a man, even while merely soulish or animal, he possesses what can be called "the spirit of the man" (v. 11), that which "knows," or his personal consciousness and mental activities ("a man's thoughts"). But since this spirit has not been regenerated by the Holy Spirit, it is, even while alert horizontally, dead vertically.

Perhaps it may be said therefore that both soul and spirit are aspects of man in his total self, but represent the two channels of communication in human nature as created: the *soulish* (social, emotional, intellectual, and aesthetic) which communicates *outward;* and the *spiritual* (religious, motivational, and axiological) which communicates *upward.* The spiritual channel is dead to God because man's receptivity is impaired through sin, and as a consequence even his soulishness is in progressive decay.

The "soul" can be saved only by saving the man as spirit. Some such distinction is implied in the assertion that the "word of God" is sharp enough to pierce "the division of soul and spirit, of joints and marrow, and discerning the thoughts and intentions of the heart" (Heb. 4:12). Joints are visible; marrow is not. Who can tell simply by studying a man outwardly whether the "marrow" of his spirit is sound? Only the Holy Spirit applying the sword of the Word can discern whether the thoughts and intentions of a man's heart are truly spiritual or only soulish.

Finally we have been reminded that "while man shares spirit with God, he shares soul with the animals (Gen. 1:21, 24 . . . and Rev. 16:3). To put it another way, spirit is attributed to man, never to animals."[20] A sound conclusion therefore is that the spirit is "that aspect of the person through which he may be related to God."[21]

20. W. T. Purkiser, *Exploring Our Christian Faith* (Kansas City: Beacon Hill Press, 1960), p. 218.
21. *Loc. cit.* As to whether spirit characterizes man as man or only regenerate

D. Heart and Conscience

The word *kardia*, "heart," is also extremely important in the biblical view of man, as its 158 instances in the New Testament would suggest. Yet closeness to some usages of "soul" might be suggested by Eph. 6:6 where *psychē* is translated "heart." It is also sufficiently akin to *splagchnon*, "bowels," to justify the translation "heart" in most modern versions. From the heart's basic denotation as the blood-circulating organ, by "an easy transition the word came to stand for man's entire mental and moral activity, both the rational and the emotional elements. In other words, the heart is used figuratively for the hidden springs of the personal life."[22]

However, its usage is more qualitative than constitutive. Such words as soul and spirit speak of the essence of human nature. Heart, on the other hand, is more expressive of character, i.e., what a man is in the hidden center of his being. Thus the term is used for man's affections (Luke 24:32; Acts 21:13), his intentions (Heb. 4:12), the seat of moral and spiritual life (Mark 7:21; John 14:1; Rom. 9:2; 2 Cor. 2:4), *et al*. The New Testament concept of heart contributes significantly to the biblical conception of man as an emotional, affectional, volitional, very vital, and dynamic being continually reacting and relating morally to life and others, whether God or men. Perhaps it could be said that the heart is the self in moral relationship.[23]

The New Testament assumes that conscience as an activity of moral self-judgment is universally characteristic of the human race (Rom. 2:15; 2 Cor. 4:2). The conscience, however, may be maimed in various degrees through sin (1 Cor. 8:7; 1 Tim. 4:2). It would appear therefore that man is a being with an ineradicable consciousness of right and wrong, who knows himself to be responsible. His many attempts to elude this awareness and to escape its claims only confirm the inherent moral dimension of his nature.[24]

---

man, see George Eldon Ladd, *A Theology of the New Testament* (Grand Rapids, Mich.: Wm. B. Eerdmans Publishing Co., 1974), p. 463.

22. W. E. Vine, *Dictionary*, 2:206 ff.

23. Faith, to be efficacious, must be from the heart (Mark 11:23; Rom. 10:10). This can only mean that believing is an action of the inner man in full sincerity, involving simultaneous endorsement of reason and conscience, and utilizing the full energy of volitional capacity.

24. Whether *suneidēsis*, "conscience," belongs to the natural image of God in man, or is the first stage through prevenient grace in the restoration of the moral image, must be decided by systematic theology. (Wesley believed the latter.)

E. Mind

Elementary also to man as viewed in the New Testament is his intellectual activity. Man is a thinking being, with faculties of imagination, reason, perception, and memory (hence his creativity and inventiveness). We are told to love God with all the *dianonia,* "mind" (Mark 12:30).

In the natural man the mind is darkened (Eph. 4:18) in the sense that it is dull to spiritual truth. It is also the tool of the flesh rather than the Holy Spirit (Eph. 2:3); hence the satiric saying is not altogether inappropriate—"The mind finds excuses for doing what the heart wants to do."

Other Greek words used commonly are *nous,* "denoting the seat of reflective consciousness" (Vine) and *phronēma,* though this word indicates not so much a faculty as the habitual disposition of the faculty, or a frame of mind.[25] It is by the *nous* that Paul serves "the law of God" (Rom. 7:25); yet a few lines later when speaking of carnal mindedness as over against spiritual mindedness, he uses *phronēma*—"disposition" or "bent."

The interaction, overlapping, and in a sense interpenetration of mind, heart, will, soul, and spirit indicate that the New Testament normally sees man holistically. Yet in some contexts Paul distinguishes between his ego and his total being (Rom. 7:14-25; cf. Gal. 2:20). It would appear that while man tends to function holistically, there is a central *self* which is responsible to act as the coordinating agent. The self keeps the body under (1 Cor. 9:27), girds the mind "for action" (1 Pet. 1:13), abstains from "passions of the flesh" which "war against your soul" (1 Pet. 2:11), sets the mind on "things that are above" (Col. 3:2), and endorses the law of God in spite of the *dwelling-in-me sin* (Rom. 7:25).

It is very significant that the scripture sees the transformation of the self to depend on the renewal of the mind (*nous,* Rom. 12:2). The renewal here *(anakainōsis)* is a making new in the sense of different. The reference is not so much to the mind as a thinking faculty as it is to a habitual orientation—one's characteristic perception of life and its values. Paul is saying that transformation depends on learning to think differently. If we would stop being conformed to the world, we

---

25. For fuller discussion of this and related words, see C. Ryder Smith, *The Bible Doctrine of Man* (London: The Epworth Press, 1951), p. 206.

must stop thinking like the world. Paul would have endorsed the implications in Harry Blamire's book title *The Christian Mind.*[26]

III. Some Particular Issues

A. A Dualistic Being

The unmistakable teaching of the New Testament is that man is essentially a spirit being. Only secondarily and temporarily does he inhabit a fleshly body. The inner self is assumed to be the real self. It can speak of its body with an astonishing detachment, as something which "I" have but can exist without. The clear promise of ultimate renewed corporeality does not change the fact that the body of "flesh and blood" we now possess is viewed as an accessory, not an absolute necessity for either manness or personhood.

This is borne out by the teachings of Jesus himself: "And do not fear those who kill the body but cannot kill the soul; rather fear him who can destroy both soul and body in hell" (Matt. 10:28). Soul cannot possibly be here the equivalent of animal life, for killing the body is destroying animal life. Jesus is saying that those who kill the body *cannot touch the real you* (cf. Luke 12:20; 23:46; Acts 7:59). It must survive. A termination of bodily life does not mean the cessation of personal being.

Paul is just as emphatic. It is after death that the person will suffer or be rewarded. He will experience the consequences of *his* choices while in the body (cf. 2 Cor. 5:10). In order to achieve the eternal salvation of a certain man as *spirit,* Paul took the radical measure of delivering him "to Satan for the destruction of the flesh" (1 Cor. 5:5). Notice further the difference between Paul and his body: "I pommel my body and subdue it" (1 Cor. 9:27). It is to him a tool, an instrument. Why? Because he is wanting to save not his body but himself: "lest . . . I myself should be disqualified." Again, his buoyancy is in the assurance that the "inner nature" will outlive the "outer nature" which "is wasting away" (2 Cor. 4:16). Its dissolution will release him into "an eternal weight of glory far beyond all comparison . . . for the things which are seen are temporal, but the

---

26. In the New Testament there seems to be no awareness of the physical brain as the organ of the mind. Yet mental illness is recognized, if we can read this much into the accounts of Mark 5:15 and Luke 8:35 that the demoniac when delivered was "in his right mind" *(sōphreneō).*

things which are not seen are eternal" (cf. 2 Cor. 5:1-8; also 2 Pet. 1:14).

The New Testament's verdict is that while "the body apart from the spirit is dead" (James 2:26), it cannot be said that the spirit without the body is dead. This, moreover, is the way man is as man, not just redeemed man. He is essentially spirit, only secondarily *bios* (biological life) and flesh. "Flesh and blood cannot inherit the kingdom of God," but *men will* (1 Cor. 15:50).

B. Being and Relation

The individual is a discrete, hidden being, whose life is qualified by his relationships but whose being is not dependent on those relationships.[27] Though a being in community, his individuality is never lost in community. Always the gospel call is to persons. "If any man would come after me, let him . . ." (Matt. 16:24), not "if any family, or city, or caste." Faith is a radically personal commitment, which may begin as a reflex of environment but must become profoundly and independently one's own.

Too much must not be read into the apparent "corporate personality" ascribed by Jesus to cities (Matt. 10:15; 11:20-24; Luke 10:10-16). When Jesus said, "Woe to you, Bethsaida!" He was really addressing himself to the people of the city who individually rejected Him. The rejection was sufficiently unanimous that their character was imputed to the city as a whole. That he was thinking of individuals is clear in his conclusion: "He who hears you hears me, and he who rejects you rejects me" (Luke 10:16). We are not to understand that a literal city, as such, will appear at the judgment, but those who comprised the city and gave to it an evil or good name (cf. Rom. 14:12; 2 Cor. 5:10; Rev. 20:11-15).

To overstress man as a being in relation is to run into the danger of failing to see the man himself. In this direction lies both determinism and pantheism. The current disaffection for ontology has created a distaste for trying to fathom man in himself as a discrete being. But the Bible does not encourage this distaste. Its assumption rather is that behind *relations* are free, uncoerced *relators.* Relationships gone awry will result in alienation, sorrow, and corruption but will not affect essential manness. The demoniac (Mark 5:1-17; cf. Matt. 8:

---

27. There is no hint in the New Testament of an *idea* of manness in the Platonic sense. Nor is there a dichotomy of preexistent soul unrelated to the material body it inhabits.

28-34; Luke 8:26-37) was a sorry specimen of manhood when all his relationships both with God and men were shattered by the legion of demons. But both before and after his healing he is called a man (vv. 2, 15). While different both in character and relationships, before and after, he was the same in personal identity. There was unbroken continuity in the midst of radical change.

What was the one irreducible quality that constituted his manness? He was a descendant of Adam. As such, his manness was not only unique and unduplicatable but inalienable.[28]

While G. C. Berkouwer stresses the relational nature of man, he guards against misunderstanding by saying:

> Nor should this be seen as choosing relation over reality, or relational over ontological, or choosing one horn of any such dilemma; for such a dilemma, such a contrast, is not at all in line with the Biblical outlook, which does not sacrifice reality to relation, but shows us reality existing as reality, full created reality, only *in* this relation to God.[29]

C. Meaning of "Nature"

The New Testament offers no systematic analysis of human nature by the use of the term *physis*, "nature"; but the few occasions where this word is used are revealing. All but one are Pauline. Conscience belongs to the nature of man (Rom. 2:14). Such disparate aberrations as homosexuality and long hair on men are classified as contrary to nature (Rom. 1:26; 1 Cor. 11:14). Obviously Paul is not speaking here of the nature of individuals, but of the nature of humanness in its standard form. He also uses "nature" in the sense of racial particularity: "We who are Jews by nature" (Gal. 2:15, KJV). To the Ephesians he speaks of the universality of a sinful nature (2:3), which is of course deformed nature rather than original nature. Especially significant is the announced privilege of men becoming through Christ "partakers of the divine nature" (2 Pet. 1:4).

Summarizing these bits of evidence, it may be said that there are irreducible attributes of human nature as such without which man would not be man, and that *one* of these irreducible attributes is

---

28. In the light of this we must be wary also of defining *person* exclusively in terms of conscious state (or a "flow" of consciousness)—which could easily exclude newborn and unborn infants and vegetating old people. Such may not have legal status as persons but they have real being which is eternal in nature and incalculably important to God. Faculties may be either unformed or decayed without the essential identity of the person as a human being thereby affected.

29. *Man: the Image of God*, p. 35.

the malleability of moral and personal nature. It is the nature of man to be capable of change. This includes the capacity to dehumanize himself by perversions, on the one hand, or to share in God's holiness, on the other. Manness in its simplest essence may be a fixed state, but humanness in personal character is not, either as sinful or as holy (though through probationary processes character may *become* fixed).

D. Freedom—Illusory or Real?

Admittedly the New Testament recognizes many limitations to man as man which constitute a degree of determinism (Matt. 6:27; Jas. 4:13-15). Yet it needs no labored proof by an array of texts to be aware of the pervasive assumption in the New Testament of man's very real freedom, especially in the area of moral and spiritual choice. Even in everyday practical matters man's freedom is varied and extensive (Mark 7:1 ff.; 1 Cor. 7:1 ff.). But supremely, his basic allegiance and his final loyalty are the quest of both God and Satan. Every entreaty, command, or rebuke presupposes the axiom that there can be no accountability without responsibility; and there can be no responsibility without some measure of real freedom, involving ability (1) to choose between moral alternatives, and (2) to grow toward one's potential.[30]

As far as freedom as a prerequisite to sin is concerned, Scott points out that action either good or evil which merely is "one integer in a complex chain of causation" is necessarily void of "the element of personal responsibility and freedom." And he quotes John S. Whale: "The attempt to trace sin back to an empirical fact which causes it, invalidates man's God-given sense that he is a will and a person. The will is *ex hypothesi* that which is *non-derivable.*"[31]

The question of *being* and *relation* finds much of its importance right here. For to overemphasize man as a creature *in* relationships is to lead to a concept of him as a creature *of* relationships. This is pure determinism. Instead of being seen as an acting agent, he is no more than a cog in relation to other parts in a monistic mechanism.

IV. CHRIST THE PERFECT MAN

Christ was perfect Man, not in the sense that through discipline He achieved perfection, but in the sense that He was the supreme Exem-

---

30. Cf. Smith, *Doctrine of Man,* p. 172.
31. Nicholls, *Conflicting Images,* p. 16.

plar of *manness,* both in human nature as it most essentially is by creation, and in mature humanity as it is intended to be. Pilate said more than he knew in his announcement, "Here is the man!" (John 19:5). All four Evangelists witness to the preference of Jesus for the title "Son of man" (Matthew 29 times, Mark 14 times, Luke 23, and John 12 times; cf. 1 Tim. 2:5).[32]

Therefore we understand best what it means to be normatively human by looking at Jesus of Nazareth. Scott understands this idea to be basic in Karl Barth's thought, "that in the perspective of the Christian faith the most decisive manifestation of the 'real' man is to be encountered in Jesus Christ." He continues: "Here it is, as Barth has told us in one after another of his massive treatises . . . that Christianity meets what is for it the definitive disclosure both of man's essential nature and of how all men would live were they to give full expression to that nature."[33]

This means that when we look at Jesus we learn that normal humanness means a life of concretized loving. It means a continuous fellowship with God as Father, and an equally continuous subjection and obedience to the Father. Withdrawal or evasion of this subordination to God is therefore as "unnatural" to true humanness as for a bird to attempt to fly in a vacuum.

The physical attributes of man in Stage One were Christ's also, the need for food, air, rest, the society of others, and the ability to verbalize. What about sex? He would not have been true flesh if sexual desires and attractions were totally lacking; nor could it have been declared that He "in every respect has been tempted as we are" (Heb. 4:15). Yet He was the one Example of perfect control, and as such demonstrates that overt sex experience is not essential to full and perfect humanness. Those who choose to remain single like their Lord for the kingdom of heaven's sake are not less manly or womanly for that fact. And ultimately manness will shed its sexuality, as a passing accoutrement to Stage One (cf. Matt. 22:30; Luke 20:35).

The testimony of the Incarnation forever exonerates human nature of the charge of intrinsic sinfulness. Jesus became man not only to redeem human nature but to exemplify it. He showed what it really is, normatively, as well as what fallen human nature could

---

32. For an excellent discussion of the entire Son of Man concept, see Alan Richardson, *An Introduction to the Theology of the New Testament* (New York: Harper and Row, Publishers, 1958), pp. 120-41.

33. Nicholls, *Conflicting Images,* pp. 12-13.

become. Flesh, in the sense of the earthly body-mind-soul unity, is not sinful in itself. If it were, Jesus could not have become flesh (John 1:14). The desires of the body and mind toward knowledge, growth, love, and procreation are not in themselves sinful. It is their prostitution in the service of self that is sinful. "To err is human" it is said, and generally this is intended to mean, "To sin is human." The saying is true in strict reference to fallen man as a caricature of his true self. But when we perceive the Christ, we perceive that sin is an abnormality and a distortion. It is more truly human to be holy.

16

Man in Sin

The developing Gnosticism of intertestamental and first-century thought saw man's problem as ignorance on the one hand, and bodily materiality on the other. In contrast, there is in the New Testament a firm continuity with the Old in tracing man's ills neither to physicality as such nor to lack of knowledge, but to rebellion against God. Man's malady is not seen as the misfortune of finiteness but as the misuse of freedom. This alone accounts for the wasteland of the human predicament.

Man's history as narrated in the Bible is an irrational tedium of disobedience and violence, with only fitful reprieves of improvement and revival. Man as God's crowning creation has been an embarrassment and a heartbreak. The Bible is the story of this moral predicament and of God's redemption (Luke 1:68-79; 4:18-19). Speaking of the seriousness of sin, C. Ryder Smith says the idea epitomizes "one half of the New Testament." He continues:

> In it sin is not only serious, but fatal. If this were not so, there would be no New Testament. The text in John (3:16) which is rightly taken as *the* synopsis of Christianity, teaches, not only that God sent His Son to save men from sin, but that without Him men would "perish." God's "love" shows itself, not in the assurance that sin "does not matter," but in the offer of salvation from it. It "matters" so much that it demands the Cross. If the Christian Church is "obsessed with sin," as some complain, so is the Christian God. To depreciate sin is to depreciate Christ. Even if He were reduced to a teacher, the Sermon on the Mount is a mani-

festo against sin. But *"we* preach Christ crucified." If sin is not
fatal, Christ is redundant.[1]

I. SIN AS PERSONAL WRONG

While the Bible describes in many ways man's abnormal condition,
and many Hebrew and Greek words are employed, the generic term
in English is "sin." Man commits sin. Because of this he is a sinner.
What does the New Testament teach about this terrible blight?

A. Some Generalizations About Sin

1. The idea of sin is fundamentally a *religious concept,* inasmuch as the
Bible sees it as primarily an affront to God (1 John 1:5-6).

2. Sin also is essentially *moral* (or ethical) *in nature,* because it is
viewed as that which is wrong instead of right, and also because it
is inseparably related to the questions of freedom and responsibility.

3. Throughout the Scriptures, sin is *universally condemned.* It is
never excused or approved, or treated as negotiable. The uniform
stance is one of intolerance.[2]

4. A fourth major assumption especially obvious in the New
Testament is the *personal and individual nature* of sin. Groups are rebuked and the plural address is often used by Jesus and others, but
this is never such an indictment of groups as to exonerate individuals. Guilt is a personal, private burden.

5. Finally, the New Testament testifies clearly to the *universality*
of sin. There are no naturally good people who have escaped its
blighting touch; for "all have sinned and fall short of the glory of
God" (Rom. 3:23; cf. v. 9; 2 Cor. 5:14; Gal. 3:22; cf. Phil. 3:6 with
1 Tim. 1:15; 1 John 1:10).[3]

---

1. *The Bible Doctrine of Sin* (London: The Epworth Press, 1953), p. 182.

2. Provision was made in the Old Testament for a so-called sin of ignorance,
and supreme provision for the sins of all is made in Christ; but this is not
permissiveness, it is redemption. The Bible offers no way whereby sin as such can be
made acceptable. When Jesus said to the woman taken in adultery, "Neither do I
condemn thee," He was not expressing tolerance but forgiveness (John 8:11; cf. Rom.
6:1, 15; 1 Cor. 15:34; Eph. 4:26; 1 Tim. 5:20; 1 John 2:1).

3. The fact that some may achieve a certain relative goodness is freely
recognized, such as Elizabeth and Zacharias (Luke 1:6) and Nathaniel ("in whom is no
guile," John 1:47). Jesus also speaks of a "good man" (Luke 6:45) and an "honest and
good heart" (Luke 8:15). But these distinctions in character bear witness to the
universal operation of God's grace on the one hand and to the scope of human choice
on the other; they are not evidences of either an innate sinlessness or a completely
spotless record.

270 / God, Man, and Salvation

B. The Identification of Sins

The approach in the New Testament is not theoretical but intensely practical and personal. The announcement of the angel to Joseph was that Jesus would save His people "from their sins" (Matt. 1:21). What follows in the New Testament is not philosophy but examples of what is meant by "sins." We see almost immediately the treachery and cruelty of Herod. Later, when the people confessed their sins under the preaching of John, it was not sin in the abstract, but concrete deeds, such as greed, civil extortion, false accusation, and covetousness (Luke 3:10-14). The sins of hardheartedness, hypocrisy, and conspiracy soon raised their ugly heads (Mark 3:2-6). Quickly thereafter came the sin of blasphemy (Mark 3:28-30). In His own village Jesus was faced with the sin of unbelief (Mark 6:1-6).

Both Jesus and Paul upon occasion compiled lists of sins. Jesus named some of the sins which arise out of a sinful heart: "evil thoughts [intentions], murder, adultery, fornication, theft, false witness, slander" (Matt. 15:19; cf. Mark 7:20). Paul also catalogued human iniquities by name (Rom. 1:28-32; 1 Cor. 6:9-10; Gal. 5:19-21; Eph. 4:25 ff.; Col. 3:5-9; 1 Tim. 1:9-10). An example of Peter's stark realism is 2 Peter 2. In the New Testament there are no less than 90 activities or attitudes which are condemned. Even a casual study of the Greek words would leave no one guessing as to the kind of behavior considered to be wrong.

Of special concern to the New Testament writers are sins *against purity*. Whereas *porneia*, "fornication," is promiscuity of any kind, *moichēa*, "adultery," is sex relationship with a married person. Condemnatory references to these sins total some 67 in the New Testament.[4] Other sex sins which when practised exclude from saving grace are homosexuality and lesbianism (Rom. 1:26-27; 1 Cor. 6:9; 1 Tim. 1:10). Certain terms in the KJV—"effeminacy," "lasciviousness," "evil concupiscence," and "uncleanness"—are related terms indicating forms of perversion such as excessive sexiness in imagination, thought patterns, language, and conduct (1 Cor. 6:9; Mark 7:22; Col. 3:5; 1 Thess. 4:5; Rom. 1:24). "Sensuality" and "unbridled passion" would convey the general idea.

Sins of *materialism* also claim a large share of attention. "Take heed," Jesus urges, "and beware of all covetousness; for a man's life does not consist in the abundance of his possessions" (Luke 12:15).

---

4. Some may refer to spiritual adultery, or unfaithfulness to God, e.g., Jas. 4:4.

Much of Christ's teaching aims at this sin. In the parable of the sower it is the "cares of the world, and the delight of riches" that create thorny soil and prevent fruitbearing (Matt. 13:22). In the parable of the wedding feast the invited guests default the great honor of the king's invitation by their trivial preoccupation with their own material affairs (Matt. 22:5). Paul frequently warns also against covetousness, which he labels as a form of idolatry—putting things in the place of God (Rom. 1:29; 1 Cor. 5:11; 6:10; Eph. 5:3-5; Col. 3:5; 1 Tim. 3:3; 6:10; cf. also Heb. 13:5; 2 Pet. 2:3, 14).

Obviously, the New Testament is pervaded by a profound sin consciousness. Anyone steeped in its ethical perspective will come to share this kind of biblical realism, no matter how depressing it admittedly is.[5]

II. THE INNER NATURE OF SIN

Why are such moral activities treated as evils? Why are they so consistently disallowed in the life of a believer? Careful examination will reveal certain common elements.

Their common character explains why Paul could say, "Those who do such things shall not inherit the kingdom of God" (Gal. 5:21). They are identifiable as *such things;* no claim is made here or elsewhere in the New Testament that every possible sin is catalogued (cf. 1 Tim. 1:10). Many modern practices may properly be called sins even though not named in the Bible, because they share sin's universal and identifiable characteristics.

---

5. Many are the possible classifications, such as sins against God, others, self. Or they may be categorized as overt, verbal, and mental. They include sins of word and deed but also sins of attitude. Some we may appropriately call "sins of the flesh" while others are clearly "sins of the spirit." Perhaps a more useful breakdown might be as follows:

Sins of the unregenerate: These are sins named as characteristic of the preconversion life—"such were some of you" (1 Cor. 6:10-11; Gal. 5:19-21; Col. 3:5-7; *et al.*).

Sins of believers: These are sins which are most apt to creep into the Church, generally relating to wrong attitudes and relationships (Col. 3:8-13). In many instances they are direct manifestation of the carnal condition of unsanctified believers (1 Cor. 3:1-3). In no case are such sins treated as normal or acceptable, but always as ultimately fatal.

Sins of backsliding: These are sins that mark the person withdrawing from Christ, first by heart-hardening (Heb. 3:12-15), persistent disobedience (vv. 16-19), careless presumption (4:1-12), and final denial and apostasy (6:4-6; cf. 2 Pet. 2:20-22).

A. The Element of Violation

The first characteristic of sin is that a divine standard of rightness is being violated. This standard is essentially the law of God, exemplified first in the commandment given to Adam, then the law through Moses, and finally the commandments of Christ and the inspired writers.[6] Even in pagans, who have not the precise law in biblical form, the element of violation is present, for they "show that what the law requires is written on their hearts, while their conscience also bears witness" (Rom. 2:14-15).

Certain basic Greek terms used for sin or in relation to it aid us here. The most common is *hamartia* in its noun and verb forms, "the most comprehensive term for moral obliquity."[7] It is the generic term for sin in the sense that it is used for the sinful nature, the sin principle, and for particular kinds of wrongdoing. Yet in spite of the variety of uses the word is never far from its classical meaning, "missing the mark."[8] It is violation in the sense of falling short of a specified duty or goal, generally through a *willfully wrong aim*. James says, "Whoever knows what is right to do and fails to do it, for him it is sin" (4:17).[9]

There are other words which more precisely convey the idea of violation in the sense of overt transgression, rather than falling short. These are: (1) *apeitheia*, "disobedience" (Eph. 2:2; 5:6; Rom. 11:30, 32; Heb. 4:6, 11); (2) *parakoē*, also translated "disobedience" (Rom. 5:19; 2 Cor. 10:6; Heb. 2:2); (3) *paraptōma*, a "lapse from uprightness" (EDNTW; so in Rom. 11:11-12; Gal. 6:1, *et al.*); (4) *paranomia*, "transgression" in 2 Pet. 2:16; and (5) *parabasis*, a willful overstepping (as in Rom. 4:15; 5:14; Heb. 2:2).

In thus violating law, sinners are fundamentally violating the rights of others. This is equivalent to saying that they are violating love, because love by its very nature is zealous for the rights of other persons. It is only as we reach this vantage point of love that we discern the inner meaning of violation. Moralism tends to see sin merely as a breaking of the rules; sin biblically is a violation of per-

---

6. Even the standard set by apostolic authority becomes binding: "Now we command you, brethren, in the name of our Lord Jesus Christ, that you keep aloof from every brother who leads an unruly life and not according to the tradition [*paradosis*, "handing down"] which you received from us. For you yourselves know how you ought to follow our example" (2 Thess. 3:6; cf. 1 Cor. 14:37).

7. Vine, *EDNTW*, 4:32.

8. E.g., Rom. 3:23; cf. Ryder, *Doctrine of Sin*, p. 143.

9. However, *hamartia* is often used of commission as well as omission.

sons. God's law is simply an expression of His Person. His law culminates in the command to love Him supremely, and then to love one's neighbor as himself (Matt. 22:36-40; cf. Deut. 6:5; Lev. 19:18). "On these two commandments depend all the law and the prophets," declared Jesus. Anything therefore which violates or falls short of the love which seeks to fulfill the inner intent of the law is sin.

B. The Element of Self-centeredness

When one pries beneath the surface of these activities and attitudes thus classified as sinful in the New Testament, one finds consistently a dominating self-reference, controlled by an inner core of self-sovereignty. Basic selfishness is being expressed in one form or another. Sinners are like Diotrephes, who "likes to put himself first" (3 John 9), and hence they tend to reject all authority but themselves. It is because they are "lovers of self" that they are "lovers of money, proud, arrogant" (2 Tim. 3:2-4). These are the natural tendencies of self-centeredness. One aspect of the sinlessness of Jesus was His refusal to "please himself" (Rom. 15:3). When Christians allow the principle of self-pleasing to control them in their mutual relations or personal practices, they have lapsed into a sinful frame of mind (vv. 1-2).[10]

C. The Element of Rebellion

While sin is seen to be an expression of selfishness, it is also an assertion of personal will in defiance of God. In sinning, men know they are doing that which God has forbidden; they are thus rejecting the Law-Giver as well as His law. This rebelliousness is illustrated by the citizens who hated their king "and sent an embassy after him, saying, 'We do not want this man to reign over us'" (Luke 19:11-27).

According to Paul, behind the specific forms of overt sin is the heart attitude that refuses to honor God "as God or give thanks" and does "not see fit to acknowledge God" (Rom. 1:21, 28). The word *asebeia*, "impiety," is the opposite of *eusebeia*, "godliness" (cf. Rom.

---

10. It is important to distinguish, however, between self-centeredness in the sense of idolatry, and *self-awareness*, a high degree of which almost always characterizes strong personalities. This self-awareness will inevitably give rise to a certain amount of verbal self-reference—as we find in both Jesus and Paul. Such self-reference is not sinful unless self instead of God is the end. In Jesus the God-man, and in Paul the apostle, self was engaged in loving the Father even when prompted by immediate circumstances to say, "I." It is not absolute selflessness which is the Christian goal, but the sanctification of the self. Failure to love self properly is as truly sin as is failure to love God and the neighbor properly.

1:18; 11:26; 2 Tim. 2:16; Titus 2:12). In comparing *asebeia* with *anomia,* "lawlessness" (cf. 1 John 3:4), Vine observes: "*Anomia* is disregard for, or defiance of, God's laws; *asebeia* is the same attitude toward God's Person."[11] This is why all sin, at base, is an expression of idolatry. As E. La B. Cherbonnier has put it: "Sin is simply another word for allegiance to a false god."[12]

D. The Element of Blameworthiness

The more common term for blameworthiness is "guilt," used in the sense of real culpability. This is the element that distinguishes sin from mistake, misfortune, and infirmity. A review of the biblical enumerations of wrong clearly indicate a divine condemnation, not just on the activities themselves, but of the persons who do them. Persons are addressed as free agents who sin willingly, and are therefore blameworthy, not merely pitiable. Paul is quick to commend whatever he can (1 Cor. 11:2); but when rebuking the Corinthians for their disorderly observance of the Lord's Supper, he says, "I do not commend you" (vv. 17, 22).

Blameworthiness, then, becomes the touchstone that identifies objective wrong as sin *per se.* The unavoidable limitations and errors that belong to human finiteness pose problems which are ethical in nature. Those errors, however, are not necessarily sinful. They become sinful only as they involve directly or indirectly the responsible attitudes and activities of free persons in relationship to God, to others, and to self.

A legalistic concept of sin defines it entirely in terms of deviation from the absolute standard, whether known or unknown, intended or unintended. An ethical concept of sin insists that while the deviation needs to be *corrected,* the doer is not *condemned* unless *along with* the violation are the factors that make him blameworthy. These factors are knowledge and volition, within the framework of normal accountability (i.e., freedom and intelligence).[13]

---

11. *EDNTW,* 4:170. Speaking of 1 John 3:4, Vine says: "This definition of sin sets forth its essential character as the rejection of the law, or will of God, and the substitution of the will of self" (2:317).

12. *Hardness of Heart* (Garden City, N.Y.: Doubleday and Co., Inc., 1955), p. 42.

13. C. Ryder Smith argues that Paul concedes the legitimacy of thus using the term "sin" legalistically, but in a strictly qualified, nonnormative sense. Commenting on Romans 5:13, he says: "In other words, the Apostle believes that 'anything contrary to God's will' is sin, but that when God comes to deal with a sinner He only takes count of the sins that *the man knew* to be sins. *For the purpose of judgment* the definition of sin is not 'anything contrary to God's will', but 'anything *known* to be contrary to

Paul's total discussion in Romans is unmistakably polarized around the ethical concept of sin. Thus the apostle could say of the heathen world, "They are without excuse." He also declares, "Though they know God's decree that those who do such things deserve to die, they not only do them but approve those who practice them" (Rom. 1:20, 32). No exoneration here due to environment! (Cf. Rom. 2:1.) Moreover, to say that "the judgment of God rightly falls upon those who do such things" (Rom. 2:2 ff.) can only mean that they who practice them *deserve* the judgment. In other words, they are blameworthy. (Cf. his converse view of virtue in 2 Cor. 8:12.)

The ethical concept of sin is also supported by the connotation of the terms used. The word *parabasis*, "transgression," always means a willful violation of a specific, known law (Rom. 2:23; 4:15; 5:14; Gal. 3:19; 1 Tim. 2:14; Heb. 2:2; 9:15; cf. *parabatēs*, Isa. 2:9; Gal. 2:18; also *parabaino*, Matt. 15:2-3; Acts 1:25; 2 John 9). The related words *anomos*, "without law," and *anomia*, "lawlessness," are also essentially ethical in their New Testament usage. Speaking of *anomos* in 2 Pet. 2:8, Vine says, "The thought is not simply that of doing what is unlawful, but of flagrant defiance of the known will of God."[14]

In addition, the terms *parapiptein*, "fall away," and *paraptōma*, a "falling away," speak of disloyalty to the law-giver. C. Ryder Smith says that the use of *parapiptein* in Heb. 6:6 "clearly speaks of a deliberate 'treachery'." Of the second word he says that in the New Testament as well as in the Septuagint, "the idea of a traitor's desertion is never wholly lost." He goes on to say:

> The Greek term occurs as a synonym for *opheilēma, parabasis,* and *parakoē* (Mark 6:12, 14; Rom. 5:14 f., 19 f.). Paul, quoting Is. 53:6, uses it where LXX has *hamartia* (Rom. 4:25; cf. Eph. 1:7). There is no doubt that in most of the passages the "falling aside" that the word literally describes is deliberate, and that it is a mistake to introduce the idea that a man does not "fall" by choice.[15]

Furthermore, the words frequently translated "disobedience" in the New Testament (*apeitheia*, "unpersuadable"; *parakoē*, "refusing to

---

His will'. It follows that *for that purpose individual* sin alone counts—and that guilt is wholly individual" (*Doctrine of Sin*, pp. 147-48). In other words, sin may be viewed only in terms of objective wrongness—which would include an error in arithmetic as well as a willful falsehood. But God looks behind the mistake of hand or head to the heart, and does not impute wrongness *as sin* if such imputation is not justified by the facts. To impute sin without regard to intentions would be a travesty on justice, and in effect reduce the "sin" idea to the misfortune of finiteness rather than to the wickedness of an accountable agent.

14. *EDNTW*, 2:317.
15. *Doctrine of Sin*, pp. 149-50.

hear") clearly indicate conscious unwillingness, hence full responsibility (Eph. 2:2; 5:6; Heb. 4:6, 11; Rom. 5:19; 2 Cor. 10:6; Heb. 2:2, *et al.*). Also, when Paul says, "Whatever does not proceed from faith is sin" (Rom. 14:23), he implies accountability, as the context indicates. The action is not one of true ignorance (hence innocence) but of presumption, which pushes aside an awareness of doubtfulness. In other words, the warning bell of conscience is disregarded.

The comparison of Matt. 5:28 with Jas. 1:14-15 provides additional insight here. When Jesus declares that the man "who looks on a woman to lust for her has committed adultery with her already in his heart," He is saying two things: First, the overt act is not the beginning of sin but its expression; the sin occurs in the heart. Second, He is saying that evil intention is in God's sight equivalent to the evil deed.

But at what point does a feeling of attraction for a woman become this kind of adultery? Some would assume Jesus to mean an involuntary movement of desire, and therefore use the statement to prove the impossibility of avoiding sin. But we must interpret the indictment in the light of James's explanation that the drawing away of attention by spontaneous desire is not in itself sin: it is only when desire has "conceived" that it "gives birth to sin." *Conception* can only refer to a union of the desire with consent; sin is the result. If the desire is decisively rejected, there is no sin. We must therefore postulate an element of evil intention in the words "to lust for her." An inner capitulation is implied which says, "I would if I could."[16]

The Johannine literature is as unmistakable in its ethical view of sin as is the Pauline. The sovereignty which belongs to God is invested in Christ; therefore the Holy Spirit will convict the world of sin, Jesus says, "because they do not believe in me" (16:9). Man's relation to Christ becomes his relation to God. But the sin is not unbelief which stems from ignorance, but from rejection. "If any man's will is to do his will, he shall know . . ." is the dictum (7:17). Again, ". . . you will die in your sins unless you believe that I am *he*" (8:24). When the Pharisees protested, "Are we also blind?" Jesus answered, "If you were blind, you would have no guilt; but now that you say, 'We see,' your guilt remains" (9:40-41; cf. 15:22). Real blindness

---

16. The infinitive phrase of *pros to epithumesai*, "to lust for," should be understood to express purpose, not result. Of course the context of Christ's words would imply that if by carelessness in the use of our eyes we needlessly expose ourselves to this sort of stimulation, we become culpably responsible for the onset of the temptation; this too would be sin. But in any case the volitional element is unmistakably present.

would imply guiltlessness; but professed knowledge allows no alibis.

As for John's Epistles and Apocalypse, only a thoroughly ethical concept of sin is found throughout. The exegetical key to 1 John 1:1-10 is 2:1, "I am writing this to you so that you may not sin." In his thinking sin is always a dread possibility but never a necessity. And the complete exclusion of sinning from the Christian life in chapter 3 is understandable only on the assumption that by sin John does not mean to include unintentional infractions. He does not confuse violations of love with infirmities which fall short of absolute perfection.[17]

Though an affirmed Calvinist, L. Berkhof recognizes the ethical nature of sin. He writes:

> In view of . . . the way in which the Bible usually speaks of sin, there can be no doubt of its ethical character. . . . Fundamentally, it is not something passive, such as a weakness, a fault, or an imperfection, for which we cannot be held responsible, but an active opposition to God, and positive transgression of His law, which constitutes guilt. Sin is the result of a free but evil choice of man.[18]

He also points out that the usual formal definition of sin as "lack of conformity to the law of God" is inadequate, unless we specify clearly the material content of law, which is "love to God." He adds: "And if from the material point of view moral goodness consists in love to God, then moral evil must consist in the opposite."[19]

III. Characteristics of Sin

A. Deceitful

A peculiarity of sin is its power to deceive (Rom. 7:11). No one could be tempted by sin unless there was seen in the enticing thing some-

---

17. John makes significant use of a major New Testament term, *adikia,* "unrighteousness." When we confess our *hamartias,* we are promised not only forgiveness of the *hamartias* but cleansing from *adikia* (1:9). Later he uses this term in a definitive-type statement: "All wrongdoing is sin" (5:17). Legalistically, this could be construed to mean that everything not technically right is sin—including unintentional mistakes and errors. But the context forbids such amoralism. The apostle obviously has in mind a moral or spiritual wrongness that is observable by others and needs their intercessory prayer; yet it may not have reached the finality of the unforgivable sin. This usage is compatible with the normal use of the word elsewhere, which essentially expresses a wilful rejection of the truth and a wrongness in opposition to the truth; hence full accountability. See Cremer, also Arndt and Gingrich, Vine; cf. Rom. 1:18; John 7:17-18; 2 Thess. 2:10-12.

18. L. Berkhoff, *Systematic Theology* (London: The Banner of Truth Trust, 1963 [1941]), p. 231.

19. *Ibid.,* p. 232.

thing that seemed to be of value. Sin has its "fleeting pleasures" (Heb. 11:25). Also, sin seems to give certain advantages, as were promised in the garden.[20] Today the argument is that only what is experienced can be understood; therefore to know life to the full one must taste of its evils as well as its virtues. In sin therefore there seems to be the promise of expansion and enrichment. Perhaps the most common facet of this deceitfulness is the phony promise of greater freedom. Peter speaks of the sensual but suave debauchee who ensnares unstable converts by "promising them freedom . . ." (2 Pet. 2:19; cf. Matt. 13:22; 2 Thess. 2:10; 2 Tim. 3:13; 1 John 3:7).

B. Enslaving

Instead of enlarging freedom, sin only contracts it and ultimately destroys it totally. Speaking of the smooth talkers who promise freedom, Peter goes on to describe them: "They themselves are slaves of corruption: for whatever overcomes a man, to that he is enslaved." Years before, Peter had heard his Lord say, "Truly, truly, I say to you, every one who commits sin is a slave to sin" (John 8:34). Every act of sin becomes a newly braided cord in the tyrant's lash, by which sin lords it over the conscience and enslaves the will. The sinner becomes increasingly free to sin, but not free not to sin, and not free to escape sin's bitter sorrows and galling chains. "Do you not know," says Paul, "that if you yield yourselves to any one as obedient slaves, you are slaves of the one whom you obey, either of sin, which leads to death, or of obedience, which leads to righteousness?" (Rom. 6:16; cf. 7:11).

C. Progressive

Sin never permits the maintenance of a stable plane of character, but is always cumulative in its hardening and depraving effects. Paul expresses it as "resulting in further lawlessness" (Rom. 6:19, NASB). The build-up of personal iniquity over the years is what is sometimes called "acquired depravity," in distinction from inborn depravity.

Sin is also progressive in another sense. At least three major passages (Genesis 1—12; Rom. 1:18-32; all of Hebrews) seem to indicate that there are what might be called root sins, from which grosser and more overt forms of sin inevitably develop. In the Genesis account we see the rise and progress of sin from innocence; in

---

20. Specifically, says William M. Greathouse, "power, pleasure, and wisdom" ("Romans," *BBC,* 8:151).

Romans we can trace the downward stages of pagan man who rejects God as Sovereign; in Hebrews we see the graduated steps of backsliding, from simple neglect (2:1-3) to final and irreversible apostasy (10:39). It is the nature of sin to consolidate and enlarge its grip on its victim, so that "evil men and imposters will go on from bad to worse, deceivers and deceived" (2 Tim. 3:13).

In the Genesis and Hebrews passages the sin of unbelief seems to be the root sin. It was not until Eve accepted the satanic slander on God's character and was persuaded to adopt her own judgment as the basis of action in the place of God's word that she deliberately disobeyed. Inner distrust comes before overt defiance. Men reject God's law because they have come to distrust His intentions. Sin thus begins in a breakdown of trusting love. Sooner or later this breakdown of love's faith will issue in a radical disobedience. Then comes an established pattern of self-sovereignty and self-idolatry, with its pride, autonomy, and bent to lawlessness; next come various forms of moral perversion, illusion, and wickedness.[21]

IV. THE CONSEQUENCES OF SIN

A. Divine Wrath

The New Testament as well as the Old portrays God as a holy being who reacts to sin, not mildly or indifferently but vigorously and punitively. "Let no one deceive you with empty words," warns Paul, "for it is because of these things that the wrath of God comes upon the sons of disobedience" (Eph. 5:6). Such reaction is seen not as vindictive or capricious but as inherent in His holiness; as properly normative, in fact, as is His love. Holiness cannot be indifferent to unholiness.

Jesus declares the love of God is so great that He gave "his only Son" (John 3:16). With equal emphasis in the same discourse He declares that the Christ-rejector will perish, because "the wrath of God rests upon him" (v. 36). The wrath of God is on him already, as

---

21. It could be summarized: *(a)* distrust of God's goodness; *(b)* rejection of God as sovereign (this rejection focuses on Christ where the gospel has been preached); *(c)* a necessary corollary, the rejection of God's Word as the criterion of truth; *(d)* the next consequent stage downward is the perversion of good for selfish ends (John 5:44); *(e)* inevitably will come thereafter a total wickedness, which Paul calls "a base mind" (Rom. 1:28), a mind utterly abandoned to the practice of sin in whatever form it presents itself; and finally *(f)* demonism, when the enemy who entered into Judas claims his own.

on every sinner in the world; Jesus is God's only appointed Way of escape from this wrath. The atonement dissipates that wrath for the believer, but only for the believer (2 Cor. 2:14-16; Col. 1:22-23; 1 Tim. 4:10; 6:12; 2 Tim. 2:11-13; Heb. 3:12; 10:39; 1 Pet. 1:9).

For the present, God's wrath is restrained in its expression and is disciplinary in its purpose. To the foreground is "His kindness and forbearance and patience" that is calculated to lead men "to repentance" (Rom. 2:4; cf. 2 Pet. 3:9). But while restrained, God's wrath is not dormant. When warning the Gentile believers against smug complacency, Paul says, "Do not become proud, but stand in awe. For if God did not spare the natural branches, neither will he spare you. Note then the kindness and severity of God: severity toward those who have fallen, but God's kindness to you, provided you continue in his kindness; otherwise you too will be cut off" (Rom. 11:20-22). The God who claims the right of vengeance (Rom. 12:19) has not thrown away the sword in this gospel dispensation, for the Scripture expressly declares that He has deputized the ruler of the state to wield the sword: "He is the servant of God to execute his wrath on the wrongdoer" (Rom. 13:4).

But while the wrath of God is restrained now, it is building up to a cataclysmic outpouring in the final consummation. Not only does the "judgment of God rightly" fall *now* upon "those who do such things" (Rom. 2:2), but persistent evildoers are "storing up wrath" for themselves against "the day of wrath when God's righteous judgment will be revealed" (Rom. 2:5). This final outpouring of wrath (Matt. 3:7) will certainly not fall on well-meaning bunglers, but rather on *recalcitrant impenitents.* "Your hard and impenitent heart," Paul says (v. 5; cf. 2 Thess. 1:5-10; Heb. 10:26 ff.; 12:18 ff.; 2 Pet. 3:7 ff.; Rev. 14:10, 19; 15:1, 7; 16:1, 19; 18:3; 19:15).

Paul speaks of the revelation of "the wrath of God" practically in the same breath as the revelation through the gospel of the "righteousness of God" (Rom. 1:17-18). Actually, knowledge of God's wrath is part of the Good News, because it discloses the terrible peril from which now there is a way of escape. But also it is part of the Good News, because it reveals the kind of a righteous and predictable God with whom we have to do. We are not left in doubt concerning His reaction to sin. The universe is moral at its heart! Therefore we may be sure we are not victims either of blind chance or irresponsible caprice. We are in an inescapable relationship with a God who offers us in Christ a share in His righteousness, but who informs us in advance that He will punish us if we choose to align ourselves with the "ungodliness and wickedness of men who by their wickedness suppress the truth" (v. 18). We therefore know exactly where we stand.[22]

Jesus as truly expresses the wrath of God as He expresses the love of God. There is something terribly prophetic about the anger with which He looked around at the hardhearted Pharisees (Mark 3:5; cf. Matt. 21:12-13; 23:12-33; John 2:13-18). Christ's wrath has no resemblance to the petty anger of sinful men—and only a carnal heart could so libel Him. Rather it is that holy wrath which will not compromise with sin; e.g., "On that day many will say to me, 'Lord, Lord' . . . And then I will declare to them, 'I never knew you; depart from me, you evildoers'" (Matt. 7:22-23; cf. Matt. 10:32-33; Luke 12:8 ff.; Rev. 8:1-13). Sentimentalists would reject this anger as being out of character. But we woefully misapprehend Jesus if we fail to see this demand for righteousness as exactly in character. Here is a wrath that is devoid of favoritism.

Furthermore, it is none other than the "Lord Jesus" himself who "is revealed from heaven with his mighty angels in flaming fire, inflicting vengeance upon those who do not know God and upon those who do not obey the gospel of our Lord Jesus" (2 Thess. 1:7-8). Most strikingly, the Revelation of John discloses an indissoluble unity between the wrath of God and the wrath of the Lamb: Frightened men will pray, "calling to the mountains and rocks, 'Fall on us and hide us from the face of him who is seated on the throne, and from the wrath of the Lamb; for the great day of their [note plural] wrath has come'" (Rev. 6:16-17; cf. 14:10; 19:11-16).

B. Death

Paul plainly declares that death is a consequent of sin (Rom. 5:12; 6:23; 8:10). However, it is not suffered simply because of the natural entropy of the human organism but is imposed as a penalty. It is this

22. Speaking of Rom. 1:18-32, Frank Stagg says that "to Paul the wrath of God is his delivering of man over to man's own choice of the way of disobedience and self-worship" (*New Testament Theology* [Nashville: Broadman Press, 1962], p. 138). Others express a similar idea in the understanding that God's wrath is simply His sovereign aloofness, His decision to respect man's moral agency and allow man's sin to wreak its own consequences. That there is a natural law of retribution in sin is undeniable, but even this is the arrangement of God (Gal. 6:7-8). The theory is true but not the whole truth, for God is positively relating himself by *giving them over* (Rom. 1:24, 26, 28). "God sends upon them a strong delusion" declares Paul, as a *direct recompense* "because they refused to love the truth and so be saved" (2 Thess. 2:10-11; cf. Rom. 3:5-8).

judicial aspect of death that invests it with unnatural horror, and causes it always to be linked with sin as an unholy duo. This link also explains the pervasive fear that plagues man, including many secondary terrors related directly or indirectly to his obsessive dread of death (Heb. 2:14-15). Human life cannot escape the uneasiness and anxiety of existence under death's shadow. Not only does redemption in Christ save from sin and death, but it offers deliverance *now* from the fears associated with them.

Primarily, death means the simple termination of physical life, and the consequent release of man as spirit. The underlying idea always is not nonexistence, but atrophy and separation.[23] By far the majority of the words for "death" (principally *thanatos*, "death," and *apothnēskō*, "to die") unmistakably refer to physical death. This is almost exclusively the case in the Synoptics.

In John's Gospel, however, we suddenly find ourselves introduced to the concept of spiritual death. The peril of being condemned to eternal damnation is clear enough in the Synoptics; in that sense the idea of spiritual death is implicit there too. But in John the present state of the sinner is viewed as a kind of death. Jesus talks about being dead while physically alive, and about being saved from such death while not yet having died physically (5:24; 6:50; 8:51-52; cf. 1 John 3:14).

When we get into the Pauline Epistles, we discover that the references to death are rather equally divided between death as a departure from the body and death as that state in which sinners now are. "For me to live is Christ, and to die is gain" (Phil. 1:21) is clear enough; but so also, on the other side, is Paul's discussion epitomized by "When the commandment came, sin revived and I died" (Rom. 7:9). While the death ascribed to Adam's sin in Romans 5:12 ff. is primarily physical, the spiritual overtones are not absent (see Chapter 17). In chapter 6 the emphasis is almost totally on spiritual death, either the emancipating death *to* sin or the deathlike corruption *of* sin (Rom. 6:2-5, 7, 11, 16, 21-23).

As we study carefully, a definition of spiritual death as a concomitant of sin begins to emerge. First, sin is existence under *condemnation* (Rom. 5:16, 18; 8:1). Correspondingly, it is a profound *alienation* from God (cf. Isa. 59:1-2 with Luke 1:79; Eph. 2:3, 12), a

---

23. That this was viewed as an abnormal and premature separation from our earthly order of existence, and never as a total extinction or destruction of the person, will be pointed out in another connection (cf. Chap. 35).

liability to eternal separation from God (Rom. 2:6-9), and a *condition* of spiritual coma (Eph. 2:1; 5:14).

The supreme peril toward which every biblical warning and redemptive provision is directed is dying physically while yet in spiritual death. When this occurs, death becomes final and eternal (Jas. 5:19-20). The word more commonly used to express this ultimate danger is *apollumi,* "to loose," "destroy," normally translated in KJV by "perish." "For God so loved the world, that he gave his only Son, that whoever believes in him should not perish, but have eternal life" (John 3:16; cf. Matt. 18:14; Luke 13:3, 5, 35; John 10:28; Rom. 2:12; 1 Cor. 1:18; 8:11; 15:18; 2 Cor. 2:15; 2 Thess. 2:10; 2 Pet. 3:9). In Revelation, the inspired writer gives this ultimate death a name: the "second death" (Rev. 20:6, 14).[24]

Depravity, degradation, and death are the products of sin. Sin when "it is full-grown brings forth death" (Jas. 1:15; cf. Rom. 6:23; 8:6). Sin is never wholesome, always poisonous; never ennobling, always debasing; never constructive, always destructive; never beautifying, always blighting. Every single form of behavior condemned in the Scriptures is inherently disruptive and damaging, with cosmic consequences. Sins of the spirit, such as envy and bitterness, divide men, and by them "many become defiled" (Heb. 12:15). Sins of the "flesh" produce personal and social decay (Gal. 6:8; 2 Pet. 1:4; Jas. 4:1-2). From the biblical standpoint, apart from God's grace, humanity is not an improving but a degenerating race.

The only thing God finds ultimately wrong with man is sin. This, and this alone, brought Christ as Redeemer into the world. Sin therefore is the enemy. Every sin dishonors God and exalts the adversary. Every sin defiles the soul, and if not covered by the blood of Christ, carries eternal personal consequences. Every sin sends into the pool of life eddies and ripples of influence, whose resistless surge never stops. Sins may be forgiven without their effects in life being erased (viz., David).

Sin is the cause of every unhappy home, every divorce, every war, every quarrel, every graveyard, and every tombstone. Even the sorrows traceable to the dislocations in the natural order are in some way related to the curse of sin (Rom. 8:18-23).

These associated evils are bad enough, but Christ really has

---

24. For further discussion, see *Projecting Our Heritage,* comp. by Myron F. Boyd and Merne A. Harris (Kansas City: Beacon Hill Press of Kansas City, 1969), pp. 69-71, incl. footnote on p. 71.

nothing to offer those who merely want salvation from sin's pains and inconveniences. The sin problem is much deeper than that. It cost God the harmony and beauty of His creation, and fellowship with His crowning creature, man. To redeem man from sin cost God His Son. Sin pierced His head with a crown of thorns and drove the nails into His hands. Christ came to redeem us from sin itself (Matt. 1:21; Heb. 7:25; 9:26-28).

17

A Racial Corruption

The New Testament supports the Old in witnessing to man's radical fallenness (Jer. 17:9). It has already been made clear that this corruption is not endemic in the sense of being native to human nature as created (see Chapter 15). The heart as the inner citadel of man's moral nature may be either corrupt (as in his fallen state) or holy. Full redemption has as its objective the cleansing of the heart (Matt. 5:8; 12:35; 1 Tim. 1:5; Jas. 4:8).

The issue now confronting us, therefore, is not what human nature may have been originally, but, When does it actually become depraved? Is the child's nature "loaded" toward sin, i.e., more prone to be evil than holy? If this is the teaching of the New Testament, then in some sense it becomes proper to speak of inherited sinfulness. But everywhere in the New Testament men are addressed as free and accountable; and so in view of the clear biblical teaching of the ethical nature of sin in itself, the idea of inherited sinfulness plunges us into complexity. It would certainly appear that a prevolitional sinfulness would have to be spoken of as "sin" in a subethical, accommodative sense. [1]

---

1. Undoubtedly, much of the phenomena of moral bondage, with its need for divine grace, could be accounted for on the supposition that man's depravity is totally acquired from environment and personal sinning. E. La B. Cherbonnier, who rejects the Reformation formulation of the doctrine of original sin, accounts for the "bondage of the will" in this way. He says, "If human freedom is only *fulfilled* in *agapē*, then, conversely, it will be progressively *destroyed* by sin." He considers that the frustrating impotence of Paul ("For I do not do the good I want, but the evil I do not want is what I do," Rom. 7:19) is a form of acquired "compulsive behavior" (*Hardness of heart*, pp. 132 ff.).

I. THE PRE-PENTECOST WITNESS

The writers of the four Gospels recall the attitudes, events, and sayings of Jesus which reflect His general view of man. This view suggests a racial solidarity in sinfulness that is unexplainable apart from a common participation in a human nature which has become morally and spiritually defective.

A. Jesus' View of Man

It is remarkable that Jesus categorized even His disciples as "evil" (Matt. 7:11; Luke 11:13).[2] In the light of this it is not unreasonable to understand His reference to "sinful men" (Luke 24:7) to be a characterization of *man* as sinful, rather than simply a particular reference to some men, as if some were sinful and others were not. Those persons not endorsing the crucifixion of Christ were those who had already allowed His redeeming power to be at work in them; apart from this invasion of grace it was the *human race* that put Jesus to death, just as it was for the *human race* that He died.

The effect that Jesus had on men was astonishingly provocative. Either they were prompted, as Peter, to acknowledge their sinfulness (Luke 5:8), or else they were hardened. Jesus' constant unmasking of the "best" people did not shame them but aroused an upsurging of their boundless iniquity. It seemed that He was to them a fire heating the caldron of their subconscious and bringing it boiling to the surface. Apparently the holiness of Jesus activated the radical unholiness of man.

Though Jesus' love for men was deep enough that He would die for them, it was never rose-tinted. "Jesus did not trust himself to them, because he knew all men and needed no one to bear witness of man; for he himself knew what was in man" (John 2:24-25). Furthermore, Jesus' declaration that "no one is good but God alone" (Mark 10:18) is a hint that if goodness belonged to the original image

---

It should be pointed out, however, that many scholars who reject "original sin" seem unaware of any doctrine other than the traditional, which identifies original sin as a full participation in Adam's guilt, on the one hand, and as an endemic moral depravity, on the other—a depravity so deep as to be an inseparable element of human nature itself. This conception of original sin is unbiblical, and we approve of its rejection.

2. The apparent acknowledgment of "righteous" and "well" (Matt. 9:12; Mark 2:17; Luke 5:31-32), says G. C. Berkouwer, is not really a reference "to some 'elite' group who are raised above the general sinfulness by a righteousness acceptable to God; it is rather a caustic criticism of the boundless over-evaluation, the failure to recognize that one is a sinner before God" (*Man: Image of God*, p. 143).

of God in man, it is now lost. If there is no goodness outside of God, then those outside of God are bereft of goodness.[3]

B. Spiritual Impotence

One indicator of man's universally sinful nature is the assertion of Jesus that no man can come to Him "unless the Father who sent me draws him" (John 6:44, 65). Here is a dual evidence of prevolitional depravity. For one thing, the implication is that if left alone, no man will have an inclination to come to Jesus. But there is also a clear indication of an impairment of moral ability, for the words are *oudes dunatai*, "absolutely unable." This acknowledgment of moral inability in the most religious people on earth to respond properly to Jesus Christ, unaided by grace, is a devastating revelation of their spiritual condition. There seems to be more here than a depravity totally acquired by personal wrong choices.

II. THE PLIGHT OF "FLESH"

The Greek word *sarx*, "flesh," as used in the New Testament, sheds light on the question of man's preconversion nature (see Chapter 15).[4]

A. Flesh and the New Birth

The ethical overtones in the biblical concept of flesh are first seen in John 1:12-13, combined with 3:6, "That which is born of the flesh is flesh, and that which is born of the Spirit is spirit." By human procreation only flesh is produced—a flesh which left to itself is incapable (*ou dunatai*, "unable, cannot") of perceiving the spiritual

---

3. It is true Jesus applies good *(agathos)* to men in other settings (Matt. 5:45; 12:35; 25:21, 23; cf. Luke 1:6; 2:25), but doubtless a grace-traced goodness is intended. Since no man would be called good by Jesus who was not devout, we may assume him to be already in the redemptive stream of divine influences.

4. *Sarx* may refer simply to the body (Acts 2:31), or to the human race with its kinship lines (Rom. 1:3), or to the understanding of the natural man (Matt. 16:17; Rom. 6:19). For further study see Lambert, *Dictionary of the Apostolic Church* (Grand Rapids, Mich.: Baker Book House, rep. 1973), 1:411 ff.; also Richard E. Howard, *Newness of Life* (Kansas City: Beacon Hill Press of Kansas City, 1975). Howard says: "In actuality when a man lives according to the flesh *(kata sarka)*, he is living *according to himself.* Because of the basic nature of man, this means that the person living *by* the flesh also lives *for* the flesh. Not only does he live by means of his own strength and resources (human means), but he lives for himself. The consequence is that to live *kata sarka* results in the improper satisfaction of the demands of the fleshly (human) body—its desires, propensities, and wishes" (p. 33).

realities of the kingdom of God. If God created man as a spirit in live relationship with God, that spiritual aliveness has been lost; it can only be recovered through a new birth by the Spirit. The need for the new birth is not therefore because *good* children have chosen to sin and have become evil; the need for the new birth is *inbred.* Clearly, human nature at birth does not have within it potential for its own holiness.[5]

John 1:12-13 supports this view. Only through Christ can men "become children of God" (v. 12). Coming *to* Christ is volitional ("as many as received him"), but the *need* is subvolitional. The biblical concept of spiritual sonship is not relationship only but also a sharing of moral likeness. This aspect of the divine image in man has been lost. To say that it can only be recovered in Christ is to say that apart from redemption all men, *as men,* are unlike Him. Jesus calls His listeners children of the devil because they are partakers of Satan's nature instead of God's nature (John 8:44; cf. John 3:8, 10).

B. Flesh as Sinful

In Paul's Epistle to the Romans the ethical concept of flesh as man-under-sin is crucial to his soteriology. The key is 8:3: "For God has done what the law, weakened by the flesh, could not do: sending his own Son in the likeness of sinful flesh and for sin, he condemned sin in the flesh." Essentially, flesh is man in his earthly mode of existence. The term "sinful flesh" denotes human nature infected by sin, which is the distinguishing characteristic of every individual as a member of a fallen race (cf. Eph. 2:1-3).

That Jesus was not sinful is evidence that flesh per se is not necessarily sinful, but that through some catastrophe flesh has fallen under the domination of sin. It is this which makes human nature morally impotent before the demands of the Law. Clearly this is not a condition resulting solely from personal choices but one in which every man finds himself.[6]

---

5. Speaking of Christ becoming flesh, Wesley says: "Christ was born frail, as well as we, and in this sense was 'flesh'; yet, being without sin, he had no need to be 'born of the Spirit'" (*The Works of John Wesley* [Kansas City: Nazarene Publishing House, reprinted from 1872 edition], 9:406-7). Wesley says flatly: "To be 'born flesh' is to be born corrupt and sinful." Since he understands flesh here to imply an antithesis to spirit (both Holy Spirit and regenerate spirit), he adds: "It is evident, to be 'born of the flesh' is to be the sinful offspring of sinful parents, so as to have need of the renewing influences of the Holy Spirit, on that account, even from our birth."

6. James Denney observes: "It does not prejudice Christ's sinlessness, which is a fixed point with the Apostle *ab initio;* and if any one says that it involves a

Whereas *sarx* in itself is neutral but may be infected by sin, Paul uses the term metaphorically in Rom. 7:5—8:13 and in Gal. 5:13-24 as standing for the sin itself. Hence, in this manner of speaking, to be "in the flesh" is to be under the domination of sin; and all men, not by individual choice but by *nature*, are in this state. As so used, flesh may be defined as human nature oriented toward sin. The phrase *phronēma tēs sarkos* (8:6), "the mind of flesh," is Paul's more precise way of saying what he sometimes means by "flesh" alone. It accents the dispositional bent of fallen human nature, in sharpest contrast to the dispositional bent of redeemed human nature. The disposition or bent is "hostile to God; it does not submit to God's law, indeed it cannot" (v. 7). Naturally, therefore, "those who are in the flesh cannot please God" (v. 8).[7]

III. THE VERDICT OF LAW

The law is more than the just basis of guilt, and its level of possession the measure of responsibility; it also serves as God's way of showing man the wickedness of his nature. Not only "through the law comes knowledge of sin" (Rom. 3:20) in *particular*, but by the law is the discovery of the deep-rootedness of man's intransigence. It was to serve this deeper function that the Mosaic law was given. Paul begins to develop this theme in Rom. 5:20: "Law came in, to increase the trespass" (cf. Gal. 3:19). The purpose clause, *hina pleonasē*, "to increase," does not mean that God wished men to sin more, but He wished to arouse their sinfulness by means of the Law that they might see it for what it is.[8] The inference is that if God's perfect law

---

contradiction to maintain that Christ was sinless, and that He came in a nature which in us is identified with sin, it may be pointed out that this identification does not belong to the essence of our nature, but its corruption" ("The Epistle to the Romans," *The Expositor's Greek Testament* [Grand Rapids, Mich.: Wm. B. Eerdmans Publishing Co., reprint 1967], 2:645). Note John 8:44 with 1 John 3:8, 10.

7. As an example of the great flexibility of *sarx*, even in Paul's hands, note Gal. 2:20 where "in the flesh" simply means "in the body." In 2 Cor. 10:3 the word is used both positively and negatively in the same verse. Speaking of *sarx* used in ethical sense, Wesley comments: "But why is this corruption termed flesh? Not because it is confined to the body. It is the corruption of our whole nature, and is therefore termed 'the old man.' . . . Not because it is primarily seated in the body; it is primarily seated in the soul. If 'sin reigns in our mortal bodies,' it is because the sinful soul uses the bodily members as 'instruments of unrighteousness'" (*Works*, 9:408).

8. James Denney says: "The offence is multiplied because the law, encountering the flesh, evokes its natural antagonism to God and so stimulates it into disobedience" (*Expositor's Greek Testament*, 2:631). See also Ladd's discussion, *Theology of the NT*, p. 508.

irritates man into multiplied infractions, something must be very radically wrong with man! Holy human nature would have no trouble with God's law. Conformity would be natural and joyous.[9]

This is precisely the conclusion Paul comes to in Romans 7. What is the source of my tendency to sin? he asks. Where is the real culprit? Is it the law (v. 7)? Is it wrong to impose law on man? The idea is unthinkable. The law "is holy, and the commandment is holy and just and good" (v. 12; cf. v. 14) in the sense that it is a reflection of the real nature of man and of the moral principles that are universally relevant to human happiness. The fact that such spiritual law arouses in man a combativeness toward it only demonstrates the unspirituality of man as he now is. That which "promised life" (v. 10)—which was a blueprint for peaceful and harmonious interrelatedness—could not possibly "result in death." In the law only those things intrinsically harmful were forbidden, and only those things intrinsically healthful were commanded.

The incredible phenomenon described in Romans 7 is not the experience of a man whose reason finds fault with the law, for he testifies, "I delight in the law of God, in my inmost self" (v. 22). Yet it is in *this* man that the law "results in death." In spite of his perception of the law's soundness he finds himself at loggerheads with it. That which fits his *created* nature like a glove is strangely uncomfortable.

The message of Romans 7 is therefore that law does much more than focus and intensify the guilt for actual wrongdoing (vv. 9-11, 13). It also discovers a depravity of nature back of the individual infractions. To become aware of this depravity is essential to man's self-knowledge. "Yet, if it had not been for the law, I should not have known sin [*tēn hamartian*, 'the sin']. I should not have known what it is to covet if the law had not said, 'You shall not covet'" (v. 7). The proclivity to covet was there already. The law did not create that, it only revealed it. It is an inner bent therefore that preconditions the soul to fight the law, and hence predetermines an irrational warfare when the law comes. In this conflict, law and reason lose.

---

9. There is no evidence that God's one restriction in the Garden was burdensome, and there would have been no disposition to break it if Eve had not been tricked by deception into a distrust of God's motives. It was acceptance of distrust that constituted the "fall"; distrust made overt disobedience psychologically possible. Inward unbelief led to outward action.

IV. THE CHARACTER OF INDWELLING SIN

Scholars have frequently noted the transition in Paul's total frame of reference from personal sins and guilt to *hē hamartia,* "the sin." This use of the article with the singular noun he introduces in 5:12; from then on, the discussion majors on this kind of sin.[10] Speaking of 5:12, Greathouse comments:

> Up to this point Paul has been dealing chiefly with the problem of sin as *guilt;* now he introduces the idea of sin as *revolt.* This is indicated by the new phrase *hē hamartia,* which occurs 28 times between 5:12 and 8:10. In each instance it refers to "the principle of revolt whereby the human will rises against the divine will" [quoting Godet]. Beet comments that *sin* here "is not a mere act, but a living, hostile, deadly power."[11]

In chapter 7, Paul is endeavoring to make clear that this sin principle is the real villain. Twice he pinpoints it precisely as "the dwelling-in-me sin" (*hē enoikousa en emoi hamartia,* vv. 17, 20). It is this sinfulness that determines the moral character of *flesh,* i.e., human nature in earthly form.

A. An Alien Force

Not only does Paul exonerate the law of God but he also exonerates the "I"—"It is no longer I that do it" (7:17, also 15-16, 19-20, 22, 25). Biblical theology will not permit us to psychologize this in modern terms and try to explain it as the bondage of the will to an evil habit. We must work from Paul's own psychology, which posits a much deeper problem. He is confronting an inner moral tyranny that is alien to man's true nature. To have blamed the law would have been blaming the God who gave it; so also it would be blaming the Creator to ascribe this inner moral dichotomy to an original defect. There is an *I* in this passage which disowns what it finds in itself, yet at the same time owns it as inwardly present. It is also clear that volitional acts of wrongdoing are not in view. We are dealing with a subvolitional tendency to fall short of an adopted, reasonable standard.

B. Its Nature as Law

Beginning with 7:21 Paul introduces a new characterization of indwelling sin: it is a *nomos,* "law," which overpowers the *law* of his

---

10. A multiple sense to what otherwise is uniformly singular is in 7:5, "the sinful passions."

11. *Beacon Bible Commentary,* 8:114.

mind (vv. 21, 23, 25; 8:2). Clearly this is not law in the sense of commandment (as is the law of God) but law in the sense of a uniform mode of operation, e.g., the law of gravitation.[12] Arndt and Gingrich use the phrase "principle of action" as explanatory of "the law of my mind."[13] Thus Paul becomes understandable:

> So I find it to be a law that when I want to do right, evil lies close at hand. For I delight in the law of God, in my inmost self, but I see in my members another law at war with the law of my mind and making me captive to the law of sin which dwells in my members. Wretched man that I am! Who will deliver me from this body of death? Thanks be to God through Jesus Christ our Lord! So then, I of myself serve the law of God with my mind, but with my flesh I serve the law of sin (Rom. 7:21-25; cf. 8:1-4).[14]

To define indwelling sin as a law in this sense is profoundly significant, for such a law always has three characteristics: (1) Its action is both uniform and predictable; that is, just as the "law of the Spirit" (8:2) is uniformly and predictably destructive of sin, so the law of sin is uniformly and predictably impelling to evil. (2) Furthermore, such a law is *found,* not enacted. The law of sin in man's nature is a propensity that the individual discovers in himself but has not personally caused. (3) Such a law is beyond man's power to control or his power to destroy. He can resist its impulse but he cannot excise it. Its operation does not depend on man's consent.

Such are the phenomena of indwelling sin. Speaking of 8:2, A. Berkeley Mickelsen says: "Both the Spirit and sin and death are called the law because of the constancy of their influence and action."[15] The unregulative, disruptive, and contravolitional nature of indwelling sin is therefore unmistakable.

---

12. Cremer comments, "That the idea of order is the prominent one, appears from the fact that *nomos* is applied to the order of tone and key in music."

13. *Lexicon,* p. 544.

14. The NASB muddies the waters by locating this law of sin in the physical body. The word *body* is not in v. 23, nor does the sense require it. Commenting on *melos,* Arndt and Gingrich say, "There is no fixed boundary between parts of the body as taken lit. and fig."; for example, they give Col. 3:5, *nekrōsate to melē to epi tēs gēs,* which "may be paraphrased: *put to death whatever in your nature belongs to the earth*" (p. 502). Paul's terms in these chapters, invested as they are with ethical meanings, such as "flesh," "our body of sin," "the body of this death," leave little doubt that "my members" refer to human propensities pervaded by sin, whether bodily, mental, or spiritual. We could paraphrase, "I see a different law in the parts of my nature, waging war against my reason, and making me a prisoner of the law of sin which is in the various parts of my nature."

15. *Wycliffe Bible Commentary,* ed. Charles F. Pfeiffer and Everett F. Harrison (Chicago: Moody Press, 1962), p. 1205.

How then can this law of sin be defined? *It is a predictable and spontaneous contrariness toward the law of God uniformly present in human nature as now constituted.* But to say "the law of God" is to say God himself. Thus the law of sin is synonymous with the carnal mind ("the mind that is set on the flesh")—the mind that is "hostile to God" (Rom. 8:7). This hostility explains why the carnal mind always leans toward rebellion against God and His law.

This is why also the perversity is such a disruptive force in the personality. What could be more schizophrenic than the situation as Paul summarizes it: "So then, I of myself serve the law of God with my mind, but with my flesh I serve the law of sin" (7:25)? There is only one self—"I myself"—but this one self experiences the stress of dual claims. It is at the same time a servant, through the reason, to the law of God, and a servant, through the flesh, to indwelling sin. But it is not an even struggle. The polarity of sin is stronger than the polarity of reason. This is the great tragedy of the human predicament. It is the onesidedness of the battle and the certainty of the outcome which prompts the cry: "Wretched man that I am! Who will deliver me from this body of death?" (v. 24).[16]

C. Sin and Desire

To speak of *the sin* as an alien quality and as having the nature of law is still not to reach its depths. For the specific law which discloses this essence turns out to be the tenth commandment, "You shall not covet" (7:7). Having learned of the law, instead of avoiding coveting as a matter of simple obedience, Paul is compelled to confess, "[the] sin, finding opportunity in the commandment, wrought in me all kinds of covetousness" (v. 8). It was not the prohibition that pro-

---

16. Who is the "I"—Paul? In the light of the rest of the Epistle it is obvious that this cannot be his personal predicament at the time of writing. In using the personal pronoun, Paul is representing universal man, insofar as man has become aware through grace of his moral dichotomy. But is it regenerate man or primarily an awakened Jew under the law? Tomes have been written on both sides. It is better to take an overview which sees Paul's concern in this scripture not with a category of people but a problem of persons—all persons who have not been cleansed of this troublesome indwelling sin. His real grappling is with the mystery of human perversity. Why do I keep on acting this way, or rather *being* this way, in spite of my wish and resolve to the contrary? This that I find in myself is irrational, immoral, unspiritual, and shameful. What is it? Why is the law impotent? Why do I find a spontaneous antagonism to that which I have at one and the same time endorsed? It is the human situation of fallen man which Paul is analyzing, inspired by the Spirit, first in relation to the law, then in relation to the higher reason, and then—thank God!—in relation to Jesus Christ, in whom alone is the remedy to be found.

duced coveting; it was *the sin.* Coveting itself is a secret sin of the heart, but here is present *a sin which is behind coveting,* as coveting's prompter and source. The intensive verb "produced," *katergazomai,* means "to work out (to the finish)," says Robertson.[17] *The sin* is a combativeness against the law that defies and overrides it, a combativeness created by a *deep priority of the self over the will of God.*

C. Ryder Smith points out, quite rightly, that *epithumia,* "desire," in itself is not sinful, but becomes ethically sinful when turned in a wrong direction by the will. In his concern to rule out any kind of nonvolitional sin, Smith says: "While Paul does teach here that he chooses a wrong desire in spite of his better self, *until* he so chooses he has not sinned."[18] True, somewhere in the picture he becomes responsible for his covetings. Only at this point do they become sins, "properly so-called" (Wesley). But Paul is not pinning the blame on desire *(epithumia)* but on *hē hamartia* which championed *epithumia's* rights against God.

To bog down in a discussion of *desire* is to miss the whole issue in this chapter. This issue is why the self from earliest accountability so perversely tends to defy the law, in spite of shame and bewilderment over the fact. If conscious choosing were the whole story, it would seem that victory and defeat might at least come out about 50-50! But it does not, and this is precisely the problem. Paul is insisting that there is something in the self which he calls *the sin.* It acts before the reason does, and tips the scales unfairly in the direction of overt sinning.[19]

---

17. *Word Pictures in the New Testament* (New York: Harper and Brothers Publishers, 1933), 4:368.
18. Smith, *Doctrine of Sin,* p. 162.
19. This does not mean that Smith is wrong in wanting to preserve the ethical content of guilt in the concept of sin per se; even that is assumed in this very passage, if we but look in the right place. Paul goes on to explain that "apart from the law sin lies dead. I was once alive apart from the law, but when the commandment came, [the] sin revived and I died" (vv. 8-9). Sin is present and the illicit coveting goes on, but under cover of ignorance and innocence. *The sin* on its own is present but does not kill; it is not imputed to us as sin. But sin in its true nature as anti-God perversity is activated by the confrontation of the law. It is when *the sin* is thus activated into deliberate transgression that we personally die, because then we have sinned guiltily. This whole discussion of nonvolitional sinfulness is in perfect harmony with the underlying assumption of the ethical nature of sin per se. It is clearly a moral defect serious enough to be called *the sin,* but it falls short of the blameworthiness requisite to sins. The possibility of being alive spiritually with this sin present, but the impossibility of remaining alive spiritually with this sin translated into overt deeds is the strongest possible evidence of this insight.

D. Sin as Self-idolatry

We cannot completely pierce the "mystery of iniquity," but the connection between *hē hamartia* and *epithumia* is clearly one of inner kinship. Perhaps there is a clue here to *the sin as an inbred bent toward self-idolatry, or self-sovereignty, that precedes conscious choosing and helps to shape it.*

Inordinate love of self creates a spontaneous supersensitiveness to one's rights, feelings, and pleasures. This sensitivity is so powerful that the awakened person is unable, on his own, to extricate himself from the stranglehold of this pervasive pattern of self-seeking. As a consequence there is a spontaneous suspicion and perhaps open antagonism against anything that threatens the autonomy of self or the priority of self-oriented values. The law—and behind the law, God—is just this kind of a threat. The point of open clash is most apt to be at the tenth commandment, because this sinful self wants what it wants with a feverish imperiousness. Soon it is wanting what God has forbidden it to have, and so we have coveting. The desired object may not be the neighbor's wife, but "your neighbor's house, his field or his manservant . . . his ox, or his ass, or anything that is your neighbor's" (Deut. 5:21).

The "anything" could include not only material goods but position, power, even prestige, as Aaron and Miriam coveted equality with Moses. Thus the sin of inordinate self-love (pride?) prompts the defense mechanism of self-assertion and combativeness, giving rise ultimately to greed, envy, and jealousy. Then, if there are obstacles in the way of doing as we please, we must outwit them with cunning, scheming, deceitfulness, and finally with ill will, hatred, lying, stealing, and murder. The whole foul brood of evil deeds spring from this activated "all kinds of covetousness" (v. 8). How apt is Peter's vivid clause, "the corruption that is in the world because of passion" (*epithumia,* 2 Pet. 1:4).

Because human nature was created with God as its Axis, this idolatrous self-love is really an eccentricity. A self that is centered in self is self off-center. This perversion affects destructively and disastrously the whole man and thus the whole world of human relations.

E. Sin as Carnal-mindedness

It is apparent that the state of man described by Paul is a state of tension between the *nous,* "mind," and the *phronēma,* "frame of mind." Those afflicted with indwelling sin are characterized by a mind-bent that is "set on the flesh" (8:5-7). The disposition is inclined toward a pampering of self in its physical and earthly life; but since the reason disapproves of such monolithic obsession, there is a tension between the rational and dispositional. On the other hand, spiritual-mindedness is rational because it is a disposition, in affection and desire, that agrees with the dictates of the *nous.*

Purity of Heart Is to Will One Thing is the title of one of the works of the Danish philosopher Kierkegaard. Purity of heart is a harmony between *nous* and *phronēma,* the reason and the affections, intellect and disposition. Purity of heart unites the propositional self and the propensive self, the approved goals and the real drives, the public commitments and secret preferences. Therefore heart purity is not only to "will one thing" but to *want* one thing. Only as the deepest desires are sanctified, and freed from their feverish service to self, can the will truly be delivered from its slavery to sin and by divine grace reign again.[20]

V. The Relation of "The Sin" to Adam

A. The Chronology of Sin

When was Paul (or any man) alive without the law, and when did he die? What is the chronology of sin? While Paul can speak of "the law of sin and death," he does not equate the two. The nature of *the* sin is such that when activated, it produces death by inducing specific acts of voluntary sinning. Wilber T. Dayton says: "Paul . . . must have been referring to the innocence of infancy, when grace was neither conditional nor resisted." He understands Paul to be saying that when he came to "moral awareness," the "dormant energies of sin awoke and killed me." According to Dayton, Paul is saying: "There was something in me that would not play fair with truth. This latent tendency to favor self and to yield to evil became my undoing."[21]

---

20. It is clear that just as Paul refuses to blame the law of God or human nature as created, so he leaves no room for "blaming" an evil environment. The attempt by some theologians to avoid any lineal transmission of sinfulness and to explain everything in terms of surrounding influences, breaks to pieces biblically on the rock of Romans 5—8. The problem is *within* every man. Each man's sinfulness is so deep that if every other man became holy and the environment ideal, his sinfulness would remain. As important as is the factor of influence, it is an inadequate explanation here.

21. "Romans and Galatians," *The Wesleyan Bible Commentary,* Charles W. Carter, ed. (Grand Rapids, Mich.: Wm. B. Eerdmans Publishing Co., 1965), 5:49.

The important thing to see is that whenever this occurred, *the sin* was already there. It was not the result of Paul's first sinful choice, it preceded it. Hence there is a kind of sin that is prevolitional, thus nonvolitional. But if it was present when Paul (or any child) came to the age of accountability, then it characterized him as a preaccountable child. It is very difficult to escape the implication that Paul is describing the kind of a being his parents procreated. "Do not men come into the world with sinful propensities?" queries Wesley.[22]

B. An Inherited Bias

The passage most crucial to the question of the relation of racial sinfulness to Adam's transgression is Rom. 5:12-21. Paul's aim there is to show that both intensively and extensively the obedience of Christ more than offsets the effects of the disobedience of Adam. But in stressing this point he clearly traces human depravity to the Garden.

From Adam's single act of disobedience streamed three consequences all summarized under the heading of death in v. 15: "If many died through one man's trespass [legally, physically, and spiritually], much more have the grace of God and the free gift in the grace of that one man Jesus Christ abounded for many." Then this generalized statement is itemized as follows: The judgment against Adam's sin resulted in condemnation for the race, *but* this is offset by "the free gift [that] . . . brings justification" (v. 16). Also as physical death "reigned through that one man, much more will those who receive the abundance of grace and the free gift of righteousness reign in life through the one man Jesus Christ" (v. 17). *The sin* (the principle of indwelling sin) constitutes the spiritual effect on *human nature* just as death and condemnation constitute *physical* and *legal* effects. It "came into the world" solely "through one man" (v. 12).

---

22. Wesley's longest and most vigorous polemic was his refutation of a Dr. John Taylor's *The Scripture Doctrine of Original Sin.* Taylor both denied that man entered the world with a sinful nature and repudiated any adverse effects suffered by the race for Adam's sin. For Wesley this was a blow "at the whole frame of Scriptural Christianity" (*Works,* 2:114). Wesley was unimpressed with Taylor's attempt to relegate Romans 7 totally to the struggle of an awakened Jew under the law, for he felt the discussion missed the main intent of the passage. "I cannot but observe, upon the whole, the question is, Does not Rom. 7:23, show that we come into the world with sinful propensities? . . . But instead of keeping to this, you spend above twenty pages in proving that this chapter does not describe a regenerate person! It may, or it may not; but this does not touch the question: Do not men come into the world with sinful propensities?" (*Works,* 9:298).

So, as *the sin* "reigned in death, grace also might reign through righteousness to eternal life through [one Man] Jesus Christ our Lord" (v. 21).[23]

Alan Richardson admits that Paul "undoubtedly thought of Adam as a historical individual," but he insists that theologically Paul was thinking of Adam as "'mankind,' 'everyman,' Paul himself." To Paul, "Adam" is merely a collective noun. "Adam represents all men, because all men have the character of Adam."[24] But this is to miss the clear fact that for Paul it is the unique historical individuality of Adam which is the pivot of his argument. There is unmistakable chronology here. Sin and death *entered* at a point in time, a definite period of time *intervened* between Adam's transgression and the giving of the Mosaic law, death reigned *from* Adam *to* Moses. These chronological notes are essential to Paul's line of thought.

There is no way we can avoid the teaching that there is a real genealogical linkage between Adam's sin and our present sinfulness as members of the human race.[25] We are sinful by inherited nature because that is the kind of nature Adam transmitted, as a result of his sin. William Greathouse says that as "a consequence of the first man's disobedience the entire race has been corrupted. This corruption consists of men's being born out of true relation with God and condemned constantly to worsen their relationship." Therefore, he concludes, man *"inherits* a situation of *death*—moral bankruptcy, weakness and corruption."[26]

There is no attempt in the Scriptures to explain how Adam so

---

23. Note the difference between the real righteousness *(dikaiosunēs)* of this verse and the forensic justification of v. 16 *(dikaiōma;* see Vine, "a sentence of acquittal"). Verse 16 emphasizes the forgiveness of "many trespasses," while v. 21 discloses that the possibilities of grace in Christ extend even to *the sin.*

24. *Introduction to the Theology of the NT,* p. 248.

25. When the inner nature and activity of indwelling sin is described in c. 7, and Paul is forced to explain everything by the simple fact, "I am carnal, sold under [the] sin" (v. 14), he is dropping back in thought to Adam. He cannot be referring to his first evil choice, for *the sin* was already there, as we have previously seen. There never was a time when Paul, as representative man, was not *"rooted in the flesh as it were"* (Thayer, *Greek-English Lexicon).* Comparing *sarkikos,* "fleshly" (as used in Rom. 7:14) with *sarkinos,* "fleshly," "carnal," Thayer says, "Unless we decide that Paul used *sarkikos* and *sarkinos* indiscriminately, we must suppose that *sarkinos* here expresses the idea of *sarkikos* with an emphasis; *wholly given up to the flesh, rooted in the flesh as it were."* This is to say that he was born this way, for he shared the common nature of a race which had been *pepramenos hupo tēn hamartian,* lit., "having been sold under sin," or "into slavery to *the sin,"* by Adam.

26. *Beacon Bible Commentary,* 8:117. Cf. Eph. 1:18-25; 2:1-3; 4:18, 22.

defiled the stream of human nature, and there are no theories respecting transmission of *the sin*. The assumption, of course, is that man comes into the world no longer either primitively holy, as was Adam, or dispositionally neutral, but premorally bent toward sin. Thayer's definition of the law of sin is: "the impulse to sin inherent in human nature" (*Lexicon*, p. 427). But the word "inherent" is objectionable, for it suggests that sin belongs to the essential constitution of man. If that were true, its removal would be an injury rather than correction. We should say therefore—indeed, saying it is hardly escapable in the light of all the scriptural data—that the law of sin, *the sin*, is an *inherited* impulse to sin, pervasively resident, but not irremediably *inherent*.[27]

C. An Impaired Moral Ability

Admittedly there is a serious paradox in the strong biblical assumption that an ethical element belongs to sin per se and the concurrent teaching that there is a sinful bent which is inherited. The peril of contradiction is avoided if inherited sin is viewed as subethical in nature, carrying in itself no personal culpability, until endorsed as the chosen set of the soul in responsible maturity.

Along with this issue comes the related question of impaired freedom. If the tyranny of inbred sin over the will is absolute, then actual sin with guilt becomes impossible, because total inability cancels accountability.[28]

---

27. It goes without saying, of course, that *the sin* is not an entity, or any kind of substance in the soul, in spite of Paul's persistent personification of it as if it were an independent agent. Its enslavement of the will would seem to suggest the nature of an entity, since it has attributes, or characteristics, with their uniform and predictable modes of manifestation. But we must insist that these are ways of describing the deep-seated perversity of this human condition, which in final analysis turns out to be the self deprived of the sanctifying Spirit from birth and hence depraved in nature. If an axle is bent, its crookedness cannot be thought of as an entity in the sense that it can be weighed, or extracted as a material thing, or exist in abstraction from the axle; notwithstanding, the moment the car begins to move, the bentness begins to manifest itself as a distinct and characteristic force creating a visible wobble in the wheel and perhaps a vibration in the entire body. It is a condition which derives its dynamic force from the activity of the car. If man were an inactive, passive being, sin (if possible at all) would be a static state, for it has no power of its own. But man is perpetually active. The eccentricity of his inborn ego-bent derives its dynamic destructive and disruptive power from the activity of the total person in life's total context. (For further discussion of inbred sin as privative yet dynamic, see Chap. 4.)

28. For further discussion of this problem see Kenneth E. Geiger, comp., *The Word and the Doctrine* (Kansas City: Beacon Hill Press, 1965), p. 113.

But the same Paul who defines the *limits* of sinful man's moral freedom in Romans 7 also defines his residue of power in Philippians. As far as the legal righteousness in the law was concerned, he was blameless. But man's ability failed at the crucial point of cleansing his nature from the persistent tendency to covet and from the latent antagonism to God. Human freedom, in the sense of power to make moral choices, *is* impaired by sin. Such impairment is the nature of sin. But through prevenient grace every man has freedom to look to Christ in whom the power of cleansing and moral victory resides.

Inbred sin therefore must be viewed as comparable, albeit in reverse, to Adam's *primitive holiness.* This primitive holiness is a created natural leaning toward God that made loving God easy, but not inevitable or irreversible. So likewise inbred sin is a primitive, subethical leaning toward self that makes self-idolatry easy, but not as an *absolute,* cause-and-effect mechanism. The overflowing abundance of grace quite overwhelms the power of *the sin.*

It is as if under Adam man's only hope of salvation would be in heroically fighting the heritage of Adam within himself—then only to fail. In contrast, the redemptive event in Christ means that while each person comes into the world with Adamic nature, he is also already within the sphere of God's grace. Prevenient grace is a pervasive influence that will shepherd him to conversion and sanctification and finally to heaven, *unless he determinedly breaks his way out.* In Adam it is impossible to be saved. In Christ—as are all men potentially—it is hard to be lost. *Yet Christ causes both Adam's influences and His own to stop short of absolute moral determinism.* We personally decide whether we shall abide in Adam or abide in Christ. At birth we are in both, but sooner or later we must choose one or the other.

D. The Question of Guilt

Rom. 5:12 leaves no doubt that *the sin* entering into the world was the product of Adam, and *death* was the product of *the sin.* Then Paul doubles back on himself to add the explanatory phrase "because all sinned." This means that all share in the death because all are guilty of sinning. The question is whether Paul means to be crediting Adam's sin to the "all." Did all sin *in Adam,* or as a *result* of Adam's sin?

Wesley, the Reformers, and many modern commentators would say that all are under the sentence of death because all (including infants) share in the guilt of Adam's sin. Death as *penalty* can be justified only on the basis of their involvement with Adam's high-handed transgression. Mickelsen says: "Paul sees men from Adam to Moses as involved both in Adam's initial sin and in its consequence."[29]

But while voluntary sinning requires personal repentance and particular forgiveness, Paul seems to say that any "guilt" accruing from Adam's sin is universally cancelled, as one of the unconditional benefits of the Second Adam. In Rom. 5:18, the "condemnation for all men" resulting from Adam was cancelled in the coextensive "acquittal and life for all men" through Christ. There is therefore no real basis for complaint. "It is nowhere said or implied," observes Barmby, "that the natural infection which they could not help will be visited on individuals in the final judgement."[30]

This view of transmitted *guilt* is not, however, shared by all. Wilber Dayton declares that Paul does not say that "sin was 'imputed' to all because of Adam's sin. Nor does he specify that all were present in Adam and participated in his act of sin." Commenting more directly on the phrase "because all sinned," he adds: "When or how? He [Paul] does not say. It may then be safe for us not to say. It is sufficient that since the first man sinned, this ghastly spirit of revolt has, in one way or another, shown itself in all the offspring. All have sinned, as was already said in 3:23."[31]

The internal movement of this passage would seem to indicate the transmission of *the sin*, but not the transmission of Adam's *guilt*. Paul immediately hastens to add that "sin indeed was in the world before the law was given; but sin is not counted where there is no law. Yet death reigned from Adam to Moses, even over those whose sins were not like the transgression of Adam" (vv. 13-14). This could be interpreted to mean that since their own sin was not imputed to them as worthy of death, Adam's must have been. But it could be

29. A. Berkeley Mickelsen, "Romans," *The Wycliffe Bible Commentary*, ed. Charles F. Pfeiffer and Everett F. Harrison (Chicago: Moody Press, 1962), p. 1198. The same sort of idea is employed by Paul in associating the entire race with Christ's death in 2 Cor. 5:14, "We are convinced that one has died for all, therefore all have died." That is, in some sense every man was with Christ on the Cross, and thus shares in the benefit, preveniently, *apart* from his choice and finally and fully *by* his choice. To thus say that all died with Christ may be the counterpart of saying that all sinned in Adam.

30. J. Barmby, "Romans," *The Pulpit Commentary*, ed. H. D. M. Spence and Joseph S. Exell (Grand Rapids, Mich.: Wm. B. Eerdmans Publishing Co., 1950 edition), p. 127.

31. *Wesleyan Bible Commentary*, 5:39. The Calvinist A. T. Robertson (*Word Pictures*, 4:358) says that *hēmarton*, "sinned," as a constative aorist of *hamartanō*, simply gathers up "in this one tense the history of the race (committed sin). The transmission of Adam became facts of experience."

equally a flat denial of the notion, for Paul expressly says that these people did not sin in the way Adam did—high-handedly transgressing a published law. Therefore *their* sin was not his; for if they sinned *in Adam,* they sinned *his sin!* To impute Adam's sin to them to whom Adam's law had not been given would be doing exactly what Paul has just said God does not do.[32]

The stumbling block seems to be that if death is *penalty* for deliberate transgression of a known law, as in Adam's case, it is unjust to condemn infants to share in this penalty unless in some way they were implicated in the sin. To say infants deserve to die is to the modern mind a contradiction in terms. Nor is it required by the text. But to concede a *legal* implication in Adam's sin as their representative, and a sharing of death as a simple consequence of belonging to a race now under sentence of death, is less objectionable. Whatever our interpretation, the stake of infants in Christ infinitely exceeds their handicap in Adam.[33]

---

32. Neither is it clear whether the "judgment" arising "following one trespass" (v. 16) *constitutes* condemnation for all, or (as NASB puts it) results in condemnation for all. If *the sin* became the spreading incubus of a sinful tendency, prompting universal *sinning,* then this sinning would occasion the condemnation. The same uncertainty is in v. 18, and also in the clause "as by one man's disobedience many were made sinners" in v. 19. Vincent says that *katestathēsan,* "were made," may mean "to declare or show to be; or to constitute, make to be." He continues: "The exact meaning in this passage is disputed. The following are the principal explanations: 1. Set down in a declarative sense; declared to be. 2. Placed in the category of sinners because of a vital connection with the first transgressor. 3. Became sinners; were made. This last harmonizes with *sinned* in v. 12. The disobedience of Adam is thus declared to be the occasion of the death of all, because it is the occasion of their sin; but the precise nature of this relation is not explained" (Marvin R. Vincent, *Word Studies in the New Testament* [Grand Rapids, Mich.: Wm. B. Eerdmans Publishing Co., orig. 1887, reprinted 1965], 3:64).

33. For careful discussion of this complex issue from the standpoint of systematic theology see H. Orton Wiley, *Christian Theology,* 2:109-40. Note especially: "His [Adam's] descendants, therefore, were born under the curse of the law which has deprived human nature of the Spirit of God, and which can be restored only in Christ. Hereditary depravity then, is not only the law of natural heredity, but that law operating under the penal consequence of Adam's sin" (p. 125).

Section Three

A Saviour, Christ the Lord

18

Jesus' Self-testimony

I. THE NEW TESTAMENT AS CHRISTOLOGICAL

It has been said that while the New Testament is theocentric, it is also Christo-normative. That is to say, Christ is definitive of all that is written in the New Testament, whether one is speaking of God, man, sin, salvation, the Church, or the future life. We cannot speak biblically about any of these matters without reference to Christ. Therefore, any preaching or teaching in the life of the Church that finally does not focus on Christ and His work is not truly Christian. So it was in the Early Church and so it has been in the Church through the ages as she has sought to propagate her faith.

With the renaissance of biblical theology came a new interest in Christology. "Vertical" revelation tended to put Christ at the heart of the faith. Until very recently with the resurgence of concern over the existence of God,[1] New Testament theology had subdued much of liberal thought which saw Jesus only as the greatest of the prophets, the prophet of love, the first great Christian, or the one who realized the highest in man's quest for God. The Harnacks of the liberal period for the most part had been quieted.

However, today's thinking about Christ has shifted to a different focus because of the vigorous debate over the nature of the Gospels—whether they are biographies giving us authentic facts of the Jesus of history, or only *kerygmata*, introducing us to the Christ of faith. Rudolf Bultmann and his followers have been largely responsible for this shift. They emphasize the Christ of faith often to the total exclusion of the Jesus of history.[2]

Scholars, both orthodox and liberal, have revolted against the Bultmannian reductionism with respect to the importance of the historical Jesus. They insist that the evidence of history, however limited it might be, is absolutely necessary if there is to be an authentic Christian faith. Pannenberg's summarizing word, following Gerhard Ebling, is correct: "It is recognized today that faith must have 'support in the historical Jesus himself.' That means, certainly, in Jesus himself as he is accessible to our historical inquiry."[3] The New Testament, he says, must be viewed not only as a "preaching text" but also as a "historical source."

A study of Christ against this background evokes a serious question for the theologian: Is the faith of the Early Church as expressed in the New Testament sufficiently grounded in the words and con-

---

1. Cf. Langdon Gilkey, *Naming the Whirlwind: The Renewal of God-Language* (Indianapolis: Bobbs-Merrill Co., 1969), p. 5: "There is, then, almost nothing in the life of the churches . . . that has not been questioned with the utmost intensity in the last few years. . . . We shall concentrate here on what we regard, from the point of view of theology, as the center of the crisis, namely the question of the reality of God and so of the possibility of meaningful language about him."

2. For concise treatments of this bit of history, cf. R. H. Fuller, *The New Testament in Current Study* (New York: Charles Scribner's Sons, 1962), pp. 25-53; "The New Testament in Current Study," *Contemporary Christian Trends*, ed. William M. Pinson, Jr., and Clyde E. Fant, Jr. (Waco, Tex.: Word, Inc., 1972), pp. 138-53. This second article is an updating of the first one. Also, cf. Charles C. Anderson, *Critical Quests of Jesus* (Grand Rapids, Mich.: Wm. B. Eerdmans Publishing Co., 1969); *The Historical Jesus: A Continuing Quest* (Grand Rapids, Mich.: Wm. B. Eerdmans Publishing Co., 1972).

3. *Jesus, God and Man*, p. 24. Cf. also Joachim Jeremias' dealing with the question, "How reliable is the tradition of the sayings of Jesus?" *New Testament Theology: The Proclamation of Jesus*, trans. John Bowden (New York: Charles Scribner's Sons, 1971), pp. 1 ff.: "In the synoptic tradition it is the inauthenticity, and not the authenticity, of the sayings of Jesus that must be demonstrated."

sciousness of Jesus of Nazareth? It has been, and still is, the conviction of traditional Christian thought that, with full acknowledgment of all the variations of expression concerning Christ in the New Testament, the Early Church faithfully transmitted the words and works of Jesus. Behind the record are trustworthy witnesses to Jesus, and especially to Jesus' self-consciousness, that is to say, what He knew himself to be.

Form history *(Formegeschichte)* has performed a valuable service in stating the nature of the New Testament as preaching; its failure has been its historical skepticism. But as Longenecker pointedly reminds us, neither catechetical, missionary, nor polemic interests were sufficiently creative to originate the tradition of Jesus:

> The powerful unity of thought from the very beginning presupposes, in addition to the activity of the Spirit, a similarly powerful creative personality. Jesus himself was for the earliest Christians both the source of their basic convictions and the paradigm in their interpretation of the Old Testament.[4]

Unquestionably, the Church preached its understanding of Christ's mission, but the historical Jesus must take priority (cf. Luke 1:1-4; John 20:30 ff.). Our faith rests first of all on Jesus himself as we know Him in the Gospels and secondarily on the interpretation of Him by the apostles. Floyd Filson sees the issue clearly and writes to it:

> If we could erase from mind and memory all concrete details that the Gospels have given us, all specific incidents which express the spirit and purpose of Jesus, he could no longer grip the imagination and command the will. He would be at best an elusive shadow whose exact identity and meaning for us we could never know. A fatal vagueness would blight the Christian faith. The gospel would not be able to speak its convincing word from within the human struggle.[5]

Several guidlines can be laid down at this point:

First, Jesus did not come to deliver a ready-made doctrine of himself, i.e., a Christology. He came to perform a redemptive deed. His was an experiential purpose—to bring man and God together in reconciliation (2 Cor. 5:19). Out of the believing response of the Early Church developed a doctrine.[6]

---

4. Richard N. Longenecker, *The Christology of Early Jewish Christianity* (Naperville, Ill.: Alec R. Allenson, Inc., 1970), p. 9.

5. *Jesus Christ the Risen Lord,* p. 95.

6. Cf. R. H. Fuller, *The Foundations of New Testament Christology* (New York: Charles Scribner's Sons, 1965), p. 15.

Second, the saving deed, in its totality, provides the basis for the Church's commitment to Christ as her Lord. This means that Incarnation, teachings, miracles, Cross-death, Resurrection, and Ascension comprise the deed. All must be taken as bearing the hope of salvation. A long time ago, P. T. Forsyth emphasized this truth:

> The whole claim of Jesus for himself is not to be determined by the explicit words he uses about himself, but also, and even more, by the claims set upon us by the whole gospel of his person and work when these had been perfected. The claim of Jesus in his cross and resurrection is even greater than the claim explicit in his mouth.[7]

Third, "the uniqueness of the person bursts all categories of the human mind and human language."[8] This character of Christ makes it extremely difficult to frame, even with all the materials of the New Testament, a fully satisfying Christology. Need we argue the point that the Church across the ages has found it so? Our primary hope is to gather together, beginning with the titles of Christ, the faith affirmations about the person and ministry of Christ, and thereby gain a reasonable understanding of His nature.

James Denney once wrote that "the fundamental thing in Christology is Christ's testimony to himself." However, such a statement calls for some judicious modifications, especially as one attempts to bring into focus all the statements of Christ concerning himself. Fuller's judgment is correct: "What we have to look for is rather in the nature of presuppositions and hints which arise from his interpretation of his destiny."[9] These presuppositions are not "proclaimed from the house-tops," but Jesus does provide "the raw materials for an estimate of his person" and believers with eyes of faith will know what to do with them. Fuller sees the titles given to Jesus as "raw material for Christology." We shall now move to examine some of the appellations which Jesus used of himself and which the Early Church employed to speak of Him.

II. Son of Man

A. The Title in the Gospels

This title appears some 69 times in the Synoptic Gospels and about 12

---

7. P. T. Forsyth, *The Person and Place of Jesus Christ* (Boston: The Pilgrim Press, 1909), p. 101.
8. Spoken by Ernest E. Saunders in a class at Garrett Theological Seminary, 1956; Adolph Harnack said much the same: "There is no generic category under which Christ can be placed, whether it be Reformer, Prophet, or Founder."
9. R. H. Fuller, *The Mission and Achievement of Jesus* (Naperville, Ill.: Allenson, 1954), p. 79.

times in John's Gospel. It is the one title that Jesus uses most frequently of himself as reported in the Synoptics. But curiously He employs it in a detached manner.[10] He does not say, "I am the Son of Man." Rather, He uses the third person in an impersonal manner, as in the case of His reply to the disciples after Peter's declaration of Jesus as the Christ: "And he began to teach them that the Son of man must suffer many things, and be rejected by the elders and the chief priests and the scribes, and be killed, and after three days rise again" (Mark 8:31; cf. also 14:62).

The only possible exception is found in John 9:35-37 where Jesus asks the blind man, "Do you believe in the Son of man?" When the man asks who the Son of Man is, Jesus replies: "You have seen him, and it is he who speaks to you." Some ancient manuscripts have "Son of God" in place of "Son of man."

Fuller has conveniently separated the Son of Man sayings into three distinct groups. (1) *Present usage*, those occurrences "where it is intended as a self-designation of Jesus present and active in His earthly ministry." A precise illustration is Mark 2:10-11: "'But that you may know that the Son of man has authority on earth to forgive sins'—he said to the paralytic—'I say to you, rise, take up your pallet and go home.'"[11] (2) *Suffering usage*, those occurrences where the passion of the Lord is in view, such as Mark 8:31 quoted above.[12] (3) *Future usage*, those occurrences which clearly refer to the exalted and glorified Son of Man. As a concluding exhortation to His call to radical discipleship, Jesus warns: "For whoever is ashamed of me and of my words in this adulterous and sinful generation, of him will the Son of man also be ashamed, when he comes in the glory of his Father with the holy angels" (Mark 8:38).[13]

B. Sources of the Title

The conclusion to which one must come after surveying these uses is that "Son of man" represented in the mind of Christ a special insight into His person. But that fact is at the same time the introduc-

---

10. With the possible exceptions of Luke 24:7 and John 12:34, all of the occurrences are attributed to Jesus himself. Furthermore it is found in all the strata of the tradition. In only Acts 7:56; Rev. 1:13; 14:14 is it employed as a Christological title, and from this limited use we are justified in saying that its usage is peculiar to Jesus.

11. Cf. 2:28; 10:45; Matt. 8:20; 11:19; 12:32; 13:37; 16:13; Luke 9:58; 12:10; 19:10; *et al.*

12. Cf. Mark 9:12, 31; 10:33, 45; 14:21, 41; Luke 22:22; 24:7; *et al.*

13. Cf. also 9:9; 13:26; 14:62; Matt. 12:40; 24:27, 37, 44; Luke 11:30; 17:22, 30; 18:8; *et al.*; cf. Fuller, *Mission and Achievement of Jesus*, pp. 96-97.

tion of a more difficult problem. What meaning did He wish to convey by it?

It has been the usual procedure of scholars to seek assistance from both the immediate cultural setting and the Old Testament in determining the way in which the Lord used the term. For example, since Jesus spoke Aramaic, the *lingua franca* of Palestine, He would have used the phrase *bar nasha,* literally "son of man." In rabbinic circles of the day this phrase was used in the generic sense of "a man" or "any man" and as a deferential circumlocution for the first person pronoun "I." As G. Vermes has demonstrated in his exhaustive study, in no place in the rabbinic usage, verbal or written, does it carry Messianic meaning.[14] Suffice it to say, with the generic usage quite prevalent in that day Jesus would have temporarily escaped opposition that might otherwise have come with a supernaturalistic meaning.

Numerous studies have sought to locate hints of the meaning of "Son of Man" in several alleged pre-Christian Jewish writings, especially 1 Enoch 37—71 and 4 Ezra 13, where the Son of Man is an apocalyptic, eschatological agent of redemption.[15] This supramundane, preexistent being who is with the Creator and who will appear as a redeemer is found all over the Ethiopic Enoch (chapters 37—71). The telling argument against the view that this might be the source for Jesus' usage is that neither Enoch nor 4 Ezra are demonstrably pre-Christian.

Turning to the Old Testament, we discover the phrase in several books. Ps. 8:4 reads: "What is man that thou art mindful of him, and the son of man that thou dost care for him?" (Cf. also Job 7:17-18; Ps. 144:3.) While the writer to the Hebrews uses this verse as a reference to Christ (2:6-8), in the Old Testament context the phrase simply emphasizes the weakness and insignificance of man, even though God cares for him. "Mere man" might well be substituted for the phrase "son of man" in these instances.

Likewise, the prophet Ezekiel employs the phrase frequently. Upon seeing the great vision of the glory of God, the prophet fell upon his face in fear. God said to him: "Son of man, stand upon your

---

14. In M. Black, *An Aramaic Approach to the Gospels and Acts,* 3rd ed. (Oxford: Clarendon Press, 1967), pp. 310-28.

15. Cf. A. J. B. Higgins, *Jesus and the Son of Man* (London: Lutterworth, 1964); H. E. Tödt, *The Son of Man in the Synoptic Tradition,* trans. by D. M. Barton (London: SCM Press, 1965). For a current survey, I. H. Marshall, "The Synoptic Son of Man Sayings in Recent Discussion," NTS, XII (1966), pp. 327-51.

feet, and I will speak to you" (2:1; see 2:3, 8; 3:1; *et al.*). Even an un-
sophisticated reading of these passages in Ezekiel would readily suggest that "son of man" conveys the idea of "a mortal man" with
limited ability to fulfill the Lord's demands. Christ is certainly the
Great Prophet, but Ezekiel's usage can hardly carry the weight of
meaning found in the New Testament where the Son of Man forgives
the sins of men (Mark 2:10) and suffers vicariously for mankind
(Mark 10:45).

Daniel 7 is another possible source of Jesus' understanding of
"Son of man." Verse 13 reads, "I saw in the night visions, and behold,
with the clouds of heaven there came *one like a son of man,* and he
came to the Ancient of Days and was presented before him." To this
"one like a son of man" was given the kingdom (v. 14). Later on in
the passage a group of persons called "the saints of the Most High"
also receive and possess the kingdom (vv. 18, 22, 25, 27).

Two important aspects of the phrase in this passage are to be
noted. First, the "son of man" is identified with the "saints of the
Most High." It appears that the phrase represents both an individual
and a people. We seem to have a corporate sense aligned with an
individual sense. The "saints" are the redeemed Israel and the "son of
man" is the embodiment of that remnant. T. W. Manson expresses
this idea as follows:

> In other words, the Son of Man is, like the Servant of
> Jehovah, an ideal figure and stands for the manifestation of the
> Kingdom of God on earth in a people wholly devoted to their
> heavenly King. . . . His mission is to create the Son of Man, the
> Kingdom of saints of the Most High, to realize in Israel the idea
> contained in the term.[16]

Jesus proved to be in truth the Son of Man. The failure of mankind or Israel to be "the saints of the Most High" left the responsibility to Jesus. He embodied in himself "the perfect human response
to the regal claims of God." At one moment He was both the Son of
Man and "the saints of the Most High." Frank Stagg's conclusion
is noteworthy: "The mystical yet real solidarity between Christ and
his people is such that not only is he the Son of man, but his people
become in him the 'Son of man'."[17]

---

16. *The Teaching of Jesus,* p. 227.
17. Frank Stagg, *New Testament Theology* (Nashville: Broadman Press, 1962), pp.
60-61; cf. C. H. Dodd, *The Interpretation of the Fourth Gospel* (New York: Cambridge
University Press, 1953), pp. 241-49, for a discussion of the individual and corporate
ideas as expressed in John's Gospel.

Second, the glorification and vindication of the "saints of the Most High" comes through suffering. In the Gospels it is recorded that the Son of Man and His disciples will share the same destiny; they will both suffer for the Kingdom but will nevertheless receive the Kingdom (Mark 8:34; Luke 22:28-30). This fusing of the individualistic and corporate concepts along with the pronouncement of glorification through suffering finds its basis in the "Suffering Servant" songs of Isaiah (42:1-4; 49:1-6; 50:4-9; 52:13—53:12).

T. W. Manson, R. Newton Flew, W. Manson, V. Taylor, Frank Stagg, Alan Richardson, Floyd Filson, and others see Jesus as pouring the meaning of the Suffering Servant into the title Son of Man. T. W. Manson observes: "It was a true instinct that found in Jesus the fulfilment of Isaiah liii, for the 'Son of Man' is the lineal descendant of the 'Servant of Jehovah' and Jesus by being the 'Son of Man' realizes the ideals contained in the picture of the Lord's Servant."[18]

The kingdom of evil shall not triumph over the kingdom of God, because the very suffering of Christ and His people will be the release of the power of the victorious Kingdom. In and through His own sufferings as the Son of Man, Christ created the "saints of the Most High," the Church. Christ's followers suffer redeemingly across the ages with the realization that it is through the suffering that glorification and vindication will come and the kingdom of God will be realized finally in its consummate glory. Just as the Son of Man will appear in power and glory in the future, so those who have become "the Son of Man in Him" will rise to dominion and glory at the divinely appointed time.

C. Usage in Other New Testament Books

Why is this term "Son of man" not used outside the Gospels except in Acts 7:56, on the lips of Stephen, and in Rev. 1:13 and 14:14? Jeremias insists that, in the transition of the Church from a Semitic to a Greek-speaking milieu, an attempt was made "to avoid the danger that native Greeks would take the title as a designation of descent."[19] This effort to avoid misunderstanding is not to suggest that New Testament leaders were unacquainted with the title. Certainly Paul was familiar with it as seen in the designation of Christ as *ho anthrōpos*

---

18. *Teaching of Jesus*, p. 231. Notice the references to the Isaianic passages in Matt. 12:18-21 and Luke 4:16-21. The Early Church understood the connection between Jesus and the Ebed Yahweh: Acts 3:13, 26; 4:27, 30; 8:32-35; 1 Pet. 2:21-25.

19. *NT Theology*, p. 265.

in Rom. 5:15 and in 1 Cor. 15:21, plus his interpretation of the Son of Man (Psalm 8) in Messianic terms in 1 Cor. 15:27; Eph. 1:22; and Phil. 3:21. Furthermore, the Adam-Christ typology in Paul could have had its genesis in the "Son of man" concept.[20]

D. Summary

In Jewish thought the title "Son of man" apparently had no fixed meaning. While it had a wide variety of meanings or usages, to some degree it carried Messianic significance and for that reason provided a medium for Christ's special Messianic meaning. Its relationship to the Jewish pattern of Messianic thought would, however, have kept it from evoking excessive hostility. Surely Jesus had to exercise caution in His use of Messianic terms not only to avoid premature antagonism from His enemies but also to keep from misleading His hearers—most of whom would tend to interpret such terms in traditional ways.

This designation was Jesus' self-chosen title. The tradition is quite consistent that the title occurs exclusively on His lips. In explicating His nature, Jesus used this appellation with its meaning in Daniel and fused it with the Suffering Servant motifs of Isaiah. Contrary to what Bultmann *et al.* have written, the meaning of "Son of man" in the Gospels is not the work of the early community. We prefer Richardson's conclusion: "The bold new teaching about the Son of Man, i.e., a Messiah who should suffer, was the original work of Jesus himself, and no other plausible suggestion has ever been put forward."[21]

Moreover the Son of Man creates in His being "the saints of the Most High." The Son and the saints share the suffering and the triumph of Kingdom life. In Pauline terms, "Son of man" suggests the introduction of a new humanity, because Jesus is the Last Adam (Rom. 5:12-21; 1 Cor. 15:20-28, 42-50). This understanding of the title precludes the simplistic definition that emphasizes only the humanity of Christ.

It is proper to affirm that Jesus is "the personal embodiment of human nature at its best." He is the Representative of the human race, and the Realization of the divine ideal in man. The "Son of

---

20. *Ibid.;* cf. Stauffer, *NT Theology,* p. 111.
21. Alan Richardson, *Introduction to the Theology of the NT,* p. 136; cf. Jeremias, *NT Theology,* p. 276, for an explanation of Jesus' use of the third person in speaking of the Son of Man.

man" nomenclature indeed suggests these aspects of His nature, but it embraces more. The Son of Man is the Eternal Son who comes into man's desperate world to suffer and identify with mankind. He is the exalted Son who will come on the clouds in the future with His saints to vindicate the Kingdom. Stauffer observes that our Lord had "an idea of the Son of Man that comprised a whole theology of history in itself. In calling himself the Son of Man Jesus had already taken the decisive step in claiming cosmic history as his own."[22]

III. SON OF GOD

A. The Title in the Gospels

The title "Son of God" *(ho huios tou theou)* or simply "the Son" *(ho huios)* is likewise a part of the self-testimony of Jesus. Peter confessed, "You are the Christ, the Son of the living God" (Matt. 16:16; Mark 8:29). The high priest inquired of Jesus: "Are you the Christ, the Son of God?" (Matt. 26:63; cf. the circumlocution in Mark 14:61). Luke records that the demons recognized the sonship of Jesus: "You are the Son of God!" (4:41). John's Gospel records frequent references to Christ as "Son of God" or "the Son" (1:49; 3:16-17; 5:19-26; 6:40; 8:36; 10:36; 14:13; 17:1). Jesus' own most explicit reference is found in John 10:36: "Do you say of him whom the Father consecrated and sent into the world, 'You are blaspheming,' because I said, 'I am the Son of God'?" (cf. 3:18; 11:27; 20:31).

In recent years it has been assumed by certain scholars that the title "Son of God" was placed upon the lips of Jesus by the church.[23] Against this position must be set such evidence as (1) the divine identification of Christ "the Beloved Son" at the Baptism (Mark 1:11 and par.) and the Transfiguration (Mark 9:7 and par.); (2) the unique parable of the wicked husbandmen in which Christ is referred to as "the beloved son" (Mark 12:1-11 and par.); (3) Christ's deep sense of filial consciousness which evoked the frequent reference to God as

---

22. *NT Theology,* p. 111.
23. Oscar Cullmann, *Christology of the New Testament,* trans. Shirley C. Guthrie and Charles A. M. Hall (Philadelphia: The Westminster Press, 1959), pp. 275 ff.; R. H. Fuller, *Foundations of New Testament Christology,* pp. 114 ff.; Wilhelm Bousset, *Kyrios Christos,* trans. John E. Steely (New York: Abingdon Press, 1970), pp. 90-91; Rudolph Bultmann, *Theology of the New Testament* (New York: Charles Scribner's Sons, 1970), 1:128-33, asserts that "Son of God" was employed by the Hellenistic-Jewish Christians but did not mean "the divinity of Christ" until the Gentile churches used it.

"Father" (Matt. 6:9; 11:25; Mark 14:36; Luke 23:34, 46; John 11:41; 12:27, *et al.*); (4) the Trinitarian formula of Matt. 28:19.

We have already noted that in the Fourth Gospel, Jesus frequently designates himself as God's Son. Therefore, it does seem valid to assert that Christ knew His divine status, and on occasion informed His listeners of that status by referring to himself as "God's Son." Richardson writes: "Though the Gospels are reticent upon the subject of the inner life of Jesus, they leave us in no doubt about his consciousness of his own special relation to the Father."[24] Thus, "his realization of God as his Father and of the Father's acknowledgement of him as Son was the basic dictum of his ministry."[25] The Early Church inherited that understanding of Christ's self-consciousness and declared it in both the Jewish and the Gentile milieu.

In discussing this title, Ethelbert Stauffer focuses on Matt. 11:25-27 in which Jesus declares, "All things have been delivered to me by my Father; and no one knows the Son except the Father, and no one knows the Father except the Son and any one to whom the Son chooses to reveal him." In opposition to scholars who deny the authenticity of this verse, Stauffer demonstrates that the Amarna Letter to the Sun from 1370 B.C. and the Qumran Psalms and the Manual of Discipline have similar phrasing. He concludes that "it can no longer be asserted that the language of this saying of Jesus would have been inconceivable among the Palestinian Jews of the early imperial age, and that therefore the saying cannot be attributed to Jesus, but must have sprung from the Hellenistic primitive church."[26] The saying certainly could have come from the lips of the Teacher from Nazareth.

Moreover, Jesus asserts that "No one knows the Father except the Son." Every Jew believed that he could know the Father only through the writings of Moses, the Holy Scriptures. This excluding declaration of Jesus is therefore unique. Stauffer concludes that "no one in the early Jerusalem Christian community, or in any other, would ever have dared to invent such a saying for Jesus. Jesus him-

---

24. *Introduction to the Theology of the NT*, p. 149.

25. Longenecker, *Christology of Early Jewish Christianity*, p. 96.

26. *Jesus and His Story*, trans. Richard and Clara Winston (New York: Alfred A. Knopf, 1960), p. 168; cf. A. M. Hunter, "Crux Criticorum—Matt. XI 25-30—a Reappraisal," *New Testament Studies* VIII (1962), pp. 241-49; P. T. Forsyth, *Person and Place of Jesus Christ*, p. 112: "Surely the Father and the Son here are both absolute terms. . . . The Father in his holy Eternity is meant and with such a Father the Son is *correlative*. Whatever is meant by the Father has its counterpart in the Son. If the one is an eternal Father the other is a co-eternal Son."

self and Jesus alone could have been so bold and so solitary, so free and independent, so absolutistic."[27] The bedrock truth in this affirmation is that a wholly reciprocal and deeply personal relationship existed between the Father and the Son.

B. Old Testament Insights

How shall the title "Son of God" be understood? The meaning in the Old Testament provides a basic insight for the New Testament interpretation. The phrase is employed there to indicate the special relationship of angels, kings, and righteous men to God. Most importantly, Israel is called God's son: "When Israel was a child I loved him, and out of Egypt I called my son" (Hos. 11:1). In the covenantal relationship God pledged himself to Israel, and the responsibility of Israel was to be obedient to God. Failure to obey resulted in the loss of sonship.

Alongside this covenantal and corporate understanding of sonship, the Old Testament speaks of the king of Israel, who is God's representative among the people, as God's son (2 Sam. 7:14; Ps. 2:7; cf. also Ps. 89:26-37). In the time of Jesus Judaism permitted the two ideas of Israel as God's son and the king as God's son to exist side by side. It would appear, as Longenecker suggests, that in Jesus "the corporate and royal Son-of-God motifs were brought together."[28] If so, He was not only Israel's Messiah King, but He was in fact the New Israel corporately because of his perfect obedience to the Father. He was the Son of God *par excellence.*

Christ becomes "the sole Israel of God" because of His unique obedience, which is clearly expressed in His prayer in the Garden of Gethsemane, "Not what I will, but what thou wilt" (Mark 14:36). Furthermore, in the parable of the wicked husbandmen (Mark 12:1-11) the "beloved son" is put to death. That act by the workers, symbolizing Israel, pictures at the same time the rejection of the Old Israel as "God's son." God's acclamation at the Baptism and the Transfiguration, "Thou art my beloved Son," might well be taken as signaling His rejection of the Old Israel and the creating of a New One in Christ.

C. The Church's Growing Understanding

It appears that the name "Son of God" bore only a Messianic mean-

---

27. *Jesus and His Story,* p. 169; cf. also Vincent Taylor, *The Names of Jesus* (London: Macmillan and Co., 1954), p. 64.

28. *Christology of Early Jewish Christianity,* p. 99.

ing for the disciples, and possibly for all the earliest followers. Certainly at the beginning of their relationship the disciples saw Jesus as a man wonderfully anointed with the Spirit for some divine purpose which they came to learn was His mission on the earth. Peter's confession includes the two terms "Son of God" and "Messiah" (Christ), but that does not necessarily mean that the disciples understood "Son of God" in the special sense that it held for Jesus. Sonship was no mere phase of His earthly existence nor just a circumlocution for Messiah. "He brought His sonship with him from heaven."

Thus Jesus himself understood fully His own nature as well as His mission, but the relationship of His person and Messianic mission did not come clear to the disciples until after His resurrection. As Son of God, Jesus fulfilled the mission of the Father in complete obedience. He was the long-awaited Messiah, but Messiahship did not make Him the Son nor vice-versa. He was both Messiah and Son in the uniqueness and absoluteness of His relationship to the Father. It was by reason of His Sonship that He was qualified for His office of Messiah. Messiahship of the type He fulfilled in His incarnate life called for One who was truly and specially a Son.

The Early Church saw the connection and began to speak of Christ in ontological terms. For example, John's Gospel, the last of the four to have been written, is an attempt to express the essential unity between the Father and the Son. The Evangelist preserves for us such explicit words as "I and the Father are one" (10:30); "that they may be one, even as we are one" (17:11); "Even as thou, Father, art in me, and I in thee" (17:21). Sonship in these instances connotes a unity of being as well as of spirit and purpose.

It is not necessary to claim with Vincent Taylor that the Messianic aspect of the name was eclipsed by the primitive community. Rather, the plus factor in the name (he sees it as being "Messianic with a plus") is illuminated by the Cross and Resurrection and thus comes to expression in the faith of the early community.[29]

The doctrinalizing process of the early community led to the free use of "Son of God" in explaining the person of Christ. For example, when Paul says that "in the fullness of the time God sent forth his Son," he has moved theologically well beyond the notion of Christ as

---

29. For discussions on the question of Christ's deity, cf. Vincent Taylor, "Does the New Testament Call Jesus God?" *The Expository Times*, LXIII (January, 1962); John A. Witwer, "Did Jesus Claim to Be God?" *Bibliotheca Sacra*, vol. 125 (April, 1968).

"the divinely commissioned national deliverer to the thought of one who comes to our world from the depths of the being of God."[30]

Also, John's use of the word *monogenēs* ("only begotten Son," John 1:14, 18; 3:16, 18; 1 John 4:9) suggests a heightened view of Christ as the Son of God. Although Leon Morris may be right when he says that we should not read too much into "only begotten,"[31] yet John is making a claim of absolute uniqueness for Jesus Christ. There is none other who has incorporated in His being the transcendent glory of God (John 1:14), just as an only son discloses what his father is like.

However, John 1:18, even with its textual problems, lifts the issue of relationship to a higher plane than just singularity. J. H. Bernard states that the terms "only," "God," and "he who is in the bosom of the Father" are three distinct descriptions of Him who makes God known.[32] So we might translate the relevant portion of the verse: "the only begotten Son, who is God, who is in the bosom of the Father, he has made him known." Contextually understood, *monogenēs*, like *prōtotokos* ("first-born," Col. 1:15), has the ring of deity in it. The participle *ōn* is a timeless present and speaks of Christ's relationship before incarnation. The word "bosom" *(kolpon)*, whether taken from the practice of friends reclining at a feast or from a father's embrace, denotes perfect intimacy. Thus, it seems impossible to avoid the idea of equality and identity of being in the word *monogenēs*. Jesus used this word in speaking of himself (John 3:16); and when the Church accepted it as meaning "divine," she was not in error.

We have acknowledged the exclusive sense in which Christ is the Son of God, but there is more. We must see that Christ "sought to be acknowledged son of God not as a result of His own authoritative

---

30. Vincent Taylor, *Names of Jesus,* p. 70.

31. "The Gospel According to John," *The New International Commentary on the New Testament* (Grand Rapids, Mich.: Wm. B. Eerdmans Publishing Co., 1971), p. 105; B. F. Westcott, *The Gospel According to St. John* (London: James Clarke and Co., Ltd., 1880), p. 12: "Christ is the One Only Son, the One to whom the title belongs in a sense completely unique and singular, as distinguished from that which there are many children of God"; cf. Richardson, *Introduction to the Theology of the NT,* p. 152, for a discussion of the relationship of *monogenēs* and *agapētos.*

32. *A Critical and Exegetical Commentary on the Gospel According to St. John* (New York: Charles Scribner's Sons, 1929), p. 31; cf. Raymond E. Brown, "The Gospel According to John," *Anchor Bible,* p. 17. On the textual problem, see Bruce M. Metzger, *A Textual Commentary on the Greek New Testament* (London and New York: United Bible Societies, 1971), p. 198.

pronouncements about Himself, but as a direct result of the unique impact of His life."³³ Stress should be laid therefore upon His redemptive acts among men as communicating His relationship to God. The dynamic nature of His life should not be overshadowed by a preoccupation with the metaphysical aspects. Jesus must be seen to be the Son of God as He "lived and moved and had His being" in the midst of men.

The Fourth Gospel expresses its purpose in such terms. "These are written that you may believe that Jesus is the *Christ*, the Son of God, and that believing you may have life in his name" (20:31). In both work and word, John hoped that his readers would see the Messianic, redeeming nature of Christ and thus come to faith in Him as God's Son. Taylor is correct when he writes, "Divinity is felt before it is named, and when it is named the words are inadequate."³⁴

IV. "I AM"

Throughout the Gospel material there are a number of references in which Jesus uses the pronoun "I" in such an emphatic way that with Jeremias we can only conclude that Jesus is saying something special about His status.³⁵ This "emphatic *egō*" appears in the six antitheses of the Sermon on the Mount (Matt. 5:21-48) in the very familiar and startling clause, "You have heard that it was said . . . but I say to you." By these words, Jesus not only sets himself above all the interpreters of the Torah, but, most importantly, above Moses. Contrary to Jeremias' claim that He set himself in opposition to the Torah, Jesus saw himself as its Fulfiller (Matt. 5:17). At one and the same time He cleansed it of the stultifying interpretations of Judaism and unfolded its deepest meaning.³⁶

When *egō* is combined with the Aramaic *'amēn* ("verily," "truly," "certainly"), we encounter an unprecedented usage. It is found 59 times in the four Gospels, with the largest number (25) in John. *'Amēn* apparently is used to add authority to the words of the speaker, and it has something of the force of the prophetic "Thus saith the Lord." In this instance, however, Jesus does not speak *for* God but *as*

33. Harry Hutchison, "Who Does He Think He Is?" *Scottish Journal of Theology*, XIV (September, 1961), p. 235.
34. *Names of Jesus*, p. 70.
35. *NT Theology*, pp. 251 ff.
36. *Ibid.*, p. 253; cf. H. D. A. Major, T. W. Manson, C. J. Wright, *The Mission and Message of Jesus* (New York: E. P. Dutton, 1938), pp. 445-46.

God. He is more than the greatest prophet; He is God incarnate, the very Source of the Word.

The "emphatic *egō*" appears in pronouncements of authority in healings (Mark 9:25); in the commissioning and sending of messengers (Matt. 10:16); in words of prophecy (cf. Luke 22:32); in the inauguration of the kingdom of God (Matt. 12:28; Luke 11:20). Also Jesus emphatically declares to His disciples, "I will build my church" (Matt. 16:18). The pronoun is not used with the verb "build" but the pronouncement is introduced with the authoritative clause, "And I tell you" *(kagō de soi legō)*.

The accusative "me" also carries the same force as the "I." It requires an exclusiveness in discipleship to Christ, even above loyalty to parents (Matt. 10:37). It also demands a full and unqualified listening to the words of Jesus (Matt. 7:24), and a recognition that Jesus is the Representative of the divine, for He says, "Whoever receives *me*, receives not *me* but him who sent *me*" (Mark 9:37, italics added; cf. also Matt. 10:40; Luke 9:48; John 12:44; 13:20). Many more intimations of this special use of *egō* are found in the Gospels, but these suffice to illuminate the self-testimony of Jesus.

The "I am's" *(egō eimi)* of the Fourth Gospel are unique, but they bear the same meaning and importance as the emphatic use of the pronoun "I" in the Synoptics. This phrase suggests Exod. 3:14, "I AM WHO I AM," the identifying declaration of Yahweh which was given to Moses. One must conjecture that Jesus in an oblique way was saying, "I am the God of Abraham, Isaac, and Jacob, and therefore the One who delivered Israel." On one occasion He declared to His Jewish opponents, "Before Abraham was, I am" (John 8:58).

Usually, the Lord cast His "I am" in the form of a metaphor which described some aspect of His saving work. Note the following from John's Gospel:

> "I am the bread of life" (6:35, 48).
> "I am the living bread" (6:51).
> "I am the light of the world" (8:12).
> "I am the door of the sheep" (10:7).
> "I am the good shepherd" (10:11).
> "I am the resurrection and the life" (11:25).
> "I am the way, the truth and the life" (14:6).
> "I am the true vine" (15:1).

Stephen Neill comments that "we might have expected Him to say, 'I give the bread of life,' 'I show you the way,' 'I tell you the truth;' but He does not. He cannot separate His message from himself. . . . He is himself the center of His own message and of the challenge that He brings."[37] These "I am" statements make the claim that Jesus can be and do for men what God alone can be and do for them. Moreover, as the affirmation "I am the good shepherd" broadly suggests, Jesus will be to His followers what Yahweh was to the people of the Old Testament, namely, the loving Protector, Guide, Nurturer, and Rescuer (cf. Ps. 23:4; Isa. 40:10-11; Ezek. 34:11-12, 18).

Ethelbert Stauffer sees in the *egō eimi* a self-revelatory formula that goes back to the ritual for the Feast of Tabernacles and the Passover liturgy in the Old Testament.[38] It is terminology used exclusively of God. Isaiah the prophet is influenced by this formula, because it appears several times in his oracles. When this theophanic formula is employed, it might simply be "I am" or "I am Yahweh" or "I am He." In the Hebrew language the words "I am He" are *ani huah* and *ani hu*; in the Aramaic *ana hu*. When translated into the Greek, they become *egō eimi.* No verb appears in the Hebrew; we have *ani* which means "I" and *huah* or *hu* which means "he." In the Semitic languages, the personal pronoun of the third person is frequently used for various forms of the copulative verb, i.e., "am," "are," "is." *Ani hu* can be properly translated, "I am He." However, in the Greek Bible the translation is preponderantly *egō eimi,* "I am."

Stauffer concludes that *egō eimi* in the Gospels is intended as a divine self-revelation. He cites Mark 13:6 as a precise example: "Many will come in my name, saying, 'I am He!' and they will lead many astray." Three times the *ani hu* formula is used by Jesus at the Feast of Tabernacles (John 8:24, 28, 58). He also employed it at the Feast of the Passover in response to the question of Caiaphas (Mark 14:62). Stauffer maintains that the source of the usage of these formulas is Jesus himself. "He wished to convey that in his life the historical epiphany of God was taking place. . . . Where I am, there God is, there God lives and speaks, calls, asks, acts, decides, loves, chooses, forgives, rejects, suffers, and dies. Nothing bolder can be said, or imagined."[39]

In conclusion, Christ's testimony about His identity rests mainly on the frequent use of the three titular phrases "Son of Man," "Son

---

37. *Who Is Jesus Christ?* (London: United Society for Christian Literature, 1956), p. 40.
38. *Jesus and His Story,* pp. 174-95.
39. *Ibid.,* pp. 192-94.

of God," and "I am." All three bear special meaning with respect to both His person and His mission in the world. Each one speaks of His singular relationship to God, including attributes reserved solely for Deity.

19

Foundation Motifs in the Early Church's Testimony

Unquestionably the Resurrection shed a bright ray of light on the person and work of the Lord. Johannes Weiss, Albert Schweitzer, and Rudolf Bultmann conjecture that the origin and development of the Christology of the New Testament must be attributed to the futuristic orientation of the Church. That is to say, the expectations and delay of the *parousia* moulded the thought of the Church regarding Christ. It is probably more correct to say that solid convictions about Christ were provoked by the impact of the Resurrection upon the minds and hearts of the early followers. Longenecker concludes, "While Jesus made a decided personal impact upon his disciples during the course of his earthly ministry, it was the fact of his resurrection from the dead, as interpreted first by Jesus himself and then by the Spirit, which was the historical point of departure in their christological understanding."[1]

The cruciality of the Resurrection for Christology is discernible in the fact that by it the disciples were able to put the Cross into perspective and to relate the whole of Jesus' ministry to it. A major element in Peter's Pentecost Day message is Christ's resurrection (Acts 2:22-36); and the Apostle Paul opens his major treatise on salvation by faith by declaring that "Jesus Christ our Lord" was "designated Son of God in power according to the Spirit of holiness

---

1. *Christology of Early Jewish Christianity*, p. 148.

by his resurrection from the dead" (Rom. 1:4). The Resurrection brought to the disciples a unified view of the life, teachings, and death of Christ, and it inspired them to be witnesses to Him. They not only knew who He was but also who they were to be as a result of this mighty deed of God.

It must be kept in mind, however, that the Resurrection as an interpreting event had its preconditioning in the teachings of Jesus. Both prior to and following the Resurrection, our Lord Jesus provided His witness to its meaning (Matt. 16:21; Mark 8:31-33; 9:30-32; 10:32-34; Luke 24:44-49; John 2:13-22). Some scholars have attributed to the Early Church almost total originality in its testimony to Christ. On the contrary, what the early community proclaimed with confidence about her Saviour was rooted in the teachings of Christ. E. G. Jay's assessment is solid: "We find it too great a psychological improbability to suppose that the early Church, or any member, or group of members of it, invented a Christology which attributed to Jesus a status of which he had given them no hint and had even denied."[2]

Two titles—"Lord" and "Christ"—became basic in the Early Church's witness to Jesus. So Peter preached, "Let all the house of Israel therefore know assuredly that God has made him both Lord and Christ, this Jesus whom you crucified" (Acts 2:36). The question as to whether "Christ" or "Lord" was the earliest and most formative affirmation of Jesus is somewhat pedantic.[3] It appears that in the post-Resurrection period several strands were woven into one grand commitment to Jesus as Israel's Saviour, and it was fully acceptable to declare either that "Jesus is the Christ" or "Jesus is Lord."

I. CHRIST-MESSIAH; SON OF DAVID

A. Christ-Messiah

The English word "Christ" is a transliteration of the Greek *Christos* which is derived from *chriō*, "to anoint." *Christos* is the term employed by biblical translators to render the Hebrew *mashiach* which means "anointed one." Transliterated, *mashiach* becomes *messiah*. The early Christians, in attaching the word "Christ" to the name "Jesus," were

---

2. *Son of Man, Son of God* (London: SPCK, 1965), p. 31.
3. Cf. Cullmann, *The Earliest Christian Confession*, trans. J. K. S. Reid (London: Lutterworth Press, 1949), pp. 27-30, 57-62; *Christology of the NT*, pp. 11, 215; Longenecker, *Christology of Early Jewish Christianity*, pp. 149 ff.

simply saying, "Jesus Messiah," or "Jesus the Anointed One." Very early, *messiah* or *christos* became a proper name. In Christian writings which are considered by scholars as being among the oldest, the appellation "Jesus Christ" is used without explanation (Gal. 1:1; 1 Thess. 1:1, *et al.*). Moreover, both Matthew and Mark announce that they are presenting the record of "Jesus Christ" (Matt. 1:1, 18; Mark 1:1). Thus, what was initially a title also became a name, the article having been dropped.

The use of *Christos* as a title is dominant in the Book of Acts, Matthew (12 times), John's Gospel (approximately 12 times), John's letters (3 times), the Apocalypse (twice), Hebrews (6 times), and in 1 Peter (5 times). *Christos* appears several times in the last two books as a name, but the most frequent usage is titular. For the most part, whenever Paul's letters are addressed to non-Jewish readers, the word is employed as a name. This is also true of Luke's writings and Mark's.

The question of major importance at this point is whether or not Jesus understood himself to be the Messiah of God and whether He openly communicated this fact to His followers.

In dealing with the question, it is necessary, first of all, to note the messianic expectations of the Jews. In Hebrew literature and especially in the Old Testament, the term *mashiach* is used to designate individuals who are called of God for special divine missions. Among this group are found patriarchs, priests (Exod. 28:41), prophets (1 Kings 19:16), but especially kings. The king in the Old Testament was denominated the Lord's "Anointed" (Ps. 18:50; cf. 1 Sam. 2:10, 35; 24:6; 26:9, 11, 16, 23). The pouring of the sacred oil upon him by the priest was symbolic of the coming of the Spirit of God upon him.

The failure of the kings of Israel to bring about the "good times of God" evoked the hope of a coming ideal King who would fulfill the hopes of Israel. Deliverance from Israel's enemies and the consequent introduction of the eschatological age of peace were the expectations of the messianism of Judaism in the period prior to Christ's coming. Within this general framework, a variety of conceptions of the nature and function of the Messiah prevailed.[4] However, the controlling notion was nationalistic, for the Jews anticipated

4. Cf. F. F. Bruce, "Messiah," *NBD*, pp. 811-18; E. Jenni, "Messiah," *Interpreter's Dictionary of the Bible*, George A. Buttrick, ed. (Nashville: Abingdon Press, 1962), 3:360-65.

a messiah who would be of the lineage of David. He would do his work upon this earth, either creating a permanent order or an interim order of peace before the inauguration of the final kingdom of God.

Because of this inflammatory dogma of the Messiah, it is understandable why Jesus avoided the use of the term in speaking of himself and cautioned others not to refer to him messianically (Matt. 17:9 and par.; Mark 1:44; 5:43; 7:36; 8:26; Luke 4:41).

However, on occasion His Messiahship was clearly expressed. When He visited His home synagogue in Nazareth, He read to His countrymen Isa. 61:1-2 in which the word "anointed" is used by the prophet (Luke 4:16-21). He announced to the people: "Today this scripture has been fulfilled in your hearing" (4:21). By using the word "anointed," He implied that He was the Messiah, the Anointed One. This particular saying, however, describes a Messiah not in keeping with the nationalistic expectations of the Jews but in keeping with the "Ebed Yahweh" (Servant of the Lord).[5]

Jesus' reticence in being called the Messiah or in speaking of himself in Messianic ways is an uncontestable fact. The three most frequently mentioned Synoptic passages upon which the evidence rests are (1) Peter's confession (Matt. 16:13-20; Mark 8:27-30; Luke 9:18-21); (2) Caiaphas' question, "Are you the Christ?" (Matt. 26:57-66; Mark 14:53-64); (3) Pilate's question: "Are you the King of the Jews?" (Matt. 27: 11-14; Mark 15:2-5; Luke 23:3; John 18:33-38). In each case Jesus shows an unmistakable element of caution. He warns the disciples, in the first instance, that they are "to tell no one that he was the Christ" (Matt. 16:20). In the two other cases, the answer is thrown back to the questioners, but Jesus does not explicitly deny that He is the Christ.

However, in the encounter with Caiaphas He goes on immediately to talk about the Son of Man. Obviously, Jesus is not trying to refute the Messianic confession; rather, He is seeking to avoid a public confrontation which an open declaration might have precipitated.

In the spiritual setting, alone with His disciples, He obliquely acknowledges that He is the long-awaited Messiah. What they proclaimed about Christ's Messiahship in the days following the

---

5. Cf. W. C. van Unnik, "Jesus the Christ," *New Testament Studies,* VIII (1962), 113-16. Jesus' application of Isa. 61:1-2 to himself and the evident anointing of the Spirit upon His life were instructive to His disciples on the matter of Messiahship.

Resurrection was predicated on such experiences with the historical Christ.

John preserves for us the remarkable conversation of Jesus with the woman at Jacob's well in Samaria (John 4:1-30). This theological dialogue at one point turns to the Messianic question. She leads: "I know that Messiah is coming (he who is called Christ); when he comes, he will show us all things." In response, Jesus straightforwardly identifies himself as the Messiah: "I who speak to you am he" (4:25-26).

Some scholars, following Wrede, assert that the "messianic secret" was a creation of Mark. In answer, it must be stated candidly that the Gospel record does not support this view. The accounts of Jesus' baptism, temptation, and transfiguration, along with His responses to Peter, the high priest, and the Samaritan woman, clearly teach that Jesus understood himself to be the Messiah of God. His ministry was thus the fulfillment of the Messianic hopes of His people.[6] His view of himself as the Messiah was devoid of the usual nationalistic element, however, though certainly not the fact of kingship. Cullmann concludes:

> In so far as Jesus was conscious of having to fulfill the task of the people of Israel, it does not contradict his conception of his vocation if he did accept also the concept of kingship in such a way that it had a new content for him—if he thought in terms of a "kingdom not of this world", as the Gospel of John describes it.[7]

B. Son of David

A corollary idea to the Messiah concept is expressed in the appellation "Son of David." The genealogies of Matthew and Luke clearly demonstrate the Davidic ancestry of Jesus (cf. Matt. 1:1). In the Gospel accounts, Jesus is hailed as the "Son of David" by blind Bartimaeus (Mark 10:47) and by the crowd on the occasion of the Triumphal Entry (Matt. 21:9; Mark 11:10). Our Lord did not attempt to stop these accolades.

The only recorded instance in which Jesus related himself to

6. Cf. W. Wrede, *Das Messiasgeheimnis in den Evangelien* (Gottingen: Vanderhoeck and Ruprecht, 1901); G. Bornkamm, *Jesus of Nazareth*, trans. Irene and Fraser McLuskey with James M. Robinson (New York: Harper and Row, 1960), pp. 171 ff.; R. H. Fuller, *Foundations of New Testament Christology* (New York: Charles Scribner's Sons, 1965), pp. 109-11; cf. Cullmann's reaction to both Wrede and Bultmann, who followed Wrede: *Christology of the NT*, pp. 124-25.

7. *Christology of the NT*, p. 133.

326 / God, Man, and Salvation

David was in the remarkable word in Mark 12:35-37. At that moment He was teaching in the Temple and He queried: "How can the scribes say that the Christ is the son of David?" He answered His own question by quoting Ps. 110:1: "The Lord said to my Lord, Sit at my right hand, till I put thy enemies under thy feet." The Master then questioned whether David would address his own son as "Lord."

While Jesus obviously was challenging the current views on the Son-of-David understanding of Messiahship, He was not denying His own Davidic descent. The issue in the challenge is that the Messiah whom David called his Lord must be greater than David. His origin cannot be from David, but must be from Someone higher than David.

Certainly, the Early Church had no doubts about Christ's lineage from David. For one thing, as we have already noted, the genealogies of Matthew and Luke demonstrate that He was the Son of David (Matt. 1:1-17; Luke 3:23-38). Paul also finds some importance in this Davidic relationship, for he uses it in his famous message at Antioch of Pisidia (Acts 13:22-23) and in listing the basic elements of his gospel concerning God's Son, "who was descended from David according to the flesh" (Rom. 1:3; cf. also 2 Tim. 2:8). The Apocalypse likewise refers to the Davidic descent in liturgical terms, heralding Jesus as having "the key of David" (3:7), and being "the Root of David" (5:5; 22:16).

It is reasonable to conclude from the New Testament materials that (1) the Davidic descent of Jesus is "firmly embedded in the Christian tradition from an early date"[8]; and (2) the Christian community sought to maintain a continuity with the Old Testament prophecy regarding the Messiah, who for them was unquestionably Jesus. According to 2 Sam. 7:16, David was promised: "Your house and your kingdom shall be made sure for ever before me; your throne shall be established for ever." Isaiah, Micah, Jeremiah, Ezekiel, and Zechariah all foster the Davidic messianology. The Early Christians viewed Jesus as greater than any of His predecessors in Israel's history, even David; but at the same time, they saw Him as fulfilling all the expectations of the Davidic, Messianic redemption of the people. To this degree a continuity exists between David the king and "the Son of David."

In the Early Church all the reserve of Jesus with respect to the use of the term *Messiah* disappears. In the light of her experience of

---

8. Longenecker, *Christology of Early Jewish Christianity*, p. 109.

His resurrection and her expectation of His second coming, the Church forthrightly declared, "Jesus is the Messiah." Moreover, as we have shown above, in His lifetime Jesus acknowledged that He was the Messiah; and so what the Early Church proclaimed regarding His Messiahship was continuous with His own self-consciousness. The Book of Acts is a major witness to the Christian proclamation of Jesus as the promised Messiah. On the Day of Pentecost, the Apostle Peter preached that David foretold the resurrection of "the Christ" (Acts 2:31) and the next day he preached that "all the prophets spoke of God's Christ needing to suffer" (3:18). The evangelistic activities of early believers are summarized in 5:42: "And every day in the temple and at home they did not cease teaching and preaching Jesus as the Christ." The leading preachers of the youthful movement made Christ the essence of their message: Philip preached "the Christ" to the Samaritans (Acts 8:5); Paul preached "the Christ" to the people in Damascus (Acts 9:22), Thessalonica (17:3), and Corinth (18:5); and Apollos preached Jesus as Christ to the people in Ephesus (18:28).

What conclusions can be drawn from this study of the Messiah motif?

1. Jesus permitted others to apply the words *Christos* and "Son of David" to himself but He cautioned them not to noise it abroad. Only on one occasion did He identify himself as "the Christ" (John 4:26).

2. He vigorously rejected the idea of a nationalistic king-redeemer, which had become attached to the title. He turned, rather, to Isaiah's "suffering Servant Songs" to describe the character of God's Messiah (cf. Matt. 16:13-23, *et al.*).

3. While He is listed in the Gospels as descended from David genetically, He is also declared to be greater than David (Matt. 22:41-45; Mark 12:35-37; Luke 20:41-44; cf. Acts 2:29-36).

4. The Resurrection experience of the followers of Christ convinced them of His Messiahship, and so they immediately began to preach openly that He was Israel's long-awaited Messiah (Acts 2:36). Their conviction concerning this rested squarely upon *His Messianic consciousness, His enduement with the Spirit, and His teachings.*

The declaration that "Jesus is the Christ" would naturally draw an angry rejoinder from the Jewish community. They took literally the scripture which reads, "Cursed be everyone who hangs on a tree" (Gal. 3:13). But the impact of Jesus' own self-consciousness and the miracle of the Resurrection enabled the Early Church to accept His crucifixion as an integral part of His Messianic nature and mission.

5. What was at first only a title soon became a permanent name. Both Cullmann and Longenecker are correct in assuming that the movement of Christianity into the Gentile world, where the Jewish preoccupation with messianism did not prevail, brought about the denominative use of the word "Messiah" or "Christ."[9]

II. LORD

The earliest creed of the Christian Church was "Jesus is Lord." Paul writes to the Romans, "If you confess with your lips that Jesus is Lord and believe in your heart that God has raised him from the dead, you will be saved" (10:9). He tells the Corinthians that this confession, "Jesus is Lord," cannot be made by anyone except by the assistance of the Holy Spirit (1 Cor. 12:3). For Paul the self-emptying and humiliation of "Christ Jesus" led to His exaltation. As a result "at the name of Jesus every knee should bow, in heaven and earth and under the earth, and every tongue confess that Jesus Christ is Lord, to the glory of God the Father" (Phil. 2:5-11). In the developing Christology of the Church, the various titles ascribed to Jesus were blended so that Paul can employ consistently the unique appellation "our Lord Jesus Christ" *(Kurios Jēsous Christos).*

A. Definition and Use of "Kurios" in the Gospels

The Greek word *kurios,* either with or without the article, occurs over 240 times in the Gospels. The importance of its frequency, however, is obscured because several English words are needed to translate its various shades of meaning.[10] Sometimes it is used as a word of respect, such as "sir" (Matt. 21:30); a title of authority, "master" (Matt. 15:27), or a title of possession, "owner" (Luke 19:33). The fundamental significance of these instances is its description of ownership or authority over persons or things, hence demanding reverence and deference.

Jesus is frequently addressed as "Lord," the vocative case, *kurie,* being employed. For example, Peter is recorded as pleading, "Lord, if it is you, bid me come to you on the water" (Matt. 14:28).

---

9. *Christology of the NT,* p. 133; Longenecker, *Christology of Early Jewish Christianity,* pp. 75 ff.

10. Werner Foerster and Gottfreid Quell, *Kurios et al.* TDNT, 3:1039 ff.

Jesus even refers to himself in this manner: "Not every one who says to me, 'Lord, Lord,' shall enter the kingdom of heaven" (Matt. 7:21). This vocative use of the word appears numerous times in John's Gospel, especially in the sections where conversations between Jesus and His disciples are recorded. Unquestionably, the vocative *kurie* represents profound respect, but on occasion it goes further and conveys a worshipful acclamation, as in the faith of the blind man cured by Jesus, "Lord, I believe" (John 9:38).

There are numerous occurrences of the word with the article *(ho kurios)* in Luke (18 times) and John (12 times). Longenecker, following Vincent Taylor, observes that the instances of "the Lord" in Luke are found in narrative sections and in John for the most part in post-Resurrection sections. Apparently the Evangelist John did not feel at liberty to use "the Lord" in its titular sense in the earlier ministry of Jesus.[11]

A most remarkable instance of "the Lord" comes from the lips of Jesus in the Upper Room: "You call me Teacher and Lord *[ho didaskalos kai ho kurios]*" (John 13:13). John's magnificent portrayal of the struggle of faith and unfaith is preserved for us in the climactic declaration of Thomas, "My Lord and my God *[ho kurios mou kai ho theos mou]*" (John 20:28).

Kurios was applied to the rabbis in that day. It is a valid assumption, therefore, that the disciples of Jesus were showing Him at least the same respect that the disciples of the rabbis accorded their teachers. Rawlinson, however, concludes that *kurios* bears more than the conventional politeness and honor due a teacher. He writes: "It implies, strictly speaking, that he [rabbi] is *more* than a 'teacher'— that he is in fact a 'lord' who has the rights of a 'lord' over his disciples."[12] Rawlinson goes on to assert, however, that it is doubtful that the disciples viewed Jesus simply as a rabbi. Rather, when they spoke of Him as "Lord," they were thinking of Him as the exalted Messiah.[13]

It appears that the Gospels, especially in the sections which give us insight into the relationship between Jesus and the disciples, preserve for us an embryonic Christology arising out of the title

11. *The Christology of Early Jewish Christianity*, pp. 130-31; cf. V. Taylor, *Names of Jesus*, p. 43.

12. A. E. J. Rawlinson, *New Testament Doctrine of the Christ* (London: Longmans, Green, and Co., 1926), p. 234.

13. *Ibid.*

"Lord." The suggestion of Rawlinson with respect to the investment of Messianic connotations in the word *kurios* is proper. Jesus' discussion of Ps. 110:1 (Matt. 22:45; Mark 12:37; Luke 20:44) strongly supports the idea that He thought of himself as "the Lord"; and furthermore, the frequent citation of this verse by the early followers indicates that it carried more than ordinary meaning. Jesus' references to himself as "Lord of the Sabbath" (Mark 2:28) and "your Lord" (Matt. 24:42), combined with the facts mentioned above, provided the raw material for a *kurios* Christology.[14] Christ's divine Lordship blossoms into explicit terms in Peter's proclamation at Pentecost, "God has made him both Lord and Christ, this Jesus whom you crucified" (Acts 2:36).

B. The Use of "Kurios" Outside of the Gospels

The title "Lord" appears in the Epistles 46 times. The central thrust is that of divine sovereignty (cf. Rom. 10:12; 14:8-9; 1 Cor. 5:4; 2 Cor. 10:8; Phil. 2:11, 19; 1 Thess. 4:6). Unquestionably the simple concept of respect or ownership has been displaced by a full recognition of Jesus' deity. Thus, the writers understand that as Lord, Jesus the Christ can rightfully claim from men an utter devotion, loyalty, reverence, and worship of the heart. So 1 Pet. 3:15 exhorts, "But in your hearts reverence [*hagiasate,* literally 'sanctify'] Christ as Lord."

Wilhelm Bousset has maintained that the application of the title *kurios* to Jesus first took place upon Greek soil. The "significant transition" is inconceivable at any stage earlier than that of Hellenistic Christianity.[15] This theory is based upon the notion that the Greek world was not unfamiliar with the *kurios* concept, for the mystery religions applied the term to their deities, e.g., *Kurios Mythra.* On official inscriptions, the Roman emperors, Nero and Caligula, were designated *Kurios.* Thus Bousset and others have concluded that the Greek-speaking church introduced the worship of Jesus as *Kurios.*

Two lines of evidence can be raised in opposition to this hypothesis. First, the Greek translators of the Old Testament (the Septuagint) fairly consistently employed *kurios* in rendering the two divine names *Yahweh* and *Adonai.*[16] Occasionally they used the Greek *Theos.*

14. Cf. David M. Kay, *Glory at the Right Hand: Psalm 110 in Early Christianity* (New York: Abingdon Press, 1973).

15. *Kyrios Christos,* trans. John E. Steely (New York: Abingdon Press, 1970), pp. 121 ff.; cf. Rudolf Bultmann, *Theology of the NT,* 1:125 ff.

16. For a thorough study of this point, cf. G. Quell, TDNT, 3:1058 ff.; Sherman E. Johnson, "Lord (Christ)," IDB, 3:151: "To an early Christian accustomed to reading the

A Greek-speaking Jew would hear the Christian missionaries calling Christ *Kurios,* the term which he would naturally associate with his God. It is most reasonable to assume with Rawlinson that the acclamation of Jesus as Lord goes back to the original Christianity of Palestine, indeed to the teachings of Jesus.[17] Furthermore, the Jewish Christians, and especially the disciples, had been nurtured on the faith of the Old Testament and thus were easily able following the Resurrection to make the application of *Kurios* to Jesus. To them He was the Divine One.

Second, in the New Testament there are several Aramaic expressions for Deity, such as *Abba,* "Father" (Rom. 8:15; Gal. 4:6) and *Eli,* "My God" (Matt. 27:46). But for this study the most important one is *Marana Tha,* "Our Lord, Come!" (1 Cor. 16:22; cf. also Rev. 22:20, *Erchou, kurie Jēsou,* "Come, Lord Jesus!").[18] This prayer is found also in the *Didache,* dated about A.D. 95. Although it appears in the Greek-speaking church, as indicated by the references in 1 Corinthians and in the Apocalypse, that does not preclude its origination in Palestine. In fact, "Since *maranatha* was preserved as an Aramaic formula even in Greek-speaking churches we must assume that it originated as a christological ascription in the early Aramaic-speaking Church."[19] This is the most natural conclusion, "for it would hardly have been retained untranslated in a Greek text had it originated as the translation of a more primary Greek term."[20]

We conclude that Jesus was called "Lord" in the Palestinian Church before the Church went out on Gentile soil. In the earliest recoverable period, Jesus is presented as the Object of man's worship. In the case of Stephen, the first martyr, prayer is addressed to Jesus: "Lord Jesus, receive my spirit" (Acts 7:59). The Eucharist soon became known as the "Lord's Supper" (*Kuriakos deipnos,* 1 Cor. 11:20), and the Christian's day of worship "the Lord's Day" (*Kuriakē hēmēra,* Rev. 1:10).

OT, the word 'Lord', when used of Jesus, would suggest his identification with the God of the OT." One cannot follow Johnson's logic, however, when he says the *Kurios* "expressed Christ's divinity without explicitly asserting his deity."

17. *NT Doctrine of Christ,* pp. 231-37; cf. his excellent refutation of Bousset.

18. Early MSS were written without separation of words, and for that reason *marana tha* could be taken as *maran atha,* "Our Lord has come." The prayer for His coming seems, however, to make better sense in the context.

19. W. Kramer, *Christ, Lord, Son of God,* trans. B. Hardy (London: SCM Press, 1966), p. 100.

20. Longenecker, *Christology of Early Jewish Christians,* p. 122; cf. Cullmann, *Christology of the NT,* p. 214.

The seedbed for the acclamation and worship of Christ as Lord is Jesus himself, and the reflections of the early Jewish Church rest upon the words of the Lord. Following the Easter event, the Early Church began to grasp what Jesus' treatment of Ps. 110:1 (Matt. 22:44; 26:64; Acts 2:34) and His use of *kurios* meant, especially as they continued to explore their affirmation that "Jesus is Lord."

The Gentile church engaged in its mission with even greater commitment to the announcement that "Jesus is Lord," and it appears from the biblical record that Christ's Lordship was more frequently employed by her than by the Jewish Christian community, which tended to emphasize the Messiahship of Jesus.

McDonald's summary of the use of the titles "Christ" and "Lord" is correct: "To the Jewish Christians Jesus was Messiah; to the Hellenistic Christian Jew He was 'The Christ'; to the Gentile Christian He was 'The Lord'. And all three are combined in the familiar name, 'The Lord Jesus Christ.'"[21]

III. THE WISDOM OF GOD

Paul develops the concept of Christ as "the Wisdom of God" primarily in Corinthians, where he struggles to set the gospel in perspective vis-a-vis Greek thought. He asserts that the Greeks seek wisdom, a creature of the mind of man. In contrast, "those who are called, both Jews and Greeks," seek "Christ the power of God and the wisdom of God *[sophia theou]*' (1 Cor. 1:24, 30; cf. the entire passage, 1 Cor. 1:17—2:16). Wisdom in this context is to be construed not as speculative understanding but rather as gifted insight. In this case, the wisdom is proffered through a person, Jesus Christ, who in the totality of His person and work reveals the mind of God. Man's search for understanding of the Beyond (his metaphysical quest) can be satisfied only in knowing Christ.

In the Ephesian letter, the apostle declares that God "has made known to us in all wisdom and insight the mystery of his will, according to his purpose which he set forth in Christ as a plan for the fullness of time, to unite all things in him, things in heaven and things on earth" (1:9-10). Moreover, Paul expresses his pastoral desires for the Christians throughout the Asian church in his Epistle to the Colossians: "That their hearts may be encouraged as they are

21. H. D. McDonald, *Jesus, Human and Divine* (Grand Rapids, Mich.: Zondervan Publishing House, 1968), p. 101.

knit together in love, to have all the riches of assured understanding *[sophias]* and the knowledge of God's mystery, of Christ, in whom are hid all the treasures of wisdom and knowledge" (2:2-3).

Paul's *Wisdom Christology* might well have been rooted (1) in Christ's allusions to himself as "Wisdom" (Matt. 11:19; Luke 11:49) and (2) in the apostolic consciousness that Christ was "the *new Torah,* the complete revelation of God's will, replacing the old law." In this connection, too, his Christological piece in Col. 1:15-20 suggests the personified and hypostatized "Wisdom" of Prov. 8:22-31. Paul's *Wisdom* functions dynamically, assisting in the creation of the cosmos (Col. 1:16-17) and providing redemption for mankind (1 Cor. 1:24, 30). When he preaches Christ, Paul really preaches "wisdom"—the spiritual insight that provides redemption. Christ is the Wisdom of God, which is further defined as "our righteousness and sanctification and redemption"[22] (1 Cor. 1:30).

IV. THE WORD

Three places in the Johannine corpus the title "the Word" *(ho logos)* or "the Word of God" *(ho logos tou theou)* is used to express the nature of Christ (John 1:1, 14; 1 John 1:1; Rev. 19:13). The principal passage is in John 1 where the *Logos* is declared (1) to have been at the creation with God (1:1); (2) to have the God nature (1:1); (3) to have functioned co-creatively with God in bringing into existence the world (1:3); and (4) to have been enfleshed and to have resided among men (1:14).

Scholars have wrestled with the intended meaning of *logos.* From the Jewish background, we receive some help from the phrase "the word of Yahweh" *(dabar Yahweh).* A *dabar,* "word," is more than a sound; it is "a unit of energy and of effective power. A word did not only *say* things, a word *did* things."[23] When God spoke, the implied action transpired. God spoke and the cosmos came into being (Gen. 1:2, 6, 9, 11, 14, 20, 24, 26). God's word goes forth to accomplish its purpose; it does not return to Him void of action (Isa. 55:11). Action is implicit in the speaking. To speak of Jesus as the Logos of God is to

---

22. Cf. David A. Hubbard, "Wisdom," *New Bible Dictionary* (Grand Rapids, Mich.: Wm. B. Eerdmans Publishing Co., 1962), pp. 113-34; W. D. Davies, *Paul and Rabbinic Judaism* (London: SPCK, 1948), pp. 147-76.

23. William Barclay, *Jesus as They Saw Him* (New York: Harper and Row, 1962), p. 422.

say that He is more than the voice of God; it is to say that He is the dynamic and creative Power of God in action.

The Greeks in hearing the word *logos* would probably think of the "mind" or "reason." The *logos* as applied to Christ would mean for them that "the mind of God" was revealed in Christ. But apart from this translation would be the image concept. A Jew with a semi-Greek mentality, such as Philo, the Alexandrian religious philosopher, might hear "image" when the word *logos* would be used.[24]

It is obvious that a certain ambiguity of definition prevails. Nevertheless, it would appear that John wished to convey dimensions of the nature of Christ which had only been hinted at earlier.[25] Christ is the Message of God to men; He is the Gospel in himself, God's Good News of redemption (cf. Heb. 1:1-2). He gives us the mind of God, which is obsessed with one objective, namely, the redemption of His creatures (1:1-13).

The Logos of God is creative, not only in establishing the universe, but in making sons unto God. At the heart of the universe is a creative, loving Person. In a summarizing response to the question, What is the Logos? Conzelmann takes note of the relationship of word to the revealer. "The point is that the word is not detached from the revealer so that it can be communicated as free content. It is based exclusively on his existence, and therefore cannot be taught and learned as knowledge. Anyone who has the person, i.e. who believes in him, has salvation."[26]

As Cullmann insists, while the Evangelist has in mind to emphasize the *function* of the Word—His *action*—he begins the Prologue by referring to the *being* of the Word before the creation. "The Word was God" means that "the Logos is God in his revelation." Also, to avoid the concept of two gods, as if the Logos were a god apart from

---

24. Cf. C. H. Dodd who concludes that John's *Logos* doctrine is similar in substance to that of Philo: *The Interpretation of the Fourth Gospel* (Cambridge: University Press, 1953), pp. 263-85.

25. Leon Morris' conclusion is judicious: "While John uses a term which was widely familiar, and which would convey a meaning to men of very diverse backgrounds, his thought is essentially Christian. When he speaks of Jesus as the *Logos* he does but put the coping stone on an edifice that was being erected throughout the New Testament." Morris finds the use of *logos* throughout the Synoptics and later portions of John's Gospel to indicate the gospel in its personalized meaning in Christ as instructive in understanding John's use of the term in his prologue. Cf. "The Gospel According to John," *The New International Commentary on the New Testament* (Grand Rapids, Mich.: Wm. B. Eerdmans Publishing Co., 1971), pp. 115-26.

26. Hans Conzelmann, *An Outline of the Theology of the New Testament,* trans. by John Bowden (New York: Harper and Row, 1969), p. 336.

God, John writes, "The Word was with God." No view of subordination is suggested here, else John would perhaps have written that "God was with the Word." Admittedly, this relationship is paradoxical, but it must stand as written that Christ was both *with God* and *was God*. The term "Logos" not only declares the divine nature of Christ but expresses also the self-revealing and self-giving redemptive action of God.

V. PROPHET

In His self-revealing and self-giving ministry, Christ fulfills prophetic, priestly, and kingly roles. As Prophet, He declares the divine truth in His life, death, and resurrection. In centuries past, God spoke through His specially called prophets, but in this age He has spoken His Word in this special One, the Christ (Heb. 1:1-2). During His earthly ministry, Jesus was acclaimed as having a ministry like the prophets. When they listened to His messages, some of His hearers thought of Elijah, others of John the Baptist, or Jeremiah (Mark 6:14-15; Luke 9:8). When Jesus rode into Jerusalem on an ass during one day of the last week of His earthly life, the crowds responded to the question, Who is this? by answering, "This is the prophet Jesus from Nazareth of Galilee" (Matt. 21:11; cf. Luke 7:16; 24:19).

The Gospel record clearly demonstrates that Jesus bore the marks of a prophet in the fact of His consciousness of having been *sent* from God, in calling men to immediate decision, and in offering a radical solution to the deteriorating religious life of the old Israel. He spoke with an inherent authority (Matt. 7:28-29) and He was recognized by Nicodemus as "a teacher come from God" (John 3:2).

The most important prophetological note (Cullmann's term) is recorded in the Fourth Gospel, following Christ's feeding of the 5,000. The people conclude, "This is indeed the prophet who is to come into the world" (6:14; 7:40). "The prophet" cannot be other than a reference to Moses' prediction of such a revealer of God's Word (Deut. 18:15, 18). Both Peter and Stephen employ the same passage in offering an *apologia* for the youthful Christian faith (Acts 3:22-23; 7:37). They apparently considered Christ the Fulfillment of the Mosaic word.

This prophetic role emphasizes Christ's divine mission. He comes from God under specific order, not only to *declare* the divine Word, but to *be* the divine Word of grace and righteousness. However, to focus only on His prophetic ministry would be to truncate the meaning of the Incarnation. Christ was indeed the climax of the prophetic succession, but He was at the same time both the Subject and the Object of prophecy. He functioned as the Bearer of God's redemptive Word; He also inspired all prophetic utterances of the past. More important, He was the Central Focus of all prophecy—the One to whom all the prophets pointed as God's eschatological word of salvation. In Him the truth of God was spoken personally, historically, and finally.[27]

VI. PRIEST

While the designation of Christ as the true High Priest is distinctive of the Epistle to the Hebrews, a plausible case can be developed for the view that in the Gospels Jesus presented himself as High Priest. Twice He refers to Psalm 110 with respect to the Messiah (Mark 12:35 ff.; 14:62). Psalm 110:1 reads: "The Lord said unto my Lord, Sit Thou at my right hand, until I make thine enemies thy footstool." Psalm 110:4b reads: "You are a priest for ever after the order of Melchizedek." Mark 12:35 may be a correction of scribal understanding of the meaning of "Son of David" and "Messiah." But, as Stagg suggests, "Possibly he also claimed here to be the 'High Priest after the order of Melchizedek,' a High Priest whom he thus related to the Christ."[28]

In John 17, which was called "the High-Priestly prayer" by Chytraeus in the sixteenth century, Jesus "sanctifies" or "consecrates" himself, in the same sense that a Hebrew priest prepared himself for office. He engages in this act in behalf of His disciples (cf. Luke 22:32). Richardson reminds us that Jesus is presented as providing access to God. He is "the way" (hē hodos, John 14:6), and He has opened up a new and living way to the Father (Heb. 10:20). It follows that the earliest Christians should naturally refer to themselves as those of the Way (Acts 9:2; 19:9; 22:4).

The idea of "access" with priestly overtones appears in the Greek word prosagōgē, which denotes an introduction into someone's presence, generally a person of some esteem. Three times the word

27. Cf. Cullmann, Christology of the NT, pp. 13 ff.; G. Friedrich, "Prophētēs," TDNT, 6:829 ff.
28. NT Theology, p. 71; cf. Cullmann's theory that Jesus at the time of His appearance before Caiaphas (Mark 15:62) strongly implied that He was High Priest, but not an earthly one (Christology of the NT, pp. 88 ff.).

appears in the Pauline writings and in each case it implies the office of a priest (Rom. 5:2; Eph. 2:18; 3:12). In Rom. 8:34, Paul declares through a rhetorical query that Christ is at the right hand of God interceding for the elect (cf. parallel in Heb. 7:25). Peter is explicit when he writes, "For Christ also died for sins once for all . . . that he might bring [prosagōgē] us to God" (1 Pet. 3:18). He goes on to assert the Son's descensus into the place of imprisoned spirits but who now "has gone into heaven and is at the right hand of God" (3:22). In the Apocalypse "one like a son of man" is clothed in the garments of a priest (1:13).

As noted above, the mediatorial activity of Christ, accomplished through his High Priesthood, is most broadly expressed in the Epistle to the Hebrews. No less than 10 times the author employs the title "the high priest" (2:17; 3:1; 4:14-15; 5:5, 10; 6:20; 7:26; 8:1; 9:11). Jesus is also designated simply "priest" in 5:6 and "a great priest" in 10:21. Following carefully his typological schema, the author asserts the eternality of Christ's sacerdotal function, for He is "a priest after the order of Melchizedek" (5:6).[29] There is no record of Melchizedek's birth or death; he appears only as a priest, and Abraham paid tithes to him. So Jesus appears without special genetic relationship or legal enactment. He "has neither beginning of days nor end of life" (7:3), thus remaining "a priest for ever" (7:3). He is therefore "able to make expiation for the sins of the people" (2:17).

The ministry of the Aaronic high priest was imperfectly exercised under the Old Covenant. The ministry of Christ, on the other hand, is completely and effectively executed because of His simultaneous identification with mankind and with the Godhead. He is tempted in every respect (kata panta) and for that reason qualifies as Mediator for mankind. He goes into the heavenly sanctuary, "taking not the blood of goats and calves but his own blood, thus securing an eternal redemption" (9:12). This is a "once for all" act on the part of the High Priest, because "he always lives" (7:24-25) and He now stands in the presence of God to intercede for us.

He will come again, not for the purpose of offering a sacrifice for sin, but to take unto himself those who have been faithfully waiting for Him (9:24-28). Enthroned at the right hand of God as Priest-

29. Cf. David M. Kay, Glory at the Right Hand, pp. 130 ff., for a full discussion on Melchizedek in Jewish and Christian traditions. Kay sees Heb. 1:3 as thematic in the Epistle's Christology. "He sat down at the right hand of the majesty on high" and, "having made purification for sins," announced the chief themes of the Epistle, i.e., exaltation and atonement, p. 143.

King, His life is one of continual intercession for us. Stagg comments: "He is not just a high Priest alone with God in the holy of holies; he is a Person, joined together with those whom he takes into the presence of God."[30]

The priestly role of Christ therefore is a profound expression of grace—the act of Christ in bestowing, by means of His mediation, the benefits of the divine love upon all who come believingly to Him.[31]

VII. KING

A. The King Concept in the Gospels

In the Gospel accounts, Jesus is declared to be the Bringer or Manifestation of the kingdom of God, but in that part of the New Testament, the concept of king is not openly applied to Him. He is presented as more than an example of one who was living under the sovereignty of God, but He is not hailed as King of the cosmos or Lord of all. Though there are passing references to Him as King, these declarations for the most part are overlaid with the contemporary Messianic concepts. For example, the Fourth Gospel includes the confession of Nathanael, "Rabbi, you are the Son of God! You are the King of Israel!" (1:49). After the feeding of the 5,000, Jesus withdrew into the mountains to escape the crowds who were about to "take him by force to make him king" (6:15). Both of these instances, however, must be interpreted in line with the prevailing interest in the establishment of the Davidic, nationalistic kingdom (cf. also Matt. 2:2).

In the Triumphal Entry, Jesus is declared King, as in the case of Luke's account of the accolades of the crowd: "Blessed is the King who comes in the name of the Lord!" (19:38; cf. John 12:13). Matthew and John quote Zech. 9:9 in emphasizing the Messianic character of this event: "Behold, your king is coming, sitting on an ass's colt" (John 12:15; Matt. 21:5). In the original context of Zechariah, the king who comes to Zion is the long-expected prince of the house of David. Bruce, however, observes a relationship between Zech. 9:9 and Isa. 40:9 and 62:11. He concludes that a salvation meaning is central in this act. Jesus wished it to be known that "he was presenting Himself to the city in that day of its visitation, not as a

30. *NT Theology,* p. 70.
31. Cf. W. R. Cannon, *The Redeemer* (New York: Abingdon Press, 1951), pp. 69 ff.

warrior-Messiah but as a peaceful prince—and indeed as Israel's shepherd-king, ready to 'devote himself for his people's salvation.'"[32] The designation of Kingship appears several times in the trial episodes. Pilate asks Jesus, "Are you the king of the Jews?" (Mark 15:2; John 18:37). Also, in the contest between Pilate and the religious leaders the Lord is referred to as King: "Do you want me to release for you the King of the Jews?" (Mark 15:9). "Then what shall I do with the man whom you call the King of the Jews?" (Mark 15:12). Stubbornly, even in the face of the religious leaders' disclaimer that Christ was their King, Pilate exclaimed, "Here is your King!" (John 19:14). Moreover, they were angry that Pilate had placed the title on the Cross, "Jesus of Nazareth, the King of the Jews." His adamant reply to their protest was "What I have written I have written" (John 19:19-22). At the Crucifixion the chief priests and the soldiers taunted Jesus by referring to His Kingship (Mark 15:32; Luke 23:37).

B. The King Concept in the Acts and Epistles

In the non-Gospel material, also, the word "king" is applied to Jesus in only a limited number of places. In Acts 17:7 the Jews at Thessalonica bring a charge against Paul and his workers that they are teaching, "There is another king, Jesus." Paul and Peter avoid this title, perhaps for politically expedient reasons. Vincent Taylor suggests that for these men what was of value in the term "could be embraced in the title 'the Lord,' with the added advantage of the liturgical associations of the Kyrios-title."[33]

John's Apocalypse, however, specifically refers to the Kingship of Christ in three passages: "Jesus Christ the faithful witness, the first born of the dead, and the ruler of kings on earth" (1:5); "for he is Lord of lords and King of kings" (17:14); "on his robe and on his thigh he has a name inscribed, King of kings and Lord of lords" (19:16). Near the end of the century when John ministered, the Christians did not enjoy a favorable relationship with the existing political order, so John's testimony to Christ as King of Kings was a challenge to the faith of the Christians.

C. The Meaning of Christ's Kingship

The Early Church believed that her Lord shared the throne of God,

32. F. F. Bruce, *New Testament Development of Old Testament Themes* (Grand Rapids, Mich.: Wm. B. Eerdmans Publishing Co., 1968), p. 107.
33. *Names of Jesus*, p. 77.

and for that reason all authority in heaven and earth was His peculiar possession (Matt. 28:18; Acts 2:33; Rom. 8:34; Eph. 1:20; Heb. 1:3, 13; 1 Pet. 3:22; Rev. 3:21). Christ already reigns in glory with the Father. Men of faith know this truth and they await joyfully the full manifestation of His Kingship at His appearing. Moreover, they themselves reign with Christ, sharing His kingly position, because they have been raised with Him (Col. 3:1).

In Rom. 5:17, Paul writes, "For if by the transgression of one, death reigned through the one, by much more shall those receiving the abundance of the grace of the free gift of righteousness reign through the one, Jesus Christ." Submission to God's sovereignty is at the same time a sharing in the reign of Christ. Peter tells his readers that as Christians they constitute "an elect race, a royal priesthood, a holy nation, a people of God's own possession" (1 Pet. 2:9). All who reign now with Christ shall reign with Him eternally (Rev. 3:21; 5:9-10; 20:6; 22:5). This paradox of our reigning with Christ is beautifully expressed by the Apostle Paul to Timothy: "If we have died with him, we shall also live with him; if we endure, we shall also reign with him" (2 Tim. 2:11-12).

The Kingship of Christ has a dual thrust, asserting in one context the eternal relationship of the Son to the Father, but in another declaring the royal character of His redemption. Through His death, resurrection, and ascension, He manifested and established the Kingdom. All rival kingdoms are evil in nature. In this present age, all who pay obeisance to Him share in His authority as Lord and are citizens of His kingdom. When the end comes, the unity of the kingdom of God and the kingdom of Christ will be manifested (1 Cor. 15:24-25). Christ's mediatorial relationship and rule will not cease, however, because He will forever exercise His power for the benefit of the redeemed and for the glory of the eternal Kingdom.

20

The Incarnation

As the Church proclaimed her gospel concerning God's Son, she naturally raised a number of profound theological questions in the minds of her converts. These queries she attempted to answer by reflection on the words of the Lord, on the teaching concerning God's activities and nature as recorded in the old Scriptures, and on her own developing experience of God's daily grace. Among these questions was the nature of Christ's incarnation and the corollary issues of His identity with the Father, His sinlessness, and His birth.

At the heart of the Christian faith is the declaration that our Lord Jesus Christ, the eternal Son of God, became man for our salvation. This affirmation is expressed succinctly in the term *incarnation*. This word is of Latin origin and simply means "invested with flesh." An acceptable synonym is "enfleshment."

The classic reference for this truth is John 1:14: "The Word became flesh and dwelt among us." In the words of F. F. Bruce, John asserts that the "one Who had His being eternally within the unity of the Godhead became man at a point in time, without relinquishing His oneness with God."[1] This confession raises several questions: (1) What was Christ's relationship to the Godhead before Incarnation? (2) Having taken on sinful flesh, is He sinless? (3) What is the intention of the birth through a virgin?

---

1. F. F. Bruce, "The Person of Christ: Incarnation and Virgin Birth," *Basic Christian Doctrines*, ed. Carl F. H. Henry (New York: Holt, Rinehart, and Winston, 1962), p. 125.

I. CHRIST'S IDENTITY WITH GOD

With the repeated confession "Jesus is Lord," there came the inevitable declaration of Christ's identification with God. As noted above, *kurios* is the word employed in the Septuagint to translate the Hebrew terms for God, namely, *Yahweh, Adonai,* and on occasion *Elohim.* The examination of this fact leads Raymond Brown to question: "If Jesus could be given this title, *kurios,* why could he not be called *theos,* which the Septuagint often used to translate '*elohim*'?"[2] Moreover, in the Hellenistic world divine attributes were usually assumed for beings who bore the title *kurios.*

With the tremendous impact of the young faith on all phases of Roman society, philosophical and especially ontological questions were naturally raised. For some people, "Who is this Jesus?" was more than a question of parentage. Early Christian preachers and teachers naturally sought to respond to this burning question. What we get in the New Testament are essentially only proclamatory statements of Christ's nature, but they do suggest the theological response of the early community. When clarification of the nature of Christ became necessary, the Early Church was not hesitant to attribute to Jesus the title *Theos.* This also included all the characteristics of Deity, as, for example, creativity (John 1:3; 1 Cor. 8:6; Col. 1:16-17). Thus in the developed faith of the Church, Jesus is God.

The passages in which Jesus is given the title *Theos* are few but decisive. For the most part they are found in the later canonical material.

A. Pauline References

1. *Romans 9:1-5.* In this passage the apostle gives expression to his soul anguish over the failure of his kinsmen to accept Christ. They were blessed in that Christ was "of their race," but they still rejected Him. Verse 5 reads in Greek: *Kai ex hōn ho Christos to kata sarka* ("from whom is the Christ according to the flesh"), *ho ōn epi pantōn* ("the One who is over all"), *theos eulogētos eis tous aiōnas, amēn* ("God blessed unto the ages, Amen").

In essence, the critical exegetical issue is whether a comma should be placed after *sarka,* thus permitting the remainder of the verse to refer to Christ. The RSV margin reads: "Christ, who is God over all, blessed for ever. Amen." Phillips, KJV, and RSV leave the

2. Raymond E. Brown, *Jesus, God Man* (Milwaukee, Wis.: Bruce, 1967), p. 29.

question of interpretation undecided. Placing a period after *sarka* makes the rest of the verse a doxology as in the RSV: ". . . according to the flesh, is the Christ. God who is over all be blessed for ever. Amen" (cf. also NEB, Moffatt). Since the original manuscripts had no punctuation, the decision between these two possibilities is difficult.

Sanday and Headlam comment that "an immense preponderance of the Christian writers of the first eight centuries refer the word to Christ."[3] Greathouse assumes, along with Sanday and Headlam, that these early writers did not arrive at their conclusion on dogmatic grounds, because the verse is rarely cited in controversy. To them the language of the text had this meaning.[4]

The course of Paul's argument in 9:3-4 leads to an enunciation of the human birth of Christ as an Israelite. But Paul does not want to be misunderstood on the matter of Christ's nature. "*To kata sarka* leads us to expect an antithesis, and we find just what we should have expected in *ho ōn epi pantōn theos.*"[5] Paul says essentially that "Christ was in human terms a Jew, but in fact God."[6] Nygren's conclusion is similar: "'According to the flesh,' *kata sarka*, Christ belongs to Israel; but 'according to the Spirit,' *kata pneuma*, He is 'God who is over all, blessed forever.'"[7]

2. *2 Thessalonians 1:12.* This verse has the familiar phrase *kata tēn charin tou theou hēmōn kai kuriou Jēsou Christou*, "the grace of our God and the Lord Jesus Christ" (RSV, KJV, NEB, NASB). The point of the division of opinion is whether the genitive construction "of our God and the Lord Jesus Christ" refers to one or two Persons. The use of only one article with the two nouns can very well be taken as meaning "of our God and Lord Jesus Christ." This restricts the grace to Christ who is both God and Lord.

Scholars who disagree with this rendering of the phrase point up the fact *(a)* that "Lord" is often used as a proper name and does not here need the definite article to bring out the double reference,[8]

3. W. Sanday and A. C. Headlam, "The Epistle to the Romans," *International Critical Commentary* (New York: Charles Scribner's Sons, 1929), p. 234.

4. William M. Greathouse, "The Epistle to the Romans," *Beacon Bible Commentary* (Kansas City: Beacon Hill Press of Kansas City), 8:200.

5. *Ibid.*

6. C. K. Barrett, "The Epistle to the Romans," *Harper's New Testament Commentaries* (New York: Harper and Bros., 1957), pp. 178-79.

7. Anders Nygren, *Commentary on Romans*, trans. C. C. Rasmussen (Philadelphia: Fortress Press, 1949), p. 356.

8. D. Edmond Hiebert, *The Thessalonian Epistles* (Chicago: Moody Press, 1971), p. 298.

and *(b)* that the context in which the phrase is located speaks of both God and Christ, thus giving the phrase a twofold character.[9] Longenecker feels otherwise. He writes: "While this may very well be the case, 'the grace of the Lord Jesus Christ' is a typically Pauline expression and allows the possibility that 'the grace of our God and Lord Jesus Christ' was but a variant and extension of thought on the part of the apostle."[10]

3. *Titus 2:13.* In this passage Paul uses the unique note, "the appearing of the glory of our great God and Savior Jesus Christ" *(epiphaneian tēs doxēs tou megalou theou kai sōtēros hēmōn Jēsou Christou).* Here we have much the same exegetical issue. Are two persons, namely, Christ and God, intended? The use of the article before the word *theos* but not before *sōtēr* does not militate against the possibility that Paul has only Christ in mind. Hendriksen comments, "Paul indicates that believers look forward to the appearing of the One who is *really* God and Savior . . . Christ Jesus."[11] A similar phraseology appears in 2 Pet. 1:1: "the righteousness of our God and Savior Jesus Christ" *(dikaiosunē tou theou hēmōn kai sōtēros Jēsou Christou).* Assuming in this instance that the Apostle Paul might have had some influence upon Peter's theological thought, we can reasonably conclude that Paul intended to ascribe the term *theos* to Jesus.

B. The Prologue of John

John's Gospel opens with the declaration that the Logos (Christ) was in the beginning with God *(ēn pros ton theon)* and was God *(theos ēn ho logos).* It has been noted that John does not use the Greek word *theios,* which literally means "divine." Raymond Brown comments:

> To preserve in English the different nuance of *theos* with and without the article, some (Moffatt) would translate, "The Word was divine." But this seems too weak; and, after all, there is in Greek an adjective for "divine" *(theios)* which the author did not choose to use. . . . The NEB paraphrases the line: "What God was,

---

9. Cf. Cullmann, *Christology of the NT,* p. 131; Leon Morris, "The First and Second Epistles to the Thessalonians," *The New International Commentary on the New Testament* (Grand Rapids, Mich.: Eerdmans Publishing Co., 1959), p. 212.

10. *Christology of Early Jewish Christianity,* pp. 138-39; cf. Vincent Taylor, "Does the New Testament Call Jesus 'God'?" *New Testament Essays* (London: Epworth Press, 1970), pp. 83-85. Taylor's restraint in the face of considerable evidence is not satisfying.

11. Wm. Hendriksen, *New Testament Commentary: Exposition of the Pastoral Epistles* (Grand Rapids, Mich.: Baker Book House, 1957), pp. 373-75; cf. also A. T. Robertson, *A Grammar of the Greek New Testament in the Light of Historical Research,* 2nd ed. (New York: George H. Doran Co., 1915), pp. 785-87.

the Word was"; and this is certainly better than "divine." Yet for a modern Christian reader whose trinitarian background has accustomed him to thinking of "God" as a larger concept than "God the Father," the translation "The Word was God" is quite correct.[12]

John's "Logos" does much more than just represent God. He is employing the highest Christological language in the New Testament when he asserts, "The Logos was God." Christ was not a *tertium quid*—God, Christ, man. Christ does not just reveal God, but God reveals himself *in* Christ. This Johannine language parallels Paul's word, "God was in Christ, reconciling the world to himself" (2 Cor. 5:19).

John 1:1 is supported by the strange yet textually attested reference to Jesus in 1:18 as "the only-begotten [or only] God" *(monogenēs theos).*[13] The Son, who exists in the "bosom" *(kolpon,* literally "the chest") of the Father, has made known or exegeted *(exēgēsato)* the Father to men.

However, John's most explicit reference is found in Thomas' surprising confession in 20:28, "My Lord and my God" *(ho kurios mou kai ho theos mou).*[14] Affirming the same view of Christ's God nature, John writes in his First Epistle (5:20): "This is the true God" *(houtos estin ho alēthinos theos).*

C. Hebrews 1

The writer to the Hebrews leads off with the concept that the Son "reflects the glory of God, and bears the very stamp of his nature" *(charaktēn tēs hupostaseōs autou).* He then refers to Ps. 45:6 in establishing the superiority of the Son over the angels. In contrast to any word spoken to the angels, God says to the Son: "Thy throne, O God, is for ever and ever, and the righteous scepter is the scepter of thy kingdom" (1:8). If *ho Theos* be taken as a vocative, then the writer seems to be calling Christ "God." The intention of the author to designate the Son as God is substantiated in the further use of Ps. 102:25-27 in 1:10, where Christ's participation in the creation of the universe is expressed.

12. Brown, "Gospel According to John 1—12," *AB*, p. 115.

13. Cf. Bruce Metzger, *A Textual Commentary on the Greek New Testament* (New York: United Bible Societies, 1971), p. 198: "With the acquisition of p. 66 and p. 75, both of which read *theos,* the external support of this reading has been notably strengthened."

14. John's Gospel, in at least two places, reports that the deity issue was part of the opposition to Jesus; cf. 5:18; 10:33.

D. The Kenosis Passage

In Philippians 2, the Apostle Paul incorporates what scholars today consider an early Christian hymn to illustrate the humility and possible sacrifice necessary to maintain a common bond of love in the Church.[15] The anticipated familiarity of the readers with the hymn would suggest that Paul did not create it. Verses 5-11 are compacted with theological thoughts but at least four ideas surface in them.

1. Christ has the "form of God" *(morphē theou);* that is to say, He shares the essential nature of Deity.

2. Christ did not consider "equality with God" *(isa theo)* a status which He must retain *(harpagmon)*[16] at any price, but He was constrained by love to live "incognito"[17] in order to redeem mankind. *Harpagmon* comes from a verb meaning "to snatch, clutch, or seize violently." In its usage here it can either refer to an act of seizing violently something that one does not now possess, or to clutching or holding onto something one now does possess. Assuming the first definition, *harpagmon* would imply that Christ did not seek equality with God in the sense of snatching for himself the honor and glory bound up with it. Assuming the second definition, *harpagmon* would imply a desperate grasping of the status which He already held with the Father.

Both the RSV and the NIV seem to favor the first sense. It seems more reasonable, however, to see the apostle saying that Christ's decision was not to hold onto His rightful "equality with God" so that men would comprehend it while He was in the incarnate state. He emptied himself of His knowability as God and, as the KJV suggests, "made himself of no reputation."

3. Christ's self-emptying *(heauton ekenōsen)* may point to His decision to suffer in His incarnate state. The verb *kenoun* means "'to pour out,' with Christ himself as the object. Thus Christ emptied himself of himself. At no time did He allow selfish considerations to dominate His spotless life."[18] Cullmann concludes, "The *Man* became *a* Man"

15. E. Lohmeyer initially proposed that Paul quotes an ancient Aramaic psalm, and this hypothesis has governed much of all succeeding investigation of this passage. While this view is attractive, it cannot be definitely proved. Cf. Lohmeyer, *Kyrios Jesus Eine Untersuchung zu Phil. 2:5-11* (1928).

16. W. Foerster, "Harpamos," *TDNT,* 1:472-74. J. B. Lightfoot, *Paul's Epistle to the Philippians* (London: Macmillan, 1913), p. 111: "... yet He did not look upon equality with God as a prize which must not slip from His grasp"; cf. also pp. 133-37.

17. Karl Barth, *The Epistle to the Philippians,* trans. James W. Leitch (Richmond, Va.: John Knox Press, 1947), pp. 60-65.

18. John A. Knight, "Philippians," *BBC,* 9:318-22.

and "he assumed the role of the *ebed Yahweh*" through obedience.[19] With respect to the self-emptying, we must not assume that a loss of divinity is implied, for as Pannenberg writes, "Attributes essential to his divinity cannot be absent even in his humiliation unless the humiliated were no longer God."[20]

4. Christ was exalted to the status of Lordship by virtue of His humiliation and obedience to the Cross. He was given the name *kurios* which belonged solely to God. As with God, every being in the cosmos must now bow in worship to Christ.

The effect of this passage is not to suggest that Jesus was other than Deity before the Incarnation. On the contrary, the *via dolorosa* was only the way of establishing before all men who He really was, namely, the Lord of Glory. Barth is correct in consistently applying the title "God's Equal" to Christ throughout his interpretation of the text. In the incarnate state, "God's Equal" lived in a state of unknowability; His glory was not known by men. Following His crucifixion and resurrection, He came to be known as what He always was, namely, "God's Equal." In the exaltation Jesus' unity with God was revealed and confirmed.

Essentially, Phil. 2:5-11 with its use of *morphē* and *isa theō* in referring to Christ is not very different from the Johannine idea of the Logos who is "in the beginning with God" and "was God." In His preexistent state, Christ held the highest possible relationship with God. As a result of His obedience, however, He is accorded the status of *Kurios*, which means He possesses the right to exercise the divine sovereignty. The Apostle Paul understood that Christ had always been *huios*, but through His resurrection, He is "the Son of God with power" (*huios tou theou en dunamei*, Rom. 1:4).

E. Colossians 1:13-20

Another Pauline passage that demonstrates the growth of theological understanding of the person and work of Christ is Col. 1:13-20. The writer reminds his readers that it is in Christ we have redemption, the forgiveness of sins. Then he characterizes Christ as "the image of the invisible God" (*eikōn tou theou*), "the firstborn of all creation" (*prōtotokos pasēs ktiseōs*), and "the fulness" (*to plērōma*). In Col. 2:9, Paul

---

19. *Christology of the New Testament*, p. 178: Along with others, Cullmann interprets this passage in the ideological framework of the "Son of Man" and "Servant of the Lord" titles.

20. *Jesus, God and Man*, p. 312.

348 / God, Man, and Salvation

declares that in Christ "the whole fullness of diety dwells bodily"
(katoikei pan to plērōma tēs theotētos sōmatikōs).

Paul declares that Christ *is* "the image of the invisible God." He
thus affirms that Christ is more than finite man, who also in one
sense bears the image of God. *Eikōn* is intended to convey essential
kinship. Christ has an incomparable relationship to God, one that
no other being is privileged to enjoy. Even in the incarnate state,
Christ "reflects the glory of God and bears the very stamp of his
nature" (Heb. 1:3).

Prōtotokos is another relational term (Col. 1:15, 18; cf. Rom. 8:
29; Heb. 1:6). It is not to be construed as indicating that Christ is a
created being.[21] "First-created" would therefore be an improper
translation; "firstborn" more nearly expresses its meaning; Hebrew
familial concepts lie behind it. The firstborn son in the Hebrew tradition bore the vitality, privileges, and responsibilities of the family.
Since Christ is the only Son "generating" from the Father, He must
be accorded the honor and reverence due Him.

If Paul had intended to declare that Christ was the first of creation, he had available to him a more precise term, namely *prōtoktistos,*
a compound of *prōtos* ("first") and *ktistos* (from *ktizō,* "to create"). J. B.
Lightfoot mentions that in the fourth century, Clement of Alexan-
dria, without reference to this passage in Colossians, contrasts the
monogenēs and the *prōtotokos* with the *prōtoktistoi,* the highest order of
angelic beings.[22]

Two main ideas are asserted by *prōtotokos:* (1) priority to all creation, thus indicating the absolute preexistence of the Son; (2) sovereignty over all creation, acknowledging in Old Testament Messianic
terms that Christ as God's "firstborn" is the natural Ruler, the
Head of God's household.[23] *Prōtotokos* is an equivalent of *monogenēs*
(John 1:18 *et al.*), which emphasizes also uniqueness of relationship
to the Father. The singularity of the Son in the Godhead as well as
the preexistence of the Son to the created order is affirmed by these
two terms. There is a cosmological note in vv. 16-17 in which Christ
is declared to be the Co-Creator and Harmonizer of the universe.

---

21. *Prōtotokos* is a compound noun developed from *prōtos,* "first," and *tiktein,* "to
beget" or "to give birth." (Cf. Matt. 1:25; Luke 2:7; Rom. 8:29; Heb. 1:6; 11:28.)

22. *Saint Paul's Epistles to the Colossians and to Philemon* (Grand Rapids, Mich.:
Zondervan Publishing House, 1961, rev. reprint), p. 147.

23. *Ibid.,* pp. 146, 174; K. L. Schmidt, "Prototokos," *TDNT,* 6:879: "What is meant
is the unique supremacy of Christ over all creatures as the Mediator of their creation."

This naturally follows from the previous declaration of the primacy and priority of the Son as the "Firstborn." He belongs to eternity. He is not created and therefore qualifies for the roles of both Creatorship and Saviourhood.[24]

The word *plērōma* is highly illuminating because it expresses the final Pauline thought on the person of Christ. It had been used by the Gnostics to distinguish God from Christ. Only God, who exists in total otherness, possesses the fullness of Deity. Christ is only an intermediary, they said—greater than man but less than God. In contradiction to that theology, Paul declares that in Christ "all the fullness of God was pleased to dwell."[25]

Plērōma means "sum total," "fullness," or even "[super] abundance" of something. The "sum total" or "full measure" of Deity dwells in Christ. Paul uses the Greek *katoikeō* and it is usually translated "dwell." But it denotes permanence, so the apostle is suggesting that all that constitutes God resides and continues to reside in Christ. Even in the incarnate state Christ's divine nature prevailed. This fact is expressed in Col. 2:9: "In him all the fullness of deity dwells bodily."

Docetism with its theory that Christ only appeared to be a man falls before this emphatic assertion. "All the fullness" means that the totality of Deity is present in Christ. *Sōmatikōs* ("bodily") can justifiably be translated "in the human body" and thus means "really, not figuratively." The union between the human and the divine was as real as the union between soul and body in man. God and man are one Christ. Or, Jesus Christ is God Incarnate. Thus, for Paul sovereignty and Saviourhood are constitutive to Christ's nature. Since He eternally generates from the Father, He shares the divine nature and therefore enters into the Godhead's passion for the reconciliation of all creation.

In summary, the Early Church, whether functioning in a Jewish or Gentile setting, exercised considerable care in expressing Jesus' identity with God. Growing opposition and the need for instruction certainly demanded the necessary theological clarification. It is sig-

---

24. A number of other expressions in the New Testament denote Christ's primacy and priority in the cosmos, such as *archē*, "beginning" (Rev. 21:6; 22:13); *archēgos*, "leader, pioneer, chief one, prince" (Acts 3:15; 5:31); *kephalē*, "head" (Acts 4:11; Col. 1:18; 2:10; 1 Pet. 2:7; *to Alpha kai to Omega*, "the first and the last."

25. Cf. F. F. Bruce, "Colossians," *The New International Commentary on the New Testament* (Grand Rapids, Mich.: Wm. B. Eerdmans Publishing Co., 1957), pp. 206-8. *Pleroma* is used 11 times in Paul's Epistles and is applied to each Person of the Trinity.

nificant that writings such as John's Gospel, Hebrews, and Peter, which come out of Jewish environments, give us the most explicit references. The Jewish encounter at the point of monotheism must have sparked these attempts at relating Christ to God. The encounter brought forth profound affirmations of Christ's deity. Paul elects to employ the word "Lord" to express the ramifications of Jesus' "godness."

II. Christ's Sinlessness

Pannenberg perceptively observes: "If sin is essentially life in contradiction to God, in self-centered closing of our ego against God, then Jesus' unity with God in his personal community with the Father and in his identity with the person of the Son of God mean immediately his separation from all sin."[26] Throughout the New Testament this fact is unquestionably affirmed.

A. The Attestation of the Gospels

Jesus was not one of the seekers after God; rather, in the totality of His life He bore witness to the very existence of God. He lived out of a deep awareness of God's presence in His own being. If ever anyone was sure of God, Jesus was that Person, and the reason lay in the fact of His unity with God.

The Gospel writers present Jesus as authentically human, yet they do not attempt to "prove" His sinlessness. They simply let the record stand. Jesus, who understood better than anyone else what sin really is, showed no awareness of sin in himself. He recognized sin in others and grieved over it. He forgave sin and finally suffered on the Cross for it. John records that Jesus even challenged His opponents: "Which of you convicts [elegchei] me of sin?" (John 8:46). McDonald states the truth succinctly: "With Him there was no memory of sin's defeat, no trace of sin's scars, no shame of a bad conscience. He lived all His days without the personal sense of sin's guilt and the personal fear of sin's consequences."[27]

Luke explored the circumstances attending the birth of Jesus and in his investigation uncovered the conversation of Mary, the mother of Jesus, with the angel Gabriel. The heavenly messenger

---

26. *Jesus, God and Man*, p. 355.
27. *Jesus, Human and Divine*, p. 39.

announced to her that the Holy Spirit would come upon her, and the child who would be born to her would be called "holy, the Son of God" (Luke 1:35).[28] Thus, Luke declares at the beginning of his account that Jesus was God's fully acceptable Son, the Sinless One.

Others detected an authentic righteousness in Jesus and were either humbled or rebuked by it. John the Baptist was ready to defer to Jesus at the time that the Master presented himself for baptism (Matt. 3:14). Also, Pilate's wife sent word to her husband to "have nothing to do with that righteous man" *(tō dikaiō ekeinō),* for she "suffered much over him . . . in a dream" (Matt. 27:19). Even Peter, who lived close to Jesus, at one moment in his life fell down before the Lord and implored: "Depart from me, for I am a sinful man, O Lord" (Luke 5:8). The Roman centurion discerned something spiritually distinctive in Christ. "Certainly this man was innocent" *(dikaios,* righteous, Luke 23:47).

According to Mark 10:18, Christ responds to the rich young man's address of Him as "Good Teacher" with the question: "Why do you call me good *[agathon]?* No one is good but God alone." This response is not to be taken as "a veiled acknowledgment of moral need" but rather as Jesus' mode of testing the young man's sincerity. It appears from the limited references in the four Gospels that generally the individuals whose minds were not calloused in opposition to Jesus viewed His spirit and behavior as above the normal for men.

B. The Affirmation of the Christian Community

From the earliest period in the Christian community Jesus' sinlessness was affirmed, and obviously the life of Jesus itself dictated the thoughts of the Church on this point. In other words, the early community confidently declared what had been sensed and said about Jesus during His brief ministry. Paul emphasized in Gal. 3:13 that Jesus was treated as a sinner by God in our stead. "Only because Jesus was himself without sin," writes Pannenberg, "can it be said that what he suffered was not the consequence of his own guilt, but that he took his suffering upon himself for our sake."[29]

Explicitly the apostle states in 2 Cor. 5:21, "For our sake he made him to be sin who knew no sin, so that in him we might become the righteousness of God." "Who knew no sin" *(ton mē gnonta*

---

28. Cf. Acts 2:27, *ton hosion sou,* which means literally "his holy one." *Hosios* bears the idea of piety and purity.

29. *Jesus, God and Man,* p. 355.

hamartian) simply means "who had done no sin." Paul is asserting
that Christ was not experienced in sinning. He was not made a sinner
in deed, but rather was made a "sin offering" that men might be
made the righteousness of God. It has been assumed by commentators that Paul is employing "the Hebrew idiom in which certain
words for sin *(hattat, asam)* mean not only sin but sin-offering."[30] The
Suffering Servant of Isa. 53:10 is made an *asary* ("an offering for sin,"
RSV; cf. Isa. 53:6). Carver comments: "Christ, who 'was innocent of
sin' (NEB), entered a sphere utterly alien to Him, that we might enter
that sphere from which we have alienated ourselves."[31]

The same truth surfaces in Rom. 8:3. God sent "his own Son in
the likeness of sinful flesh [*en homoiōmati sarkos hamartias*, 'in our sinful
condition of existence'] and for sin [*peri hamartias*, RSV margin, 'as an
offering for sin'], . . . [in order that He might condemn] sin in the
flesh," that is, in its own realm.

The rest of the New Testament follows Paul's line of thought
regarding Jesus' sinless character. Hebrews portrays Christ as our
High Priest, who is well able to represent us before the altar of God
because He was tempted "in every respect [*ta panta*] as we are, yet
without sinning [*chōris hamartias*]" (4:15; cf. 7:26; 9:14). Negatively
He kept himself free from all sin, but positively He completely
obeyed the Father. The influence of the "Suffering Servant" song in
Isaiah 53 with its image of the "Perfect Lamb" is seen in 1 Pet. 2:22-
25. Peter writes: "He committed no sin; no guile was found on his
lips" (2:22). Also, "For Christ also died for sins once and for all, the
righteous for the unrighteous, that he might bring us to God" (3:18;
cf. Acts 3:13; 4:27, where "Child" can be read "Servant"). In his First
Epistle, John forthrightly avers, "In him there is no sin" (3:5).

These references to the moral perfection of Christ are not numerous, but they do indicate the breadth of the tradition on this
aspect of the primitive Church's understanding of Christ. Pannenberg's question on this matter is cogent: "And indeed, how could the
first Christians hold their own against their Jewish opposition without stressing this point?"[32] Though "very man of very man," as the
later creed affirmed, Jesus still fulfilled all the divine demands and
lived out the love and righteousness of God himself. H. R. Macintosh
asserts that Jesus is

30. F. F. Bruce, "1 and 2 Corinthians," *New Century Bible* (London: Marshall,
Morgan, and Scott, 1971), p. 210.
31. Frank G. Carver, "2 Corinthians," *BBC*, 8:556.
32. *Jesus, God and Man*, p. 355.

aware that He needs no cleansing. Even in the article of death He knows it. There is no consciousness of sin; there is no memory of sin; there is no fear of sin as a future contingency flowing from the weakness or shortcoming of even the most distant past. Sinlessly one with God, all His life he moved among men, uttering the word of pardon to the guilty, and uttering it with Divine effect.[33]

Macintosh's further word is appropriate: "No miracle of Christ equals the miracle of His sinless life. To be holy in all thought and feeling; never to fail in duty to others, never to transgress the law of perfect love to God or man, never to exceed or to come short—this is a condition outstripping the power of imagination."[34]

III. The Virgin Birth

From primitive times, the Church has confessed that the Lord's incarnation came through conception in the womb of Mary by the power of the Holy Spirit. This conviction is expressed by Ignatius, Justin, Irenaeus, and Tertullian. It also appears in the eucharistic service of *The Apostolic Tradition,* in the *Te Deum Laudamus,* and in Tatian's *Diatessaron.* However, only two New Testament writers, Matthew and Luke, refer to the Virgin Birth, and this fact has led some interpreters to discredit the tradition.

Why did not Paul and John include a word about this phenomenon in their extensive writings? William Childs Robinson is convinced that "what is explicit in Matthew and Luke is implicit in Paul and John." He defends his position by a reference to "the argument from silence" in Paul and "the argument from analogy" in John.[35] The evidential value of Robinson's study is limited, but we are compelled to assert that other New Testament writers, while not mentioning the Virgin Birth, say nothing to contradict it.

Matthew records that Mary "was found to be with child of the Holy Spirit" (*heurethē en gastri echousa ek pneumatos hagiou,* 1:18): The angel's word to Joseph was "That which is conceived in her is of the Holy Spirit" (*to gar en autē gennēthen ek pneumatos estin hagiou,* 1:20). Matthew then adds the prophetic note from Isa. 7:14.

Luke asserts the virginity of Mary and includes the angelic word: "And behold, you will conceive in your womb and bear a son,

33. *The Person of Jesus Christ* (London: SCM, 1918), p. 28.
34. *Ibid.*
35. "The Virgin Birth—A Broader Base," *Christianity Today,* Dec. 8, 1972, pp. 6-8.

and you shall call his name Jesus" (1:26-31). Mary reminds the angel that she has no husband, but the angel replied, "The Holy Spirit will come upon you *[pneuma hagion epeleusetai epi se]*, and the power of the Most High will overshadow you; therefore the child to be born will be called Holy, the Son of God" (1:34-35).

What do these accounts affirm about the birth of Christ?

1. The virginal conception of the Lord is sheer miracle. The Virgin Birth, as J. K. S. Reid avers, is not an explanation, it is "the affirmation of mystery and miracle. It affirms that here God is at work. . . . The Virgin Birth is unequivocally supernatural."[36] The birth is the result of the activity of the Holy Spirit as the creative power of God (cf. Gen. 1:2). The conception is not by the natural means of copulation with a male but by special action by the Holy Spirit (*ek pneumatos hagiou,* Matt. 1:18, 20). Luke's words are "will come upon you" *(epeleusetai epi se)* and "will overshadow you" *(episkiasei soi).* They express the same fact of miraculous Spirit involvement. These biblical accounts affirm that Christ was supernaturally conceived. James Orr, at the end of his long study, *The Virgin Birth of Christ,* concludes, "This miracle is not simply an *inward* or *spiritual* miracle, but has a *physical* side as well."[37]

2. Especially in Matthew, the story has an apologetic purpose. The concern is not so much with what the birth of the Son of God may mean in and of itself and for His mother. The purpose is to establish the salvation role which this One will play in human redemption. Against the doubts of Joseph and skeptical Jews, Matthew by reference to prophecy demonstrates that Christ is the Messiah, and the primal proof scripturally is Isa. 7:14. This miraculous deed is thus "a fixed part of the divine plan of salvation."[38]

Viewed apologetically, the Virgin Birth is a sign of God's special activity in salvation. So Richardson writes that it is "the sign of the inauguration of the Last Things, the first results of the outpouring of the Holy Spirit in the latter days, when the new creation was being inaugurated in the day of Israel's redemption (Isa. 32:15; Ezek. 36: 26ff.; 37:14; cf. Ps. 51:10ff.; Joel 2:28ff.; etc.)."[39] Through the birth

---

36. "Virgin Birth," *A Theological Word Book of the Bible,* ed. Alan Richardson (London: SCM Press, 1950), p. 277.

37. (New York: Charles Scribner's Sons, 1907), p. 217; cf. also J. Gresham Machen, *The Virgin Birth of Christ* (New York: Harper and Bros., 1930), pp. 380 ff.

38. Hans von Campenhausen, *The Virgin Birth in the Theology of the Ancient Church* (Naperville, Ill: Alec R. Allenson, Inc., 1962), p. 26; von Campenhausen's study on this point merits serious study.

39. Richardson, *Introduction to the Theology of the NT,* p. 174.

there has been set into motion a series of saving events, both historical and personal, which will eventuate in the final victory of God.
This birth is the promise of all these other events.

Inherently, therefore, the Virgin Birth has rootage through the
old Scriptures to all the past of Israel's history. But at the same time
it has a uniqueness of its own relating to the new work of God. With
respect to this latter fact, one cannot find parallels to it in the Old
Testament or in the pagan religious environment. Moreover, "it is
unique because it holds the once-only place reserved for the coming
of the Saviour in the divine economy of salvation, of which the OT is
the advance proclamation and the NT is the evidence of fulfillment."[40]

3. The Virgin Birth only suggests the sinlessness of Christ or His
moral purity. There is a common assertion that in Jesus' virginal
conception through the Holy Spirit "the entail of sin was broken
within the human family." But Reid's reaction to this merits consideration: "An account that would plausibly break the entail of sin
would have to be much more clever than to leave him connected
on even one side of his parentage with the human race and thus so
far involved in corrupt human nature."[41]

Von Campenhausen's comment that Luke's account is more dogmatic and touches on the metaphysical question of substance and
nature has merit. The angelic word to Mary that the child shall be
called "holy" or "that holy thing" *(hagion)* might imply freedom from
the taint of sin. But even here the evidential character of material is
limited because *hagion* can also be taken to mean "separation for
divine service."

Perhaps the record was not intended to emphasize Christ's sinlessness so much as to declare that Jesus is the Head of a new race.
Wiley writes that *hagion* implies that a change was to be wrought in
the very constitution of humanity:

> Jesus was not, therefore, merely the origin of a new individ-
> ual in the race, but a pre-existent One coming into the race from
> above; He was not merely another individualization of human
> nature, but the conjoining of the divine and human natures in a
> new order of being—a theanthropic person. . . . In Jesus there is
> the birth of a new order of humanity, a new man, which after God
> is created in righteousness and true holiness.[42]

40. *Ibid.*, p. 175.
41. "Virgin Birth," *Theological Word Book*, p. 277.
42. Wiley, *Christian Theology*, 2:148; cf. Rom. 5:12-21.

Two additional thoughts must be introduced with respect to the Virgin Birth and Christ's sinlessness. According to Von Campenhausen, the issue of sinlessness was not prominent in apostolic teaching until the time of Ambrose.[43] Furthermore, the teaching of the Virgin Birth must be interpreted within the broader framework of Christology. James Orr's conclusions are judicious: "The perfect sinlessness of Christ, and the archetypal character of His humanity, imply a miracle in His origin. The doctrine of the Incarnation of the pre-existent Son implies a miracle in Christ's origin."[44] The Virgin Birth is integral to the entire gospel and cannot be fully understood apart from the theology of the entire New Testament. When the full truth about the Lord is understood, the birth both in its divine and human aspects is found to be in line with God's workings unto salvation in history. As one has written, "The Virgin Birth is not, therefore, a discovery of faith but a disclosure to faith."

4. A relationship exists between the birth of our Lord and the Christian's spiritual birth. The Holy Spirit, the power of the Most High (Luke 1:35), is the life-giving Agent in the birth of the new man, Jesus Christ. So Richardson can write, "Christ was born, as Christians are born, 'not of blood, nor of the will of the flesh, nor of the will of an husband *(aner)*, but of God' (John 1:13)."[45] The Creator-Spirit incarnated the Word and gave "life" to mankind; now the Spirit working through the Incarnate Christ enables individual men to become the children of God (John 1:12). The Apostle Paul writes: "Thus it is written, 'The first man Adam became a living being'; the last Adam became a life-giving spirit" (1 Cor. 15:45).

Minimally interpreted, the Birth Narratives and the Virgin Birth accounts in particular proclaim that Christ's presence among men is divinely initiated and is the beginning of a new age in the history of salvation.

---

43. *Virgin Birth*, pp. 76-80.
44. *Virgin Birth of Christ*, p. 229; cf. Reid, "Virgin Birth," p. 277.
45. *Introduction to the Theology of the NT*, p. 174.

21

Christ's Death, Resurrection, and Ascension

I. THE SCANDAL OF CHRIST'S DEATH

At this point in our study, it is wise to introduce the response of the Early Church to the death of Christ. The secular mind of the day probably viewed the Crucifixion as an unfortunate end to a brilliant evangelistic career. The sharp interpretative light of the Resurrection, however, enabled the disciples to place it in true perspective. They did not seek to rationalize it; they simply proclaimed it as having been predetermined by God. On the Day of Pentecost, Peter preached that Jesus was "delivered up according to the definite plan and foreknowledge of God" (Acts 2:23; cf. 3:18; 13:26-27; Eph. 1:9-10; 1 Pet. 1:18-20, *et al.*). In the earliest recoverable tradition the death of Christ was interpreted as a planned act of God.

Moreover, the death was seen as an atonement for sin. The clue came from Jesus himself who instructed His disciples: "The Son of Man also came not to be served but to serve, and to give his life as a ransom for many" (Mark 10:45). The atonement does not come through as clearly in Acts as in other New Testament books, but Peter on the Day of Pentecost and subsequently called men to repentance after having spoken of the meaning of Christ's death (cf. 2:37-38; 3:18-19; 4:10-12).

It is Paul who expressly states the atoning character of our Lord's death. To the Corinthians he writes: "Christ died for our sins in accordance with the scriptures" (1 Cor. 15:3), and to the Romans he writes that God put forward *(proetheto)* Christ "as an expiation by his blood" (3:25; cf. 1 John 2:2). The heart of the Book of Hebrews is the redemptive nature of the death of Christ (Heb. 9:26-28). At the final judgment, where the central issue is Christ's death and human sin, only one Person is qualified to "open the scroll and break its seals" of judgment, namely, "the Lamb that was slain" (Rev. 5:6-14).

The Apostle Paul was particularly sensitive on the point of the interpretation of Christ's death. He knew the Hebrew revulsion to cross-death (cf. 1 Cor. 1:23), because the Law commanded this form of death only for extreme crimes. Deuteronomy says explicitly, "For a hanged man is accursed by God" (21:23).

Writing to the Galatians, Paul dares to assert, "Christ redeemed us from the curse of the law, having become a curse for us—for it is written, 'Cursed be every one who hangs on a tree'" (3:13). Thus, the very act signifying criminal activity became in Christ the way of deliverance from crime and every form of divinely detested behavior. Christ came under *(hupo)* the Law (Gal. 4:4) in order to redeem those who were under *(hupo)* the Law (Gal. 4:5)—and thus under *(hupo)* a curse (Gal. 3:10)—from *(ek)* the curse of the Law (3:13) by becoming a curse for *(huper)* us (Gal. 3:13). The obedience of Christ unto death, even the death of the Cross (Phil. 2:8), was part and parcel of His atoning intention. By so doing, He wiped out the death-dealing impact of sin by opening up an access to the righteousness of God. God made Him to be a sin offering "so that in him we might become the righteousness of God" (2 Cor. 5:21).

II. THE IMPACT OF CHRIST'S RESURRECTION

Floyd V. Filson begins his study of the thought of the New Testament with the following preamble:

> The entire New Testament was written in the light of the resurrection fact. To all its writers, Jesus is the central figure of history, and they understand and interpret his career in the light of his resurrection. They regard his resurrection not merely as a possibility or even as a probability; it is for them the one rock-bottom fact upon which the solid structure of Christian faith and life is built.[1]

This judgment of Filson is sound. We cannot assume that there is "a Gospel which stands upon its own feet and may be understood

---

1. *Jesus Christ, the Risen Lord* (New York: Abingdon Press, 1956), p. 31.

and appreciated before we pass on to the Resurrection."[2] That was not the approach of the disciples. For them "the Gospel without the Resurrection was not merely a Gospel without its final chapter; it was not a Gospel at all."[3] In the earliest preaching we hear a repetitive note on the Resurrection: "But God raised him up" (Acts 2:24); "whom God raised from the dead" (3:15; 4:10); "but God raised him on the third day" (10:40); "but God raised him from the dead" (13:30). Paul tells the Corinthians that Christ "was buried" and "was raised on the third day in accordance with the scriptures" (1 Cor. 15:4).

Thus the Resurrection becomes an "article of faith" in the developed New Testament thought. Salvation depends upon confession with the lips "that Jesus is Lord" and upon believing in the heart "that God raised him from the dead" (Rom. 10:9; cf. Gal. 1:1; Eph. 1:20; Col. 2:12; 1 Thess. 1:9-10; 2 Tim. 2:8; 1 Pet. 1:21). The Resurrection becomes "the living center" of the Christian faith.

Hugh Anderson comments, "Easter, therefore, is no mere addendum to other factors in the story of Jesus Christ; it is constitutive for the community's faith and worship, its discipleship and mission to the world."[4] So it is that Paul could write to the Corinthians, "If Christ has not been raised, your faith is futile and you are still in your sins" (1 Cor. 15:17).

A. The Resurrection Appearances

The accounts of the Lord's appearances following His resurrection are fairly extensive, but they can be summarized in three groups: (1) to the disciples, and particularly Peter; (2) to the immediate family of Jesus. James is mentioned by the Apostle Paul (1 Cor. 15:7); Luke records that "Mary the mother of Jesus, and his brothers" were gathered with the disciples in a private house in Jerusalem following the final Resurrection appearance, an incident from which we might assume that they were present at the appearance (Acts 1:14). (3) Appearances to women who according to the records shared Jesus' mission (Mark 16:1-8; Luke 23:55-56; John 20:18). The revelation to Paul (1 Cor. 15:8-9) was perhaps three years later, but it must be included in the group of disclosures to the apostles. Paul in this account obviously places himself among the apostles though "the least" of them.

---

2. Michael Ramsey, *The Resurrection of Christ* (London: Geoffrey Bles, 1946), p. 7.
3. *Ibid.*
4. *Jesus and Christian Origins* (New York: Oxford Press, 1964), p. 187.

What can we make of these appearances? First, the enumeration is clearly intended to give proof for the historicity and objectivity of the Resurrection. "The risen Christ was a vital personality who acted according to a definite plan, bearing witness to himself by appearing whenever, wherever, however and before whomever he pleased."[5]

Second, in His new form, Jesus' being was both physical and pneumatic.[6] He was identifiable as One with flesh and bones, but He was also able to set aside the normal laws of nature so that He could pass through closed doors. All this was inexplicable to the disciples, and they did not indulge in unnecessary rationalistic explanations; they simply proclaimed His resurrection as miracle.[7] The Gospels emphasize that the tomb was empty and that Jesus indeed was raised from the tomb. But the affirmation in New Testament preaching was not *ek taphou*, "from the tomb," but rather *ek nekrōn*, "from the dead." Nonetheless, as Paul Althaus has asserted, the Resurrection kerygma could not have been continued in Jerusalem if the fact of the empty tomb had not been firmly established.

The appearances of the Lord following the Resurrection were only to those who were in a position to recognize Him and to those who had had a relationship with Him in the past. There is no record that Jesus' foes or critics were encountered by Him. Saunders reminds us that "He does not appear to a Sadducee or to Herod Antipas or to Caiaphas."[8] This fact leads only to the conclusion that faith played an important role in the Resurrection appearances: their facticity is bound up with the experiences of the men involved.

We are confronted with an "inner dimension" to these events centering in the experiences of the early believers with the risen Christ. Simple, positivistic modes of historical studies will not reveal the total meaning of the Resurrection. But, as Saunders remarks, "We must accept seriously the apostolic testimony that they are real en-

---

5. Ethelbert Stauffer, *Jesus and His Story*, trans. by Richard and Clara Winston (New York: Alfred A. Knopf, 1960), pp. 151-52.

6. For a full discussion on this aspect of the Lord's appearances, cf. J. A. Schep, *The Nature of the Resurrection Body* (Grand Rapids, Mich.: Wm. B. Eerdmans Publishing Co., 1964), pp. 107-81; the Apostle Paul is the best guide on the nature of Christ's risen form, 1 Cor. 15:42-50.

7. On the reliability of the empty tomb accounts, cf. Stauffer, *Jesus and His Story*, pp. 143-47.

8. E. W. Saunders, *Jesus in the Gospels* (Englewood Cliffs, N.J.: Prentice-Hall, Inc., 1967), p. 294.

counters, not just rearranged viewpoints or dawning insights without other ground than subjective reflection."[9]

Pannenberg, who asserts that history is the exclusive medium for revelation and thus provides the sole basis for faith, is confident that the resurrection of Jesus did occur. The Resurrection appearances and the empty tomb were not figments of the apostles' imagination. The Resurrection episode could not have been fabricated, even considering their disoriented state of mind following the tragic Cross experience. They could not have talked themselves into believing that Jesus was raised from the dead. Pannenberg concludes that the appearance tradition and the grave tradition came into existence independently but they mutually complement each other, and in so doing "they let the assertion of the reality of Jesus' resurrection . . . appear as historically very probable, and that always means in historical inquiry that it is to be presupposed until contrary evidence appears."[10]

B. The Faith of Easter

It is hardly proper to isolate the Resurrection theologically and assign to it all the meaning of the gospel. While it merits special consideration, it must be kept contextually legitimate; it must be related to the complex of events that includes the Cross, the Ascension, and Pentecost. The New Testament gives broad expression to the meaning of the Resurrection.

1. The Resurrection was and is the vindication of Jesus. By it the identity of Jesus and the truth of His mission were forever established. The Jews thought He was a pretender and the disciples grew doubtful of His authenticity as the events of the last week unfolded. But the Resurrection and the subsequent acts attendant to it certified Christ's credentials as God's Elect One. So Peter could preach at Pentecost, "Let all the house of Israel therefore know assuredly that God has made him both Lord and Christ, this Jesus whom you crucified" (Acts 2:36).

Paul, writing to the Romans, confesses that "Jesus Christ our

---

9. *Jesus in the Gospels,* p. 295.

10. *Jesus, God and Man,* p. 105; for a thorough and contemporary study of the issue of the Resurrection and historical reasoning, with deft criticisms of various authors including Pannenberg, cf. Daniel P. Fuller, *Easter Faith and History* (Grand Rapids, Mich.: Wm. B. Eerdmans Publishing Co., 1964), pp. 145-87; also, Merril C. Tenney, "The Historicity of the Resurrection," *Jesus of Nazareth, Saviour, and Lord,* ed. Carl F. H. Henry (Grand Rapids, Mich.: Wm. B. Eerdmans Publishing Co., 1966), pp. 135-44.

Lord" was "designated Son of God in power according to the Spirit of holiness by his resurrection from the dead" (Rom. 1:4). This is not some form of adoptionism; this is confirmation and vindication. Anderson writes, "In the Resurrection, who he really was, is now confirmed."[11] Moreover, the Christ of the Resurrection is not some new being thrust upon the world, but the same Jesus whom the disciples knew earlier. *This same Jesus* was now enthroned in His glory, and His kingdom was being realized through His believing followers. The Resurrection is, as someone has said, "the fullness of faith in Jesus."

2. The Resurrection declares the triumph of God through Christ over the forces of sin and death and consequently the triumph of believers. "Lawless men" put Christ to death (Acts 2:23); the "pangs of death" (*ōdinas*, "agony of death," NASB) were His experience, but God "raised him up, having loosed the pangs of death." God, by delivering up His Son to the Cross, to the machinations of men possessed of evil, and to the "destroyer," had permitted the Lord to suffer all. But the divine act of Resurrection despoiled all sinful efforts and wrested from death its power.

So Paul can write confidently, "'Death is swallowed up in victory. O death, where is thy victory? O death, where is thy sting?' The sting of death is sin, and the power of sin is the law. But thanks be to God, who gives us the victory through our Lord Jesus Christ" (1 Cor. 15:54-57). To the Colossians he writes that God "disarmed the principalities and powers and made a public example of them, triumphing over them in him" (2:15).[12] Obviously the reference is to the Cross, but it presupposes the Resurrection. As Anderson writes, "A *theologia resurrection* is the inescapable presupposition of a *theologia crucis.*"[13]

The writer to the Hebrews says that Jesus shared our nature "that through death he might destroy him who has the power of death, that is, the devil" (2:14). The triumph signalized in the Death-Resurrection is both Christ's and God's, but it is also the triumph of men who receive Christ in faith. The power of sin and death in the life of men can be destroyed through the resurrected life of Christ. Paul writes that believers "reign in life through the one man Jesus Christ" (Rom. 5:17).

---

11. *Jesus and Christian Origins,* p. 209; cf. his resume of the interpretation of Rom. 1:4, pp. 209, 338-39.
12. *En autō* can also be translated "in it," that is, the Cross.
13. *Jesus and Christian Origins,* p. 185.

Taking up the symbolism of baptism, the Apostle Paul says, "We were buried therefore with him by baptism into death, so that as Christ was raised from the dead by the glory of the Father, we too might walk in newness of life" (Rom. 6:4). "The believer, having died with Christ symbolically in baptism, shares in the new risen life of Christ, which He as 'the life-giving spirit,' imparts to the believer."[14] They are "more than conquerors" in this through Him (Rom. 8:37). Christ was the "first fruits of those who have fallen asleep" (1 Cor. 15:20) and "the very idea of firstfruits meant that there are later fruits. . . . Christ's resurrection accordingly carries with it the resurrection of those that are in Christ."[15]

3. The faith of the Resurrection carries with it the realization that a new age has dawned. When the Early Church began to put it all together—the Cross, the Resurrection, the Ascension, and Pentecost—they understood that the last age (the *eschaton*) had dawned. Christ the Messiah was indeed ruling and His kingdom was being established. The Petrine interpretation on the Day of Pentecost locked in on Joel 2:28, which carries the prophecy that at the last time God would pour out His Spirit upon all flesh. The apostle unhesitatingly declared, "This is it!"

Richardson sees the Resurrection as "the exodus event in the salvation-history of the New Israel, the mysterious and supernatural act by which God has brought his people out of the land of bondage into the realm of promise, over which his beloved Son reigns forever more (cf. Col. 1:13)."[16] According to Paul in 1 Cor. 10:11, the old age is still with us, but the new age is overlapping it. From another point of view, the Resurrection announced the beginning of a new humanity because the new Adam was identified (1 Cor. 15:20-23).

The Early Church has a whole new perspective of history because of the Resurrection. She can now look back to the centuries of God's dealings with Israel and identify herself; she can look at Jesus of Nazareth and understand who He was and the meaning of saving acts in her behalf. But the future is opened to her also. In fact, the future with its hopes is rushing upon her. In this is born her great expectation of the Parousia.

---

14. S. H. Hooke, *The Resurrection of Christ as History and Experience* (London: Darton, Longman, and Todd, 1967), p. 60. Hook has produced an excellent work on the teaching of the entire New Testament on the Resurrection.

15. Leon Morris, *The Cross in the New Testament* (Grand Rapids, Mich.: Wm. B. Eerdmans Publishing Co., 1965), p. 258.

16. *Introduction to the Theology of the NT,* p. 197.

Peter writes to a people who are in the midst of tribulation and reminds them of the resurrection hope. "Blessed be the God and Father of our Lord Jesus Christ! By his great mercy we have been born anew to a living hope through the resurrection of Jesus Christ from the dead" (1 Pet. 1:3). Through what God has done in raising Jesus from the dead, they are endowed with a hope that will not fade away because God tenderly guards them with His power (1 Pet. 1:5).

The current theology of hope, represented in Pannenberg and Moltmann, makes much of the Resurrection.[17] This theology asserts that "the end of history is present proleptically in Jesus of Nazareth. In his resurrection the final end of universal history has been anticipated; it has occurred beforehand."[18] Hope theologians, however, shred somewhat the cord of hope; they say that "the ultimate divine confirmation of Jesus will take place in the occurrence of his return. Only then will the revelation of God in Jesus become manifest in its ultimate, irresistible glory."[19] Granted the eschatological character of resurrection faith, the validity of New Testament faith is more centrally focused in the past event of Christ's resurrection and its realized meaning now through the Church's proclamation than in an apocalyptic event of the future. The Church's confidence that her Lord lives today is the earnest of future resurrection and glory. The future is more consummation than confirmation.

4. As a final note, it bears repetition to say that without the Resurrection, the work of Christ would have remained unfinished and salvation-history would have been only a fleeting hope. Stauffer concludes, "Without Easter there can be no *kyrie eleison!* For the Christ to whom the Church lifts up its need is the exalted Christ, the heavenly king and priest."[20]

III. The Ascension

The biblical material on the Ascension is brief. Neither the First nor the Fourth Gospel mentions it. Mark's account is in the disputed

---

17. Jürgen Moltmann, *The Theology of Hope* (New York: Harper and Row, 1967); W. Pannenberg, *Jesus, God and Man;* "Redemptive Event and History," *Essays on Old Testament Hermeneutics,* ed. Calus Westermann (Richmond, Va.: John Knox Press, 1964); Martin E. Marty and Dean G. Peerman, eds., *New Theology No. 5* (London: Macmillan Co., 1968), *et al.*

18. Carl E. Braaten, "Toward a Theology of Hope," *New Theology No. 5,* p. 105.

19. Pannenberg, *Jesus, God and Man,* p. 108.

20. *NT Theology,* p. 137.

ending of chapter 16. It is Luke, therefore, who gives us the record of the ascent of the Lord: "While he blessed them, he parted from them" (Luke 24:51). In Acts 1:9 we are told, "And when he had said this, as they were looking on, he was lifted up, and a cloud took him out of their sight."

In this later, longer account in Acts it is recorded that a cloud received Jesus and the men watching saw Him no more. Then two angels announced to them that "this Jesus, who was taken up from you into heaven, will come in the same way as you saw him go into heaven" (1:11). To complete the record, we must add to these accounts the references in John's Gospel where Jesus speaks of His "going away" (John 13:3; 14:2, 28; 16:7).

For Christ, ascension signalized three things: (1) *exaltation,* the reward of the long experience from heaven to hell to the right hand of the Father (Eph. 4:8-9; 1 Tim. 3:16; 1 Pet. 3:22); (2) *intercession,* the saving function on behalf of His followers (Rom. 8:34; 1 John 2:1); (3) *gift,* the pouring out of the Holy Spirit upon Christ's disciples and the future Church (Acts 2:33; cf. John 15:26; 16:7).[21]

---

21. Cf. G. C. Berkouwer, *The Work of Christ,* trans. Cornelius Lambregtse (Grand Rapids, Mich.: Wm. B. Eerdmans Publishing Co., 1965), pp. 202 ff.

Section Four

Salvation Through Christ

———•———

22

The Provision of Salvation

Paul's famous summary of the *kerygma* in 1 Cor. 15:3-4 begins with the declaration that "Christ died for our sins in accordance with the scriptures." The setting for this creedal statement is a passage in which Paul defends the Christian's hope of resurrection. For Paul the validity of the gospel itself is at stake in any skepticism about the Resurrection. His defense includes a clear expression of the meaning of Christ's death, namely, He died "for our sins" or "on account of our sins" *(huper tōn hamartiōn hēmōn)*.

Historically one would have no problem with the simple statement "Christ died," because it could easily be verified. But to say that "Christ died for our sins" introduces a new set of considerations which are more than historical.[1] They involve the deepest theological

---

1. Cf. Peter's explicit word in 1 Pet. 2:24: "He himself bore our sins in his body on the tree."

assumptions. The cross-death of Jesus of Nazareth was a saving act. James Denney says it cryptically, "We do not preach that Jesus died, but that He died for us, and in particular that He died for our sins."[2] Herein is what C. F. D. Moule dares to call

> a vehement form [of] the "scandal of particularity"—this claim that an obscure man, put to death like two other condemned men at the same execution, and like, alas, millions of poor wretches at one time or another, achieved by his death something of such potency that its effects stretch infinitely far . . . both backward and forward—backward so as to take all past history into its embrace, forward to the length of the human race that is to be.[3]

In 1 Cor. 1:23, Paul speaks of Christ's crucifixion as a *skandalon,* "a stumbling block," to the Jews and *moria,* "foolishness," to the Greeks. There are other aspects of the gospel that pull men up short, but hardly any is more scandalous than the Crucifixion. Nevertheless, here is the foundation, because Christianity's message of salvation rests on this point. God's offer of salvation includes more than the acceptance of the words and the ethically impeccable life of His Son; it demands submission to Christ's cross. The salvation which God offers mankind is realizable only through the cross of Christ.

Before exploring the theme of the provision of salvation through atoning death,[4] it seems wise to deal with several background topics, namely: (1) the quest for salvation, (2) the experience and the preaching of the Cross, and (3) the development of the teaching of the provision of salvation in the New Testament.

I. THE QUEST FOR SALVATION

Universally man seeks salvation; he reaches out for rescue "from a life-condition which he knows to be contradictory to his true na-

2. *The Christian Doctrine of Reconciliation* (London: James Clarke and Co., n.d.), p. 20; Stauffer, *New Testament Theology,* p. 131: "The *pro nobis* which Jesus uses in the words of institution of the eucharist straight away took the lead in formulating the soteriological thinking of the early Church"; A. M. Hunter, *The Message of the New Testament* (London: SCM Press, 1943, pp. 92 ff.).

3. *The Sacrifice of Christ* (Philadelphia: Fortress Press, 1964), p. 9. The phrase "the scandal of particularity" *(das Ärgernis der Einmaligkeit)* was first used by Gerhard Kittel, the eminent German lexicographer.

4. The technical theological term *atonement* is not strictly a NT term. The KJV translates the Greek word *katallage* in Rom. 5:11 with the word "atonement," but the literal meaning of the Greek is "reconciliation." The concept of atonement comes through the OT, where the Hebrew *kaphar* carries that meaning. Cf. the Greek

ture." He longs for restoration to a freedom which will accord him the privilege of expressing his true nature.

In the Old Testament, salvation is expressed by a word meaning literally "to be wide," "spacious," "to develop without hindrance," and thus "to be safe, sound, or victorious." The real concern of the Old Testament in its story of salvation is to tell how sinful, unreconciled man strives for personal security and freedom in his world, but discovers to his astonishment that his salvation historically and personally cannot be known by personal achievement but only by the work of God.

At the Exodus deliverance, which expresses historically the salvation of God, Moses exhorts the people: "Fear not, stand firm, and see the salvation of the Lord [yeshuath Yahweh], which he will work for you today" (Exod. 14:13). In very personal language, David prays for salvation and asks God to "restore to me the joy of thy salvation and uphold me with a willing spirit" (Ps. 51:12). In the case of Israel in Egypt and David in his palace, life was threatened and in both instances salvation was essentially rescue from the oppressive situation.[5]

First-century man, both Gentile and Jew, longed for *sōtēria,* "salvation." Among the Gentiles, the mystery cults peddled their "gospels" of salvation through esoteric liturgies while the intellectual philosophies of Epicureanism and Stoicism offered the populace the freedom of *ataraxia* (self-sufficiency, moderation) and *apatheia* (passivity, contentment).[6]

The Jewish world was no less interested in salvation, and the sects of Judaism were proclaiming their salvation hopes—from the Sadducees in Judea to the Essenes in their desert home at Qumran. The Jews of the Diaspora, from the Hasmonean ascendancy to A.D. 70, engaged in extensive missionary activities. "In Paul's own time, Jewish proselytism must have reached its heights. The summons to salvation . . . rang out far and wide into the world."[7]

---

hilaskesthai and its derivatives, the meanings of which are highly disputed; the term "atone" hardly does justice to them. A. G. Hebert, "Atone, Atonement," *A Theological Word Book of the New Testament,* pp. 25-26; Friedrich Buchsel, "*hilaskomai, hilasmos,*" TDNT, 3:301-23.

5. For a discussion of the salvation of God in the OT, cf. F. F. Bruce, *The New Testament Development of Old Testament Themes* (Grand Rapids, Mich.: Wm. B. Eerdmans Publishing Co., 1969), pp. 32-39.

6. James Denney, *The Christian Doctrine of Reconciliation* (London: James Clarke and Co., n.d.), pp. 4-5.

7. H. J. Schoeps, *Paul,* trans. Harold Knight (Philadelphia: The Westminster

For some Jews this present order was evil and that was well represented by the presence of ubiquitous Roman forces. Many people, especially the "humble" ones, the *am ha'aretz,* no longer looked for their salvation collectively or personally in this present order, political or religious, but rather expected the supernatural Messianic intervention of God. Then evil would be destroyed and freedom—"spacious" and "secure" existence—would be theirs.

Luke, with his great sense for reading history, picks up this quest in the birth narratives of John the Baptist and Jesus. John's father, Zechariah, sings, "Blessed be the Lord God of Israel, for . . . he raised up a horn of salvation for us" (Luke 1:68-69; cf. also vv. 71, 77). Mary, the mother of Jesus, breaks out in a hymn, "My soul magnifies the Lord, and my spirit rejoices in God my Saviour" (1:46-47). To the shepherds on the hillsides, the angel of the Lord announced, "Behold, I bring you good news of great joy which will come to all the people; for to you is born this day in the city of David a Saviour, who is Christ the Lord" (2:10-11). And the theme of Paul's Roman letter centers in *sōtēria:* "For I am not ashamed of the gospel: it is the power of God for salvation *[eis sōtērian]*[8] to every one who has faith, to the Jew first and also to the Greek" (1:16).

Certainly, it is a warranted assumption that Paul felt his gospel was a response to a deep longing in the human spirit for salvation. Speaking of the New Testament doctrine of the atonement, V. Taylor writes, "It is nothing less than the doctrine of how man, feeble in his purpose and separated from God by his sins, can be brought into a relationship of true and abiding fellowship with Him, and thus can be enabled to fulfill his divine destiny, both as an individual, and as a member of the community to which he belongs."[9] In keeping with the nature of salvation as understood throughout the Bible, salvation embraces both negative and positive factors. It is both deliverance from sin and the blessing of reconciliation with God.

In the centuries before Christ and in the entire period of the Early Church's ministry, men everywhere despaired of salvation in the present order. Life was so sin-ridden that it could only come

Press, 1961), p. 228; cf. Matt. 23:15: "Woe to you, scribes and Pharisees, hypocrites! for you traverse sea and land to make a single proselyte."

8. "A divine activity or power leading to salvation," C. K. Barrett, "The Epistle to the Romans," *Black's New Testament Commentaries* (London: Adam and Charles Black, 1957), p. 28.

9. *The Atonement in New Testament Teaching,* 3rd ed. (London: The Epworth Press, 1958), p. 167.

under condemnation. But the message of Christ and His followers of the first century brought great expectation of a new life.

II. EXPERIENCE AND THE CROSS

A certain theological naiveté might be charged in Denney's insistence upon "the experimental basis" of the doctrine of the atonement, but a profounder truth is evidenced than might be readily appreciated. He writes: "A reconciled man, preaching Christ as the way of reconciliation, and preaching Him in the temper and spirit which the experience of reconciliation creates, is the most effective mediator of Christ's reconciling power."[10] Having once been estranged from God, the writers of the New Testament effectively communicated the message of reconciliation because they were themselves reconciled to God through Christ.

Thus, when we go to the New Testament, "we never see the death of Jesus as a mere spectacle, a purely objective or external event. We see it through eyes which have felt it, which have filled with tears as they gazed upon it."[11] Denney is appealing to the hermeneutical principle which insists that "eyes of faith" are needed if one is to comprehend the truth of the death of Christ and to effectively communicate it. A sense of the finality or absoluteness of the teaching, and the minimizing of speculation on it are possible because of this experimental approach to the atoning work of Christ.

Such experience is the basis of Paul's argument in 1 Cor. 1:26— 2:16. He writes that not many of the Corinthians are wiser or powerful or of noble birth, but they are redeemed men and they possess the divine wisdom. "He is the source of your life in Christ Jesus, whom God made our wisdom, our righteousness and sanctification and redemption" (1:30).[12] Experience therefore is a teacher in regard to the atonement, because experience partakes of the larger revelation of God's purposes of salvation and the provision of that salvation through Christ's cross.

III. THE DEVELOPMENT OF THE TEACHING

Vincent Taylor has reiterated a hermeneutical principle that should be applied in every exploration of the teaching of the New Testa-

---

10. *The Christian Doctrine of Reconciliation*, p. 8.
11. *Ibid.*, p. 19.
12. Cf. Stauffer, *NT Theology*, p. 126: "But it is not the wise who gather round

ment: "The story of the primitive faith of the Church is that of a vital process, sustained by the illumination of the Spirit, and enriched by the experiences and perceptions of individuals within the life of the worshipping society."[13] Serious investigation of the New Testament references to the saving work of Christ reveals a kind of developing understanding of it in the life of the Church. Continual reflection on the life and teachings of Christ and observation of the power of the preaching of the Cross led to enlarged perception of its meaning.

In our study we recognize the doctrinal process, which had at least two aspects:

1. Preaching in the earliest days of the Christian movement announced the efficacy of the death of Christ, but did not include theorizing about it. Unhesitatingly Peter told the members of the Sanhedrin, "And there is salvation in no one else, for there is no other name under heaven given among men by which we must be saved" (Acts 4:12; cf. 5:31). Paul's message at Antioch in Pisidia is a proclamation of salvation as it relates to the Old Testament background. He declares that *(a)* out of the Davidic lineage God provided a Saviour, Jesus (Acts 13:23); *(b)* through the family of Abraham and all God-fearers has come "the message of salvation" (v. 26); and *(c)* upon the rejection of the truth by the Jews, the message of salvation was taken to the Gentiles (v. 47; cf. the quotation from the Servant Song in Isa. 49:6).

Apparently at this time in the life of the Church, soteriology as a developed teaching is somewhat subordinate to Christology. The invitation to salvation is predicated more on who provided it than upon the rationale of its provision through the death of Christ. It is a reasonable assumption that questions of many sorts were raised by this preaching and teaching. These questions led, in turn, to more developed statements on the nature of the suffering of Christ, as for example, the Book of Hebrews. Jeremias sees this Epistle as providing us "with the most extensive interpretation of the cross."[14] Also, Paul's attempt to write somewhat systematically about the Cross in Romans is another illustration of theological growth.

Jesus (cf. Matt. 11:25; Luke 5:31); it is rather the learners, who know about the final depths of human existence, about the hardships of man's toil and the burden of his guilt. To such as these Jesus reveals in himself a wisdom that is not of this world (cf. 1 Cor. 1:26ff.; 2:6ff.)."

13. *Atonement in NT Teaching,* p. 49.

14. J. Jeremias, *The Central Message of the New Testament* (New York: Charles Scribner's Sons, 1965), p. 31.

2. The several New Testament books provide a variety of insights on salvation. It has been common among scholars in pursuit of the meaning of the death of Christ to state in summary propositions the salient points of the atonement. Leon Morris lists 14:

a. all men are sinners;

b. all sinners are in desperate peril because of their guilt;

c. salvation takes place only because God in His love wills it and brings it about;

d. salvation depends on what God has done in Christ;

e. both the Godhead and the manhood of Christ are involved in the process;

f. Christ was personally innocent;

g. While the importance of the life of Christ is not to be minimized, central importance is attached to His death;

h. in His death Christ made himself one with sinners; He took their place;

i. by His life, death, resurrection, and ascension Christ triumphed over Satan and sin and every conceivable force of evil;

j. not only did Christ win a victory, but He secured a verdict; He wrought salvation powerfully, but also legally;

k. in His death Christ revealed the nature of God as love;

l. in His death Christ is man's supreme Example;

m. men are invited to make a threefold response in repentance, faith, and holy living;

n. there is a cross for the Christian as well as for the Christ.[15]

Morris' list presupposes both diversity and agreement as to the significance of the Cross. The individual New Testament writers have their particular emphasis, but there is no conflict. "What is very impressive," Morris writes, "is the way in which with their varied backgrounds, and their very different way of putting things they should agree so closely on the great central thing, that we are saved, if we are saved at all, only through the death of Jesus Christ for us."[16] This fact points up the vital process provoked and sustained by the Holy Spirit, and enriched by the experiences and perceptions of persons within the Church, which brought the faith to mature and inspirational expression.

---

15. *The Cross in the New Testament* (Grand Rapids, Mich.: Wm. B. Eerdmans Publishing Co., 1965), pp. 364-93; cf. V. Taylor's list, *The Atonement in NT Teaching,* pp. 50-51; G. C. Berkouwer, *The Work of Christ,* trans. Cornelius Lambregtse (Grand Rapids, Mich.: Wm. B. Eerdmans Publishing Co., 1965), pp. 253 ff.

16. *Ibid.,* p. 397.

The importance of this "pluriformity of approaches to Christ's work" is seen in the history of dogma where a number of theories of the atonement have been proposed, each one giving special attention to particular aspects of Christ's ministry at the Cross. The New Testament material indeed suggests variety, and so it is incumbent upon the interpreter to deal fairly with all the material. Taylor's word accurately describes the New Testament's developmental picture and should be taken as a viable guide for the study of Christ's work: "As we have recognized from the outset, it is more plausible that some ideas would be emphasized more than others at different centers, that some aspects of the doctrine would remain in abeyance and that others would become prominent only as time passed and the range of experience grew."[17] Further, each writer has his point of view that is dictated by the concerns which lead him to compose his book along with the factors which gave birth to his own experience of Christ's salvation.

IV. JESUS' TEACHINGS ABOUT HIS DEATH

It is a basic premise of this study that Jesus is the Fount of Christian truth. Despite the theological developments which evolve in the New Testament, the central theses are rooted in the words and work of Christ. For that reason, it is necessary to examine the words of the Lord on His mission in death before venturing to a composite picture of the teaching of the entire New Testament on the atonement.

A. Expectations of His Death

If the Gospels make any point clear about Jesus, it is that throughout His brief ministry there was a mounting opposition to Him. He was reproached by the religious authorities on many counts, particularly for transgression of the Sabbath laws (Mark 2:23-28), the cleansing of the Temple (Mark 11:15-19, and par.), assuming the prerogatives of Deity (Mark 2:1-12; John 5:18; 10:30), and performing exorcisms which could only be attributed, in their judgment, to demonic relationships (Matt. 12:22-24). These were high crimes in their book, and death was the only rightful punishment.[18]

John's Gospel has two notes that show the caution of Jesus in His movements about the land during His ministry. "After this Jesus

---

17. *Atonement in NT Teaching*, p. 49.
18. Mishna. Tractate Sanhedrin, 7, 4.

went about in Galilee; he would not go about in Judea, because the Jews sought to kill him" (7:1). Following the raising of Lazarus, the Sanhedrin met to determine what to do with Jesus because of the numbers of people who were turning to Him. Caiaphas, the high priest, expressed the principle upon which death was legitimized: "You do not understand that it is expedient for you that one man should die for the people, and that the whole nation should not perish" (11:50). A few verses later John records that "from that day on they took counsel how to put him to death" (11:53). Jesus was aware of these intentions, so He retreated to Ephraim, a town near the wilderness, and remained there with His disciples until His sense of mission led Him back into the city (11:54).

Jeremias makes much of the fact that Jesus repeatedly reckoned himself among the prophets, and martyrdom was expected as an integral part of the prophetic ministry. Honoring prophets by adorning their final resting places was something of an "expiation of their murder" (cf. Matt. 23:29; Luke 11:47). John the Baptist stood in that illustrious line and his coming was in preparation for Christ's coming in the power of the Kingdom (Matt. 11:9-13). When the Pharisees told Jesus that Herod Antipas was seeking to kill Him and that for safety He should leave the environs of Galilee, Jesus said in reply: "Nevertheless, I must go on my way today and tomorrow and the day following; for it cannot be that a prophet should perish away from Jerusalem" (Luke 13:33).[19] The lament of Jesus over Jerusalem immediately follows in Luke's account (13:34-35). Christ's redemptive ministry included death at Jerusalem and He knew this. We are therefore not surprised to find insights into this fact in the Gospels.

B. Announcements of His Death

On two occasions in the Synoptic record Jesus explicitly spoke of His death.

1. After Peter's confession at Caesarea Philippi, "You are the Christ," Jesus "began to teach them that the Son of Man must suffer many things, and be rejected by the elders and the chief priests and

---

19. Cf. Jeremias, *Central Message of the NT*, p. 41; Alfred Plummer, "A Critical and Exegetical Commentary on the Gospel According to St. Luke," *The International Critical Commentary* (New York: Charles Scribner's Sons, 1910), pp. 350-51; H. D. A. Major, T. W. Manson, and C. J. Wright, *The Mission and Message of Jesus* (New York: E. P. Dutton and Co., 1938), p. 569: "Herod must not be greedy: for Jerusalem has first claim on the blood of God's messengers."

the scribes, and be killed, and after three days rise again" (Matt. 16: 21; Mark 8:31; Luke 9:22). This was the first time that Jesus plainly shared with them the secret that His divine vocation would take Him through death to resurrection. But the prophetic prediction of His redeeming future was to be shared with the disciples on later occasions (Mark 9:31; 10:33-34 and par.). The little Greek word *dei,* "must," as employed in these announcements, expresses the divine necessity. Jesus taught that He *must* go to Jerusalem and die.

Denney sees a double significance in Christ's use of the word "must." It may indicate either "outward constraint," since hostile forces were arrayed against Him, or "inward constraint," suggesting that "death was something He was bound to accept and contemplate if the work He came to do was to be done, if the vocation with which He was called was to be fulfilled."[20] These two senses are not incompatible, but the inward necessity is more fundamental. "The divine necessity for a career of suffering and death is primary; . . . it is not deduced from the malignant necessities by which He is encompassed; it rises up within Him, in divine power, to encounter these outward necessities and subdue them."[21] This "*dei* of divine necessity" surfaces again in Gethsemane when Jesus agonizingly prays, "Father, yet not what I will, but what you will" (Mark 14:36).

2. At the house of Simon the leper in Bethany, a woman anointed Jesus; and in response to a question of wasting such valuable ointment, Jesus said, "She has anointed my body beforehand for burying" (Mark 14:3-9; cf. Matt. 26:6-13). At that juncture in His brief life, Jesus' mind, no doubt, was gripped by the impending events of His death, and the act of love by the woman comforted Him. Remarkably He takes the occasion to speak again about His death.

The gospel of John has preserved sayings of Jesus in which He speaks of being "lifted up" (*huposōthēnai dei,* 3:14; 8:28; 12:34) and of waiting for His "hour" (*hē hōra mou*) (2:4; 12:23, 27; 13:1; 17:1; cf. Matt. 26:18, 45). These references carry theological overtones. They announce His coming death and at the same time imply the special character of that death. Christ was "lifted up" on a cross but that act was also His hour of glory. Morris comments:

---

20. James Denney, *The Death of Christ* (New York: A. C. Armstrong and Son, 1903), pp. 23, 30.
21. *Ibid.,* p. 31.

It is part of John's aim to show that Jesus showed forth His glory not in spite of His earthly humiliation, but precisely by means of those humiliations. Supremely is this the case with the Cross. To the outward eye this was the uttermost in degradation, the death of a felon. To the eye of faith it was (and is) the supreme glory.[22]

C. The Purpose of His Death

Jesus spoke guardedly about His death for reasons that are quite obvious. The religious intrigue was such that He could not hope to complete His ministry if He openly taught the meaning of His death.

It must be established, however, that Jesus, through His own teachings about His death, laid the foundation for all future interpretation of it by the Church. We cannot accept the idea that some of these interpretive sayings *(logia)* are after the event *(post eventum).* Rather, they are the pre-Easter words of Jesus.

Several passages unfold the meaning of Christ's death.

1. Mark 10:35-40 contains Jesus' answer to James and John when they requested the places at His right and left hands in the Kingdom. The symbols of the "cup" and "baptism" express our Lord's acceptance of His sacrificial vocation as well as the unspeakable agony of the coming Cross. Later He prayed, "My Father, if it be possible let this cup pass from me," but He yielded finally, "Not as I will, but as thou wilt" (Matt. 26:39, par.). His death was no ordinary demise. It bore a special divine meaning, and the disciples were informed in this incident that they would share in its purpose through their later service to the Master (cf. Matt. 20:23, par.).

2. The accounts of the Lord's Supper indicate the significance of His death. Both Denney and Jeremias view the subtle references to Isaiah 53 by Jesus as important for any exposition of meaning of His death.[23] On the basis of this premise, Jeremias[24] takes note of Mark 14:24; "This is my blood of the [new] covenant, which is poured out for many *[huper pollōn].*" The phrase "for many" probably reflects Isa.

22. Leon Morris, "The Gospel According to John," *The New International Commentary on the New Testament* (Grand Rapids, Mich.: Wm. B. Eerdmans Publishing Co., 1971), p. 226; cf. V. Taylor's discussion on these verses in *Atonement in NT Teaching,* p. 147.

23. Denney, *Death of Christ,* pp. 34-35; Jeremias, *Central Message of the NT,* pp. 45 ff.; also *NT Theology,* pp. 276 ff.; cf. T. W. Manson, *Teachings of Jesus,* p. 231; V. Taylor, *The Cross of Christ* (London: Macmillan Co., 1956), pp. 18-23.

24. *Central Message of the NT,* pp. 45 ff.

53:12. "Many" without the article conveys the inclusive sense of "the great number," or "all."

3. In Mark 10:45 the servant concept is very clear: "For the Son of man also came not to be served but to serve, and to give his life a ransom for many." This verse emphasizes the voluntary character of the death—He "came to give." He elected willfully to engage in this deed.

His "life" is the price He pays for "ransom." This metaphor should not be drawn out but taken simply for what it means on the surface. Christ was not thinking of "buying freedom by bribing the devil, or paying a debt to God or to the moral law. Man is in slavery: Jesus is giving His life to set him free."[25]

4. In Luke 22:35-38 Jesus suggests that His disciples buy swords. A quotation from Isa. 53:12 is offered by Jesus to support the recommendation: "I tell you that this scripture must be fulfilled in me, 'And he was reckoned with transgressors'; for what is written about me has its fulfillment."

Jeremias thinks we "strike the bed-rock of tradition" in this saying, primarily because of the reference to the "imminent beginning of the apocalyptic tribulation" and the unglossed statement of the disciples about carrying two swords.[26] This latter assertion points up their total lack of understanding. What is important is Jesus' declaration of His impending death interpreted within the context of the sacrificial teaching of Isaiah 53.

5. In Mark 14:27-28 Jesus said to them, "You will all fall away; for it is written, 'I will strike the shepherd, and the sheep will be scattered.' But after I am raised up, I will go before you to Galilee." The Old Testament reference is Zech. 13:7-9, where "the death of the shepherd ushers in not only the eschatological tribulation of the flock but also the gathering of the tried and purified remnant within the kingdom of God."[27] The language of the shepherd in Mark 14:28, "to go before" *(proaxō)*, is related to John 10, where it is said, "The good shepherd lays down his life for the sheep" (cf. vv. 11, 15). Jeremias thinks this passage from John is understandable only against the background of Isaiah 53.

6. In Luke 23:34 we have Jesus' prayer, "Father, forgive them; for they know not what they do." Jeremias is confident that we

---

25. Hugh Martin, *The Claims of Christ* (London: SCM Press, 1955), p. 97.
26. *Central Message of the NT*, p. 47.
27. *Ibid.*, p. 48.

have in this prayer an implicit interpretation of our Lord's death. He contends that a condemned man before his execution must offer the expiatory vow, "May my death expiate all my sins." Jesus, to the contrary, "applies the atoning virtue of his death not to himself, as was the custom, but to his executioners."[28] Once again, Isaiah's prophecy is the background, especially 53:12, which reads, "He made intercession for the transgressors."

In conclusion, Jesus exhibited a deep sense of mission in life, which reached back to His baptism and temptation, if not earlier. That mission involved the giving of His whole life for the redemption of God's people. Paul's *kenosis* passage (Phil. 2:5-11) expresses it most poignantly. At a designated time, Jesus began to instruct the disciples concerning His impending death and resurrection. The three predictive passages in the earliest tradition affirm this fact (Mark 8:31; 9:31; 10:33). Concurrently He began to interpret His death as being more than a martyrdom; it was a vicarious sacrifice, a representative deed, and an act of the will of God.

These ideas, as Jeremias, Denney, and others have clarified for us, arise out of the majestic Suffering Servant Hymn in Isaiah 53. The Lord's Supper focalizes several of these original ideas concerning Jesus, especially in the areas that speak of a "broken body," "poured out blood," and salvation "for many." He was surely sacrificing His life for others. With these ideas, the Early Church moved into her world to proclaim the Cross and to probe its meaning both for herself and for the evangelization of the world.[29]

The real purpose of the atoning work of God in Christ was to bring salvation *(sōtēria)*. That salvation is defined in a variety of ways but basically it is redemption *(apolutrōsis)* or deliverance from sin. Redemption includes the putting away of sin (Heb. 9:26); the bearing away of sin (John 1:29); purification of sin (Heb. 1:3); cleansing from sin (1 John 1:7); expiation or propitiation for sin (Rom. 3:25; Heb. 2:17; 1 John 2:2); and forgiveness (Matt. 26:28; Eph. 1:7; Col. 1:14).

Deliverance includes freedom from the demonic powers which are the sources of sin (John 12:31; Col. 2:14-15; Heb. 2:14-15); freedom from the law as a self-merit system of salvation (Romans 7; Gal. 2:15-21; Eph. 2:8-10; Phil. 3:7-10); freedom from the fear of

28. *Ibid.*
29. Cf. V. Taylor's paragraphs on "How Jesus Interpreted His Cross," *Cross of Christ*, pp. 18-23.

death because through Christ we have passed from death into life (John 3:15-16; 5:24; 6:51; 10:27-28; Rom. 5:21; 6:5-11; 1 Corinthians 15; Col. 3:4; Heb. 2:14-15; 9:12; Jas. 1:12; Rev. 7:9-17). Salvation through Christ is thus total rescue from the clutches of sin's power and the enjoyment of a sound and wholesome existence.

Our attention is now turned to drawing together the variety of expressions of the saving work of Christ in the rest of the New Testament, in order to answer the question: How shall we describe Christ's saving deed?

23

The Efficacy of Christ's Death

Any discussion of the atonement must begin with God, a fact made abundantly clear in the New Testament. It is God who initiates the Incarnation and the subsequent death and Resurrection. "For God so loved the world that he gave his only begotten Son, that whosoever believeth in him should not perish but have everlasting life" (John 3:16). "But God shows his love for us in that while we were yet sinners Christ died for us" (Rom. 5:8).[1] Again Paul writes, "He who did not spare his own Son but gave him up for us all, will he not also give us all things with him?" (Rom. 8:32). It is God's love that moves Him to this extraordinary action.

Donald Baillie comments, "There is an atonement, an expiation, in the heart of God Himself, and out of this comes the forgiveness of our sins."[2] This means that God alone bears the costs. He suffers more than man does for his sins, not alone because He has been wronged, but because the shame of what we have done weighs so heavily on His heart. Herein is the objective reality of the atonement, namely,

---

1. Cf. A. M. Hunter, *Message of the NT*, pp. 89-90; speaking of Rom. 5:8: "That noble sentence needs only some such supplement as 'in order to reconcile us to himself,' to be a fine summary of what the New Testament has to say about the Atonement. It originates in the gracious will of God; it is necessitated by men's sin; its means is Christ, and especially Christ crucified; and its purpose is reconciliation, or restored fellowship, with God."

2. *God Was in Christ* (New York: Charles Scribner's Sons, 1948), p. 175.

that God made an offering of himself in Christ. Paul's word to the Corinthians is expressive: "God was in Christ reconciling the world to himself" (2 Cor. 5:19). The subjective phase of the work of atonement is man's assurance of forgiveness and restored relationship with God on the basis of faith in Christ.

I. JUDGMENT UPON SIN

The little phrase "for us" is axiomatic in this study of the atonement of Christ. To declare that Christ died for us is to raise the question of our condition which made the Cross-death necessary. Sin in the human heart is the answer. Paul passes along the faith of the Church when he says that "Christ died for our sins according to the scriptures" (1 Cor. 15:3; cf. also Rom. 5:6, 8; 6:10; Gal. 1:4; Eph. 2:5; Titus 2:14; Heb. 9:26; 10:12; 1 Pet. 2:24; 1 John 1:7, "the blood of Jesus"; 2:2, "propitiation for our sins," KJV; Rev. 1:5, "by his blood").

The most explicit word from the Lord which provides foundation for Paul's assertion comes out of the Supper episode. Jesus said, "For this is my blood of the covenant, which is poured out for many for the forgiveness of sins" (*eis aphesin hamartiōn,* Matt. 26:28). Christ took the *via dolorosa* in order to provide a means of forgiveness *(aphesis)* of sins.[3]

The Cross does not figure largely in Christ's forgiving ministry in the Gospels; neither is there a strain of interpretation of the Cross in relationship to forgiveness introduced by the Gospel writers. It is proper to assume that the event of the Cross needed to transpire before the implicit truth could be exposed. We have stated before that the Cross and the Resurrection shed illuminating rays of light on the events of Christ's life. While the love of God originated the saving deed of the Cross, the sin of mankind necessitated it. Man's need for atonement, moreover, involves his helplessness to put himself right with God. He is "estranged and hostile in mind, doing evil deeds" (Col. 1:21), "without God in the world" (Eph. 2:12), and alienated from the life of God" (Eph. 4:18). This state of affairs is due to man's sin, which the holy God cannot tolerate.[4] Thus after the Resurrection there was never a period, not even a very short one, when the saving significance of the Cross was not implicitly recognized.

---

3. *Aphesis* means "remission," "sending away," or "letting loose without exacting payment." Cf. Leon Morris, "Forgiveness," NBD, pp. 435-36. Morris notes that forgiveness is more usually linked directly with Christ himself (Eph. 4:32; Acts 5:31), but he warns that the work of Christ cannot be separated from the person of Christ.
4. Cf. C. L. Mitton, "Atonement," IDB, 1:311.

The point of major importance is the note of condemnation of sin sounded through the Cross. John and Paul reflect this emphasis. John 3:19 reads: "This is the judgment, that light is come into the world, and men loved darkness rather than light." Darkness is symbolic of sin. As Jesus approached His death, He said, "Now is the judgment of this world, now shall the ruler of this world be cast out; and I, when I am lifted up from the earth, will draw all men to myself" (John 12:31-32). A confrontation between God and the evil order, both cosmic and individual, took place at the Cross. Since that time "the prince of the air" and sinful mankind stand condemned unless a faith response to Christ's atoning death has transpired.

To the Romans, Paul wrote: "For God has done what the law, weakened by the flesh, could not do: sending his own Son in the likeness of sinful flesh and for sin, he condemned sin in the flesh" (8:3). Seen within the framework of God's eschatological purposes, the work of Christ was the beginning of their fulfillment, and one of the effects was the condemnation of sin. Barrett writes, "Judgment has begun, and the Cross left no doubt of the attitude of God towards sin."[5]

In the greatness of His love for men, Christ in a true sense bore the weight of the judgment upon sin. This truth is not easy to understand, but we know that it is possible for one who is not personally subject to the penalty for a wrongdoing to endure some of its consequences. Parents, for example, suffer when their children commit wrong and suffer thereby. In such a way, Christ might experience in indescribable ways the judgment which has fallen upon sinful mankind.

Vincent Taylor writes that "we are not debarred from pressing this analogy because Christ Himself was sinless. . . . Only saints in the making can bear the sins of another; only Christ can bear the sins of the world." He goes on to assert that "there does not seem to me to be any good reason why we should hesitate to think of Christ as submitting to the judgment which overtakes human sin."[6] Denney asks rhetorically if we are not compelled to say that in the dark hour of the Cross, Christ "had to realize to the full the divine reaction against

---

5. *Epistle to the Romans*, p. 157; John Wesley comments on Rom. 8:3 that God "gave sentence that sin should be destroyed, and the believer wholly delivered from it," *Explanatory Notes upon the New Testament* (Naperville, Ill.: Alec R. Allenson, 1966, reprint), p. 546.
6. *Forgiveness and Reconciliation* (London: Macmillan and Co., 1956), p. 211.

sin in the race in which He was incorporated, and that without doing so He could not have been the Redeemer of that race from sin, or the Reconciler of sinful men to God."[7]

The judgment on sin is very personal, too, for as J. S. Whale comments, "The events of Holy Week are the final measure of us all, and we are all found wanting."[8] The world which put Christ to death is our world. In the light of Calvary, the good things about us, even our fairly successful attempts to be righteous, are seen for what they really are, "ever perverted by the deep-seated wrongness, the *permanens infirmatas,* of human nature." Paul's conclusion about mankind's spiritual status is irrefutable: "For I have already charged that all men, both Jews and Greeks, are under the power of sin, as it is written: None is righteous, no, not one" (Rom. 3:9-10; cf. 3:23).

The word "wrath" *(orgē)* is a strong New Testament term that expresses the divine reaction to sin. "The wrath of God is revealed from heaven against all ungodliness and wickedness of men who by their wickedness suppress the truth" (Rom. 1:18). Those who do not obey the Son fall under the wrath of God (John 3:36). Paul tells the readers of Ephesians not to be deceived, "for it is because of these things that the wrath of God comes upon the sons of disobedience" (5:6). According to the Apocalypse, even the Lamb is possessed with a wrath that is poured out upon rebellious man at the end of time (6:16; 11:18; 15:1; 16:1, 19; 18:8; 19:15).

The most extensive expression of the wrath of God comes at the beginning of Romans, where Paul characterizes the condition of obstreperous mankind and the *divine permissio.* Three times Paul says that God "gave them up" *(paredōken,* 1:24, 26, 28) to pursue the ways they had already chosen.[9]

The wrath of God comes to its fullest revelation in the cross of Christ. Reason causes us to resist any notion that the wrath of God fell upon Christ, yet at the Cross a full exposure of the divine displeasure against sin took place (Mark 15:34). John Calvin asks in puzzle-

---

7. *Christian Doctrine of Reconciliation,* p. 273.
8. *Victor and Victim* (Cambridge: University Press, 1960), p. 64.
9. For a discussion on the wrath of God, cf. D. E. H. Whiteley, *The Theology of St. Paul* (Philadelphia: Fortress Press, 1966), pp. 61-72; Richardson, *Introduction to the Theology of the NT,* p. 76: "In Paul, as in the NT generally, though the expression is used absolutely, it always means 'the wrath *of God'* and not a kind of impersonal 'inevitable process of cause and effect in a moral universe'; we can rationalize the idea in that way, if we like, but it would be a mistake to suppose that the NT writers did so"; cf. John Deschner on Wesley, *Wesley's Christology* (Dallas: Southern Methodist University Press, 1960), pp. 150-52.

ment, "How could He be angry with the beloved Son, with whom His soul was well pleased?" And yet Calvin can go on to speak of Christ as abandoned and forsaken of God.[10] Whale reminds us of this "huge paradox, the outrageous originality of the gospel of our redemption that the divine judgement on man's whole evil situation falls upon the divine judge."[11]

In typical antithetical style, the Apostle Paul speaks to the Roman Christians of the redemptive effects of Christ's work at the Cross, one of which is deliverance from the wrath of God: "Since, therefore, we are now justified by his blood, much more shall we be saved by him from the wrath of God. For if while we were enemies we were reconciled to God by the death of his Son, much more, now that we are reconciled, shall we be saved by his life" (5:9-10; cf. 1 Thess. 5:10).

H. R. Mackintosh discusses three ways that man's sin is judged in the cross of Christ. First, "sin is condemned in the cross because there it is permitted fully to expose its true nature." Perfect goodness and perfect love represented in Christ set in sharp contrast the terrible character of our sins. Second, "sin is judged in the cross by Jesus' attitude to its intrinsic evil." Instead of seeking the easy way for himself, Jesus denounced sin, refused to compromise with it, and elected to shed His blood for its eradication. Third, "sin is judged in the cross of Jesus because the connection between sin and suffering is there made utterly clear."[12]

Numerous scriptures bear out this connection: Mark 10:45; Rom. 3:25-26; 2 Cor. 5:14-15, 21; Gal. 1:4; 3:13; 1 Tim. 2:5-6; 1 Pet. 1:18-21; 2:24-25; 3:18. Peter's word expresses it explicitly: "He himself bore our sins in his body on the tree, that we might die to sin and live to righteousness" (1 Pet. 2:24; cf. Isa. 53:4-6). The Innocent One suffered for the guilty, or as Barth says, "The Judge was judged in our place." In the delicate relationships between persons, sin brings pain; and reconciliation can be experienced only when that pain is borne by both the sinner and the one sinned against. Mackintosh thus concludes: "For the very reason that he [Christ] was related to the sinful with such profound intimacy, the judgment of God on their sin struck *him*."[13]

---

10. *Institutes*, II, XVI, 10.
11. *Victor and Victim*, p. 67; cf. Stagg, *NT Theology*, p. 138.
12. *The Christian Experience of Forgiveness* (London: Nisbet and Co., 1927), pp. 198-206.
13. *Ibid.*, p. 204.

The judgment of God upon sin in the Cross is at the same time the vindication of the divine righteousness. By this very act of His cross-judgment of sin, God provides deliverance from sin's otherwise ineradicable condemnation. In the Cross He makes possible a life of righteousness through faith in Christ's atoning work (Rom. 3:24-26; 2 Cor. 5:21).

II. A VICARIOUS DEED

Not only was the cross of Christ a judgment upon sin, it was also a vicarious act on the part of Christ. The word "vicarious" is a transliteration of the Latin *vicarius* which means literally "substituted." It denotes "taking the place of another." A vicar is a deputy or substitute minister; he acts as a representative of another minister. Metaphorically, in our study, "vicarious" connotes an experience that is "endured, suffered, or performed by one person in place of another." To describe Christ's death as vicarious is to declare that He in some manner endured or suffered an experience which was due us. In vicarious suffering, the effects or benefits accrue to someone other than the sufferer. It is endured on behalf of others, doing for them what they are not able to do for themselves.

A. Christ's Teachings

Once again, Jesus' words are instructive, for He sets forth the view that His death has vicarious value. The Lord's application to His ministry of the teaching of the Suffering Servant from Isaiah 53 was intended to demonstrate His vicarial role. Two logia are quite explicit.[14] Mark 10:45 reads: "For the Son of man also came not to be served but to serve, and to give his life a ransom for many *(anti pollōn)*." Mark 14:24 is taken from the Eucharist ceremony. "This is my blood of the covenant, which is poured out for many *[huper pollōn]*." The little phrase "for many" has produced much debate because of the different prepositions used, *anti* and *huper*. Are they equivalents? *Anti* implies substitution, an idea offensive to many scholars, whereas *huper* merely implies representation.

Anti means "instead of" or "in place of." According to Vincent

14. See John 10:15, "I lay down my life *(huper)* the sheep"; also Caiaphas' "unconscious prophecy" in 11:50-51: "You do not understand that it is expedient for you that one man should die for the people, and that the whole nation should not perish." He prophesied that Jesus should die for the nation.

Taylor it should not be treated as a synonym of *huper*, which means "in behalf of."[15] Arndt and Gingrich, on the other hand, list three meanings for *anti*, one of which parallels *huper*: (1) to indicate one person or thing is to be replaced by another, *instead of, in place of* (Matt. 2:22); (2) to indicate that one thing is equivalent to another, *for, as, in place of* (Matt. 5:38, "an eye *for* an eye"; 1 Cor. 11:15); (3) to indicate *in place of, for* (Matt. 17:27; 20:28; Mark 10:45). Based upon a study of Gen. 44:33, these two eminent lexicographers apparently conclude that in the case of Mark 10:45, the idea of vicarious activity is expressed by the use of *anti*.[16] The meaning is that in the act of deliverance the "many" not only benefit but receive what they cannot gain for themselves. As noted earlier, "many" may carry the meaning of "all." But here it contrasts the vicarious act of the One with all those for whom it was done.

In a biblical view of atonement, the idea of substitution is inescapable. The Septuagint uses the word "ransom" *(lutron)* 140 times, generally with the thought of the payment of compensation, deliverance from prison, or the offering of a substitute. Christ's hearers would have understood that He meant substitution.[17] In the ancient world, "ransom" was related to freedom from imprisonment, the payment of a ransom effecting release.

Thus, Christ was saying that His death was the price paid to release the penitent sinner shackled by sin. As a result the sinner is a free man. Once he lived under the sentence of death because of sin, but Christ by the surrender of His own life liberated him. Christ brought him back to God on the condition of faith in Christ's work. Denney writes:

> A ransom is not wanted at all except where life has been forfeited, and the meaning of the sentence unambiguously is that the forfeited lives of many are liberated by the surrender of Christ's life, and that to surrender His life to do them this incalculable service was the very soul of his calling."[18]

B. The Teachings of the Epistles

The writers of the New Testament lift up this theme of self-giving for others and deepen its meaning for Christian teaching. The preposi-

15. *Gospel According to St. Mark*, p. 444.
16. *Greek-English Lexicon of the NT*, pp. 72-73.
17. Cf. David Hill, *Greek Words and Hebrew Meanings: Studies in the Semantics of Soteriological Terms* (Cambridge: University Press, 1967), pp. 77-81; Leon Morris, *Cross in the NT*, pp. 52-54.
18. *Death of Christ*, p. 45.

tion *huper* with its introduction of the idea of vicarial service appears again and again. Paul writes in Romans that "while we were yet helpless *[asthenōn]*, at the right time Christ died *for [huper] the ungodly*" (5:6). He follows this declaration with the grander truth that "God shows his love for us in that while we were yet sinners Christ died *for us*" (5:8).

The death of Christ, which expressed the love of God for mankind, was also a deliberate act of God. "He did not spare his own Son but gave him up *for us all*" *(huper hēmōn pantōn*, 8:32). Our salvation was obtained "through our Lord Jesus Christ, who died *for us*" (1 Thess. 5:9-10), and it is personalized for those who "have been crucified with Christ" (Gal. 2:20).

This self-giving act of Christ includes more than emancipation from the power of sin; it creates through purification a "people of God's own possession." Paul writes to Titus that Christ "gave himself for us to redeem us from all iniquity and to purify for himself a people of his own who are zealous for good deeds" (2:14).

In Tim. 2:6 we find a Pauline parallel to Jesus' words in Mark 10:45. The apostle writes that Christ gave himself "as a ransom for all" *(ho dous heauton antilutron huper pantōn)*. The prefix *(anti)* to the word *lutron* suggests the notion of substitution.[19] However, basing one's interpretation on the appearance of *anti* in this verse, care should be taken not to overstress the idea of substitutionary ransom in Paul. The apostle does not use *anti* in a prepositional phrase; *huper* is his preference. Paul does speak of a substitutionary act, but it arises in a different set of scriptures. It must be kept clear that he views Christ's saving deed as a self-giving act, the benefits of which, including deliverance from sin and incorporation into God's people, accrued to those who believed in Christ.

The Epistle to the Hebrews also represents Christ's death as a work *for us*. A key verse says that by the grace of God, Christ tasted death "for every man" *(huper pantos*, 2:9). Jesus is called the "forerunner" who has gone *on our behalf* behind the curtain to intercede *for us* (6:19-20). He acts at the Cross *on our behalf* and *for every man*.

The First Epistle of Peter likewise highlights the vicarious nature of Christ's work. Christ was "destined *[proegnōsmenou]* before the foundation of the world but was manifested at the end of times *for*

---

19. Leon Morris, *The Apostolic Preaching of the Cross* (Grand Rapids, Mich.: Wm. B. Eerdmans Publishing Co., 1955), p. 48.

your sake [di' humas]." That manifestation was for the purpose of providing a ransom through His precious blood (1 Pet. 1:18-20).

Peter's most pointed word is found in his appeal to Christlike living in 1 Pet. 2:21. There he resorts to Christ's example at the Cross: "Christ also suffered *for you [huper humon]*, leaving you an example, that you should follow in his steps." He moves on to assert in clear terms that Christ "bore our sins in his body on the tree, that we might die to sin and live to righteousness" (v. 24).

John likewise supports this vicarious concept of the nature of Christ's death in his First Epistle: "By this we know love, that he laid down his life *for us [huper hēmōn]"* (3:16).

The vicarious character of Christ's work illuminates the whole nature of Deity. God's eternal love was willing to pay any price to reestablish relationships with mankind. The gracious spirit of the Father which "gave up" the Son to death was matched in equal measure by the Son's gift of himself in death for sinful man. This deed at Calvary was totally selfless. The benefits accrue overwhelmingly to the sinner who responds to it in faith. It was "on behalf" of man that this supreme act of self-giving transpired.

C. His Death and Ours

The vicarious deed of the Lord involved the experience of death *for us,* and obedience to God *for us.* This deed by Christ included going the way of death and resurrection. Speaking of righteousness, the central result of Christ's work, Paul declares, "It will be reckoned to us who believe in him that raised from the dead Jesus our Lord, who was put to death for our trespasses and raised for our justification" (Rom. 4:24-25). In other places Paul asserts that Christ voluntarily "gave himself for us" (Titus 2:14); here in Romans he says that Christ was "put to death" *(paredothē).*[20] This "putting to death" refers to the intentional divine involvement in the Cross—not to the fact that Christ's contemporaries crucified Him outside Jerusalem's walls. Evil men could not have put him to death for our trespasses *(dia ta paraptomata hēmōn).*[21] Only God himself could have done that.

There exists a penal relationship between sin and death. Paul declares this fact in Rom. 6:23, "the wages of sin is death," and in 1 Cor. 15:56, "the sting of death is sin." Death in mankind's history

---

20. *Paredothē* means "delivered" but in this case it metaphorically means "put to death," for the context includes the "raising" of Christ. The Cross and Resurrection are considered two aspects of a single deed of salvation.

thus stands as the symbol of the tragic alienation between God and man because of sin. Even as far back as Genesis 3, death is described as the outcome of Adam's fall. Through all of his history man has lived with this expected result of his sinfulness. One might justifiably conclude that because death is so certain and irreversible, it controls the meaning of the life of the sinner; it is the ultimate issue for thoughtful man. To live is to die.

Christ's vicarious act takes Him all the way into man's existence and that includes tasting death (cf. Heb. 2:14-15). He destroyed the power of death over man's life and demonstrated through the God-initiated Resurrection that sin can really be overcome. Other interpretative factors are part of the meaning of the Cross, but in this case Christ's experience of death paradoxically declares that through death we can be victorious.

It has been said that "the death of Christ transforms our thinking about death." Indeed it transforms our understanding of our existence; it is no longer moving "from life to death" but rather "from death to life." All must die, but if we have died spiritually with Christ, "death is swallowed up in victory" (1 Cor. 15:54).

Paul's *kenosis* passage emphatically speaks of the Lord's action in "emptying" and "humbling" himself as the supreme example for the Christian life. Paul calls the readers to unity, sympathy, selflessness, and humility like Christ's. "Have this mind among yourselves, which you have in Christ Jesus" (Phil. 2:1-11). "This mind" accepts the "divine death" as the way to exalted life. If we are united with Him in His death, we will also share His victory over death.

D. His Obedience and Ours

Paul and the author of Hebrews emphasize that Christ acted in obedience to God's demands, and in doing so the benefits accrued to mankind. In the representative deed of the Cross, Christ's obedience provided the possibility for our obedience and salvation. "In the days of his flesh, Jesus offered up prayers and supplications, with loud cries and tears, to him who was able to save him from death, and he was heard for his godly fear. Although he was a Son, he learned obedience *[emathen . . . tēn hupakoēn]* through what he suffered; and being made perfect he became the source of eternal salvation to all

---

21. *Dia* with the accusative in this case indicates the reason why something happens, so He was put to death "because of our sins," or "for the sake of our sins." Cf. Arndt and Gingrich, *Lexicon*, p. 180.

who obey him, being designated by God a high priest after the order of Melchizedek" (Heb. 5:7-10).

"Learning obedience" on the part of the Son must be related to His priestly work, namely, to His death in behalf of mankind. It does not relate to the normal education of a child in obedience to a parent. The will of the Father controlled His mind and spirit throughout His ministry. He finally cried out in the Garden of Gethsemane, "Not my will but thy will be done." That obedience opened up the way for God to be reconciled to His creatures. It also qualified Christ as High Priest to bring to God all who through His power are enabled to make a similar believing and obedient response to the will of God. He is thus "the source of salvation to all who obey him" (Heb. 5:9). Christ's death as an act of obedience was on our behalf, because now through our obedience to Christ's call we are reconciled to the Father.

Paul regards the human race as represented by two persons, Adam and Christ (Rom. 5:12-21; 1 Cor. 15:21-22, 45-50). These persons, as it were, "incorporate the human race, or sections of it, within themselves, and the dealings they have with God they have representatively on behalf of their fellows."[22] The religious history of mankind is determined by relationship to these two representatives.

Obedience and disobedience to God determine the character of the humanity which these two persons create. Adam disobeyed God and thus mankind inherited sin and death. To be one with Adam is to share the "primal wretchedness" of disobedience, the urge to patricide against God, and the life of alienation and fear (Rom. 5:19).

Christ, on the other hand, obeyed God, and the new humanity He creates enjoys justification and life. Identification with Christ places the individual in a radically different situation. Since Christ has been obedient unto death, His resurrection is the assurance that all who share in His obedience in the life of His body, the Church, share also His righteousness and victory over death. Paul summarizes: "Then as one man's trespass led to condemnation for all men, so one man's act of righteousness leads to acquittal and life for all men. For as by one man's disobedience many were made sinners, so by one man's obedience many will be made righteous" (Rom. 5:18-19). Christ submitted to the Father's call to death and became the

22. C. K. Barrett, *From First Adam to Last* (New York: Charles Scribner's Sons, 1962), p. 5; cf. also Karl Barth, *Christ and Adam*, trans. by T. A. Small (New York: Harper and Bros., 1957).

Head of a new humanity. The Second Adam by obedience regained for us what was lost by the first Adam. Our obedience to the obedient Son is our hope of salvation.

III. THE SACRIFICIAL DEATH

No fair-minded reader of the New Testament can deny the widespread belief of the Early Church that the death of Christ was an act of self-giving on His part. Culpepper comments, "Indeed, sacrificial ideas pervade every segment of the New Testament."[23]

A. The Idea of Sacrifice

Jesus himself initiated the explanation of His death as a sacrifice, for He interpreted His mission in the world in terms of the fulfillment of the spiritualized concept of sacrifice found in Isaiah 53. By numerous figures He anticipated the sacrifice of His life for others. For example, to Andrew and Philip, on the occasion when the Greeks wished to see Jesus, the Master declared, "Truly, truly, I say to you, unless a grain of wheat falls into the earth and dies, it remains alone; but if it dies, it bears much fruit. He who loves his life loses it, and he who hates his life in this world will keep it for eternal life" (John 12:24-25). The Master was not only calling His disciples to sacrificial living and dying; He had His own future death in mind.

The several records of the Lord's Supper contain four sacrificial terms that relate to cultic practices in the Old Testament: (1) blood (Lev. 17:11); (2) covenant (Exod. 24:8); (3) poured out (Lev. 4:7-8); and (4) body (cf. 1 Cor. 11:23-26; Mark 14:22-25; par.). The explicit references to Christ as "our paschal lamb" (1 Cor. 5:7) and "a lamb without blemish or spot" (1 Pet. 1:19) suggest that sacrificial notions were broadly attached to the death of Christ (cf. Rev. 5:6, 8, 12).

Thusia, "sacrifice," is used for Jesus' death in Eph. 5:2: "And walk in love, as Christ loved us and gave himself up for us, a fragrant offering and sacrifice *[thusian]* to God." Hebrews, in which the category of sacrifice is an important key for interpreting the life and work of Christ, uses *thusia* in four places (7:27; 9:26; 10:12, 26).[24] The

---

23. Robert H. Culpepper, *Interpreting the Atonement* (Grand Rapids, Mich.: Wm. B. Eerdmans Publishing Co., 1966), p. 68. This is one of the finest brief surveys of the biblical and theological aspects of the atonement.

24. Johannes Behm, *Thusia,* TDNT, 3:185: "When Hebrews compares the atoning sacrifice of Christ with its OT model, it does not present us with a caricature which remains within the sphere of a religion of law. It goes back to the original conception and purpose of sacrifice in the OT, namely, that it is a means of personal

language of 9:26 is especially expressive: "But as it is, he has appeared once for all at the end of the age to put away sin by the sacrifice of himself" (dia tēs thusias autou). The central theme of this Epistle is that Christ is the eternal High Priest. By offering himself once for all (hapax) in perfect sacrifice for sin, He does what could never be accomplished under the old order, namely, the securing of eternal redemption. However, the sacrifices of the past presaged and made understandable the truly efficacious character of Christ's offering. So the author proclaims, "For it is impossible that the blood of bulls and goats should take away sins" (Heb. 10:4), but "we have been sanctified through the offering of the body of Jesus once for all" (10:10).

B. The Lamb of God

John retained for us a note from the Judean phase of Jesus' life when he records that John the Baptist twice introduced Jesus as the "Lamb of God" (ho amnos tou theou). John 1:29 reads, "The next day he saw Jesus coming toward him, and said, 'Behold, the Lamb of God.'" Markus Barth sees these Johannine passages as summaries of all the cultic, servanthood (Isaiah 53), and redemption motifs of the Old Testament. The official high priest of the old order did not die for the sins of the people; the sacrificial animals died. On the contrary, in the New Testament view "only the faithful servant of Isa. 53 laid down his life, and was thus priest and victim in one person."[25] John tells us that:

1. Christ's sacrifice is a "gift of God." The title "Lamb of God" cannot mean "godly lamb" or "lamb given to God"; it means the lamb "provided by God" or the lamb "acceptable to God," "glorified by God." The removal of our sins and the reestablishment of our relationships with God are thus benefits of God's grace.

2. John also emphasizes the purpose of the Lamb's death—to "take away the sin of the world" (ho airōn tēn hamartian tou kosmou).

---

intercourse between God and man. This original purpose of sacrifice is finally fulfilled in the personal act of Christ, in the voluntary and unique offering up of His life. Sacrifice is thus brought to an end in Him. Cultic sacrifice is not merely transcended but ended by the unique self-offering of Christ (10:18; cf. 9:8) because the person of Christ as High-priest is unique." Cf. Behm's fine discussion of the "Old Testament Presupposition" of sacrifice, p. 183.

25. Barth, Was Christ's Death a Sacrifice? (Edinburgh: Oliver and Boyd, 1961), p. 39. Speaking of the entire NT, Barth comments that "the main competition to 'sacrificial' soteriology seems to come from the Isaianic, prophetic, or psalterial environment of Isa. 53" (p. 7).

Airō has a variety of meanings in the Septuagint and even in John's Gospel, but the essential meaning is that of "removal" or "blotting out." In these two verses it means the removal of sin at the expense of another's life. "It costs no less than the life of God's chosen Servant to free the people from sin."[26]

As the Lamb of God *(Agnus Dei)*, Christ makes atonement for the whole world without distinction of race or religion. The sacrifice of the Lamb makes universal redemption possible.

3. The wider context of the Fourth Gospel makes it quite plain that the sacrifice of the Lamb is His glorification. Throughout the Gospel, Christ's death is called ascent into heaven, exaltation, or glorification (3:13 f.; 12:32, 34; 17:4 ff.). This "glory" He possesses is not one that He "takes" or "seeks from men" (5:41, 44; 8:50), but, rather, He holds it with the Father (17:1, 4 ff.). However, both the Father and Son are glorified in the sacrifice of the Lamb. The Son, by His death, is disclosed as the Son of God.

The Book of Hebrews has parallel expressions: "But we see Jesus . . . crowned with glory and honor because of *[dia]* the suffering of death, so that by the grace of God he might taste death for every one" (2:9). Thus, the sacrifice of Christ is an epiphany, a revelation of both the nature of God and the Son. Once again we see the inevitable intertwining of Christology and soteriology.

It seems clear, as Jeremias asserts, that the early community, along with Jesus himself, viewed Jesus as the Servant of the Lord described in Isaiah 53. According to Isa. 53:7, the Servant who suffers patiently is compared to a lamb. This comparison is expressly related to Jesus in Philip's discussion with the Ethiopian eunuch in Acts 8:32. Jeremias ventures that Isa. 53:7 "might well be the origin of the description of Jesus as *amnos.*"[27]

Peter also speaks of the efficacy of Christ's death as due in a measure to His sinlessness, for he was "a lamb without blemish or spot" (1 Pet. 1:19).

A second group of references compare Jesus to the Paschal lamb. John notes that the Roman soldiers did not break the legs of the dying Christ and that this was a fulfillment of scripture regarding the Passover lamb, "Not a bone of him shall be broken" (19:36; cf. Exod. 12:46; Num. 9:12). Writing to the Corinthians, Paul explicitly refers to Christ as "our paschal lamb" (1 Cor. 5:7). Jeremias concludes

26. *Ibid.*
27. *Amnos,* TDNT, 1:339.

that while the comparison of Jesus with the Passover sacrifice might well have resulted in His description as *amnos*, "more likely the two lines of influence interacted."[28] The references from Isaiah remind us that Christ went to His death with the patience of an innocent sacrificial lamb. We are also reminded that the effect of that death was the conditional cancelling of sin for the whole of humanity. The time of salvation had come. As Peter declares, this Lamb "was destined before the foundation of the world, but was made manifest at the end of the times for your sake" (1 Pet. 1:20). As the Passover lamb figured in the emancipation from Egypt's bondage, so Christ, the Paschal Lamb of the new covenant, has accomplished redemption (*elutrōthēte*, 1 Pet. 1:18) from the bondage of sin.

C. Romans 3:21-26

This brief paragraph is introduced by Paul to assert the continuity of the Old Testament law and the prophets with what is now revealed in Christ. At the same time it affirms the discontinuity of the Christian revelation with the then current Jewish misunderstanding of the law (v. 21). The paragraph also introduces the next major section of the Epistle which deals with the righteousness of God now revealed through Christ Jesus for all who believe (3:21—11:36). The divine decision in the face of the universal sinfulness of man is that freely all can be made righteous by faith through the redemption which is provided in Christ Jesus (vv. 22-24).[29] The ground of God's verdict is given in vv. 25-26: "God put forward [Christ] as an expiation by his blood, to be received by faith. This was to show God's righteousness . . . to prove . . . that he justifies him who has faith in Jesus."

Several characteristics of Christ's sacrifice surface in this comprehensive passage:

1. *Redemption and sacrifice are inseparable (v. 24).* Redemption *(apolutrōsis)* is an important word in the New Testament salvation vocabulary. It appears seven times in the letters of Paul, twice in the letter to the Hebrews, and once in Luke's Gospel (Luke 21:28; Rom. 3:24; 8:23; 1 Cor. 1:30; Eph. 1:7, 14; 4:30; Heb. 9:15; 11:35). Being one of the *lutron* words of the New Testament, the compound *apolutrōsis* suggests the idea of "ransoming *away* (*apo*, 'away from'),

28. *Ibid.*
29. M. Barth, *Was Christ's Death a Sacrifice?* p. 28.

with emphasis on the resulting deliverance rather than on the method of redemption."[30]

This redemption requires the price of Christ's blood (*en tō autou haimati,* Rom. 3:25; Eph. 1:7, *et al.*); for this reason *apolutrōsis* still bears a large measure of the idea of ransom. A slavery context lies behind the word. It thus implies that the former state of existence was one of bondage from which there has come deliverance. We are redeemed from the slavery of sin, and this experience of redemption is enjoyed as forgiveness (Eph. 1:7; Col. 1:14; Heb. 9:15). Barth concludes that redemption and sacrificial atonement "retain different names but mean one and the same." He refers to 1 Cor. 1:30, where Paul says that God is "the source of your life in Christ Jesus, whom God made our wisdom, our righteousness and sanctification and redemption *[apolutrōsis]*."[31]

2. *God himself is the initiator of the sacrifice of Christ.* God put forward *(proethētō)* Christ as an expiation by His blood *(hilastērion dia pisteos).* A variety of interpretations have been offered for *proethētō,* ranging from God's resolution in time and eternity to God's proclamation through His appointed ambassadors. But as Barth concludes, "In any case, God Himself is the Agent and Subject, who brings and proclaims the sacrifice of Christ. The sacrifice of Christ is a gift of God's love for sinners."[32] This is Paul's way of saying that "the atonement is made in the heart of God." D. M. Baillie reminds us that the objective reality of the atonement rests in the fact that God made an offering of himself in Christ; God was really putting himself forth in sacrificial love to emancipate His creature from the bondage of sin.[33]

3. *The sacrifice is described as a hilastērion.* God put forward Christ "as an expiation" (RSV); "to be a propitiation" (KJV); "propitiatory sacrifice" (margin, NASB); "sacrifice of atonement" (NIV). The mention of blood in the same context *(en tō autou haimati)* unmistakably indicates that Paul has sacrificial concepts in mind when speaking of this action of God.

The Greek word *hilastērion* has evoked extensive research to determine what Paul had in mind in employing it here. It appears in Heb. 9:5 and obviously means "mercy seat." The verb *hilasakesthai* occurs in Heb. 2:17, where Christ is called "a merciful and faithful

30. Hill, *Greek Words and Hebrew Meanings,* p. 71.
31. *Was Christ's Death a Sacrifice?* p. 30.
32. *Ibid.,* p. 31; cf. John 3:16; Rom. 5:8; 8:32; Eph. 2:4; 1 John 4:9-10.
33. *God Was in Christ,* pp. 197-99.

high priest in the service of God, to make expiation for the sins of the people" (RSV; "to make reconciliation," KJV). The substantive *hilasmos* occurs in 1 John 2:2 and 4:10.

Generally New Testament scholars see three possible translations of *hilastērion*:

a. Mercy seat. The mercy seat was the cover of the ark of the covenant upon which the high priest sprinkled blood on the Day of Atonement to atone for the sins of the people (Exod. 25:18-22; Lev. 16:2, 13 ff.). Christ therefore is the true Mercy Seat, where deliverance from the guilt of sin takes place, where reconciliation with God is experienced. Across the years this translation has received favorable acceptance by such scholars as Cremer, Thayer, Vincent, Charles Hodge, T. W. Manson, Brunner, F. F. Bruce, Alan Richardson, and Godet. The major argument against it is the fact that Paul does not elsewhere employ Levitical symbolism in the Epistle to the Romans.[34]

b. Expiation. This is defined as an act or means for "extinguishing," "covering up," or "annulling" sin. Expiation is not directed chiefly toward the offended party. Rather, it is directed towards that which has caused the breakdown in relationship; it deals with sin and guilt; it is concerned with making reparations for the offence. The sacrifice of Christ, therefore, made it possible for God to forgive sin and thus effect a reconciliation between himself and man.

This interpretation of *hilastērion* seems to have had its inception with C. H. Dodd:

> The Greek word *(hilasterion)* is derived from a verb which in pagan writers and inscriptions has two meanings: (a) 'to placate' a man or a god; (b) 'to expiate' a sin, i.e. to perform an act (such as the payment of a fine or the offering of a sacrifice) by which its guilt is annulled. The former meaning is overwhelmingly the more common. In the Septuagint, on the other hand, the meaning (a) is practically unknown where God is the object, and the meaning (b) is found in scores of passages. Thus the

---

34. Cf. V. Taylor, "A Great Text Reconsidered," *New Testament Essays* (London: Epworth Press, 1970), p. 130: "It should be recognized that in all these cases the rendering 'mercy-seat' *(Gnadenstuhl)* is misleading; it suggests a place where grace is dispensed ... The article is wanting and the context does not suggest the idea; indeed, its introduction in the passage would be exceedingly abrupt and confused." Alan Richardson writes: "All indicate that St. Paul is putting forward the view that Calvary is the Christian 'mercy-seat' and that Good Friday is the Christian Day of Atonement. Or, to put the matter in another way, Christ, sprinkled with his own blood, is the true propitiatory of which the 'mercy-seat' in the holy of holies was the antitype and foreshadowing. This would be the meaning both of St. Paul and Auct. Heb." *(Introduction to the Theology of the NT,* p. 225).

biblical sense of the verb is 'to perform an act whereby guilt or defilement is removed'.[35]

Since Dodd's publication, numerous scholars have followed his line of thinking, including Vincent Taylor, John Knox, C. K. Barrett, Arndt and Gingrich, A. M. Hunter, R. H. Culpepper, Eric Rust, Markus Barth, and Allan Richardson.

According to these interpreters, *hilastērion* is not an act of placating an angry, wrathful deity but an act of covering sin or annulling its guilt. By setting forth Christ as an atoning Sacrifice, God at once demonstrated His love for the sinner and also judged his sin. But in so doing, He called the sinner into a reconciled relationship with himself. This seems to be the meaning of *hilasmos* in 1 John 2:2 and 4:10. We read in 1 John 4:10: "In this is love, not that we loved God but that he loved us and sent his Son to be the expiation for our sins."

Frequently, supporters of the translation "propitiation" (see below) will call attention to 2 Cor. 5:18-19: "All this is from God, who through Christ reconciled us to himself and gave us the ministry of reconciliation; that is, God was in Christ reconciling the world to himself." The usual response, as Frank Carver states it, is:

It is man who must be reconciled, not God, as in Judaism, for God does the reconciling. Involved certainly is the wrath of God against the sin of men (Rom. 1:18; 2:5), or else their trespasses would not be counted against them. God in holy love took the initiative. In the Cross of Christ, He became the Aggressor and invaded estranged human life with forgiving love (Rom. 5:10, 15, RSV).[36]

The major argument against the expiation view is that it fails to give proper place to the wrath of God (cf. Rom. 1:18; 5:9; 1 Thess. 1:10) and to the need for full satisfaction of the divine nature. Wiley writes:

God's nature being that of holy love [and these two attributes in harmony], He cannot exhibit this love apart from righteousness, and therefore, must maintain the honor of His divine sovereignty. This He does, not from any external expediency, but from His essential and eternal nature. Furthermore, love cannot be exhibited apart from holiness.[37]

Stevens asks the question, Who is propitiated? and he replies, "The answer can only be God."[38]

35. *The Epistle of Paul to the Romans* (New York: Harper and Bros., 1932), p. 54.
36. Carver, "2 Corinthians," *BBC*, 8:555.
37. *Christian Theology*, 2:284.
38. *Theology of the NT*, p. 413.

c. *Propitiation, propitiatory sacrifice, or means of propitiation.* This view asserts that the sacrifice of Christ was an act to placate or to satisfy God's righteous nature.[39] Paul means by this word that the action is directed toward God to offset His wrath upon sin and thus to evoke His favor (cf. Rom. 1:18; 5:9; 1 Thess. 1:10). Jesus was crucified to enable God to be reconciled to His creatures, forgiving their sins but at the same time maintaining His justice (2 Cor. 5:18-19). Curtis concludes, "The death of Jesus Christ is the sacrificial means by which God is rendered propitious to one having faith."[40]

Leon Morris rejects the translation of *hilastērion* as "mercy seat" or "place where God shows mercy to man": "It is to be contended that the balance of probability is strongly in the direction of seeing in *hilastērion* in Rom. 3 a general reference to the removal of the wrath of God, rather than a specific reference either to the mercy-seat or to the Day of Atonement."[41] "Means of propitiation" is therefore his choice for the translation.

David Hill has concluded that the word can be given a propitiatory significance if it is related to a noncultic passage in 4 Macc. 17:22 where the death of seven sons is referred to as follows: "They having become as it were a ransom for the sins of the nation; and through the blood of these righteous men and their propitiatory death *(tou hilastēriou thanatou)* the divine providence delivered *(diesōsen)* Israel which had hitherto suffered evil."[42]

The major argument against "propitiation" is that it seems to contradict the pervasive Pauline notion of the initiatory grace of God. God put forward *(proethētō)* Christ as a sacrifice. Such passages as Rom. 5:8 and 8:32, in which the free flow of the love of God is emphasized, militate against this interpretation of *hilastērion*. The argument goes that God did not need to be reconciled; in fact, He functioned as the Reconciler drawing men unto himself by His loving act in Christ.

W. M. Greathouse seems to accept a mediating position somewhat following Richardson's interpretation that propitiation must be thought of as more or less synonymous with expiation. "Propitiation has a Godward reference: through the death of Christ God's wrath

---

39. For a discussion of the adjectival use of this word, cf. V. Taylor, "A Great Text Reconsidered"; Sanday and Headlam, "Romans," ICC, p. 88; see also Hill's conclusions, *Greek Words and Hebrew Meanings,* pp. 36 ff.

40. Olin A. Curtis, *The Christian Faith* (Grand Rapids, Mich.: Kregel Publications, 1905), p. 302.

41. "The Meaning of *Hilasterion* in Rom. 3:25," NTS, 2 (1955-56): p. 43.

42. *Greek Words and Hebrew Meanings,* pp. 41 ff.

is overcome and His justice is demonstrated. Expiation has a manward reference: Christ's sacrifice removes the guilt of man's sin."[43] Usually scholars have espoused one or the other of the above interpretations, but we can readily see that *hilastērion* is a multifaceted concept.

4. *The sacrifice of Christ was a revelation of the righteousness of God (dikaiousunē theou)*. Verse 21 reads, "But now the righteousness of God has been manifested apart from the law"; and verses 25*b*-26 add, "This was to show God's righteousness . . . ; it was to prove at the present time that he himself is righteous and that he justifies him who has faith." This sacrificial act reveals that God in himself is righteous and that His all-consuming purpose for man is to make him righteous. The Cross-deed is a salvation act.

Paul sees a juridical dimension to this sacrificial deed; it is intended to demonstrate that God is trustworthy "though every man be false" (Rom. 3:4). Ultimately God's righteousness is at stake in the present sinfulness of the world. In the Cross God is vindicated because sin is dramatically condemned. Man's justification is dependent on the established and proclaimed righteousness of God himself (3:25; 4:25).[44] The Cross settled conclusively the issue of God's justice.

5. *Christ's sacrifice is an efficacious act in man's behalf*. It changes his situation before God. Verse 26*b* reads: "He justifies *[dikaiounta]* him who has faith in Jesus." Sinners are not only "justified," but also made righteous. By faith, sinners are acquitted, understood in courtroom terminology. Undoubtedly, Paul has a forensic view of justification, but he also has what Jeremias calls "a soteriological understanding of *dikaiounta*." Justification does not consist merely in a change of God's judgment. If so, we come dangerously near to the misunderstanding that justification is only an "as if."

> God's acquittal is not only forensic, it is not an "as if", not a mere word, but it is God's word that works and creates life. God's word is always an effective word. . . . It is the beginning of a new life, a new existence, a new creation through the gift of the Holy Spirit.[45]

The new situation of the sinners is characterized by peace: "Therefore being justified by faith we have peace with God" (Rom. 5:1). Barth comments that "Christ's sacrifice has a nature and power

---

43. Greathouse, "Romans," *BBC*, 8:92.
44. Barth, *Was Christ's Death a Sacrifice?* p. 34.
45. Jeremias, *Central Message of the NT*, p. 64.

that 'effects what it shows,' i.e. the end of the old, the beginning of new life."[46]

D. The Blood of Christ

Special attention needs to be paid to the frequent use of the word "blood" in expressing the character of Christ's sacrifice. Paul writes that God "put forward" Christ "as an expiation by his blood" (Rom. 3:25). Approximately three dozen references to the blood of Christ are found in the New Testament. What does "blood" symbolize when it is used in connection with Christ's death?

One view equates blood with life. The *locus classicus* in the Bible for this interpretation is Lev. 17:11: "For the life of the flesh is in the blood; and I have given it for you upon the altar to make atonement for your souls."[47] Vincent Taylor explains, "The victim is slain in order that its life, in the form of blood, may be released. . . . The aim is to make it possible for life to be presented as an offering to the Deity. . . . The bestowal of life is the fundamental idea in sacrificial worship."[48] The slaughter is necessary but the death plays no part in the sacrifice. Westcott understands blood to suggest "a life liberated" and made available for men.

Another view of the significance of blood focuses on the idea of death. Moffatt, Denney, Behm, and Morris conclude that death is the central notion in atonement, so that it is *the taking of life which atones.* In the original Passover (Exod. 12:13) blood was splashed upon the door lintel, symbolizing that a death had taken place. There was no thought that the sign would indicate that a life was being presented to anyone. Moreover, there are 25 references in the New Testament where violent death is intended by the word "blood." Both "blood" and "death" appear in parallel passages in Rom. 5:9-10: "Since, therefore, we are now justified by his blood, much more shall we be saved by him from the wrath of God. For if while we were enemies we were reconciled to God by the death of his Son, much more, now that we are reconciled, shall we be saved by his life" (cf. also Heb. 9:14 ff.; 13:11 ff.).

Behm reminds us that "'blood of Christ' is like 'cross of Christ,' only another clearer expression for the death of Christ in its salvation meanings."[49] Denney's question is pertinent: "What relevance is

---

46. *Was Christ's Death a Sacrifice?* p. 34.
47. Cf. also Gen. 9:4; Deut. 12:23.
48. *Jesus and His Sacrifice* (New York: Macmillan and Co., 1937), p. 54.
49. *Haima, TDNT,* 1:174.

there to the power of the risen Lord if death is not the important thought in the term blood?"[50] It was the giving up of his life in violent death, a real sacrifice of life, that provided our redemption.

The interest of the New Testament writers does not rest in the material blood of Christ but rather in what it stands for, namely, the provision of salvation through the death of the Son of God. The phrase "blood of Christ" is a "pregnant verbal symbol for the saving work of Christ."[51] Surely Paul and John would not countenance any blood mysticism, such as was found in the mystery religions. "The blood of Christ" equals in soteriological meaning "the cross of Christ."

E. The Idea of Substitution

Was Christ's death in any way a substitute for something that was due mankind? Substitution in this frame of reference means that the guilty party goes completely free, relieved of the threat of punishment which he would have eventually sustained.

The sacrifice of Christ did something for us that we could not do for ourselves. Passages like 2 Cor. 5:21; Gal. 3:13; 1 Pet. 2:24 and 3:18 most naturally fall into the pattern of substitutionary atonement.[52] Christ's death was "in place of" or "instead of" man's rightful death. The Righteous One died instead of the unrighteous one. Paul says that for our sake God made Christ "to be sin, so that in him we might become the righteousness of God" (2 Cor. 5:21).

God's justice would not permit sin to go unpunished, so His judgment fell upon all sinners. But to overcome the impasse between His justice and His love, He substituted the cross of Christ, He "made him to be sin" that reconciliation between himself and His creatures might be realized. Forgiveness of the sinner becomes a genuinely moral possibility since God's honor and law are maintained.

"Made him to be sin" is a unique phrase in the biblical record.

50. *The Death of Christ*, p. 149.
51. Behm, *Haima*, TDNT, 1:175.
52. Twice in Corinthians Paul tells his readers, "You were bought with a price" (*ēgorasthēte gar timēs*), 1 Cor. 6:20; 7:23; cf. Gal. 3:13; "Christ redeemed *[exēgorasen]* us from the curse of the law"; Gal. 4:5, "to redeem *[exagorase]* those who were under the law." These statements belong in the same general context as the payment of a ransom. But, as C. L. Mitton concludes, the Corinthian passages especially emphasize, "not so much the means by which an end is achieved, as the end which is attained. In this case it is the truth that man now belongs utterly to God ('you are not your own')" ("Atonement," IDB, 1:313).

402 / God, Man, and Salvation

Christ was not made to be a "sinner" but to be "sin." Because He was not a sinner, that is, He did not participate in sinful actions, He could not have borne personal punishment. Bengel suggests that "He was made sin in the same way that we are made *righteousness*."[53] The *en autō* corresponds to the *huper hēmōn*. Christ embraced what was not deservedly His, namely, sin, just as we embrace what is not deservedly ours, namely, righteousness. To repeat Carver's comment quoted in an earlier chapter: "Christ, who 'was innocent of sin' (NEB), entered a sphere utterly alien to Him, that we might enter that sphere from which we have alienated ourselves."[54] A similar thought is expressed in Gal. 3:13 where Paul writes that Christ became "a curse for us."

Quite obviously, a penal element is present in this act,[55] but its precise nature does not lend itself to easy statement. Christ did not enter into our sinning and thus could not suffer a universal punishment or make a universal confession of our sins. 1 Peter 2:24 says that He "bore our sins in his body on the tree," a quotation from Isa. 53:12 in the LXX, where the Greek wording is identical. Hebrews 9:28 expresses the same idea: "So Christ having been offered once to bear the sins of many, will appear the second time."

Albert Barnes has dealt at some length with the Hebrews passage, as well as with 2 Cor. 5:21. He concludes that the idea of "bearing the sins of many" means simply "that Christ endured sufferings in his own person which, if they had been inflicted on us would have been the proper punishment of sin. He who was innocent interposed, and received on himself what was descending to meet us, and consented to be treated as he would have deserved if he had been a sinner."[56]

---

53. J. A. Bengel, *Gnomon of the New Testament*, trans. James Bryce, 7th ed. (Edinburgh: T. and T. Clark, 1895); cf. Curtis, *Christian Faith*, p. 310: "Jesus Christ, then, according to Saint Paul, was one (sic) not a sinner and yet one constituted a sinner. . . . In himself, Christ was *not* a sinner, but as a substitute, standing for men, he was a sinner. . . . How could Jesus be—how was he—a substitutional sinner? Why simply in the one fact that he *died*. Death, this bodily death, was the exact, historic, divine penalty for human sin. . . . Christ was thus treated as a sinner is treated; by substitution he was 'numbered with the transgressors'—he was placed in the category of sin."

54. "2 Corinthians," *BBC*, 8:556.

55. Cf. Rust's discussion, "The Atoning Act of God in Christ," *Review and Exposition* (January, 1962), pp. 68-70.

56. Albert Barnes, "Hebrews," *Notes on the New Testament* (Grand Rapids, Mich.: Baker Book House, 1949), p. 217; cf. also J. N. D. Kelly, "A Commentary on the Epistles of Peter and of Jude," *Harper's New Testament Commentaries* (New York: Harper and Row, 1969), pp. 122-23.

There is justification for the position that even the God-man could not know the guilt and shame of sin, and because of His sinlessness could not be punished. On the other hand, His vicarious involvement would exceed anything we might experience in similar situations. The only reasonable conclusion to which one can come is that, if there is a penal substitutionary dimension to the sacrifice of Christ, it rests in the fact that He experienced judgment as only God can experience it. This was possible because He knew holy love and fully comprehended the nature of sin and the just punishment due sinners. On the Cross He suffered because He knew the facts of our alienation from the Father. His sufferings therefore were substituted for our deserved punishment. To that degree we can speak of penalty in this substitutionary deed.

Rust follows P. T. Forsyth in concluding that

> our Lord did not undergo punishment, but he did fully experience the consequences of our sin and the alienation from the Father which goes with them. . . . He carried the penalty but not the punishment. This was the depth of the agony of the Cross. . . . By his deep sympathy with us men he confessed the holiness of divine love and the justice of our condemnation, of God's judging sin to its very death.[57]

IV. RECONCILIATION

The salvation purchased by Christ's sacrifice is also characterized as reconciliation. Justification is the acquittal of the sinner from all guilt of sin, while reconciliation is the restoration of the sinner to fellowship with God. Understood in the broader context of New Testament thought, sin is alienation; it disrupts fellowship and introduces hostility between persons. More specifically, sin has broken the relationship between God and His creatures. The work of Christ on the Cross was to the end of reconciliing man and God.

This concept is peculiarly Pauline. Christ spoke of reconciliation between persons as necessary before worship can be acceptable; Paul also used it in these terms in 1 Cor. 7:11 (wife being reconciled to her husband). But the soteriological idea of reconciliation is found only in four places in Paul's writings (Rom. 5:10; 2 Cor. 5:18-19; Eph. 2:16; Col. 1:20).

The Greek word *katallassein* (to reconcile) literally means "to

---

57. "The Atoning Act of God in Christ," pp. 69-70; cf. P. T. Forsyth, *The Work of Christ* (London: Hodder and Stoughton, 1910), pp. 139 ff.

change" or "to exchange." It is noteworthy that Paul intensifies the meaning of the word in Ephesians and Colossians by adding the prefix *apo (apokatallassein)* "to exchange completely."[58] Reconciliation therefore means, for Paul, a complete change in man's relationship to God. The cross of Christ has made it possible for men, through faith in Christ's work at Calvary, to exchange one set of relationships with God for a new set of relationships. Before faith, there is hostility between God and man because of sin; after faith there is life, righteousness, hope, love, and peace. Man needs this change of relationships in order to avoid spiritual death, and so God provides the possibility through the death of Christ.

Reconciliation is a work of God in Christ. "God was in Christ reconciling the world to himself" (2 Cor. 5:19). "We were reconciled to God by the death of his Son" (Rom. 5:10). "And you, who were once estranged and hostile in mind, doing evil deeds, he has now reconciled in the body of flesh by his death" (Col. 1:21-22). Through the Cross, Christ has reconciled both Jew and Gentile to God (Eph. 2:15-16).

Reconciliation initiated by the love of God, has man as its object. It is man, not God primarily, who needs to be reconciled. The sinner is helpless and thus cannot overcome the alienation between himself and God. He can know reconciliation only by the act of God's love (Rom. 5:8). Even when we were enemies *(echthroi),* we were reconciled to God by the death of His Son (Rom. 5:10). The little phrase in 2 Cor. 5:19, "not counting their trespasses against them," expresses the objective character of this reconciliation. Men may now know that God no longer considers them enemies or objects of His wrath. The barrier of sin has been obliterated by the Cross, and consequently freedom from guilt and the burden of sin is now man's hope.

This is the objective phase of reconciliation, this righting of wrong relationships between God and man. Reconciliation therefore makes a difference both for man and God.

When we are forgiven through the gracious act of God in Christ, as Denney writes, not only are we reconciled to God, but God is reconciled to us. "He is not reconciled in the sense that something is won from Him for us against His will, but in the sense that His will to bless us is realized, as it was not before on the basis of what

---

58. *Apokatallassein,* which occurs only in these passages in the NT, is found nowhere in the LXX or other Greek versions of the OT or in classical authors.

Christ has done, and of our appropriation of it."[59] When the sinner accepts in faith Christ's atoning work, this two-way reconciliation takes place. A whole new set of spiritual and ethical relationships prevail in the context of grace. Hostility is gone and loving submission is generated. This is the subjective phase of reconciliation.

V. Christ's Death in Relation to Holiness

The death of Christ provides not only the possibility of the forgiveness of sins (Eph. 1:7), justification (Rom. 5:9), reconciliation (Rom. 5:11; 2 Cor. 5:18), and eternal life (John 3:16; 10:10); it also makes possible a life cleansed and lived in holiness. Jesus prayed for His disciples: "For them I sanctify myself, that they too may be truly sanctified" (John 17:19, NIV). That is to say, "I set myself apart to the Cross that they may know the cleansed and separated life in reality." Earlier in the chapter He petitioned the Father on their behalf, "Sanctify them by the truth, your word is truth" (v. 17, NIV).

The writer to the Hebrews uses an illuminating analogy of the Christian faith based on the Old Testament sacrificial system. He speaks of Christ, like a lamb, suffering outside the city gate "in order to sanctify the people through his own blood" (13:12). In Ephesians 5 we have Paul's magnificent picture of the Church as the bride of Christ. It provides a basis for instruction in marital relations, but it also speaks of the work of Christ for the sanctification of His people (vv. 25-27).

At one point Paul exhorts the husbands to love their wives, "as Christ loved the church and gave himself up for her, that he might sanctify her, having cleansed her by the washing of the water with the word, that he might present the church to himself in splendor, without spot or wrinkle or any such thing, that she may be holy and without blemish" (5:25-27; cf. also 1:4). To the Colossians he wrote: "He [Christ] has now reconciled [you] in his body of flesh by his death, in order to present you holy and blameless and irreproachable before him" (1:22). Christ's death was to the end of redeeming (emancipating) us from all iniquity *(anomias)* and of purifying for himself a people of his own possession who are zealous for good deeds (Titus 2:14).

The Apostle Paul is quick to link baptism with the death of

59. James Denney, *The Christian Doctrine of Reconciliation* (London: James Clarke Co., Ltd., 1971), p. 238.

Christ as a type of the experience of the Christian who has to come into newness of life and freedom from sin. "Do you not know that all of us who have been baptized into Christ Jesus were baptized into his death? We were buried therefore with him by baptism into death, so that as Christ was raised from the dead by the glory of the Father, we too might walk in newness of life" (Rom. 6:3-4).

Paul also depicts the old life *(ho palios anthrōpos)* as being crucified with Christ "in order that the body of sin might be destroyed and that we might no longer be enslaved to sin *[tē hamartia]*" (Rom. 6:6). God has made the crucified Christ "our wisdom, our righteousness, and sanctification and redemption" (1 Cor. 1:30). The Cross-Resurrection event is the focus of Christian theology, and it is the only hope of full deliverance from the guilt and pollution of sin. John writes, "The reason the Son of God appeared was to destroy the works of the devil" (1 John 3:8). All who have fellowship with the Son by walking in the light enjoy the cleansing power of His blood, which means freedom from sin (1 John 1:5-10).

VI. Faith and Christ's Self-giving

Christ's death at Calvary was objective and once for all, efficacious for all men at all times. His sacrifice need not be repeated (Heb. 7:27; 9:12); it is a finished work (John 19:30). In the Cross God so identified himself with sinful humanity that He drew the whole race into it. Christ was the "man for others" not only in life but also in death. His deed avails for all of us potentially, but its saving effect is actualized only through faith. His love identifies Him with us and in a complementary sense our faith fulfills that identification. Thus, the benefits of the Cross are experienced only by faith (John 3:16; Acts 16:31; Rom. 3:25-26; 5:1; Gal. 2:19-20; Eph. 2:8-10; 1 Pet. 2:21-25).

Faith is the saving response to the proclamation of the Cross. It includes repentance for sins committed and also trust in Christ. Faith accepts Christ's call of the Cross as a personal act; faith says, "It was for me!" Faith sees the Cross as the judgment of God upon sin; it also discerns that Christ's death arose out of divine love. Faith is abandonment to Christ. "Just as a gull driven by the wind, comes to rest upon the shelving rock, so the soul drops its wings and rests in the breast of God."[60]

Thus Christ is the Substance of faith. "Faith is not a purely sub-

---

60. Taylor, *Cross of Christ,* p. 97.

jective response; it is objectively controlled by the fact of Christ. Its character is determined by what He is and by what He has done."[61] Bultmann reminds us that faith is simultaneously obedience to the proclamation about Christ, and *confession* of Christ as Lord. Faith is "faith in . . . that is, it always has reference to its object, God's saving deed in Christ."[62]

Faith brings a new life because it brings freedom from the guilt and power of sin. But that faith is not self-creating and sustaining; it is generated and maintained in the reconciled relationship with God in Christ. Paul can thus write, "The life I now live in the flesh I live by faith in the Son of God, who loved me and gave himself for me" (Gal. 2:20).

In the Incarnation God identified with our wayward humanness; in the Cross He amazingly dealt with that waywardness. Faith, born at the Cross, is the portal to restored relations with God.

VII. CONCLUSION

Any attempt to bring together all the strands of New Testament teaching on the work of Christ at Calvary will likely overlook some aspects of the deed. However, it seems wise to summarize in a few statements the insights of the various writers.

1. *Christ's death on the Cross was an objective, once-for-all historical event.*[63] When speaking of the death of Christ, we are affirming that something happened in history that does not need to be repeated. The writer to the Hebrews makes this abundantly clear in the use of the phrase "once for all" *(ephapaxi)* in 7:27; 9:12; 10:10. Peter understood it as such: "For Christ also died for sins *once for all [hapax]*, the righteous for the unrighteous, that he might bring us to God" (1 Pet. 3:18, italics added).

Furthermore, the objectivity of the atonement includes the fact that God is specially involved. His righteousness is upheld because the Cross deals with the penalty which sin evokes. This objectivity is related to the necessity of atonement on the part of God. While

---

61. *Ibid.*, p. 98.
62. *Theology of the NT*, 1:314 ff.
63. Cf. Karl Barth, *Church Dogmatics* (Edinburgh: T. and T. Clark, 1956), 4:1, 245-48: "It is a matter of history. Everything depends upon the fact that this truth as it comes from God for us men is not simply imagined and presented as a true teaching of pious and thoughtful people, but that it happened in this way, in the space and time which are those of all men."

men are influenced deeply by the demonstration of love at Calvary, they must also come to terms with the wrath of God against sin which is revealed at the Cross. The sacrificial nature of the Cross is not an abstract or sentimental idea; it is a historical deed which deeply affects the relationship of the holy Creator to His sinful creatures.

2. *The cross of Christ, with the full salvation which it provides, was initiated by God and is the profoundest expression of His love.* Culpepper writes: "The cross of Christ was not given by man to change God, but given by God to change man."[64] "For God so loved the world that he gave his only Son" (John 3:16). It was God who "did not spare his own Son but gave him up for us all" (Rom. 8:32). Moreover, God set forth the righteous and sinless One for the unrighteous and sinful. Man was unworthy of this act, and he was unable by any means of his own to reverse his relationship to God.

Paul employs four strong words to emphasize this fact. Christ died for us when we were *helpless, ungodly, sinners,* and *enemies* (Rom. 5:6, 8, 10). John enunciates the same truth: "In this is love, not that we loved God but that he loved us and sent his Son to be the expiation *[hilasmon]* for our sins" (1 John 4:10). The Trinity functions in a unity (John 17). Therefore, to speak of either the love of God or the love of Christ as it relates to the atoning deed is to express the same divine truth. The Cross is the amazing demonstration of the loving care of the Eternal God.

3. *Through the sacrifice of Christ, God dealt a decisive blow to the power of evil in the cosmos and to the power of sin and death in the life of man.* The Cross is a victory. John acknowledges that "the whole world is in the power of the evil one" (1 John 5:19), but he is also ready to proclaim that the Son of God appeared "to destroy the works of the devil" (1 John 3:8). To a Jerusalem crowd Jesus declared, "Now is the judgment of this world, now shall the ruler of this world be cast out; and I, when I am lifted up from the earth, will draw all men to myself." John adds, "He said this to show by what death he was to die" (John 12:31-33).

Evil spiritual powers are at work in the cosmos, but the Cross is the supreme instrument used by God to overthrow them (Col. 2:14-15). So Aulen confidently writes:

The evil powers appear to have won the victory. But Christ wins the victory in apparent defeat and triumphs in his death.

64. *Interpreting the Atonement,* p. 131.

Divine love is victorious in self-giving and sacrifice. This decisive victory creates a new situation and changes the estate of both man and the world. A new age has begun. The finished work signifies the victorious coming of divine love. Christian faith is born with a paean of praise in its heart: "In all this we are more than conquerors."[65]

For man, the Cross means deliverance from the guilt and power of sin. Christ "gave himself for us to redeem us from all iniquity and to purify for himself a people of his own who are zealous for good deeds" (Titus 2:14). Christ was made "a sin offering" that we "in him might become the righteousness of God" (2 Cor. 5:21). Victory over death has been realized in Christ's death. In the Cross-Resurrection deed "death is swallowed up in victory" (1 Cor. 15:54; cf. 2 Tim. 1:10). The sting of sin, which is death, and also the power of sin have been abolished in Christ's sacrifice. The Jew put his confidence in the Law but discovered that law only intensified his knowledge of and anguish over sin. The Cross exposed the "legalism" of that form of salvation and opened up to the Jew the way of faith. In Col. 2:14, Paul declares that the bond of legal demands was nailed to the Cross. To the Galatians, who were about to submit to the Law at the insistence of the Judaizers, he wrote: "Christ redeemed us from the curse of the law, having become a curse for us" (Gal. 3:13; cf. Rom. 10:4).

The Cross therefore is a victory of universal scope. Faith brings assurance of this fact now, but the full realization of that victory over sin, death, and judgment will come at the consummation of this new age into which the Cross has brought us. This is the message of the Book of Revelation. The Lamb finally wins all (Revelation 21—22).

---

65. Gustav Aulen, *The Faith of the Christian Church* (Philadelphia: Muhlenberg Press, 1948), p. 228.

24

Grace, Faith, and Divine Sovereignty

The biblical theologian does not need to prove that there are radical dislocations among men. The Bible's unique and indispensable contribution is not in disclosing that something is wrong, but in its diagnosis and solution. Bearing real guilt, man is alienated from God and derelict from the kingdom of God. He needs to be saved. This need is admirably stated by Frank Stagg:

> Salvation in its nature must answer to the plight of man as it actually is. Man's plight as sinner is the result of a fatal choice involving the whole man in bondage, guilt, estrangement, and death; salvation thus must be concerned with the total man. It must offer redemption from bondage, forgiveness for guilt, reconciliation for estrangement, renewal for the marred image of God.[1]

I. God's Initiative and Man's Response

A. Grace—Initiating and Enabling

The consistent witness of the New Testament is that salvation proceeds from God's grace. "For the grace of God has appeared for the salvation of all men . . ." (Titus 2:11). At once we are confronted not only with a key word but a root theological idea. Paul's thought

---

1. *NT Theology*, p. 80.

is dominated by the grace concept. The word "grace" *(charis)* is not found in Matthew or Mark. It appears only 7 times in the Johannine writings, 8 times in Hebrews, and twice in James, but in the Pauline literature it occurs 100 times. The fact that Luke uses the word 24 times in Luke and Acts may reflect the influence of Paul. Only in Peter's Epistles do we find the word with greater frequency per chapter (11 times). But while Peter speaks of grace with full understanding of its centrality, Paul more systematically expounds the doctrine.[2]

The basic meaning of *charis* as used in the New Testament is twofold. First, it is God's love in action in Christ; and second, God's power in action in the believer. The first is generally expressed by the idea of favor (Luke 1:30), a favor completely unmerited, without legal claim. Grace is God's compassion as He expresses that compassion through His redemptive provision in Christ.[3]

B. The Enabling Grace

The second meaning of grace is just as basic, though frequently ignored. God looks with favor on us in order that He may infuse us with His own moral energy. There is therefore a grace toward us and a grace within us. Grace is intended to change us; it does not leave us where we are. It is God's remedy for man's moral impotence. Grace operates through awakening, repentance, regeneration, sanctification, illumination, discipline, and ultimately glorification.

In Rom. 5:20-21, Paul vigorously contends that grace is an imparted power to overcome sin. He develops this theme in the following chapter. Grace, he says, abounds much more than sin; not just with a commensurate balance of the guilt, but in an intensive changing power, that "grace also might reign through righteousness to eternal life through Jesus Christ our Lord."

This assertion is followed at once by a vigorous denunciation of two possible misunderstandings of his meaning. One is the notion that in order to exhibit the munificence of grace, it is legitimate to continue in sin (6:1); the other is that since we are not under law but under grace, we can therefore revert to sinning with impunity

---

2. While the word is normally translated "grace," there are other words used in the KJV, such as "gracious," "favour," "pleasure," "liberality," "gift," and several instances of "thanks." "Returning thanks" and "saying grace" are linguistically akin.

3. A helpful survey of the New Testament use of *charis* in comparison to the Old Testament is given by Richardson, *Theology of the NT*, pp. 281 ff.

(v. 15).[4] Paul indignantly repudiates both distortions. Grace is not in any sense a license to sin. It cannot be construed as a divine indulgence. The precise opposite is the case: It is a divine energizing through the Spirit whereby sin may be overcome.[5] The idea is fundamental in both Pauline and non-Pauline writings (John 1:17; Acts 20:32; Rom. 5:2, 20-21; 6:14-15; 1 Cor. 15:10; 2 Cor. 1:12; 9:14; 12:9; Heb. 4:16; Jas. 4:6; 2 Pet. 3:18).

C. The Response of Faith

It is just as clear that the changing power of grace is conditional. Paul expresses his conviction that the gospel is "the power of God for salvation through faith for faith; as it is written, 'He who through faith is righteous shall live'" (Rom. 1:16-17). Paul never permits his readers to forget that faith is the essential God-ordained catalyst which releases the power of God's grace in the soul (Rom. 3:22, 25-26, 28; 5:1; cf. the similar teaching in Hebrews and the letters of Peter).

Grace therefore is not an irresistible and magical infusion but a divine activity that can be rejected by unbelief. Therefore while salvation depends entirely upon God's initiative, it is not imposed. Man must open the door of his heart (Rev. 3:20). According to John, the fundamental purpose in recording the Gospel was to inspire faith: "These are written that you may believe" (John 20:31; cf. 19:35).[6]

However, saving faith in the New Testament is more than believing God in principle, though this is where it must begin (Heb. 11:6). It is believing specifically what God has done in Christ for me a sinner. Moreover, though believing in God is certainly a righteous act, just as disbelieving in God is a sinful act, we are not to infer that we are saved by this righteous act on the basis of its own merit. The matter is concisely stated by Joachim Jeremias:

> Thus faith replaces works. But then the question arises: Are we again confronted with some achievement on the strength of which God is gracious, if the justification follows because of faith?

---

4. Cf. A. T. Robertson, *Word Pictures*, 4:363 ff.

5. While Sanday and Headlam (*ICC*) discount this aspect of grace, reports Alan Richardson, he acknowledges it as "the divine prompting and help which precedes and accompanies right action" (*Theology of the NT*, p. 283). See also F. F. Bruce, *Tyndale New Testament Commentaries* (Grand Rapids, Mich.: Wm. B. Eerdmans Publishing Co., 1963) on Romans 6:14 (p. 140).

6. The four Gospels do not constitute some irrefutable and overpowering demonstration that obviates the volitional element in faith. Enough evidence is given in the New Testament to provide logical grounds for believing, but not enough to remove faith from the arena of moral choice. Man voluntarily disbelieved himself away from God; it is only right that he should be required to believe his way back.

The answer here is: Yes! We are, in fact, confronted with an achievement. God does in fact grant His grace on the basis of an achievement. But now it is not my achievement, but the achievement of Christ on the cross. Faith is not an achievement in itself, rather it is the hand which grasps the work of Christ and holds it out to God.[7]

In the Pauline corpus the "faith way" is always the antithesis of the "works way." The corresponding contrast is between faith and law. When Paul places law over against faith, he is not referring to the obligation to do right or to what he calls being under law to Christ (1 Cor. 9:21); he refers to the Mosaic law system as the supposed means of becoming justified before God. Paul refuses to accept any compromise that would in effect blend law (which in this sense is virtually synonymous with works) with faith.

This is naturally a blow not only to the cultic mentality of Judaism but to the pride of the moralist. It is hard for man to accept the fact that he cannot make himself fit for God's society. This is an affront to his ego, hence he tends subconsciously to resist to the last ditch. Tenaciously he clings to the delusion that there is something he can do to merit the favor of God. He wants to be self-made, because only in this way can he redeem his self-esteem on his own terms.[8] But in the New Testament view of things, faith is a complete and final turning away from all self-righteousness and self-salvation. It is the abandonment of oneself to God's merciful provision in Christ as the sole and adequate ground of hope.

On the divine side, therefore, God's merciful initiative is called grace. But it is also from the divine side that the response of faith is required as a condition for the saving operation of grace. These two concepts are found side by side in the teaching of the New Testament. They are not contradictory or mutually exclusive. On the contrary Paul explains that salvation "depends on faith, in order that the promise may rest on grace" (Rom. 4:16).

II. THE CRUCIAL FAITH-WORKS CONFLICT

The New Testament reflects sharp tension in the Early Church concerning the true nature of saving grace. The focal issue for the

---

7. Jeremias, *Central Message of the NT*, p. 56.
8. We see the evidence of this in the universal proneness either to compromise the Christian way of faith or to postpone it as long as possible. Virtually all non-Christian religions are "works" religions.

surfacing of this tension was the question of Gentile circumcision. Confrontation led to the first great church council (Acts 15), and later prompted the letter to the Galatians.

A. The Circumcision Controversy

Resolving the issue was vital to the very survival of Christianity. Simply stated, the question was whether or not Gentile believers must become Jewish proselytes by being circumcised (Acts 15:1).

In the background of the controversy was the deeply rooted Jewish conviction that whatever salvation the Gentiles were to experience was conditioned on their coming under Mosaic authority. The Judaizers sensed that to permit the free evangelization of Gentiles without their subordination to Moses would be the death knell for Judaism. On the opposite side Paul and his party saw just as clearly that to demand of the Gentiles circumcision and its implied law-order would be fatal to Christianity.[9]

B. The Jerusalem Verdict

The conflict erupted at Antioch, when unauthorized members of the Judaizers, purporting to represent the true teachings of the mother church, infiltrated the Christian community. "And when Paul and Barnabas had no small dissension and debate with them, Paul and Barnabas and some of the others were appointed to go up to Jerusalem to the apostles and the elders about this question" (Acts 15:2). Paul and Barnabas took several Antiochians, including Titus, as samples of uncircumcised believers, and departed (Gal. 2:1, 3).

After "there had been much debate" (Acts 15:7), Peter stood up, followed by Paul and Barnabas. All three argued from experience, Peter from the Cornelius episode, and Paul and Barnabas from the "signs and wonders God had done through them among the Gentiles" (v. 12). The argument in both cases was that since God had already manifestly put His seal upon the salvation of the Gentiles without circumcision, why say they could not be saved except they

---

9. Even the circumcision of Jews was unavailing as to salvation (Rom. 2:28-29; 3:30; Gal. 6:15); yet Paul did not oppose its practice among them. In fact, as a matter of expediency, he circumcised the half-Jew Timothy, in order to make him acceptable to the Jews in "those parts" (Acts 16:1-3). Since they knew that his father was a Greek, Timothy had to be identified religiously as a Jew if Jews were to listen to him. But this had no bearing in Paul's mind on Timothy's salvation. What Paul did as strategy he would not tolerate when demanded under the category of a soteriological requisite.

be circumcised? Or why impose a burden God himself evidently did not require? Peter pleads: "Now therefore why do you make trial of God by putting a yoke upon the neck of the disciples which neither our fathers nor we have been able to bear?" (v. 10). James, the half brother of Jesus, as president of the council, strengthened this stand by supporting it from Scripture, the final court of appeal, then closed the debate with his epoch-making decision.

James's sentence and the official letter which followed disclaimed all Jerusalem responsibility for the subversive agitation, and vindicated Paul and Barnabas as "men who have risked their lives for the sake of our Lord Jesus Christ" (v. 26). Thus was concluded what E. M. Blaiklock calls "a great turning-point in the history of Christianity and the world."[10]

C. The Theological Implications

While both Peter and James saw that circumcision was not necessary to salvation through Christ, Paul saw that its imposition on Gentiles was *incompatible* with salvation through Christ. The sentiment of Peter and James was, Why bother them? (v. 19). Paul's conviction was that "if you receive circumcision, Christ will be of no advantage to you" (Gal. 5:2; cf. vv. 3-4; 6:12-15).[11]

1. *Faith Versus Ritual.*

Just what were the life and death implications for Christianity which Paul saw? Robertson calls the issue "one of the great religious controversies of all time . . . that between spiritual religion and ritualistic or ceremonial religion."[12]

The Spirit-inspired achievement of Paul was in proving that grace-works systems are not compatible. One cancels the other. If we are children of the free woman, then the bondwoman and her son must be cast out (Gal. 4:30). If under faith, we are no longer under the schoolmaster, law (Gal. 3:24-25). If righteousness comes by the

---

10. "The Acts of the Apostles," *Tyndale New Testament Commentaries* (London: The Tyndale Press, 1963), p. 115.

11. From one aspect it was the struggle between grace and law-works. From another view it was the struggle between sectarianism and catholicity, or narrow provincialism and worldwide evangelism. From yet another angle it was the struggle between bondage and freedom. "For you were called to freedom," asserts Paul (Gal. 5:13).

12. *Word Pictures*, 3:222. He adds: "It [the controversy] is with us yet with baptism taking the place of circumcision." See also Archibald M. Hunter's interpretation of Paul's view of the sacraments, *Introducing New Testament Theology* (Philadelphia: The Westminster Press, 1957), pp. 98 ff.

law, then it cannot come by grace (Gal. 3:21-22). If salvation begins in the Spirit, it cannot be established in the flesh (Gal. 3:3). Paul's whole thesis is that true salvation, with its concomitants of grace, catholicity, and freedom, is entirely of Christ; all other systems are either shadows, forerunners, or counterfeits. To seek salvation to any extent whatsoever in the law system, or to append Christ to either Moses or Plato, is to imply the insufficiency of Christ, and thereby in effect to deny Him altogether.

Circumcision was both the symbol and the initiation of the whole law system, so that whoever was circumcised was "bound to keep the whole Law" (Gal. 5:3). Therefore Paul's flat pronouncement that if they insisted on circumcision, Christ would profit them nothing. Here we have the first great historical example of the principle declared by Jesus that since new wine would burst old bottles, the attempt must not be made to contain it in old bottles. The Mosaic regime must be seen as a passing preparation for Christianity, a *phase* in God's progressive revelation which was both climaxed and dissolved in Christ.

The controversy has carried over into Christendom in various subtle forms. Is entrance into the Kingdom by sacraments and ritual or by repentance and faith? By priestcraft or by preaching? If we are to take Paul seriously in his rejection of ritual circumcision, as constituting in itself a badge of divine approval (Rom. 2:25-29), we must extend the principle. We must say that in Christ Jesus not only does circumcision avail nothing, but purely as rites neither do water baptism, confirmation, church membership, or the Lord's Supper. It is only "a new creation" that counts (Gal. 6:15).

2. Liberty, not License.

On the other hand there has been in every age of the Church the real danger of entirely misinterpreting Paul's letter to the Galatians by allowing antinomianism to replace Judaism. There is little value in getting rid of legalism if there is nothing left but license. When Paul was pleading for freedom from the law, he was not pleading for lawlessness. He was showing the inability of the Mosaic ceremonial and sacrificial system either to save the soul (except in anticipation of Christ) or to achieve holiness; but he of all men knew that there could be no escape from the eternal obligation of ethical conduct. To save ourselves from such a fallacy, we need only inquire if our faith is the kind that works "through love" (Gal. 5:6), and whether our liberty is *in Christ,* or in fleshly desire which engenders a worse bondage by far than Moses. Paul's solemn warning is timeless: they who practice the works of the flesh "shall not inherit the kingdom of God" (Gal. 5:21).

Paul was not advocating therefore an emancipation to anarchy, but an emancipation to a new allegiance. "I have been crucified with Christ; it is no longer I who live, but Christ who lives in me; and the life I now live in the flesh I live by faith in the Son of God, who loved me and gave himself for me" (2:20). Here is obedience without enslavement, submission without coercion, bonds without bondage. Here is a new fullness because of a new enthronement. As Ladd says, "The man indwelt by the Holy Spirit and thus energized by love is enabled to fulfill the Law as men under the Law never could."[13]

III. THE NATURE OF FAITH

Strictly speaking, the New Testament offers no definition of faith, though the descriptive statement of Hebrews comes close: "Now faith is the asurance of things hoped for, the conviction of things not seen" (11:1). Faith is thus the activity of the soul which perceives spiritual and eternal realities outside the phenomenal order. Faith accepts as true that which is not yet experienced or seen (2 Cor. 5:7). As such, it is the bridge between present experience and future hope.

However, this grasp of the future is mere wishful thinking unless it is based upon a firm confidence in God. Without such confidence God cannot be pleased: "For whoever would draw near to God must believe that he exists and that he rewards those who seek him" (Heb. 11:6).[14] The question of belief or unbelief is not only a question of God's existence, but also of His integrity. For man to slander God by any degree of unbelief is sin, and constitutes an insurmountable barrier to fellowship and a moral ground of condemnation. Until man removes this barrier by beginning to accept God as true, no other barrier can be touched. Hence faith is the key that unlocks the divine resources in behalf of men. "According to your faith be it unto

---

13. *Theology of the NT*, p. 510.
14. Here is a clear insistence on a faith which is theistic, in sharpest distinction from a deistic or pantheistic faith. The God who is the Object of biblical faith is both transcendent and immanent. Moreover He is an intensely personal Being who concerns himself with men and will respond to those who seek Him.

you" (Matt. 9:29, KJV) is the faith principle to which the entire New Testament bears unmistakable witness.[15]

A. Faith and Divine Revelation

That which distinguishes valid faith from presumption, superstition, or mere "wishful thinking" is its rational basis. While faith lays hold of that not yet experienced, it does so on the basis of what is experienced. Biblically, this can only be the prior action of God in some form of self-revelation, mediated persuasively to man's consciousness. Abraham's faith is an illustration. The faith by which he emigrated from Haran to Canaan was a response to God's initiative (Heb. 11:8 ff.). How God communicated to Abraham we are not told; the mode is not important but the fact is all-important. Faith therefore, biblically conceived, is not a hunger for God, or a vague belief in a divine power, or the spiritual quest of the naturally religious man. It is a rational acceptance of a positive revelation. Faith does not initiate but responds to God's initiative. If God had not in "many and various ways" spoken to the fathers, and finally "by a Son," biblical faith could never have arisen (Heb. 1:1).

B. Trust in the Promises

Faith in God cannot be dissociated from faith in His word; this indeed is the real test of professed faith. The front line of this faith concerns God's promises. This was the faith which God credited to Abraham for righteousness (Gen. 15:6; Rom. 4:3 f.; Gal. 3:6-9). The gallery of faith-saints displayed in Hebrews 11 is a panorama of lives lived in total confidence that what God said He would do, would sooner or later be done. Faith for them was expectation. It was thus teleological.

This aspect of faith is strong in the New Testament. A classical example is Paul's declaration of confidence during the storm: "So take heart, men, for I have faith in God that it will be exactly as I have been told" (Acts 27:25). The measure of such faith is the degree to which one is able to rest on the word of God alone, without supporting sense-evidence. It was this ability that Jesus called "so great faith" (Matt. 8:10, KJV) in contrast to the usual feeble faith which leaned on the crutch of the miraculous (John 4:44-48).

---

15. To faith is ascribed healing (Matt. 8:13; 9:22; Mark 9:23), justification (John 3:16; Rom. 3:22-26; 5:1), sanctification (Acts 15:8-9; 26:18; Rom. 5:2-5; cf. 2 Thess. 2:13), and all the grace gifts of the Christian walk (Hebrews 11).

C. From Promise to Event

However, the New Testament represents a radical change in the direction of faith, from expectation to acceptance and appropriation. This is still faith in God's word, but now not so much promise as fulfillment. God's word is in and through Christ (Heb. 1:1-3). Calvary in its full redemptive meaning becomes the required object of faith. Instead of being primarily teleological and eschatalogical, faith is now primarily historical; it is a firm confidence—indeed, a *trust*—not only in what God will do, but in what He has done. Christian faith therefore is more than "assurance of things hoped for"; it is assurance of things now available. It is thus that faith is perfected, for the Old Testament saints "though well attested by their faith, did not receive what was promised, since God had foreseen something better for us, that apart from us they should not be made perfect" (Heb. 11:39-40; 12:2).[16]

This faith in God that focuses on His action in Christ is universally declared to be the condition by which we personally receive the benefits of Christ's death and resurrection (John 3:14-18, 36; 6:40; 11:25 ff.; Rom. 1:16; Heb. 10:39; 1 John 5:4-12; *et al.*).[17] For one thing, the God who *could* raise Jesus from the dead, and who *did* so, can safely and rationally be believed. Implicit here also is the reminder that only the God who raised Jesus from the dead is to be the Object of our faith. Faith in any other god is misdirected, and as such is idolatrous, delusive, and impotent.

D. Faith As Wholistic Action

Faith is that which men possess only insofar as it is that which they do. When the Philippian jailor asked, "Men, what must I do to be saved?" Paul answered, "Believe in the Lord Jesus" (Acts 16:30-31), a command to action. The whole man must choose to accept the gospel message as true, and he must act accordingly. The inner accep-

---

16. Strong faith is still independent of immediate phenomenal proof, as Jesus intimated to Thomas: "Have you believed because you have seen me? Blessed are those who have not seen and yet believe" (John 20:29).

17. Usually the preposition used is *en* ("in"), implying firm belief or trust in a person, doctrine, or cause—in this case, Christ. Occasionally the preposition is *epi* ("upon"), such as when Paul declares that righteousness will be reckoned to "us who believe in [*epi*, 'on,'] Him that was raised from the dead Jesus our Lord" (Rom. 4:24). This preposition may stress the *rest* of faith, as a quiet confidence established on a solid foundation.

tance is as much a voluntary action as is the outward behavior that follows.

The "word of faith" which Paul preached demanded a twofold response, the inward motion of believing "with the heart," and the outward confession "with the mouth" (Rom. 10:8-10). So-called faith that is merely an intellectual assent without obedience is spurious, as James makes clear (2:14-26). Paul, in opposing faith to works, consistently meant works of merit or of ritual by which salvation could be achieved. He would just as vigorously repudiate a mere assent of the mind as would James. Assent of the mind to the testimony of history is indeed a kind of faith by which knowledge is obtained (Heb. 11:3)—in fact, much of our knowledge comes this way; but *saving* faith carries into commitment the whole man, not just the mind (Heb. 11:4-7).

Alan Richardson correctly rejects the notion that James and Paul are at loggerheads: "James says that 'faith without works is dead' (2:26); for Paul, faith without works is impossible." He explains further, "For James it would have been of no avail if Abraham had believed God, but had been unwilling to put his faith into action by obeying God's command; on Paul's view, for Abraham to have refused obedience would have been the same thing as to have disbelieved."[18]

E. Faith and Knowledge

In one sense faith is a kind of knowledge (Heb. 11:1), and he "who believes in the Son of God has the testimony in himself" (1 John 5:10). This, however, is a "full assurance of faith" (Heb. 10:22), in which believing has become persuasion. This is far beyond the first halting attempts to exercise faith, attempts which may be trembling and vacillating because of contrary feelings and apprearances (Matt. 8:26; 14:31; Mark 9:24). To believe properly is to reach ultimately the ability to say, "I know," with all doubt and uncertainty banished. Before that point the desperate soul may have to echo the cry of the distraught father, "I believe; help my unbelief" (Mark 9:24).

But just as faith is a kind of knowledge, so also does it depend on the possession of *prior* knowledge. There must be some understanding of what is to be believed. When Jesus said to Bartimaeus, "Your faith has made you well," He implied not only *decision* which

---

18. *Theology of the NT*, p. 241. He also observes the similarity between *hē pistis sunērgei tois ergois*, Jas. 2:22, and *pistis di' agapēs energoumenē*, Gal. 5:6.

issued in loud, determined supplication, but some previous knowledge, sufficient to convince him that Jesus could help him. When and how Bartimaeus acquired this knowledge we do not know (probably from stories told him by others); but that he possessed it is evident from the fact that when he was told the identity of this Passerby, he instantly sprang into action.

So likewise behind the Spirit-baptism of Cornelius was a considerable degree of knowledge about Jesus (Acts 10:36-38). The primary function of Peter's preaching was to supply the missing links in this knowledge. Similarly, the Philippian jailor could not believe in a Christ of whom he was completely ignorant (Acts 16:30-31). The name had to be given content. It is probable that he was already aware of some rudiments of the preaching of Paul and Silas. In any case, Paul did not command "Believe on the Lord Jesus" and leave it at that. The next verse says, "And they spake the word of the Lord to him together with all who were in the house." Soon his knowledge was sufficiently substantial for intelligent believing to become possible (Rom. 10:17).

Having chosen to believe, one's faith is strengthened and confirmed by additional knowledge. Most importantly, this knowledge is personal acquaintance as well as objective information; indeed, turning knowledge of the gospel into personal acquaintance is the dynamic effect of the right kind of believing (cf. Eph. 1:13). Then, because this new Friend is so absolutely trustworthy, our faith in Him grows as our acquaintance deepens. Thus Paul could say after many years of walking with Christ, "For this reason I also suffer these things, but I am not ashamed; for I know whom I have believed and I am convinced that He is able to guard what I have entrusted to Him until that day" (2 Tim. 1:12, NASB).

IV. FAITH AND REPENTANCE

A. The Necessity of Repentance

The proclamation of both John the Baptist and Jesus opened with the command to repent (Matt. 3:2; 4:17). To call men to repent was at the heart of Jesus' mission (Luke 5:32). "To repent" *(metanoeō)* means to change one's mind not only in the sense of opinion but in the sense of intention. This is made abundantly clear by the various contextual situations. Repentance includes both a confession of sins (Matt. 3:6; Mark 1:5) and purpose of amendment (vv. 7-8; cf. Luke

3:4-14). Implied is a new commitment to God—"I accept the will of God, instead of my own, as regnant in my life."[19] References to such a spirit of change, penitence, and surrender permeate the Gospel records even where the word is not used (cf. Matt. 5:3-6; 16:24; 18: 3-9; 19:21; Luke 18:9-14). True repentance issues in obedience, not just words (Matt. 21:28-32). As a condition of salvation it is as mandatory as faith (Luke 13:1-5). This also belongs to man's response to God's overtures; without repentance any other response lacks basic morality and sincerity.

The emphasis on repentance was not the least abridged by the apostles after Pentecost (Acts 2:38; 3:19; 5:31). Furthermore, this requirement was not confined to the Jews. Evidence for this is made clear by Paul's declaration to the Athenians (Acts 17:30), and the resume of his message given to the Ephesian elders (Acts 20:21). Christ's commission to Paul made it clear that unless sinners *turn*, there will be no forgiveness (Acts 26:18-20). In these passages there is no prior regeneration to induce repentance, though of course prior awakening is assumed. Stress rather is on the kind of preaching that enlightens and persuades, as the means of prompting the action of which all sinners are capable, through prevenient grace.

The Epistles also are unanimous in their assumption that repentance is essential to any sound conversion, and is equally demanded if sin recurs after conversion. Since they are letters to Christians, naturally the initial command to repent would not be in the foreground; but the insistence that there must be repentance for postconversion sin is clear enough. Even in Romans where Paul's polemic is against a works-justification and where he most vigorously affirms *sola fide* (cf. 3:27-28; 4:1-5), he will not permit an antinomian misunderstanding (6:2). It is the "unrepentant" heart which stores up wrath for itself (Rom. 2:5).

Though the man in Corinth guilty of immorality (1 Cor. 5:1) may have been truly converted at some time, he is now called a "wicked person" who is to be removed from their fellowship (v. 13). Dual repentance is called for. Those involved, especially those who sanctioned this evil deed, must repent of their arrogance in the face of this deplorable situation (they should have "mourned," v. 2), and demonstrate repentance by prompt discipline; the culprit also must be brought to repentance. To effect this Paul delivers the

---

19. William Douglas Chamberlain, *An Exegetical Grammar of the Greek New Testament* (New York: The Macmillan Co., 1960), p. 141.

man "to Satan for the destruction of his flesh *[sarx],* that his spirit may be saved in the day of the Lord Jesus" (v. 5, NASB).[20]

That Paul defines repentance as including amendment and likewise as essential to salvation is confirmed by his reference in his second Corinthian letter to another occasion of offense (2 Cor. 7: 8-12). The "sorrow" which belongs to true repentance can be distinguished from "the sorrow of the world." The first sorrow "produces a repentance that leads to salvation and brings no regret." "For see what earnestness this godly grief has produced in you, . . . what indignation, what alarm, . . . what zeal, what punishment!" (v. 11). Similar and equally thorough repentance of the offender is implied in 2:5-11 of the same letter. There is a vast difference between the *remorse* of Judas *(metemelēthē),* the *regret* of worldlings *(metamelomai),* and the *repentance* unto salvation *(metanoian),* which is "change of mind and life" (Robertson).

B. The Relation of Repentance to Faith

But what is the relation of repentance to faith? Three views are possible.

1. They are incompatible as conditions of salvation, and to protect *sola fide* repentance must be soft-pedaled.[21]

2. They are two distinct and coequal requisites for salvation. Paul's distinction, "repentance to God and of faith in our Lord Jesus Christ" (Acts 20:21), would seem to suggest this. God is the Sovereign whose laws have been violated and whose Person has been despised; repentance toward Him therefore must be the first step. But Christ is the divinely appointed means of salvation; therefore added to the repentance must be believing, trusting acceptance of the proffered door of mercy.

3. Faith alone is the condition of salvation, but the kind of faith which can arise only from a spirit of penitence. Without repentance, faith is a mere intellectual assent, impotent and impudent. This is the biblical position. It is, on the one hand, psychologically impossible to believe in Christ as a personal Saviour without a real desire for the salvation our faith is professing to appropriate. To desire salvation

---

20. A. T. Robertson observes, "Note the use of *to pneuma* in contrast with *sarx* as the seat of personality" (*Word Pictures,* 4:113).

21. So states Frederick D. Bruner, who insists that repentance is "not something to be done" but is God's gift, by which one is prompted irresistibly to be baptized (*A Theology of the Holy Spirit* [Grand Rapids, Mich.: Wm. B. Eerdmans Publishing Co., 1970], p. 166).

from hell without salvation from sin is immoral and hypocritical. The attempt therefore to exercise faith in a Saviour whose salvation is only partially or lackadaisically wanted, is an exercise in futility.[22] On the other hand, repentance cannot save, only Christ can do that. Therefore it is still *sola fide*. But unless men repent, they cannot believe (cf. Matt. 21:32).

C. Repentance as Voluntary

There is a sense in which repentance may be said to be a gift of God, without denying its nature as the action of sinners. This is in the sense that grace itself, and indeed the whole network of saving influences, is the gift of God. To say therefore that "Then to the Gentiles God has granted repentance unto life" (Acts 11:18) is the astonished Judaizers' way of conceding that the awakening grace which makes repentance possible is offered to all men.

Yet when Peter dealt with the mercenary Simon, he urged, "Repent therefore of this wickedness of yours, and pray to the Lord that, if possible, the intent of your heart may be forgiven you" (Acts 8:22). The gravity of Simon's sin was such that Peter was not sure of its forgivability, but he was sure at least that there would be no forgiveness without repentance; and his assumption that Simon *could* repent is the normal standpoint of the Scriptures. The decision was Simon's. Even when viewed as a "gift," repentance is not a state dropped irresistibly in the soul. Men who have been granted repentance by God may still elect not to repent.[23]

V. THE DIVINE INITIATIVE—ITS NATURE AND EXTENT

A. Terms and Their Meaning

The New Testament uses three terms significantly in relation to be-

---

22. Dorothy L. Sayers observes that "grace abounds only when there is genuine repentance, and we cannot ... simultaneously will sin and repentance, since this involves a contradiction in terms" (*A Matter of Eternity*, ed. Rosamond Kent Sprague [Grand Rapids, Mich.: Wm. B. Eerdmans Publishing Co., 1973], p. 64).

23. In the light of the plain insistence in the New Testament that repentance and obedience, not only initial but ongoing, are essential to saving faith, it is incredible that scholars such as Bruner should confuse these requisites with the "works" Paul rejects as being inimical to faith. Such a view fragments not only the New Testament but the Epistle in which "works" are most vigorously repudiated, Romans. Of course "no human being will be justified in his sight by works of the law" (3:20). But it is not repentance which is incompatible with faith, but the works-merit system, represented by circumcision.

lievers: *election, foreknowledge,* and *predestination.* Believers are called the *elect* (*eklektos,* "picked out") throughout the literature (Matt. 24:22, 24, 31; Mark 13:20, 22, 27; Luke 18:7; Rom. 8:33; Col. 3:12; 2 Tim. 2:10; Titus 1:1; 1 Pet. 1:1; 2:9). The noun *eklogē,* "a selection," is also used of believers, as, "For we know, brethren beloved by God, His choice of you" (1 Thess. 1:4, NASB; cf. Rom. 11:5, 7; 2 Pet. 1:10). The verbs "foreknow" and "predestine" are used together in Romans 8:29: "For those whom he foreknew he also predestined to be conformed to the image of his Son." Here the predestination is to Christlikeness; those so predestined are those whom God foreknew.[24]

The verb *proginōskō,* "to foreknow," may have overtones of foreordination, as in the case of Israel as God's chosen people (Rom. 11: 2) and in the case of Christ (1 Pet. 1:20), but never as an arbitrary foreordaining of individuals to eternal salvation. Speaking of the divine foreknowledge (cf. Acts 2:23; 1 Pet. 1:2), Vine comments: "Foreknowledge is one aspect of omniscience; it is implied in God's warnings, promises and predictions. See Acts 15:18. God's foreknowledge involves His electing grace, but this does not preclude human will. He foreknows the exercise of faith which brings salvation."[25]

When Peter brings together "His calling and choosing you" (2 Pet. 1:10, NASB), he may have been remembering his Lord's words, "For many are called, but few are chosen" (Matt. 22:14). Obviously this saying of Jesus implies that calling may not issue in election. Therefore, either the calling is insincere, or the call is intended to become election only when accepted; without personal response the calling is abortive.[26] Peter links the election with not only initial response but continued diligence (KJV; "be the more zealous," RSV). The certainty ("sure," KJV) is expressed by *bebaian.* "The word has a legal sense," says R. H. Strachan. "*Bebaiosis* is the legal guarantee, obtained by a buyer from a seller, to be gone back upon should any third party claim the thing. Here the readers are exhorted to produce a guarantee of their calling and election. This may be done by the cultivation of the Christian graces."[27]

---

24. Since the predestination is based on the foreknowledge, the two terms obviously cannot be synonymous. Vine comments that *proorizō,* to "predestine," "is to be distinguished from *proginōskō* 'to foreknow;' the latter has special reference to the persons foreknown by God; *proorizō* has special reference to that which the subjects of His foreknowledge are predestinated" (*Dictionary,* 3:203).

25. *Ibid.,* 2:119. See also Vine's discussion of *horizō,* "to determine," 1:305.

26. "Calling" is also used of the Christian's vocation (cf. Rom. 11:29; Eph. 4:1).

27. R. H. Strachan, "The Second Epistle General of Peter," *The Expositor's Greek Testament* (Grand Rapids, Mich.: Wm. B. Eerdmans Publishing Co., reprinted 1967),

At first reading, Acts 13:48 would seem a clear declaration of an exact correspondence between believing and foreordination to believe. When Paul turned from the Jews in Pisidian Antioch to the Gentiles, they greatly rejoiced; "and as many as had been appointed to eternal life believed." Though this is not *protassō*, "foreordain," as in 17:26, the perfect tense, passive voice would seem to give it that sense. But R. J. Knowling acknowledges a body of scholarly opinion which takes the word as being in the middle voice, not passive, which would suggest, "As many as had set themselves unto eternal life." This would fit the context perfectly and make excellent sense. Obviously the Jews had not properly set themselves to obtaining eternal life; rather by their willful rejection of the truth had judged themselves "unworthy of eternal life" (v. 46). But even if the word is to be taken in its strongest sense, "there is no countenance here," Knowling observes, "for the *absolutum decretum* of the Calvinists."[28]

B. Principles of the Divine Plan

Two major passages strongly accent God's sovereign action, so much so that the relation of free will to divine election has become a major theological issue. Those passages are Ephesians 1 and 2 and Romans 9, 10, and 11. They need to be examined in greater detail.

In a dramatic and sweeping manner Ephesians views salvation from the side of God's initiative. Every facet of the redemptive scheme is traced to God's mercy and goodness, "according to the purpose of his will, to the praise of his glorious grace" (1:5-6). Not only is salvation the free gift of God's love, but God's power in implementing His design is unlimited: ". . . who accomplishes all things according to the counsel of his will" (v. 11).

5:128. It is difficult to see the justification for the NASB rendering, "Therefore, brethren, be all the more diligent to make certain about His calling and choosing you." God's calling and choosing of us is not in doubt, but our confirmation of the calling and election is what is in the balance and what needs to be settled by our diligence. Robertson (*Word Pictures*, 5:153) understands *eklogēn*, "election," in 2 Pet. 1:10 to mean "actual acceptance."

28. *The Expositor's Greek Testament*, 2:300. A. T. Robertson's comment is helpful (*Word Pictures*, 3:200): "The Jews had voluntarily rejected the word of God. On the other side were those Gentiles who gladly accepted what the Jews had rejected, not all the Gentiles. Why these Gentiles here ranged themselves on God's side as opposed to the Jews Luke does not tell us. This verse does not solve the vexing problem of divine sovereignty and human free agency. There is no evidence that Luke had in mind an *absolutum decretum* of personal salvation. Paul had shown that God's plan extended to and included Gentiles. Certainly the Spirit of God does move upon the human heart to which some respond, as here, while others push him away." See also John Wesley, *Notes, in loco.*

The participation of the Ephesians in the inheritance is ascribed directly to their "having been predestined according to His purpose." Furthermore, their regeneration is explained as being the effect of the direct action of God upon them: "But God, who is rich in mercy, . . . even when we were dead through our trespasses, made us alive together with Christ (by grace you have been saved)" (2:4-5). To cap it off and make doubly sure they do not claim the tiniest fragment of credit, Paul reminds them: "For by grace you have been saved through faith; and this is not your own doing, it is the gift of God— not because of works, lest any man should boast" (2:8-9).

Since to a remarkable degree Ephesians is a microcosm of the New Testament,[29] we can reasonably expect to find in it the underlying principles of God's redemptive activity.

1. God's initiative is prior to anything man does or can do (Eph. 1:1-6).
2. The focus of all redemptive activity and resources is in Christ, including our predestination "to be his sons" (1:5-7) and even God's mysterious will concerning the future (1:9-10).
3. God designs that the Church shall constitute the community of the redeemed, and at the same time the instrument of evangelization (1:22-23; 2:19-22; 3:8-10; 4:1-16).[30]
4. There is also the faith principle, which stipulates that our access to the blessings of redemption is not by striving or meritorious works but solely by the act and attitude of believing (1:13, 15; 2:8).
5. A further principle is that the substance of the redemption has been predetermined by God. It includes His design that we be "holy and blameless before him," our adoption "to be his sons," and the "forgiveness of our trespasses"—this much at least (1:4-5, 7; cf. 2:22; 3:16-21; 4:12-31; 5:25-27).[31]
6. Yet another principle of the sovereign pattern is the inclusion of the Gentiles in full equality with the Jews. This is "the mystery of Christ," hidden to previous generations but now revealed: "the Gen-

29. F. F. Bruce considers Colossians and Ephesians to be "the climax of Pauline theology" (*The Message of the New Testament* [Grand Rapids, Mich.: Wm. B. Eerdmans Publishing Co., 1972], p. 42).
30. F. F. Bruce observes that in Ephesians "we are presented with a vision of the church as being not only God's masterpiece of reconciliation here and now, but also God's pilot scheme for the reconciled universe of the future" (*Ibid.*, p. 40).
31. Conformity to the image of Christ ("an inward and not merely superficial conformity"—Robertson) is the way Paul summarizes it in Rom. 8:29.

tiles are fellow heirs, members of the same body, and partakers of the promise in Christ Jesus through the gospel" (3:1-6).[32]

7. A seventh principle governing the divine mode of operation is the assignment to the Holy Spirit of the province of direct action upon man in effecting personal salvation.[33]

These basic principles are clear enough. But they bring us full circle. The original knotty problems remain concerning the exact relationship of God's initiative to man's response. Is the faith, too, implanted by the Spirit? Is the action of the Spirit always effectual? Is the redemptive influence of the Spirit qualitatively and purposefully different in those who respond unto salvation from what it is in those who do not respond?

C. The Universality of God's Design

One side of the coin of sovereignty is sketched in Ephesians 1 and 2, as if this were the only side. The other side, however, is made entirely clear by the New Testament as a whole. So much is this true that an eighth principle can be stated: *Salvation is the divinely willed destiny for all men, but a destiny which can be thwarted by unbelief chosen in freedom in spite of the divine overtures and provisions.* This can be seen when we examine the following scriptures.

1. *Openness of the Call.*

Having rejoiced over the election of the Thessalonian believers (as noted below in fn. 33), Paul explains: "To this he called you through our gospel, so that you may obtain the glory of our Lord Jesus Christ." God did not call from heaven, a particular irresistible call, singling out His elect by name; He called them *through the gospel* ("by means of our Gospel preaching," Berk.). The gospel was preached to all who would hear, without partiality or discrimination, and its hope was offered equally to all.

---

32. Yet the plan goes beyond the mere "inclusion" of the Gentiles; it is nothing less than the abolition of the barrier which divided Gentile from Jew, and the creation of "one new man," neither Jew nor Gentile but Christian. Remaining racial differences no longer matter, for the new unity in Christ transcends them (2:14-16).

33. This is a constant reference in the New Testament. The "new birth" is by the Spirit (John 3:5). It is by the Spirit that we are inducted into the body of Christ (1 Cor. 12:13), and also sanctified (2 Thess. 2:13; cf. 2 Cor. 3:3, 18; Titus 3:5). Here sanctification accomplished by the Spirit and faith on the human side are declared to be the means by which the purposed salvation becomes reality (cf. 1 Pet. 1:2). As for Ephesians, it is by the Spirit that we are "to be strengthened with might . . . in the inner man" (3:16), and it is by being "filled with the Spirit" (5:18) that we rise to the heights of holy and victorious living.

Whether Paul included John 3:16 in his preaching or not, it belongs to the gospel: "For God so loved the world that he gave his only Son, that whoever believes in him should not perish but have eternal life." Paul did announce that God "now commands all men everywhere to repent" (Acts 17:30). Is not the call to repent a call also to believe? It was Jesus himself who preached to all, "Repent, and believe in the gospel" (Mark 1:15). Could He have been guilty of double-talk, knowing that some who heard would be irresistibly caused to believe because they were intended to, while others would be left in unbelief because the call was not for them? Is the universal call inherent in the gospel proclamation authentic for some but in-authentic for others?

When Jesus told the parable of the king who sent his servants to bring into the wedding those who had been invited, it is clear that those who were first called were really on the king's list. Jesus gave no hint that the king knew in advance their refusal and engineered it. The simple wording is "Those invited were not worthy" (Matt. 22:8).

Unquestionably the unrestricted proclamation of the gospel call implies an equally unrestricted desire in the heart of God for a favorable response (cf. 1 Tim. 2:4-6; 2 Pet. 3:9). Whatever the terms *predestination* and *foreordination* mean, they do not imply a final division of men predetermined arbitrarily by divine decree.

2. *The Freedom of Faith.*

The nature of faith is discussed elsewhere in this volume. But at this point we need to face the question, Is believing covertly the action of God or really the free action of the repenting sinner?

At the outset it must be stated that "the gift of God" of Eph. 2:8 relates not to faith but to salvation (see margin, NASB). As A. T. Robertson says, "'Grace' is God's part, 'faith' ours."[34] This is consistent with the New Testament usage which everywhere commands believing as that which man can and must do (Mark 1:15; John 1:12; 8:16, 24; 12:36; 16:31; Rom. 3:22; 10:9). Faith may be made impossible by clinging to sin or to selfish motives: "How can you believe, who receive glory from one another and do not seek the glory that comes from the only God?" (John 5:44). To suppose such inability is to be

34. *Word Pictures,* 4:525. He explains further: "*And that (kai touto).* Neuter . . . and so refers not to *pistis* (feminine) or to *charis* (feminine also) but to the act of being saved by grace conditioned on faith on our part."

ascribed to the secret design of God would be little short of blasphemous.

Consider the appeal of the writer to the Hebrews. He pleads with his readers to take care lest there should be in any one of them "an evil, unbelieving heart, leading you to fall away from the living God" (Heb. 3:12). Is there anything here but the obvious assumption that the choice lay within their power? While not responsible for the redemptive activity of God, they were responsible for whether or not they accepted it in faith.

Even Ephesians, so strong on divine sovereignty, assumes a real responsibility incumbent on the believer. Note the exhortation, "Be strong in the Lord and in the strength of his might" (6:10), and more particularly in the specific command, "Stand therefore, . . . taking the shield of faith, with which you can quench all the flaming darts of the evil one" (vv. 14-16).

While Paul insists that knowledge is indispensable to faith (Rom. 10:14, 17), he equally grants to the knower the choice of faith —"But they have not all heeded the gospel" (v. 16).[35]

3. *The Action of the Spirit.*

Most of the references in the New Testament to the ministry of the Holy Spirit relate to His activity in and upon believers. One is amazed to discover how little there is expounding the nature of His action on the unsaved. In the case of Lydia in Philippi, the opening of her heart is ascribed not to the Spirit but to "the Lord" (Acts 16:14). Also, Jesus spoke of the drawing power of His crucifixion (John 12:32); note its universality—"I . . . will draw all men to myself." Earlier, using the same word (*helkuō*, "to draw out" or "toward"), Jesus had said: "No one can come to me unless the Father who sent me draws him" (John 6:44).[36] But what about the Holy Spirit?

---

35. It is astonishing that Richardson should say that faith is "not something that we do, but is itself a *charisma pneumatos* (1 Cor. 12:9)" (*Theology of the NT*, p. 283). The special gift of faith listed by Paul as one of the panoply of the Spirit's enablings has to do with Christian work on the part of those already Christians—who already have *saving* faith. To confuse this "gift" of faith with justifying faith is to imply that only *some* believers are justified!—for the "gift" is designated as God's will for some, not all.

36. While this does not bear directly on our present inquiry concerning the action of the Holy Spirit, it is the clear affirmation of man's inability to respond to Jesus apart from grace, and that the Father is sovereign in determining the basis on which men can become believers. However, the context makes it clear that the Father's drawing is not an arbitrary selectivity. "For this is the will of my Father, that every one who sees the Son and believes in him should have eternal life" (v. 40). But who will actually and savingly believe? The answer is in v. 45: "Every one who has heard and learned from the Father comes to me." This was spoken to the Jews who were rejecting Jesus on the basis of a profession of loyalty to God. Jesus is saying

Though not stated, we can assume from other teachings that the Lord opened Lydia's heart by means of the Holy Spirit and likewise by the same Spirit draws men to Jesus.

Perhaps most definitive is John 16:8-11: "And He, when He comes, will convict the world concerning sin, and righteousness, and judgment" (NASB). The word "convict" *(elenchō),* in this instance, means "to convict, confute, refute, usually with the suggestion of putting the convicted person to shame."[37] It thus is stronger than "convince" (RSV). The *New Testament in Basic English* says: "Will make the world conscious of sin."[38]

The direct action of the Spirit is declared by the apostles to be the secret of their effectiveness. Paul says that it was "by word and deed, by the power of signs and wonders, by the power of the Holy Spirit" that Christ worked through him "to win obedience from the Gentiles" (Rom. 15:18-19). Similar claims are made by Paul to the Corinthians (1 Cor. 2:4), and to the Thessalonians (1 Thess. 1:5). Peter similarly declares to his readers that the gospel was preached to them "through the Holy Spirit sent from heaven" (1 Pet. 1:12). Apparently the truth is not enough. The truth must be thrust into the conscience and enforced upon the mind by the Spirit.

The main object of our inquiry is now open. Is there any hint in the Scriptures that the Spirit's endorsing and convicting activity is either *selective* or *irresistible?*[39] "You men . . . are always resisting the

that a true relationship with the Father would inevitably open their eyes to himself. Their rejection of Jesus only demonstrated their alienation from the Father. There is no particular ordination to salvation in this passage.

37. Vine, *Dictionary,* 1:239.

38. In saying "when he comes," Jesus did not imply that the Spirit's convicting activity among men would begin with His advent on the Day of Pentecost, for the Old Testament indicates this ministry from the time of the Fall. Rather, He meant (1) that the Spirit would more officially and effectively take over where Jesus himself left off; and (2) that the Spirit's striving would now be especially in relation to the crucified Christ. That the Spirit had been "drawing" previously through conscience is indicated by Stephen when he accused his listeners of always resisting the Holy Spirit, then adding, "As your fathers did so do you" (Acts 7:51).

39. To sustain a Calvinistic understanding of "effectual calling" and "irresistible grace," George Smeaton labors hard to confine the convicting ministry of the Spirit to the elect (*The Doctrine of the Holy Spirit* [London: The Banner of Truth Trust, orig. 1882, rep. 1961], pp. 172-83). His argument is that the awakening of the Spirit is such as to be necessarily effective, infallibly resulting in conversion. But such a position would never be read into this passage except on a priori grounds. The Bible says the "world" is the subject of the Spirit's convicting ministry, and never divides this world into two classes, those to whom the Spirit ministers with sufficient power to assure effectiveness and those to whom the Spirit ministers with designedly insufficient power. All such refinements are speculative developments of historical theology but they are not biblical theology.

Holy Spirit," said Stephen, implying the striving of the Holy Spirit—a striving which is never a mockery, never a kind of divine feint. Further, the fact that man is able to blaspheme against the Holy Spirit (Mark 3:28-30), to insult "the Spirit of grace" (Heb. 10:29), and to "nullify the grace of God" (Gal. 2:21), indicates a freedom in response to the Spirit's movings which leaves no doubt that in the end decisive responsibility belongs to the sinner, not to God. Without the awakening of the Spirit, man would never arouse from his moral and spiritual torpor. With the Spirit's awakening, repentance and faith are now possible but still optional. The grace granted to all through the Spirit restores that measure of freedom which makes a real choice possible; it does not overwhelm the will. A real choice is no more possible in irresistible divine influence than in the moral impotence of abandoned depravity.

D. The Teaching of Romans 9—11

No doubt this is the most crucial passage for a biblical understanding of the relation of the divine sovereignty to election. The immediate problem is apparent failure on God's part (9:6) in keeping His promises to the Israelites, a failure which seems to cast a shadow on both God's integrity and power. In his inspired defense of God's integrity, Paul soon is grappling with the underlying principles of divine sovereignty.

In the whole of c. 9 Paul is steering his course between the extremes of no sovereignty and arbitrary sovereignty. While these waters are too deep for our complete understanding, they are at least the channel. Only by keeping to this channel can we escape shipwreck on the reefs of either divine weakness or implied tyranny.[40]

1. *In Defense of the Divine Integrity.*

On the one hand is the rock of divine weakness: the problem of the apparent breakdown of God's sovereignty (and by implication, His integrity). For centuries promises had been read, recited, and believed concerning the glory that was to be Israel's when the Messiah came. To the Israelites pertained "the sonship, the glory, the covenants, the giving of the law, the worship, and the promises" (9:4).

---

40. In the words of Olshausen, the apostle "neither intends by the grace of God to take away from man the free determination of the will, nor by the latter the all-sufficiency of grace; his object is to establish both in reciprocal connexion" (Hermann Olshausen, *Biblical Commentary on the New Testament* [New York: Sheldon, Blakeman and Co., 1858], 4:73).

But now the Messiah *has* come—yet look at the wretched condition of blind Israel! Has God failed? Is God to confess defeat by casting off His chosen people utterly? Moule asks, "Has God done with the race to which he guaranteed such perpetuity of blessing?"[41] Paul quickly steers away from this reef by saying: "It is not as though the word of God has failed" (9:6).

He then proceeds at once to show that the promises were never intended to mean the unconditional inclusion of every blood-born Jew. "For not all who are descended from Israel belong to Israel and not all are children of Abraham because they are his descendants: but through Isaac shall your descendants be named. This means that it is not the children of the flesh who are the children of God, but the children of the promise are reckoned as descendants" (9:6-8). Just as genealogically the supernatural children of the promise (not Ishmael and his posterity but Isaac) are counted as the true seed of Abraham, so now the spiritual inheritors of the promises in Christ are accounted as the true Israel. This is made clear when Paul returns to complete the argument in verse 25. Even Isaiah supports him in his thesis that the fulfillment of the promises is to be realized by the remnant, not the whole mass of Israelites (v. 27). Paul sees "in the whole past a long warning that, while an outer circle of benefits might affect the nation, the inner circle, the light and life of God indeed, embraced 'a remnant' only."[42]

But between verses 9 and 24, the apostle turns aside slightly to show that God's sovereignty is intact not only in the revelation of His will through the *promises* but in the revelation of His will in *election.* He exemplifies by citing two familiar cases: *(a)* His will that Jacob rather than Esau be the progenitor of the Israelitish line; *(b)* His will that Pharaoh be an instrument in his self-disclosure to the human race. He further strengthens his defense of the divine sovereignty by the analogy of the clay and the potter: "Has the potter no right over the clay, to make out of the same lump one vessel for beauty and another for menial use?" (v. 21). Paul has no doubt that God's *will is decisive.* The apparent breakdown of His sovereignty as seen in the plight of the Jews is not real: Its supposition can only be due to a misunderstanding of God's program.

On the other hand Paul just as carefully veers away from the

41. II. C. G. Moule, "The Epistle of St. Paul to the Romans," *The Expositor's Bible,* ed. W. Robertson Nicoll (New York: A. C. Armstrong and Son, 1905), p. 246.
42. *Loc. cit.*

rock on the other side of the channel: the injustice latent in the arbitrary and perhaps even capricious exercise of sovereignty. The human mind leaps from one extreme to the other. The extreme interpretation of Paul's position is indicated in the question: "Why does he still find fault? For who can resist his will?" (9:19).[43]

2. *In Defense of Divine Justice.*

Let us take the references in order. There is no final election of individuals to salvation or damnation in the choice of Isaac over Ishmael, or of Jacob over Esau. Sanday and Headlam approvingly quote Gore: " 'The Absolute election of Jacob,—the "loving" of Jacob and the "hating" of Esau,—has reference simply to the election of one to higher privileges as head of the chosen race, than the other. It has nothing to do with their ultimate salvation.' "[44] So likewise write Wesley, A. T. Robertson, Garvie, and Moule. "No personal animosity is in question," says Moule, but only a "relative repudiation."[45]

The strong statements of verses 15-16 and 18, climaxing with "He hardens the heart of whomever he wills," must be seen in the light of the context, and especially in the light of the example Paul expressly cites as illustrative of the principles here enunciated: Pha-

---

43. Three considerations require our understanding:

(1) The Jews had no *moral* claim on God's special favor, by virtue of any superior worthiness or works of their own. It was no merit of Isaac's that he and not Ishmael was the son of the promise. Nor was it on any merit of Jacob's that he was chosen rather than Esau; "though they [the twins] were not yet born and had done nothing either good or bad, in order that God's purpose of election might continue, not because of works but because of his call, she was told, '*The elder will serve the younger*' " (11-12, italics added).

(2) There is the categorical assumption. Paul does not give a direct reply to the question "Why does he still find fault?" but rules out the question as being improper. "But, who are you, O man, to answer back to God? Will what is molded say to its molder, 'Why have you made me thus?' " (v. 20).

(3) There is also the theological impasse. If Paul means to teach that God's sovereignty, with the hardening and softening and unconditional election, extends to the final salvation or damnation of the soul, then the question "Why does he still find fault?" will not be dismissed, and no amount of adroit dodging or pious shaming will elude it.

44. William Sanday and Arthur C. Headlam, "The Epistle to the Romans," *ICC*, p. 245, referring to *Studia Biblica*, iii:44.

45. H. C. G. Moule, *Expositor's Bible*, p. 250. Of the expression "the purpose of God according to election" (KJV) found in v. 11, Garvie writes: "The salvation of mankind has been the intention of God from the beginning, and this intention has guided His action throughout the ages" (*The New Century Bible*). He thus interprets Rom. 8:28 and Eph. 1:9-11 also. And Sanday and Headlam significantly concede: "The gloss of Calvin *dumdios ad salutem praedestinat, alios ad aeternam damnationem* is nowhere implied in the text" (*ICC*).

raoh. A. E. Garvie writes of him (commenting on the clause in v. 17, "For this very purpose I raised you up"): "The words in their original context mean that Pharaoh had been spared in the plague of boils, as God had further intentions in dealing with him, to use him as an instrument for the release of Israel from bondage."[46] Concerning the use of the word "hardeneth" (KJV) he further comments: "Paul is here dealing with only one aspect of God's action; his aim is to assert the Divine sovereignty over against all human arrogance; it is altogether to misuse this passage to derive from it any doctrine of divine reprobation to eternal death."[47] Moule admirably summarizes the case:

> Pharaoh's was a case of concurrent phenomena. *A man* there on the one hand, willingly, deliberately, and most guiltily, battling with right, and rightly bringing ruin on his own head, wholly of himself. *God* was there on the other hand, making that man a monument not of grace but of judgment. And that side, that line, is isolated here, and treated as if it were all.[48]

Similar modifications of an extreme view of divine sovereignty are implicit in vv. 21-23.[49]

Though Paul for the moment is emphasizing God's sovereignty, even in this strongest of all passages on the subject he is not caught on the rock of divine tyranny any more than on the rock of divine weakness. More conclusive than any of the observations above is the emphatic denial of Paul that there is unrighteousness with God (v. 14). This assurance underlies his whole position and renders incorrect any interpretation of his words that would imply the contrary. The case is firmly established when we interpret this passage in the light of the entire Epistle—which is not only our right but our obligation to do. As Olshausen says: The doctrine of the predestination of the wicked "loses all semblance of truth" as soon as 9:14 is viewed in connection with 11—to say nothing of cc. 8 and 10.[50]

---

46. "Romans," *New Century Bible*, p. 215.

47. *Ibid.*, p. 216.

48. *Expositor's Bible*, p. 253.

49. Garvie thinks that "vessels" (v. 21) refers to earthly use, not to eternal destiny; in which case Jacob and Esau would be a perfect example, for they were made, one unto honor and the other unto dishonor, out of "the same lump," i.e. the same parentage (*ICC*, p. 261). Sanday and Headlam, Wesley, Robertson, Garvie, Moule, Denney, Olshausen, and Weiss all are emphatic in asserting that neither the context nor the clause itself, "prepared for destruction," require us to ascribe to God's design their evil condition. Of all sources examined, only Meyers dissents from this view.

50. *Biblical Commentary on the NT*, p. 74.

E. A Biblical Concept of Sovereignty

Taking the whole of Romans 9—11, we discover a fourfold exercise of divine sovereignty:

1. In the divine *choice of earthly instruments,* as in the cases of Isaac, Jacob, Israel, Moses, Pharaoh, and so on down through every king, prophet, and priest whom God particularly uses in carrying forward His designs. Why God raises up one through historical providences and sets another down, why He chooses David to be king rather than his more promising brothers, why only one in a family is called to preach the gospel, is not for us to know; such matters lie within the veil of God's omniscient wisdom and belong to the prerogatives of His own will.

2. In the divine *appointment of means and methods;* and here is seen the harmony of the entire Epistle. Throughout the letter Paul is arguing a salvation obtained by faith, not works; based on grace, not merit; procured by Christ, not Moses. But the mass of Jews were unsaved because they *rejected this method,* not because God predestined them to be unsaved. "For being ignorant of the righteousness that comes from God, and seeking to establish their own, they did not submit to God's righteousness" (10:3). They were broken off, not by arbitrary design, but "because of their unbelief" (11:20). To say that God foreordained their unbelief and our faith is to make meaningless all warnings, such as the one immediately following: "For if God did not spare the natural branches, neither will he spare you. Note then the kindness and the severity of God: severity toward those who have fallen, but God's kindness to you, provided you continue in his kindness; otherwise you too will be cut off" (11:21-22).

3. In the divine *initiation of salvation.* The whole plan of redemption is God's down-reach to lift fallen man. It is not man's device whereby salvation may be *achieved,* but God's design whereby salvation may be *received.* Therefore what we have is given, not earned. It is mercy, not justice. It is divine, not human. And it leaves us in eternal indebtedness to God, the Author of our salvation.

4. The divine *guarantee of ultimate triumph.* It is a mistake to assert "God has never lost a battle." He has. But He is going to win the war, and that is what counts in the end. As Garvie says, "God's purpose must be carried out, and can be thwarted, by man's freedom."[51] Thwarted, but not ultimately defeated. God has exercised a self-limited sovereignty out of respect to the free creature He has created in

---

51. *New Century Bible,* p. 201.

His own image, but He has not surrendered His sovereignty. Individual destinies have been prostituted by individual wills, but the certainty that the final outcome of history will be His outcome has not been weakened.

To repeat: He remains the Potter and will overrule where He cannot rule, even to making the wrath of man to praise Him, and using in His intricate maneuverings wicked men as His unwitting servants. In this sense He used Pharaoh—"that my name may be declared through all the earth." He didn't will the wickedness but He willed to use the wickedness. Countless adjustments divinely manipulated along the way will keep human history moving forward. Human losses constitute the heartbreak of God but never the conquest of God.

We may conclude therefore that *while the sovereignty of God is absolute in its prerogatives, it is self-limited in its exercise.* Since God "made the world and everything in it," He is "Lord of heaven and earth" (Acts 17:24). This is His unlimited right, and any rival claim is both fraudulent and wicked. His sovereign right to rule extends to personal agents as well as impersonal forces. Therefore He has sole claim on the allegiance, affections, and energies of every personal being. "You shall worship the Lord your God, and him only shall you serve," quoted Jesus in His confrontation with Satan (Luke 4:8).

In the exercise of this sovereignty God does whatever He chooses to do. Mary exclaimed, "He has filled the hungry with good things, and the rich he has sent empty away" (Luke 1:53). And Jesus said to Pilate, "You would have no power over me unless it had been given you from above" (John 19:11). Behind every secondary cause is the will of God, either determinative or permissive. The will of God shall be done. Paul quotes Isaiah 45:23: "As I live, says the Lord, every knee shall bow to me, and every tongue shall give praise to God" (Rom. 14:11; Phil. 2:10).

However, God's sovereign will *includes* His purpose to grant to man the power to say no. A measure of autonomy in man, with the potential of becoming a focal point of rebellion, is within the total scope of the divine plan. It is God's will that man should choose in decisive freedom. That he is able to resist God is clear from the Lord's prayer, "Thy will be done, on earth as it is in heaven" (Matt. 6:10). Obviously His will is not now being done on earth as it is in heaven.

The sad prospect therefore of persistent rebellion on the part of some cannot be interpreted as a failure in the divine sovereignty, if it is seen once for all that this scheme of things is part of that sovereignty. On the side of divine love, which seeks to persuade instead of manipulate, God's will is frustrated by every lost soul; but on the side of the divine respect for human freedom, His will is inviolable. From the standpoint of what constitutes a demonstration of successful sovereignty, the gospel call and the wooing of the Spirit will pose no problems in relating *call* to *election* if our thinking moves within the framework of a biblical view of sovereignty.

"O the depth of the riches and wisdom and knowledge of God! How unsearchable are his judgments and how inscrutable his ways! ... For from him and through him and to him are all things. To him be glory for ever. Amen" (Rom. 11:33, 36).

25

A New Man in Christ

The salvation theme consistently governs the New Testament. Mary's Child is to be called Jesus, "for he will save" (Matt. 1:21). The angels announce to the astonished shepherds "a Savior who is Christ the Lord" (Luke 2:11). Zacharias in prophetic ecstasy sings of the redemption to be accomplished by the Lord's "horn of salvation" (Luke 1:68-79). Simeon declares with great elation his readiness now to die in peace, "for mine eyes have seen thy salvation" (Luke 2:28-32). While many were blind to any dimension in the expected salvation other than political and physical, those who saw with spiritual eyes into the mission of Jesus marked a grander and farther horizon (cf. Luke 18:23 ff.). Not just the Jews but the world was under divine sentence, and Jesus came that "the world might be saved through him" (John 3:17).

However, the cosmic dimensions of salvation are not our immediate inquiry. Rather, what happens when sinners repent and believe the gospel? When Jesus explained the parable of the sower, He said that the devil snatches the gospel seed away from the wayside hearers "that they may not believe and be saved" (Luke 8:12). Obviously the end of believing is being saved. In the mind of Christ, what is the content of this salvation?

In the Synoptics certain basic answers are found, which become enriched and deepened by metaphor and picture in John, illustrated in the Acts, and expounded in the Epistles.

I. What Jesus Taught About Salvation

A. Recovery and Deliverance

First of all, in salvation the lost are recovered. Jesus said: "For the Son of man came to seek and to save the lost." Confrontation with Jesus brought Zacchaeus, the straying tax collector, to a sudden spiritual awakening, in which he saw life's relationships once again in proper perspective (Luke 19:1-10). "Today salvation has come to this house," Jesus announced.

We miss the perspective of Jesus if we see lostness only in its subjective aspects. Ultimate lostness has a dimension outside this world. Jesus declared that the gaining of a whole world cannot compensate for the loss of one's soul (Matt. 16:26; Mark 8:35). Because the essence of lostness is alienation from God, it can only lead to final and eternal banishment from His presence. Lostness is not a plight of unknown location, but of complete waste, like a lost hour or a lost opportunity—an absolute and irrecoverable loss.

While the lostness experienced by men in this world is real, it is not yet final. The lost soul may be found, the alienation cease, the waste be stopped, the bewilderment ended. It was for this that Jesus came. No one remains lost who is found by Jesus; no one remains found who departs from Jesus. But it must be stressed that this is recovery, not just discovery. Salvation is more than being found; it is being brought home by Jesus Christ. It includes a restoration both of position and condition (Luke 15:5-7, 24).

B. Transformation

In this life-shaking confrontation with Jesus, which is salvation, profound changes occur in the believer. He begins to experience the kinds of change that Jesus came to accomplish (Luke 4:18). The mighty deliverance experienced by the Gadarene demoniac (Mark 5:15) is symbolic of every conversion. The command suddenly makes sense: "Go home to your friends, and tell them how much the Lord has done for you, and how he has had mercy on you" (v. 19). A saved person has a testimony. He has entered the narrow gate of repentance and has set resolute foot on the narrow way that leads to life (Matt. 7:13-14; cf. Mark 8:35). God acknowledges him as His own because he has ceased the practice of evil (Matt. 7:23). He has begun to experience the true inward righteousness, in motive and spirit, without which final and eternal access to the Kingdom is impossible (Matt. 5:20).

The radical nature and extent of this change is intimated by Jesus in one of His solemn absolutes: "Truly, I say to you, unless you turn and become like children [*paidia,* very young children], you will never enter the kingdom of heaven" (Matt. 18:3). True conversion involves a transformation that is like a return to childhood; it is in fact a return to childlikeness.[1]

C. Forgiveness

In a sense forgiveness underlies and is the condition for all else. When the angel promised that Jesus would be a Saviour by saving His people from their sins (Matt. 1:21), he meant first of all salvation from the *guilt* of those sins. Sin has a claim on the sinner, which tortures his conscience and alienates him from God. No human atonement will suffice, no attempt to deny or hide will succeed, no reformation will balance the score. Only one hope is offered: forgiveness.

The necessity of forgiveness is implied by Jesus' warning that in trifling with the Holy Spirit men are in danger of committing an unforgivable sin (Mark 3:28-30), thus destroying all hope. Furthermore, an authentic relationship as a disciple of Christ cannot be established apart from the forgiveness of sins (Mark 4:11-12; cf. Matt. 11:28-29). The converse is just as true: No one can be forgiven who refuses to trust in Jesus as the ground of forgiveness—"for you will die in your sins unless you believe that I am he" (John 8:24).

1. *The Baptism of John.*

The use of water as a ritual was secondary to the essence of baptism, which was "a baptism of repentance for the forgiveness of sins" (Mark 1:4; cf. Acts 13:24; 19:4). John was God's appointed instrument for introducing the Jewish people to a new way of receiving forgiveness that bypassed the Temple but which included repentance and faith as conditions.[2] Thus John's ministry was introductory to the gospel order, and to Jesus the heart of the gospel.

The forgiveness of sins which John mediated was a true reconciliation with God, not merely a ceremonial cleansing. Those who

---

1. A small child is sinful, but not corrupted or hardened. Jesus is saying that sinners who are saved are cleansed of the accretion of their own personal depravity, and once again know something of the innocence, wonder, wholesomeness of outlook, and spiritual responsiveness of an unspoiled child.

2. Those seeking water baptism without showing evidence of true repentance were rejected by John (Matt. 3:7-8). But faith was necessary also, for Paul interpreted John as "telling the people to believe in the one who was to come after him, that is, Jesus" (Acts 19:4).

were forgiven could now enter directly into the new regime with a clear record, enjoying peace with God and peace in their hearts. They could at once begin to follow Jesus as disciples, precisely as many did. This is the reason that when calling out disciples who should be with Him, Jesus did not first demand of them repentance and baptism. They were spiritually qualified already and felt therefore a natural inclination to respond promptly to the Lord's call. That their response was limited by their imperfect understanding, and continued to deepen as they continued to walk with Christ, does not invalidate the repentance or the completeness of their forgiveness. They were already new men, standing in a new relationship to God, to their past, and to the future.

This reveals the true interpretation of Zacharias' inspired prophecy. John as forerunner was appointed to "go before the Lord to prepare his ways; to give knowledge of salvation to his people in the forgiveness of their sins" (Luke 1:76-77). It was by the forgiveness of their sins that they came to know the nature of the salvation which the Messiah was to bring; indeed this experience of forgiveness was their initial experience of salvation.[3]

2. A Conditional Forgiveness.

Those thus initiated into the mysteries of the Kingdom were made to understand that their forgiveness was related to Jesus as Messiah, but it was not necessary for them to understand the means by which Jesus made their forgiveness possible. They had no concept yet of Christ's atoning death. They could not therefore be infected by a presumption of forgiveness so objective and absolute as to include sins of the future as well as sins of the past. On the contrary the teachings of Jesus so clearly declared the contingent nature of forgiveness that it would seem impossible for the wholesale pardon notion ever to arise. The fact that a prayer for forgiveness is included in the disciples' model prayer would suggest that the forgiveness received under John was not a paid-up moral insurance policy. Renewed sinning demanded renewed repentance and new forgiveness.

Furthermore, the renewed forgiveness is contingent on maintenance of a forgiving spirit toward others (Matt. 6:8-15). This prin-

3. Only in respect to the technical formula prescribed in the Great Commission (Matt. 28:19) could John's baptism (or the later baptizing of Christ's disciples, John 4:1-2) be called sub-Christian. Not the formula, but the *experience* accompanying, determines the participant's relation to God. That experience was forgiveness, based on repentance and faith, of which the water rite was the public witness.

ciple is reaffirmed by Jesus in a later discourse, when He answered Peter's question, "Lord, how often shall my brother sin against me, and I forgive him?" (Matt. 18:21 ff.). The parable that follows closes with the solemn application: "So also my heavenly Father will do to every one of you, if you do not forgive your brother from your heart" (v. 35). Forgiveness is cancelled if the forgiven become unforgiving.[4]

3. *Forgiveness and Justification.*

The relation of forgiveness to justification is crucial to New Testament theology. Therefore it is important to search for clues in the teachings of Jesus. The critical word *dikaioō,* "to justify," so frequent in Paul's writings, is found only twice in Matthew, five times in Luke, and not at all in Mark or John.

The word *vindicated* is the closest parallel to *dikaioō,* and fits almost every example, either as a true vindication of rightness or an attempt to establish a pseudo-vindication (Matt. 11:19; 12:37; Luke 7:29, 35; 10:29). Self-justification—the attempt to set oneself right in the eyes of others—is particularly odious to Jesus (Luke 16:15).

The life and death issue is: How can sinful man be justified before God? The Synoptics provide an answer by means of *dikaioō* in only one passage, the parable of the Pharisee and the publican. "I tell you, this man"—this humble, repentant, sin-confessing publican—"went down to his house justified rather than the other" (Luke 18: 10-14). Clearly this was divine justification. But what was its nature? The usual meaning of *vindication* could not be appropriate here. He did not go down to his house exonerated, but pardoned. Because forgiven, he was now acceptable to God. Here is a clue for a sound, biblical doctrine of justification.

D. Discipleship

The transition from John the Baptist to Jesus permitted an initial salvation activated by faith in the soon-coming Messiah, but this faith had to become open alignment with Jesus if the salvation was to be confirmed and sustained (Matt. 10:32-39). Jesus identified him-

---

4. Unfortunately the Judaean populace provided a mass example. Thousands were baptized by John and his assistants, and we may assume that at least a majority of them actually experienced the joy of forgiveness. Yet relatively few allowed forgiveness to lead them into ongoing discipleship. Could Matt. 12:43-45 have a bearing here? When the exorcised spirit returns to its former abode and finds it "empty, swept, and put in order," it goes and "brings with him seven other spirits more evil than himself, . . . and the last state . . . becomes worse than the first. So shall it be also with this evil generation."

self as the One whom John had been announcing, and claimed a total transfer of allegiance. Becoming His disciples was not expected merely of the special followers called away from their vocations, but equally of all who would be saved. Not only were those who "labor and are heavy-laden" promised rest if they would but come to Jesus, but they were challenged to take His yoke and learn from Him (Matt. 11:28-30). This challenge they would understand as the usual invitation of a rabbi to become a learning follower.

However, it soon became apparent that Jesus meant far more than simply accepting and acknowledging His tutorial guidance; He meant nothing less than accepting His absolute authority as Lord. He not only taught "as one who had authority," but insisted on more than lip service to that authority; it must be acknowledged by obedience (Matt. 7:21-29).

In a later discourse also, Jesus left no doubt concerning the absolute demands of discipleship. Allegiance to Him must be so unconditional that disciples accept without qualification even a possible rupture with father and mother (Matt. 10:34-39; cf. Luke 12:51-53; 14:26-33). Still later, when Peter presumed to correct Him, Jesus not only rebuked Peter soundly, but reiterated once again the terms of discipleship: "If any man would come after me, let him deny himself [renounce his claim to self-sovereignty] and take up his cross and follow me" (Matt. 16:24).

Being saved, therefore, means becoming Jesus' disciple not tentatively or tepidly but radically and unreservedly. Jesus will claim as "his people" (Matt. 1:21) only those who openly and boldly identify with Him. Only the "repentance" and "believing" that lead to this kind of discipleship will bring lasting benefits.

E. Entry into the Kingdom

Being saved means being in the kingdom of God. When Jesus declared the difficulty of a rich man entering "the kingdom of God," the disciples exclaimed, "Who then can be saved?" (Matt. 19:24-25), indicating that in their minds being saved and in the Kingdom were equivalent. There is further evidence that initial salvation did not merely give hope for access to the Kingdom ultimately, but inducted believers into the Kingdom immediately. When explaining to the puzzled disciples His use of parables, Jesus said: "To you has been given the secret of the Kingdom of God, but for those outside everything is in parables" (Mark 4:11). He thus implied that *they* were *inside.* Again He encouraged them to rejoice because their names were written in heaven (Luke 10:20)—implying heavenly citizenship.[5]

This new Kingdom was not *fully* revealed until the Day of Pentecost, so that from John the Baptist to Pentecost was a transition period. Yet even then the Kingdom was open through preaching (like an offer of charter membership), and any man could press in with bold faith (cf. Matt. 11:11-12; Luke 16:16).[6]

II. THE JOHANNINE METAPHORS

Under the inspiration of the Holy Spirit, John selects elements in the teaching of Jesus which stress (1) sonship and the gift of a new kind of life, and (2) the mystical, inner union of the believer with Christ. Perhaps the emphasis may be said to be more on regeneration and less on forgiveness. The meaning of discipleship is also sharpened. A further advance is the revelation of the Spirit's activity in effecting the changes inherent in salvation and in creating this real union with Christ. Herein, also, is the promise of that fuller redemptive ministry to be made available to believers by the Spirit's coming at Pentecost.

A. A Spiritual Birth

The supreme "right" which Christ gives those who take Him as Saviour and Lord is the privilege of becoming "children of God" (John 1:12). Obviously, the relationship of creature to Creator does not constitute this special relationship of child to father. The first is already fact. The reestablishment of the Father-child relationship is the

---

5. While conversion and becoming like little children seems in Matthew to suggest a prior condition for future entry (18:3), in Mark the entry is actually shown to be concomitant: "Whoever does not receive the kingdom of God like a child shall not enter it" (10:15).

6. This does not mean that those in the pre-Kingdom era would necessarily be eternally lost or that Jesus would not be the ultimate ground of their salvation. Acceptability under the law was on the basis of its prefigurement of Christ. The law, in and of itself, could not effect regeneration. And when the new order was announced by John and Jesus, no one was automatically in it because of who he was, or because of his relationship to the old order, not even John. Wesley quotes the following with approval: "Whosoever . . . is least in the kingdom of heaven, by Christian regeneration, is greater than any who has attained only the righteousness of the law, because the law maketh nothing perfect." Wesley adds his own comment: "It may further mean, the least true Christian believer has a more perfect knowledge of Jesus Christ, of His redemption and kingdom, than John the Baptist had, who died before the full manifestation of the Gospel" *(Explanatory Notes upon the New Testament).*

objective of redemption. The "children of God" category is thus not coextensive with humanity, but is a special family within the human race (John 11:52).[7]

Becoming children of God is not simply a human resolve to be like God. A supernatural change must occur, a "becoming" which is a real begetting of God (John 1:13). And this is the substance of Jesus' announcement to Nicodemus, "You must be born anew" (3:7)—not a second physical birth, but a birth of spiritual life, embracing a divine likeness and a divine kinship. To be born of "water and the Spirit" is to be made spiritually alive by the joint action of the Word (symbolized by water, cf. John 15:3; Eph. 5:26; 1 Pet. 1:23; 1 John 5:7-13) and the Spirit.[8]

If we forget that the birth figure is a metaphor, we will be in danger of over-literalizing the concept. We must not suppose that the "new birth" is exactly like physical birth. The new birth is not an irreversible, uncancellable procreation of a new person, of the same metaphysical nature as its male and female parents. Furthermore it is not such a "birth" as to be inconsistent with the equally biblical concept of "adoption." Rather, a person, who, having been procreated in the flesh, and being of the same nature and substance as his parents, is *morally and spiritually* transformed by the inward action of the Holy Spirit. He becomes not a little god but a spiritual son. Spiritual life which was lost is regained; a new godlikeness of nature is imparted; and there is a reinstatement with God and readmittance into the heavenly family. Being saved is indeed a new beginning, involving a "birthday" and a family celebration.[9]

B. Possession of Eternal Life

The *life* everywhere promised in John's Gospel as integral to salvation

---

7. The concept is fundamentally a matter of moral and spiritual likeness. Jesus admitted that racially the Jews were Abraham's "descendants" (John 8:37, 56); but morally and spiritually they were unlike Abraham (vv. 37-40). When they claimed not only Abraham but God as their father (v. 41), Jesus bluntly said, "You are of your father the devil" (vv. 41-44). Not human blood lines or religious pedigree but likeness is the acid test.

8. Speaking of *gennaō*, to "beget," passive voice, thus being used metaphorically, Vine says that in the "writings of the Apostle John [it is] of the gracious act of God in conferring upon those who believe the nature and disposition of 'children' imparting to them spiritual life, John 3:3, 5, 7; 1 John 2:29; 3:9; 4:7; 5:1, 4, 18" (*Dictionary*, 1:109).

9. It is equally important to avoid allowing the metaphorical figure to blur the reality of a true inner change, or of its divine nature. The new birth is far more than the subjective psychological effects of either repentance or believing.

is qualitatively new. Jesus declares, "I came that they may have life, and have it abundantly" (10:10). What life was intended to be—free, secure, and fulfilling—Christ came to make possible. This is a new fullness of natural life, here and now. It becomes possible through a new *kind* of life that is spiritual. Spiritual life is the upward dimension of human experience. This dynamic participation in the very love and wholeness of God makes human life complete and saves it from the banality of mere existence. No one made alive by Christ ever wonders what life is all about.

Both wine and water suggest metaphorically the qualities of this new life (John 2:1-11; 4:14; 7:37). As wine, it is sparkling and exhilarating without being debilitating (in contrast to the wine of worldliness). As water, it is refreshing, cleansing, renewing, sustaining, beautifying—God's perfect answer to the feverish thirst and parched aridness of the sin-sick soul. "These things I have spoken unto you, that my joy may be in you, and that your joy may be full" (15:11).

This generation of a new kind of life—a new dimension of experience—is described also by the metaphor of resurrection. The references to life beyond the grave are unmistakable and are to be taken seriously (5:28-29; 11:25-26). But unmistakable also is the declaration that those who have eternal life through believing have "passed from death to life" (5:24-25). Robertson comments: "Not the future resurrection in verse 23, but the spiritual resurrection here and now."[10] Thus the concept of the new birth is enriched to include the idea of a spiritual restoration from the dead.

But while the concept of eternal life in the New Testament is primarily qualitative, and must never, therefore, be reduced to mere endlessness, neither must its endless duration be missed. The inference here is clear that Jesus is talking of a transtemporal dimension as well as trans-physical. "He . . . who hates his life in this world shall keep it to life eternal" (12:25, NASB). Life eternal is a life beyond this world.

C. Union with Christ

In John's Gospel some very graphic pictures are used to portray the inwardness of salvation, not only in personal changes, but in a mystical oneness with the indwelling Christ.

---

10. *Word Pictures,* 5:86.

1. *A Well of Water.*

Baptismal waters are external; but to the woman of Samaria, Jesus identified himself as the Giver of a kind of water which would not only perpetually slake spiritual thirst, but become in one "a spring of water welling up to eternal life" (John 4:14).[11]

2. *Bread and Blood.*

To others later, Jesus said, "Do not labor for the food which perishes, but for the food which endures to eternal life" (6:27). While first naming himself as the Giver, He quickly declares himself to be the Bread (vv. 35, 48-51). We might suppose the metaphor to refer to His teachings and the beautiful example of His life, which inspire us as we meditate upon them. Jesus, however, does not permit such an inoffensive interpretation; the bread is His "flesh" and it is by means of His self-giving on the Cross that it becomes available for eating. If up to this point His hearers were puzzled, they were now shocked: "How can this man give us his flesh to eat?" (v. 52). Jesus proceeds to turn shock into outrage: "Truly, truly, I say to you, unless you eat the flesh of the Son of man and drink his blood, you have no life in you" (v. 53; cf. vv. 54-58).[12]

Such a vigorous metaphor would not permit Jesus' hearers to see the believer's union with Christ as social only. Disciples must experience something more than the pleasant connection that exists between a rabbi and a little coterie of admiring followers. Those who up to this time were such disciples "drew back and no longer went about with him" (v. 66). External discipleship on the natural plane they understood. But internal union, which drew eternal life out of His blood-shedding, was a dimension they could not comprehend.

3. *The Vine and Branches.*

The kind of discipleship that belongs to salvation is specified by Jesus: "By this my Father is glorified, that you bear much fruit, and

---

11. Later, on the last great day of the Feast of Tabernacles, Jesus identified himself not only as the Giver but the Water (John 7:37); only now the well becomes rivers, and the drinker enjoys not a solitary satisfaction, but becomes himself an inexhaustible source of supply for others (v. 38). By so much does the Gift of the Spirit enlarge the ministry of the indwelling Saviour (v. 39).

12. Jesus here is not only pinpointing His blood atonement as the means of our salvation. He is saying *this* must be the specific focus of our faith. Effectual faith is an internalizing of both Christ's person and His death so that He *in us* becomes (in a sense) *us*, and His power and holiness become ours, very much like the food we eat turns within us into energy and sinew.

so prove to be my disciples" (15:8). The difference is that while followers of a teacher on the natural plane can transmit his ideas, they cannot recreate or transmit his spirit. The bond between Jesus and His disciples must be closer—as close as that of the vine to the branches. What disciples produce is by means of inner life, not fleshly labor. No metaphor more aptly conveys the complete dependence of believers on Christ, or the vital nature of their union with Him.

Yet metaphor it remains, because the *difference* between believers and branches is as striking as the *similarity*. In the natural order branches have no choice, whereas the believer's relationship to Christ as the Vine remains voluntary and individual. Not only may the *life* of the vine be forfeited, but also one's *place* on the vine. Indeed, severance is possible in two ways: failing to bear fruit (v. 2), and failing to abide (vv. 4-7)—failure to continue drawing life from the Vine.[13]

III. Salvation in the Early Church

The Philippian jailor well represents the controlling concern of awakened sinners in their confrontation with the gospel; "Men, what must I do to be saved?" The reply expresses the consistent answer of the Church: "Believe in the Lord Jesus, and you will be saved, you and your household" (Acts 16:30-31). Whatever the jailor had in mind by the term "saved," the more important question is, What did Paul and the Apostolic Church mean by it?[14]

"The salvation of the new people of God by the Messiah is the

---

13. F. Godet is correct when he says: "Faith in Christ is usually supposed to be fact accomplished once for all, and which should necessarily and naturally display its consequences, as a tree produces its fruits. It is forgotten that in the spiritual domain nothing *is done* which does not require to be continually done again, and that what is not done again today, will tomorrow begin to be undone. Thus it is the bond of the soul to Christ, whereby we have become His branches, relaxes the instant we do not re-form it with new active force and begins to break with every unpardoned act of infidelity. The branch becomes barren, and yet Christ's law demanding its fruitfulness remains (John 14)" (*St. Paul's Epistle to the Romans,* tr. by A. Cusin [Edinburgh: T. and T. Clark, 1884], 2:54).

14. There is every reason to believe that the salvation of which the jailor felt himself to be so urgently in need was moral and spiritual. A jailor who does not lose a single prisoner in an earthquake has no cause for anxiety about either his job or his head. He undoubtedly knew the announcement of the slave girl that these men were "servants of the Most High God, who proclaim to you the way of salvation" (Acts 16:17). An uneasy conscience and hungry heart were suddenly brought to sharp focus by these startling events.

chief theme of the New Testament," correctly observes Alan Richardson.[15] The salvation motif dominates the Epistles as well as the Gospels and the Acts. It is because the gospel is "the power of God for salvation" that Paul finds no need to be ashamed of it (Rom. 1:16). The specific purpose of the grace of God, as revealed in Christ, is to make salvation available to "all men" (Titus 2:11). The salvation now disclosed is that to which the prophets pointed but did not fully understand (1 Pet. 1:10-11).

A. Safety and Soundness

There are two major notes to this salvation, corresponding to the two meanings of *sōtēria,* as well as the verb *sōzō, viz.,* "safety" and "soundness." The concept includes deliverance from immediate objective peril and preservation in this safety. It also includes deliverance from a subjective peril consisting in a fatal condition of unsoundness. Careful examination of the concept will disclose yet a third dimension. There is a cosmic salvation from sin's scars and from a sin-infested environment, in which not only all believers will be glorified, but the earth itself shall be redeemed. This is the grand, irreversible, and nonforfeitable consummation of all the salvation events and processes which have gone before. Thus salvation is viewed teleologically.

B. Salvation's Stages

There is basic agreement among the writers in the second half of the New Testament not only concerning the substance of salvation but concerning its stages. It is biblical to say, "I am saved, I am being saved, and I shall be saved." There is an immediate salvation that one enjoys upon experiencing justification by faith (Rom. 10:9-13; 11:11; 1 Cor. 10:33; 2 Cor. 6:1-2; 7:10; Eph. 2:5, 8; 6:17; 1 Thess. 2:16; 2 Thess. 2:10; 1 Tim. 2:4; 2 Tim. 3:15). There is also an ongoing salvation, a being saved, which includes both process and crisis. The emphasis here is not objective but subjective, a restoration to soundness, which comes under the general heading of sanctification (1 Cor. 1:18; 2 Cor. 2:15; 2 Thess. 2:13; Heb. 10:39; 1 Pet. 1:2, 9; 2 Pet. 1:1-4; 10-11).

Finally, there is the eschatological aspect to salvation. When Paul says, "For salvation is nearer to us now than when we first be-

---

15. *Theology of the NT,* p. 81.

lieved" (Rom. 13:11), he is seeing salvation not as a present experience but as a future hope (Rom. 8:23-27; cf. Rom. 5:9; 1 Cor. 3:15; 5:5; Phil. 1:28; 1 Thess. 5:8-10; Heb. 1:14; 5:9; 9:28; 1 Pet. 1:5; Rev. 12:10). In some cases, to be sure, the term "salvation" is timeless, referring to the totality of God's provision in Christ (Rom. 1:16; Eph. 1:13; 1 Tim. 1:15; 2 Tim. 2:10; 2 Pet. 3:15; Jude 3).

C. Salvation and Redemption

The concept of salvation parallels that of redemption *(apolutrōsis)*. Richardson says the two are synonymous.[16] When Paul says, "They are justified by his grace as a gift, through the redemption which is in Christ Jesus" (Rom. 3:24), he is using redemption as a synonym for salvation, and referring to the total experience (cf. 1 Pet. 1:18). Elsewhere, as with salvation, there is a redemption realizable now (Eph. 1:7; Col. 1:14; Titus 2:14; Heb. 9:15) and a future redemption which is the culmination of all that has gone before (Rom. 8:23; 1 Cor. 1:30; Eph. 1:14; 4:30; Heb. 9:12 *[lutrōsis]*; cf. Luke 21:28). While the verb *lutroō*, "to loose by a price" (Titus 2:14; 1 Pet. 1:8) emphasizes the means of our redemption, *sōtēria* and *apolutrōsis* emphasize its substance.

It is a deliverance, Peter says, not only from guilt, but "from the futile ways inherited from your fathers" (1 Pet. 1:18-19). The new way of life made possible by this redemption is *holiness* "in all your conduct" (v. 15). Redemption of the firstborn in the wilderness at five shekels a head (Num. 3:44-51) was a restoration of the right to live. Redemption through Christ's blood is a restoration of power to live right. The substance of the redemption as greatly exceeds mere extension of physical life as the cost exceeds five shekels.[17]

IV. The Substance of Initial Salvation

In addition to this brief survey of salvation concepts in the Epistles, a more detailed examination of certain key passages is necessary.

A. A New Creation

"Therefore," Paul writes, "if any one is in Christ, he is a new creature

---

16. *Ibid.,* p. 80.
17. The fundamental ideas of redemption in the Old Testament are deliverance and restoration. The *means* of redemption, whether money, blood, or sword, varied, and was incidental to the objective of deliverance. Especially significant was the redemption of the firstborn (Exod. 13:10-13; Num. 18:15, 17).

[margin, 'there is a new creation']; the old has passed away, behold, the new has come" (2 Cor. 5:17). That such a statement is pivotal is obvious; but what does it mean?

1. *In Christ.*

This phrase expresses the personal union with Christ pictured by the Johannine metaphors of eating and drinking, and the Vine and the branches. Here too, individuals are in mind—"any one . . . he is." We do not acquire this relationship with Christ corporately or parentally, but privately, personally, and individually.

Being "in Christ" is the counterpart of "Christ in you, the hope of glory" (Col. 1:27). It is hence a salvation bond and surety—a declaration of relationship. At the same time it is a possession, in fellowship, of a real presence. The Spirit responding to our repentance and faith unites us with the living Christ as personal Lord and Saviour. Speaking of the some 200 times Paul uses this phrase, Archibald M. Hunter observes that in most cases "it means 'in communion with Christ,' pregnantly describing that fellowship with a living Lord which is the very nerve of Paul's Christianity."[18]

But being in Christ also means being in the corporate body of Christ, the Church. The Spirit who joins us to Christ inducts us into the organism as a living, functioning member of the whole (1 Cor. 12:13). While we are united to Christ individually, we do not remain isolated members but share this union with all others who are in Him. Hence all who are in Him are in each other also, in a reflective but real sense. Hunter says that "in passage after passage the phrase carries a corporate meaning. To be 'in Christ' signifies to be 'in the community of Christ', to be a member of the new people of God of which He is the Head."[19]

2. *Personal Newness.*

In this passage Paul speaks of "a new creation" or "a new creature." The word *ktisis* may be translated "a making" or "thing made." In the first instance we have the idea of a *creation,* in the second of the *creature,* hence the uncertainty of the translations. The adjective *kainos,* "new," suggests that the man in Christ is the subject of a new creative act and as a consequence is the new creature. The kind of newness indicated by *kainos,* says Vine, is not so much temporal, i.e.,

18. *Introducing New Testament Theology* (Philadelphia: The Westminster Press, 1957), p. 96.
19. *Loc. cit.*

recent or "brand new," as it is a newness "of form or quality, of different nature from what is contrasted as old."[20] What Paul is saying therefore is that being in Christ means to be transformed. Apart from thus being radically altered, no religious rite or religious facade is of any value (Gal. 6:15).

Human nature is fixed in some areas, malleable in others. As God-created *manness*, with its normal propensities and faculties, human nature is not altered by salvation; it is only captured, purified, and redirected. "Nature" may also refer to the inherited peculiarities of the individual, as for instance largeness or smallness, mental and temperamental endowments. The newness which is in Christ does not significantly alter this dimension of nature either, except as modest modifications may gradually be accomplished through training or discipline.

But when we start describing the person's moral and spiritual nature, we begin using such words as *selfish, greedy, lustful;* or *generous, kind,* and *magnanimous.* Immediately we know that we have touched the real essence of human personhood. These are qualitative and relational terms. We have penetrated into the realm of character. We know this is the all-important area of humanness, and this is what most needs to be changed. In this inner being of character it may be said of the man in Christ: "The old things passed away; behold, new things have come." Old directions, old values, old goals, which belong to the preconversion life, have vanished. They have been displaced by a new direction, a new value system, a new orientation toward Christ, and by a new destiny, consciously chosen and constantly pursued.

The concept of the new birth finds its home in this transformation. To be made new is to be regenerated, to be made alive. In the New Testament, the term "regeneration" is used only once in this sense (Titus 3:5). Here the phrase "washing of regeneration" seems to be equivalent to the cleansing and rejuvenation which occurs in the new birth.

While *palinggenesia* ("regeneration") is not common, the idea is common enough. Such phrases as "alive from the dead" *(ek nekrōn zōntas)* and "raised up" *(sunēgerthēte),* as well as "newness," are governing concepts with Paul (Rom. 6:13; cf. v. 11; Eph. 2:5; Col. 2:12; 3:1; see also Eph. 5:14; Col. 2:13). To the Ephesians Paul writes, "God . . . when we were dead through our trespasses, made us alive together

---

20. *Dictionary,* 3:109.

with Christ" (2:4-5). Our union with Christ's death assures us of a future resurrection *(anastasis)* like His, but in the meantime we are enabled to "walk in newness *[kainotēti]* of life" (Rom. 6:4-5). It is life of a "new quality" (Vine).

3. *Newness Both Actual and Potential.*

While the newness is both instantaneous and radical, its full realization is not immediately complete. The Corinthians were "in Christ," but only *babes.* The "old" had not yet all passed away, for they were "still fleshly" (1 Cor. 3:1-3). The Hebrews also knew something of the newness in Christ, but not to the measure of God's design, so they were urged to "press on to maturity" (Heb. 6:1, NASB; margin, "perfection"); to enter confidently, as regenerate believers, into "the holy place" (10:19-22); to "lay aside every encumbrance" and "the sin which so easily" entangled them (12:1); to go after peace and holiness, and guard carefully against falling short of this available grace (12:12-17).

Clearly, being in Christ implies and demands total newness; but there are postconversion stages in its full realization, involving further decision on the believer's part and ministrations of grace on God's part (see C. 26).[21]

B. A New Righteousness

With Paul a new kind of righteousness is inseparable from being "in Christ." Another crucial passage therefore is his personal manifesto: "I count everything as loss . . . that I may gain Christ and be found in him, not having a righteousness of my own, based on law, but that which is through faith in Christ, the righteousness from God that depends on faith" (Phil. 3:8-9). In rejecting a righteousness of his own, Paul does not mean that he does not want to be personally righteous. The exact opposite is true. He desires personal righteousness far deeper and more thorough than would ever be possible by his own efforts to conform to the legal requirements of the Law. He knew well the impotence of the Paul-law team to make the inner

---

21. The Galatians, too, were "in Christ," yet Paul experienced renewed "labor pains" in his intercession for them; "until Christ is formed in you," he said (Gal. 4:19). The Ephesians also were in Christ, yet if Christ were really to be at home in their hearts, and if they were going to be able to "be filled up to all the fullness of God," they needed the decisive empowerment "in the inner man" by the Holy Spirit (3:14-19). Furthermore, they were exhorted to put off their "old nature" (4:22-24; cf. Col. 3:9; Rom. 6:6) and to be "filled with the Spirit" (5:18).

difference his soul craved. He needed, and perceived in Christ, One who was adequate as Saviour precisely because He was adequate as Sanctifier.

The righteousness that comes from God is related to "the righteousness of God" which in the gospel is revealed from "faith for faith" (Rom. 1:17). God's righteousness makes possible a true righteousness in the believer. In this connection it is important that we grasp the full sweep of Paul's use of *dikaiosunē,* "righteousness, rectitude, godliness." A. T. Robertson points out that this word controls the thought of the Epistle to the Romans, and that in Paul's usage it means both justification and sanctification.[22]

1. *Justified by Faith.*

In Rom. 5:1 we are given the epitome of the previous four chapters. To understand this verse is to understand them at least accurately, if not wholly. Our initial experience of salvation brings us by faith into a new relationship with God. Elsewhere Paul calls it reconciliation (2 Cor. 5:18-21). In that passage Christ's death is seen as God's appointed substitute for the penalty of the world's transgressions, the way whereby He can erase the record of "their trespasses against them." This is what God has done through Christ. Now the challenge comes to the sinner, not just to listen to "the word of reconciliation" with mere mental assent, but to "be reconciled to God."

In the discussion in Romans the objective work of Christ is individualized by the sinner's accepting it for himself. This includes both an acceptance of the indictment "for all have sinned" (3:23) and an acceptance of the blood of Christ as the sole remedy for sin's guilt and consequences. It is by this kind of faith that we are "justified" and thus brought into the relationship of peace with God. This peace is infinitely beyond a truce; it is a real acceptance and a real fellowship.

A proper understanding of this initial justifying is basic to New Testament theology. To be "just" *(dikaios)* before God by means of the Law is possible only by observing it faultlessly (Rom. 2:13). This is possible theoretically but not practically because of man's inherited sinfulness. Because sin is already a fact, this door is shut: "No human being will be justified in his sight by works of the law" (3:20). Once infractions have occurred, no amount of law-keeping or cultic observances thereafter can really set one right (Heb. 10:1-4). But in Christ,

22. *Word Pictures,* 4:327.

God's righteousness is displayed in two ways (3:21-31): (1) His righteousness is vindicated by the public display of Christ "as a propitiation" (Rom. 3:25, NASB); and (2) it is displayed in the gift of righteousness in which man is "justified by his grace as a gift, through the redemption that is in Christ Jesus" (v. 24).

To justify *(dikaioō)* means "to declare or make *dikaios*" (Robertson), i.e., *righteous*. God's justification is both the *declaration* and the *making*. "No man is justified by faith whose faith does not make him just" is a sound aphorism. After expounding justification as a *declaration* in cc. 2—4, Paul proceeds through cc. 5—8 to explain that the righteousness available from God is also a complete renovation, i.e., sanctification.

To be justified in the sense of being *declared* righteous is forensic. This means it is the change of status in relation to God's law. The guilt and condemnation attached to transgressions are lifted. But in laying hold of a sound theology at this point, it is also important to see this declaration of righteousness not as a mere reckoning contrary to fact but as the state of one who is forgiven.[23] This forgiveness is a complete remission of penalty on the basis of faith in Christ's substitutionary death; it is not a simple *transference* of credit (cf. Acts 13: 38; 26:18; Eph. 1:7; Col. 1:14; also cf. Jas. 5:15; 1 John 1:9; 2:12).[24]

Nowhere is Christ's death or righteousness said to be imputed to us in a legalistic fashion. While *logidzomai*, to "count" or "calculate," is a common word with Paul, its theological use in the sense of an

---

23. Misunderstanding here has wrought untold mischief. If the relation is seen as an absolute transference of the sinner's guilt to Christ who in His death paid fully the penalty due, and at the same time the absolute transference (by imputation) of the obedience of Christ to the sinner, then the sinner of necessity must be *seen* by God as both innocent and righteous, even though in fact he is neither. In such a scheme we are dealing with legal fictions. Furthermore forgiveness is ruled out, since penalty *paid* needs no forgiveness.

The two primary words translated "forgiveness" are *aphiēmi* and *charizomai*. Vine considers the first more directly related to atonement in Paul's thought. He says that it (and the noun *aphesis*) signifies "the remission of the punishment due to sinful conduct, the deliverance of the sinner from the penalty Divinely, and therefore righteously, imposed," and also "it involves the complete removal of the cause of offence; such remission is based upon the vicarious and propitiatory sacrifice of Christ" (*Dictionary*, 2:122 ff). For Paul's use of verb *aphiēmi* and noun *aphesis* see Rom. 1:27; 4:7; 1 Cor. 7:11-13; Eph. 1:7; Col. 1:14. For his use of *charizomai* see Rom. 8:32; 1 Cor. 2:12; 2 Cor. 2:7, 10; 12:13; Gal. 3:18; Eph. 4:32; Phil. 1:29; 2:9; Col. 2:13; 3:13.

24. The interpretation of justification as being declared "not guilty" in *The Living Bible* (Rom. 3:22, 24) can be grossly misleading. To be justified is rather to be declared guilty but forgiven.

imputed righteousness is found only in Romans 4. And even in this passage there are *two* bases on which God accounts a man righteous.

First, faith in contrast to works.[25] Abraham's *faith* was reckoned to him for righteousness, and similarly our faith in Christ will be reckoned (imputed) to us (vv. 3, 5, 9, 22-24). This means that our right standing with God depends, not on our working for it, but by simply believing what God has said and by accepting what He offers to us in Christ.

Second, *forgiveness* is the basis of such reckoning. Paul cites David as also teaching the reckoning of righteousness apart from works (v. 6). But when we read the passage (vv. 7-8) from Ps. 32:1, we discover that God is not imputing righteousness by a legal fiction but on the ground of forgiveness. When a sinner is forgiven, his sins are no longer charged against him. In summary, a sinner is accounted righteous by God when he believes and when he is forgiven. But these are the human and divine sides of the same event.

A forgiven man is a righteous man in his relation to God and the Law, but he is under moral obligation to proceed from that point to be righteous in heart and life (cf. Rom. 6:12-16). He has no nonforfeitable legal title to a standing of innocence on the basis of an objective transaction in his behalf, the benefits of which are imputed to him unconditionally. Such an arrangement would mean that what he did subsequent to forgiveness would have no bearing on his final salvation. Such "salvation" would be a barren mechanism and a moral mockery.

2. Initial Sanctification.

The purpose of reconciliation, therefore, is "that in him we might become the righteousness of God" (2 Cor. 5:21). The kingdom of God is "righteousness and peace and joy in the Holy Spirit" (Rom. 14:17). This is *dikaiosunē*—a real righteousness of life and character as well as a justification through forgiveness. Peter's understanding tallies exactly. Christ bore our sins, not as a substitute for our righteousness, but "that we might die to sin and live to righteousness. By his wounds you have been healed" (1 Pet. 2:24). Obviously the heal-

---

25. The reference in 2 Cor. 5:19 is negative, "not imputing their trespasses unto them," which is a statement of God's universal offer and provision in Christ; but an offer which to result in eternal salvation must be validated by personal response; hence, "we are ambassadors for Christ, as though God were entreating through us; we beg you on behalf of Christ, be reconciled to God" (v. 20).

ing which is here declared in the atonement is moral and spiritual, not physical.[26]

In conversion the giving of the new character is markedly begun. When the Corinthians are said to have been "sanctified in Christ Jesus, called to be saints" (1:2), not only is their positional holiness affirmed, but also their ethical obligation and vocation. They are called to be as *holy* in life as they are *separate* and *hallowed* by virtue of their relationship to Christ. The measure of the *real change* that had already occurred is indicated in 6:11—"And such were some of you. But you were washed, you were sanctified, you were justified in the name of the Lord Jesus Christ, and in ['by,' KJV] the Spirit of our God." Here indeed are both real and relative changes, traceable to the objective atonement of Christ and to the subjective ministry of the Spirit.[27]

A second look will show the precise nature of the depravity from which they were cleansed. It was not their *inherited* sinfulness but those habits and patterns of evil that they had *acquired* through their own choice (1 Cor. 5:9-11—"And such were some of you"). Manifestations of the remaining self-centeredness were still present in less serious ways (1 Cor. 3:1-3, *et al.*). The cleansing of life which had occurred was profound and real; but it fell short of complete cleansing or entire sanctification. To speak of the cleansing of *acquired* depravity as initial sanctification would seem to express accurately the facts as found in this passage.[28]

C. A New Assurance

The love, peace, and joy which the New Testament consistently attaches to being in Christ are in the realm of conscious experience.

---

26. Paul in Romans 5 affirms the needlessness of continuing in sin, while in c. 6 he shows its moral impossibility for one in true union with Christ. John, both in his Epistles and in the Revelation, declares the impossibility of reconciling the possession of eternal life with a pattern of willful sinning (1 John 1:6—2:2, 4, 6, 9, 11, 15; 3:1-10, 14-15, 24; 5:2, 18, 21; Rev. 2:5 *et al.*; 22:11-15). The letters of James, Peter, and Jude concur.

27. We cannot accept fully the position of A. Oepke in Kittel that these "three distinctive Christian words" ("washed," "sanctified," "justified") are "virtually synonymous" (4:304). They are related as concomitants of the distinct first work of grace to which the three aorists point; but each word expresses different aspects of this great change. Robertson separates the washing from the sanctification and the justification, saying that the first refers to baptism as the outward symbol of the other two (*Word Pictures*, 4:20). Metz sees the self-washing (middle voice) referred to as their own part in repentance (*BBC*, 8:298).

28. See Wiley, *Christian Theology*, 2:475-80; Wesley, *Works*, 5:150 ff.; 8:285.

They strongly imply that possession of forgiveness and eternal life are matters of personal certainty. Rejoicing in God is declared our privilege (Rom. 5:11), but this is possible only when we have an assurance of God's presence and approval. According to apostolic teachings, this assurance begins in the new birth and is created by two subjective experiences.

1. *The Witness of the Spirit.*

An awareness of physical experience, either pleasurable or painful, is mediated through the bodily senses; but an awareness of spiritual facts can come only by direct revelation of Spirit to spirit (1 Cor. 2:12). This is twofold: a revelation of *objective truth* and a revelation of *personal standing.* In respect to the first, the axiom is "No one can say, 'Jesus is Lord,' except by the Holy Spirit" (1 Cor. 12:3; cf. 1 John 4:2 ff.; Matt. 22:43). Since anyone can parrot the words, the statement obviously means to say, "Jesus is Lord," with full sincerity and persuasion of the truth. Reason should do its best to sort out evidence and thus avoid credulity and superstition. But the mind on its own cannot pierce the barrier of mystery and uncertainty. The Holy Spirit must—and will if the seeker is honest (John 7:17)—reward searching with direct perception. In this moment of revelation, at least, doubt is not only banished but is virtually impossible. This is more than human intuition; it is direct divine illumination (cf. John 20:27-29).

In respect to the second revelation—personal standing—the Holy Spirit creates an awareness that not only have I accepted *Him* but He has accepted *me.* The faith that claims pardon through Christ becomes through the Spirit a sense of "peace with God" (Rom. 5:1). The war is over, the estrangement is past. But the Spirit has an even more glorious word, *viz.,* that God has made us "children of God," and to this stupendous fact the "Spirit himself beareth witness with our spirit" (Rom. 8:16, KJV).

The intensive pronoun *himself* reminds us that this good news is not secondhand or mediated through men; it is a personal persuasion created in us directly by the Holy Spirit himself. This is direct and sure, firsthand and deeper than intellectual understanding. It is an immediate impression on our spirit, too far down for us to be able fully either to verbalize or intellectualize it. It is both *to* our spirit and *with* our spirit. We discover that our spirit, as personal, immaterial being, has been infused with "the spirit of sonship," and we are now enabled by the Spirit to cry, "'Abba! Father!'" (v. 15). The disposition of a child to approach his father in spontaneous, artless, and glad recognition is now the disposition that governs our approach to God. Such is the import of the Aramaic "Abba"—the intimate "Papa" of a child who is sure of his identity and standing (Mark 10:36; Gal. 4:6).

Wesley concedes that he cannot explain "how the divine testimony is manifested to the heart." But he insists on the *fact* that "the Spirit of God does give a believer such a testimony of his adoption, that while it is present to the soul, he can no more doubt the reality of his sonship, than he can doubt of the shining of the sun, while he stands in the full blaze of his beams."[29]

2. Awareness of Change.

The quickening of spiritual life (Eph. 2:1-5) which is the new birth must in the nature of the case be knowable. A quickened person knows himself to be different. He can say, "Something has happened to me." This observable difference is both religious and moral. The religious difference focuses in the new attitude toward God, and with it the new movement of the soul towards spiritual things in general. But the moral difference is so endemic to the whole that where the moral difference is lacking, the religious difference may be said to be spurious. We see this in the context of the Ephesian reference: The making alive is a raising up "with him" from our "trespasses and sins" to a new kind of life (vv. 1-4). The new birth is not the animation of continuing corruption; we are not alive spiritually while yet dead morally (cf. Rom. 6:1-23).[30]

Therefore the observable evidences of a change wrought by grace and a present continuing state of grace may be summarized as follows:

a. A disposition and a determination to obey God (Matt. 7:21; 1 John 2:4; Rom. 8:14).

b. A radical break with the old life (Rom. 6:1-2; 1 Cor. 6:11; Eph. 5:3-10; 2 Tim. 2:19; 1 John 2:15; 3:6-10).

c. A reorientation of life around God and spiritual things, (the obvious teaching of the Acts, the Epistles, and Revelation).

---

29. *Works,* 5:117 (Sermon: "The Witness of the Spirit").

30. The matter is put most strikingly in Romans 8. The necessary moral difference is stated *before* the declaration of the Spirit's direct witness. Being children implies *sonship,* which, as we have seen, carries the meaning of likeness as well as kinship. Those who "are led by the Spirit of God, are sons of God" (v. 14). The ultimatum is: "If you live according to the flesh you will die, but if by the Spirit you put to death the deeds of the body you will live" (v. 13). Once again we confront the conditionality of salvation in Christ.

d. A love of the brethren with the church becoming the social hub of life (a special emphasis in 1 John, as for instance 3:14-17).

We may know therefore our immediate standing with God both by the inner witness of the Spirit and by honest self-examination. "Examine yourselves, to see whether you are holding to your faith. Test yourselves. Do you not realize that Jesus Christ is in you?— unless indeed you fail to meet the test!" (2 Cor. 13:5).

26

Salvation and Holiness

The true wisdom, Paul says, is not to be found in Greek philosophy, but only in Christ: and that not speculatively but experientially. To those who by faith are "in Christ Jesus" He becomes "wisdom from God—that is, our righteousness, holiness and redemption" (1 Cor. 1:30, NIV).[1] There can be no theology of the divine wisdom, as manifest in Christ, which neglects a theology of sanctification; nor can this true wisdom be personally known apart from the experiencing of sanctification.[2]

I. The New Testament Concept of Holiness

Paul's linking of sanctification ("holiness," NIV) with righteousness and redemption as the trilogy of our privileges in Christ is true to the consistent view of the New Testament. We have been chosen "to be saved through sanctification by the Spirit" as well as by our personal faith in the truth (2 Thess. 2:13). God's design for us in Christ "before the foundation of the world" was "that we should be holy and blameless before him" (Eph. 1:4).

---

1. Note that the three blessings are expanded concepts of wisdom. Cf. Lightfoot, Robertson, Moffatt, Phillips, *et al.* Cf. Jas. 1:5-7 with 3:17.

2. The importance which Paul attaches to sanctification can be explained by the commission which he received directly from Christ at the moment of his conversion. That commission was so to preach that men would "turn from darkness to light and from the power of Satan to God, that they may receive forgiveness of sins and a place among those who are sanctified by faith in me" (Acts 26:18).

"Sanctification" and "holy" are *hagiasmos* and *hagios*, respectively. They are two of a family of five Greek terms from the old Greek word *hagos*, meaning the object of religious awe, reverence. While *hagos* is not itself in the New Testament, several of its derivatives are important New Testament terms. They have to do *first* with *(a)* the awesome sacredness of God's person and *(b)* the purity of His moral character; and *second*, with *(a)* the sacredness of persons or things in relation to God, and *(b)* the required moral character of men. The frequency of these words is impressive; but the statistics alone cannot convey their crucial centrality in expressing God's provision and requirement in Christ. Two axioms underlie all else: God's own holiness is His reason for requiring holiness in men; and God's own holiness is the pattern for man's holiness (1 Pet. 1:15-16; cf. Lev. 11: 44-45; 19:2; 20:7-8).[3]

---

3. The following brief word study (based on Arndt and Gingrich) may be useful as an overview:

hagios, adj. "dedicated to God," "holy," "sacred," as Matt. 4:5; "pure," "perfect," "worthy of God," as Rom. 12:1; Col. 1:22 (125 times; plus 15 instances of noun form *hagion*).

hagiotēs, noun, "holiness," only once, Heb. 12:10 ("share in his holy character"); possibly also 2 Cor. 1:12 (see textual note in *USB* Greek Text).

hagiosunē, noun, "holiness," three times, Rom. 1:4; 2 Cor. 7:1; 1 Thess. 3:13; denotes ethical purity; cf. Kittel, 1:115.

hagiadzō, verb, "make holy," "consecrate," "sanctify" (including to "purify" in some instances), as Rom. 15:16; Eph. 5:26 (29 times).

hagiasmos, noun, "holiness," "consecration," "sanctification"; "the use in a moral sense for a process or, more often, its result (the state of being made holy) is peculiar to our literature." Ten times only: Rom. 6:19, 22; 1 Cor. 1:30; 1 Thess. 4:3-4, 7; 2 Thess. 2:13; 1 Tim. 2:15; Heb. 12:14; 1 Pet. 1:2. (From the verb *hagiadzein*, according to Procksch in *TDNT*.)

Another family of words is built on the *hag* root, as follows:

hagneia, noun, "purity," "chastity," twice: 1 Tim. 4:12; 5:2.

hagnos, adj., "pure," "chaste," "innocent," eight times: 2 Cor. 7:11; 11:2; Phil. 4:8; 1 Tim. 5:22; Titus 2:5; Jas. 3:17; 1 Pet. 3:2; 1 John 3:3.

hagnidzō, verb, "purify," ceremonially or ethically; seven times: John 11:55; Acts 21:24, 26; 24:18; Jas. 4:8; 1 Pet. 1:22; 1 John 3:3.

hagnismos, noun, "purification" (ceremonial), Acts 21:26 only.

Other words are *hieros*, "sacred," 2 Tim. 3:15; *hosios*, "holy," "devout," 1 Tim. 2:8; Titus 1:8; *hosiōs*, adv. "holily," 1 Thess. 2:10; *hosiotēs*, "holiness" (combination of piety and purity, Luke 1:75; Eph. 4:24). For further word studies see Wiley, *Christian Theology*, 2:464 ff.; Turner, *The Vision Which Transforms* (Kansas City: Beacon Hill Press, 1964), pp. 114 ff. See also Kittel, *TDNT*, 1:88-115. The view that "sanctification" is the act or process by which we are made holy and "holiness" is the resulting state, is a refinement of systematic theology, but is difficult to support from the New Testament usage of the words. "The Bible makes no distinction between sanctification and holiness," writes W. T. Purkiser (*Sanctification and Its Synonyms* [Kansas City: Beacon Hill Press, 1961], p. 84, fn. 4; cf. p. 14).

A. Holiness and Righteousness

Where a distinction is implied, as in 1 Cor. 1:30, *dikaiosunē,* "righteousness," has particular reference to the legal and relational change of justification, while *hagiasmos,* "sanctification," refers to an inner change of character. However, in many cases *dikaiosunē* includes practical righteousness and thus the two terms are closely related. The "righteousness which comes from God on the basis of faith" (Phil. 3:9, NASB) cannot be restricted to a mere imputation of legal justification; neither can the "righteousness of God" which we are to seek first (Matt. 6:33; cf. 5:6, 8, 20), or the "righteousness" which is disclosed in the gospel (Rom. 1:17). In these passages righteousness is virtually a synonym for holiness.

The special emphasis of righteousness in its practical, moral sense is justice or rectitude in our manner of life ("right action," Vine, EDNTW, 3:298), while the special emphasis of sanctification is consecration to God and purification from sin. In the deepest sense there can be no complete righteousness without sanctification, and sanctification is illusory without righteousness (cf. Romans 6).

B. Christ the Source

It is Jesus Christ "whom God made our wisdom," and thus our dependence is solely on Him for the components of that wisdom. New Testament holiness is at the farthest pole from any form of humanistic moralism, or a "do it yourself" kind of goodness. The teachings of Jesus in the Gospels, as for instance in the Sermon on the Mount, lift up the standard without always explaining the basis of the necessary moral power. However, New Testament writers leave no room for uncertainty at this point. Whereas sanctification is the will of the Father, its realization in personal experience is one of the express objectives of the atonement (John 17:19; Eph. 5:25-26; Heb. 10:10, 14, 29; 13:12). It is significant also that while the expiatory provisions of His death have sinners in view primarily, the sanctifying provisions are specifically designated for His people (John 17:9; Eph. 5:25-26; Heb. 13:12).

This much is certain: The New Testament concept of holiness is neither a natural goodness in man nor a personal attainment, but a goodness available solely through Christ.

C. Christ the Pattern

While God's holiness as man's pattern has already been declared axiomatic, some qualification is nevertheless necessary. Our holiness is derived from God and is therefore an acquirement, while God's holiness is His essential and eternal nature. Our holiness, furthermore, is amissible (may be lost); God's is not. Again, God's holiness includes His majesty and divine glory—qualities man can rejoice in but cannot share.

These various differences may be summarized by saying that man may enjoy the holiness of the creature, God the holiness of the Creator; man the holiness of a subject, God that of the Sovereign. Between God as God and man as man are corresponding differences in propriety and suitability. Holiness in man will include submissiveness, humility, obedience, and reverence. In the relationship between God and man, these traits are essential to man's side, for they inherently belong to his role as creature and subject. But the same traits do not belong to the holiness of God.

In God the exercise of sovereignty is perfectly compatible with His holiness, for such sovereignty belongs to His person as Creator and Governor. God's demand for the throne of our hearts, then, belongs to His holiness; *our* demand for that throne belongs to iniquity. Indeed the very essence of unholiness in man is a secret resentment of God's sovereignty (cf. Rom. 8:7). We conclude therefore that while holiness in God includes His sovereign rule over us, holiness in us includes not only our acceptance of that rule but an inner adjustment so thorough that we are happy in it.

It is in these respects that Jesus Christ as Son of Man is our pattern. This is to say that the holiness we see in Jesus is primarily the holiness which belongs to man. He said, for instance, "I am gentle and lowly in heart" (Matt. 11:29). As a youth He subjected himself to His parents. He lived in constant dependence on the Father and equally constant obedience (cf. John 5:30).

The content of Christian holiness can best be understood therefore in terms of Christlikeness. While this means a pattern to be followed (John 13:13-15), it also means an inward conformity to the very "image of his Son, in order that he might be the firstborn among many brethren" (Rom. 8:29; cf. Gal. 4:19). The full perfection of this conformity is yet ahead (1 John 3:2); yet our purity may be like His (v. 3) and our love may be perfected. In this respect, "as He is so are we in this world" (1 John 4:16-17). Though *outward* Christlikeness in personality may fall short in this life (because of the infirmities and limitations of our present state), we can at least be in possession now of the mind (*phronēma,* "frame of mind," "disposition") of Christ

(Phil. 2:5-8). According to Wesley, this mind is the essence of that holiness "without which no one will see the Lord" (Heb. 12:14).[4]

D. The Heart of the New Covenant

The writer to the Hebrews explains that Christ mediates a better covenant, "since it is enacted on better promises" (Heb. 8:6). They are better promises because they promise better spiritual privileges than were available under the old covenant (John 4:23-24; Rom. 9:30—10:4; Heb. 7:18-19, 22, 25; 9:13-14; 10:14-22; 13:20-21).

The "new covenant" was seen by Jeremiah as a new and radical conformity of heart to the complete rule of God (Jer. 31:31-34). In the letter to the Hebrews it is explained twice that the fulfillment of Jeremiah's prophecy is the core of what is provided in Christ (8:10; 10:15-17). Specifically: "I will put my laws into their mind, and write them in their hearts." This means an adjustment of human nature to fit the righteousness of the law. Peter, too, links the better promises to this inner change. Speaking of "his precious and very great promises" which have been given to us, he explains their content: "That through these you may become partakers of the divine nature" (2 Pet. 1:4).

E. Both Positional and Personal

There is a sense in which all believers are holy in Christ, and may be called such. The repentant sinner who gives himself to Christ enters into a holy relationship, and the believer takes on a holiness or sanctity which derives from this relationship (cf. Matt. 23:19). This is sometimes spoken of as *positional* holiness, and explains the customary designation of believers as *hagioi*, "holy ones, saints," in the Early Church.[5] It is equivalent to the primitive *qadosh*, "dedication" or "separation"; that which was devoted was not to be desecrated by common use. Both times and things could be thus holy "by virtue of their relation to God."[6] It is highly proper, therefore, for Christians to be gripped by the solemn awareness that as the tithe, the Sabbath, and the house of God are sacred because especially devoted to God, and therefore any misuse is a desecration, so *much more* are Christians hallowed and separate.

However, the New Testament does not permit a sanctity which

---

4. *Works*, 10:364.
5. Some 55 times in Acts, the Epistles, and Revelation.
6. Turner, *Vision Which Transforms*, p. 21.

remains positional only. "Become what you are" is the demand. Saints must be saintly. Believers are "called to be saints" (Rom. 1:7; 1 Cor. 1:2)—not by appellation only, but by vocation. While the saints will judge the world, those who have been "saints" in name only will not (1 Cor. 6:2, 9-10). To suppose otherwise is to be "deceived" (v. 9; cf. 10:1-13; 11:31-32). In fact, it is not an exaggeration to say that the entire Corinthian correspondence is an explication of the ethical practicalities of the Christian's vocation as a "saint."[7]

The notion held by some that Christ Jesus becomes to us "righteousness and sanctification" by imputation only is without sound exegetical basis. Archdeacon Farrar writes: "The text is a singularly full statement of the whole result of the work of Christ, as the source of 'all spiritual blessings in things heavenly' (Eph. 1:3), in whom we are complete (Col. 2:10)."[8] To assume that those who are in Christ participate in His sanctification in the sense that it is *credited* to them by virtue of this union without being *accomplished* in them, is to miss the redemptive genius of our Lord, who makes us like himself. Leon Morris writes: "He is our sanctification, for we could never attain holiness in our own strength. Sanctification is accomplished only in the divine power."[9] Through contact with the Cross, says Dods, "We become direct recipients of the holiness, the love, the power of God."[10] It is plain therefore that Christ is our *Source* of holiness, not our *substitute* for holiness.

F. The Antithesis of Sin

The elemental fact implied and asserted consistently is the radical incompatibility between holiness and sin.[11] Any degree or kind of sin

---

7. Elsewhere the church is reminded that even needless discussion of "immorality and all impurity or covetousness" is inherently improper among saints (Eph. 5:3; cf. Rom. 16:2; 1 Cor. 1:2; Rev. 19:8). According to the Revelator the true saints are those who "keep the commandments of God and the faith of Jesus" (Rev. 14:12). Apparently, the Early Church considered that basic inner holiness with a life that matched was part and parcel of what it meant to be a Christian (cf. 1 Cor. 5:8; 2 Cor. 1:12; Eph. 2:1-10; 4:1; 5:1-2; Phil. 1:10; 2:12-15; 2 Pet. 3:11).

8. *Pulpit Commentary*, 19:9.

9. "First Corinthians," *Tyndale New Testament Commentaries* (London: The Tyndale Press, 1966), p. 50.

10. *One Volume New Testament Commentary* (Grand Rapids, Mich.: Baker Book House, 1957), *ad loc.*

11. While the cultic and ceremonial concept of purity and holiness loomed large in the Mosaic economy, it is rare in the NT (cf. 1 Cor. 7:14). As Otto Procksch says: "Already in the Sermon on the Mount Jesus fills out the concept of purity with ethical content . . . and this became normative for primitive Christianity (1 Tim. 1:5; 2 Tim. 2:22; Titus 1:15; John 1:17; cf. Matt. 23:26, etc.)" (Kittel, *TDNT*, 1:108). Speaking of

is a degree or kind of unholiness. The perfecting of holiness demands a thorough cleansing from "every defilement of body and spirit" (2 Cor. 7:1; cf. context, 6:14-18). The word for holiness here is *hagiō-sunē*, meaning a moral quality of life and character; hence an absence of defilement, and by implication, complete devotion to God. It is used two other times: in Rom. 1:4, "the Spirit of holiness," and in 1 Thess. 3:13, "so that he may establish your hearts unblamable in holiness before our God and Father, at the coming of our Lord Jesus with all his saints [holy ones]."[12] To be *unblamable* in holiness would imply being perfected in holiness, the precise objective of Paul's exhortation to the Corinthians. In both cases sin is decisively ruled out.[13]

The antithesis between holiness and sin which is expressed so forcefully in the Corinthian letters is equally clear in the other Epistles (1 Thess. 4:4-8; Eph. 1:4; 1 Pet. 1:14-15). Everywhere the standard is absolute. Not a single verse makes allowance for a defective holiness as the norm, even temporarily. Whenever defective holiness is seen, the instruction is always for immediate correction. This is especially striking in the passages that specify holiness as essential for heaven (Rom. 6:19, 22; Heb. 12:14 [*hagiasmos* in all three cases]; 1 Pet. 4:18; 2 Pet. 3:11, 14, *et al.*; cf. Matt. 5:8, 20). As E. P. Elly-son says, "Christianity has no standard of experience or living lower

---

hagiasmos, he says that it "is always distinguished from *hagios* and *hagiadzein* by the emphasis on the moral element" (p. 113).

12. The translation of *en* (in) by "at" might seem to imply an accomplishment of holiness not *before* but *when* the Lord comes. But NEB catches the sense: "May he make your hearts firm, so that you may stand before our God and Father holy and faultless when our Lord Jesus comes with all those who are his own" (cf. 5:23).

13. To interpret the present participle of 2 Cor. 7:1, "make holiness perfect," as a switch from the crisic cleansing (aorist of *katharidzō*), obligatory now, to a gradual perfecting of a personal holiness subsequently, is doubtful exegesis, in spite of its espousal by Daniel Steele and others. Ralph Earle (in personal note to author) says:

"Let us cleanse" is in the aorist (hortatory) subjunctive, suggesting an instantaneous crisis of cleansing, rather than a process. "Perfecting" is a present participle, indicating action simultaneous with that of the main verb—"let us cleanse." The clear sense of the Greek is that "perfecting holiness" is synonymous, or at least concomitant, with the crisis of cleansing.

See also William Greathouse in *Exploring Our Christian Faith,* ed. W. T. Purkiser (Kansas City: Beacon Hill Press, 1960), p. 341; Turner, *Vision Which Transforms,* p. 123; Arndt and Gingrich—"to perfect holiness = become perfectly holy, 2 Cor. 7:1."

than holiness. Man was created holy; hence his normal state is holy."[14]

G. Holiness and Love

Since on the two great commandments "depend all the law and the prophets" (Matt. 22:40; cf. Mark 12:28-31; Luke 10:25-28), no biblical concept of holiness could be unrelated to this standard. All particularized moral duties or prohibitions are subsumed under the requirement to love. Holiness does not consist of the religious commitment to this standard, but rather of that Spirit-wrought disposition which fulfills it. Holiness is loving God and man in the way pleasing to God; it is not rapturous sentiment about love.

The Epistles constantly reinforce and expound this (Rom. 12:9-19; 13:8-10; Phil. 2:1-5; 1 Pet. 1:22; 1 John 4:7-21, *et al.*). While *hagiasmos*, "sanctity" (NASB), is distinguished from love and faith in 1 Tim. 2:15 (cf. 4:12), and while love seems at times to be isolated as simply the brightest star in a galaxy of virtues (Gal. 5:22; Col. 3:12-14; 2 Pet. 1:5-7), the usual assumption is that *agapē* ("love") is the essence and sum of the whole, and its enthronement the substance of holiness.

Whether the stress is on heart purity (as in Matt. 5:8) or on perfect love (as in 1 John 4:17-18), the synthesis always supports the conclusion that Christian love is holy and Christian holiness is loving. It is primarily in love before God that we are to "be holy and blameless" (Eph. 1:4).[15] Love may be said to be the dynamic aspect of holiness, while holiness is the "quality control" of love. As "religion that is pure" includes the two hemispheres of purity and benevolence (Jas. 1:27), so biblical holiness includes the same two hemispheres; indeed holiness is virtually synonymous with "pure religion" (KJV).

On the one hand true love keeps the commandments, i.e., submits to the rule and authority of Christ (John 14:15; 2 John 6, *et al.*). On the other hand a mark of the purified is zeal for good works (Titus 2:14). Holiness therefore is not a state unrelated to action, and loving is what holiness does. When it ceases to love, it ceases to exist,

14. *Bible Holiness* (Kansas City: Beacon Hill Press, rev. 1952), p. 22. This uncompromising wholeness and thorough soundness characteristic of New Testament holiness is also seen in certain vividly descriptive passages, which clearly delineate the substance without using the word, such as Rom. 13:12-14; Gal. 5:6, 13-14; 1 Tim. 1:5; Titus 2:11-14; Phil. 2:14-16; Col. 3:5-8; *et al.*
15. If we are to follow the UBS Greek text in connecting *en agapē* to the previous clause instead of to the following, as in RSV and NASB.

and shrinks into sterile moralism.[16] If we define holiness as a *pure heart*, a *good conscience*, and *faith* without hypocrisy (1 Tim. 1:5) we are promptly reminded that this is the matrix of love, the real aim of proper gospel preaching; it is this kind of love which alone fulfills the specification of normal Christian experience. In respect to God, it is undivided in its allegiance (from a "pure heart"); in respect to men, it is uncompromising in its conduct (a "good conscience"); and in respect to its nature, it is a divine activation through faith (out of a "sincere faith"). It is therefore a love which is pure in motive, conscientious in action, and divine in its source. Because it is supremely directed to God, it loves all that honors God and hates whatever dishonors God (Rom. 12:9; 1 Thess. 5:21; Titus 1:8; Heb. 1:9).[17]

II. The Relation of Holiness to Maturity

There are two ways in which holiness may be linked with maturity—the common factor in both being that maturity requires growth and therefore cannot be the instant product of a "work" of grace. The first view assumes that growth in holiness constitutes a corresponding decrease in unholiness. This is tantamount to growing *into* holiness. In the second view, holiness is linked with maturity only as its necessary prerequisite, in the sense that open-ended growing takes place within the sphere of holiness. There is a growth *in* holiness without such growth constituting a growth *of* holiness. The *perfected*

---

16. This is clear if *(a)* we think of holiness as *freedom from sin,* and then remember that sin is some form of self-directed instead of God-directed love; or *(b)* we think of holiness as *obedience* to God, and then are reminded that the great commandments are to love God and our fellows with a devotion and service which (on the Godward side) are boundless in their claims. This kind of love will work no ill to the neighbor (Rom. 13:10); and at the same time, because God is holy and our brother's welfare is at stake, will escape the "hypocrisy" of sentimentality by *abhorring* "what is evil" and *cleaving* to "what is good" (Rom. 12:9; cf. Heb. 1:9; see Wiley, *Christian Theology,* 2:492); or *(c)* we think of holiness as *consecration.* If this last, we will need to see that it must be a *loving* response to God's "mercies" or the consecration is duty-driven and fear-inspired, without warmth or power (Rom. 12:1-2).

17. The inseverability of love and holiness is seen also in such clauses as "faith working through love" (Gal. 5:6); "a spirit . . . of power and love and discipline" (2 Tim. 2:7); "He who has my commandments and keeps them, he it is who loves me" (John 14:21); "walk in love, just as Christ also loved you" (Eph. 2:4); "Since you have . . . purified your souls for a sincere love . . . fervently love one another" (1 Pet. 1:22); "By this love is perfected with us, . . . because as He is, so also are we in this world" (1 John 4:18); "and they did not love their life even to death" (Rev. 12:11). It is equally true that unholiness may be defined as misdirected love (John 3:19; 12:43; 1 Tim. 6:10; 2 Tim. 4:10; 2 Pet. 2:15; Rev. 22:15).

holiness of heart thus becomes the dynamic for *perfecting* full-orbed Christian character and personality. This we believe to be the biblical teaching.[18]

A. Holiness Not Maturity

The true opposite of holiness is sinfulness, not immaturity (Rom. 6:15-22). Therefore, if growth in holiness is growth out of unholiness, it is necessarily growth out of sinfulness. An increase in holiness will in this case be a gradual reduction of sinfulness. At what point will the process be complete? If such a point is unreachable in this life, then no man can be entirely holy in this life. Such a view does not tally with the biblical commands and provisions for holiness. Nor does it tally with the dogmatic statement that holiness *(hagiasmos)* is essential for seeing the Lord (Heb. 12:14; cf. Matt. 5:8). This biblical assertion certainly implies that if holiness is not experienced before death, it will not be afterward.[19]

The most consistent position therefore is that holiness in New Testament teaching is immediately possible and perpetually obligatory; but persons who have been made holy are expected to "grow in the grace" (2 Pet. 3:18; cf. 1:1-11). This is intended to be a growth within holiness, not growth toward its attainment. Jesus, too, as a boy "increased in wisdom and in stature, and in favor [*charis,* 'grace'] with God and man" (Luke 2:52); but this can hardly be construed as an improvement in His holiness.

Holiness is (negatively) the antithesis of sin and (positively) full devotement to God. Within this relationship there are *constant* elements. Love should never be compromised by hate, obedience by dis-

---

18. The "babyhood" that characterizes carnal Christians (as with the Corinthians, 1 Cor. 3:1-4) is not the innocent childhood of the newborn—the proper stage for weakness, ignorance, and unskillfulness—but arrested development. The fault is not legitimate immaturity but carnality, manifested in jealousy and strife. This requires cleansing to remedy, not the temporal process of growth. See also Wiley, *Christian Theology,* 2:507.

19. The problem would vanish if the statement in Hebrews could be construed to make seeing the Lord depend on simply the *pursuit* of holiness, but the Greek will not allow this. Contextually, holiness here is a state related to peaceableness with men but demanding more—an inner rightness with God, which excludes bitterness, impurity, and secularism (vv. 15-17). This kind of holiness is "the grace of God," concerning which we are warned not to "fail to obtain" (v. 15). Obviously the total implication is of a holiness, which, on the one hand, is the central *sine qua non* in God's sight, and on the other, is immediately available. Its *pursuit* must be seen as that kind of endeavor which has the immediate attainment of holiness as its objective and expectation.

obedience, consecration by withholding, faith by unbelief; yet these are the essential notes of holiness. But on these *foundations* we build the *variables*, such as knowledge, ethical insight, strength, skill, and all the outward qualities which we recognize as mature Christlikeness.

To suppose holiness in this life cannot be "entire" because of plaguing infirmities and consequent imperfections is to confuse the issue. W. T. Purkiser has pointed out: "God forgives our sins (1 John 1:9). The blood of Christ cleanses from all sin (1 John 1:7). But the Holy Spirit helps us with our infirmities (Rom. 8:26)."[20] Paul would never have gloried in his infirmities (2 Cor. 12:9) if he had confused them with sin, or had viewed them as an impediment to entire holiness.[21]

B. Growing in Love

In one sense only can we properly speak of developing in holiness. This relates to one's growth in love, when love is viewed as an element of holiness. However, extreme caution is necessary here. The growing, dynamic, fervent love is from the root of a pure heart. Timothy was exhorted to "aim at righteousness, faith, love ... with those who call upon the Lord from a pure heart" (2 Tim. 2:22; cf. Luke 8:15; 1 Pet. 1:22). Holiness (conceived as purity) is essential for love to function as it ought. As Mildred Wynkoop says: "Only a pure heart can love properly."[22] The impediments to love must be removed, or it cannot thrive. To whatever degree love is not pure it is not holy; to whatever degree it is not holy it is crippled—and crippled love is not pleasing to God.

In summary, purity as a present quality may be sound and firm, while the love that is thereby set free is open-ended. It can keep on deepening and expanding as long as we continue to grow in our experience and capacity as persons (cf. Col. 3:12-14).[23]

---

20. *Herald of Holiness,* Oct. 13, 1965.
21. Peter does not admonish us (1 Pet. 1:15), "As he who has called you is wise and mature so you are to be wise and mature." This is important, but the call is to be holy.
22. *A Theology of Love* (Kansas City: Beacon Hill Press of Kansas City, 1972), p. 265.
23. Two passages have been seriously advanced in recent years to prove gradualism in the attainment of holiness, but neither applies. The first, 2 Cor. 7:1, has been discussed above. The second, 1 John 1:7, has been interpreted as referring to a gradual or repetitive cleansing, on the ground that "cleanses us" is in the present tense. The present cleansing is from all sin, *now,* on the basis of walking in the light as "he himself is in the light"—*now;* and "in him is no darkness at all." If we try to combine walking with God with walking in darkness, "we lie and do not practice the truth" (v. 6). Yet this is the exact import of interpreting "cleansing" as either a

III. The Possibility of Entire Holiness

The initial crisis of the new birth has been examined. We must now inquire whether the new birth marks the limits of instantaneous change, with only development following, or whether it is preparatory and complementary to a yet deeper change, indispensable to a whole salvation.[24]

A. The Incompleteness of Initial Sanctification

That initial sanctification is not complete has already been noted. The sinful deficiencies in the spirit of the disciples before Pentecost are patent. The same kind of carnal spirit surfaced again in the church at Corinth. The very exhortation to perfect holiness (2 Cor. 7:1) implies a degree of true but partial holiness previously, a condition which compelled Paul to pinpoint their spiritual problem: "You are not restricted by us, but you are restricted in your own affections" (2 Cor. 6:12). In the same vein, Paul's prayer that God sanctify the Thessalonians "wholly" (1 Thess. 5:23) could only imply that their sanctification up to that time was not entire. The same double-mindedness, with its carnal manifestations, is the subject of James's rebuke and exhortations (1:5-8). The vacillation of the Hebrew Christians prompts the writing of a hortatory Epistle to entice them from the swamps to the highlands. However we explain these various defects, it is evident that Christians may be holy without being entirely holy (cf. 1 Thess. 1:3-6 with 3:10; 4:3 and 5:23; also cf. Heb. 3:1 with 3:12; 5:11 ff.; 12:1 ff.). Yet whole holiness is wanted, and its possibility everywhere assumed and affirmed.

B. The Nature of Sin in Believers

It has been previously seen that the practice of overt sinning is not

---

perpetual expiation of perpetual sinning (which would be walking in darkness), or as a gradual accomplishment of purity. For further discussion see Purkiser, *Sanctification and Its Synonyms*, pp. 45-46.

24. What Wesley found in the Bible shaped his theology of holiness. He wrote: "In 1729, two young men, reading the Bible, saw they could not be saved without holiness, followed after it, and incited others so to do. In 1737 they saw holiness comes by faith. They saw likewise, that men are justified before they are sanctified; but still holiness was their point. God then thrust them out, utterly against their will, to raise a holy people" (*Works*, 8:300). (This quotation was from a tract on Methodism published repeatedly, with various revisions, between 1744 and 1789. This is from the final revision, two years before Wesley died. He here claims to have learned from the Bible his doctrine of entire sanctification subsequent to justification. See also his sermon "The Scripture Way of Salvation," *Works*, 6:43 ff.).

characteristic of the believer and cannot be reconciled with what it means to be a Christian. What we actually see, however, are traits of unsanctified egos, still beset with a remaining tendency to self-sovereignty. Christians under apostolic jurisdiction who reverted to open sins of the flesh were either excommunicated or threatened with such action. But Christians whose spirit was sub-Christian, who in the midst of a certain sincere loyalty to Christ were acting unlike Him in their interpersonal relationships, were rebuked, warned, instructed, prayed for, and their condition diagnosed.

What we see in the disciples, therefore, is their jockeying for position, their bickering and vindictiveness, their recurrent spiritual dullness, their cowardice in danger, and Peter's defensiveness even after the Resurrection. We see Ananias deceived by his craving for possessions (Acts 5:1 ff.), Demas by his lurking love of the world (2 Tim. 4:10), and Diotrephes by his carnal lust for power (3 John 9). Here are three directions the inner self-sovereignty is apt to take when permitted to gain the upper hand. We see the party spirit, rivalry, envy, and jealousy dividing the Corinthians; the proneness to unbelief in the Hebrew Christians; the cliquishness, pride, warring desires, the hankering to be like the world which prompts the sharp, searching words of James. These are all traits seen commonly in Christians, both in Bible times and now, which reflect a deep malady of spirit.[25]

In Romans Paul presents the "mind set on the flesh" and the "mind set on the Spirit" as irreconcilable opposites, the one leading to death, the other to life and peace. Yet it is clear from his designation of the Corinthians as "yet carnal" (1 Cor. 3:1-3) that there can be, temporarily, a warring, soul-rending condition of doublemindedness (*dipsuchos*, "double-minded," Jas. 1:8; 4:8). The life of the Spirit to which believers have committed themselves has not yet been able entirely to dethrone self and enthrone Christ. This is certainly a substandard state of affairs. Remaining carnality is the natural egoism fighting for its supremacy—and its life. But in the end the opposite principle must prevail: "He that will save his life shall lose it"; and "Except a grain of wheat fall into the ground and die, it abideth alone."

---

25. As the manifestations of this self-centered spirit become more flagrant, they in some cases mark spiritual retrogression or backsliding.

C. Our Lord's Prayer

It is against this background of spiritual limitation that Jesus prays the "High-Priestly prayer" (John 17). He prayed not only for the immediate band of disciples but "also for those who are to believe in me through their word" (v. 20). He asks that they be kept from the "evil one" (v. 15), that they be perfectly united with each other and in Him (vv. 21-23), and that they may ultimately be with Him in glory (v. 24). But his key petition is for their sanctification (v. 17). As Donald S. Metz puts it, these are the "central words of the prayer" and constitute "a revelation of what Jesus desired and willed for men."[26] If this petition is answered, the other answers will follow.

1. *A Need of Believers.*

It is evident that what our Lord is profoundly concerned about is to see a change subsequent to conversion. Earlier in the evening Jesus had pronounced the disciples "clean" by the word which He had spoken to them (John 15:3). He had declared their union with himself to be as close as that of branches to a vine. Now, in this prayer, He says they belong not to the world but to the Father and to the Son (vv. 6-16). Yet it is clear that He perceives in them a need for a deeper work of grace. They need to be qualified spiritually to fulfill their mission: "As thou didst send me into the world, so I have sent them into the world" (v. 18). This commission demands their sanctification as its only hope of success.

That such a crucial experience of sanctification is a normal and universal need of believers is indicated in the Epistles. Many commands, promises, exhortations, and prayers are directed to the Christians to whom the letters are being written, urging them to enter decisively into a higher level of Christian experience. While described in various ways, this higher experience corresponds in substance to what Jesus had in mind (Rom. 6:13; 12:1-2; 1 Cor. 6:19-20; 2 Cor. 7:1; 13:9, NASB; Eph. 3:14-21; 4:22-23 [cf. NEB]; 5:18-21; Phil. 1:9-10; 2:5-8; 3:15; Col. 1:9-13, 28; 3:1-10; 4:12; 1 Thess. 3:10-13 [cf. NEB]; 4:3-7; 5:23-24; 1 Tim. 1:1-5; 2 Tim. 2:19-21; Titus 2:11-14; Heb. 3:12—4:11; 5:12—6:2; 10:19-25; 12:12-17; Jas. 1:1-8 with 3:17; 4:1-8; 1 Pet. 1:14-16; 2:1-5; 2 Pet. 1:4; 3:11-12, 14; 1 John 1:5-7; 3:1-3; 4:17-18).

26. *Studies in Biblical Holiness* (Kansas City: Beacon Hill Press of Kansas City, 1971), p. 109.

2. The Meaning of Sanctification.

Exactly what did Jesus mean when He prayed for the sanctification of His disciples? Even without any word study we are safe in assuming that, being painfully aware of their self-centeredness, He was asking for its correction. He wanted them to experience a consecration and yieldedness to God that would make them totally available to the deployment of the Father and completely subject to the control of the Holy Spirit.

The verb *hagiadzō*, "to make holy," essentially means to *separate (a) to* God, and *(b) from* sin. The necessity of the second part grows out of the implications of the first. Total consecration is acceptable only as that which is consecrated is made clean (2 Chron. 29:5, 15-19).[27] An attempt to consecrate a defiled offering, unsubmitted for cleansing, is insincere, insulting, and condemned (Rom. 12:1—note "holy"; cf. the prohibition against defective sacrifices in Lev. 22:21-25; Deut. 15:21; Mal. 1:8).

It is apparent that while the disciples had already experienced a cleansing at one level, they were in dire need of cleansing at a deeper level, at the very center of the self. It surely was this deeper cleansing which Jesus had in mind in His concern that they be sanctified "in truth" (v. 19). A holiness was necessary which was real rather than fictitious, thorough rather than partial, and which cleansed the heart from the lie that is latent in the carnal mind. There must be an inward conformity to the truth.

But Jesus had in mind an enablement as well as a cleansing. Cowardice needed to be replaced by courage, lassitude and passivity by dynamic aggressiveness in the things of God. Sanctification is a work of grace that creates a surging spiritual drive—"a zest for good works" (Titus 2:14, Moffatt). This kind of inner spiritual initiative the disciples lacked at the time of Christ's prayer, but demonstrated in abundant measure after experiencing the fullness of the Holy Spirit.

3. The Means of Sanctification.

In this passage three means of sanctification are specified:

a. The Father himself is the Sanctifier. The Bible indicates the necessity of a self-sanctification in the sense of self-presentation and self-cleansing (Rom. 12:1; 2 Cor. 7:1; Jas. 4:8; 1 John 3:3), and the requirement of personal faith for sanctification (Acts 26:18). But at

---

27. Cf. James Hastings, ed., *The Great Texts of the Bible* (Grand Rapids, Mich.: Wm. B. Eerdmans Publishing Co., n.d.), 12:294 ff.

the deepest level, God himself must act. This truth is seen by Paul
also: "May the God of peace himself sanctify you wholly" (1 Thess.
5:23-24).

   b. The instrumental means is *the truth* (not "in the truth," RSV,
but "by means of the truth," cf. Phillips, NEB). This truth is identified
by Jesus: "thy word is truth." Generally, the "word" here is understood to be the oral or written revelation of God's will for His people,
by which they are led into the experience. There is implicit also a
reference to God's word as fiat: when He speaks, it is done (Matt.
8:2-3). The Spirit turns promise into experiential reality (Acts 20:32;
2 Pet. 1:4). On the other hand, Oscar Cullmann suggests that the
word is a reference to Jesus himself. He says: "The Word of God
which is identical with Jesus' proclaimed *logos* is 'truth' (17:17); but
Jesus himself is the truth in person (14:6). Thus in this respect the
ordinary Johannine use of the word *logos* directly clarifies the designation of Jesus as Logos."[28] However, we cannot ignore Jesus' own
emphasis on the spoken word (John 4:48-50; 5:24; 6:63, 68; 8:31;
12:48; 15:3).

   c. Jesus identifies His own self-presentation as a further means
of their sanctification. "And for their sake I consecrate myself, that
they also may be consecrated in truth" (v. 19). The purpose of Christ's
death in relation to the world can be seen in John 3:16, but here it is
seen in relation to His disciples. There is in the atonement a provision, therefore, for the thorough sanctifying of God's people as well
as their free justification (Eph. 5:25-27; Heb. 10:7 with 10; 13:12).

D. The Answer to Romans 7

Paul's purpose in Romans 7 is to show that the real impediment to
successful law-keeping is an inherited bent to sinning, which he calls
the law of sin, or the "dwelling-in-me sin." The subvolitional nature
of this inner disorganizing force answers perfectly, not only to the
universal overt sinfulness we see in the race, but also to the phenomena we witness in Christians. There is a self which keeps turning
back into itself. Actions and traits are produced which are not deliberately chosen by the Christian, but which keep dogging his steps as
an acute embarrassment to him.[29]

---

28. *Christology of the NT*, p. 260; cf. p. 106.
29. The effort to confine Paul's discussion to the awakened Jew under the law
does not fully meet the facts of the case. Godet is helpful here. He says: "Paul speaks
of the unregenerate man without concerning himself with the question how far the
unregenerate heart still remains in the regenerate believer." Paul is not describing

There is no possible way of missing the connection between 8:1-4 and the deep human problem discussed in c. 7. The complete escape from condemnation (v. 1) assumes deliverance from sin on both levels, not only from personal guiltiness through forgiveness, but also from the thraldom of inbred sin. The deliverance from the "law of sin and of death" by the "law of the Spirit of life in Christ Jesus" can only mean total solution to the abject bondage of the wretched man who said, "I am carnal, sold under sin" (Rom. 7:14).

The power of the Spirit to effect such a loosing is ascribed directly to the action of Christ on the Cross in condemning "sin in the flesh." The word "condemn" (*katekrine,* literally, "to judge down") means far more than disapprove; Christ did not need to die for indwelling sin to be merely disapproved. The term implies not only power to pass sentence but also power to execute the sentence. The nature and extent of this action is revealed by the purpose: "in order that the requirement of the Law might be fulfilled in us." The law requires us to be righteous and holy by loving God and our neighbor. This obligation is not abrogated by Christ's death, but its fulfillment is made possible by providing a radical inner correction of that perversity which hitherto prevented it. Clearly the righteousness which eludes us in chapter 7 because of indwelling sin is now possible, with a new naturalness, fullness, and freedom. Since "the law of sin" which infects human nature is the sole obstacle, the accomplishment of the righteousness implies the removal of this obstacle.

This is nothing less therefore than a radical renovation, which makes the perfect will of God the believer's delight, not only at the level of the reason (7:22) but at the level of affection. Self is finally dethroned and the tyranny of excessive egoism broken. That lurking disposition to suppose that ownership is somehow *shared* between Christ and self is purified (cf. Titus 2:14). Thus the true "freedom" of the Christian becomes apparent. In the words of Mary McDermott Shideler, "The gift of the Spirit is not liberation from the divine pattern, but liberation within it."[30]

---

a chosen way of life, but an irrational, unwanted tendency to keep reverting to a rejected way. "Here," comments Godet, "is the *permanent essence* of human *nature* since the fall outside the action of faith. Thus is explained the use of the *present,* without our saying that Paul describes his present state" (*Commentary on St. Paul's Epistle to the Romans,* 2:36).

30. *Christian Century,* Oct. 11, 1972. Cf. Hans Conzelmann's declaration: "We have no freedom to sin" (*An Outline of the Theology of the New Testament,* trans. John Bowden [London: SCM Press, Ltd., 1969]).

This liberation is the answer, not only to the problem of universal sin, but more especially to the problem of the carnal disposition in believers. Its source is inherited sinfulness; as such it requires neither repentance nor forgiveness when the awakened sinner comes to Christ. But *afterward*, since it is crippling and arresting, the Spirit begins to focus the spotlight of His attention upon it. Only a forgiven, regenerated believer can perceive the remains of this perversity within himself, with such clarity and understanding that it can become the subject of specific spiritual struggle and confrontation. Only a regenerated ego can willingly die to the remains of its own carnal defenses (cf. Rom. 6:13). This puts the deeper cleansing on a thoroughly moral, conscious, and responsible basis. But in this available remedy for the spiritual core of racial depravity we see with new perspective the true scope and adequacy of the overwhelming power of the last Adam to reverse the damage perpetrated on the human race by the first Adam (Rom. 5:12-21).

IV. The Relation of Holiness to Perfection

It is impossible to ignore the pronounced emphasis on perfection in the Bible, whether in the Old or New Testaments.[31] Two words are used which carry strong theological significance.

A. Adjustment for Service

In his final remarks to the Corinthians, Paul expresses the prayer-wish that they be "made complete" (NASB) and then almost immediately changes the prayer-wish to a command, "Be made complete" (2 Cor. 13:9, 11, NASB). He uses *katartisis*, as an action noun, and its verbal cognate, *katartizō*, meaning "to fit" or "adjust thoroughly." Thus Paul ends his second letter to this divided church on the same note with which he began his first: "I appeal to you, brethren, . . . that all of you . . . be united [be made complete, NASB] in the same mind and the same judgment" (1 Cor. 1:10).

This idea is made vivid by the translation *mend*—"mending their

---

31. There is, first of all, perfection in the sense of *accuracy*, expressed by *akribēs*, which may be comparative and thus subject to increase. Four times in Acts (KJV) is found the expression "more perfectly" (18:26; 23:15, 20; 24:22). The idea of perfection is also expressed by *artios*, "fitted," as "all scripture is . . . profitable . . . that the man of God may be adequate" (2 Tim. 3:16-17; KJV, "perfect"). Once *pleroō*, "to fill," "make full," is translated "perfect" (KJV); but in NASB, "for I have not found your deeds completed in the sight of my God" (Rev. 3:2).

nets" (Matt. 4:21; Mark 1:19). Torn and tangled nets could not be used; nor can Christians who are in spiritual disrepair be useful in the Lord's work. It is this kind of perfecting that is mediated by the clergy, "for the equipment of the saints, for the work of ministry, for building up the body of Christ" (Eph. 4:12; cf. Matt. 21:16; Luke 6:40; Heb. 13:21).[32]

B. Completeness and Fulfillment

By far the most common word for perfection is *telos* and its various cognate forms. Literally *telos* means "end," or "point aimed at as a limit" (cf. Rom. 6:21; 1 Tim. 1:5). To be *teleios*, "perfect," is to have reached or fulfilled the point aimed at. Thayer says: "wanting nothing necessary to completeness; perfect" (cf. 1 Cor. 13:10; Jas. 1:4, 25; 1 John 4:18).[33] Obviously, since the point aimed at is variable, perfection is equally variable and can be determined solely by relating performance to the objective. This means that what may be perfect at one level may be imperfect at another; or what completely fulfills one goal may do so in the midst of many surrounding imperfections. If one's goal is to memorize 10 chapters of scripture, then completeness (fulfillment), at that particular point, is the memorizing of 10 chapters. But the memorizing of 10 chapters is not perfection if the goal is 15 chapters. This helps us to see that the concept of *telos* is both precise and flexible. The term may properly be used in spite of a sliding scale of measurement criteria.

1. *The Present Perfection.*

There is a class of Christians who in distinction from others are called perfect in the sense that they are complete in their consecration, devotion, and spiritual-mindedness (1 Cor. 2:6, cf. vv. 11-16; Phil. 3:15). The specific perfections which together comprise the total perfection are the perfection of *faith* by obedience (Jas. 2:22) and the perfection of *love* (Matt. 5:48; John 17:23; 1 John 4:17-18).[34]

---

32. Obviously the term embraces spiritual adjustment as well as training and equipping. Spiritual adjustment is especially germane to Paul's concern for the Thessalonians in expressing his earnest prayer that he may "see you face to face and supply what is lacking in your faith" (1 Thess. 3:10; cf. 1 Pet. 5:10; cf. NASB).

33. *A Greek-English Lexicon of the New Testament* (Grand Rapids, Mich.: Zondervan Publishing House, reprinted 1963), p. 618.

34. It is not always faithful to the intended definiteness in this word to translate it *mature.* This is true because maturity is difficult to pinpoint by precise criteria. Christians are forever in the process of maturing and can never be said to have finally reached the end point; but within the total process they should know at all times by experience the meaning of complete love for all men and complete obedience to God.

There is thus a present perfection available at every stage of the Christian life; indeed it is the *norm* for Christians. When James said, "Let steadfastness have its full effect," he was thinking of the *present* possibility which was the duty of every Christian, "that you may be perfect and complete, lacking in nothing" (Jas. 1:2-4). In this case the perfection of patience that is the index to spiritual wholeness is the inward surrender which makes it possible to confront trials with joyfulness. This is more a matter of *holiness* than of skill or growth.

2. *Perfection as a Goal.*

There is also a kind of perfection which is always a goal. Here the term *maturity* becomes more appropriate. When James speaks of stumbling Christian workers, he says: "If any one makes no mistakes in what he says he is a perfect man, able to bridle the whole body also" (3:2). Here he is describing a highly advanced maturity—an attainment, indeed, which few could claim. Commenting on the sentence, "For we all stumble in many ways," R. Duane Thompson says:

> Stumbling is not the prerogative of the favored few; it is common to all men. . . . This is not to be regarded as sin in the sense of deliberate deviation from God's will; it may rather be thought of as "intellectual and moral mistakes and blunders; which is true enough of the wisest and holiest of us."[35]

It is possible that Paul's concern in the letter to the Ephesians represents an intermediate level of perfection, which involves growth and yet is definitely attainable: "Until we all attain to the unity of the faith and of the knowledge of the Son of God, to mature [perfect] manhood, to the measure of the stature of the fullness of Christ" (Eph. 4:13). The possibility of definite attainment is suggested by the following verses which outline the results of reaching this fullness. Even though process is involved here, yet such a goal cannot be reached apart from the crisis of definite cleansing of the heart from the impediments to such maturity.

3. *The Ultimate Perfection.*

This is the perfection which Paul disclaims in writing to the Philippians: "Not that I have already obtained this or am already perfect; but I press on to make it my own, because Christ Jesus has

---

35. "James," *The Wesleyan Bible Commentary,* ed. Charles W. Carter (Grand Rapids, Mich.: Wm. B. Eerdmans Publishing Co., 1966), 6:220. Words quoted by Thompson are from Whedon's *Commentary.*

made me his own" (3:12 ff.). The perfection that he has not yet attained is "the resurrection from among the dead" which he has already stated to be his goal.[36] The prize "of the upward call of God in Christ Jesus" is transtemporal and celestial. Yet in using the one word (adjectival and verbal forms) to indicate a perfection *not* yet experienced, and in the same paragraph a perfection which may be properly claimed, Paul does two things: On the one hand he is silencing all who would deny any kind of Christian perfection realizable in this life; and on the other hand he cautions those who would arbitrarily interpret such perfection as an absolute, implying no need for continued growth and development.

C. Perfection and Holiness

It is increasingly clear that holiness and perfection are often virtually equivalent. In a footnote, Turner gives this significant reminder: "A rabbinic aphorism, 'be ye therefore perfect,' was a paraphrase of 'Be ye therefore holy.'"[37] Certainly the perfection indicated in Matt. 5:3-48 is the substance of what the New Testament means by holiness. It is universal love which fulfills the spirit of the law by going beyond its letter, and a morality which is as inward as it is outward.

As has already been noted, *perfect* means *holy* when it is a synonym for *spiritual* (1 Cor. 2:6, cf. v. 15; 3:1-3; Gal. 6:1) or *spiritually minded* (Rom. 8:6, KJV). Moreover, when Jesus prayed that His disciples might be "perfected in unity," He must have intended something akin to what He had in mind when He prayed that they might be "sanctified in truth." One prayer could not be answered without the other. That Jesus was asking for real possibilities in both cases is unmistakable. Indeed the realization of these possibilities would be necessary to properly represent Him before the world. To speak of such an experience as "Christian perfection" can hardly be avoided.

Yet perfection may be more (or even less) than entire sanctification, depending on what the "end" or goal is. If the goal is repentance and faith in Christ as Saviour, the witness of the Spirit is evidence that completeness prevails at this level. If the goal is the

---

36. To twist this resurrection to mean the joy of living a victorious life seems like an attempt to avoid the implied contingency. *The Living Bible* and *Amplified* cannot be defended here.

37. *Vision Which Transforms,* p. 155, fn. 88. See also Oscar Cullmann; commenting on Heb. 10:14, he says that *teleioō,* "to make perfect," is "almost a synonym for *hagiadzō* (to sanctify)" (*Christology of the NT,* trans. by Guthrie and Hall [Philadelphia: The Westminster Press, 1959], p. 100).

spiritual unity and holiness of heart which was the burden of Christ's prayer, then perfection is realized through the answer to that prayer. If the goal is maturity—a degree of stability, character strength, and wisdom which is definable and recognizable—such perfection is attained through growth.

If the goal is *finality* of judgment, knowledge, and skill as a Christian, then perfection in this life is impossible, for such a goal is always receding. If the goal is irreversible redemption from "our lowly body" (Phil. 3:20-21) and from a sinful environment, then perfection awaits the next life.

Clearly the sphere of Christian perfection which corresponds to holiness is the heart, not the whole man. When we move from the heart to the head and the hand, perfection may no longer be claimed. In this case holiness moves *toward* perfection and cannot be equated with it.[38]

We conclude that the New Testament concept of *holiness* includes perfect love and perfect purity of heart. But the New Testament concept of *perfection* is more elastic; it embodies an emphasis on completeness and the satisfactoriness of some specific attainment. Therefore, to speak of acceptable perfection in the midst of many imperfections is biblical, but an attempt to combine acceptable holiness with unholiness is not.

---

38. See H. Orton Wiley on Heb. 10:14; 11:39-40; and 12:23, in *The Epistle to the Hebrews* (Kansas City: Beacon Hill Press, 1959), pp. 324 ff., 380 ff., 404 ff.

27

Holiness and the Holy Spirit

.

In the unfolding drama of redemption the most crucial events to date are the Incarnation, Crucifixion, Resurrection, Ascension, and finally the outpouring of the Holy Spirit on the Day of Pentecost. These events represent a series of progressive stages, both in revelation and redemption. Christmas speaks of God *with* us; Good Friday, Easter, and the Ascension speak of God *for* us; while Pentecost speaks of God *in* us. In respect to personal salvation, available in this life, it may be said that Pentecost is the climactic day to which the others point. They were necessary in order that this day might be. The recovery of unobstructed fellowship between the human spirit and the divine Spirit must surely be central to every other facet of God's redemptive program. It is in this recovery that we find the true significance of the outpouring of the Holy Spirit.

I. THE SIGNIFICANCE OF PENTECOST

We have previously affirmed that holiness is the heart of the new covenant. If this be true, it is reasonable to suppose that a careful study of the mission and ministry of the Holy Spirit in this dispensation would either confirm or disprove that thesis.

A. The Significance of the Day

In the Jewish calendar Pentecost was the second major annual feast. It began 50 days after the Passover (hence the name, "Pentecost"). It was a Hebrew harvest festival, called "Feast of Weeks," with emphasis on the "first fruits." This was symbolized by two large loaves of bread offered by the high priest on the first day of the feast. Only after this act could the worshippers begin to use the grain of the new harvest. The feast also was believed by the Jews themselves to be a commemoration of the giving of the Law on Mount Sinai. Thus can be seen in the day not only the symbolism of harvest but of holiness.[1]

Ten days[2] after Christ ascended, the Jewish Pentecost became a Christian Pentecost. In the remarkable events of that day we have the perfect fulfillment of both symbols: (1) The 3,000 conversions represent the firstfruits of the new harvest, and (2) The remarkable transformation in the 120 who were filled with the Holy Spirit answers to the meaning of Sinai, and hence signals the personal realization of the new covenant. Immediately there began to be seen and manifested *(a)* a new norm of religious experience; *(b)* a new universality of access and privilege; *(c)* a new mode of religious life, including worship and service; and *(d)* a new method of religious expansion, or evangelism.

B. The Fulfillment of Promise

The event of Pentecost was related to what John the Baptist and Jesus called the baptism with the Holy Spirit (Matt. 3:11-12; Mark 1:8; Luke 3:16; John 1:33; Acts 1:4-5). Attention is early focused on a divine "promise" of the Spirit to be received crucially as a gift. This would not only be an epochal experience but would constitute the most normative and distinguishing mark of the Christian era. What begins as a rivulet in the Synoptics becomes a stream in John and a river in the Acts. The Epistles vary, but on the whole they assume and corroborate what is more explicit in the historical documents. The promise was voiced by Joel (2:28-32; cf. Isa. 44:3; Ezek. 11:19), reiterated by John the Baptist and Jesus, and reaffirmed by Peter. The source of the promise is the Father, who said through Joel, "I will pour out my Spirit upon all flesh" (Acts 2:17).

God designs that as a consequence of Christ's work as our High Priest a new inwardness of His own presence shall be possible. This is linked by Ezekiel with the new righteousness as its inner dynamic

---

1. See Charles W. Carter, *The Person and Ministry of the Holy Spirit* (Grand Rapids, Mich.: Baker Book House, 1974), pp. 148, 150 ff.

2. Some authorities say *eight*.

(36:25-27). But it is also a new fellowship. This is the idea Jesus most wanted to convey in His designation of the promised Holy Spirit as *parakletos*, "Comforter" or "Helper" (John 14:15-17, 26; 15:26; 16:7).

If the writing of the Law on the tablets of the heart is central to the new covenant, this which Jesus calls "the promise of the Father" is the other side of the same coin. It is God's appointed means of implementing the new covenant.

C. The Spirit as a Gift

Constantly the New Testament represents *the promise* as being the reception of the Holy Spirit as a gift, specifically in His strengthening, cleansing, and enduing fullness. Jesus taught that if we as fallen men know how to give good gifts, "How much more will the heavenly Father give the Holy Spirit to those who ask him?" (Luke 11:13). The gift nature of the Spirit's coming is accented also in John (7:39; 14:16), the Acts (2:38; 5:32; 8:20; 10:45; 11:17), and the Epistles (Rom. 5:5; 1 Cor. 2:12; 1 Thess. 4:7; 1 John 3:24; 4:13).

Is there any special significance in this sharp emphasis on the Spirit as a special gift? Five notes may be suggested. (1) It is clear that the coming of the promised Spirit is a unique event, different from the Spirit's previous relationship to men. (2) It is an experience that is knowable, as clearly so as gift giving and gift receiving usually are. (3) It is an individual experience, even when received simultaneously with other persons (Acts 2:3-4; 8:16-19). (4) The cumulative inference is that the gift is conditional, thus not available to those who do not meet the conditions stipulated. Its availability stems from God's sovereignty and Christ's atonement, which means clearly specified moral terms. (5) It is a crisic and instantaneous experience.[3]

D. The Relation of the Gift of the Spirit to the New Birth

Some suppose that the special promise of the Spirit finds its fulfill-

---

3. The action indicated by *lambano* ("to receive") is normally active and volitional. When we read in John 1:12, "To all who received him," we are certainly to understand that a deliberate taking of Jesus is meant; the reference is not to passive recipients but active acceptors, who believe on Jesus in the sense that they choose to take Him as Christ and Lord. It is justifiable to interpret Paul in the same sense in his forceful questioning of the Ephesians, "Did ye receive the Holy Spirit, having believed" (Acts 19:2, NASB), meaning, "Did you take the Holy Spirit?" When Jesus "breathed" on His disciples and said "Receive the Holy Spirit" (John 20:22), it was not the immediate impartation of the Spirit but a command to *take* the Spirit. The verb is ingressive aorist active imperative, hence a command to incisive action, not a statement of present fact. The command thus bears a close relationship to Luke 24:49.

ment in the birth of the Spirit. Yet there is every evidence that Jesus considered His disciples to have already experienced what He urged upon Nicodemus (cf. John 14—17).[4] It was to these very disciples that the promise of the Spirit, to be received as a gift, was particularly made, both in symbolic act (John 20:22) and verbal command-promise (Luke 24:49). In view of this we are compelled to conclude that the term "gift" in relation to receiving the Spirit refers primarily to the coming of the Spirit as indwelling Comforter. It is the goal of God's gracious movements in the soul, by which the peace with God in justification becomes fully restored fellowship with God. Moreover, the sharp distinction between the baptism with water and the baptism with the Spirit, and the preparatory nature of the first for the second, must prevail as long as both baptisms are to be experienced.[5]

What then is the relation ōf the newborn child of God to the Holy Spirit? Is the Spirit in any sense imparted at conversion? Jesus' statement to the disciples, "You know him, for he dwells with you, and will be in you" (John 14:17) is a clue.[6] The world has no part in the Spirit because "it neither sees him [with spiritual eyes] nor knows him," but in contrast to the world, Jesus adds, "you know him." Did He mean that in himself—in His own person—visible among them, they knew the Spirit? Jesus never identifies the Spirit with himself in this way. Rather, He said, "It is to your advantage that I go away, for if I do not go away, the Counselor will not come to you; but if I go, I will send him to you" (16:7). In 14:17, He says, "He dwells with you"; now He says, "I will send him to you." Two things are evidently true. First, the presence of the Spirit among the disciples before Pentecost was not simply the presence of Jesus. The Spirit was working with them in His own right. Second, the coming of the Spirit after Christ's departure would obviously be in a relationship different from what they now knew. We are forced back to the exact way Jesus put it: "He dwells with you [is constantly by your side] and will be in you."[7]

---

4. See Carter, *Person and Ministry of the Holy Spirit*, p. 154.

5. See Turner, *Vision Which Transforms*, p. 151. See also Purkiser, *Sanctification and Its Synonyms*, pp. 28-37.

6. The UBS text gives *en humin estin* ("is in you") instead of *en humin estai* ("will be in you") but with only a D rating (signifyiṅg a "very high degree of doubt"). Both NASB and NIV follow RSV here. This is compatible with Christ's promise that the Gift of the Comforter would be *given*, i.e., an anticipated event, implying a relationship with the Spirit not yet experienced.

7. As spatial terms, *with* and *in* are figurative; but a real difference is intended,

Surely the Spirit is the active Agent in regenerating a sinner. The believer knows *(ginōskō)* Him relationally, through Jesus, though without full understanding *(epiginōskō)*. The Spirit is with that person thereafter, prodding, guiding, so that "all who are led by the Spirit of God are sons of God" (Rom. 8:14). Yet in this very passage Paul seems to acknowledge the difference between having the Spirit, in this elementary relationship, and the Spirit being "at home" in them: "However you are not in the flesh but in the Spirit, if indeed the Spirit of God dwells in you," i.e., makes *His home* in you (vv. 9, 11; cf. Berk.). Sanday and Headlam say that the expression "denotes a settled permanent penetrating influence inseparable from the higher life of the Christian." Commenting on v. 9 they observe: "This amounts to saying that all Christians have the Spirit in greater or less degree" (cf. Rom. 12:1-2).[8]

Clearly one may have the Spirit as a Christian without having been baptized with the Spirit or without being filled with the Spirit. When the apostles stipulated that the deacons should be "men of good repute, full of the Spirit and of wisdom" (Acts 6:3), they implied that not all believers were filled with the Spirit, just as not all had reputation or wisdom.

The presence and activity of the Spirit in every Christian, plus the subsequent experience of His fullness, has prompted some to speak of the gift as twofold, in some degree similar to the twofold gift of a young woman to her fiance, first in engagement then in marriage. But the documents themselves seem to confine the terms "promise of the Spirit" and "gift of the Spirit" to the special outpouring *upon believers,* first witnessed on the Day of Pentecost.

E. The Sanctification of Believers

The evidence is cumulative that what happend to the 120 on the Day of Pentecost was at its heart the fulfillment of the Lord's high-priestly prayer, "Sanctify them" (John 17:17). What Jesus meant by the prayer surely included what they obviously needed: purging, consecrating, reinforcing, empowering. These acts of divine power would be needed to repair and prepare them inwardly so they could be exposed to the world's evil without contamination; could work to-

---

nevertheless. It is not psychologically possible for men to yield their hearts to the Spirit's full, inward, sanctifying presence and power until they become *aware* of this possibility through the preparatory mission and teaching of Jesus.

8. Sanday and Headlam, "Romans," *ICC,* pp. 196-97.

gether in the rough and tumble of life in the bond of love, and would have an inwrought bent to persevere in steadfast loyalty and faith. These are the precise needs so profoundly met when the Holy Spirit came upon them. This was a second experience of inner change, the first having occurred in the beginning of their discipleship. While that first change made them true devotees of Jesus, it did not sufficiently make them like Jesus.

It was at this very point that we see the greatest glory of Pentecost. There was an instant enlargement of vision, a new and radical kind of spiritual-mindedness, an insight into spiritual realities, and even more significantly, a thorough purification of the disciples' inner motives. The quality of their spirit (attitude, frame of mind) was altered profoundly and permanently. They were indeed not only renewed men but renovated and rectified men. Here we see in practical personality *change* everything that could be intended by the formal definition of *hagiadzō*, to "consecrate," "purify."

F. Inaugural Signs and Lasting Essentials

1. *Wind—Power.*

The substance of the sanctifying power of the Holy Spirit which characterized the first Pentecost experience is seen further in the remarkable signs that accompanied the event. These were outward signs both of the new dispensation and of the normative work of grace which the dispensation introduced. The gentle winds of the Spirit of which Jesus spoke (John 3:8), signifying the invisible, mysterious movements of the Spirit on the souls of men, now is a sound as of a rushing mighty wind, filling all the house where the waiting 120 are sitting. Here we have the picture of adequate power possessing every atom of their being and permeating their personalities at every level of relationship.[9] Charles W. Carter says:

> The "noise like a violent [or, 'mighty'] rushing wind" on the Day of Pentecost is vividly suggestive of the power (*dunamis*, from which the English word "dynamite" comes) of God in His relation to man. This . . . is the symbolical fulfillment of Christ's words to His disciples: "And behold, I send the promise of My Father upon you; but stay in the city, until you are clothed with power [*dunamis*] from on high" (Luke 24:49).[10]

---

9. It was not an "irresistible grace" but a God-possession that created an unavoidable impact on the world around them; as, for instance, Stephen, who, "full of grace and power, did great wonders and signs among the people" and they "could not withstand the wisdom and the Spirit with which he spoke" (Acts 6:8, 10).

10. *Person and Ministry of the Spirit.* p. 162.

While there are several purposes in this power, two primary ones are suggested by Carter: "First, the indwelling Spirit's power is the assurance of the sanctified Christian's victory over the powers of temptation and sin." It is fundamentally a moral power. But second, "the power of the Spirit is an effective enablement to the execution of the Christian witness."[11] The promise of such power is seen in Acts 1:8 and its fulfillment noted in Acts 4:33. That such power is not bestowed in conversion is implied by Paul's deep concern for the Ephesian Christians. He writes: "For this reason I bow my knees before the Father, that . . . he may grant you to be strengthened with might [dunamis] through his Spirit in the inner man . . . that you may be filled with all the fullness of God" (Eph. 3:14-19).

2. *Fire—Purity.*

The "tongues as of fire" which distributed themselves resting upon each of the 120 became the sign of fulfillment of words spoken by both Malachi and John the Baptist (Mal. 3:1-3; Matt. 3:11-12). As fire is a deeper cleansing agent than water, so the fire of Pentecost speaks of inner purification beyond the expiation of water baptism (cf. Isa. 6:6-7 with Acts 15:8-9). As "a consuming fire" (Heb. 12:29) God in His awful holiness will either consume sin from the heart or consume the depraved soul in judgment. He will have a purified people. He can safely use no other kind.

The symbol of fire forbids any thought of cold, sterile holiness. Those who are purified by the Spirit are "zealous for good deeds" (Titus 2:14). The holy heart is a burning heart. "The 'tongue like as of fire' is the symbol of aggressive Christianity," says Thomas Walker.[12] J. Brice observes: "It is the transition from formalism to fervour that marks the miracle of Pentecost." And he quotes his former mentor, Samuel Chadwick: "Men ablaze are invincible. Hell trembles when men kindle. The stronghold of Satan is proof against everything but fire. The church is powerless without the flame of the Holy Ghost."[13]

3. *Tongues—Communication.*

The spontaneous speaking in the languages of the many pilgrims at the feast was symbolic of the new method of conquest: the preaching of the word, anointed by the Spirit, in the dialects of the people.

---

11. *Ibid.,* p. 166.
12. *The Acts of the Apostles* (Chicago: Moody Press, 1965), p. 29.
13. *Pentecost* (Salem, Ohio: Convention Book Store, repr. 1973), pp. 73-76.

The Kingdom would be extended throughout the world by word of mouth and by word of pen. The Church was thus launched on a speaking mission. Spirit-baptized believers were commissioned not to become political reformers or economic sages or social servants primarily. They were sent out simply to witness everywhere by word and life—and if need be by death—to man's only hope in Christ. They were commissioned to "make disciples of all nations" (Matt. 28: 19-20; cf. Acts 14:1).[14]

It is disastrous for the Church to confuse the sign with the thing signified, or to miss the lasting essentials in a frenetic attempt to recapture signs. The lasting essentials are spiritual and moral power, inward and outward holiness, anointing for communication and evangelism, all in and through the indwelling Holy Spirit. The recognized norm in the primitive Church was "fullness" (possession of and by the Spirit); the external expressions were variable.

II. THE SPIRIT AS SANCTIFYING AGENT

While the sanctification of believers is the will of the Father, and the provision of the Son, its personal accomplishment is the direct work of the Holy Spirit. He may therefore be said to be the immediate Agent. Christ "gave himself up" for the Church in order "that he might sanctify her" (Eph. 5:25-26); but what He accomplished was a possibility, not a fact of experience. On the basis of His atoning death He is now able to accomplish our sanctification by the outpoured Holy Spirit.

The same can be said of the declaration in Heb. 13:12: "So Jesus also suffered outside the gate in order to sanctify the people through his own blood." Through His blood (*dia* with the genitive) the people of God (the worshippers) may be thoroughly cleansed from their sin.[15]

But while the Blood is the means, the Spirit is the Effector. The verse then, according to H. Orton Wiley, speaks of "the power of

---

14. The so-called second Pentecost of Acts 4:23 ff. was marked not by foreign languages, for such were not needed, but boldness to speak the Word of God (v. 31). The miracle of languages was rarely repeated; it was the courageous faithfulness which was the real norm of Spirit-filled believers in the new dispensation. See Richard S. Taylor, *Tongues: Their Purpose and Meaning* (Kansas City: Beacon Hill Press of Kansas City, 1973); and W. T. Purkiser, *The Gifts of the Spirit* (Kansas City: Beacon Hill Press of Kansas City, 1975).

15. The sanctifying here is much more than declaring the people holy forensically by an objective expiation.

Jesus to sanctify, and the actual accomplishment of this purpose through the baptism with the Holy Spirit."[16] In Titus also the sanctifying purpose of the atonement is declared: Jesus "gave himself for us to redeem us from all iniquity and to purify for himself a people of his own who are zealous for good deeds" (2:14). Again such redemption and purification are made possible by His death, but made actual by the Spirit (cf. Rom. 15:13, 16; Eph. 3:16 ff.; 1 Thess. 4:8; 2 Thess. 2:13; 1 Pet. 1:2; Titus 3:5).

A. The Spirit and the Word

When Jesus prayed that the disciples be sanctified "by the truth" (Phillips),[17] He immediately added, "Thy word is truth." The word here is "message" (TCNT), both about Christ and by Christ (see Chapter 26). It is erroneous to say that the authority is in Christ's person only, and not in the word; for He who said, "I am . . . the truth" (John 14:6), also said, "If you continue in my word . . . you will know the truth, and the truth will make you free" (8:31-32). But it is the Holy Spirit, "the Spirit of truth" (14:17), who recalls those words to the mind and interprets them to the soul (14:26; 15:26; 16:12-15). This He did first of all by shaping the teachings of the Apostolic Church, and through that Church producing the New Testament as the written Word.

Christ's words written—and also the inspired interpretative words of the apostles—are fully as much the *Word of God* as were those words at the moment they fell from His (and their) lips. Writing them down did not alter either their power, truth, or authority. Whether being preached by the apostles or being read in the twentieth century, the Holy Spirit takes the words which are already His and uses them as His instrument in sanctification. Through this composite Word He discloses our need (Heb. 4:12); through the Word He shows us the provision (Acts 20:32); through the Spirit, in turn, we are enabled to purify our souls in "obedience to the truth" (1 Pet. 1:22).[18] Indeed, it is through faith in the Word that we receive the Spirit himself (Gal. 3:2).[19]

---

16. *Epistle to the Hebrews*, p. 417. See also Carter, *Person and Ministry of the Holy Spirit*, pp. 314 ff.

17. To interpret *en* as instrumental, with, or by, makes more sense than to assume the locative, *in* the truth.

18. While the addition of *dia pneumatos*, "through the Spirit" (KJV), lacks full manuscript support, the idea can reasonably be said to be implied.

19. The Spirit is not only the Executive of the Godhead in internalizing promises and provisions, but in executing the divine word as fiat. Just as God said, "'Let there

B. The Spirit and Faith

Jesus frequently pinpointed faith as the key to divine blessings. But here too the Spirit plays the dynamic part, for He not only is the Executive of the Godhead in effecting the change within, but is also the Helper of faith. If faith comes "from what is heard, and what is heard comes by the preaching of Christ" (Rom. 10:17), it is the Spirit who quickens the Word to our minds and inspires faith.

This is the principle governing faith by which we are sanctified as well as pardoned. In numerous passages faith is cited as the activating catalyst, from the human side, in the experiencing of a deeper work of grace (Rom. 5:2-5 plus Gal. 3:2, 5 and Eph. 3:17; Acts 15:9 with 26:18; Rom. 15:13; 1 Thess. 3:10; Heb. 4:1-3; 10:22; 2 Pet. 1:4-5).

The *prayer* of faith is expectant, definite petition (Luke 11:9-10, 13). The *work* of faith is obedience (Acts 1:4-5; 5:32; Jas. 1:22-25; 2:26). The *reward* of faith is experience, including both fact and assurance (Acts 15:8-9; cf. 26:18). The *simplicity* of faith is symbolized by opening a door (Rev. 3:21). Yet present in every movement of faith is the enabling and prompting of the Holy Spirit. He reminds us of the Word, helps us to claim a specific promise until it is experientially fulfilled, and at every point honors the Word which is both Christ's and His.

God has chosen us to be saved through the sanctification of the Spirit and our belief in the truth (2 Thess. 2:13; cf. 1 Pet. 1:2). It is clear, however, that it is not our faith which sanctifies; rather it is our faith in the *truth* that makes possible the Spirit's sanctifying. Here again it would be artificial to sever faith in Christ from faith in the Word. The *truth* is both Christ the living Word and the Bible the written Word. To Paul, Jesus specified "faith in me" as the source of sanctification (Acts 26:18), yet the *truth* revealed to us in the Scriptures is that Jesus *is* Sanctifier, through the Spirit. And while Peter ascribed the direct work of sanctification to the Spirit (1 Pet. 1:2), he also ascribed to Christ the granting of "precious and magnificent promises, in order that by them you might become partakers of the divine nature" (2 Pet. 1:3-4, NASB).[20]

---

be light,' and there was light" (Gen. 1:3), so Jesus said to the leper, "'I will; be clean.' And immediately his leprosy was cleansed" (Matt. 8:3). Yet while the *exousia*, "authority," was in Jesus' word, the Holy Spirit validated this authority by constituting in himself the *dunamis* ("power"). The actual physiological change in the body of the leper was accomplished by the Spirit in response to Christ's pronouncement.

20. The word of Christ cannot be separated from His person; but neither can the Person be separated from the word. The integrity of the Person is equally in the word.

The secret *modus operandi* of the Spirit in effecting inner sanctification is not explained by the Scriptures, and any attempt to do so would be speculative. It is safe to say, however, that His work must not be so reduced to a mere influence that it virtually ceases to be a "work of grace." Without the direct action of the Spirit upon the soul no believer is sanctified wholly. Yet this action is not like the operation of a surgeon upon a patient while under anesthesia. It is a work interacting with the believer as a yielding, asking, obeying, believing participant, fully awake and fully aware of what is going on.

III. THE MEANING OF SPIRIT-BAPTISM

A. The Baptizing Agents

Baptizing, whether literal or metaphorical, involves an agent, a subject, and a medium of baptism. In the "baptism of John" (Matt. 21: 25), John was the agent, repentant people were the subjects, and water was the medium. In the baptism with the Spirit, Jesus is the Agent, believers are the subjects, and the Spirit is the medium with *(en)* which they are baptized. (*En* may be translated "in," "with," and sometimes "by.")

Yet the Spirit does have His own baptism: "For by one Spirit we were all baptized into one body" (1 Cor. 12:13; cf. NEB), an event which occurs in regeneration. But this is obviously not the further baptism which John promised Jesus would administer to those qualified by the baptism of repentance. Christ's baptism was administered to the Church on the Day of Pentecost and to Cornelius and his household (Acts 11:16-17). Peter specifically identifies this baptism as the promised gift of the Spirit.[21] "There is a manifest distinction," writes James Elder Cumming, "between the Spirit baptising men into Christ and Christ baptising men with the Holy Ghost."[22]

---

21. Wiley interprets baptism by the Spirit in 1 Cor. 12:13 as a reference to the baptism with the Spirit. He says: "We not only must have new life, but being members of a race we must have a new social nexus. For this reason the baptism with the Spirit which purifies the heart is very closely associated with the Spirit in His charismatic (or gift-bestowing) relation as shown in the text, 'For by one Spirit are we all baptized into the one body.' Only when we are cleansed from all sin by the baptism with the Holy Spirit, and that Spirit takes up His abode in our hearts may it be said that we are fully in the body of Christ—that is, in the sense of the New Covenant relationship. Otherwise we are but children under the covenant. (Gal. 4:1-2)." (From personal letter to A. E. Sanner, Northwest Nazarene College.)

22. *Through the Eternal Spirit* (Minneapolis, Minn.: Bethany Fellowship, Inc., 1965, reprint), p. 86.

B. The Baptism Metaphor

In the New Testament the concept of baptism is as thoroughly metaphorical as it is cultic. In fact, in many instances the term is used without any reference whatsoever to an external baptismal rite. There are three metaphorical emphases found in the New Testament: cleansing, death, and induction. The idea of *cleansing* is seen in the symbols of water and fire (Matt. 3:11; Acts 22:16; cf. Mark 7:3-4; John 2:6). The meaning of baptism as a *death* is seen in Christ's identification of His own coming death as a baptism (Mark 10:38-39), and in Paul's reminder, "Do you not know that all of us who have been baptized into Christ Jesus were baptized into his death?" (Rom. 6:3).

The idea of *induction* is also a distinct emphasis in the New Testament, indeed it is implicit in the earliest sense of *baptidzō*, "to immerse." While "baptism" is used in reference to the experience of Pentecost, the event is spoken of also as a *pouring* (Acts 2:17-18; 10:45) and likewise an *infilling* (Acts 2:4, *et al.*), neither one an "immersion" in the cultic sense. However, both baptism as outpouring and as infilling are compatible with immersion seen as a *metaphor*, suggesting induction or initiation for permanence.[23]

The metaphorical sense of "baptism" is far more frequent in the New Testament than has been generally recognized, and the blanket assumption that the word is in every case a reference to the baptismal rite with water is at least questionable.

These three metaphorical emphases are relevant both to the new birth and to the baptism with the Holy Spirit. Water is the symbol of the *"washing"* of regeneration (John 3:5; Acts 22:16; Titus 3:5); *death* to sin is the implication of regeneration (Rom. 6:2-4; Gal. 5:24; Eph. 2:1-2); and certainly there is an *immersion* or induction into a new kind of life, focused on Jesus Christ himself (Acts 8:5 ff.; 2 Cor. 5:17; Phil. 1:21; Col. 3:1-3, 9-10; 1 Thess. 1:4).

---

23. In classical Greek *baptō* meant "dip" and could and would have been used by the New Testament writers if that was the idea they intended to convey. On the other hand *baptidzō* suggested immersion for permanence, either into the water resulting in drowning or in some other form of complete commitment and absorption. It was in this sense that Paul spoke of the Israelites being "baptized into Moses in the cloud and in the sea" (1 Cor. 10:2). They were immersed, that is *inducted*, into the Mosaic regime; but this is not a reference to a baptismal *mode*, as such, for being baptized "in the sea" was without water (only the Egyptians got wet!) and there is no evidence that the reference to the cloud suggested that they were rained on (that would have been sprinkling!). Cf. Kittel, *TDNT*, 1:530. The modern concept of "total immersion" language schools should aid us in seeing baptism as symbolic of complete induction into Christ and the baptism with the Spirit as "total immersion" in Christ.

All of this is intensified and expanded in content at the crisis point of the baptism with the Holy Spirit. Fire is now the symbol of the *cleansing* (Acts 2:3; cf. Mal. 3:1-3; Matt. 3:11-12); that which is cleansed is neither guilt nor acquired depravity but the egoistic principle of the carnal mind—dross and chaff (cf. Acts 15:8-9). There is also a deepened experience of spiritual *death,* but at this level a death to the sinful claims of the self-nature (Rom. 12:1-2; Eph. 4:22-23; Phil. 2:5 ff.; 2 Tim. 2:11). This is sometimes spoken of as crucifixion, or death to self (Gal. 2:20; cf. Acts 20:22-24; Gal. 6:14, 17).

In entire sanctification there is also the completion of the *induction* process. Here the emphasis is on the enduement of power by the direct infilling of the Holy Spirit whereby the entire personality comes under the unreserved and uncompromised direction of the Spirit of Christ (Acts 7:55; 13:52, *et al.;* Eph. 5:18 ff.). This may be said to be a full induction or immersion into the complete rule of the Spirit, who establishes Christ on the throne of the heart, forms in the human spirit the image of Christ (Eph. 3:16-21), and creates that spiritual-mindedness which is "life and peace" (Rom. 8:1-6). This is properly called the baptism *with* or *in* the Spirit.

C. Relation to Spirit-Fullness

It is perfectly clear from a comparison of Acts 1:5 and 11:16 with 2:4 that to be baptized with the Spirit is to be filled with the Spirit. Those who identify the *baptism* with the Spirit with the *birth* of the Spirit are saying that all regenerate persons are Spirit-filled. Not only do the facts of experience repudiate such a notion, but the Scriptures do also, by inescapable implication (Acts 6:3; 8:12-17; 9:17; Eph. 3:16-19; 5:18).

That the Scriptures do not repudiate the idea directly would suggest that it was not an issue in the New Testament Church. Two deductions are justified: (1) The birth of the Spirit and the baptism with the Spirit are neither equivalent nor concomitant; and (2) all who are baptized with the Spirit are thereby filled with the Spirit.

However, we immediately run into difficulty if we assume the reverse to be true—that all who in the Scriptures are said to be filled with the Spirit have been baptized with the Spirit. The fullness which accompanies the baptism with the Spirit is unique to our dispensation. It brings a basic purging of nature and an intimacy of relationship not included in the pre-Pentecost fullness.

It is this distinction that prompts Delbert R. Rose (following Daniel Steele) to remind us that *charismatic* fullness, *ecstatic* fullness, and *ethical* fullness, while they may overlap, are not the same. Bezalel, John the Baptist, and both his parents experienced charismatic fullness (Exod. 28:3; 31:3; 35:30-31; Luke 1:15, 41, 67). Therefore the display of charismata is not unique to this age, nor is it proof of having been baptized with the Spirit. Similarly the disciples experienced ecstatic fullness before Pentecost (Luke 24:52-53; cf. John 3:29).

The fullness of those baptized with the Spirit is essentially an ethical fullness, the indispensable element of which is the purifying of the heart (Acts 15:8-9). Delbert Rose writes:

> In a word, to be baptized with the Holy Spirit is a fullness of a specific kind. This experience may or may not be accompanied by "an emotional high" or by some one of the spiritual gifts. Neither "ecstasy" nor any one of the Spirit's "charismata" is essential to, or evidence of, the Saviour's baptizing work.[24]

A further relationship between baptism and Spirit-fullness may be observed in the idea inherent in baptism as a crisic event with lasting consequences. Believers are baptized with the Spirit into a condition of Spirit-fullness, a relationship with the Spirit which may be *renewed* (Acts 4:31), and must be *maintained* (Eph. 5:18, present tense) with much care and prayerfulness.

IV. DISPENSATIONAL ISSUES

The significance of Pentecost as the beginning of the dispensation of the Holy Spirit has prompted some to explain that this apparently fixed timetable was what prevented the disciples from being baptized with the Spirit earlier. Admittedly (so the argument runs) they received the gift of the Spirit *after* their conversion, but their experience cannot be advanced as the norm. From the Day of Pentecost a new order prevailed, and from that day forward the full gift of the Spirit was coincident with the new birth. But this approach runs into some serious difficulties.

A. The Example of Jesus

Surely the experience of Jesus bears some relation to Christians as a divinely designed model. His baptism at the hands of John was "to

---

24. "Distinguishing Things That Differ," *Wesleyan Theological Journal*, vol. 9, spring, 1974, p. 12. Speaking of 1 Cor. 12:13, Rose observes, "It seems definitely not to have been identical with the baptism with the Holy Spirit (and with fire) which John the Baptist prophesied Jesus would bestow, and which Jesus himself promised to disciples, and which Peter personally possessed and preached. For the Spirit-baptism Jesus administered was heart-cleansing and power-bestowing for holy living and serving."

fulfill all righteousness" (Matt. 3:15), and thus to identify himself with sinful man. But also that baptism was to qualify symbolically for the coming of the Holy Spirit upon Him which immediately followed. Wiley points out that this was not only the divine "attestation to the Messiahship of Jesus" but the "official anointing of the Spirit by which He was consecrated to the holy office of Mediator."[25] It was not a sanctifying baptism with the Spirit in the sense of cleansing from sin any more than the water baptism indicated an expiation of personal guilt. But we do have here in close conjunction the two baptisms. They are not only Christ's official inductions into mediatorial ministry, but they also represent the two corresponding steps in our personal salvation and equipping. As such they reveal an inherent and timeless logic both in their distinctiveness and their sequence.[26]

B. The Teachings of Jesus

In our Lord's discussion of the promised Comforter there seems to be an implication of a basic principle: The Holy Spirit in this specific office is available only to those who have a prior spiritual fitness. There must be spiritual life, sufficient to condition one into some degree of intelligent readiness and receptivity. Such qualifying life could be nothing less than that love for Jesus which prompts obedience to Him (John 14:15, 21, 23; cf. Acts 5:32).

It is for this reason that the world is ruled out. The world "cannot receive" Him, *not* because Pentecost has not yet come, but because the world "neither sees him nor knows him" (v. 17). This disqualification is as true of the world after the Day of Pentecost as before. Since the "world" as Jesus used the terms in this discourse meant nonbelievers, we are compelled to conclude that before one is ready to receive the Spirit as Comforter, he must cease to belong to the world, whether before Pentecost or after.[27]

C. The Experience of the Early Church

The above inference is what we find confirmed by the post-Pentecost

---

25. *Christian Theology,* 2:152.

26. An inference may be drawn that a great gap of time between the baptism of repentance and the baptism with the Spirit should not be viewed as the norm.

27. Perhaps there is an inherent logical correspondence between the necessary stages in the revelation of the Godhead and those stages as they are personalized in the believer. Just as the soteriological offices of the Son could not be revealed until those of the Father had been, so the soteriological offices of the Spirit could be revealed only subsequently to the unveiling of the Son.

developments. Peter insisted that his Jewish listeners could not receive "the gift of the Holy Spirit" until they qualified by first repenting and then being baptized "in the name of Jesus Christ for the forgiveness of your sins" (Acts 2:38). A sequence of events is implied here. Whether they received the gift one minute after, two hours after, or the next day is irrelevant. It was still a subsequent experience, and it is inescapable that the instructions Peter gave them were the conditions which they must meet in order to become eligible. Furthermore, the conditions were essentially the same which had been laid down by both Jesus and John the Baptist. The advent of the new dispensation had not changed this fundamental order (cf. v. 39; John 17:19-20).

Furthermore, this was the consistent order after Pentecost. The visible rite of baptism with water might be administered after the baptism with the Spirit (cf. Cornelius, the Ephesians, and possibly Paul), but the qualifying repentance and faith in Jesus always occurred prior to the baptism with the Spirit. Therefore Peter's "Ye shall receive" did not mean an automatic bestowment at the instant of faith and forgiveness.[28] The Samaritans complied with the instruction to repent and to be baptized. They were filled with "great joy" but did not receive the fullness of the Spirit until the apostles came from Jerusalem to pray for this specific experience. Paul capitulated to Christ on the Damascus road, but was filled with the Spirit three days later. The case is clear also with the Ephesians, especially in the light of Acts 19:4.[29]

---

28. The RSV, NIV, and NEB are singularly unfortunate in ignoring the time sequence implied in the Greek of Acts 11:17. Their rendering seems to give credence to the position of Frederick Dale Bruner (*A Theology of the Holy Spirit*, p. 195) that in this verse we have evidence "that the apostles considered Pentecost to be the 'terminus a quo' of their faith, hence the date of their conversion." In the first place it is necessary for him to ignore the aorist participle and translate "when we believed" instead of "after we believed." While occasionally "the aorist participle expresses simultaneous action," it "normally describes action antecedent to that of the main verb," says W. D. Chamberlain (*Exegetical Grammar of the Greek New Testament*, p. 171). In this case the plain historical facts would dictate the normal usage. These facts are that the disciples were regenerate before Pentecost and considered themselves as such. A simple reading of Acts 1 will make this apparent; also John 14—17; cf. Luke 10:20. Turner's conclusion is sound: "After weighing the relevant evidence it seems clear that the disciples experienced a personal Pentecost, subsequent to their being 'born of water and of the Spirit'" (*Vision Which Transforms*, p. 153).

29. Some suppose Cornelius and his household to be an exception. However, when the pros and cons of the data are weighed, the arguments for such a conclusion are not compelling. At the very least, Peter's report (Acts 15:8-9) implies that God does not give the great gift of the Spirit unless and until He finds a *ready* heart. This the Lord found in Cornelius. That he possessed some degree of prior spiritual life and

D. Crisis in the Epistles

The experiential discreteness between the birth of the Spirit and the baptism with the Spirit can be quite clearly established from the Gospels and the Acts. It is often said, however, that the pattern of secondness in respect to entire sanctification is absent, or at least vague, in the Epistles.

It has already been noted that the Epistles unmistakably delineate the standard of Christian experience which is God's will for believers and which is possible in this life. Also they deal constantly and in many ways with the symptoms and problems of Christians who have not reached that standard. This simple fact would argue that conversion does not induct one at once into his full privileges in Christ. Further, it needs to be observed that the normal approach of the writers is to see the standard as an absolute for all believers and to constantly urge upon Christians the appropriation of this standard, without presenting the matter systematically as a one-two series of steps.[30]

Moreover, the life-setting *(Sitz im Leben)* may help us. If Paul customarily was as zealous respecting the fullness of the Holy Spirit as he was at Ephesus (Acts 19:1-6; cf. *WBC* on Rom. 15:16), the assumption is reasonable that basic indoctrination concerning the baptism with the Spirit has been given by him in person. This may explain why it is not systematically treated in the letters. Not only may prior indoctrination be assumed, but the probability is strong that most of his converts would very soon have been led by Paul into this deeper experience. Paul had done this for the Ephesians just as

---

even knowledge of Jesus is evident from Acts 10:2-4, 15, 22, 34-38. See Ralph Earle's suggested explanation in *BBC*, 8:383.

30. Turner writes: "There are some who emphasize the difference in emphasis between the Synoptic-Acts tradition and that of the Pauline Epistles. The alleged difference is that in Acts the external *effluence* of the Spirit is stressed (in wind, fire, tongues, power) while in Paul it is the internal influence of the Spirit which is experienced (in purity, love, joy, etc.). That there are differences of emphasis is admissible: in the Synoptics and Acts the emphasis is upon the *power* of the Spirit in witnessing and service; in Paul's letters the emphasis is upon the moral effects of the Spirit's indwelling; while in the Johannine writings the emphasis is upon the Spirit as Revealer, Interpreter, and Bearer of the truth. Thus from these three sources the Spirit is presented respectively as giving *power, purity,* and *knowledge of Christ;* in the Synoptics and Acts the charismatic, in Paul the ethical, in John the intellectual" *(Vision Which Transforms,* pp. 149 ff.). This is helpful as long as we see these varying emphases as complementary and in no sense contradictory or corrective. The doctrine of secondness in the baptism with the Holy Spirit derived from the Gospels and Acts is neither cancelled nor weakened by the different emphases of the Epistles.

Ananias had done it for him. The apostles early led the Samaritans into this experience; later Priscilla and Aquila instructed Apollos.

Since all of the churches, at the time they were addressed in writing, were in a fluid and mixed state, they undoubtedly included the full spectrum of both spiritual attainments and spiritual needs. While some members were sanctified wholly, others were "yet carnal," and still others had reverted to sin in various forms of scandalous conduct. The letters, therefore, because addressed to different levels of spiritual needs and a variety of problems, cannot be analyzed neatly into discrete categories of experience.

Nevertheless evidence of twofoldness in the Spirit's saving ministry is found in the Epistles.

1. *The Need of the Thessalonians.*

A study of the first letter to the Thessalonian Christians suggests that Paul had not been with this particular group long enough to indoctrinate them or lead them into the fullness of the Spirit.[31] This is suggested *(a)* by his deep concern that he might see them again and "supply what is lacking" in their faith (3:10); *(b)* his declaration of the will of God as their sanctification, and the relation of that will to the gift of the Holy Spirit (4:3, 8); and *(c)* his final prayer that the very God of peace would sanctify them "wholly" (5:23).[32] The assurance is voiced in verse 24, "He who calls you is faithful, and he will do it." By no means is this verse a stall. Paul is rather saying, "God is ready when you are."[33] The actual sanctifying is here ascribed to the God of peace himself and inwrought by the Holy Spirit. This is made clear in 2 Thess. 2:13 where *hagiasmos* is the action noun indicating the *sanctifying* for which Paul prays in his use of the aorist verb *hagiadzō.*

2. *Twofoldness in Romans.*

While the handling of Romans 5:1-5 is open to honest diversity of opinion, it is difficult to fault NASB: "Therefore having been justi-

---

31. See Ralph Earle, ed., *Exploring the New Testament* (Kansas City: Beacon Hill Press, 1955), pp. 453-56.

32. In respect to 5:23, it is extremely questionable exegesis to weaken this strong expression of their need and of God's will be identifying the aorist tense of *sanctify* as a constative aorist, thus relating entire sanctification primarily to God's total and timeless ministry in the Church, and thereby minimizing its urgency and immediate availability in personal experience.

33. Probably also the timing of their full sanctification, which is God's declared will and their need now, is somehow related to "completing what is lacking" in their faith (3:10), whether *via* Paul or another, or even *this letter.*

fied by faith, we have peace with God through our Lord Jesus Christ, through whom also we have obtained our introduction by faith into this grace in which we stand; and we exult in hope of the glory of God." The next three verses, climaxing with a reference to the out-poured love of God possessing our hearts through the Holy Spirit who is given to us, describes the victory that characterizes "this grace in which we stand."

This passage seems to be the real transition in Paul's thought from initial justification by faith to a deeper relationship with God which is available to believers through the Holy Spirit. This is confirmed in the thought-development of cc. 5—8. Not only was the guilt of our sins nailed with Christ on the Cross, but also "our old self" was nailed there for the specific purpose "that the body of sin might be done away with, that we should no longer be slaves to sin" (6:6, NASB; cf. 7:24).

Further, the *presentation* of the body, balanced by the thorough *renewing* of the mind (Rom. 12:1-2), is clearly a crucial advance; but it is urged upon believers, not unregenerate sinners. The changes delineated in this exhortation are in some respects a completion of previous changes and in other respects new in kind.[34]

3. *The Spirit in Ephesians.*

In this Epistle there is recognition of the Spirit's preliminary reception at the time of repentance and faith in Christ. But there is also a subsequent norm of fullness, which some of them had experienced and to which others were urged. Eph. 1:13, for instance, clearly indicates the sealing "with the promised Holy Spirit" as having been experienced subsequent to their initial believing (cf. Phillips, NASB). This is very possibly a reference to Paul's original contact with the first nucleus of the Church, recorded in Acts 19:1-7.

Also in this Epistle there is the prayer that they might be strengthened with power "through his Spirit in the inner man" and that Christ might dwell in their hearts "through faith" in order that

---

34. The *lordship* of Jesus is an integral element of a true conversion experience. The acknowledgement of this lordship is essential to repentance and faith. However, its full implications are not normally seen when the sinner accepts Christ as a Saviour. The carnal *mind (phronēma,* cf. Rom. 8:6-7) is that disposition to drag the feet in facing up to those implications. It is that deep reluctance to be thoroughly honest in implementing the lordship of Christ, not only in the major matters of vocation and relationship, but in life's practical details. All of this discloses an aberrant disposition which characterizes a "mind" *(nous)* only partially renewed.

they might be "filled with all the fullness of God" (3:14-19). Likewise there is the command to "be filled with the Spirit" (5:18). Here is an imperative that speaks of a continuous norm but by implication demands an initial infilling. Undoubtedly therefore there were persons to whom this letter was addressed who knew by experience the baptism with the Holy Spirit and others who needed to move up to and into this experience.[35]

4. *The Corinthian Problem.*

A further issue concerns the Corinthians who had so many evidences of the Holy Spirit's presence and ministry in their midst and yet who perhaps more than any other church fell short of the normal evidences of entire sanctification.

Paul refuses to see the gifts of the Spirit as evidence of a deep experience in Christ—as the entire first letter bears witness. In this he has support from the Gospels and from Acts. *Before* the Day of Pentecost the disciples had remarkable gifts, all of which could be ascribed to the Spirit; yet they were not baptized with the Spirit. When Paul questions: "Do you not know that you are God's temple and that God's Spirit dwells in you?" (1 Cor. 3:16), he is speaking to them collectively. He is not describing them as Spirit-filled Christians. Rather, he is reminding them that because the Church is the temple in which the Holy Spirit dwells, it is a serious thing for any man to destroy that temple. Furthermore, the general assertion "Your body is a temple of the Holy Spirit" (1 Cor. 6:19) could be said of any Christian without implying that he was a fully cleansed and Spirit-possessed temple.

One might be tempted to ask, Why then does not Paul bluntly say in his letter: "What you Corinthians need is to be sanctified wholly through the baptism with the Holy Spirit"? Undoubtedly such precise doctrinal language would make things easier for the biblical theologian. However, the Corinthians already were overzealous of experiences which they ascribed to the Holy Spirit. This may explain, at least in part, why Paul tried to cool their fever at that point and direct their attention rather to the *substance* of perfect

---

35. The sanctification of the Church for which Christ died has as its express objective the presentation of the Church "before him in splendor, without spot or wrinkle or any such thing, that she might be holy and without blemish." This presupposes a *prior* cleansing *(expiatory),* "having cleansed her by the washing of the water with the word" (5:26-27, note aorist participle).

love (1 Cor. 13:1-13) and to challenge them to thorough self-cleansing (2 Cor. 7:1).

5. The Galatian Letter.

Paul challenges the Galatian Christians, "Did you receive the Spirit by the works of the law, or by hearing with faith?" (3:2). Explaining the sense in which Christ redeemed us "from the curse of the law," he says it was "that in Christ Jesus the blessing of Abraham might come upon the Gentiles, that we might receive the promise of the Spirit through faith" (3:14). The blessing of Abraham has been unmistakably defined as justification by faith. He now says this blessing of justification is a means to a further end—the reception of the Holy Spirit in the full measure which has been called "the promise."

V. Raymond Edman comments on 3:2: "Just as salvation is by faith . . . so by simple faith we receive the fullness of the Holy Spirit."[36] This entire section relates to 5:16-25. Walking by the Spirit (v. 25) is consistent with having "crucified the flesh with its passions and desires" (v. 24). It completely excludes the "deeds of the flesh" (vv. 19 ff.) and results in the "fruit of the Spirit" (vv. 22 ff.). This "walking by the Spirit" is equivalent to the spiritual-mindedness of believers in whom the Spirit is "at home" (Rom. 8:9, Berk.). It is also equivalent to the *fullness* of the Spirit, spoken of in Eph. 5:18 ff. In the case of the Galatian churches also, some members enjoyed the fullness of the Spirit (6:1), while others either had not come this far or had reverted to legalism, and through legalism to an abnormal, debilitating conflict between the Spirit and the flesh (5:7-24).

6. Passages in Other Epistles.

The twofoldness of salvation is seen also in Titus. Here the purpose of Christ's death is said to be both our deliverance from the guilt of every evil deed, and our inward purging from everything incompatible with God's perfect ownership (Titus 2:14; cf. 3:5).

In Hebrews the argument climaxes with the grand declaration that Christ as High Priest has opened a way into the holiest, i.e., into complete unbroken fellowship in the immediate presence of God. We are urged to avail ourselves of our full privilege in Christ, but with the prior qualifications of having "our hearts sprinkled clean from an evil conscience and our bodies washed with pure water" (Heb. 10:

---

36. *They Found the Secret* (Grand Rapids, Mich.: Zondervan Publishing House, 1968), p. 154.

22)—clear references to the preparatory exercises at the entry of the first sanctuary which symbolized regeneration.[37]

James also indicates the distinction between the cleansing of the hands which sinners are commanded to do through repentance and faith, and the purification of the heart which is a challenge to the "double-minded" (*dipsuchoi,* 4:8).

Many have seen in 1 John 1:5-10 a duality of need and a duality of provision. There is forgiveness and initial cleansing from acquired depravity, based on confession (v. 9); and there is also thorough and continuous cleansing from inner sinfulness, subject to continuous walking in the light.[38]

All of these indications of twofoldness match perfectly our Lord's fundamental commission to Paul to preach a gospel that would result in receiving the forgiveness of sins and "a place among those who are sanctified" (Acts 26:18).

E. The Challenge of the Imperative

Challenges to specific crisis action, by which believers are to bring their spiritual state up to par, are found in Rom. 6:13, 19; 12:1-2; 13:14; 2 Cor. 7:1; Eph. 4:31; 5:8 ff.; Col. 3:5, 10; 2 Tim. 2:21; Heb. 6:1; Jas. 4:8; *et al.*

The significance of the imperative mood in Pauline literature is pointed out by both Richard E. Howard and Rob L. Staples. Howard says: "The indicative mood depicts a simple assertion, in past, present, or future time—this is, was or shall be. The imperative mood depicts a commanding assertion—this must be."[39] Building on this principle, Staples comments:

> In his letters, Paul is writing to believers. When he speaks of what his converts "were" or "are" (even "shall be") it is the indicative; when he tells them what they "must do or be" it is the imperative. Moreover, the imperative is based on the indicative. Because of the indicative, Paul could command the imperative; because of what they were, he could point them to what they must be and do.

Applying this principle to Romans 6, Staples continues:

> These two crises depicted by the indicative and the imperative may be called (1) self-emancipation and (2) self-presentation —terms which are both psychological and Pauline. In the first crisis, the self is set free from the old life of sin; in the second this

37. See Wiley, *Epistle to the Hebrews,* pp. 338 ff.
38. For elaboration, see W. T. Purkiser, *Sanctification and Its Synonyms,* pp. 45-46.
39. "Galatians," *BBC,* 9:23; cf. pp. 90, 93, 111.

free self is presented (i.e. committed, dedicated, consecrated) to
God in a decisive act "resulting in sanctification" (v. 19).[40]

VI. Summary and Conclusions

It is the ministry of the Holy Spirit to translate the provisions of
Christ into personal experience. These provisions include both regeneration and entire sanctification, as well as subsequent guidance
and discipline. There is adequate basis in the New Testament for
linking together entire sanctification and the baptism with the Holy
Spirit. This baptism is distinct from and subsequent to the birth of
the Spirit.

The normal relationship of the believer is unhindered fellowship with God in Christ through the fullness of the Holy Spirit as
Comforter. However, the Spirit's inward presence is not a fusion of
two beings into one in a metaphysical sense. The human ego is
cleansed and empowered but not overridden or destroyed.

The New Testament evidence for two works of grace in the
divine plan, though not found in dogmatic form, is adequate for the
development of such a doctrine. As Rob Staples says, the "structure"
as well as the "substance" of sanctification "can be found in the Scriptures—providing we approach the Scriptures with an understanding
of what it is we are seeking there."[41] By this he means, not isolated
"proof texts," but the kinds of evidence appropriate to the nature of
the documents.

The New Testament will not support a theology of salvation
that abstracts the ministry of the Spirit *in* the believer from the objective work of Christ *for* the believer. Nor will it support a "declarative
grace" that brings justification independently of the success or failure
of the Holy Spirit in His ministration of "operative grace"—the grace
that brings life and sanctification.

The true New Testament doctrine is that the salvation provided
by Christ is dispensed "through sanctification by the Spirit" (2 Thess.
2:13; 1 Pet. 1:2) and is ultimately unrealizable otherwise. The saving
offices of Christ and the Spirit are interlocked and interdependent.

---

40. "Sanctification and Selfhood: A Phenomenological Analysis of the Wesleyan
Message," *Wesleyan Theological Journal,* vol. 7, no. 1, spring, 1972, p. 3. For elaboration,
see Richard E. Howard, *Newness of Life* (Kansas City: Beacon Hill Press of Kansas City,
1975).
41. *Ibid.,* p. 13.

We cannot expect Christ's benefits without the Spirit's regenerating and sanctifying power. The Spirit is as essentially involved in our final and eternal salvation as is Christ the Son. To permit a theology that implies a dichotomy is a landmark error—but one which underlies vast systems of doctrine in our day.

Section Five

The Life of a Saved People

28

Toward Christian Maturity

It was in Antioch that "the disciples were for the first time called Christians" (Acts 11:26). Here Barnabas exhibited the instinctive sense of responsibility toward new converts that gripped the Early Church, exhorting "them all to remain faithful to the Lord with steadfast purpose" (v. 23). Babes were not abandoned; they were nurtured. Their growth and final salvation were never taken for granted (Acts 8:14 ff.; 13:43; 15:36).

But what is evident in Acts becomes dominant in the Epistles. All of the letters are directed to Christians and clearly have as their aim precisely what Paul specifies as the function of "all scripture." The Epistles were designed to be not only "profitable for teaching" but also for "reproof, for correction, and for training in righteousness, that the man of God may be complete, equipped for every good work" (2 Tim. 3:16-17).

What happens after the crisis experiences of salvation is clearly therefore of major importance in the New Testament perspective.

Two burdens run parallel. One is that a vital and growing relationship with the Lord be maintained; the other, that the Christian's relationship with his fellows be exemplary. The first we may call Christian devotion; and the second, Christian ethics.

The mature Christian is one who has attained to a high degree of stability and credibility in both areas. This chapter will be devoted primarily to the progress of the soul—without implying that this can be a real experience apart from simultaneous and corresponding attention to ethics. Using Micah's trilogy (6:8) we will consider the last first: "to walk humbly with your God." Only by so walking can the "salt of the earth" retain its "saltness" (Matt. 5:13).

I. THE RESPONSIBILITY OF THE BELIEVER

While the Early Church leaders carried a heavy sense of responsibility toward converts, it was no stronger than the sense of responsibility urged upon the believer himself. "But grow in the grace and knowledge of our Lord and Savior Jesus Christ" was Peter's final command (2 Pet. 3:18), an injunction epitomizing the viewpoint of the New Testament. Apparently growth is not inevitable or automatic. Growing is what the believer does by choice (cf. 2 Pet. 1:5-10). While the grace available is so adequate that dismay is never justified, it is not so overwhelming as to justify trifling or presumption. For "how shall we escape if we neglect such a great salvation?" is the unanswerable challenge to those among the Hebrews who already had tasted salvation's power (2:1-4; cf. 3:12-14; 5:12—6:12; 10:26-29, 35-39; 12:1-17).

While we must guard against a humanistic self-reliance by remembering that we "by God's power are guarded" (1 Pet. 1:5), we must not fail to add what the Bible adds: "through faith." Jude strikes the balance by saying, "Now to him who is able to keep you from falling" *after first* commanding, ". . . keep yourselves in the love of God" (24, 21). John says, "Look to yourselves, that you may not lose what you have worked for, but may win a full reward" (2 John 8). Paul insists that while "God is at work" in us "both to will and to work for his good pleasure," our task is to "work out" our own "salvation with fear and trembling" (Phil. 2:12-13). "This exhortation," says A. T. Robertson, "assumes human free agency in carrying on the work of one's salvation."[1] And the same apostle who is sure that

---

1. *Word Pictures*, 4:446.

Christ "is able to guard until that Day what" He has "entrusted to me" admonishes Timothy, almost in the next sentence, "Guard the truth that has been entrusted to you by the Holy Spirit" (2 Tim. 1:12, 14; cf. Heb. 2:1; Jas. 1:25).

Perhaps the most frequent and urgent admonitions are given by Jesus himself. The imperative "Take heed" is found no less than 12 times in His sayings, exclusive of parallels. And when "many believed in him" following one of His controversial discourses, He said to them simply: "If you continue in my word, you are truly my disciples" (John 8:30-31). There is no way to minimize or escape the total and consistent New Testament teaching on the importance of going forward in the Christian life; nor that this essential progress is squarely up to the believer (cf. Eph. 2:10).[2]

II. The Province of Growth

It has been apparent that some deficiencies in the Christian are unacceptable and are therefore to be corrected immediately, by confession, self-cleansing, consecration, prayer, and faith. No allowance is made or license given to love God with less than our whole being at any moment, or to love our brother less than ourselves, or to be walking behind light, or to fail to be spiritually minded. Nor are worldly-mindedness and lukewarmness treated as innocent weaknesses which the Christian is exhorted to overcome gradually.[3]

---

2. When a Christian worker builds with "wood, hay, and stubble," yet *on Christ* as the Foundation, his salvation is not forfeited, only his work (1 Cor. 3:10-15). But when a believer has reverted to overt sinning, the final salvation of his spirit is in jeopardy (1 Cor. 5:1-5). The Epistle to the Galatians groans with an agonizing distress in Paul which reflects a real fear for their ultimate salvation (2:15-21; 3:1-4; 4:8-9, 19-20; 5:1-4, 7, 15, 16-26; 6:1-8). Timothy is urged: "Take heed to your teaching; hold to that, for by so doing you will save both yourself and your hearers" (1 Tim. 4:16; cf. 2 Cor. 7:10; Phil. 2:12; Col. 1:22-23; Jas. 1:21-22; 2:14; 5:20; 1 Pet. 4:18).

3. Indeed the immediate privileges, to which believers are urged at once, are staggering. Paul travails that Christ be "formed" in them (Gal. 4:19); he expects that the crucifixion of the flesh to which they are committed be a subjective reality (Gal. 5:24); that they be identifiable as "spiritual" (Gal. 6:1); as "perfect" in the sense of total commitment (2 Cor. 13:9, 11, KJV); that the mind of Christ be established in them as their governing motivation (Phil. 2:5); that Christ dwell in their hearts by faith through the strengthening of the Spirit's dynamic power (Eph. 3:16); that they be thoroughly renewed in the spirit of their minds (Rom. 12:2; Eph. 4:23); that they exhibit the fervency in good works which marks the redeemed and purified (Titus 2:14); that they know the perfect love which flows from a pure heart and a good conscience and faith unfeigned (1 Tim. 1:5). Here is the norm, not the far-off goal. It is from this base that growth proceeds.

Yet the New Testament has much to say about progress in the Christian life. What are the areas which are legitimately matters of growth and development but that require time and process? It is important that we "rightly divide" here, lest we confuse the two categories and suppose that some facets of Christian deficiency that God designs to correct crucially are proper subjects of growth, or that areas properly in the sphere of growth are to be struggled over under the illusion that they are subject to instant correction.

The matter is clearly expressed by Donald S. Metz:

> The Corinthians had accepted the gospel as a new and revolutionary way of life. Yet many problems persisted in the church. In the Christian life some problems, such as actual sins and transgressions, are solved in the new birth (1 John 3:8-9). Other problems, such as carnal affections and attitudes, are solved by the cleansing power of the Holy Spirit in the crisis of entire sanctification (1 Cor. 3:3; 2 Cor. 7:1; Eph. 5:25-26). Other problems not related to sin or to the carnal mind are solved by spiritual maturity, growth in grace, and enlarged understanding. The problems of the church at Corinth were due primarily to the carnal mind, although some, such as the problem of marriage and celibacy, may have been due to lack of understanding.[4]

It is important therefore that we give careful attention to passages that plainly mark out the areas which belong to the sphere of progress and growth.

A. Christlikeness of Personality

While a holy man is Christ-centered, and while his Christian witness is not tarnished by sinning, he is only relatively Christlike in total personality. There may be many crudities and blunderings, even ill-advised reactions, which on the surface do not remind others of Jesus.

The veil of spiritual blindness that lies over the heart of unbelievers has been removed. Paul writes: "We all, with unveiled face, beholding the glory of the Lord, are being changed into his likeness from one degree of glory to another; for this comes from the Lord who is the Spirit" (2 Cor. 3:18). The image of Christ is the important lodestar. The general meaning of "image" *(eikon)* is visible, recognizable likeness to or of an original, perhaps now invisible (cf. Matt. 22:20; Rom. 1:23; 1 Cor. 11:7; 15:49, *et al.*). The inner likeness or conformity *(summorphous)* to this image is the predetermined goal of the divine calling (Rom. 8:29).

---

4. *BBC,* 8:313.

The inner conformation is essentially ours through regeneration and sanctification, fitting us for eternal exhibition of triumph when Christ stands as "the first-born among many brethren" (Rom. 8:29; cf. Heb. 2:11). But the *metamorphosis,* the complete transformation of character, includes the translation of the inner conformity into outward personality, and in this respect is a gradual process.⁵ We are to take on Christlikeness "from glory to glory," or from one degree of visible resemblance to another. A high degree must have been recognizable in the personality and face of Commissioner Samuel Brengle when after a visit to the home a little girl said to her mother, "Would Jesus have looked like Brother Brengle if he had lived to be 75?"

The import of the present tense in Rom. 12:2 might be debatable. There we are dealing not with a simple statement of fact, as in Corinthians, but a command, which seems to be the counterpart of "Do not be conformed to this world." This too is present tense, but the sense of crisic immediacy is obvious.⁶ If, however, the transformation of Romans is to be given a progressive sense (as is clearly the import of the Corinthian reference), then we may understand the "renewing of your mind" to constitute the inner change immediately possible and obligatory. The transformation would be the external change in life-style, taking shape increasingly, as new light comes; yet the *pattern* of conformity with the world is to stop at once. The renewing of the mind is brought about by the sanctifying of the Holy Spirit (Titus 3:5; cf. Eph. 4:23); but a truly renewed mind will gladly stop any remaining worldly conformity and will progressively translate its own thorough renewal into whatever outward changes are consonant with it (cf. Phil. 2:12). The result of such progress will be a growing recognizability of Christlikeness.

B. Acquiring Maturity

The function of the special ministries within the Church, Paul says, is "for the equipment of the saints,⁷ for the work of ministry, for building up the body of Christ" (Eph. 4:12). The goal of this edifying is

---

5. Only the verb form is in the New Testament, Matt. 17:2; Mark 9:2; Rom. 12:2; this passage. The punctiliar sense of the aorist tense respecting the transfiguration of Jesus is obvious from the event; here the tense is present, hence "our being transformed." But in either case the emphasis is on the visible, recognizable likeness.

6. See Robertson, *Word Pictures,* "Stop being fashioned"; cf. NIV, "Do not conform any longer." No license is given to stop gradually over a long period of time.

7. *Hagioi,* "holy ones," a general designation for all believers, similar to "Christian."

mature manhood in spiritual things, a maturity which is defined as a "measure of the stature of the fullness of Christ" (Eph. 4:13). The "equipment" *(katartismos)* includes as a presupposition whatever *mending* is necessary, the possible nature of which is suggested elsewhere in the Epistle (1:18 ff.; 3:13 ff.; 4:1-3, 20-32; 5:15-21, 25-27). This mending may be either internal (sanctification) or external (manner of walk, ethics). But the "perfecting" (KJV) does not stop with complete and satisfactory spiritual adjustment. It includes that nurturing and training which leads to two indispensable marks of maturity: *doctrinal stability* and *smooth functioning* in the Body. Both ideas are interwoven here and are interdependent. This kind of progress occurs only as the Christian learns to combine verbal fidelity to the truth with love (v. 15).[8]

III. MARKS OF MATURITY

From one standpoint maturity is open-ended, therefore difficult to define. Even relatively mature Christians are still growing. Self-satisfaction with one's attainments is fatal. Yet when John addressed all as "little children," then subdivided into young men and fathers (1 John 2:12-14), he must have had in mind categories that were recognizable.[9]

Christian perfection as holiness, or a sanctified frame of mind, is the disposition to count all things but loss for Christ, and to "press on in order" to lay hold of the ultimate goal (Phil. 3:7-16, NASB). This is the foundation. But what are the marks of Christian perfection conceived as *maturity?* Doctrinal stability and adjustment within the body of Christ have already been noted. But there are other marks.

A. Contentment

Paul's own testimony furnishes the main clues. In spite of imprisonment and impoverishment he says: ". . . I have learned, in whatever state I am, to be content" (Phil. 4:11). This is not the contentment of indifference or of vegetation, which neither desires nor prays for change. It is rather a sanctified self-sufficiency, which has

---

8. A Christian who is out of joint, and hence fails to achieve that harmony which belongs to the "proper working of each individual part," needs yet a lot of "perfecting," if not crisically by purging, at least by much discipline and instruction.

9. For further discussion see Harvey J. S. Blaney, *BBC* 10:367 ff.

inner resources in Christ for the hour of adversity.[10] Yet this level of unflappable composure is in part the acquirement of years of "learning experience." While such learning is a process, often painfully slow, the constative aorist tense here would suggest that Paul has learned his lesson well. It does not have to be relearned every'time something goes wrong. Emotional stability is a mark of Christian maturity.

B. Discernment

There are several facets of Christian discernment.

1. One is mature perception of doctrinal truth in distinction from error (Eph. 4:14; Heb. 5:11-14). The mature Christian is not easily fooled. This insight into truth also extends to ethical issues (Eph. 5:11-17).

2. Another important facet is a discernment of true spirituality. To inculcate a proper concept of spirituality could almost be said to be the whole of Paul's burden in both Corinthian letters. The Corinthians measured spirituality in terms of gifts, the showier and more spectacular the better. This, Paul chided, was thinking like children, not like spiritual adults (1 Cor. 14:20). Paul measured spirituality (negatively) in terms of freedom from carnal traits (1 Cor. 3:1 ff.), and (positively) in terms of perfect love (1 Corinthians 13), which fosters stability, faithfulness, and patience.[11]

Paul reminds the shallow Corinthians that he had "visions and revelations" which put all their gifts in the shade. But he refuses to glory in these lofty experiences; instead he says, "I will all the more gladly boast of my weaknesses, that the power of Christ may rest upon me" (2 Cor. 12:9). What power? To perform miracles? No, the power to be victorious over thorns. Superficial Christians would have measured Paul's spirituality by whether or not he received healing. True spirituality perceives that the greater miracle is not deliverance from the thorn but deliverance from preoccupation with it. True spirituality is exhibited in that pure devotion to Jesus which gladly accepts the grace rather than the miracle, the moment one perceives that in this path lies greater glory to the Lord.

3. A yet further aspect of discernment is acquaintance with the

---

10. When Christ is the Center, nothing else can be, neither money, health, nor happy circumstances (2 Tim. 1:7).

11. When Christians become infected by a lust for religious excitement, simple goodness gradually begins to seem tame. The passion for holiness is displaced by a passion for religious fireworks. This quickly degenerates into pseudo-spirituality.

movings and leadings of the Holy Spirit (1 Cor. 2:9-16). Walking "in the Spirit" is the essence of the normal Christian life (Gal. 5:25); but it takes time to learn the art of such walking as will teach a Philip how to recognize the voice of the Spirit when He prompts action (Acts 8:29), and will teach a Paul and Silas the meaning of the Spirit's restraint (Acts 16:6-7). The anointing "by the Holy One" (1 John 2:20, 27; 4:1-3) is through the Spirit, who touches our eyes and gives spiritual insight, generally into truth, sometimes into people (Acts 5: 1-5). As we grow, our sensitivity to the reproof or promptings of the Spirit grows apace (Eph. 4:30; 1 Thess. 5:17).

C. Balance

Peter provides one of the most comprehensive expositions of personal progress in spiritual matters to be found in the New Testament (2 Pet. 1:5-7). His emphasis is on the development of all the essential graces, that the character may become full-orbed.[12] Regenerating and purifying *faith* is the foundation. By faith we escape the "corruption that is in the world because of passion," and by it we are made "partakers of the divine nature" (2 Pet. 1:4). Faith, however, must be supplemented with *aretēn*, which is not "virtue" in the modern sense of the term, but "resolution" (Moffatt). For a believer to become complacent is to prevent all spiritual progress, if indeed any holiness at all can be maintained (cf. Phil. 1:10; 2:12 ff.; 3:13-15).

To our resolution we are to add *knowledge.* We must be intelligent in our zeal, remembering always the peril of "zeal without knowledge." Good religion is made better by the addition of common sense.[13]

Similarly, our knowledge must be supplied with *self-control,* for the man who knows much without applying that knowledge to his own life is self-condemned. Our self-control, if it is to be complete, must be supplemented with *steadfastness,* because the need for discipline is not temporary. We shall not reach a place where we can afford to become flabby or to let down our spiritual and moral guard.

---

12. The translation of *epichorēgēsate* by "add" (KJV) misses the full strength of this aorist imperative. It rather signifies "to supply, furnish, present" (Thayer), and is so translated with slight variations by ASV, Moffatt, and NASB. But Goodspeed, Williams, and NEB, as well as RSV, use the word "supplement," which probably most accurately expresses the idea. The inference is that unless this process of supplementing goes on, the character will become lopsided and perhaps even distorted.

13. Knowing God is primary, but we must also know *about* Him, otherwise we will foolishly misrepresent Him. The same word is used in 2 Pet. 3:18, where we are told to grow in the "knowledge of our Lord and Savior Jesus Christ."

Our *perseverance*, however, must be supplied with *godliness*, i.e., habitual prayerfulness and piety, lest it degenerate into a mere human tenacity and unbending stubbornness. Dogged persistence without warmth or flexibility ceases to be a Christian virtue. On the other hand, our prayerfulness and piety must be supplemented by *brotherly kindness*, which in this case is a true liking for people, a fraternal sociability essential to happy human relations. This sociability must at the same time avoid unseemly levity or frivolity which would breed compromise and grieve the Spirit (cf. Eph. 4:29; 5:4).

But "brotherly kindness" *(philadelphia)* will fall short if it is permitted to stand alone. Sooner or later, natural liking for people will break down, especially when we discover things about them that we do not like, or when we become victims of some rascality. Therefore brotherly love can be perfected and preserved only by a massive infusion of *agape*—Christian love—available through the constant supply of the indwelling Holy Spirit. Such love transcends the natural dimensions. Going far beyond the joys of congeniality, it actively seeks the welfare of others, even when at times congeniality must give way to pain (cf. Col. 3:12-14).

"For if these qualities are yours and are increasing, they render you neither useless nor unfruitful in the true knowledge of our Lord Jesus Christ" (2 Pet. 1:8, NASB). In the light of the extreme gravity of the issues at stake, according to vv. 1-11, the word increasing should be underscored. It is in these specific qualities of Christian character, and particularly in the symmetry of their development in relation to each other, that we find the marks of growth and maturity (cf. Gal. 5:22-23; Phil. 4:8; Col. 3:12-16).

IV. Growth Through Prayer

If we are to "grow in grace," how are we to go about it? According to Jude we keep ourselves "in the love of God" by building ourselves up on our "most holy faith, praying in the Holy Ghost," and "looking for the mercy of our Lord Jesus Christ unto eternal life" (vv. 20-21, KJV). Here is deliberate self-development, combined with a specific kind of praying and a maintained attitude of expectancy. Titus also combines this expectancy with holy living. The "grace of God" teaches us that we should "live sober, upright, and godly lives in this world, awaiting our blessed hope, the appearing of the glory of our great God and Savior, Jesus Christ" (2:12-13). The upward look is a stance of eager anticipation combined with sober awareness of present obligation.[14]

A. The Meaning of Prayer

There seems to be no attempt in the Bible to defend the validity of prayer, any more than to prove the existence of God. Nor is there an attempt to expound systematically a theology of prayer. Praying is assumed to be a normal activity of believers. In His instructions Jesus did not say, "If you pray," but "When you pray."

One fundamental concept underlies whatever else is taught: Prayer is communion with a Person. God desires to be to the one who prays a Father, in every way that the word is meaningful at its highest and best. What could be more natural, or need less defense, than a child talking to his father! Whatever form of prayer may be in view—supplication, intercession, or praise and adoration; public or private—this assumption of a person-to-Person communion is never absent. No priestly proxies or mechanical aids, such as prayer wheels or ringing of bells, so characteristic of other religions, can be found in biblical Christianity (cf. Matt. 6:7). This means, of course, that prayer is much more than wishful daydreaming or even vague aspiration; it is the deliberate and conscious directing of our thoughts or words to God.

But while prayer is viewed as entirely natural, it is also easily neglected, and therefore frequently urged upon believers as a duty. Jesus told "a parable, to the effect that they ought always to pray and not to lose heart" (Luke 18:1). The peril of losing heart may arise out of physical weariness (Mark 14:38), worldly distractions (Luke 21:34-36), or more commonly because of apparent failure or mysterious delays in answers to prayer (Luke 18:7-8). In spite of the assurance that God cares and will answer, Jesus wonders: "Nevertheless, when the Son of man comes, will he find faith on earth?"[15]

---

14. The daily duties therefore are to be performed always in the light of the Second Coming. "Who then is the faithful and wise servant," Jesus asks, "whom his master has set over his household . . . ? Blessed is that servant whom his master when he comes will find so doing" (Matt. 24:45-46). It was because the one-talent steward forgot the day of accounting, and his responsibilities at hand in the light of that day, that he was rebuked so scathingly and cast into "outer darkness" (Matt. 25:24-30).

15. The faith which is in doubt is primarily a vital faith in a God who answers prayer. A Church that has lost confidence in prayer as a key to the supernatural is a Laodicean church (Rev. 3:14-21).

B. Prayer Principles Taught by Jesus

The gist of our Lord's instructions to His disciples concerning prayer can be briefly summarized.

1. The sanctity of prayer as a private affair between us and God must be preserved by the shut door (Matt. 6:1-5); yet this must not be pressed to the unwarranted conclusion that only private prayer is acceptable (Matt. 21:13; Acts 1:14; 13:2-3; 16:13, *et al.*). Jesus is simply enforcing the necessity of pure motives. Prayer must never be prostituted into a means of cheap religious display.

2. Prayer should not be a matter of strained or loud wordiness, as if God were either deaf, asleep, or indifferent; "for your Father knows what you need before you ask him" (Matt. 6:7-8).

3. The approach should be simple and direct. Both the order of our approach and a list of items that are always proper to pray about are given in the Pattern Prayer (Matt. 6:9-13).[16]

According to this pattern, a proper approach to God should be worship, intercession, and petition, in that order. As for petition, it is always legitimate to ask for daily needs, forgiveness, and deliverance from evil.[17]

4. In our asking, seeking, and knocking, we should credit God with already having the desire, as a true Father, to "give good things to those who ask him!" (Matt. 7:7-11; Luke 11:9-13). It is apparent that our prayer life will be meaningful and satisfying only if our concept of God is biblical.

5. There is compounded certainty in *corporate* praying: ". . . if two of you agree on earth about anything they ask, it will be done for them . . ." (Matt. 18:19-20). The presupposition is that they are in harmony with the living Lord in their midst (v. 20) and that the agreement is Spirit-inspired conviction rather than mere human willfulness.

6. For prayer to be successful, it must be backed by steadfast, unwavering faith (Matt. 21:22; Mark 11:24).

7. Prayer to the Father must be in the name of Jesus (John 14:

---

16. The clause "For thine is the kingdom, and the power, and the glory, forever. Amen" is not in the earliest manuscripts, though no reasonable objection can be raised to its use.

17. This prayer was not intended to be formalized and repeated by rote as the daily prayer of Christians; nor is any doctrine of daily sinning and daily repenting to be construed from it. It was given by Jesus to illustrate the simplicity of prayer in contrast to the meaningless emotional jargon of the heathen, and to suggest the proper order of approach and the proper areas of subject matter.

13-14; 16:23-24). This means approaching God in full awareness of the mediatorship of the Son and of the free access opened by the Son. It implies an abandonment of any conceit that we are worthy to approach a holy God on our own merits. It also means coming in harmony with the *character* of the Son—always implied by *name,* in biblical usage. We thus avoid petitions that are "out of character." Finally, it means coming in dependence upon the *authority* of the Son. Merely to append "in Jesus' name" at the end of every prayer is not, in itself, what Jesus is talking about.

8. In close connection with the proper use of the Name is the idea of *abiding* as a prerequisite for successful praying: "If you abide in me, and my words abide in you, ask whatever you will, and it shall be done for you" (John 15:7). If there is spiritual union with Christ, there will be compatibility in the nature of our petitions.

Jesus also made it perfectly clear that some things thwart prayer: particularly an unforgiving spirit (Matt. 6:15), a wrong motive (6:5), a lack of persistence (Luke 11:5-13), a spirit of self-righteousness (Luke 18:10-14), a lack of obedience (Matt. 7:22), and a dislocated relationship with a brother which we are making no honest effort to mend (Matt. 5:23-24).

C. The Spirit and Prayer

In the *teachings of the Early Church* on prayer a significant new emphasis is introduced: the aid of the Holy Spirit. Jude speaks of praying "in the Holy Spirit," and Paul also insists that "all prayer and supplication" must "at all times" be "in the Spirit" (Eph. 6:18). It is by means of the Spirit that Christ fulfills His promise to be with us; and the peculiar office of the Spirit is to carry forward the tutelage begun by Jesus in response to the disciples' request, "Lord, teach us to pray." The Holy Spirit prompts us to prayer and directs us in our petitions. But even more, He "intercedes for us with sighs too deep for words" in those times when we feel the prayer urge but "do not know how to pray as we ought" (Rom. 8:26-27). Thus the Spirit supplies the divine dimension to our prayer life and saves it from becoming a barren, humanistic self-psychology.

To pray "in the Spirit" requires spiritual, mental, and emotional harmony with the Spirit. To this end Paul exhorts us to "keep alert" (Eph. 6:18). This relationship with the Spirit is delicate, and many things can impair it, such as unholy hands, wrath, and dissension (1 Tim. 2:8), or even domestic harshness (1 Pet. 3:7). One object of prayer is to keep us from sin; and, conversely, obstinate sin will keep us from prayer.

The relationship of prayer to the Spirit-filled life is exemplified in Acts. Instead of the inward fullness of the Spirit diminishing the disciples' sense of the need for prayer, it greatly increased it. So obvious is this that we can say categorically: A spiritual church, truly apostolic, is a praying church. It was through prayer that the 120 became ready for the outpouring of the Spirit on the Day of Pentecost (Acts 1:14). After Pentecost the believers "devoted themselves to the apostles' teaching . . . and the prayers" (2:42). It was because Peter and John were faithful to "the hour of prayer" that they had occasion to offer healing to the lame man at the gate of the Temple (3:1 ff.). Prayer was their spontaneous resort and refuge when threatened with persecution (4:24 ff.). It was their keen awareness of the priority of prayer, and their fear of being distracted from it, that prompted the apostles to suggest the election of the first board of deacons (6:1-5). The first official missionary advance was born in a prayer meeting (13:1-3). And so throughout the record, everything done in public was undergirded by constant prayer in private.

V. The Milk and Meat of the Word

The apostles refused to become immersed in administrative details, not only because of the priority of prayer, but equally because of the priority "of the word" (Acts 6:4). By this they meant the content of their teaching. It was this content, which Paul elsewhere calls "my gospel," that he has in mind when he testifies to having declared "the whole counsel of God" (Acts 20:27). Then, as a benediction, he commends the little band of Ephesian elders "to God and to the word of his grace which is able to build you up and give you the inheritance among all those who are sanctified" (v. 32).

A. An Instrument of Grace

It is important to notice the close conjunction between God and "the word of his grace." Through this word God acts redemptively. Therefore if believers are to know God deeply and intimately, it will be through the word. Again we are confronted by the believer's responsibility. If it is the task of preachers to expound the word, it is the duty of believers to hear it, to read it, to understand it, and to obey it. This the primitive Church did, from the very start: "And they devoted themselves to the apostles' teaching" (Acts 2:42; cf. 17:11).

Because the word is so indispensable to the ministration of God's grace, Peter's admonition is timelessly urgent: "Long for the pure spiritual milk, that by it you may grow" (1 Pet. 2:2). Clearly, healthy growth depends on healthy appetite but also upon unadulterated truth. The word must not be watered down if "newborn babes" are to thrive.[18]

B. Reasons for Incapacity

Believers are responsible for so assimilating the milk of the word that they can within reasonable time handle strong meat. Before the Day of Pentecost even the Lord had to adjust His teaching for the disciples (John 16:12). But when Pentecost came, they grew years in a day. A similar release had not widely occurred in the Corinthian church. As a result, their infantile incapacity for solid food was needlessly prolonged, justifying a rebuke (1 Cor. 3:1-3). The same arrested development had stunted the Hebrew believers (Heb. 5:12-14). It would appear therefore that failure to understand the deeper truths of Christ (1 Cor. 2:6) is due to *(a)* failure to feed on the milk of the word in the formative days of the Christian life, and *(b)* failure to seek the illuminating fullness of the Spirit. Only then can the new Christian understand the word of Jude concerning building ourselves up on our "most holy faith" (Jude 20).[19]

When combatting Satan in the wilderness, Jesus set an example by wielding the sword of the written Word (Matt. 4:4, 7, 10; cf. Eph. 6:17-18). In this conflict He reaffirmed the principle that must govern all believers: "Man shall not live by bread alone, but by every word that proceeds from the mouth of God" (v. 4; cf. Deut. 8:3). No Christian can be a match for the stratagem of Satan if he knows neither the Word nor how to use it.

C. The Word, Oral and Written

The New Testament places on the believer a responsibility to feed on

---

18. Lit., "logical, unadulterated milk." Spiritual food must involve the activity of the mind, and be undiluted by humanistic sentiment. That which feeds the emotions only will not produce sound growth.

19. The emphasis on the authoritative, revealed word of the gospel found in the primitive Church echoed a corresponding emphasis in the teachings of Jesus. This was the true hearing from the heart for which Jesus constantly pleaded: "He who has ears to hear, let him hear . . ." (Matt. 7:24-27; 11:15; cf. Mark 4:9, 23; 7:16; 8:18; Luke 9:44; 14:35).

the word. This includes regular and frequent listening to apostolic preaching and teaching. However, it must not be supposed that the "word" refers only to speaking. The word, which focuses in Christ and His salvation, is authenticated in the New Testament by constant appeal to the written Scriptures. This is true both of Christ himself and His apostles.[20] The Christ-event is seen as the fulfillment and continuation of the only Bible which believers then had. It is therefore not only a proclamation of the recent salvation acts of God which the apostles define as "the ministry of the word," but always that proclamation in relation to its biblical roots. Believing in Christ did not result in the Old Testament being displaced, but in its being confirmed.

It is also hinted that as the oral word of Christ and the apostles became written, it too was taken as the authentic Word of God, along with the older Scriptures. And why not? If the message preached was the word, why wouldn't the message written be equally authentic? Peter classifies Paul's Epistles along with "the other Scriptures," and declares that distorting these new Scriptures would bring spiritual "destruction" (2 Pet. 3:16; cf. Paul's own claim, 1 Cor. 14:37).[21]

The conclusion is inescapable that if there is to be spiritual growth, there must be immersion in the word, both as *written* and as *spoken;* but that if discrepancy develops between the oral word and the Bible, loyalty to the Bible must prevail (Matt. 22:29).

VI. FUNCTIONING IN THE BODY

A. As Practiced in the Early Church

An invariable and seemingly spontaneous concomitant of being saved, if we are to judge by the Acts, is a joyous sense of oneness with other believers: "And the Lord added to their number day by day those who were being saved" (Acts 2:47).[22] We thus see the nat-

---

20. While Jesus radically corrects the rabbinical accretions and sophistical interpretations, He never corrects the Old Testament Scriptures themselves.
21. It is intriguing to observe that when the phrase "He who has an ear, let him hear" is repeated in Revelation, it is applied to "what the Spirit says to the church." The word to be "heard" was never orally proclaimed at all, as far as we know; it was solely in writing from the outset (Rev. 2:1, 7). Apparently the "hearing" enjoined is a spiritual activity of the soul, whether the message comes through the eye gate or the ear gate.
22. No one formally joined the church, except insofar as baptism was interpreted

ural living out of the relationships implicit in Jesus' metaphor of the Vine and branches. The phenomenon that we see in the Acts is a gravitation to each other around a common center without destroying the integrity of the person. The word *community* is far too feeble to do justice to the intensity and depth of the cohesion. There is a real social, yet *spiritual,* organism into which they are inducted by the Spirit-birth (cf. 1 Cor. 12:13).[23]

The apostles became the center around whom the new lifestyle of the early converts revolved. It was no longer the Sanhedrin, rabbis, or even the synagogue (Acts 2:42; 5:12-13; 6:1-6). Later the phenomenon continued, perhaps to a lesser degree, around the local elders. Another sign of this common church-mindedness was the spontaneous disposition to share. This was manifested not only by a happy socializing from house to house but also by a pooling of material resources (2:44-46; 4:32-35). Yet there is no evidence of pressure or compulsion; this openhandedness was quite voluntary and natural, as if flowing out of a new inner life and love—which indeed it was.

B. As Admonished in the Epistles

Since the centrifugal forces of life are great, and Satan's strategy is to alienate and isolate Christians, the believer must deliberately foster fellowship and group worship. He must be "eager to maintain the unity of the Spirit in the bond of peace" (Eph. 4:30), and carefully consider "how to stir up one another to love and good works." Believers must not neglect "to meet together, as is the habit of some" (Heb. 10:24-25).

The importance of finding one's divinely assigned place in the church and filling it cheerfully and faithfully is clearly outlined in Romans 12, Ephesians 4, and 1 Corinthians 12. While the placement is God's, the fulfillment is the believer's. He can reject, neglect, or

---

as accession; they were being joined together by the Lord as an integral element of their salvation.

23. A significant characteristic of this new family consciousness seems to be an awareness of a radical break with those social and religious units that previously had claimed their loyalties. As early as the Pentecost exhortation, Peter implied that this would be involved: "Save yourselves from this crooked generation!" (2:40). Salvation evidently consisted of an escape from the demonic world order, either Jewish or Gentile, as well as entry into the kingdom of God—a kingdom now concretized by local units of close-knit believers called churches. From the Day of Pentecost forward, conversion to Christ meant this radical and open transference from the polarity of the world to the polarity of the Church.

abuse his function in the church; or he can recognize this opportunity for spiritual growth. He can accept it, improve it, and faithfully use it. This is clearly the import of these passages. Whatever one's gifts for ministry in the church may be, their purpose can be fulfilled only if the Lord's work is done not in rivalry and vainglory, but in love, the "more excellent way" (1 Cor. 12:31). A spiritually diseased member of the body may infect and disrupt the whole (cf. Heb. 12:15).[24]

The same teaching is found in Paul's metaphor of the Church as a temple. The foundation, Christ, is already laid by the apostles; but "let each man take care how he builds upon it" (1 Cor. 3:10-17). A worker's knowledge of the message may be wood instead of gold; his judgment may be hay instead of silver; his methods may be stubble instead of precious stones. No matter how loyal a man is to Christ, the superstructure he builds may not endure the flames of divine judgment. An honest bungler may himself be saved. However, if his spirit is so bad that he actually destroys God's temple, "God will destroy him" (v. 17). As A. T. Robertson puts it: "The church-wrecker God will wreck."[25]

C. By the Exercise of Faith

The nature of saving faith has been discussed earlier (in Chapter 23). However, "faith" *(pistis)* is used in ways related to our usefulness in the Church. We may speak of these ways as faith *of* God, faith *with* God, and faith *for* God.

1. The Early Church used *pistis* to describe the faith that a sinner exercises toward Christ for his salvation. In the post-Pentecost era, she therefore began to think of "the faith" as the body of truth that was to be believed. This is frequent in the Acts, as, for example, the statement that "a great many of the priests were obedient to the faith" (6:7; cf. 13:8; 14:22; 16:5; 24:24).

The phrase here includes not only an espoused creed but a personal commitment to the new way of life. When Jude many years later appeals to Christians to "contend for the faith which was once for all delivered to the saints" (v. 3), he was concerned about the purity of the content of the *kerygma* and *didache*, both doctrine and

24. For a helpful discussion of the gifts, see Charles W. Carter, *The Person and Ministry of the Holy Spirit* (Grand Rapids, Mich.: Baker Book House, 1974), pp. 270-89; and Purkiser, *Gifts of the Spirit.*

25. *Word Pictures,* 4:99.

ethics. A. R. Fausset observes, "No other faith or revelation is to supersede it, a strong argument for resisting heretical innovators (v. 4)."[26] Clearly they were to be constantly on guard against the corruptions and dilutions of heresies, ethical as well as doctrinal (cf. v. 10; Gal. 1:23; Phil. 1:27; 1 Tim. 4:1). The responsibility of Christians *in* the Church includes a responsibility *for* the Church.

2. There is also faith *with* God. When Paul in his final imprisonment triumphantly testifies, "I have kept the faith" (2 Tim. 4:7), he is saying, according to A. T. Robertson, "He has kept the faith with Christ."[27] This is that Christian integrity or faithfulness that is one of the fruits of the Spirit (Gal. 5:22). Without this personal faith, an intellectual adherence to a system of doctrine is no better than the faith of demons (Jas. 2:19; cf. Rom. 16:26; 2 Cor. 13:5; 1 Tim. 1:5, 18-20; 3:9; 5:12; 2 Tim. 3:8, 10). Our adherence to creeds must not become a dead formality that hides a disloyal heart.

3. Faith is not only the key that unlocks saving grace but also the condition for *achievement* in the work of God. In the presence of the demon-possessed child, the disciples asked Jesus, "Why could we not cast it out?" Jesus answered, "Because of your little faith" (Matt. 17:19-20). He then announced the famous principle: "If you have faith as a grain of mustard seed, you will say to this mountain, 'Move hence to yonder place,' and it will move; and nothing will be impossible to you" (Matt. 17:20). We assume that this "mountain" is symbolic of whatever obstacles need to be removed in order to accomplish God's will.

Much that follows in New Testament history demonstrates the validity of this faith principle. It was by this kind of faith that the Old Testament warriors "conquered kingdoms . . . stopped the mouths of lions, quenched raging fire, escaped the edge of the sword, won strength out of weakness, became mighty in war" (Heb. 11:33 ff.). Such faith is one of the "gifts" of the Spirit (1 Cor. 12:9; cf. Jas. 5:15). Paul may have had such achieving faith in mind when in writing to the Thessalonians he recalls their "work of faith and labor of love" (1 Thess. 1:3).

This kind of faith—faith *for* the work of God—is illustrated by Noah who, "being warned by God concerning events as yet unseen, took heed and constructed an ark for the saving of his household"

---

26. Robert Jamieson, A. R. Fausset, David Brown, *A Commentary on the Old and New Testaments* (Hartford: S. S. Scranton & Co., n.d.), 2:543.

27. *Word Pictures*, 4:631.

(Heb. 11:7). What is here called an act of faith is simply an act of obedience to a clear and distinct direction of God. Achieving faith is not man taking the initiative; it is man responding to God's initiative.

When Jesus instructed Simon to put "out into the deep and let down your nets for a catch," Simon answered, "Master, we toiled all night and took nothing! But at your word I will let down the nets" (Luke 5:5). Peter was perhaps not very aware of "achieving faith," but he was aware of a direct command and he responded with obedience. This kind of faith always accomplishes things for God (cf. Acts 6:5; 11:24).

29

Toward Exemplary Living

In the New Testament view of life a believer's personal spiritual growth cannot occur in isolation from his daily walk. The word *peripateō*, "to walk around," is used in the Epistles 34 times in direct reference to the Christian's behavior. There is a uniform insistence that the outward life must match the inward grace. Believers must live not only *as* Christians but *like* Christians. Failure to translate religious experience into ethical living is considered by the New Testament writers as evidence of a spurious faith. Paul and John, for example, give us such admonitions as: "Let every one who names the name of the Lord depart from iniquity" (2 Tim. 2:10; cf. Matt. 7:23), and "He who says he abides in him ought to walk in the same way in which he walked" (1 John 2:6). Eric Sauer writes: "If we are now the royal children of the Most High, then we are under obligation to walk royally."[1]

Approximately one-third of all the sayings of Jesus found in the Gospels relate to Christian behavior. The fullest ethical statement is undoubtedly the Sermon on the Mount, but there are many other passages that enlarge and apply its basic principles. In the Epistles, fully half of the material concerns practical instruction in righteousness. It is true that most of the pronouncements express principles rather than "rules of thumb," but there are enough applications to specific situations confronting the Early Church to provide guidelines for Christians of every generation.

---

1. *The King of the Earth*, p. 188.

I. PRINCIPLES OF ETHICAL TEACHING

A. Sources of Authority

The assumption of the New Testament is that God's self-revelation in Christ constitutes the rule of life for the believer (Heb. 1:1-3; 2:1-3). We are not inducted into a democracy but into a kingdom, an "absolute monarchy" (Luke 6:46; Acts 1:3). The biblical ethic therefore is an authority ethic. In no sense is the Christian a law unto himself. Paul said that as an evangelist he could identify with Gentiles outside the sphere of Hebrew law, but this did not mean that he was without "law toward God"; rather he was "under the law of Christ" (1 Cor. 9:21).[2]

While the ultimate Authority is God, the Early Church saw four divinely ordained mediums of His authority in determining what constituted Christian behavior.

1. *The Bible.*

First was the Old Testament Scripture, which Jesus claimed as His support (Matt. 21:12 ff.; 15:1-9; Mark 12:24; Luke 19:45 ff.). Paul, the apostle who most vigorously sought to cut the umbilical cord of Judaism, nevertheless appealed to the Scriptures when settling ethical issues (cf. Rom. 12:19). No one saw more clearly than Paul that the basic moral standards governing the Israelites and the standards governing the Church were essentially the same. When listing the works of the flesh that would keep one out of the Kingdom (Gal. 5:19-21), he listed forms of behavior prohibited directly or indirectly in the Old Testament (cf. also Peter's appeal to Ps. 34:12-15 in 1 Pet. 3:10 ff.).

2. *Jesus.*

The supreme Source of authority was Jesus himself. His example was considered ethically definitive (1 Pet. 2:21-24). But also His sayings were a final court of appeal. The Gospels themselves witnessed to this authority of Jesus, both as external evidence and by internal testimony (cf. Matt. 7:29).

3. *The Holy Spirit.*

The third Source of authority was the Holy Spirit, as He guided

---

2. Every moral agent in the universe is properly under the authority of God the Creator. The very essence of sin is the rejection of this authority—or even irritation with it. The carnal mind is at enmity with God precisely because of God's unbending claim over the totality of life (Rom. 8:7).

the apostles and early writers. Jesus promised this guidance (John 14:26; 16:8-15). The "all truth" into which the "Spirit of truth" would guide them most certainly included ethics as well as soteriology and Christology. An example of this aid was the decision made in Jerusalem concerning the rules to be imposed on the Gentile converts: "For it has seemed good to the Holy Spirit and to us to lay upon you no greater burden than these necessary things" (Acts 15:28).

In an important sense the Holy Spirit has proved to be the immediate Authority, inasmuch as it was He who supervised the writing of the New Testament literature and the fixing of the canon. He therefore determined the basic slant of the teachings of the Church by supervising the selection and inclusion of ethical materials. In this way the three Sources of authority for the Early Church merge into one for us: the New Testament.[3]

4. *The Church.*

As the community of the new covenant, the Church is both under authority and possesses authority, and thus the Church becomes a secondary Source of guidance. The authority possessed is given to the Church by her living Lord, and its nature is defined by the Scriptures. That authority is implied in the Great Commission, to "make disciples" not only by baptism but by "teaching them to observe all" that Jesus commanded (Matt. 28:19-20). The early history as recorded in Acts reflects the awareness of this obligation and the faithfulness of the Church in discharging it. This awareness is even more noticeable in the Epistles; indeed in great measure they exercise this authority in ethical matters.[4]

B. The Viewpoint of Christian Ethics

1. *Life a Probation.*

While it may be misleading to speak of the Christian's standard of conduct as an "interim ethic,"[5] it would be appropriate to call it a

---

3. While God's supreme and final self-revelation is in Christ, only in the Scriptures is the factual and conceptual substance of this revelation transmitted to us. See Wiley's discussion, *Christian Theology,* 1:136-42.

4. This is apparent not only in the sheer mass of ethical subjects and admonitions but in specific directives for the discipline of offenders (1 Cor. 5:1-13; 2 Cor. 2:4-11; 10:8-11; 13:1-3; 1 Thess. 5:14; 2 Thess. 3:6-15; *et al.*).

5. As believed by Albert Schweitzer. See article on "Interim Ethics" by George E. Ladd, *Baker's Dictionary of Christian Ethics,* ed. by Carl F. H. Henry (Grand Rapids, Mich.: Baker Book House, 1973), p. 332.

"pilgrim ethic." The viewpoint from which ethical standards are developed is that of the total philosophy of life found in the New Testament. This philosophy sees life on this earth, not as an end in itself, but as a means to an end. Thus the viewpoint is thoroughly eschatological. On virtually every page Christians are taught to look ahead, and live as men who are on probation, destined for the judgment and eternity (Titus 2:11-14).

2. *Life a Stewardship.*

God's ownership and our stewardship are twin presuppositions that govern the whole of New Testament teaching. This viewpoint is so pervasive that documentation would be superfluous. What is right therefore is always determined not only by what is legally permissible, but by what advances the Kingdom. In the biblical view of things, personal liberties which disregard the stewardship of possessions, talents, time, or influence become unethical conduct. It is to be expected therefore that the Christian will be governed by an ethic sharply discordant with the prevailing standards around him.

C. The Basis of Christian Ethics

No man can be right with his fellows who is not right with God. If the vertical relationship is wrong, the horizontal will be also; perhaps not in any external defect, but in the inner spirit which is essential for the relationship to be fully Christian. This prior necessity of a right relationship with God is presupposed in all of the Scriptures that deal with ethical matters. The record of the revival under John the Baptist, characterized by repentance and the remission of sins, comes before the Sermon on the Mount. The Epistles do not launch directly into homilies on practical duties but first lay an evangelical foundation of salvation. This explains the soundness of L. Harold DeWolf's listing of repentance, faith, and obedience as special emphases in the ethics of Jesus.[6] Turning from sin to God in Christ, followed by continuous submission to the rule of God, are indispensable foundation stones for Christian ethics.

D. Love the Motive

Kant was not original in enunciating the principle that for a choice to be moral it must not only be right in itself but must be done in the right spirit and for the right reason. This inner *why* is the constant

---

6. *Responsible Freedom* (New York: Harper and Row, Publishers, 1971), pp. 58 ff.

probing of the New Testament. A murderous spirit makes a murderer, even when there is no overt act (Matt. 5:22; 1 John 3:15). Inner adultery of the will and mind is real adultery in God's sight (Matt. 5:28). Religious acts are of value only as they are performed to please God rather than for show before men (Matt. 6:1-2, 16). Love, and love alone, will give to an act that quality of spirit which is Christian, and provide a motive which is acceptable. A Christian spirit is a loving spirit; and the aim of love is the glory of God and the good of man. Above all, therefore, the Christian ethic is a love ethic (Rom. 13:8-10). Whatever else this may mean, it certainly implies that the inner dynamic of acceptable behavior is our desire to please God and do right. True Christian conduct is not motivated by fear, self-interest, or cultural conditioning.

Love is the "fulfilling of the law," not in the sense that it sets law aside, as being above it. Rather, love fulfills the law by seeking to reach the heart of the law's intent, and thus fulfilling the law from the heart.

E. The Redemptive Principle

Ethics to be Christian must be grounded in the atoning work of Jesus Christ. Only in this way can that unique union of justice and mercy which is the genius of Christian ethics find its rationale. Mercy can be had at the expense of justice, or justice can be had at the expense of mercy; both can be had only at Calvary. It is impossible to develop a Christian ethic in abstraction from the Cross; to attempt to do so is to produce a moralistic system of sentimental platitudes.

The redemptive principle is seen when we begin to read the extras that belong to Christian ethics—putting God and others first, blessing our tormentors, going the second mile, refusing to fight for petty personal rights, modesty and submission, in honor preferring one another, subordinating profits to people, avoiding materialism, having a forgiving spirit.[7] If strict justice alone is the aim, some of these traits and attitudes seem flabby and irresponsible. Is it right to suffer personal injustice and do nothing about it? No—not apart

---

7. That Jesus' unqualified and radical absolutes (Matt. 5:38-42) are not to be taken in complete literalness, should be clear to all who understand the nature of figurative language and who interpret these sayings against the background of Scripture. Jesus' instructions were symbolic of a spirit and a way of life; His followers are not to retaliate, nor habitually to invoke the rigors of the law. They are to react in a nobler way: to return good for evil, to be generous and magnanimous in dealing with the enemy.

from the Cross. It is right, however, when we see that God in Christ has already done something about it.

A forgiving spirit on the basis of the Cross is not weakness. It is, rather, an identification with the offender, as being one equally guilty, but forgiven, facing another who also may be forgiven. The evil deed is never simply being ignored when it is consciously and prayerfully referred to Calvary. All are doomed if ruled by justice alone, and all are in need of mercy. Therefore Christian ethics must be forever pointing men, not to the law for redress, but to an atoning Saviour.

The perfect biblical illustration of the stance appropriate for the Christian is found in Jesus' parable of the unmerciful servant (Matt. 18:23-35). Forgiving the huge debt of 10,000 talents was not costless. In effect, the creditor "forgave" by *paying the debt to himself.* This was what cancellation meant. The creditor himself absorbed the loss.

The ethical principles appropriate to men who stand in this kind of a relationship to God must be like the love that creates an undeserved free atonement. To receive thus so freely from God, and then proceed to be legalistically stringent in our man-ward relationships, is to be ungodlike. If we persist in this attitude, God's mercy is retracted. "And in anger his lord delivered him to the jailers . . . So also my heavenly Father will do to every one of you, if you do not forgive your brother from your heart."

It is important that order be preserved in society, but the Christian is motivated by a higher concern—not simply "law and order" but total redemption. The man who injures another may need to be punished; but the Christian is not preoccupied with that need. Far more, the culprit needs to be set right with God. The Christian will be glad to forego his "pound of flesh" if he can help the offender bury his guilt in the blood of Christ. That will be the true redress and the perfect justice.[8]

II. THE RELATION OF LOVE TO LAW

That love is both the touchstone of Christian ethics and its inner spring is unquestionably the teaching of the New Testament. Much uncertainty has arisen, however, when the attempt has been made to

---

8. This does not cancel the obligation of the state to deal with offenses, nor does it rule out the possibility that at times it may be my Christian duty to cooperate with the state.

expound the exact relationship between love and law. Some have supposed that love completely supersedes law. The counterpart of this is the further misunderstanding that Paul's doctrine of justification by faith implies a salvation "apart from law" (Rom. 3:21) in the sense that the righteousness prescribed by the law is no longer necessary. In this direction is a sort of supranomianism which soon becomes antinomianism.[9]

The issue is sharpened by the watershed declaration: "For the law was given through Moses; grace and truth came through Jesus Christ" (John 1:17). The unfortunate "but" in the KJV has misled many into seeing here an opposition between law on the one hand and grace and truth on the other, as if grace and truth dispensed with the law. Rather the idea is that whereas the standard of holy living was delivered to men through Moses, the ability actually to live this way came through Jesus. Thus Christ's work is an enabling, not a supplanting. Grace is God's way of bringing law and truth together in living experience.

A. Jesus and the Law

In the Sermon on the Mount, Jesus defines the kind of righteousness acceptable (Matt. 5:20-48). His examples drive straight to the heart of the sixth and seventh commandments (and indirectly to the ninth also, vv. 33-37). Acceptable righteousness is much more than the avoidance of overt, legal murder. It can be no less than right attitudes and adjusted relationships right across the board (vv. 21-26). Similar rigorous interpretations are applied to adultery and truthfulness. No hint is given here that Jesus' program called for the least modification of these commandments, to say nothing of their cancellation (cf. Matt. 15:3-9).

Jesus' support of the law is seen even more directly and simply in His declaration of "the great and first commandment": "You shall love the Lord your God with all your heart, and with all your soul, and with all your mind . . . [and the] second is like it, You shall love your neighbor as yourself. On these two commandments depend all the law and the prophets" (Matt. 22:34-40; cf. Mark 12:28-31; Luke 10:25-28).

Four things stand out here: (1) These are commandments, i.e., laws. (2) They are both quoted from the Pentateuch (Deut. 6:5; Lev.

---

9. As suggested in the unfortunate paraphrase "Love is the only law you need" (Rom. 13:10, TLB).

19:18). (3) They constitute not the displacement of the "law and the prophets" but their distilled essence.[10] (4) They are still binding.

B. Jesus and Retributive Justice

The law defined by its broad principles and representative applications the kind of behavior acceptable to God, but it also specified the principles to be followed in dealing with infractions. Jesus deals with this vexing problem as recorded in Matt. 5:38 ff. and 43 ff. The rabbinical gloss had it: "You shall love your neighbor and hate your enemy." The command to love was Mosaic (Lev. 19:18, 33) but not the command to hate. Jesus declared, "But I say to you . . ." As usual, He brushed aside the false interpretation by directing their thoughts to the universality and impartiality of the Father's love. This is the true standard (v. 48).

Then are we to understand Jesus to be completely repudiating the retributive system of justice? It is more in harmony with the overall New Testament teaching to suppose that He is intending two things.

First, Jesus is correcting the abuse of the law. He sets aside as unworthy that spirit of vengeance which had been adopted as a rule of life in personal relations, supposedly with the sanction of Moses. We say "supposedly," because the Mosaic instructions clearly made the administration of the *lex talionis* strictly the responsibility of the judges (Exod. 21:22). The law for the private citizen was "You shall not take vengeance" (Lev. 19:18).[11]

Depriving civil authorities of their duty to impose the law and enforce penalties as needed to carry out the duties of responsible government must not be read into Jesus' teachings. This becomes even clearer when Matt. 5:38-48 is viewed in the light of the retributive principle that still pervades God's moral government over men (Matt. 6:1-4, 14-15; 7:1-2, 22-23; 18:23-35; 25:31-46; Luke 16:19-25; Rom. 11:22; 2 Cor. 5:10; Gal. 6:7-8, *et al.*).

Second, Jesus is introducing the principle that is to govern the reactions of children of the Kingdom toward injuries suffered at the hands of children of the evil one. God's people, whose primary allegiance is now in a different order, must act in the new way, not the

10. What Jesus corrected was the prevailing narrow bigotry in defining "neighbor" as a fellow Jew. This He did by the parable of the Good Samaritan (Luke 10:29-37).

11. An exception was in the case of premeditated murder, Num. 35:11-34.

old way. This higher way is for those who know how to love and are willing to lose some civil rights in their fidelity to a higher allegiance. The whole frame of reference concerns believers (1) acting as private persons, and (2) as living under Kingdom rule. The teaching of this passage from Matthew says nothing about the duties of the state. Officially, at the civil and public level, some system of retribution must still stand, made necessary by the hard reality of defiant sinfulness.

III. UNIVERSAL MANDATES FOR CHRISTIANS

It is apparent that the ethics of Romans 12 and 13 differ from 14 and 15. In 12 and 13 Paul is dealing with universal Christian obligations, mandatory for everyone.[12] No Christian is exempt from a single duty or restraint discussed here. In sharp contrast, the specific problems of chapters 14 and 15 are flexible and unlegislated. Some ethical matters are relative to the time, place, and circumstances, as interpreted by the individual or community conscience. When Scripture does not speak with a clear meaning, its principles must be applied by sanctified common sense. Differences of opinion and practice which remain must be absorbed by mutual love, respect, and tolerance.

Let us note the clear mandates found in Romans 12 and 13.

A. Consecration

The Christian cannot be ethical unless he begins by correcting what is defective or supplying what is missing in his Godward relationship. The presentation of their bodies to God as "a living and holy sacrifice" is urged upon the Roman Christians. This is not as a "counsel of perfection" but as an ethical obligation—"by the mercies of God ... your reasonable service" (v. 1, KJV). It is entirely proper therefore for treatises on Christian ethics to include "duties to God." Not only do His mercies create obligations, but even more fundamentally His eternal sovereignty as Creator and Ruler places responsibilities on us.

The Christian duties of prayer and worship are part of the larger duty of adjusting fully to the claims of total consecration and stewardship. A renewed mind thinks like a Christian instead of like a

---

12. The declaration of some that Galatians is the "Magna Charta of Christian liberty" is a truth frequently perverted into an unbiblical libertarianism. If freedom is misunderstood as a license to indulge the flesh, the consequence will be eternal bondage, because "those who practice such things shall not inherit the Kingdom of God" (Gal. 5:21).

half-Christianized pagan. Such a thorough and deliberate extension of the renewal begun in conversion is the only guarantee of cheerful alacrity in conforming to the ethical admonitions which follow in this passage of Scripture.

B. Separation

The universal mandate "Do not be conformed to this world" (v. 2) demands not only a radical alienation from the spirit of the world, but also a refusal to allow the world to write the fine print of daily standards. The Christian has forgotten who he is if his life-style, appearance, speech, and pastimes bear the obvious impress of non-Christian pacesetters, or anti-Christian subcultures. The Christian with the renewed mind never takes his ethical cue from the crowd, nor does he defend a practice on the ground that "everyone does it." He knows that he is different. His life-style will not hide this difference but reveal it.

C. Responsibility

Every Christian is ethically obligated to be faithful and diligent, both in religious duties and secular. The exercise of gifts is to be "in liberality . . . zeal . . . cheerfulness" (Rom. 12:8). We should not "flag in zeal" but by being "aglow with the Spirit, serve the Lord" (v. 11). Elsewhere: "It is required of stewards that they be found trustworthy" (1 Cor. 4:2); and "Look carefully then how you walk . . . making the most of the time" (Eph. 5:15-16; cf. 2 Cor. 8:11; Eph. 6:5-8; 2 Thess. 3:6-12; 1 Tim. 4:14-16; 1 Pet. 3:13-16, *et al.*). Christians therefore are to live responsibly and industriously in proportion to their ability.

Although there is nothing that would label leisure as wrong, the tone of the New Testament would imply that its misuse would be sin. Fundamentally the Christian ethic is a work ethic. "If any one will not work, let him not eat" is the ultimatum (2 Thess. 3:10; cf. context, vv. 6-15). It is not Christian to be a drone when physical health and mental soundness permit involvement in constructive and productive living. Christians should not rely on social welfare as a voluntary way of life, nor should they permit themselves to drift into a disposition of dependence. On the contrary the New Testament standard is for Christians to be self-reliant, earning enough not only for themselves but for others who are weak (1 Thess. 5:14; cf. Titus 3:8, 14).

D. Sincerity

Every Christian must guard against insincerity. "Let love be genuine" (Rom. 12:9). This genuineness will show itself in hospitality and benevolence (v. 13). It will also be seen in a Christlike spirit to those who wrong us (vv. 14-21; cf. James 2:14-16; 1 John 3:17-18). The sincerity of love is also proved by a spirit of equality. Paul writes: "Live in harmony with one another . . . [without being] haughty . . . [or unwilling to] associate with the lowly" (v. 16). This rules out both class snobbery and racial discrimination (Jas. 2:1-9).

E. Love of Good

While the admonition to "hate what is evil, hold fast to what is good" (v. 9) has primary reference to moral evil and good, it indirectly includes aesthetic evil and good also. It is an ethical obligation to choose beauty over ugliness, order instead of disorder, and quality over shoddiness. These choices are binding on Christians because they bear on our usefulness and happiness. Since God is a God of beauty and order, beauty and order will be prized by the godly. "Finally, brethren, whatever is true, whatever is honorable, whatever is just, whatever is pure, whatever is lovely, whatever is gracious, if there is any excellence, . . . think about these things" (Phil. 4:8).

F. Integrity

Honesty in handling goods as well as truthfulness in speech are strictly required in the New Testament, as in the Old (Mark 10:19; 2 Cor. 4:21; Eph. 4:25-28; Col. 3:9; 1 Thess. 2:12; 4:6; Heb. 13:18; 1 Pet. 2:12; cf. Zech. 5:3-4). Paul urges the Philippians to keep truth, honesty, and justice ever before their minds (Phil. 4:8).

There runs through the Epistles the twin concerns that integrity will be both real in God's sight and obvious in the sight of man. The inspired writers are very particular that at all costs the honor of the Lord's name be guarded. This is what prompted Paul to be so careful that the handling of the offering for the saints in Jerusalem be beyond any possible suspicion: "We intend that no one should blame us about the liberal gift which we are administering, for we aim at what is honorable not only in the Lord's sight but also in the sight of men" (2 Cor. 8:20-21). To the Romans he writes, "Take thought for what is noble in the sight of all" (12:17).

Clearly business dealings and social relationships must be more than minimally legal; they must be honorable. Christians must not only be honest but seem to be. Taking unfair advantage, through technicalities in the law, or through the other person's ignorance or perhaps his desperate plight, is therefore not Christian. There is no place for trickiness or duplicity in the Christian ethic. The appearance of shoddiness should be avoided as carefully as shoddiness itself, because we bear the Lord's good name in our hands.

G. Good Citizenship

Obedience to the "governing authorities" is another principle universally binding on all Christians (Rom. 13:1-7; cf. Titus 3:1). Good citizenship is not optional. Two things the Christian needs to see: First, the underlying divine authority of civil government, as God's deputy over the affairs of men. Paul does not argue the inherent social necessity of government but simply affirms its divine ordination. Rebellion against government is rebellion against God: "Therefore he who resists authority has opposed the ordinance of God . . . for it is a minister of God." For this reason, accepting civil authority for the Christian must be not just a matter of expediency but of conscience (v. 5). To be careless in observing civil law is to fall seriously short of Christian ethics.[13]

Elsewhere we learn that prayer support as well as submission is a duty incumbent on Christian citizens (1 Tim. 2:1-2). Peter also urges that believers be law-abiding (1 Pet. 2:12-17), but emphasizes the good name of their cause as a reason: "Maintain good conduct among the Gentiles, . . . For it is God's will that by doing right you should put to silence the ignorance of foolish men." While Christians are to "act as free men," they are not to interpret freedom to mean anarchy or as a divine license to disregard the common standards of good citizenship. In Roman times it was the "free men" who bore the civic responsibilities.

Clearly the New Testament assumes that citizenship in the kingdom of God does not cancel our secular obligations. Not only to the Pharisees but to us too Jesus is saying, "Render therefore to Caesar the things that are Caesar's . . ." (Matt. 22:21).[14]

---

13. The Christian also needs to see what specifically are declared to be his duties. "Pay all of them their dues, taxes to whom taxes are due, revenue to whom revenue is due, respect to whom respect is due, honor to whom honor is due" (v. 7).

14. The fact that Paul's unqualified endorsement of the institution of government was made to Christians in Rome in the first century, implies that the Christian's obligation does not depend upon a particular political system.

The possible abuse of civil authority, as when rulers oppress the innocent instead of punishing wrongdoers, or when they usurp powers that belong to God only, is not in view in Paul's discussion. What Peter commands servants might be relevant in such cases: "Servants, be submissive to your masters with all respect, not only to the kind and gentle but also to the overbearing" (1 Pet. 2:18).

But that such submission should stop short of violating divine law may be implied in his next sentence: "For one is approved if, mindful of God, he endures pain while suffering unjustly" (v. 19; cf. Matt. 5:10-12). Peter's own experience should furnish an example, when before the Sanhedrin he accepted the possible consequences of disobedience to them rather than disobey God's command to preach (Acts 4:19). When rulers so exceed their proper authority that a choice between obeying God or man is forced upon the Christian, his duty is clear.

Paul would have stood with Peter here. Yet neither would have conceded that this unusual situation in any way invalidated the general obligation of Christians to be law-abiding citizens. How far on the basis of Peter's experience modern Christians can go in building a rationale for "civil disobedience" in today's context is highly debatable. Certainly they cannot point to Paul for a precedent, for though his presence sometimes precipitated riots, there is not one instance in the New Testament where he openly disobeyed a law or defied civil authority. His frequent beatings and imprisonments were forms of persecution, not penalties for crimes.

H. Basic Morality

Paul's way of linking love to the Ten Commandments leaves no possibility of a "Christian love" that might in some situations permit adultery, murder, stealing, or coveting (Rom. 13:8-10). There are no allowances for either exceptions or exemptions. The so-called love which would temporize is not the kind Paul is writing about.[15]

"Let us conduct ourselves becomingly as in the day," Paul summarizes, "not in reveling and drunkenness, not in debauchery and licentiousness, not in quarreling and jealousy." The biblical standard for the Christian is total abstention from the world's vices. To "put

---

15. Paul would not concede that the use of the "sword" by civil authorities, which he has just endorsed (v. 4), is in any way inconsistent with what he is now saying about love. Obviously he did not consider capital punishment a violation of the sixth commandment.

on the Lord Jesus Christ" rules out making allowance for any such fleshly activities (v. 14). While separation from the world is not to be interpreted as isolation (1 Cor. 5:10), it is to be ethically radical (2 Cor. 6:14-18; Eph. 4:17-32; 5:3-14, *et al.*).

I. The Duty of Good Works

When we read that love "does no wrong to a neighbor" (Rom. 13:10), we might suppose that love is content merely to avoid inflicting injury. The New Testament does not permit one to stop with such a negative harmlessness. There are duties owed our neighbor in practical compassion and concern—in seeking his maximum spiritual and physical welfare. These are so elemental to the human situation that to fail here is to *wrong* our neighbor. Neglect also may injure as profoundly as vicious acts. By the admonition "Contribute to the needs of saints, practice hospitality" (Rom. 12:13), we are reminded that social concern is mandatory.

The Early Church learned this from Jesus "who went about doing good" (Acts 10:38). It was Jesus who made feeding the hungry, providing for the stranger, clothing the naked, and visiting the sick and imprisoned a basis for final judgment (Matt. 25:31-46). Judas' complaint that Mary's "pound of costly ointment" should have been sold and the money given to the poor, might suggest that giving to the poor was their custom (John 12:3-8).

Jesus' concern for the weak and needy was always practical, as witnessed by feeding the multitudes and healing the sick. But He did not allow His disciples to forget that the greatest need of the poor was spiritual, and that good works were first of all religious in nature (Matt. 11:5; Mark 6:34).

That the post-Pentecost Christians were like their Lord in this concern for the suffering and underprivileged is seen throughout the Book of Acts (2:45; 3:2-7; 4:32, 34; 5:15-16; 6:1-3; 9:32-34, 36-39; 10:4; *et al.*; cf. Gal. 2:10). From these experiences of the Church some clearly enunciated principles emerged.

1. The Church accepted responsibility for social welfare as part and parcel of its "body life." The importance it attached to this work is seen *(a)* in its institution of a distinct order of the ministry, the diaconate, ordained specifically for this very thing (Acts 6:1-3); and *(b)* its insistence on very high qualifications for this office (Acts 6:3; 1 Tim. 3:8-13).

2. Official responsibility was limited to helping members of the Church who had no other resources. The counterpart of this position

was that assistance was to be viewed as family responsibility first; the Church assumed responsibility only when all possible family resources were exhausted (1 Tim. 5:4-16). It is therefore unchristian for believing families with adequate means to shift the care of needy relatives to the Church—or, by implication, to the state. The insistence here is so sharp that it elicits one of Paul's most stinging rebukes: "If any one does not provide for his relatives, and specially for his own family, he has disowned the faith and is worse than an unbeliever" (1 Tim. 5:8).

3. Christians were to do as much practical good to all men as opportunity permitted, but with the household of faith being given priority (Gal. 6:10). Apparently "charity begins at home" but is not intended to stop there. When one considers the usual callousness in the ancient world, this warm benevolence and practical care was a new spirit released among men. It undoubtedly made a profound impression on the observing pagans—especially those who were the objects of such loving-kindness.

4. Able-bodied Christians were to engage in gainful occupations in order to be able, not only to support their own, but to "help cases of urgent need" (Titus 3:8, 14).[16]

IV. AREAS OF PERMITTED DIVERSITY

In chapters 14 and 15, Paul insists that some conduct should be left to personal conviction. The fact that Paul refrains from settling such differences by apostolic mandate suggests that in some areas we should not legislate. The Church is to accept the sincere believer with his variant views on secondary matters without "passing judgment" (Rom. 14:1).

A. Unregulated Matters

Wide latitude is allowed for dietary peculiarities. This includes not only the variation between meat-eating and vegetarianism (14:2), but between the eating of food classified as "clean" (kosher) and that classified as unclean. This was a two-pronged problem. It concerned

---

16. Such activity in the Early Church was a spontaneous and largely unstructured involvement in the needs of men. It was prompted by the love of Christ, on a person-to-person, local basis. Paul introduced the larger vision of care for needy fellow believers at a distance, thus fostering the sense of universal oneness in the body of Christ (Acts 24:17; Rom. 15:31; 2 Corinthians 8—9).

Jewish believers who still thought in Old Testament terms concerning forbidden and acceptable kinds of food. But it was also an issue for the Gentile converts who wondered what to do about meat bought in the market which had first been offered to idols (cf. 1 Corinthians 8 and 9).

Another unregulated issue is the question of holy days. "One man esteems one day as better than another, while another man esteems all days alike" (14:5). This too doubtless reflects the mixed Jew-Gentile composition of the church at Rome. Whether Paul was speaking of special Jewish feast days only or was also thinking of the Sabbath is a question raised by some.[17] The consistently Christian view is to see every day as equally holy in the sense that every day is a gift of God and is to be lived wholly for the Lord. Wrongdoing or worldly compromise is no more acceptable on Monday than on Sunday, but purely commercial or recreational pursuits are.

This position does not rule out the unique sanctity of the Lord's Day as a day especially reserved for those forms of corporate worship and service not practical on other days. The preservation of the Church in its corporate worship and serving, as well as the well-being of persons both physically and spiritually, constitute sufficient ethical grounds for treating the Lord's Day as the Sabbath and keeping it "holy" in this special sense. If the Sabbath was made for man (Mark 2:27), it must have been because man needed it. Dispensational transitions would not alter this need.

In other areas also the Church is to allow relative variation in practice. There is even a measure of flexibility concerning marriage and sex within a firm periphery of purity and fidelity (1 Corinthians 7). Also, a divine policy is affirmed respecting the support of the ministry, but deviation from it in some circumstances is not considered to be sin (1 Cor. 9:14; cf. context).

B. Harmonizing Rules

The underlying principle is for believers ever to keep in mind the nature of the kingdom of God. Negatively, it is "not eating and drink-

---

17. Matthew Henry, Adam Clarke, and John Wesley limit the reference to Jewish festivals. Clarke comments: "That the Sabbath is of lasting obligation may be reasonably concluded from its institution (see the note on Gen. 11:3) and from its *typical* reference . . . the word *alike* should not be added; nor is it acknowledged by any MS. or ancient *version*" (*Commentary* [New York: Abingdon Press, n.d.], 6:151).

ing" (Rom. 14:17, NASB).[18] Positively, it is "righteousness and peace
and joy in the Holy Spirit." This is the touchstone for distinguishing
essentials from nonessentials.

In the background was a very deep and crucial issue: the perpetuation or termination of the Mosaic ceremonial and cultic law.
Paul knew perfectly well that in respect to food, "nothing is unclean
in itself" (Rom. 14:14). The Old Testament distinctions were never
intrinsic, only pedagogical, and as such had served their day. But
Paul was willing for the inborn feelings of his fellow Jews to be re-
spected. He was willing for the whole edifice to crumble gradually,
provided both sides were charitable and refrained either from judgmental scorn or authoritarian imposition of personal views.

The tone in the Galatian letter is radically different. But in that
case Paul was confronting the adamant stand of the Judaizers that
the Gentiles must conform to Jewish ritual. Since they did not allow
matters of opinion to remain such, but made the Jewish cultus, particularly circumcision, into a condition of salvation, Paul had to deal
with the issue on that level. It could have been both/and; but when
the Jews made circumcision a this-or-else issue, Paul accepts the
gauntlet and declares that if circumcision is accepted as a necessity,
the sufficiency of Christ is in effect cancelled (Gal. 5:1-4). They have
"fallen away from grace."[19]

Specifically, the following principles may be drawn from Paul's
discussion:

1. When one has strong convictions about these practical matters, he should observe them conscientiously as to the Lord, no
matter what others do (Rom. 14:5-8, 23).

2. As long as his scruples cannot be proven by scriptures which
express a universal rule, a believer must not judge others as lax because they do not have identical convictions (vv. 3, 10, 13).

3. Conversely, Christians who do not share all the scruples of

---

18. The reference here is eating and drinking as they relate to questions of cultus
and ritual; it is unrelated to the basically ethical issues of health and temperance. As
temperance is a fruit of the Spirit, so intemperance is a work of the flesh (Gal.
5:21, 23).

19. The difference is tersely summarized by Matthew Henry: "The apostle
seemed willing to let the ceremonial law wither by degrees, and to let it have an
honorable burial; now these weak Romans seemed to be only following it weeping to
its grave, but those Galatians were raking it out of its ashes" (*Commentary* [Wilmington,
Del.: Sovereign Grace Publishers, 1972], 2:996).

another must not belittle him, no matter how mistaken they believe him to be (Rom. 14:1, 3-4, 10; 15:1-7).

4. Neither side must permit their differences to become hindrances to mutual worship, work, or fellowship. Equally they should avoid allowing them to become subjects of endless discussion and debate (vv. 1, 13).

5. The Christian whose conscience permits greater latitude has a special responsibility before God. He is to exercise his freedom always with a careful regard for the effect such freedom may have on others. "Do not let what you eat cause the ruin of one for whom Christ died" (v. 15); and "It is right not to eat meat or to drink wine or do anything that makes your brother stumble" (v. 21). This principle is so basic that Paul returns to it several times (Rom. 15:1-2; 1 Cor. 8:7-13; 10:23-31). Do all "to the glory of God," he concludes (1 Cor. 10:31); obviously he means that the glory of God cannot be had without the good of our brother. This ability to exercise self-restraint in one's liberties for the sake of others is the very hallmark of true spirituality and Christian love. "If your brother is being injured by what you eat, you are no longer walking in love," he affirms (Rom. 14:15). He also reminds us pointedly: "Knowledge puffs up, but love builds up" (1 Cor. 8:1).

C. Ethical Insight

Beyond the basic principles of mutual respect, the Christian must develop such a *sense* of ethics that he can discern what is really nonessential and what is intrinsically vital. Somewhere a line must be drawn. Love will tend by nature to draw the line on the conservative side, because it is genuinely concerned about ultimate consequences of acts as well as immediate appearances. But love needs the aid of sound judgment. A careful study of 1 Corinthians 8—10 may help us in cultivating this sense of discrimination. Some things are always off limits. Others may be innocent in themselves but not expedient (1 Cor. 10:23). Still others may be permissible in some circumstances but not in all (1 Cor. 10:25-29). Mature Christians are those who "have their faculties trained by practice to distinguish good from evil" (Heb. 5:14).

Today the province of "mutable morality" and individual conviction includes issues quite different from kosher foods or meat offered to idols. But the variables among Christians are as numerous as ever—the details of Sunday observance, personal appearance, permitted recreation, cost and quantity of possessions, social and cultural standards. The hope of preserving "the unity of the Spirit in the bond of peace" (Eph. 4:3) lies in remembering that while the issues are different, the principles by which they may be transcended are the same.

V. THE CHURCH AND PRIVATE CONSCIENCE

What is called the conscience is (1) both the capacity and activity of a moral agent in perceiving right from wrong, and (2) the intuitive knowledge that he ought to do what he believes to be right.

The clash between community mores and private conscience can be very acute. It seems axiomatic that no one should be compelled to do what he sincerely believes to be wrong, or prevented from doing what he is convinced he ought to do. Nevertheless, autonomy of personal conscience cannot be absolute. Sin in the heart and in the environment, plus personal variables in intelligence and maturity, have impaired the ability of the moral agent, *acting purely on his own,* to perceive the right with universal accuracy. A sincere moral judgment in a specific situation may fall so far short of mature perception and clash so directly with the rights of others, that the person's "conscience" must be denied.

Regardless of theory, in actual practice through established law, society claims the right to compel certain basic behavioral conformities without always deferring to private conscience. This is a kind of regulatory compensation for (1) personal immaturity and/or (2) perversion of conscience.

The vexing question of the relation of the Church's authority to the individual Christian arises at this point. The Church is assigned a teaching function to the believer. Thus is provided a sort of "collective conscience" by which the immature or untrained conscience of the private Christian can be both formed and nurtured—within, of course, a thoroughly biblical context.

The Church must never pose as sole interpreter of the Scriptures, thus preempting the office of the Holy Spirit; but the private Christian, on the other hand, must never ignore the Church's voice. A true illumination of the Spirit will prompt a humility and teachableness that respects the larger treasury of wisdom and experience resident in the whole Body. A private conscience that scorns the collective conscience is as unbiblical as a collective conscience that becomes oppressively imperial. All of this is implied in such passages as Eph.

4:1-3, 15-16; 5:21; Phil. 2:1-5, 12-15; 3:17-19; 1 Tim. 1:3-11; 2:8-11; 3:1-7, 15; 5:17, 20; Titus 1:7-13, *et al.*

It is the duty of the Church therefore to teach and require the "universal mandates." It is also the duty of the Church to respect those areas assigned to private opinion and to variant practice. But we have inadequately examined the data if we fail to see a third situation. This is the gray area in which the ethical position is not clearly defined by Scripture and is more relative to circumstances, times, or culture than intrinsic. In such an area the issue may be sufficiently serious to obligate the Church to speak, perhaps even to legislate. At times certain matters even in the gray area cannot be left altogether to private opinion.

When discussing the marks of appropriate conduct in the house of God, Paul draws the reins rather tightly. The basic principle is that all things must be done "decently and in order" (1 Cor. 14:40). But Paul did not leave his readers to apply this rule entirely according to their own judgment. He gave some very specific instructions concerning attire (1 Cor. 11:1-6); proprieties of the Lord's Supper (1 Cor. 11:17-34); and the exercise of gifts in public service (1 Cor. 14:1-40). There was still much room for spontaneity and freedom but within certain nonnegotiable limits.

Especially illustrative of this principle is Paul's directive to the women in the church at Corinth, forbidding them to come to the public service unveiled (11:1-16). To twentieth-century westerners this would seem to be so relatively unimportant that Paul would have said, "Let the women do as they think best."

But there was more involved in this case than simply the right of private opinion. A broader viewpoint sees the church in a culture, and representing the Lord Jesus Christ in terms of that culture. Paul saw that Christian women could rejoice in their newfound liberty and equality. They must not, however, interpret this as a right to disregard the social conventions in a way that would bring misunderstanding and possible reproach upon the church. Personal rights must not be asserted at the expense of the prior needs of the community. The Corinthian women, while truly "liberated," were in an even more fundamental sense stewards of the grace of God. They must therefore exercise their stewardship in such a way as to enhance the cause they represented, instead of tarnishing its image and thereby weakening its influence—even though the issues themselves might be local and temporary.

There are practical and profound implications of this relationship of the authority of the Church to private conscience. Timeless moral principles must be interpreted and applied in each age in ways that are relevant to the problems and culture in which the believer lives. These include such areas as the sanctity of the home, the sanctity of the body as the temple of the Holy Spirit, personal integrity, and race and sex equality in Christ. There seems no way to avoid standards, rules, requirements, and discipline. Also the Church must, through its pastoral and corporate leadership, provide directives in the area of non-absolutes. This must be done in the interests of maximum unity and community witness. The obligation of the Church in the nebulous, thankless, thin-ice area of "mutable morality" cannot be dodged.

Yet in discharging this obligation the Church must avoid turning the relative into an absolute. We must never transfer these rulings from the category of mutable morality into the category of the eternal and unchangeable. It probably was not intended by the Holy Spirit that the rules and regulations laid down by Paul in such purely cultural matters as women wearing veils should become ironclad laws for all generations. It is the failure of the Church to see the difference between cultural morality and the unchangeable mandates that has caused confusion and led to needless tension.

VI. MARRIAGE AND FAMILY

The references in the New Testament to marriage naturally reflect the ordinary customs and laws prevailing in Palestine. These customs were recognized by Christ, as witnessed by two parables depicting familiar wedding scenes, and by His own presence and miracle at the marriage in Cana of Galilee (John 2:1-11). But the Christian view of marriage goes deeper than local customs.

A. What Constitutes Marriage

Marriage, then and now, is at once (1) a contractual, formal union regulated by civil and religious law, and (2) a conjugal and domestic union. On the legal side marriage was not simply a merging of two people who decided to live together. The idea of casual unions prompted by affection which could be dissolved just as casually when the affection waned is foreign both to the New Testament and to the Jewish culture. There was not an evasion of legal bonds but a glad, public assumption of them.

A betrothal which preceded full legal marriage, such as Joseph had with Mary, was the usual order. Even this betrothal involved a legal document declaring the intended dowry and other agreements. According to Edersheim, at the wedding ceremony itself a further "formal legal instrument was signed, which set forth that the bridegroom undertook to work for her, to honor, keep, and care for her, as is the manner of the men in Israel."[20] The marriage procedure required long and careful preparation, was festive yet solemn, and involved many witnesses. In some respects it was the business of the entire community.

But living together as man and wife is equally essential to true marriage. This is implied in Paul's instructions concerning the wife who leaves her husband: "Let her remain unmarried or else be reconciled to her husband" (1 Cor. 7:11, NASB). We have here the strongest reaffirmation of the duality of marriage. Separation disrupts the marriage but does not destroy it. A separated person would be living in an unmarried state; but that she still had a husband proves the continued legal existence of the union, including its obligations. As long as this situation prevailed, a second marriage would not be permissible.

B. Normative Standards

Both Jesus and Paul based their high view of marriage on the original order of creation, by quoting Gen. 2:24: "For this reason a man shall leave his father and mother and be joined to his wife, and the two shall become one" (Matt. 19:5; Mark 10:7 ff.; Eph. 5:31). This view implies four things:

1. The Normalcy of Marriage.

The New Testament recognizes fully the original design in creating male and female. First it was to fill a need: *companionship and aid;* second, to perform a function: *populating the earth.* Marriage is expected to form the social matrix for procreation and nurture of children. In view of this, to marry was the expected and normal thing. In the Hebrew culture, a man or woman must have special reasons for celibacy. The burden of proof was on them. In response to the disciples' exclamation, "It is not expedient to marry," Jesus said, "Not all men can receive this precept, but only those to whom it

20. Alfred Edersheim, *Jesus the Messiah* (Grand Rapids, Mich.: Wm. B. Eerdmans Publishing Co., 1967), p. 70.

is given" (Matt. 19:12). He then designated three classes of eunuchs, but clearly all three were recognized as exceptions to the rule.

Paul discusses the pros and cons of marriage versus the single state in 1 Corinthians 7. For the majority, who do not have the special "gift" of unmarried contentment, marriage is recommended (vv. 1-9). Those who are capable of remaining single would find some advantages in doing so, partly in view of "the impending distress" (v. 26) and partly because of the greater freedom possible in serving the Lord (vv. 32-35).

Paul's apparent preference for the single state over the married is due to practical considerations, not to a belief in the intrinsic superiority of celibacy. This chapter needs to be balanced with Paul's instruction that the younger widows "get married, bear children, keep house . . ." (1 Tim. 5:14) and his position that to forbid marriage is a mark of apostasy (1 Tim. 4:1-3). Also, he assumes that elders and deacons will be married (1 Tim. 3:2, 12). That he believes marriage to be the proper norm is seen further by his summary statement to the Ephesians: "Let each one of you love his wife as himself, and let the wife see that she respects her husband" (Eph. 5:33).

2. *Monogamy.*

Although polygamy was legal among the Jews, it was not customary. God created one Eve, not several, and said a man should cleave to his wife, not wives. Whether this simple principle of religious and biological history shaped Jewish thinking or not, it was obviously determinative of the Christian norm. Every reference in the New Testament to marriage and family implies one wife and one husband. Jesus said, "Whosoever putteth away his wife, and marries another . . ." When New Testament writers discuss duties within the family, a simple monogamy is everywhere assumed (1 Cor. 7:2 ff.; 9:5; 11:11; Eph. 5:31, 33; 1 Pet. 3:1-7).[21]

3. *Permanence.*

Jesus explicitly drew from the Genesis pronouncement the logical conclusion of lasting obligation: "Consequently they are no longer two, but one flesh. What therefore God has joined together, let no man separate" (Mark 10:8-9, NASB). The union is doubly indissoluble. On the human side the consummation of marriage in

---

21. The expressed limitation of bishops and deacons to one wife obviously disqualifies any man in a polygamous relationship from these high offices (1 Tim. 3:2, 12; Titus 1:6).

sexual union means "one flesh"—a joining of psyches as well as bodies—which can never be violated without irreparable damage to both parties. But Jesus further ascribes their union to God, so that any attempt to dissolve it is a direct affront to God who ordained the institution of marriage.

Jesus is not saying that couples in common-law liaisons are "joined together by God." Perhaps in the Judaic context, the endorsement of God is through the legal and civil procedures and ceremonies which seek to regulate marriage in harmony with God's revealed law. By observing these regulations, improper and unlawful marriages would be avoided.

Paul makes it clear that physical union alone does not constitute legitimate marriage even though it establishes the "one flesh" relationship: "Do you not know that he who joins himself to a prostitute becomes one body with her?" Here too the proof is in Gen. 2:24: "For, as it is written, 'The two shall become one'" (1 Cor. 6:16). Obviously it is the sexual union that creates the one flesh. Yet Paul would not add, "What therefore God hath joined together let not man put asunder"! Such an unchristian union is psychically inerasable but should not be perpetuated. Jesus implied as much in saying to the Samaritan woman, "He whom you now have is not your husband" (John 4:18).

We are compelled to conclude therefore that the obligation for permanence presupposes a union not only physically but legally and divinely valid. Sex is a right that is as dependent on vows as it is on urges. It must accept responsibilities as well as privileges.[22]

4. *Sanctity.*

The sanctity of marriage enforced in the New Testament was not new to the Jews of Jesus' day.[23] It is not surprising therefore that

---

22. Naturally the question arises whether all couples joined legally are *ipso facto* joined together by God. Jesus' sweeping rejection of unjustified divorce as a legal basis for remarriage would certainly exclude such second marriages from divine sanction. A marriage that Jesus plainly brands as an act of adultery could hardly claim to be a marriage "made in heaven" (Luke 16:18). That it might become one through forgiveness and grace is an entirely different question.

Paul granted that separation might in some circumstances be permissible, but instructed that the Christian who took such initiative should remain available for a reconciliation (1 Cor. 7:10-11). Even though believers are instructed to marry "in the Lord" (1 Cor. 7:39), failure to do so in and of itself does not render the marriage invalid in God's sight (1 Cor. 7:14).

23. Edersheim says: "It must be borne in mind that marriage conveyed to the Jews much higher thoughts than those merely of festivity and merriment. The pious

Paul is inspired to see in the sacrificial love of Christ for the Church a model for Christian marriage (Eph. 5:25-32).

Furthermore the undeviating position of Scripture is that marriage as a sexual union is in itself a holy relationship; it is in no sense sinful or shameful. Even in the midst of Paul's strongest exhortation to caution, and perhaps to delay or even to total self-denial, he hastens to add, "But if you marry, you do not sin" (1 Cor. 7:28). In Hebrews we read, "Let marriage be held in honor among all, and let the marriage bed be undefiled; for God will judge the immoral and adulterous" (13:4). Clearly it is not the conjugal relation which defiles the marriage bed but fornication and adultery.

C. Duties Within the Family

1. *Between Husband and Wife.*

The principle of hierarchical orders of authority and function is universally endorsed in the Bible; it is never cancelled by the counter-balancing and equally revealed principle of equality. In this there is the reflection of the Trinity. As "the head of Christ is God," so the head of "every man is Christ," and "the head of a woman is her husband" (1 Cor. 11:3). These three headships are inherent, not arbitrary. Rebellion of the wife against this very natural order, or rebellion of the man against the headship of Christ, should be as unthinkable as would be the rebellion of Christ against God. The introduction of tension in these relationships is evidence of the beginning of sin. Only sinful hearts would see injustice or discrimination in orders that are God-given and necessary to a balanced and efficient pattern of relationships.

a. Love and Leadership. Therefore the wives are to submit to their husbands, "as to the Lord" (Eph. 5:22). A true submission to the Lord will demand a proper submission to the husband. This should be natural and joyous, and will be if the woman is surrendered to the Lord, and if her husband is equally obedient to God's command, "Husbands, love your wives" (v. 25). The standard of this love is Christ's self-giving love for the Church. It also should be the kind of love a man has for himself (vv. 28-29). This mutual, loving consideration will assure orderliness, harmony, and happiness in a home.

---

fasted before it, confessing their sins. . . . It almost seems as if, the relationship of Husband and Bride between Jehovah and His people, so frequently insisted upon, not only in the Bible but in Rabbinic writings, had always been standing out in the background" (*Jesus the Messiah*, pp. 70 ff.).

The duty of submission grows out of the purpose of creation. "For the man is not of the woman; but the woman of the man. Neither was the man created for the woman; but the woman for the man" (1 Cor. 11:8-9, NASB). This is not anti-female bias, it is simply a recital of historical fact. Eve was created to be a companion and helpmate for Adam.[24]

This natural hierarchy is always implicit and undoubtedly implies a certain practical division of responsibility (1 Tim. 5:14). The ideal for Christians, however, is teamwork in most areas. Co-partnership seems to be implied in what the Bible has to say about Mary and Joseph, Elizabeth and Zacharias, Priscilla and Aquilla. Yet even in teamwork it is the husband primarily who is held responsible for an orderly household (1 Tim. 3:4-5).

Christian wives of unsaved husbands are particularly charged with the duty of submission "so that some, though they do not obey the word, may be won without a word by the behavior of their wives" (1 Pet. 3:1). Clearly in this case the subjection of the wife is not annulled by the fact that a man is not a Christian and may therefore fall short of the Christian standard of husbandhood. The responsibility on her is doubled, for she bears in her hands both the honor of the Lord's name and the soul of her husband. Extra care in being an ideal wife will increase her power and with it the likelihood of his salvation.

b. Sex Within Marriage. The New Testament recognizes that marriage is fundamentally a sexual relationship and that sexual duties are mutual. References are delicate, as is to be expected for something as private and intimate, but not prudish, as to imply something abnormal or shameful. When we read that Joseph kept Mary "a virgin until she gave birth to a son" (Matt. 1:25, NASB) we are being given important information for the doctrine of the Virgin Birth; but the additional inference is that cohabitation was the normal and expected seal of their marriage.[25] The extended posponement would not have occurred except for the special circumstances.

---

24. The phrase in Col. 3:18, "In the Lord," is understood by Lightfoot (quoted with approval by Vincent) not as a limitation of her obligation to submission, but "an essential *a priori* obligation" (Vincent, *Word Studies in the NT*, 3:507).

25. "Knew her not" is literally "was not knowing her." The imperfect tense suggests not a one-time-only act, as was the marriage ceremony, but a repeated affirmation of union which was a normal constituent element of the marriage relationship.

Nothing could be more down to earth than the advice on sex relations in 1 Cor. 7:1-7. Paul says he wishes every man were as capable of living without sex comfortably as he was (v. 7). But he recognizes this as not so much a mark of superior holiness as a special gift which not all have. He therefore advises what is proper for most people: marriage within which regular sex relations are more normal than abnormal. Obviously there is considerable latitude in this matter, all within the boundaries of holiness.

The fundamental principle is mutuality. Nowhere in the Bible is the basic equality of male and female more graphically affirmed—and the Holy Spirit used the celibate Paul to affirm it. It is clear that where great disparity exists between the natural desires of the husband and wife, they are mutually to endeavor to adjust toward each other, each one subordinating his own desires to the happiness of the other. The husband, however, should seek to obey Peter's injunction to live with his wife according to knowledge, and show her special honor (1 Pet. 3:7). He will voluntarily out of the tenderness of his love give special deference to her feelings, knowing that her emotional nature is more sensitively balanced, and she is the one who will bear the children resulting from such free union. Therefore while the wife has no right to deprive her husband, he has a noble Christian right to deprive himself out of loving consideration. Such a husband will have the undying respect and devotion of his wife.

Even though God grants considerable freedom and latitude, the spirit of self-discipline is revelatory of one's spiritual depth. Lack of grace in this area, Peter says, will hinder a man's prayers. God observes the way men treat their wives. A wife is God's crowning gift to a man; he who misuses or dishonors the gift is affronting the Giver.[26]

2. *Between Parents and Children.*

The presence of children in the home is uniformly taken for granted in the New Testament. There is no hint that questions of family planning, birth control, abortion, or overpopulation ever arose. Embarrassment would come, not from having too many chil-

---

26. Two further conclusions may be drawn: (1) A normal sex life within marriage is not what the New Testament calls carnality; (2) The attempt on the part of either husband or wife to impose strict abstinence for any length of time, in the name of some holiness ideal, is not only being "wiser than what is written," but defying what is written, and may result in disaster through needlessly exposing the other party to excessive temptation.

dren, but from having no children, as in the case of Elizabeth and Zacharias. Issues in these areas that confront modern Christians must be settled on underlying biblical principles, such as belief in God's active concern and the leadership of the Holy Spirit in every area of our lives. The fact that Zacharias prayed for a child (Luke 1:13) simply reflected his nurture in the Old Testament faith. This was not ignorance of the biological processes of procreation; even the virgin Mary understood perfectly well that babies are conceived through the implantation of male seed (Luke 1:34). The faith of the Israelites, reflected in the New Testament, was that God was in control of the biological forces; He could open and close wombs.[27]

The New Testament would encourage a Christian philosophy of the family which sees children as very important in God's sight and sees parenthood not only as a privilege but a very high responsibility; a way, indeed, of serving God. "Whoever receives one such little child in my name receives me" (Matt. 18:5; cf. v. 10; Mark 9:37; 10:13-16; Luke 9:48). The warning against causing a child to stumble is particularly applicable to careless parents (Matt. 18:6).

a. The Role of Fathers. Fathers are to take the lead in both family religion and training. "Fathers . . . bring them up in the discipline and instruction of the Lord" (Eph. 6:4). It is a shame to shift total responsibility to the mother; it is equally a shame when the parents pull against each other in disciplinary matters. Far better for there to be unity without perfect wisdom than for either the father or mother to sabotage the other's efforts because of variant opinion (except, of course, in cases of real cruelty).

But the father who can rightfully insist on obedience from the children and cooperation from his wife must be careful to avoid provoking the children "to anger" (Eph. 6:4). In Col. 3:21 the reason is added: "lest they become discouraged." Discipline must reinforce the child's good intentions and preserve his self-esteem. It must not be so exacting and impossible in its demands that discouragement is the result, with the bitterness and rebellion which is almost sure to follow. Minor infractions should be treated as minor. It is the father's duty to see to it that the home atmosphere is not one of constant scolding and belittling; and a disciplined child should never have reason to wonder if his father loves him.

---

27. Some modern issues would be easier to handle if Christians today had this kind of faith. Scientific sophistication has weakened faith by exaggerating the finality of second causes.

b. The Duty of Obedience. While parents are to be conscientious and wise, children are to obey: "For this is right," Paul says to the Ephesians; and "this pleases the Lord," he explains to the Colossians. Apparently Paul considers the Ten Commandments still valid, even for Gentile believers, for he bases his instructions to children on the fifth commandment (Eph. 6:1-2; cf. Col. 3:20). This subordination to parents is right, both because it is an explicit, divine command, and also because it is inherently reasonable in the nature of things. Children who are permitted to snatch authority and parents who weakly abdicate theirs are making an orderly, happy family life impossible. The breakdown of family discipline always results in general social decay, and being "disobedient to parents" is one of the marks of the anarchy and disorder of a dissolute society (Rom. 1:30; 1 Tim. 3:3).[28]

The validity of the fifth commandment and of the natural order in the parent-child relationship is not specifically dependent on the parents being Christians. A child is not authorized to disobey simply because they are not. Christian children can best serve the Lord by being exemplary in this duty as well as in others. Unsaved parents would deeply resent and discount a religion that encouraged in a child the spirit of disobedience.

Yet because sin always dislocates the natural order, a Christian child would doubtless be justified in disobeying if the parental authority demanded what the child knew to be forbidden by God. But no leeway is given here for children to disrespect parents simply because the child perceives their fallibility. Here, if anywhere, Christian children (including teenagers) should follow Jesus their Lord, who at 12 years of age returned to Nazareth with His parents and remained subject to them.

D. The Question of Divorce

Under Roman law divorce dissolved a marriage and permitted remarriage, and could be initiated by either wife or husband. Under Jewish law divorce was equally a dissolution of the union with the

---

28. The family that fails in becoming a loving, close-knit unit based on Christian principles is likely to furnish an example of the heartbreaking betrayal predicted for the last days: "And brother will deliver up brother to death, and a father his child; and children will arise up against parents and cause them to be put to death" (Mark 13:12). Such is the dreadful power of sin to alienate. "Without natural affection" is the way the KJV aptly puts it (Rom. 1:31; 2 Tim. 3:3).

added stipulation that a marriage once dissolved by divorce could never be reestablished (Deut. 24:1-4). Apparently the writing of the divorce bill was the prerogative of the man, though doubtless restless Jewish women had ways of maneuvering their husbands into accommodating them if they so desired.

The grounds for divorce stipulated by Moses was confined to the discovery of "some uncleanness" in the wife. Since literally the Hebrew says a "matter of nakedness," some sexual defect is implied. The Jews found in the ambiguity of the phrase sufficient ground for endless debate over what various wifely defects might be included. In the time of Christ the debate was lively between the school of Rabbi Shammai who argued for divorce only on the grounds of actual impurity, and the school of Hillel whose elastic interpretation would include such peccadillo as burning his biscuits for breakfast.[29]

1. *The Exceptive Clauses.*

It is this background which offers a reasonable explanation for the fact that only Matthew relates the sayings of Jesus on divorce specifically to the problem of what constitutes a legitimate ground. Only the Jews (for whom Matthew was particularly writing) would be acutely concerned about the matter. There is no serious textual basis for doubting the genuineness of these exceptive clauses; nor is it logical to allow their absence in Mark and Luke to annul their authority for either the Jew or the Christian. Matthew is inspired scripture too.

Clearly Jesus outdoes Shammai in strictness. The "matter of nakedness" mentioned by Moses could have been simply uncleanness in the care of her person, or unsatisfactoriness as a marriage partner. Jesus pins the matter down to "fornication" *(porneia),* a general term covering any kind of sexual immorality whether adultery, incest, homosexuality, lesbianism, or any other real deviation. Apparently sexual immorality is the only valid ground for the breakup of a marriage. No other failure violates so devastatingly its deepest vows, rights, and loyalties. By inference a divorce for other causes is disallowed.

Matt. 5:31-32 implies that to divorce a woman was virtually to compel her, in that economy, to become another man's wife; but in so doing both she and the man who married her would be committing adultery. The union might be legal under civil law but not

---

29. Robertson, *Word Pictures,* 1:153.

morally right in God's sight. It is clear that civil law in such matters does not automatically carry divine endorsement. While the Christian is required to obey the law of the land, he may be required to go beyond the law and recognize additional restrictions imposed by the law of God. What is legal is not necessarily right. Therefore Christians look beyond the state to the Bible for their standards in these areas.

Some have argued that the fornication which Jesus named as the one ground of divorce referred only to an irregularity within the relationship of betrothed persons. Thus the divorce allowed was merely the dissolution of the betrothal. The error in this reasoning is that the discussion in Matthew 19 cannot be made relevant to betrothal. The argument used by Jesus for the ideal of permanence is the "one flesh" of full marriage, based on Gen. 1:27. Moreover the counter question, "Why then did Moses command one to give a certificate of divorce and to put her away?" shows unmistakably that the subject is a consummated marriage (cf. Deut. 24:1-4). The plain teaching is that once a marriage is both legal and consummated, there is to be no divorce and remarriage except for the one cause of immorality. That the disciples so understood Jesus is indicated by their exclamation, "If the relationship of the man with his wife is like this it is better not to marry" (Luke 19:10).

2. *Expedients of Hardheartedness.*

The flat statement in Mark 10:11 (cf. Luke 16:18), "Whoever divorces his wife and marries another, commits adultery against her," suggests that Jesus here refers to the case where a man divorces his wife with another woman in mind. To cohabit with the other woman while married would of course be adultery and subject to the penalty of the Law; but a divorce certificate will secure him from trouble and sanctify the new union! Jesus is here brushing aside such a technicality as cruel, coldhearted sophistry. A divorce that is merely a contrivance of unfaithfulness is odious to God who sees the secret intents of the heart.

Jesus explained Moses' comparative leniency as a lesser-of-two-evils accommodation to "hardness of heart" (Matt. 19:8). His reasoning points in two directions. First, men outside of grace are still beset by this sinful condition. If such hardness made divorce a necessary social expedient then, it is reasonable to suppose that the same unregenerate hardness might require the same sub-Christian adjustment today. It is probable therefore that Jesus would see the state as

Moses' successor in making concessions, for the sake of legal protection and orderliness. But such legal divorce falls far short of the divine intention and ideal.

The second hint in Jesus' indictment is for Christians. He is calling His followers to God's original pattern. Anything less is sin. For professed Christians hastily to resort to divorce is to demonstrate the same hardness of heart that Jesus diagnosed in the Jews—a hardness that does not belong to the new order of the kingdom of God. Even too great an alacrity in claiming a divorce on grounds of fornication is to fall short of the Christian spirit, which should seek in every way to be redemptive.

3. *Apostolic Regulations.*

As already indicated, Paul reaffirms the Lord's high standards for His followers. His position can be summarized briefly. (1) If Christians separate, let them stop short of divorce, avoiding remarriage, and keeping themselves available for reconciliation (1 Cor. 7:10-11). (2) Neither husband nor wife should divorce an unsaved mate, or refuse to live with them as man and wife, on religious grounds alone (vv. 12-14). Evidently some Corinthian believers must have thought that religious division was as serious an impairment of marriage as adultery. Or they may have supposed that primary loyalty to Jesus would be compromised by such intimate relation with an unbeliever. (3) If the unbeliever insists on dissolving the marriage, "let it be so; in such a case the brother or sister is not bound" (v. 15).

Exegetes are divided in their understanding of Paul here. Is he telling them to not fret? The next verse might suggest this: "For how do you know, wife, whether you will save your husband? Or how do you know, O husband, whether you will save your wife?" (v. 16, NASB). Or is he saying that such desertion is tantamount to infidelity, and that they are free to remarry? Speaking of these verses Ryrie says: "In some circumstances when two unbelievers had married and one of them subsequently became a Christian a divorce was allowed."[30]

A conclusion probably is that if the desertion is tentative, as would be the case of the unbeliever who remained not only unmarried but in friendly communication, the redemptive thing for the Christian to do would be to remain single also, regardless of legal

---

30. *Biblical Theology of the NT,* p. 207.

"rights" in the matter. But if the desertion is final, as when the unbeliever disappears completely or is known to have remarried, the believer's freedom may be interpreted as total.

4. *Possibilities of Grace.*

If to enter into a forbidden marriage is an act of adultery, is the continuation of the marriage a perpetuation of the adultery? Some take this position. However, if the second marriage is legal, it must be accepted as the only marriage which exists.

A marriage legal before the state but initially adulterous before God does not necessarily remain adulterous in God's sight. If the parties seek forgiveness for this as well as their other sins, it is reasonable to suppose that God validates their present marriage vows. He absorbs what should not have been into His redemptive will, even as He once chose Solomon out of a marriage that should never have occurred.

In the New Testament this position cannot be proved by chapter and verse, but it may be assumed from the compassionate love of God and from the absence of anything definite in the Scriptures to the contrary. Undoubtedly scores of first-generation, post-Pentecost converts were in exactly this sort of predicament. There is no inference whatever that any legal and stable marriages were repudiated or homes broken up by apostolic zeal because of past marital history. All Christians were to be faithful and pure from now on, in their present family and social setting. The past was under the Blood.

Section Six

The Society of the Saved

————◆————

30

New Testament Descriptions of the Church

New Testament theology, in its contemporary expression, has recovered not only the profound affirmations about Christ and His saving grace but also the inescapable declarations concerning the nature of the Church of Jesus Christ. Hunter is correct in seeing the unity of the New Testament in *Heilsgeschichte*, "the story of salvation." This story includes chiefly three elements: Christology, soteriology, and ecclesiology. "In other words," Hunter writes, "the *Heilsgeschichte* treats of a Saviour, a saved (and saving) People, and the means of Salvation. And these three are at bottom one—three strands in a single cord, a trinity in unity."[1]

Western, Greek-oriented religious thought tended to lose sight

---

1. *Message of the NT*, p. 9.

of the ecclesiology of New Testament teaching, mainly because of its heavy commitment to the primacy and freedom of the individual man. Needfully, there has been a return to the Bible teaching on the centrality of peoplehood, which in the New Testament is to be understood as the Church. Christ calls men to new life; simultaneously He calls men to life in community. Whenever a person begins to live "in Christ," he at the same time is incorporated into the people of God.

The New Testament teaching on the saved and saving community is the development of the Old Testament theme. Christians are heirs of the covenant made to Abraham. According to Gen. 17:6-8, *El Shaddai* (the Almighty God) established His covenant with Abraham and undertook to make him the father of a multitude of nations. "I will be your God, and you shall be my people" was the essence of that covenant. Mary in the Magnificat struck the same note. "He has helped his servant Israel in remembrance of his mercy, as he spoke to our fathers, to Abraham and his posterity forever" (Luke 1:54-55).

The coming of Christ was the fulfillment of the covenant with Abraham (cf. Acts 3:25 ff.). Paul sees the promises "made to Abraham and his offspring" as being realized in the Christian community because "the offspring" is not one "of the flesh" but "of the spirit," namely, Christ (Gal. 3:16 ff.).[2] Abraham's offspring is primarily Christ and then the sum total of those who belong to Christ. If one is Christ's, then he is Abraham's offspring, an heir according to the promise.

The Church is thus the New Israel which is embodied in Christ, and all who are "in him" constitute the true Israel, the Church. When Jesus chose 12 men to be with Him, their very number implied representation of the faithful remnant of Israel. The Master promises that they along with Him will judge "the twelve tribes of Israel" (Matt. 19:28; cf. Luke 22:30; Eph. 2:12-19). Bruce reminds us, however, that when the crucial test came, "the faithful remnant was reduced to one person, the Son of Man who entered death singlehanded and rose again as his people's representative. With him the people of God died and rose again: hence the New Testament people of God, while preserving its continuity with the Old Testament

---

2. The Greek word *sperma*, "offspring" or "seed," is singular, and can therefore refer to a single person as well as to a group of descendants.

people of God, is at the same time a new creation."[3] The rite of baptism, which signifies death and resurrection with Christ, declares that believers are incorporated into this new community, of which Christ is the very Life.

As Old Testament Israel was "chosen" by God, not for privileged status but spiritual service (Gen. 12:3; 15:6; Deut. 7:6; Hos. 1:1; Amos 3:2; et al.), so the New Testament Israel is chosen (Romans 9—11; Eph. 1:4; 1 Pet. 2:4-10) to live a holy life (1 Pet. 1:13-16) and to "bless the nations" (Luke 24:46-48; Acts 1:8; cf. Isa. 43:10, 12; 44:8). The Church as God's elect shares Christ's redemption-through-suffering role of bearing the reconciling Word of God to the nations. Another New Testament characterization of this saving role embraces the concept of priesthood. Peter calls the Christians "a royal priesthood" (1 Pet. 2:9), and John declares that the churches of Asia were made by Christ "a kingdom of priests" (Rev. 1:6). Christ's Church has been appointed to function as a priest for a sinful world, to intercede in its behalf to the end that it might be forgiven and transformed. The Church has a proclamatory responsibility, "to declare the wonderful deeds of him who called her out of darkness into his marvelous light" (1 Pet. 2:9). But she has also a priestly responsibility of suffering, if need be, to bring all men to Christ, who is her very spiritual Existence.

The Church is thus a saved and a saving community. She is a new order in society, not living aloof from the world, but living with a consciousness of her redemption and with a passion to share that redemption with those outside (John 17:14-16, 21).

I. THE EVENT OF CHRIST AND THE CHURCH

The word *event* denotes a happening that has extraordinary meaning for the person or persons involved. Life-styles, in some cases, are radically changed by an event. Whole societies sometimes experience new motivations for existence because of these special occurrences.

When we speak of the Church as event, we are not only denoting her coming into being at a particular time in the history of salvation, whether at the time of the Lord's choice of the Twelve, the Resurrection, or Pentecost, but also her continued "happening" in history. *Event* as used here connotes the saved people's profound

---

3. Cf. F. F. Bruce, *NT Development of OT Themes*, pp. 51-57.

awareness of the Lord's presence at any given time. One of the most instructive statements on the nature of the Church comes from the Lord himself and appears in a passage dealing with the resolution of personal conflicts in the life of His early followers: "For where two or three are gathered in my name, there am I in the midst of them" (Matt. 18:20).[4] On any given occasion when two or three persons come together "in the name of Christ," He presents himself to them and *there is the Church,* the true people of God. That tryst with Christ is an eventful moment because, wherever Christ appears, redemptive things happen.

Such a view of the nature of the Church emphasizes its contemporary reality because her existence depends upon the presence of the risen Lord. Moreover, as Robert Adolfs asserts, "The Church is a continuing event that is being accomplished in history and through people."[5] This is because the Church is a redeemed people moving across history and participating in the saving mission of Christ. Her viability relates to her authentic witness to the presence of her Lord; her maturation depends on her responses to the Lord's correction, direction, and call to serve needy men.

R. Newton Flew predicated his famous volume, *Jesus and His Church,* on the thesis that the Church is a new creation of Jesus. "It is old in the sense that it is a continuation of the life of Israel, the People of God. It is new in the sense that it is founded on the revelation made through Jesus of God's final purpose for mankind. It begins with the call to the first disciples."[6] The thesis of Flew is sound. However, the matter should be pressed theologically and it should be affirmed that the appearance of the Church is of the substance of the mighty deed of God in Christ. Viewed from the standpoint of holy history, the incarnation of Christ was at the same time the inauguration of the Church.[7]

It is most natural and proper to give proclamatory and theolog-

---

4. Cf. H. D. A. Major, *et al., The Mission and Message of Jesus* (New York: E. P. Dutton, Inc., 1947), p. 503, for a solid exegesis of the passage. Jeremias, in *NT Theology,* p. 170, says, "The *only* significance of the whole of Jesus' activity is to gather the eschatological people of God."

5. *The Church Is Different* (New York: Harper and Row, Inc., 1966), p. 3.

6. R. Newton Flew, *Jesus and His Church,* 2nd ed. (London: Epworth Press, 1943), pp. 97-98.

7. Cf. Richardson, *Introduction to the Theology of the NT,* p. 310: "Christ is not so much the 'founder' of the Church as he *is* himself the Church." For Richardson, the specific time of the founding was the outpouring of the Holy Spirit by the risen and ascended Lord.

ical primacy to Christology, that is, to preaching and teaching about
the person and work of Christ. The propriety of this tendency cannot
be argued. However, the meaning of the event of Christ is truncated
if there is neglect in declaring the relationship of Christ's coming to
the creation of the Church. To reiterate, when Christ appeared, the
Church appeared. So Brunner writes: "The *Ecclesia*, the Christian
society, thus itself belongs to the substance of the revelation and
constitutes the true end of the latter."[8] Ignatius' well-remembered
words are explanatory: *"Ubi Christus, ibi ecclesia"*—"Where Christ is,
there is the Church."

Israel of old was an event, having been called into existence by
God. The Old Testament, for the most part, has to do with the
election and creation of Israel, the people of God. When Adam
sinned and all subsequent generations pursued the same path of
rebellion, God turned to raising up a people who would serve Him in
love and obedience. So He called Abraham to be the father of a new
race of men. The Genesis writer in c. 12 pictures God as leading
the patriarch out of his security in Ur of the Chaldees to a strange
land where he was to father a blessed people, a new community of
believers. This surprising insinuation of God into the life of Abraham
was a redemptive event. Moreover, the emancipation of Israel from
Egypt and her establishment as a covenant people at Sinai were
integral to the redemptive nature of the Old Testament community
of faith.

When Israel forsook the divine covenantal life and turned to
idolatry, the prophets began to preach of a remnant *(she'ar)* of the
people whom God would bless and keep to himself.[9] Even that hope
proved elusive for centuries but was finally actualized in one Person,
the obedient Son, Jesus Christ. Matthew recalls, in connection with
the divine family's flight into Egypt, the arresting prophecy, "Out of
Egypt have I called my son" (Matt. 2:15; cf. Exod. 4:22, Hos. 11:1).

8. Emil Brunner, *The Misunderstanding of the Church,* trans. by Harold Knight
(Philadelphia: The Westminster Press, 1953), p. 14. Cf. Anders Nygren, ed., *This Is the
Church,* trans. by Carl C. Rasmussen (Philadelphia: Muhlenberg Press, 1952), p. 4: "In
the fact that Christ exists, the Church exists as his body." Also, this is the precise point
which John Knox makes but turns to fit another thesis, *The Church and the Reality of
Christ* (New York: Harper and Row, 1962), p. 26: "This being true, must we not say
that the Event we are concerned with, the only Event we can be crucially concerned
with, is simply the historical beginning of the Church itself?"

9. For a recent and illuminating discussion of "remnant," cf. Gerhard F. Hasel,
The Remnant: The History and Theology of the Remnant Idea from Genesis to Isaiah (Berrien
Springs, Mich.: Andrews University Press, 1972).

Jesus bore the destiny of the people of God alone. When Jesus Christ climbed toward Golgotha, He *alone* was the people of God. He bore the whole weight of God's work for this world.

Just like the old Israel, the Church is an event miraculously called into existence and sustained by God himself. Christ as the New Israel draws about himself those of like obedience to God the Father. In Him was and is created "the true Israel of God" (Gal. 6:16; cf. Rom. 9:6-8), an elect race, a royal priesthood, a holy nation, a people of God's own possession (1 Pet. 2:9; cf. Exod. 19:5-6). The Apostle Paul sees this development clearly. As noted above, he writes to the Galatians: "Now the promises were made to Abraham and to his off-spring. It does not say, 'And to offsprings,' referring to many; but referring to one, 'And to your offspring, which is Christ'" (Gal. 3:16). Paul then goes on to declare, "And if you are Christ's then you are Abraham's offspring, heirs according to promise" (Gal. 3:29).

The reality of Christ is the reality of the Church. The action of God in which He disclosed himself fully in Christ was simultaneously the action by which He called into being a people of obedience, the Church. Karl L. Schmidt concludes that "over against all sociological attempts to comprehend the Church, it must be noted that for Paul, for those who followed him, and for the Fourth Evangelist, ecclesiology and christology are identical."[10] If the two are not "identical," at least they are interlocked, so that one cannot be understood fully without the other.

This thesis finds support in certain leading ideas in the New Testament.

II. THE KINGDOM OF GOD

Jesus presented himself as the Power and Life of the kingdom of God (Matt. 12:28; Luke 17:21). He was, in His incarnate being, the primal evidence of the reign of God in the midst of the world. The "realized" character of the Kingdom has a necessary correlative in the Church.[11] The Church is "the vanguard of the kingdom to come,"

---

10. Karl L. Schmidt, *The Church*, trans. by J. R. Coates (London: Adam and Charles Black, 1950), p. 21.

11. Flew, *Jesus and His Church*, p. 13; Purkiser *et al.*, "The Kingdom of God," *Exploring Our Christian Faith*, pp. 519-37; R. O. Zorn, *Church and Kingdom* (Philadelphia: Presbyterian and Reformed Publishing Co., 1962); John Bright, *The Kingdom of God* (Nashville: Abingdon-Cokesbury Press, 1953).

or, "the community of the interval" between the "kingdom's inauguration in the event of Christ and its consummation at the eschaton."[12]

As the community of the new age of the kingly rule of God, broken open by the event of Christ, the Church lives in a tension. She experiences joy in what God has done and is doing in and through her, and yet she yearns for the complete victory of God over the kingdom of Satan. She possesses the life of the new age now through Christ who has brought and continues to bring that life to her, but she looks forward to the fulfillment of God's purposes of redemption in the age to come (cf. 1 Cor. 10:11; Heb. 12:22; 13:14). This life in the Church, created and nurtured by the Spirit of Christ, the embodiment of the sovereign power of God, as Brunner has depicted it, is "life on the threshold—one foot has already passed it, the other is still here."[13]

The Church is an inseparable part of the Kingdom but not "differentiated from it in the same way that an organ of the body, though part of it, is nevertheless to be distinguished from the whole." She is the community where the redemptive gifts and powers of the Kingdom, insofar as they are already present, are known and enjoyed. This means that the Church is not only the creature of the event of Christ, but is also the place where the redemptive glories of that event are made continuous in mankind's history.

III. THE ECCLESIA

Ecclēsia is another expression in the New Testament signifying the new people of God called into existence by the event of Christ.[14] Commonly translated "church" in the New Testament and widely used throughout certain books, the term does not appear in Mark,

---

12. A parallel concept is found in the phrase "a colony of heaven." Phil. 3:20: "But our commonwealth is in heaven, and from it we await a Savior, the Lord Jesus"; cf. Eph. 2:12, 19. *Politeuma* in Phil. 3:20 denotes (1) a colony of foreigners in a foreign country, or (2) the capital or native city which keeps the citizen residing in distant lands on its registers. Perhaps the second view is better. Though residing in a world of noncitizens of heaven, the Church possesses a relationship to the capital city of God which cannot be taken from them. Cf. "Politeuma," in Arndt and Gingrich, *Greek-English Lexicon of the NT,* p. 692.

13. Brunner, *The Misunderstanding of the Church,* p. 57.

14. Cf. also "The True Vine," John 15; "God's Temple," 1 Cor. 3:16-17; Eph. 2:21; "The Household of God," Eph. 2:19 (see "house of Israel," Heb. 8:8; "house of God," Heb. 10:21; 1 Pet. 4:17); cf. Paul S. Minear, *Images of the Church in the New Testament* (Philadelphia: The Westminster Press, 1960).

Luke, John, 2 Timothy, Titus, 1 and 2 Peter, 1 and 2 John. In Heb. 2:12 it is used in a quotation from Ps. 22:22, and in 12:23 where the reference is to "the heavenly Jerusalem," or the Church in heaven.

Extensive study has been made of the etymology of this word and its significance in Christian usage. Literally, the *ecclēsia* means "the called out" or "the assembled." It derives from a Greek compound *ek*, meaning "out of" or "from," and *kalein*, meaning "to call." The word was employed in secular Greek to express this literal meaning of assemblage, especially to denote a gathering of people for political purposes. It referred to the citizenry *(demos)* of a Greek city-state *(polis)* who had the privilege of voting. This particular use of the word is found in Acts 19:32, 39-40, in the account of the Apostle Paul's struggles with the silversmiths in Ephesus. In these verses, *ecclēsia* is used of a gathering of the people, i.e., a secular assembly.

K. L. Schmidt sees special significance in this derivation of *ecclēsia*, since the *demos*, the assembled citizens, are the *ecclētoi*, "the called out ones," who have been summoned by the *kērux*, the herald. The picture here is that of a people in a given city, who upon hearing the sound of a trumpet, hastily gather at an appointed meeting place to transact community business. They are a political unit, a company of the concerned, who are aware of their responsibility to remedy the situation which has arisen in their community. Schmidt says that this "naturally suggests that in the Bible the reference is to God in Christ calling men out of the world."[15]

In common usage, as far as we know, no religious associations were attached to *ecclēsia*. Perhaps this accounts for the Septuagint translators employing it to render the term *qahal Yahweh*, meaning "the congregation of the Lord." The expression refers to Israel as assembled before the Lord. This translation appears about 100 times in the Septuagint. *Qahal* derives from the Hebrew root meaning "to call." When it is modified with the addition of *Yahweh*, it takes on the special religious meaning. Israel is the "called out people of the Lord."[16]

---

15. *The Church*, pp. 28 ff.
16. Sometimes the LXX uses *synagōgē* to translate *qahal*, especially in the first four books of the Pentateuch. *Synagōgē* also means "assembly" or "gathering." The OT refers to Israel as *'edhah*, which comes from a verb meaning "to appoint." Israel as *'edhah Yahweh* is "the properly constituted congregation of the Lord." In the LXX *'edhah* is translated regularly by the Greek *sunagōgē*. Richardson's judgment is probably correct: "In general use *qahal* and *'edhah*, like *ecclēsia* and *sunagōgē*, are synonyms" (*Introduction to the Theology of the NT*, p. 285).

Despite the ramifications of the derivation of the term, the essential element defining the nature of the Church is quite simple.[17] The Church as *ecclēsia* is the summoned community responding in obedience to the call of God's Herald, Jesus Christ, yielding herself to His will, and living out His life in the world. The Church exists where men obediently respond to the summons of the Word, where they gather to worship under the direction of the Word, where they know themselves to be separated from the world because of the radically life-changing power of the Word.

When the Church ceases to respond obediently and joyfully to Christ, settling for something less than the responsive life to the Word, as for example, to live as a society in harmony with the spirit of the times, she is not the *ecclētoi*. Furthermore, when she no longer gathers "in His name"—when she fails to confess before all the world that she has no other reason to assemble than to worship Him and to permit His power to renew her for His service—she has no right to call herself the Church.

The term *ecclēsia* is also used in the New Testament to express the unique oneness of the Church. In Acts 8:1 there appears an explicit reference to the *ecclēsia* in Jerusalem, but in 9:31 the word *in the singular* is used not merely for the Jerusalem community but for all the Christian communities in Judea, Galilee, and Samaria. Although the plural *ecclēsiai* is also used to designate all the churches (Acts 15:41; 16:5), there is a fairly consistent use of the singular to express the Church at large. A congregation in any given place is called *ecclēsia* with the understanding that it represents the Church of God. Paul exhorts the elders of Ephesus: "Take heed to yourselves and to all the flock, in which the Holy Spirit has made you guardians, to feed the church of the Lord" (Acts 20:28).

The Church is not the sum of all the congregations. Each community, even a house church, represents the total community, the Church. Paul is explicit on this point. For example 1 Cor. 1:2 and 2 Cor. 1:1 read: "to the Church of God, which is at Corinth" *(tē ecclēsia . . . tē ousē en Korinth)*. The proper translation of the Greek is not "the Corinthian congregation" but "the Church as it is in Corinth." The Church in Corinth is not part of the Church of God; rather it *is* the

---

17. Cf. Schmidt, *The Church*, p. 24. Cf. F. J. A. Hort, *The Christian Ecclesia* (London: Macmillan and Co., 1897); G. Johnston, *The Doctrine of the Church in the New Testament* (Cambridge: University Press, 1943); Alfred F. Kuen, *I Will Build My Church*, trans. by Ruby Lindblad (Chicago: Moody Press, 1971), pp. 45-55.

Church of God. Schmidt writes, "Ornamental epithets are never employed; the only attribute, so to speak, is the genitive, 'of God,' which comes from the OT."[18]

This strong sense of oneness was not accidental. It arose out of the early Christians' common experience in Christ. In Christ, there could be only one people of God, one *ecclēsia*. Though expressed in local fellowships of believers, the Church remained always and singly "the Church of God." Even today Christians are accustomed "to speak of the Church of God but not of the congregations of God."

The *ecclēsia*, in conclusion, is "God's gathering."[19] It is a new people brought into being through God's act in Christ Jesus. Thus, wherever the Church exists, God is at work in Christ Jesus calling men into reconciling fellowship with himself. This is the salvation event, in its initial and continuous character. The Church is the evidence that salvation through Christ is happening.

IV. THE BODY OF CHRIST

This exclusively Pauline term (1 Corinthians 12; Eph. 1:22-23; 2:16; 4:12-16; Col. 1:18) carries notions of unity in diversity, mutuality, and headship.[20] One of the central thrusts of this metaphor is expressed in 1 Cor. 12:27: "Now you are the body of Christ and individually members of it." "The community is, therefore not *like* the Body of Christ," writes Nelson, "but *is* the Body of Christ on earth."[21] Eduard Schweizer underscores this thought: "Paul therefore knows and takes earnestly the fact that the Body of Christ is at the last nothing else but Christ Himself, living in the community. The community is the secondary, special form of the existence of Christ."[22]

The phrase has a unique duality. On the one hand, it denotes our *incorporation* in Christ, and on the other hand, our *extension of the incarnation* of Christ. We are in Christ (2 Cor. 5:17) but we are also

---

18. *The Church*, p. 7; 1 Cor. 10:32; 11:22; Gal. 1:13; 1 Tim. 3:5, 15.

19. Leslie Newbigin, *The Household of God* (New York: Friendship Press, 1954), p. 21.

20. J. Robert Nelson, *The Realm of Redemption* (Greenwich, Conn.: Seabury Press, 1951), pp. 27-76. This book is one of the most exhaustive studies on this metaphor. Cf. also J. A. T. Robinson, *The Body: A Study in Pauline Theology* (Chicago: Henry Regnery Co., 1951); Alan Cole, *The Body of Christ* (Philadelphia: The Westminster Press, 1965); E. Schweizer, "Soma," *Theological Dictionary of the NT*, 7:1024-94.

21. *Ibid.*, p. 75.

22. Eduard Schweizer, *Das Leben des Herren in der Gemeinde und ihre Dienste* (Zurich, 1946), p. 51.

"the supreme agency of mediation following upon that of the Incarnate Son of God Himself."[23] Robinson touches upon the event nature of the Church when he writes that she "represents that point in the creative and redemptive activity of God where He is revealed; and as such it is a continuation of that process of showing forth of himself which was begun when the Word 'was in the world . . . yet the world knew him not.' "[24]

The Church exists as "an embodiment and perpetuation of the saving work Christ himself began in the flesh."[25] The acts of the Church are really the acts of Christ.

To speak of the Church as *to sōma tou Theou* (the Body of God) is to emphasize the living, dynamic, organismic character of the community. But it must be remembered that the Church also has an institutional existence. This fact is made plain in the New Testament in the references to the appointment of persons to maintain and to promote the Church as a human social order. It is also underscored in the struggles and persecutions which the Church experienced as a social structure within the existing cultural and political order of the first century. Nevertheless, her event character is primary in the definition of her being.

Colin Williams thus writes, "The Church is a movement—a pilgrim people moving across time and space in participation in the mission of Jesus Christ. It is an event because this participation has to happen, and that happening is not something that is guaranteed in the institutional heritage."[26] At times the Church must be freed from culturally conditioned, structural forms in order to authentically express Christ's life in the world. The same Lord who continues to create the Church also equips her with the needed, though temporary, forms of her servanthood.[27]

---

23. J. S. Whale, *Christian Doctrine* (New York: The Macmillan Co., 1941), p. 140. Alan Cole takes issue with the idea of the Church as the extension of the Incarnation. In his judgment it is an "illegitimate extension of metaphor" (*The Body of Christ*, pp. 69-71).

24. Wm. Robinson, *The Biblical Doctrine of the Church* (St. Louis: Bethany Press, 1948), p. 71.

25. Zorn, *Church and Kingdom*, p. 43. Cf. E. Stauffer, *New Testament Theology*, tr. by John Marsh (London: SCM Press, 1955), p. 156: "The Church is the body of Christ. In the story of her suffering and her glorification the destiny of Jesus Christ in his passion, death, resurrection comes to its conclusion."

26. *The Church: New Directions in Theology Today* (London: Lutterworth Press, 1969), 4:27.

27. Williams acknowledges that event and institution are inseparable, but often

V. THE KOINONIA OF THE SPIRIT

A concept concomitant with the "body of Christ" image is that of the Church as a *koinōnia* or fellowship. In 2 Cor. 13:14, Paul concludes his Epistle with a benediction in which appears the phrase "the fellowship of the Holy Spirit." In an appeal to sensitive Christian living, Paul again uses the phrase in Phil. 2:1. Elsewhere he speaks of Christians being "called into the fellowship *[koinōnia]* of his Son, Jesus Christ" (1 Cor. 1:9).

This important word *koinōnia* has several meanings according to the way it is used in the New Testament. Students are divided as to where the stress should be placed. But Nelson's conclusion is judicious:

> There is a fundamental residue of agreement among them as to the *koinōnia* experience of the early Church. The strong brotherly feeling which was so real among them was not a solidarity necessitated by their circumstances . . . but was due to the positive bonds of love which derived from God, who gave the gift of His Spirit.[28]

Apart from the *agapē* love of God, which He pours into our hearts through the Holy Spirit (Rom. 5:5), the biblical concept of *koinōnia* is completely unintelligible. The Church is not specifically called "the fellowship of the Spirit," but the use of the term *koinonia* describes "the inner life of the *ecclēsia*."[29]

The faithful are bound to each other through their common sharing in Christ as the Body of Christ, and in the Holy Spirit (1 John 3:24). *Koinōnia* thus signifies common participation, togetherness, and community life, all created by the presence of the Holy Spirit. *Koinōnia Christou* and *koinōnia pneumatos* are synonyms, because Christ dwells in His Church through His Spirit.

---

he says they develop a severe tension. His conclusion is sound: "Institution is at the service of event, and where the form of the institution is standing in the way of the happening of contemporary obedience to God's call to his people to move on with him in history, then the priority of event must be recognized (Gal. 3:5-29)" (*ibid.,* 28).

28. *The Realm of Redemption,* pp. 57-58; cf. also J. Y. Campbell, *"Koinonia* and Its Cognates in the New Testament," *Journal of Biblical Literature,* LI (1932), p. 353; F. Hauck, "Koinonia," *TDNT,* 3:797-808.

29. Frank Stagg, *New Testament Theology* (Nashville: Broadman Press, 1962), p. 198. Cf. his definition of sharing as participation in the whole of something, as "belonging" to a family, and his discussion of *koinōnia* as gift and demand, pp. 198-200. Brunner speaks of the Spirit as supplying the *dynamism* of the *Ecclesia.* The most extensive survey of the meaning of *koinōnia* as it relates to the Church is L. S. Thornton, *The Common Life in the Body of Christ* (London: Dacre Press, 1950); cf. pp. 59 ff. on 2 Cor. 13:14.

The Book of Acts clearly indicates that the earliest Christians knew themselves as the community of the Spirit. Pentecost involved several experiential elements that were integral to the creation of the Church. But the most important fact is that the little company of believers in Jerusalem "experienced an extraordinary access of new power which they identified with the Spirit of God mediated by the exalted Christ."[30] Someone has commented that the word "And they were all filled with the Holy Spirit" (Acts 2:4) is the most important sentence in the history of the Christian Church.

The early Christians interpreted the Pentecost occasion as the fulfillment of Old Testament prophecy, primarily Joel 2:28-32 (Acts 2:14-21). That prophecy declared the introduction of the Age of the Spirit. The early Christians believed that the Age had dawned and that they were enjoying its blessings. By the Spirit operating in and through it, the Church belonged to the world to come.[31] Through the power of the indwelling Holy Spirit they were able to speak in "other tongues" or "languages" (2:4), to heal the sick (3:1-10; 5:12-16), to respond knowledgeably to their opponents, as in the case of Stephen (c. 7), and to be employed in other unusual ways for the furtherance of the Word of grace, as in the case of Philip (Acts 8:39).

Most important, they sensed among themselves an unexpected and remarkable unity, which properly can be called the *koinōnia* of the Spirit. Acts 2:42 reads, "And they devoted themselves to the apostles' teaching and fellowship *[koinōnia]*, to the breaking of bread and the prayers." Besides spiritual power (4:33), faith (6:5), and wholehearted sharing of material goods in that time of need (2:43-45; 4:32-37), their youthful fellowship was characterized by boldness (*parrēsia,* 4:31). Moreover, periodically these early Christians were conscious of the renewal of that fellowship by special infillings of the Spirit (4:8, 31; 13:52).

Through the entire account of the Church in the Book of Acts it is the common life in the Spirit that not only identifies the Church but also impels and directs her outreach into the Mediterranean world. Acts 9:31 reads: "So the church throughout all Judea and Galilee and Samaria had peace and was built up; and walking in the fear

---

30. Hunter, *Message of the NT,* pp. 62-63.
31. Cf. Suzanne de Dietrich, *The Witnessing Community* (Philadelphia: The Westminster Press, 1958), p. 165, where she speaks of "The Church 'between the times.'"

of the Lord and in the comfort *(paraklēsei)* of the Holy Spirit it was multiplied."

The mission to the Gentiles developed out of this *koinōnia.* While the people of the church at Antioch were "worshiping the Lord and fasting, the Holy Spirit said, 'Set apart for me Barnabas and Saul for the work to which I have called them.' Then after fasting and praying they laid their hands on them and sent them off" (13:2-3).

During his second missionary journey, Paul and his evangelistic companions decided to double back through Asia Minor after they had reached the western extremity of Asia but were forbidden by the Holy Spirit. They were directed to cross the Aegean to Europe (16: 6-10). All this emphasizes that the Church was the place where the Spirit was acting. The Church would have been, and is today, lifeless without the Spirit. This life was evidenced in the communion prevailing among the members. They were one in the bond of love produced by the indwelling Spirit.

A word from Brunner's *The Misunderstanding of the Church* is instructive. Since the Holy Spirit is "the very life-breath of the Church, the Church participates in the special character of the holy, the numinous, the supernatural, in the hallowing presence of God: for that reason the Christian society itself is a miracle."[32] The *communio sanctorum* is more than a cooperative venture of men of common interests, highly religious as they might be. It is more than a congenial and loving society of persons responding to human needs. It is a "happening," like Pentecost, brought about by the Holy Spirit who by His presence infuses hearts with the risen life of the Son, and thereby creates a *koinōnia.* Brunner says that the Church is itself a miracle whenever and wherever it exists because it is a creation of the Spirit.

In conclusion, when time has run its course and the Eternal Father has determined to bring to an end His work of redemption, the Son of Man will return to this earthly order to catch away His waiting Bride, the Church. Though the Church will have suffered indignities at the hands of evil men and will have struggled, sometimes cowardly, sometimes valiantly, against the *civitas diaboli,* she will come forth as a Bride adorned for a wedding. This will be the final and sustained expression of the Church—the Church in eternal happening, because her Lord will be in the midst of her eternally.

---

32. Brunner, *Misunderstanding of the Church,* p. 12.

"Then I heard what seemed to be the voice of a great multitude, like the sound of many waters and like the sound of many thunder-peals, crying, 'Hallelujah! For the Lord our God the Almighty reigns. Let us rejoice and exult and give him the glory, for the marriage of the Lamb has come, and his Bride has made herself ready; it was granted her to be clothed with fine linen, bright and pure—for the fine linen is the righteous deeds of the saints.' And the angel said to me, 'Write this: Blessed are those who are invited to the marrage supper of the Lamb'" (Rev. 19:6-9).

31

The Church as
Sacramental Community

The Church in her being is an event. Whenever Christ comes into the presence of a people, there He creates a community of faith which is the Church. But the Church has an ongoing life as faith is kept alive, and this continuance is to be understood in functional terms. The Church becomes and remains a sacramental community, both receiving grace and mediating grace.[1] As she responds to the presence of Christ, she both maintains her existence in grace and seeks to share her life with others. Christ is peculiarly with His Church but He is also reaching out through His people to the unredeemed that they might know salvation by grace through faith. What the Church really does is to live so as to make the saving event a possible and continuous experience. The promise of success rests in her Lord, who declared that "the gates of hell shall not prevail against" His Church (Matt. 16:18, KJV).

The Church's ministry has its genesis and *raison d'etre* in the in-

---

1. By definition, "sacramental" means "pertaining to sacraments or sacred rites." In the Christian communion it refers to particular holy acts, such as baptism and Eucharist. A sacrament, technically defined, is an act in which divine grace is signified and received. Any rite therefore that witnesses to or brings God's grace to men is sacramental. Broadly speaking, the Church's life is sacramental in that God's grace is proclaimed, mediated, and experienced in and through it. We are therefore justified in concluding that the whole life of Christ's Church is "a means of grace." "Sacramental" is employed in this sense in this study.

timate relationship between Christ and His disciples. During Christ's earthly ministry, He sent His disciples out, vested with power and authority, to minister in the same way He was ministering. They were to proclaim the coming of the kingdom of heaven, work miracles of healing and exorcism, and invoke peace, the hallmark of the Messianic kingdom (Matt. 10:1-15). Reception or rejection of these disciples was tantamount to the reception or rejection of Christ himself. The Lord reminded them that the very same Spirit which endowed Him for mission would labor through them (Matt. 10:20). In His valedictory prayer, Christ shares with the Father: "As thou didst send me into the world, so have I sent them into the world" (John 17:18). Following the Resurrection, the disciples received the gift of the Holy Spirit in full measure and were equipped for the fulfillment of Christ's ministry in and through their lives (cf. John 20: 22 ff.; Acts 1:8; 2:4 ff.).

Riesenfeld writes: "To represent Christ means to be like Him, to become as He was, not in some novel way which they devise for themselves, but by letting His mission speak through their whole course of life."[2] This ministry might result in persecution (Matt. 10: 21-23) and sacrifice (Matt. 10:38) like the Lord's, but "the servant is not above the Master." Thus, the ministry of the Church is a visible, authentic, and authoritative extension and continuation of Christ's own ministry and work. His salvific activity was indeed unique and definitive, including "revelation, expiatory sacrifice, and victory over the powers of evil." But all the redemptive power of that work flows on through Christ's chosen community as He lives and functions through her. There are three special sacramental functions of the Church which need exploration: namely, witnessing, baptism, and the Lord's Supper.

I. Witnessing

Suzanne de Dietrich, in *The Witnessing Community*, properly characterizes the Church by that title. She writes, "The church's primary function is to proclaim his deeds to every generation, to confess its faith in him, and to laud him for what he has done."[3] As the Book of Acts makes abundantly clear, the early apostles joyfully shared with their

---

2. Harald Riesenfeld, "The Ministry in the New Testament," *The Root of the Vine* (Westminster: Dacre Press, 1953), p. 111.

3. (Philadelphia: The Westminster Press, 1958), p. 149.

generation the good news that Christ is *Christus Victor* and therefore God's saving work is complete in Him. Clearly, the Church is "not simply a company of witnesses, it is itself the witnessing community."[4] This means that the Church was brought into existence by the gracious act of God in Christ; and, furthermore, she is the continuing expression of God's grace to men. In her collective character she declares the salvation of God.

The Church's role as a witnessing community relates also to the commission given her by the Lord. "Go therefore and make disciples of all nations, baptizing them in the name of the Father and of the Son and of the Holy Spirit" (Matt. 28:19; cf. Mark 16:15). The fulfillment of this commission is possible through the empowering ministry of the Holy Spirit. Christ prophesied the effects of Pentecost on the small group of believers. "But you shall receive power when the Holy Spirit has come upon you; and you shall be my witnesses *[martures]* in Jerusalem and in all Judea and Samaria and to the end of the earth" (Acts 1:8).

Martures in this instance does not refer to any witnesses to the events of the life of Jesus; rather the disciples are persons who have experienced for themselves the life-changing power of the life, death, and resurrection of the Lord. Their testimony is more than a recounting of the events; it is in itself the divine message of salvation. When the Church is truly the Church, she feels a compulsion to witness to her Lord's redeeming grace.

Peter and John reflected this compulsion arising out of new life when they said to the religious leaders in Jerusalem, "Whether it is right in the sight of God to listen to you rather than God, you must judge; for we cannot but speak of what we have seen and heard" (Acts 4:19-20). The witnessing Church is thus deeply and joyfully involved with her Lord. She is ready to pay any price, being martyred if need be, in order to give her witness to His redeeming grace.

Witnessing, sacramentally understood, takes many forms— worshiping, teaching, personal testimony, preaching, performing miracles, and "helping" (1 Cor. 12:4-11, 27-30). In Ephesians Paul depicts the ascending Christ as giving gifts to the Church: "And his gifts were that some should be apostles, some prophets, some evangelists, some pastors and teachers, for the equipment of the saints, for

---

4. Daniel T. Niles, *The Preacher's Task and the Stone of Stumbling* (New York: Harper and Bros., 1958), p. 110.

the work of ministry, for building up the body of Christ" (4:11-12). These specially endowed persons give leadership to the entire community, assisting it in mediating grace to the world.

A. Worship

Worship is the joyful celebration of Christ's presence. But here again this activity is not a self-serving activity, but rather a witness to the world that the Church's commitment to her Lord is "a service to God." Stauffer emphasizes this point. Christian worship is giving glory to God but it is also "most certainly, a service to the world. . . . Christian worship rooted men out of their self-centered individualism into an *extra nos*—away from all that is subjective—up to that which is simply objective. This was its service to humanity. It summoned the nations to worship the crucified. This was its service to God's glory."[5] By preaching and intercession she carried out this obligation.

1. *Words for Worship.*

The very words used for worship convey the concepts of service and ministry. In the Old Testament, the general word used is *'abodah,* from *abad,* "to labor, to serve." It is usually translated "the service of God." The specific act of worship is expressed in the word *hishtahawa,* which derives from *shaba,* "to bow, to prostrate oneself." The concept here is one of obeisance for the purpose of service. In the New Testament the word corresponding to the Old Testament term *'abodah* is *latreia.* This originally meant "servitude" or "the state of a hired laborer or slave." By broader usage, especially with respect to cultic practices, it came to denote "the service of God" or divine worship. The New Testament word corresponding to the Old Testament *hishtahawa* is *proskunein.* This means literally "to kiss the hand to [towards] one" and metaphorically "to prostrate oneself, to make obeisance or worship." *Proskunein,* which appears about 60 times, also carries in its etymology the concept of service to the object of worship.[6]

The blending of the concepts of what we call worship and service prevails also with regard to the verb *leitourgein.* Acts 13:2 uses a

---

5. *NT Theology,* p. 201.

6. Cf. H. Strathmann, "latreuō, latreia," *TDNT,* 4:53-65: these terms referred to cultic worship, particularly in the OT, but in the NT they are spiritualized and have to do with the whole life as an act of worship or service to God. H. Greeven, "proskuneō," *TDNT,* 6:758-66.

participle form *(leitourgountōn)* to express the idea of worshipping, while Paul employs an infinitive form *(leitourgesai)* to indicate service. He tells the Romans that the Gentiles, who received spiritual blessings from the Jerusalem Christians, ought also to be of "service" to them in material blessings, that is, to raise an offering to alleviate their poverty (Rom. 15:27).

The noun *leitourgia* can refer to the ministrations of a priest, as in the case of Zechariah, the father of John the Baptist (Luke 1:23). The word can also mean ministry in its broadest sense (Heb. 8:6), or the act of worship itself (Heb. 9:21), or sacrificial deeds for others (Phil. 2:17; cf. 2 Cor. 9:12). The minister is a *leitourgos,* essentially a servant of the people. Paul writes to the Roman Christians that because of the grace given to him by God he was made a "minister *[leitourgon]* of Christ Jesus to the Gentiles in the priestly service of the gospel of God" (Rom. 15:15-16). Christ, our High Priest, is also a minister *(leitourgos)* in the heavenly sanctuary for us (Heb. 8:2).[7]

What is important in these terms is the background of ministry or service to God. In Jesus' instructions to His disciples before His death, He warned them that their opponents would put them out of the synagogues; "indeed, the hour is coming when whoever kills you will think he is offering service *[latreian]* to God" (John 16:2). The Apostle Paul appeals to the Roman Christians to present their bodies "as a living sacrifice, holy and acceptable to God, which is your spiritual worship *[latreian]*" (Rom. 12:1; cf. KJV, "service"). To the Philippians he writes: "For we are the true circumcision, who worship *[latreuontes]* God in spirit, and glory in Christ Jesus, and put no confidence in the flesh" (3:3). In the Apocalypse, John sees a great unnumbered multitude assembled from all nations worshiping *(prosekunēsan)* God (7:11). When he asks about their identity, the elders respond that they are the survivors of the tribulation who had washed their robes in the blood of the Lamb. "These are . . . before the throne of God and serve *[latreuousin]* him day and night within his temple" (7:14-15).

Worship is adoration, reverence, and communion. But it is, at the same time, an offering of oneself in service to God. It is identification with God through the Spirit for *maturation* in love and for the *ministry* of love to mankind.

---

7. R. Mayer and H. Strathmann, "elitourgeō, leitourgia," *TDNT,* 4:215-31.

2. Worship Patterns.

Christianity's worship patterns developed slowly, but from the New Testament record certain basic characteristics are discernible.

a. As to place, at first the Christians gathered in the Temple, in accordance with the Jewish custom and Jesus' habits (Mark 14:49; Acts 2:46; 5:42). Also, simultaneously at the beginning they met in homes, probably in the house of the mother of John Mark, where the Last Supper and Pentecost took place (Acts 1:13; 12:12; cf. Luke 24:33). The expression *kat'oikon* in Acts 2:46 and 5:42 might be translated "from house to house" (NIV), possibly suggesting that several houses became worship centers.[8] Paul's churches were also house churches (Rom. 16:5; 1 Cor. 16:19; cf. also Col. 4:15; Philem. 2).

b. Services took place daily, according to Acts 2:46; 5:42; but soon the services were specifically marked out for the Lord's Day, the first day of the week, in commemoration of the Lord's resurrection (Acts 20:7; Rev. 1:10; "the Lord's day"; cf. also Didache 14, 1). Cullmann writes, "Each Lord's Day was an Easter Festival."[9]

c. Taking their clues pretty much from their Jewish heritage, the Christians carried on instruction, preaching, praying, and breaking of bread when they met together (Acts 2:42, 46; 20:7). From the fragmentary references in the New Testament we can discern a sort of reformed synagogue pattern of worship. Preaching, a basic activity in worship, will be treated at length later. Praying was no doubt free at first but later took on some liturgical form, as when the Christians might have recited together the Lord's Prayer (cf. the use of "Abba" in Rom. 8:15; Gal. 4:6). Another liturgical prayer was the Aramaic *Maranatha,* "Come, Lord Jesus," in 1 Cor. 16:22 and Rev. 22:20. In the New Testament we find benedictions and doxologies employed by the early Christians. For example, note, "The grace of our Lord be with your spirit" (Gal. 6:18; Phil. 4:23), or "be with you" (1 Cor. 16:23), or "be with you all" (Rev. 22:21), or "the grace of the Lord Jesus Christ and the love of God and the communion of the Holy Spirit be with you all" (2 Cor. 13:14).

The doxological formulas are introduced either with "blessed" (*eulogētos,* Rom. 1:25; 9:5; 2 Cor. 11:31) or "glory" (*doxa,* Rom. 11:36; Gal. 1:5; Phil. 4:20). "Amen" appears frequently in the New Testa-

---

8. Oscar Cullmann, *Early Christian Worship,* trans. A. Stewart Todd and James B. Torrance (London: SCM Press, 1953), pp. 9-10.

9. *Ibid.*

ment and we assume that it was employed in the worship of the Church. With doxologies it occurs in Rom. 1:25; 9:5; 11:36; 16:27; Gal. 1:5; Eph. 3:21; Phil. 4:20; 1 Tim. 1:17; 6:16; 2 Tim. 4:18; Heb. 13:21; 1 Pet. 4:11; 5:11; Jude 25. Worship in heaven by the four living creatures includes "Amen" (Revelation 5). At the very end of the book the response to the solemn assurance of the Lord's return is "Amen. Come, Lord Jesus!" (22:20). These elements of prayer might well have been fashioned from Jewish modes of worship.

Freedom prevailed in the worship of the early community. In Acts 4:24-31 we read of a sudden outburst of praise, singing, and prayer upon the release of Peter and John by the Sanhedrin. Paul encouraged his people to sing together "psalms, hymns, and spiritual songs" (Eph. 5:19; Col. 3:16; cf. also 1 Cor. 14:26). The Apocalypse contains several psalmlike Christian hymns, acclaiming God and Christ as King (4:8, 11; 5:9-10; 11:17; 19:1, 6). Some scholars view Phil. 2:5-11 and Col. 1:15-20 as early Christian hymns.[10] Other possible hymn fragments are Eph. 5:14; 1 Tim. 3:16; 2 Tim. 2:11-13; 1 Pet. 3:18-22.[11] Some of the most remarkable hymns are found in Luke's birth narratives: The Magnificat (1:46-56); The Benedictus (1:67-79); the Gloria (2:14); the Nunc Dimittis (2:29-32). Pliny, writing about A.D. 112, comments that the Christians of Bithynia sang "hymns to Christ as God," a note suggesting an established feature of Christian worship.[12]

In Christian services there were also healings, other miraculous manifestations of divine power, and informal and spontaneous speaking (1 Corinthians 12—14). All of these occurrences were considered signs of the ministry of the Holy Spirit among Christ's people.

The posture for prayer in worship was varied, sometimes kneeling (Luke 22:41; Eph. 3:14), sometimes prostration (Mark 14:35; 1 Cor. 14:25), but most often standing (cf. Mark 11:25; Luke 18:11, 13). This posture, often with uplifted hands and face turned upward, was very common among both pagans and Jews. Christians probably adopted the standing position, as suggested by 1 Tim. 2:8.

---

10. Cf. R. P. Martin, *Carmen Christi. Philippians ii. 5-11 in Recent Interpretation and in the Setting of Early Christian Worship* (Cambridge: University Press, 1967), pp. 17-23.

11. Cf. C. F. D. Moule, *Worship in the New Testament* (Richmond, Va.: John Knox Press, 1961), pp. 67-81, on "The Language of Worship."

12. *Epistles*, X, 96.

B. The Breaking of Bread

Another worship practice of the early Christians was the breaking of bread *(hē klasis tou artou).* In Acts 2:42, this term "breaking of bread" is employed as if it were a common practice (cf. Acts 2:46). According to Acts 20:7, 11, following a sermon by the Apostle Paul, the people engaged in the rite of bread breaking.

It is the opinion of many scholars that the joyful breaking of bread is to be connected with the Eucharist. Higgins writes: "'The breaking of bread' became a name for the Christian Lord's Supper because Jesus at his last Passover meal imposed a new and un-exampled significance and importance on the bread. It was the earliest name for the Eucharist as the successor of the Jewish Passover."[13] He also sees the phrase "the bread which we break" in 1 Cor. 10:16, where Paul instructs the Corinthian Church about her behavior at the Eucharist, as definitely indicating the relationship.

Acts 2:42-47 is not so clear on the point of eucharistic elements, but the argument from silence should not determine the case.[14] Moule's conclusion is cautious and more nearly correct: "There is no need to believe that every meal explicitly carried this significance (that is, sacramental): no doubt there was an uninstitutional freedom and flexibility. But if the Pauline tradition is a true one, it is difficult to believe that there was not, from the very first, a vivid awareness of this aspect of Christian breaking of bread also."[15]

It might well be, in keeping with Jewish meal requirements, that the rite of "breaking bread" preceded the actual eating and it served the function of thanksgiving for the food and acknowledgement of the risen Lord's presence. The "bread-breaking" occasions were therefore times of fellowship with some sacramental meaning.

1. Since the early believers were bound together by the Holy Spirit and shared a common spiritual life, these times of eating together served more than secular ends.

---

13. A. J. B. Higgins, *The Lord's Supper in the New Testament* (Chicago: Alec R. Allenson, Inc., 1952), p. 56; I. Howard Marshall, *Luke: Historian and Theologian* (Grand Rapids, Mich.: Wm. B. Eerdmans Publishing Co.), p. 206: "The breaking of bread and the Lord's Supper are names for the identical meal." Oscar Cullmann finds a very close connection between the Eucharist and "the breaking of bread," especially at the point of the "rejoicing" characteristic of both the communal meal and the Eucharist (*Early Christian Worship*, pp. 14-20); J. Jeremias, *The Eucharistic Words of Jesus*, trans. Norman Perrin, 3rd ed. (New York: Charles Scribner's Sons, 1966).

14. *Ibid.*, p. 57.

15. C. F. D. Moule, *Worship in the NT Church*, pp. 21-22.

2. The apostles remembered the sharing of food with the Master; in some cases there had been miracles of the multiplication of the loaves. The record makes it clear that they shared bread and fish with the Lord after His resurrection (John 21; Luke 24:13-35). Cullmann comments: "The coming of Christ into the midst of the community gathered at the meal is an anticipation of his coming to the Messianic Meal and looks back to the disciples' eating with the risen Christ on the Easter days."[16]

3. On occasion the Eucharist was celebrated during or after the meal. Evidence for this conclusion is to be found in 1 Cor. 11:17-34, where the issue of proper behavior at the weekly meals is dealt with by Paul; also in the reference to love feasts in Jude 12 *(agapai)* and possibly in 2 Pet. 2:13 *(agapais)*, in the Didache 9:1—10:5; 14:1, and in the letters of Ignatius of Antioch. These "agape feasts" no doubt were practiced regularly for some time. They served to renew faith in the Lord to whom the Christians were committed, to develop a consciousness of their identity and ministry in the world, and to strengthen them in the face of persecution.

Paul's instructions to the Corinthians regarding eating at home perhaps prepared the way for the separation of the *agapē* meal from the Eucharist. This separation was complete by the time of Justin (ca. A.D. 150), who gives us a description of a Sunday gathering of the community (*Apol.* 1, 67).

After sifting through all the references to worship, one cannot help but agree with Bartlett's conclusion that worship for the Early Church was considered "the extended event of Jesus Christ."[17] The risen Christ was living amongst His people and manifesting himself to them in power as they met together. Worshiping meant that God was still in Christ reconciling; and when that word was proclaimed, the redeeming work of Christ went on.

II. PROCLAMATION

Proclamation or the heralding of Good News is a central mode of witnessing in the Church. Suzanne de Dietrich correctly evaluates its importance when she writes that "it is the *preaching* of the gospel

---

16. *Early Christian Worship*, p. 16; cf. also Moule, *ibid.*, p. 21.
17. Gene Bartlett, "Worship: Ordered Proclamation of the Gospel," *Review and Expositor*, LXII, no. 3 (Summer, 1965), pp. 286 ff.

which lays the foundation of the community."[18] At the appointed
moment, Jesus began His ministry in Galilee, "preaching the gospel
of God" (Mark 1:14; Luke 4:18-19, 43-44). While Jesus spent time in
what might be strictly classified as teaching, His central ministry
was that of being a herald *(kerux)*, announcing the presence and the
power of the kingdom of God.[19] The distinctive feature of His ministry was the prophetic note of the fulfillment of ancient promises.
"He does not announce that some things will happen. His proclamation is itself event. What he declares takes place in the moment of its
declaration."[20]

In the early chapters of Acts, the missionary work of the
apostles is that of "teaching and preaching" *(didaskontes kai euag-
gelizomenoi, Acts 5:42).*

The essence of the apostles' preaching was a rehearsal of the
story of salvation. The focus was on the "the mightiest deed of God,"
the enfleshment of himself in Christ. On the Day of Pentecost, Peter
set the occasion in scriptural context by referring to Joel's prophecy.
He then moved immediately to speak of the significance of the life,
death, and resurrection of Christ as it related to the long sweep of
Israel's history (Acts 2:14-40). The same pattern of proclamation
persisted throughout those early days, according to the homilies of
Acts 1—11.[21]

This form of preaching was basically missionary or evangelistic,
but we can assume that in their own meetings the Christians heard
expositions or homilies based upon the teachings and life of Jesus
with appropriate reference to relevant passages of the Old Testament. Some of this type of preaching is found in the New Testament
letters of Hebrews and 1 John. These sermons, delivered to believers,
are more instructional and inspirational than those found in Acts
1—11.

---

18. *The Witnessing Community*, p. 149.

19. On the relationship between preaching and teaching in the NT, cf. C. H.
Dodd, *The Apostolic Preaching and Its Developments* (New York: Harper and Bros., 1936);
Everett F. Harrison, "Some Patterns of the Testament Didache," *Bibliotheca Sacra*,
vol. 119, no. 474 (April, 1962); Robert C. Worley, "Preaching and Teaching in the
Primitive Church," *McCormick Quarterly*, vol. XX (Nov., 1966), Friedrich Büchsel,
"Kēryssō," *TDNT*, 3:713.

20. Gerhard Friedrich, "Kēryssō," *TDNT*, 3:706.

21. Cf. Dodd's study of these sermons in *Apostolic Preaching*, pp. 21-24; cf. R. H.
Mounce, *The Essential Nature of NT Proclamation* (Grand Rapids, Mich.: Wm. B. Eerdmans
Publishing Co., 1960); Werner Kümmel, "The Main Types of NT Proclamation,"
Encounter, XXI (1960), 161-80.

Preaching for the early preachers was not considered a human function; it was essentially the work of the Spirit of Christ in them. They remembered what their Master had said to them, "He that heareth you heareth me" (Luke 10:16). Christ was speaking through them when they proclaimed Him. "Hence true proclamation is not just speaking about Christ. It is Christ's own speaking. . . . Christ himself is the Preacher in the word of man."[22]

The Apostle Paul's preaching and his understanding of that function paralleled that of the original apostles (Acts 13:14-41). By necessity, much of Paul's preaching was missionary in character. Proclamation was designed to bring about the conversion of sinners: "But how are men to call upon him in whom they have not believed? And how are they to hear without a preacher?" (*kerussontos*, Rom. 10:14). For Paul the preacher's responsibility was to declare that "Christ died for our sins in accordance with the scriptures, that he was buried, that he was raised on the third day in accordance with the scriptures, and that he appeared to" a great number of His followers (1 Cor. 15:3-8). Christ's mission therefore was to be set in the context of the old Scriptures, and then emphasis was to be placed upon His crucifixion and resurrection (1 Cor. 2:2).

Paul attempted another approach to preaching in Athens, but some scholars hold that he was not as effective as he had been elsewhere and that he returned to the central truths of the gospel at Corinth (cf. Acts 17:22-34). Writing later to the Corinthians, he reminds them that he sought to preach in the demonstration of the Spirit and power, for he well knew that it was the divine Spirit who "searches everything, even the depths of God" (1 Cor. 2:10) and brings about conversion. The Spirit interprets spiritual truth to those who possess the Spirit (1 Cor. 2:13), and this provides the basis for communicating the Word. Paul dares to say that the spiritual Christian has "the mind of Christ" (2:16), a basic spiritual requirement for ministry.

Proclamation is a special task for divinely called persons, whom we call "preachers." But, broadly understood, proclamation is the essential function of the Church. D. T. Niles calls the Church "a Messenger, which the gospel brings into being, and the Body within which the gospel is continuously experienced."[23] The Church therefore is "a community placed under Revelation and built up by hear-

---

22. Friedrich, *TDNT*, 3:708.
23. *Preacher's Task and the Stone of Stumbling*, p. 86.

ing the Word of God, built up by the grace of God in order that it may live."[24] The Church lives by her own proclamation, but at the same time she ministers to those outside her existence for evangelistic purposes.[25] She must continuously hear the gospel if she hopes to herald effectively the truth to the unbelieving world.

Through the variety of her functions, preaching, teaching, healing, serving, as a community of grace the Church tells the story of Jesus in its historical and experiential fullness. She actually represents Christ to herself and to those on the outside and thus evokes decision for or against Him. In so doing, she is ministering sacramentally. Whenever the Church views preaching simply as a rehearsal of ideas or propositions, her preaching ceases to have redemptive quality. But when she faithfully discharges her proclamatory function, she brings to men the word of emancipating grace.

Bonhoeffer correctly relates Christ the Word and preaching: "Christ is not only present *in* the word of the church but also *as* the word of the Church, i.e. as spoken word of preaching. . . . Christ's presence is his existence as preaching. The whole Christ is present in preaching, Christ humiliated and Christ exalted."[26] Put in these terms, preaching shares the scandal of the gospel. The amazing, yet paradoxical truth is that "the Word of God has really entered into the humiliation of the word of man." The ramifications of this truth are many; they baffle the mind and humble the preacher. Nevertheless, neither the Early Church nor the Church of any age could survive if she did not possess this identification with Christ in her proclamation. Thus, Bonhoeffer's statement brings pause: "If the whole Christ is not in the preaching then the church breaks into pieces."[27] She ceases to be a medium of grace.

III. BAPTISM

In the Christian community, baptism was undoubtedly practiced from the very first (Acts 2:38, 41; 19:5; *et al.;* Rom. 6:3; 1 Cor. 1:14-17;

---

24. Karl Barth, *The Preaching of the Gospel,* trans. B. E. Hooke (Philadelphia: Westminster Press, 1963), p. 31.

25. Cf. William Barclay's discussion of Paul's preaching, "Comparison of Paul's Missionary Preaching and Preaching to the Church," *Apostolic History and the Gospel,* ed. W. Ward Gasque and Ralph P. Martin (Grand Rapids, Mich.: Wm. B. Eerdmans Publishing Co., 1970), pp. 156-65; Bo Reicke, "A Synopsis of Early Christian Preaching," *The Root of the Vine,* pp. 143-53.

26. Dietrich Bonhoeffer, *Christ the Center,* trans. John Bowden (New York: Harper and Row, 1966), p. 52.

27. *Ibid.,* pp. 52-53.

12:13). It would be incorrect to conclude that the rite was simply a carry-over from the ministry of John the Baptist. The Christian community was simply following the Lord, who submitted to baptism by John (Mark 1:9-11), practiced baptism himself (John 3:22; 4:2), and commissioned His disciples to baptize (Matt. 28:18-20; Mark 16:16). The whole context of baptism in the New Testament is a reflection of Christ's own ministry, including His baptism, special endowment by the Spirit, life of service, death, and resurrection. Moule concludes that "this, which is the 'pattern' of the Gospel-story, is the 'pattern' also of Christian baptism."[28]

A. Baptism as Witness and Commission

Baptism, as a witness, concerned both the individual and the Church. For the receiver it was a sign of his personal salvation. This is the effect of Paul's use of the concept of baptism to explain the Christian's victorious life. "Do you not know that all of us who have been baptized into Christ Jesus were baptized into his death? We were buried therefore with him by baptism into death, so that as Christ was raised from the dead by the glory of the Father, we too might walk in newness of life" (Rom. 6:3-4; Col. 2:12). Cullmann says that Christ's baptism must be considered a "General Baptism: which looked forward to and derived its meaning from the Cross." This insight is highly instructive, because it binds the Christian's baptism to that of his Lord.[29]

Baptism was not understood to be "regenerational" or "faith creating" in the usual theological sense. Just as Christ's baptism was a sign of His previous commitment to the life and death of man, so baptism for the believer is a sign of his previous repentance, faith, and commitment to the Christ life. Repentance and faith *precede* this rite; they are not *born* there. John the Baptist, according to Matt. 3:6, baptized only those who were "confessing their sins." Ralph Earle comments: "This preacher required the candidates to acknowledge that they were sinners, and to expose themselves as such before he would baptize them."[30]

On the Day of Pentecost Peter exhorted his listeners to "repent,

28. Moule, *Worship in the NT Church*, p. 48.
29. Oscar Cullmann, *Baptism in the New Testament*, trans. J. K. S. Reid (London: SCM Press, 1950), pp. 18 ff.; cf. Stauffer, *NT Theology*, p. 161: the death of Christ places "the baptized person under ths sign of the cross"; baptism was "the marking of men with the name of Jesus."
30. "Matthew," *BBC*, 6:46.

and be baptized every one of you in the name of Jesus Christ *for the forgiveness of your sins [eis aphesis tōn hamartiōn humōn]'* (Acts 2:38). This baptism was distinctly Christian because it was "in the name of Jesus Christ."[31] It was not "to the end or purpose of the forgiveness of your sins" but rather "*on the basis of* the forgiveness of your sins." Though the construction in Greek (*eis* with the accusative) usually denotes result, in this instance a causal usage is intended.[32] Probably the phrase "for the forgiveness of your sins" should be taken with "repent" rather than "be baptized." "Forgiveness followed repentance, not baptism. Baptism was a means of portraying the repentance, a public confession of faith in Jesus."[33] God surely reserves sovereign power over even the sacraments, and He is ready to save whenever men place their faith in Christ.[34]

Christian baptism was not only a witness to faith in Christ but also to one's sense of commission as a disciple of Christ. At baptism the Christian assumed the redemptive role with His Lord (Mark 10:38; Luke 12:50). "The commission to missionary activity is bound up in all four Gospels with baptismal motifs (Luke 24:47, Mark 16:16; John 20:22; Matt. 28:19)."[35]

B. Baptism as Acceptance into the Church

It is very clear that the Early Church practiced baptism as a sacrament of initiation into the community (Acts 2:38, 41; 8:12-13, 16; 9:18; 16:15, 33; 19:5; 1 Cor. 1:14-17). The fact that Christ was himself baptized and practiced baptism through His disciples (John 3:22; 4:2) as part of His movement supports this view. By accepting John's baptism, Jesus was initiated into John's movement, which was "the

31. Cf. F. F. Bruce, "The Book of the Acts," *The New International Commentary on the New Testament* (Grand Rapids, Mich.: Wm. B. Eerdmans Publishing Co., 1954), p. 76: "It is administered 'in the name of Jesus Christ'—probably in the sense that the person being baptized confessed or invoked Jesus as Messiah (cf. ch. 22:16). In addition, the person who baptized the convert appears to have named the name of Christ over him as he was being baptized (cf. ch. 15:17; Jas. 2:7)."

32. Frank Stagg, *The Book of Acts* (Nashville: Broadman Press, 1955), pp. 62, 58; cf. Matt. 12:41; Ralph Earle, "Acts," *BBC*, 7:288; A. T. Robertson, *Word Pictures in the NT* (New York: Richard R. Smith, 1930), 3:34.

33. Stagg, *Book of Acts*, p. 63.

34. Richardson, *Introduction to the Theology of the NT*, p. 347; see William Hull's (Southern Baptist) response to Beasley-Murray's *Baptism in the New Testament*, in "Baptism in the New Testament: A Critique," *Review and Expositor*, vol. LXV (Winter, 1968), pp. 3-12.

35. Stauffer, *NT Theology*, p. 160; Barth also sees in baptism the believer being "commissioned for special duty."

way of righteousness" (cf. Matt. 3:15). Paul expresses in exact terminology the relationship of baptism to community admission: "For by one Spirit we were all baptized into one body—Jews or Greeks, slaves or free—and all were made to drink of one Spirit" (1 Cor. 12:13).[36] The identical thought appears in Gal. 3:27-28. "For as many of you as were baptized into Christ have put on Christ. There is neither slave nor free, there is neither male nor female; for you are all one in Christ Jesus." Baptism marked the Christian as a member of the new covenant community and set him off from other men. He was baptized "into" Christ—that is, became a Christian, a follower of Christ's "way," and henceforth belonged to Him.

The Church has a special stake in the baptismal act. She exists where the Spirit of Christ reigns; she is the community of grace; she is the Source of life for all men as Christ functions through her. Baptism is a sign of her efficacy, as the resurrection power of the Holy Spirit brings her into existence, sustains her, and operates through her. And as far as the Spirit is operative through her, to that degree the Church effects incorporation of believers. Appropriately therefore we can speak of "baptismal grace" which is mediated through the Church.[37]

C. Infant Baptism

Infant baptism has been much debated in recent decades in the church. Karl Barth's oft-repeated statement expresses the fury of the debate. "Infant baptism is the symptom of a very serious sickness from which the Church is suffering and which is multitudinism."[38] Several facts bear upon the issue.

---

36. On the interpretation of this verse, cf. Donald Metz, "1 Corinthians," *BBC*, 8:432. Also, C. K. Barrett, "The First Epistle to the Corinthians," *Harper's NT Commentaries*, pp. 288-89: "There is no reason to think that *we were baptized* refers to anything other than baptism in water (together with all that this outward rite signified)."

37. On the much debated question of the possible relationship of baptism to the Jewish rite of circumcision, see J. Jeremias, *Infant Baptism in the First Four Centuries*, trans. David Cairns (London: SCM Press, 1960), pp. 39, 47; R. Meyer, *TDNT*, 6:81 ff.; *contra*: H. H. Rowley, *The Unity of the Bible* (London: Carey Kingsgate Press, 1953), pp. 157 ff.; W. H. Lampe, *The Seal of the Spirit*, 2nd ed. (Naperville, Ill.: Allenson, 1967), pp. 56, 62, 85; George A. Turner, "Infant Baptism in Biblical and Historical Context," *WTJ*, vol. 5 (Spring, 1970), pp. 11 ff.; R. P. Martin, *Colossians* (Grand Rapids, Mich.: Zondervan, 1972), pp. 84 ff.

38. *The Teaching of the Church Regarding Baptism* (London: SCM Press, 1948), p. 45; others who reject infant baptism are Kurt Aland, Emil Brunner, J. R. Nelson, Alfred F. Kuen, and George A. Turner. Cullmann is one of the few present-day theologians to defend it. Cf. also Filson, Richardson, and Stauffer.

1. Infant baptism is not explicitly taught in the New Testament. However, as Filson reminds us, adult conversion was necessarily the means by which the Church arose and spread, and this might explain the failure to mention children.[39]

2. Family units were brought into the Church (Acts 8:12-13; 10:24, 43-44, 47-48; 16:14-15, 33-34; 18:8; 1 Cor. 1:16); so if the prevailing concept of the solidarity of the family played any part in directing the Early Church, we can assume that children were also baptized. When the head of a household accepted Christ, he committed his entire house (oikos); he was a "representative man."

3. While nothing can be proved about the practice of infant baptism from the concern of the Lord with children (Mark 10:13-16), that fact along with the incorporation of whole families at least opens the way for intimating the practice.

4. There is also the important theological fact that since the Church is a medium of God's grace and since the child does enjoy the blessings of that grace in his years before accountability, the Church by baptizing the child acknowledges God's grace upon his life. It also assumes responsibility along with the family for the child's spiritual development.[40]

D. The Mode of Baptism

The mode of baptism has been much disputed, and in all likelihood will not be settled satisfactorily to all concerned. The Greek verb baptizō derives from baptō, and has been transliterated into English. It has the basic meaning "to dip, immerse, swamp, plunge."[41] After allowing for the few instances in the New Testament where the idea of washing is intended (Mark 7:4; Heb. 6:2; 9:10), both the verb and the noun forms (baptisma, baptismos) denote immersion (cf. Acts 8:38-39; the reality of burial with Christ in Rom. 6:4). Throughout the history of the Church this mode has been mainly employed.

The Teaching of the Twelve Apostles has a preference for "living," that is, running water, such as the Jordan River in which the Lord was baptized. If a person cannot stand the plunge into the cold water,

---

39. *Jesus Christ the Risen Lord,* p. 218.

40. The first protest against infant baptism was raised by Tertullian in the second century. That fact assumes that it may have been an established rite well before his time.

41. Cf. Arndt and Gingrich, *Lexicon,* and R. R. Williams, "Baptize, Baptism," *A Theological Word Book of the NT,* pp. 27-30; A. Oepke, "Baptō, baptizō, baptismos, baptisma," *TDNT,* 1:529-46.

he can be baptized in warm water, or he can have water poured upon him three times, but only in the case of emergency (c. 7).

In conclusion, the ceremony of baptism was not and is not an incidental sacrament in the life of the Church. It carries both personal and communal dimensions. For the individual believer, baptism meant that he had repented of his sins, had received Christ as Saviour, and had been infused with the Holy Spirit. The rite witnessed to the reality of this experience. Moreover, baptism introduced the believer into the church. Richardson sees faith and baptism as complementary, for faith leads to "baptismal incorporation into Christ's body."[42] The believer now belongs to the "blameless children of God" (Phil. 2:15) in which there are to be no racial distinctions because everyone had been baptized into Christ.

From what we know about the ministry of the Early Church, baptism was required of everyone. In her practice of baptism, the Church was functioning sacramentally; she was acting as a divine medium of God's grace.

IV. The Lord's Supper

The sacrament of the Lord's Supper has been called in the several branches of the church by a variety of names—Eucharist,[43] Holy Communion, and the Mass. It ranks with proclamation as one of the most important grace-mediating acts of the Church. Apparently the sacrament was instituted immediately in the life of the Church and was participated in weekly, if not daily. However, a large segment of Christianity today has reserved this activity to infrequent times, preaching having assumed a primary role in its worship.

A. The Lord's Prophetic Act

During the last week of His life the Lord engaged in three prophetically symbolic acts: (1) the Triumphal Entry into Jerusalem (Matt. 21:1-11); (2) the cleansing of the Temple (Matt. 21:12-13); (3) the eating of the Passover meal with the disciples and the institution of the Lord's Supper (Matt. 26:26-29; Mark 14:22-25; Luke 22:15-20; 1 Cor. 11:23-26).

---

42. *An Introduction to the Theology of the NT,* p. 348.

43. This title is taken from the Greek *eucharistia,* which means "thanksgiving" and suggests the Lord's act of offering "thanks to the Father before the distribution of the elements; also the thanks of believers for these symbols and their meaning."

The "founding meal," as Jeremias calls it, is described in the New Testament accounts with a number of differences, but "the substance of all four independent texts is in complete agreement."[44] The phrases of common agreement are: "this is my body," "my blood of the covenant," or "the covenant in my blood," as well as "for many" or "for you." The significant addition from the Synoptics is the note of hope of a future meal with Christ: "For I tell you that from now on I shall not drink of the fruit of the vine until the kingdom of God comes" (Luke 22:18; cf. Mark 14:25; Matt. 26:29); "For as often as you eat this bread and drink the cup, you proclaim the Lord's death until he comes" (1 Cor. 11:26). Paul and Luke retain the reference to the new covenant (kainē diathēkē), "This cup is the new covenant in my blood" (1 Cor. 11:25); "This cup is poured out for you in the new covenant in my blood" (Luke 22:20).[45] The unique Pauline contribution is the exhortation: "Do this in remembrance of me" (1 Cor. 11:24-25).

As indicated above, Jesus instigated this memorial. The prophetic actions of the Lord were several: (1) He sent the disciples to prepare for the meal (Matt. 26:17, 19); (2) He took a small loaf of bread, offered thanks over it, broke it with His hands, distributed it among the disciples, and announced, "This is my body." (3) He took a cup of wine, blessed it, passed it among the disciples, and declared, "This is my blood of the new covenant." (4) He exhorted them to

---

44. *The Eucharistic Words of Jesus;* cf. Hans Lietzmann, *Messe und Herrenmahl, eine Studie zur Geschichte der Liturgie* (Berlin: Walter de Gruyter, 1955), in which the author proposes that there were two different strands of tradition, one a Jerusalem tradition, represented in Mark; the other Pauline, represented in Pauline-Lukan-Johannine materials. The first strand related to table fellowship and unrestrained joy over the presence of the risen Lord. The second strand was characterized by Hellenistic sacrificial concepts. The Apostle Paul received these insights by special revelation (1 Cor. 11:23, *apo tou kuriou*). Cf. Eduard Schweizer, *The Lord's Supper According to the New Testament,* trans. John M. Davis (Philadelphia: Fortress Press, 1967), p. 25: "Therefore, although in one instance the emphasis gravitates toward one type and in another instance toward the second type, it is impossible to establish the existence of two wholly distinct and independent types of the Lord's Supper in the early church, such as Lietzmann and Lohmeyer had in mind. If these two factors—the eschatological and the proclamation of Jesus' death—did not belong together from the very beginning, then they must certainly have merged very early in the Palestinian church."

45. On the textual problem in Luke 22:17-20, cf. Bruce M. Metzger, *A Textual Commentary on the Greek New Testament* (London: United Bible Societies, 1971), pp. 173-77. Speaking for the committee, Metzger writes: "The majority, on the other hand, impressed by the overwhelming preponderance of external evidence supporting the longer form, explained the origin of the shorter form as due to some scribal accident or misunderstanding."

engage in this act in remembrance of Him. (5) He announced that He would not drink from the cup in this manner again until "the kingdom of God comes." Through the various textual and ecclesiastical traditions these salient features of the event have been preserved.

B. The Significance of the Supper

1. *Proclamation of Christ's Death.*

Taken collectively, the accounts of the Lord's Supper give expression to three redemptive themes. First, with respect to the past, they proclaim the death of Christ. Paul makes this emphasis. "For as often as you eat this bread and drink this cup, you proclaim the Lord's death until he comes" (1 Cor. 11:26).

Despite the numerous aspects of the debate as to whether Jesus' last meal was a celebration of the Passover, the above-listed statements from the several traditions clearly suggest the background of the Passover. Dom Gregory Dix's conclusion must stand: "The *whole sequence,* Supper, Crucifixion, and Resurrection, took place for the apostles upon the background of Passover."[46] So, in this prophetic act we hear sacrificial terminology, Jesus describing himself as a sacrifice, as the eschatological Lamb (cf. 1 Cor. 5:7), whose death brings into force the new covenant which was prefigured in the making of the covenant on Sinai (Exod. 24:8) and prophesied for the time of salvation (Jer. 31:31-34). Moreover, the use of the phrase "for many" *(huper pollōn),* which roots exegetically in Isaiah 53, speaks indisputably of the redemptive meaning of His death. His was a "representative death for many."[47] To His disciples, Jesus made plain His deep dedication to their salvation in all its present and future dimensions, and He employed the setting and language of the Passover to convey that meaning.

The Supper is not a "commemorative meal for the dead," as some have tried to suggest on the basis of Hellenistic meals held in memory of the dead. It is not a time of mourning but of reverence and thanksgiving. The death of Jesus is proclaimed in all four Gospels, in fact, as a death which took place *for* the participants. The two

---

46. *Jew and Greek* (New York: Harper and Bros., 1953), p. 101; cf. also A. Gilmore, "The Date and Significance of the Last Supper," *Scottish Journal of Theology* (September, 1961), pp. 260-64; A. J. B. Higgins, *Lord's Supper in the NT;* V. Taylor, *Jesus and His Sacrifice,* pp. 114 ff., 181; Jeremias, *The Eucharistic Words of Jesus.*

47. Jeremias, *NT Theology,* pp. 290-91.

phrases in Luke 22:19-20: "which is given for you" *(to huper humōn didomenon)* and "which is poured out for you" *(to huper humōn ekchunnomenon)* contain the familiar *huper,* which means "in behalf of." Jesus said to the disciples that the breaking of His body and the shedding of His blood was to the end that the benefits of emancipation and reconciliation might accrue to them. The Early Church so understood the Communion. In participating they not only remembered and proclaimed the death of Christ, they also witnessed to their faith in the atoning benefits of that death.

    2. *Celebration of Christ's Fellowship.*

    With respect to the present, the Lord's Supper is a celebration of Christ's continued fellowship with His people. It is a time when the risen Christ meets with believers. Also, all who share faith in Christ are bound together in love at the meal. Paul's attack upon the schismatic behavior of the Corinthians at the Lord's Supper was justified because of the nature of the supper as a fellowship meal with Christ (1 Cor. 11:17-22). Earlier, in the same Epistle, Paul makes it clear that "the cup of blessing" and "the bread we break" signalize the "participation" *(koinōnia)* of the blood and body of Christ. This being the case, all who eat and drink are "one body" *(hen sōma,* 1 Cor. 10:16-17).

    Perhaps the famous invitation of "the Christ at the door" in Rev. 3:20 refers to this same fellowship in the Lord's Supper: "Behold I stand at the door and knock; if any one hears my voice and opens the door, I will come in to him and eat with him, and he with me."

    Grant's word on this element of present fellowship is instructive. He does not argue the issue of partaking of the "spiritual" or "real" body of Christ. However, he concludes that what has kept the Eucharist "alive and growing has been the realization of what is supernaturally and really present *here,* not some historic commemoration like the anniversary of a battle or of the Declaration of Independence."[48] Fundamentally, the Lord's Supper is a rite of fellowship, of union and communion, first with Christ, then with one another; in Him. According to the early Christians, the risen Christ was present at His table.

    Both Luke and Paul include the reference to the "new covenant" (Luke 22:20; 1 Cor. 11:25). The *kainē diathēkē* was not the introduction of a new doctrine or a new law, but a new disclosure and presence of God himself through Christ. Jeremiah records the divine

---

48. *Introduction to NT Thought,* p. 286.

word: "I will put my law within them, and I will write it upon their hearts; and I will be their God and they shall be my people" (31:33). Christ's presence at the meal was the assurance of the covenantal relationship, and His death has sealed the new covenant. They celebrated the Lord's death and rejoiced in their new covenantal relationship.

The question of how Christ is present in the Lord's Supper has been raised on the basis of John 6:51-58. There Jesus said, "I am the living Bread," and "He who eats my flesh and drinks my blood abides in me, and I in him." The use of the copula "is" in the Lord's institution of the rite likewise raises the question. Jesus said, "This is my body" and "This is my blood" (Matt. 26:26, 28).

Schweizer's answer to this profound question seems the most satisfying. As a governing principle, Christ is present in His word, in the word of the Church which proclaims Him. Paul records Jesus as saying, "As oft as you eat this bread and drink this cup, you proclaim the Lord's death until he comes" (1 Cor. 11:26). Schweizer continues, "One would never speak in the New Testament of the word as something 'merely' proclaimed, as if proclamation did not have the character of an event *(Tatcharakter),* but were merely something 'spiritual' intended for the intellect. It is Christ who comes in the word: 'He who hears you hears me, and he who rejects you rejects me' (Luke 10:16; also Matt. 10:40)."[49] The word begets the Church (1 Cor. 4:15; Jas. 1:18; 1 Pet. 1:23); the word imparts the gift of the Spirit (Gal. 4:15).

Schweizer sees this "word presence" in Paul's account of the Supper. It is the "blessing" of the cup and the "breaking" of the bread that is decisive, not the eating and drinking. He concludes that "the real presence of Christ in the Lord's Supper is exactly the same as his presence in the word—nothing more, nothing less. It is an event, not an object; an encounter, not a phenomenon of nature; it is Christ's encounter with his church, not the distribution of a substance."[50] Christ must never become an object at the disposal of the Church.

The event of preaching, however, is dependent on the words of man. Understood in this way, the presence of Christ at the table is indeed a real and visible word, as Augustine once taught. The early

---

49. *The Lord's Supper,* pp. 34-35.
50. *Ibid.,* pp. 37-38.

disciples in participating in this rite were deeply aware of the Lord's presence because they were hearing His word of salvation.

   3. *Anticipation of the Messianic Banquet.*

   According to the Synoptic account, in the future the Lord will drink the fruit of the vine in the Kingdom with His people (Mark 14:25 ff.; cf. 1 Cor. 11:26). This eschatological note implies that in sharing in the Supper the believer is participating proleptically in the future Messianic Banquet. The saying shows that at the Last Supper, Jesus looked forward, beyond death, to the perfect fellowship of the consummated Kingdom. Thus, for the disciple "the drinking of the cup is a present participation in that fellowship so far as it can exist here now."[51] This fact accounts, no doubt, for the joy which was manifested among the Early Church as they feasted together (Acts 2:46). The joy of knowing the presence of Christ at the Eucharist was "a foretaste of the final reunion in the Kingdom of God."

---

51. Vincent Taylor, *The Gospel According to St. Mark* (New York: St. Martin's Press, 1966), p. 547.

32

The Church as an Organized Community

The Church as event speaks of its nature; the Church as a sacramental community speaks of its saving functions; the Church as an organized community speaks of its visibility and sense of responsibility in the world. History shows that the Church became in time an institution with which both religious and political authorities had to deal. She gained status in society and with it came institutionalization as the Church sought to maintain her position in the world.[1] As her visibility increased, she struggled to be what she was created to be through her Lord. An investigation of the development of the Christian community's organization and of the creation of the various forms of leadership as recorded in the New Testament will assist in ascertaining what might be considered the normative patterns of church government and leadership.

I. PETER AND THE CHURCH

The Gospel writers record only two passages in which Jesus uses the word *ecclēsia*. In Matt. 18:17 He gives instruction as to how to handle occasions when one member sins against another. The final arbiter is

---

1. Cf. Bruce M. Metzger, "The Development of Institutional Organization in the Early Church," *Ashland Theological Bulletin,* VI (Spring, 1973), pp. 12 ff.

to be the Church. Jesus says that if settlement is not achieved, then the sinner is to be "to you as a Gentile and a tax collector."

The other passage is the response of the Lord to Peter's confession of Him as "the Christ, the Son of the living God." "And I tell you, you are Peter *[Petros]*, and on this rock *[petra]* I will build my church, and the powers of death shall not prevail against it" (Matt. 16:18).[2] Jesus goes on to say, "I will give you the keys of the kingdom of heaven, and whatever you bind on earth shall be bound in heaven, and whatever you loose on earth shall be loosed in heaven" (16:19; cf. 18:18).

Much debate has centered on the identification of "rock" in this passage. Is it Peter? Or is it the confession of Christ as the Christ, the Son of the living God? After careful study of the text, Oscar Cullmann decides that Peter is the rock on which the Church is built, that is, as apostle and not as bishop or first pope.[3] Ralph Earle, following Alan McNeile, identifies the rock as the truth which the apostle had proclaimed, namely, the Lord's Messiahship. The wordplay, however, does not preclude that Peter is the rock.[4]

Several facts must be kept in mind in any interpretation of this passage.

1. It is *Christ who builds the Church.* But as Frank Carver comments,

> Peter belongs to the building only as the foundation stone belongs to the house that rests upon it. He is the rock upon whom Jesus founds His Church as a man to whom God has revealed who Jesus is, as a man with an inspired witness to God's saving presence in Jesus-Peter and men with the same personal discovery of the Son of God.[5]

2. God's work through the centuries has been uniquely bound up with specially called men—Abraham (cf. Isa. 51:1 ff.), Moses, Joshua, David, the prophets, and John the Baptist. Why not Peter? To take this position in no way espouses a doctrine of "apostolic succession" or invests Peter with infallibility.

2. In the Aramaic language, which Jesus probably used, the same play on words comes through: "You are *Cephas*, and upon this *Cepha* I will build my church." Cf. Jesus' prophecy about Peter in John 1:42.

3. *Peter: Disciple-Apostle-Martyr,* trans. Floyd V. Filson (Philadelphia: The Westminster Press, 1953), p. 215. Cf. also *Introduction to the Theology of the NT,* p. 309. For a contemporary Catholic study of the papal claims, see Hans Küng, *The Church,* trans. Ray and Rosaleen Ockenden (New York: Sheed and Ward, 1967), pp. 444 ff.

4. *Matthew,* BBC, 6:155.

5. Frank G. Carver, *Peter, The Rock-Man* (Kansas City: Beacon Hill Press of Kansas City, 1973), p. 43.

3. The gift of "the keys of the kingdom of heaven" and the power of "binding and loosing" speak of the unique relationship of Peter's ministry to the building of the Church. Carver writes, "The key is the Father's revelation of His Son which when shared through the Spirit-inspired witness of man to man fulfills Jesus' promise: 'Whatever you shall bind on earth shall have been bound in heaven, and whatever you shall loose on earth shall have been loosed in heaven.'"[6] Peter used this key on the Day of Pentecost and 3,000 were added to the Church. A new period in God's saving work began with Pentecost, and Peter, who had lived close to Christ, played the major role.

II. The Development of Church Order

Historical evidence shows that the Early Church underwent a gradual, but not necessarily a haphazard, organizational development. The Early Church was authentically charismatic both in its worship and organization. That is to say, it was governed by the direct guidance of the Holy Spirit (cf. Acts 1:15-25; 13:2). Lightfoot's three-tier development theory merits consideration. Because of certain events in the Church he hypothesizes that the organization grew from deacons to presbyters (elders) to bishops.[7] However, a study of the data leads us to conclude a less formal development. It would appear that the positions of the deacons and the elders were established very early in the life of the Church, and the two functioned side by side in the specific areas of service assigned to them. The bishopric arose in the elder's office in a natural manner by virtue of a need for leadership.

Certain inner forces controlled the fashioning of the Church's government. First, the Church possessed a deep sense of responsibility regarding her mission in the world. She knew that the source of her life and mission was the Lord himself. *Her* ministry was *His* ministry. As T. W. Manson correctly observes, and undoubtedly the Early Church fully realized, "There is only one 'essential ministry in the Church,' the perpetual ministry of the risen and ever-present Lord himself."[8] Since the Church's ministry was derivative, it was natural

6. *Ibid.*
7. J. B. Lightfoot, *Saint Paul's Epistle to the Philippians*, rev. ed. (London: Macmillan Co., 1913), pp. 181 ff.
8. T. W. Manson, *The Church's Ministry* (Philadelphia: The Westminster Press, 1948), p. 107.

for her to become very protective of that ministry as she found herself in decision-making experiences related to church order.[9]

Second, the Church's rise in the Jewish context afforded a model for her own organization. The Church in Jerusalem appears to have adapted the structuring of the synagogue council of elders with the apostles as a separate authoritative group.[10] The church at Antioch became concerned about the interpretation of the gospel, so they appointed Paul, Barnabas, and others "to go up to Jerusalem, to the apostles and the elders" to discuss the issue (Acts 15:2, 4, 6). Paul includes a note in Galatians in which he mentions James, Cephas, and John as being "pillars" *(stuloi)* in the Jerusalem church (2:9).[11]

This dependence on the synagogue model was natural, since the Church was at first only a sect within Judaism. Properly, as Grant suggests, they were "Christian Jews," not "Jewish Christians." They had accepted Christ as the Messiah. As in the synagogue, the Christians selected older men in the community to function as "elders," and along with the apostles, these two groups handled the serious questions that arose in the Church. However, the Church introduced modifications as she broke away from the Jewish influence and moved into the Hellenistic world.

A third important factor in the development of church order, especially at first, was the priesthood of the laity. The first-century Christians did not distinguish between clergy and laity. All the members of the Church, men and women, were "priests unto God" (Rev. 1:6; 5:10; 20:6; cf. 1 Pet. 2:9). The responsibility of every member was to gather faithfully for worship and to offer his life in sacrificial service to God. As members of the *laos tou theou* they had "ministerial" responsibilities; they could not surrender the functions of evangelism and pastoral care to a professional clergy. Baptism in effect was "an ordination to the ministry of the Church" (cf. 1 Cor. 12:13 in its context).

There was a democratic mood that tempered any tendencies to radical decisions on church government. For example, in solving the

9. Cf. Floyd V. Filson, *Jesus Christ the Risen Lord,* p. 200: "Any way of organizing and administering the life of the Christian community must keep this lordship of Christ central and be consistent with it. This principle his disciples recognized."

10. On the organizational pattern of the synagogue, cf. Floyd V. Filson, "Synagogue, Temple, and Church," *The Biblical Archaeologist Reader,* ed. G. Ernest Wright and David Noel Freedman (New York: Doubleday and Co., 1961), pp. 185-200.

11. Clement also uses *stuloi* to refer to the apostles and leaders of the primitive Church, 1 Cl. 5:2.

problem of the distribution of food to the Greek widows, "the twelve summoned the body of disciples" and instructed them to pick out from among themselves "seven men of good repute, full of the Spirit and of wisdom" whom they could appoint to this duty (Acts 6:2-3). A democratic procedure prevailed in the selection of the candidates, but the apostles formally appointed them to the task.[12] At the first council of the Church (Acts 15) the apostles and elders of the Jerusalem congregation apparently exercised great restraint in the debate. Paul and Barnabas were outstanding leaders in their own right by virtue of their ministry among the Gentiles and thus had right to free expression of their views. Withal, there seems to have been a genuine attempt to arrive at a people's resolution of the issue at hand.

The evolution of church government was slow, and on the basis of the available data one cannot dogmatically assert that a particular form obtained from the beginning. B. H. Streeter writes: "In the Primitive church there was no single system of Church Order. . . . During the first hundred years of Christianity, the Church was an organism alive and growing—changing its organization to meet changing needs."[13] Canon Streeter concludes that each of the various areas of the Church had its own type of ministry, some carefully patterned, others freely structured, but "none bound by any preconceived or officially designated order which had been planned in advance." Perhaps, as Grant reacts, Streeter went too far in the direction of freedom, but "the general argument of his famous book is incontrovertible."[14]

At this point in scholarly analysis of the Church no one can argue convincingly for "one sole and exclusive type of ministry." It would be very difficult to maintain that the Early Church was "congregational," "presbyterian," or "episcopal." It has been suggested that the early chapters of Acts reflects a mixture of governmental patterns. Peter presides somewhat like a "bishop," suggesting the "episcopal" form; the apostles function like a collegium, suggesting

---

12. *Katastēsomen*, from *kathistēmi*, which means "to put in charge"; it does not carry the notion of ordination or special sacred appointment, 6:3.

13. B. H. Streeter, *The Primitive Church* (New York: The Macmillan Co., 1929), p. 267. Stagg's personal ecclesiastical commitments may slightly prejudice his conclusions, but his statements are sound: "Some evidence may be found in the New Testament for various subsequent developments. To find the roots of a particular system in the New Testament is not necessarily to find the system itself there," *NT Theology*, p. 265.

14. *Introduction to NT Thought*, pp. 273-74.

the presbyterian form; the whole community functions in a demo-cratic manner, suggesting the "congregational" pattern.[15]

The eschatological hope may have kept the community from taking serious steps toward organization, for they expected daily the return of their Lord. Whatever pattern of leadership prevailed must have been functional and expedient. It was designed to meet the existing needs, as in the case of the election of the seven in Acts 6:1-6.

On their first missionary journey, Paul and Barnabas gathered groups of believers in Lystra, Iconium, and Antioch. Before returning to their home base, they backtracked through these towns, "strength-ening the souls of the disciples, exhorting them to continue in the faith and saying that through many tribulations we must enter the kingdom of God." Then they appointed elders *(presbyteroi)* in the in-fant churches (Acts 14:21-23). This action on the part of the mis-sionaries was perhaps designed to help new Christians in these cities to maintain their faith in the event of persecution. Settlement of differences between members or churches, and the relationship of the community to the existing political authorities, probably were handled by specially designated persons at the time problems arose.

III. LEADERSHIP GROWTH

Simultaneously with the development of government and organiza-tion in the Church came the growth of leadership. Scholars readily agree that there was no fixed pattern of leadership in the first cen-tury, but incipient forms are discernible in the New Testament.

A. Apostles

When speaking of leadership, we must begin with the Twelve who are called "apostles."[16] The Lord had chosen them (Mark 3:13-19) that they might "be with him" and "be sent out to preach and have authority to cast out demons" (vv. 14-15). Following Jesus' resur-rection He appeared to them to give them instruction and to com-mission them (Matt. 28:16-20; Acts 1:1-11). When they were first formally identified as "apostles" cannot be settled; no doubt their

---

15. Bo Reicke, *Glaube und Leben der Urgemeinde* (Zurich: Zwingli-Verlag, 1957), pp. 25 ff.

16. "Apostle" means "sent one," deriving from the Greek *apostellein* (to send); cf. Mark 3:14; 6:7, 30.

sense of having been sent by the Lord contributed to this identification.[17] Moreover, Jesus' careful instruction of the Twelve and His post-resurrection visits with them confirmed in their minds that they had been set aside for a special role in the new community (Matt. 28:19; Acts 1:8).

Immediately following the ascension of Christ, the embryonic apostolate met to replace Judas, and the result of their action was the election of Matthias (Acts 1:26). This episode gives further information as to the meaning of "apostle." The Eleven decided that the successor to Judas must have "accompanied us during all the time that the Lord Jesus went in and out among us—beginning from the baptism of John until the day when he was taken up from us—one of these men must become with us a witness to his resurrection" (Acts 1:21-22).[18] The definition of "apostle" at this time was limited. Later on, the apostolate expanded to include others who could not qualify under these specific requisites. In that company were Barnabas and Paul (Acts 14:14), Andronicus and Junias (Rom. 16:7), James the brother of the Lord (Gal. 1:19), and Epaphroditus (Phil. 2:25, Greek text).[19]

Quite obviously, there is a narrow and a broad definition of the word "apostle." The broad definition is suggested in 2 Cor. 8:23; 1 Thess. 2:6; Rev. 2:2; 21:14. Paul's close associates, Silvanus and Timothy, are included with him as "apostles of Christ" (1 Thess. 1:1; 2:6). The reference in Rev. 21:14, "the twelve apostles of the Lamb," however, can only be taken as a limitation on the definition. Campbell's conclusion has merit: "All that can be said is that, after Paul, the Church soon came to restrict the use of the title to the Twelve and Paul himself. Paul's apostleship, however, seems to have been regarded as exceptional."[20]

The basic responsibility of the apostles was to give witness to Christ, especially to His resurrection (Acts 1:21-22; 1 Cor. 9:1). Paul viewed his chief work as preaching Christ (Gal. 1:16) or the gospel

17. Cf. Millar Burrows, *An Outline of Biblical Theology* (Philadelphia: The Westminster Press, 1956), p. 257: "The term may have been used informally during Jesus' ministry for those whom he sent on preaching missions."

18. Cf. F. F. Bruce, *The Book of Acts,* pp. 50 ff.

19. On the question of Paul's apostleship, cf. J. Munck, "Paul, the Apostles, and the Twelve," *Studia Theologica,* 3 (1949), 96-110; Walter Schmithals, *The Office of Apostle in the Early Church,* trans. John E. Steely (Nashville: Abingdon Press, 1969); J. Y. Campbell, "Apostle," *Theological Word Book of the Bible,* pp. 20-21.

20. *Theological Word Book of the Bible,* p. 21: Cf. F. F. Bruce, *The Epistle to the Ephesians* (New York: Fleming H. Revell Co., 1969), p. 85.

(1 Cor. 1:17). As far as the Twelve were concerned, general oversight of the community was given by them. They went on missions to other areas for purposes of evangelism (Acts 8:14-25; 9:32; 10:48; Gal. 2:11-14). The activity of the apostles was essentially that of service (*diakonias*, "ministry"; Acts 1:17; 20:24; Rom. 11:13; 2 Cor. 6:3 ff.). As servants of Christ and the Church they gave themselves to whatever responsibility called for their ministry despite the personal cost involved. Apparently in the absence of Peter in Jerusalem, James, the brother of Jesus, emerged as the leader. It was he who presided at the first conference of the church in Jerusalem while Peter served as evangelist (Acts 15).

In conclusion, "the task of the apostles was a unique first-century task; they gave witness and initial guidance to the church; their witness is better preserved in the New Testament than in the numerous curious ecclesiastical developments of later centuries."[21] It seems proper to say that theirs was a universal leadership, preaching and teaching throughout the burgeoning Christian community.

B. Evangelists

The message of Jesus is characterized in the New Testament as "good news" *(euangelion).* The preaching of this gospel is "declaring good news" *(euangelizesthai).* All proclaimers of the Christian gospel can be called evangelists, and the apostles followed their Master in this activity. However, the term "evangelists" is not applied to the apostles in the New Testament. A few times it refers to a person who is not an apostle but an itinerant missionary. Philip is called "the evangelist" in Acts 21:8; Paul urges Timothy "to do the work of an evangelist" (2 Tim. 4:5). In Eph. 4:11, Paul mentions evangelists along with apostles and prophets. We cannot conclude, however, from these few references that there existed in the Early Church an office known as "evangelist."[22]

C. Prophets and Pastor-Teachers

Paul in 1 Cor. 12:28 speaks of apostles, prophets *(prophētai),* and teachers *(didaskaloi),* whom God had appointed *(etheto)* in the Church. He also speaks in Eph. 4:11 of apostles, prophets, evangelists, pastors,

---

21. *Jesus Christ the Risen Lord,* p. 203.
22. Cf. George Johnstone, ed., "Ephesians, Philippians, Colossians and Philemon," *The Century Bible* (Greenwood, S.C.: Attic Press, 1967), p. 19.

and teachers. At Antioch five persons are designated "prophets and teachers" (Acts 13:1), among whom are Barnabas and Saul. The only acceptable conclusion that can be drawn from the New Testament materials is that which Niebuhr and Williams have drawn, namely, that we do not have two distinct classes of servants or offices represented in these names. It is very possible that these functions of prophesying and teaching could be carried on by the same person (1 Cor. 14:6).[23] In fact, one person, as in the case of Paul, could fulfill the roles of apostle, prophet, evangelist, and teacher. Thus, Stagg along with others, avers that the New Testament emphasizes function rather than office.[24]

Prophecy was preaching of a special kind. It was Spirit-inspired witness for the edification of the Church (Acts 11:27 ff.; 21:4, 9; 1 Cor. 14:1 ff.; Eph. 3:4; 2 Pet. 1:19; Rev. 19:10). However, "the prophets were not sources of new truth to the Church, but expounders of truth otherwise revealed."[25] Toward the end of the Apostolic Age it became increasingly necessary to examine the claims of prophets, to determine whether they spoke by inspiration of the Spirit of God or by a false spirit (1 John 4:1 ff.; Rev. 2:20).

The ministry of the prophets could at times be didactic. However, there were also pastor-teachers (Eph. 4:11)[26] whose primary function was to instruct the community of believers and to give attention to the spiritual growth of young converts. Burrows suggests that because the rabbis were primarily teachers, and because Jesus was considered a teacher, His followers would tend to exalt the position of the teacher in the Church.[27]

Specific terminology is lacking for the identification of those individuals known in Protestantism as pastors. A study of New Testament materials reveals that the appellations "elder," "bishop," and "deacon" or "shepherd" are employed to designate the one who has local pastoral obligations. Thus, the stated obligations of elders,

---

23. H. Richard Niebuhr and Daniel D. Williams, eds., *The Ministry in Historical Perspective* (New York: Harper and Bros., 1956), p. 13: cf. also Didache XI, 3 ff.; 13:1; 15:1-2.

24. *NT Theology*, p. 262; cf. Maurice Goguel, *The Primitive Church*, trans. H. C. Snape (London: George Allen and Unwin, 1964), p. 111.

25. J. A. Motyer, "Prophecy, Prophets," *NBC*, p. 1045.

26. Bruce, commenting on Eph. 4:11, asserts that "the two terms 'pastors' (shepherds) and 'teachers' denote one and the same class of men," *The Epistle to the Ephesians*, p. 85. It seems wise to use the hyphen between these words.

27. *Outline of Biblical Theology*, p. 258.

bishops, and deacons are essentially those of pastors. There is no evidence of formal ordination of leaders except that of "laying on of hands."

D. Elders and Bishops

The English word "elder" is the translation of the Greek word *presbuteros,* which has been transliterated into English and used to designate a certain type of church official. Elder and presbyter refer to the same New Testament office. 1 Tim. 4:14 employs the word "presbytery" *(presbuterion),* suggesting at least a semiorganized company of elders or presbyters. They laid their hands on Timothy to ordain him.

The word "presbyter" or "elder" is found frequently in the Gospels, referring to the Jewish leaders. The use of "elder" is in keeping with the Old Testament and with Judaism. The elders were simply the older men of the community who were especially endowed with wisdom and therefore qualified for leadership roles in the spiritual life of the people.

The term first appears as a title for officers in the Early Church in Acts 11:30. An offering raised by the church at Antioch for the Christians in Judea was delivered "to the elders *[presbuterous]* by the hand of Barnabas and Saul." As noted earlier, on the swing back through Lystra, Iconium, and Antioch on their first evangelistic tour, Paul and Barnabas "appointed elders *[presbuterous]* for them in every church" (Acts 14:23). Acts 15 speaks of the leadership in the Jerusalem church as "apostles and elders" (cf. Acts 21:18). The decrees issuing from the council were also declared to be the decrees of "the apostles and elders" (Acts 16:4). At the end of his third missionary journey, Paul stopped at Melitus near Ephesus and summoned the elders *(presbuterous)* of the church to meet him (Acts 20:17). When Paul returned to Jerusalem for the last time, he made a special visit to James and "all the elders were present" (Acts 21:18).

The most significant note about the title "elder" in the New Testament is that Paul does not use it in his "Pillar Epistles" (Romans, Galatians, 1 and 2 Corinthians). However, he clearly defines the role of elders and their qualifications in the Pastoral Epistles (1 Tim. 5:17-22; Titus 1:5-6). The rest of the books of the New Testament with the exception of 2 Timothy, 1 John, and Jude employ the term. Despite its absence from the major Pauline writings, the title appears to have been universally used throughout the first-century Church to designate a particular office.

The "elder" in the New Testament probably came out of the

synagogue framework. The office grew in importance in the Early Church to the extent that Paul, in his Pastoral Epistles, was able to give instructions concerning its functions and responsibilities in the churches.

First, it is to be generally assumed that the elder was an older man. Second, he was appointed by other leaders in the church to take general oversight in local congregations (Acts 14:23; Titus 1:5). Third, the elder preached and taught and, in return, received his livelihood from the community (1 Tim. 5:17-18). He engaged in ordaining young ministers, as in the case of Timothy (1 Tim. 4:14; cf. 5:22). The only reference to elders in James appears in an exhortation for the sick to call upon them to pray for them, anointing them "with oil in the name of the Lord" (5:14). This suggests that these office-bearers were regarded as spiritually minded and gifted men. Fourth, each church had a group of elders who probably functioned much like a local church board. It is noteworthy that the singular is never used in referring to this office in a local congregation; one does not read of the "elder" but the "elders." John, however, used the singular form in speaking of himself (2 John 1; 3 John 1).

In conclusion, the role of the elder was important in sustaining the early communities. However, the office did not develop in prestige and power as did the office of bishop except perhaps in certain areas such as Jerusalem (cf. Acts 21:17-26). Nevertheless, frequent reference to "elders" in the New Testament justifies the conclusion that here we see a fairly well established form of ministry.

Another developing office in the New Testament Church was that of "bishop" *(episcopos)*. The word literally means "overseer."[28] It is used only six times in the New Testament, five times by Paul (Acts 20:28; Phil. 1:1; 1 Tim. 3:1-2; Titus 1:7) and once by Peter, where the reference is to Christ (1 Pet. 2:25). Whereas the term "elder" appears to have come out of the Hebrew background, the term "bishop" arose out of the Hellenistic milieu; it is applied only to officers in Gentile churches.

Government and temple officials in Greek-speaking circles were called *episkopoi* (bishops) and *diakonoi* (deacons). The terms are employed interchangeably. In Acts 20:28 Paul calls the Ephesian leaders "bishops" but earlier he has called them "elders" (20:17). However, in listing the qualifications of a bishop in Titus 1, Paul im-

28. Herman Beyer, "Episcopos," *TDNT,* 2:608; H. J. Carpenter, "Minister, Ministry," *Theological Wordbook of the Bible,* p. 150.

plies that the bishop is one of the group of elders to which he has already referred (cf. 1:5, 7). This passage suggests that the bishop emerged from among the elders as a special leader.

The qualifications of bishops, according to Paul's letters, are several.

1. They must be men of unimpeachable character—above reproach, the husband of one wife, temperate, sensible, dignified, hospitable, not drunkards, not violent but gentle, not quarrelsome, and not lovers of money (1 Tim. 3:2-3; Titus 1:7-8).

2. A bishop must have managerial abilities. Paul asks the question, "If a man does not know how to manage his own household, how can he care [epimelēsetai] for God's church?" (1 Tim. 3:5). In Titus 1:7, the apostle refers to the bishop as "God's steward" (oikonomos, "manager" or "administrator"). The elders at Ephesus are exhorted to fulfill their responsibility "to feed the church of the Lord" (Acts 20:28). Paul here employs the word poimainein, which means "to guide, rule, lead, or tend," as in the case of a shepherd leading sheep to a pasture. Arndt and Gingrich point out that in Acts 20:28 the symbolism has retreated into the background and the concept of "the administration of a congregation" comes to the foreground.[29] The bishop really is a pastor. The interchange between these two concepts is demonstrated in 1 Pet. 2:25, where Jesus is called ton poimena kai episkopon tōn psychōn humōn, "the Shepherd [Pastor] and Guardian [Bishop or Overseer] of your souls."

3. The bishop must have ability to teach (1 Tim. 3:2). Titus 1:9 reads: "He must hold firm to the sure word as taught, so that he may be able to give instruction in sound doctrine and also to confute those who contradict it." Thus, instruction—whether through kerygmatic or didactic means—and administration are the two areas for service in the Church in which a man must show capabilities if he is to rise to the office of bishop. Apparently bishops, like elders, were supported by the local churches. Speaking a proverb, Paul tells Timothy that "the laborer deserves his wages" (1 Tim. 5:17-18; cf. also 1 Cor. 9:6-14; Gal. 6:6).

E. Deacons

The term "deacon" (diakonos) means literally "servant." It refers to one who does menial service for others. The origin of this class of

---

29. Lexicon, p. 690.

leadership in the Church remains obscure, but there are some hints as to the reason for its creation. For example, in His ministry Jesus put a great deal of emphasis upon service. In response to the request of the sons of Zebedee to occupy prominent positions in the Kingdom, Jesus talked about servanthood and reminded them, "Whoever would be great among you must be your servant *[diakonos]*" (Mark 10:43). Our Lord characterized His own ministry in the world in terms of servanthood: "For the Son of man also came not to be served *[diakonethēnai]* but to serve *[diakonēsai]*, and to give his life a ransom for many" (Mark 10:45; Rom. 15:8). To some Greeks who came to see Him, Jesus offered a word on servanthood. "If any one serves *[diakonē]* me, he must follow me; and where I am, there shall my servant *[diakonos]* be also; if any one serves *[diakonē]* me, the Father will honor him" (John 12:26).

It might well be, also, that the seven men chosen to serve the Greek widows in the Early Church, while not called deacons, provided a model of service for others in the Church.[30] These men spent considerable time evangelizing, particularly Stephen and Philip. Strictly speaking, they can be categorized as elders, but their assigned ministry was the distribution of funds to the poor from monies collected by the Church. Stagg's judgment seems sound: "This part of the elder's function may gradually have come to be assigned to men called deacons."[31]

Little reference is made to the diaconate in the rest of the New Testament, except in Phil. 1:1 and 1 Tim. 3:8-13. In the latter passage, the apostle sets forth the qualifications of the deacon, which for the most part parallel those of the elders, but there is no mention of preaching or teaching. Paul's stated requisites for the deacon and deaconess would be most important in persons moving about from house to house, serving the physical and material needs of members of the community. Onesiphorus, according to 2 Tim. 1:16-18, functioned in this manner in behalf of Paul. The deacons were not all men, for Paul speaks of Phoebe, a deaconess of Cenchreae, a town near Corinth (Rom. 16:1; cf. 1 Tim. 3:11).

In several references the Apostle Paul employs *diakonos* to designate the office of ministry in general. For example, in Eph. 3:7 he

---

30. Acts 6:1-6. The word *deacon* does not appear in the passage, yet the corresponding verb and substantive, *diakonein* and *diakonia*, are repeated more than once.

31. *NT Theology*, p. 264.

writes: "Of this gospel, I was made a minister *[diakonos]*" (cf. Col. 1:23, 25). His special helpers he calls *diakonoi:* Tychicus (Eph. 6:21); Epaphras (Col. 1:7); Timothy (1 Tim. 4:6). Apparently the apostle used *diakonos* for its "servant" meaning, for even when he refers to his ministry in response to his opponents at Corinth, he employs it (1 Cor. 3:5; 2 Cor. 3:6; 6:4; 11:15, 23). Paul understood himself to be under the control of his Master, Christ, and was thus prepared for any service that his Master might ask of him.

In conclusion, one is impressed with the fact that in the New Testament there is no description of a priesthood in the Christian community. Bishops, elders, and deacons teach, preach, administer the organization, and serve the personal needs of the communicants, but they fill no special priestly role except that which is accorded to every member. Each believer is a priest unto God and collectively the Church is a royal priesthood (1 Pet. 2:9).

Neither is there an institutional hierarchy such as developed in the church in later centuries. Although local communities are led by apostles, teachers, elders, or bishops, the Church as a whole is described as "a brotherhood" (1 Pet. 2:17; 5:9). All who belong to Christ are to be equipped for ministry (Eph. 4:12). Hans Küng's provocative book, *The Church,* illuminates this very point:

> The priesthood of all believers consists in the calling of the faithful to witness to God and his will before the world and to offer up their lives in the service of the world. It is God who creates this priesthood and hence creates fellowship among believers. . . . The priesthood of all believers is the fellowship in which each Christian, instead of living to himself, lives before God for others and is in turn supported by others. "Bear ye one another's burden and so fulfill the law of Christ" (Gal. 6:2).[32]

There are no formal or legal concepts of succession, but there is continuity through the Holy Spirit with all the Church of the past and with all contemporary expressions of the Church. The monarch of the Church is the Lord himself.

It is only fair to say, however, that the growth of the Church led to the introduction of special offices and forms of order. Walker correctly observes, "Leadership, in any case, by a committee of equals is unworkable for any protracted time, and small congregations were doubtless unable to provide for more than one full-time official."[33]

---

32. Hans Küng, *The Church,* trans. Ray and Rosaleen Ockenden (New York: Sheed and Ward, 1968), p. 381.
33. Williston Walker, *A History of the Christian Church,* rev. ed. (New York: Charles Scribner's Sons, 1959), p. 42.

Unfortunately, in some cases, the response to this need brought about the creation of hierarchal forms of ministry and government which gradually dissipated the consciousness of the Church as the people of God *(laos tou theou)*.

Section Seven

The Future in Salvation History

33

The Kingdom of God

Whatever God's original plan for man on earth might have been, we know that sin played havoc with the total human order. Not only is man's own degeneration traceable to sin, but also the dislocation in his physical environment (Rom. 8:19-25). Nothing is as God originally intended. But by far the most serious consequence of sin, as seen through the eyes of Scripture, is postmortem. Not only is earth devastated, but sin's effects are borne by man in full consciousness beyond physical death. Sin created not only an earthly morass but eternal doom. As vicious as are sin's temporal consequences, it is its eternal results that are most terrifying.

Therefore it is apparent that God's saving deed in Christ is essentially both temporal and transtemporal. Redemption is indeed the master concept. The whole plan is the recovery of a lost world and the restoration of a wandering and degenerate race. Human history can be described as the struggle between God's redemptive operation and sinful resistance, both human and satanic. The goal of history is the final and satisfactory consummation of redemption. This consummation will be such that God's original purpose in creating man will be achieved, and His decision to create will be vindicated. The difference between the redemptive goal and the original ideal is in the historical journey, which now is a *via dolorosa* past a hill called Calvary.

I. A Theology of Hope: An Overview

Nothing is clearer in the New Testament than that the Cross means victory for God and hope for man. Because the early Christians were oriented to Calvary and to Easter, they could also be oriented to the future. The prospect for man was changed from deepening gloom to expanding sunrise.

It is also clear that the New Testament sees a *telos* that is climactic and punctiliar. As a climax, it is the culmination of a prescribed series of historical developments and apocalyptic events. It is punctiliar in the sense that the events converge on the final day of judgment—which is not only final for every man but terminal for the earthly order as we know it. Human history is thus not open-ended; someday it will be closed. Probation is a period of time with a beginning and an end, both for individuals and for man on earth. There will finally be a "shut door" (Luke 13:25).

The broad outline is ordained by God and to some degree the details are revealed. The plan includes the evangelization of the world by the Church in the power of the Spirit made available at Pentecost. This will be climaxed by the second coming of Christ, which will be accompanied by the resurrection and followed (immediately or ultimately) by the judgment. This judgment will declare the eternal destiny of every son of Adam. From it there will be no reprieve or appeal, and the possibilities are only two: eternal life or eternal death (1 Corinthians 15).

There is also a school of interpretation which sees in the Scriptures a period of literal, political reign of Christ on earth. This they see as a necessary element of His mission to "destroy the works of the devil" (1 John 3:8). In this reign the redemption of individuals from sin would find its logical issue and fulfillment in the purging of society. Human history would thus climax with a demonstration of life on earth as it was meant to be (Acts 3:21). Although held by some, such a view is by no means unanimous among evangelicals.

Much of the world's redemptive program is assured by God's

sovereignty. But the implementation is flexible, in both detail and timing. This undetermined side is due to man's freedom, to which God accommodates himself in continuous interaction. Sinful man, aided and abetted by Satan, is in rebellion against God's rule. In a real freedom, men exercise considerable power to delay and sabotage God's plan—and also to exclude themselves personally from the final victory.

While the New Testament leaves no doubt concerning the ultimate outcome, it promises no universal redemption. Instead, the final picture is always one of division between the wheat and the tares, the sheep and the goats—those on the inside of the door and those on the outside. It follows then that while the sinner cannot block God's sovereign design in history, he can exclude himself from participation in it. In some sense this may appear to be less than a perfect conquest for God. But any other kind of conquest would be by coercion, which would be no divine victory at all.[1]

Such is a brief overview. A more detailed examination will disclose that the eschatological teachings of the New Testament revolve around four recurring themes: (1) The Kingdom of God; (2) The Second Coming of Christ; (3) The Resurrection and Final Judgment; (4) The Eternal Order.

II. The Concept of the Kingdom

Terms and basic ideas of the kingdom of God have been discussed elsewhere (see Cc. 13 and 19). It is the concept in its eschatological connections which now claims our attention. In the broad sense the Kingdom is first and last the kingdom of God; as such it is nothing new. Its locale is wherever God rules in unshadowed perfection over His creatures. The Bible consistently refers to this realm as heaven. We are taught this basic premise in the prayer, "Thy kingdom come, thy will be done, on earth as it is in heaven"; and Paul was sure that he would be preserved "for his heavenly kingdom" (2 Tim. 4:18). Whatever may be said about a specific kingdom of Christ as it relates to men and this earth, it must never be forgotten

---

1. Apparently also the unfolding of God's eschatological schema can be modified in timing to some degree by the faithfulness of the Church; at least Peter gives us a hint of this sobering possibility: "Since all these things are thus to be dissolved, what sort of persons ought you to be . . . waiting for and hastening the coming of the day of God" (2 Pet. 3:11-12).

that the kingdom of God is the great cosmic reality in the background. That Kingdom is the source of any earthly manifestation, and it alone is our ultimate goal. God's kingdom is in no sense dependent on the Cross for its existence. Only the *redemptive form* of this Kingdom, as a spiritual realm into which sinners may reenter through new birth, was introduced among men by Christ.

A. A Stolen Province

The great need of redemption, requiring a Cross, is also disclosed in the Lord's Prayer. Why should it be necessary to pray, "Thy kingdom come," and why should there be any difference between the completeness of God's rule "on earth" and "in heaven"? Because through duplicity Satan stole the allegiance of man and wrested this earth and the race upon it from God's kingdom. The total plan of redemption can now be expressed in two words: repossession and restoration. It is God's action to bring this segment of creation back into His kingdom. But the devastation concerned both a race of men and the planet on which they lived; therefore the restoration must include both (Rom. 8:18-23). In respect to men, the Kingdom is the realm of God's rule into which they enter by faith and which enters them by the Spirit. In respect to the earth, the Kingdom is an order that must be visibly and victoriously established, so that this planet becomes the seat of God's glory. Anything less would be but a partial reconquest.

B. A Delegated Task

The task of recovering the earth and its inhabitants to God's kingdom has been delegated to the Son. His specific mission is itself called the kingdom of God, and He reigns as Deputy King. Thus we can speak of the "eternal kingdom of our Lord and Savior Jesus Christ" (2 Pet. 1:11; cf. Col. 1:13). But this is a part for the whole: *it is that specialized form of the Kingdom which is redemptive.* As a redemptive scheme Christ's kingdom is unique because, as far as we know, no other creature or place has been lost from God.

Furthermore, the kingdom of the Son is temporary. While Peter calls Christ's kingdom "eternal," Paul says that the "end" will be when Christ "after destroying every rule and every authority and power . . . delivers the kingdom to God the Father . . . that God may be everything to every one" (1 Cor. 15:24-28). We may say then that from the standpoint of Christ as Eternal Son the everlasting Kingdom is His coequally with Father and Spirit; but from the standpoint of

Christ as Redeemer His kingdom is an episode in the vast breadth of eternity. The last sentence of its history will one day be written, and all heaven can rejoice with the Son with the ringing cry, "Mission accomplished!"

Insofar, therefore, as Christ is the King, the Kingdom "comes" when He does, and exists where He is (Luke 17:21; John 18:37; Mark 9:1). Insofar as the Kingdom is the rule/realm of God among men, it "comes" when men enter it one by one by faith and obedience, and permit its rule to enter them (Matt. 4:23; John 3:3, 5; Rom. 14:17; Col. 1:13; 1 Thess. 2:12). Insofar as the Kingdom is a social order to be established on earth in complete power, it is yet to come; this "coming" is the goal of history (Matt. 25:31; Mark 14:25; Luke 21:31; 22:18; Rev. 11:15). Insofar as the Kingdom is the eternal realm of the Father, we may speak of entering it at death (1 Cor. 15:50; 2 Tim. 4:18). By thus discerning the Kingdom in its various forms, we can understand the perfect consistency of the different ways the New Testament talks about it: It is "within you," or "among you"; it is near; it is coming; and we are urged so to live that when we die we shall have an abundant entrance "into the eternal kingdom of our Lord and Saviour Jesus Christ" (2 Pet. 1:11).

It is unfortunate that a false antithesis has been introduced by some interpreters between the Kingdom as present and the Kingdom as future. Typical is the "thoroughgoing eschatology" of Albert Schweitzer over against the "realized eschatology" of C. H. Dodd. According to Schweitzer, Jesus' concept of the Kingdom was entirely apocalyptic and future. Dodd, on the other hand, places all his interpretive weight on the passages which stress the Kingdom as a present reality.[2] A conservative approach, which accepts the various strands of emphasis as equally authentic, interprets accordingly and discovers a unifying synthesis. Such a synthesis is expressed by Robert H. Culpepper:

> Our position is that in the teaching of Jesus the kingdom of God is rooted in the eternal sovereignty of God; that it is manifested in history, in acts that reveal the divine sovereignty, particularly in the Christ-event, and is thus a present reality; but that it reaches its consummation in the future in the supramundane world that will be disclosed at the second advent

---

2. Cf. Albert Schweitzer, *The Mystery of the Kingdom of God* (London: Adam and Black, 1950; first German ed., 1901), and *The Quest of the Historical Jesus* (New York: The Macmillan Co., 1961; first German ed., 1906); Dodd, *The Apostolic Preaching and Its Developments.*

(parousia) of Jesus Christ. We believe that this is a position in keeping with the New Testament witness, and that only by arbitrary exegesis can one arrive at the interpretation of the kingdom as either exclusively future or exclusively present.[3]

III. STAGES IN THE RECONQUEST

The accomplishment of the Son's task is unfolded in stages in exact accordance with the divine plan (Acts 2:22-23; 3:18-26; 1 Tim. 3:16; Heb. 1:1-3). As has been indicated, the final double goal is the redemption of men and the establishment of Christ's rule on earth. Three stages are disclosed in the Scripture in the achievement of this project: *preparatory, mediatorial,* and *apocalyptic.*

A. The Preparatory Phase

The preparatory stage extends from the protoevangelium (Gen. 3:15) to the birth of Christ. In the divinely interpreted holy history *(Heilesgeschichte)* of the Old Testament we can trace God's steps in choosing a "seed" and fashioning a chosen people. Eventually they would transcribe into a book God's self-revelation in history, law, and prophecy (Rom. 3:1-2). In the fullness of time they would also cradle the Messiah (Rom. 9:4-5).

It was in this long history that the vision of the kingdom of God became dominant. John Bright is convinced that this is the fundamental theme of the Old Testament.[4] The events of Israel's history combined with the messages of the prophets made the Israelites increasingly kingdom conscious. A great longing and a great hope were created for an ideal king and an ideal reign, wherein would be perfect peace, safety, and righteousness. It would be Davidic in dynasty and reminiscent of David's kingdom in power yet greatly exceed David's kingdom in its perfection and permanence.

All of this was Israel's hope and became its great obsession. When John the Baptist and Jesus began talking about the kingdom of God, they were using a familiar term. But unfortunately, it was only partially understood because much of God's preparatory mes-

3. *Interpreting the Atonement* (Grand Rapids, Mich.: Wm. B. Eerdmans Publishing Co., 1966), p. 49. It has already been noted that evangelicals are divided as to whether the future Kingdom will be solely in the eternal "supramundane world," as suggested by Culpepper, or whether there will be an intermediate stage, earthly and political, yet ideal.

4. *The Kingdom of God* (New York: Abingdon-Cokesbury Press, 1953).

sage had been unheard. The Jews had missed two notes that should have opened their minds to the kind of a Messiah they found in Christ.

1. *A New People.*

One note was the emphasis on a people as well as king. In the new order this people would have to be new in kind, made new by the implementation of a new covenant (Jer. 31:31-34; Ezek. 36:25-27). The popular notion identified the people of the Messianic order solely in terms of their descent from Abraham. When Jesus announced that the long-awaited Kingdom had at last arrived, a national restoration of a Jewish state in Davidic glory was the natural assumption. The hope of the Jews in Jesus waxed and waned precisely as He seemed to fan this hope or dash it. One is not surprised that the Pharisees asked "when the kingdom of God was coming" (Luke 17:20 ff.). But we begin to grasp the tenacity of the illusion when the disciples, even after the Resurrection, were asking, "Lord, will you at this time restore the kingdom to Israel?" (Acts 1:6).[5]

2. *A Suffering Saviour.*

The other strong note which the people missed in their reading of the Scriptures was the mysterious link between power and meekness, victory and apparent defeat, a Messiah who would be both King and Suffering Servant.[6]

God's preparatory methods should have been adequate to equip the men of Christ's day with a better understanding of the Kingdom than they had. This is testified to by Jesus himself in two post-Resurrection conversations recorded in Luke 24:25-27 and 44-48. "Was it not necessary that the Christ should suffer these things and enter into his glory?" (v. 26).

---

5. Yet only the stubborn blindness of a fanatical obsession could have missed the verdict of the OT. God had already rejected national Israel as the Kingdom. That dream had long since been demolished by the preaching and writing prophets. The Kingdom would belong to a new Israel, based on a new covenant, and its citizenship would not be determined by the accidents of birth but by faith and obedience. Even the later chapters of Isaiah which seem to revive the nationalistic hope, do so on a new supernatural and nonracial base (45:20-23). Bright comments: "The true Israel of God is not racially determined, but includes those of any race who obey Him" (*ibid.,* p. 146). See also J. Barton Payne, *Theology of the Older Testament,* pp. 471-73.

6. See Robert H. Culpepper, *Interpreting the Atonement,* pp. 30-38; also Payne, *ibid.,* pp. 274-81.

B. The Mediatorial Stage

1. *The Priestly King.*

The mediatorial stage began with Christ's birth. Uniting in himself what seemed to be antipodal roles, that of Priest as well as King, Jesus' life and death constituted an enigmatic offense. The confusion lay in the failure of even the most devout Israelites to understand that the Kingdom must be composed of a new race, transformed by the *power of atonement*, before it could be openly established in political and social power. Also, individual redemption from sin must come first not only logically but chronologically. If Christ was to rule over men, they must become changed men. It would be as a Priest, therefore, that He would begin to rule; for only in a priestly function could He reconcile men to God and bring about the inner change that would fit them for the Kingdom (cf. Zech. 6:13).

The crowning offense to His countrymen was that in assuming the function of Priest, Christ went further and became the Sin Offering. Before Pentecost even the disciples could not put together the pieces of this puzzle—King, yet a King who would "give his life as a ransom for many" (Matt. 20:28).

2. *The Promised King.*

The parallel but enigmatic priestly and kingly strains are found side by side in the New Testament. To underscore this, we need first to see how unmistakably Christ is identified as the promised King of Israel. All four Gospels are emphatic in this in their first chapters. Luke gives the earliest announcement in the chain of events, that of the Angel Gabriel to Mary: "He will be great, and will be called the Son of the most high: and the Lord God will give to him the throne of his father David: and he will reign over the house of Jacob for ever; and of his kingdom there will be no end" (Luke 1:32-33). Matthew at once establishes Jesus' Davidic lineage by speaking of "his people," and the wise men query, "Where is he who has been born king of the Jews?" (1:1-7, 21; 2:2). It took Mark just 14 verses to reach the theme of our Lord's preaching: "The time is fulfilled, and the kingdom of God is at hand; repent ye, and believe in the gospel" (Mark 1:15; cf. Matt. 3:1-2; 4:17).[7]

---

7. In the first chapter of John's Gospel, Jesus as King is presented first in His cosmic relations, as the Divine Word, the Light, the Source of grace and truth, the Revelation of the Father. As a king "he came to his own home, and his own people

What the writers called the gospel was clearly the "good news" that the long-awaited kingdom of God was "at hand." There has been much discussion over the exact meaning of the last two words. The verb used *(enggizō)* means "to approach" or "draw near." It has been applied to an impending event, a Kingdom "just around the corner." But often it is used in the Scriptures as an idiomatic equivalent for arrival.[8] The perfect tense in this instance combined with the clear declaration that the "time is fulfilled" would support such an interpretation here.[9]

The evidence seems unmistakable that the birth of Christ was a turning point in history because it was the inauguration of a new order, and that new order was the kingdom of God. Insofar as the Kingdom is linked with future events, Archibald Hunter's expression "inaugurated eschatology" is apt.[10]

While Jesus did not say flatly in His public ministry, "I am the King you have been waiting for," He immediately began demonstrating kingly authority—in His teaching (Matt. 7:29), and in His power over demons, sickness, and the violent forces of nature (Matthew 8). What a strange kind of kingship is here! Later, in striking ways He identified himself: by giving to Peter "the keys of the kingdom" (Matt. 16:19), by admitting to the two sons of Zebedee that there would be a throne (Matt. 20:24), and by acknowledging to Pilate that He was the King of Israel (John 18:36-37).

3. *The Suffering King.*

Yet Jesus chose to discourage any expectation of an immediate earthly kingdom. In many ways He tried to correct His power-struck

---

received him not" (1:11; cf. NEB). Very soon we read of the early recognition by His first disciples of His Messiahship. "We have found the Messiah," exults Andrew to his brother Simon. That this term was understood by the Jews to refer to the Divine King is indicated by Nathaniel's testimony: "Rabbi, you are the Son of God! You are the King of Israel" (John 1:40).

8. Beck translates it, "God's Kingdom is here"; Phillips: "The Kingdom of God has arrived" (cf. NEB).

9. Archibald M. Hunter writes that since C. H. Dodd's insistence that *ēngiken* "has the force of 'arrived,' a linguistic battle has raged. Dodd's critics contend that 'is at hand,' not 'has arrived' is the true translation." But Hunter casts his vote at this point with Dodd, believing that *ēngiken* in Mark 1:15 has the "same force as *ephthasen* in Luke 11:20" (see Chap. 13). He adds: "Even those who boggle at this translation usually concede the main point, that Jesus believed the Kingdom to be a present reality in himself and His ministry. Indeed the evidence of the Gospels leaves us no option" (*Introducing NT Theology,* p. 27).

10. *Ibid.,* pp. 27, 46.

disciples and prepare them for what was ahead. Following His answer to the ambitious Zebedee duo, He explained, "Whoever would be first among you must be your slave; even as the Son of man came not to be served but to serve, and to give his life a ransom for many" (Matt. 20:27-28). In His answer to the Pharisees He implied His kingship by saying, "The kingdom of God is in your midst." He then proceeded to sketch for His disciples the future coming of "the Son of man." He hastened, however, to add, "But first he must suffer many things and be rejected by this generation" (Luke 17:20-25).

Later, on the day of the Triumphal Entry, Jesus accepted the homage of the crowds who called Him King—"the Son of David" (Matt. 21:9). But He deliberately presented himself as the kind of Ruler described by the prophet: "Your king is coming to you, humble, and mounted on an ass and on a colt, the foal of an ass"—the symbol of a peaceful prince, not a martial conqueror. He was no threat to Rome; this was what infuriated the Zealots and frustrated Jesus' misguided friends. Finally, before Pilate He acknowledged that He had a kingdom but flatly dissociated it from the kind Pilate knew and about which the Jews dreamed. He said, "My kingship is not of this world; if my kingship were of this world, my servants would fight that I might not be handed over to the Jews; but my kingship is not from the world" (John 18:36-37). Robert H. Culpepper says:

> As the New Testament witnesses, Jesus came forth proclaiming the Kingdom of God and asserting that the sovereignty of God in human history was being established through him. But . . . he regarded himself as a spiritual king, not a political ruler. He believed the sovereignty of God would be realized through the fulfillment of the role of the Suffering Servant, not that of military conqueror of the Davidic line.[11]

Some believe that Christ's primary program was the establishment of the literal Davidic kingdom at His first coming, and that He would have done so if the Jews had accepted His bona fide offer. According to this view, the Cross, followed by the Church Age, was a backup plan or adaptation necessitated by the rejection of the Jews, the consequence being the postponement of the literal Davidic kingdom. This view not only creates an artificial disjunction between the Kingdom and the Church,[12] but more seriously depreciates the cen-

---

11. *Interpreting the Atonement*, p. 33.
12. Hunter comments: "When men say . . . that Jesus never intended to create a church, they show that they do not understand what the Kingdom of God means. The

trality and necessity of Christ's atoning death for the race. It misses
the inherent necessity of the mediatorial stage of the Kingdom
coming before the apocalyptic—an order as necessary for Jews as for
Gentiles. As Oswald T. Allis aptly says: "It was not as King but as
Priest-King that Jesus entered Jerusalem. He came to die that He
might reign; not over Israel only, but that He 'might gather together
into one the children of God that were scattered abroad' (John
11:52)."[13]

4. Why First the Cross?

Why the order of the kingship inaugurated by humiliation,
meekness, and death? The answer lies in the nature of the Kingdom
which Christ came to introduce. When we understand this, we will
know why the first stage among men must be priestly and mediatorial.

a. Because the kingdom of Christ was an extension downward
of the eternal kingdom of God, there must be a moral basis for
entering it. Men are rebels; they must be set right with the eternal
Creator-King before citizenship in His realm can be restored. All of
this makes an atonement necessary as the way to the throne. Because
of sin the way back into the kingdom must be by way of the Cross.

b. Because men are evil in nature, they must become fit for the
Kingdom by the new birth (John 3:3-5) and by the inward sanctification of the Spirit. The new Kingdom has only true sons in it.
Between King and subjects is the bond of the new covenant (Heb.
8:6-12; 10:14-18; 12:18-29). Experiencing this covenant and being
in the Kingdom are the same (Rom. 14:17). Its basic notes are the
forgiveness of sins, the imprint of God's very nature on our nature,
and a personal acquaintance with the Lord—"they shall all know me,
from the least to the greatest." But this can only be experienced
personally as Christ mediates our cause with the Father, and as the
Spirit mediates His grace in our hearts.

---

idea of the *Ecclesia* has deep roots in the purpose of Jesus. His message of the Kingdom
implies it. His doctrine of Messiahship involves it. His ministry shows him creating it"
(*Introducing NT Theology*, p. 34).

13. *Prophecy and the Church* (Philadelphia: The Presbyterian and Reformed
Publishing Co., 1945), p. 79. For further careful and fair summary of the contrasting
views see R. Ludwigson, *A Survey of Bible Prophecy* (Grand Rapids, Mich.: Zondervan
Publishing House, 1973), pp. 37-82. For a modified dispensationalist position see John
F. Walvoord, *The Church in Prophecy* (Grand Rapids, Mich.: Zondervan Publishing
House, 1964).

c. The kingdom inaugurated by Christ is not only spiritual in nature but voluntary. Its extension is not by coercion but by persuasion. Christ becomes King of society only by becoming King of persons, who choose to bow to His scepter (Heb. 1:9). This necessitates preaching, a Church with a mission, and the quiet, unseen wooing of the Holy Spirit. It is in this way a kingdom incognito; in the world, yet not of the world; conquering, yet by weapons of its own which are spiritual rather than carnal. With divine power it penetrates and infiltrates itself among the kingdoms of this world. The sword with which Christ came is the dividing blade of truth. That sword separates men, one by one, day after day, year after year, until finally every man chooses either to be part of Christ's kingdom or part of the demonic forces in eternal opposition.

d. Because its extension is by persuasion, Christ's kingdom advances by infiltration into enemy territory. During this period of conquest the Holy Spirit is the special Deputy of Christ, just as Christ is the Deputy of the Father.

The disciples were still under an illusion before the Day of Pentecost. But once illuminated by the Holy Spirit, they were given immediately a divine insight into God's program. They knew that the King had gone from their immediate presence to obtain for himself a kingdom which would be won by the Spirit working through the Church. They understood therefore that during this period Christ's rule would be mediatorial. Thus Peter in his first sermon was able to speak of Jesus being "exalted at the right hand of God." In his second recorded discourse he said that Jesus must remain in heaven "until the time for establishing all that God spoke by the mouth of his holy prophets from of old" (Acts 2:33; 3:21).

While Christ is acknowledged as King, it seems to be the function of the Father and the Spirit to establish His rule on earth. It is "God," says Peter later, who "exalted him at his right hand as Leader and Saviour" (Acts 5:31). He goes ahead to say, "And we are witnesses to these things, and so is the Holy Spirit whom God has given to those who obey him." When Stephen, the first martyr, was being stoned, he looked up steadfastly into heaven, being "full of the Holy Spirit," and saw "the glory of God." He said, "Behold, I see the heavens opened, and the Son of man standing at the right hand of God" (Acts 7:55-56). In this regal Person at the right hand of the Father, Stephen did not see a future king but a present Sovereign who, in the words of Paul, "must reign until he has put all his enemies under his feet" (1 Cor. 15:25).

34

The Second
Coming of Christ

The constant backdrop of everything said, done, and written in the Early Church was the expectation of the personal return of the Lord in power. In the Gospels every effort is made to show that beyond immediate events is a glorious distant event. In Acts, Luke is very careful to forestall any idea that the outpouring of the Holy Spirit was the second advent of Christ. The Epistles also are clear in keeping before the fledgling churches the coming of the Lord as their sustaining hope. As for the Revelation of John, this is its primary theme.

I. The Certainty and Nature of His Coming

A. Survey of Biblical Pointers

1. *Jesus in the Synoptics:*
    Jesus directed the attention of His disciples to an immediate event of suffering death, and an ultimate event of coming to the earth in power and glory. The two events were unmistakably distinct in nature, purpose, and time. A typical saying is "For as the lightning flashes and lights up the sky from one side to the other, so will the Son of man be in his day. But first he must suffer many things, and be rejected by this generation" (Luke 17:24-25; cf. Matt. 16:27; Mark 8:38; Luke 8:26). He spoke in parables of a future appearance so sudden that there would be no time for last-minute adjustments,

and so final that by it destinies would be fixed (Matt. 25:1-13; Luke 12:40).[1]

2. *According to John.*

Christ's immediate withdrawal from His disciples as a prelude to a permanent union with them is seen also in John. The coming of the Spirit as a Comforter to preside in Christ's absence is not equivalent to the assurance of Jesus' personal return. Our Lord promised, "In my Father's house are many rooms; if it were not so, would I have told you that I go to prepare a place for you? And when I go and prepare a place for you, I will come again and will take you to myself, that where I am you may be also" (John 14:2-3). Even the final conversation recorded by John refers to this future coming: "If it is my will that he remain until I come, what is that to you?" (John 21:23).

3. *The Viewpoint of the Acts.*

In Acts, the promise of the angels at the Ascension is a key statement (1:9-11). Biederwolf amplifies the promise: "This Jesus—the same that you have just seen go into Heaven—will come in just the same way—bodily, visibly, and of course in His glorified humanity."[2]

Nor did the Church in apostolic days make any effort to relate this promise to the advent of the Spirit at Pentecost. In explaining Pentecost, Peter said, "This is what was spoken by the prophet Joel"; he never said, "This is what was promised by the angels 10 days ago." Rather, Jesus is still "exalted at the right hand of God" and it is He who "has poured out this which you see and hear" (2:32-33). Obviously, this is not that great event which is yet to come. A reason urged by Peter upon the Jews for repentance (3:19-21) was that such repentance might hasten the return of Christ: "That he may send Jesus, the Christ appointed for you, whom heaven must receive until the period of restoration of all things, about which God spoke by the mouth of His holy prophets from ancient time of old."[3]

---

1. That Jesus was referring to himself when speaking of this future coming of the Son of Man is established convincingly by Stauffer, *NT Theology,* pp. 1, 107, 111: "In calling Himself the Son of Man, Jesus had already taken the decisive step in claiming cosmic history as His own."

2. William Edward Biederwolf, *The Millennium Bible* (Grand Rapids, Mich.: Baker Book House, 1964), p. 402.

3. Obviously not all that was predicted and promised in the OT was entirely fulfilled in the death and resurrection of Christ; there were also the Pentecostal outpouring and the Church Age.

4. *The General Epistles.*

Years later, when Peter knew that his own death predicted by Jesus was near (2 Pet. 1:13-14), he sounded a strikingly similar note. Holy believers not only were to wait for the Lord's return, but could *hasten* it. Furthermore, they were to be waiting for "new heavens and a new earth" (3:12-13) as well as the visible return of Christ. But first he vigorously reaffirmed the certainty of the Second Coming itself. Here again he related this to "the predictions of holy prophets" (3:2). The complacency and scepticism born of long delay (v. 4) is ill-founded. It forgets that God's time perspective is not the same as man's (cf. Jas. 5:7-9; 1 Pet. 1:5, 7, 10-11; 1 John 2:28; 3:2; Jude 14-15).[4]

5. *The Pauline Hope.*

As for the Apostle Paul, his written thought was never far from his lodestar, the coming glory of Christ. Out of 89 chapters ascribed to him, there is direct reference to the Second Coming in 23 and allusions in at least 16 more.[5] While the heaviest emphasis is in two of his earliest letters (1 and 2 Thessalonians), the hope is not muted in his last. At least 16 years have intervened, and he is now convinced that personally he will not live to see "the day." But there is no wavering in his certainty. In his next to last letter he writes: "Awaiting our blessed hope, the appearing of the glory of our great God and Savior Jesus Christ" (Titus 2:13; cf. 1 Tim. 6:13-15).

In the very last Epistle, doubtless written shortly before his martyrdom, he says, "I charge you in the presence of God and of Christ Jesus who is to judge the living and the dead, and by his appearing and his kingdom" (2 Tim. 4:1).

B. The Purpose of His Coming

1. *To Reveal His Glory.*

God has purposed to glorify the Son, as the One in whom "the whole fulness of deity dwells bodily" (Col. 2:9), and as the rightful ruler of man. Great glory was manifest in His life, death, and

---

4. Note also the distinction between past appearance and future appearance in 1 John 3:2 and 8.

5. Plus numerous other eschatological references to the resurrection, judgment, etc. Paul's perspective is not earthbound; his entire theology rests on two foundation stones: what God has done in Christ, and because of that, what He designs to do in the future.

resurrection, and even greater glory during the Interregnum when He rules from the right hand of the Father. But this glory must reach its full manifestation in the Second Coming. God is determined so to exalt His obedient Son that "at the name of Jesus every knee should bow, in heaven and on earth and under the earth, and every tongue confess that Jesus Christ is Lord, to the glory of God the Father" (Phil. 2:10-11; cf. Rom. 14:10-12; Eph. 1:10).

Therefore the biblical references to the future coming of Christ describe Him as coming "in the glory of his Father" (Matt. 16:27) and as sitting "on his glorious throne" (Matt. 19:28). Here is Christ fully revealed, in His power, majesty, and divine regnancy. This is not the king "gentle, and mounted upon a donkey," but the Lamb sitting on a "white cloud," having "a golden crown on his head, and a sharp sickle in his hand" (Rev. 14:14; cf. 1:13-18). This is a universal revelation observed by all men who live or have lived—"every eye will see him, every one who pierced him" (Rev. 1:7).

2. To Divide Men.

Already men are dividing themselves, but in Christ's coming the division will be open, official, and irreversible. "The Son of man will send his angels, and they will gather out of his kingdom all causes of sin and all evildoers" (Matt. 13:41). Again: "The angels will come out and separate the evil from the righteous" (v. 49). The classifications will be only two; there will be no intermediate position for the half-way Christian. "Then two men will be in the field, one is taken and one is left" (Matt. 24:40-41). "When the Son of man comes in his glory," all nations (all peoples everywhere, not political entities) shall be gathered before Him, and "he will separate them one from another as a shepherd separates the sheep from the goats" (Matt. 25:31-32).

3. To Terminate Probation.

The idea that those left when Christ returns shall be saved during the tribulation (assuming the rapture precedes it) finds little support in the Scriptures. The "goats" are not given a second chance (Matt. 25:46). When the door is "shut," it is not opened as a merciful concession to the foolish virgins—who waited just a little too long to secure a fresh supply of oil (Matt. 25:10 ff.; cf. Luke 13:25). Paul's constant concern was that his converts might be ready at the coming of the Lord; he held out no hope of any possible correction afterward (1 Thess. 2:19; 3:13; 5:23; 2 Thess. 1:7-10; 2:1-11). And Peter urged us to "count the forbearance of our Lord as salvation" (2 Pet. 3:14-15).

He implied that our claim on salvation must be established before Christ's coming, because it could not be afterwards.

4. *To Judge the Wicked.*

General judgment is almost uniformly associated in the New Testament with the Lord's coming. For example, "The Son of man is to come with his angels in the glory of his Father, and then he will repay every man for what he has done" (Matt. 16:27). The servant who instead of being faithful through the last hour begins to behave wickedly is in for a surprise: "The master of that servant will come on a day when he does not expect him and at an hour he does not know, and will punish him, and put him with the hypocrites; there men will weep and gnash their teeth" (Matt. 24:45-51). This is implied also in all three major passages of Matthew 25, including the judgment of the nations.

When "the Lord comes," says Paul, He will "bring to light the things now hidden in darkness and will disclose the purposes of the heart" (1 Cor. 4:5). "When the Lord Jesus is revealed from heaven with his mighty angels in flaming fire," He will deal out "vengeance upon those who do not know God and upon those who do not obey the gospel of our Lord Jesus" (2 Thess. 1:7-9; cf. 2 Tim. 4:1). And how could it be declared more clearly than Jude expresses it: "Behold, the Lord came with his holy myriads to execute judgment on all, and to convict all the ungodly of all their deeds of ungodliness which they have committed in such an ungodly way, and of all the harsh things which ungodly sinners have spoken against Him" (14-15).[6]

5. *To Redeem His People.*

The gift of the Holy Spirit is eschatological in that He is "the guarantee of our inheritance until we acquire possession of it" (Eph. 1:13-14). This means that redemption is only partially available in this life. Paul, always looking toward "the day," reminds us that "salvation is nearer to us now than when we first believed" (Rom. 13:11). The fullness is on the other side, either of death or of the Second Coming.

The deliverance of the saints which is simultaneous with the Lord's return is threefold:

a. It is a deliverance out of an oppressively wicked environment and out of probationary uncertainties. Christ's coming takes us

---

6. Even though *ēlthen* is aorist, and hence may be translated *came*, the prophetic idea is better preserved by KJV, "the Lord cometh." See also NEB, TCNT, Phillips.

beyond any further torment by or seduction from the devil (2 Thess. 1:7, Amp.; 1 Pet. 1:4-13).

b. It is a gathering to Jesus himself. As iron filings leap to the magnet, so will all the redeemed both in heaven and in earth gravitate to the side of Jesus; "and so we shall always be with the Lord" (1 Thess. 4:17).[7] Again: "When Christ who is our life appears, then you also will appear with him in glory" (Col. 3:4). Paul expresses it both eloquently and simply in his letter to the church at Thessalonica, when he writes of "the coming of our Lord Jesus Christ and our assembling to meet him" (2 Thess. 2:1).

c. It is a deliverance from the limitations of flesh and blood. We are told plainly that "flesh and blood cannot inherit the kingdom of God" (1 Cor. 15:50). As a biological organism, fashioned of dust, man is not fitted for a celestial order of existence until changed into his glorified being. Whether by death or rapture "we shall all be changed . . . For this perishable nature must put on the imperishable, and this mortal nature must put on immortality" (vv. 51-53; cf. 1 John 3:2).

It is in the redemption and gathering of His people that our Lord will find His own glory perfected. Christ comes not only in the "glory of His Father" and of the angels; His coming is more than a glory of trumpets and power and vindication. The supreme glory of Christ's coming is the glory of an accomplished mission in the countless throngs of redeemed men. He died that "the church might be presented before him in splendor, without spot or wrinkle or any such thing, but she might be holy and without blemish" (Eph. 5:27). If when He came there were no such Church, all hell would mock and jeer, the trumpets would be muted, the praise of angels would be a hollow substitute. This is why Paul uses the pregnant clause: "When he comes on that day to be glorified in his saints" (2 Thess. 1:10). Every redeemed son of Adam will be an eternal testimonial to the power of the redeeming Blood and will be a vindication of both the creation and the Incarnation.

C. The Manner and Time of His Coming

1. *Suddenly.*

The coming of Christ will be similar to His ascension, declared

---

7. Some passages ascribe the gathering function to the angels, as in the Olivet Discourse: "And he will send forth his angels . . . and they will gather his elect from the four winds, from one end of the sky to the other" (Matt. 24:31)—clearly including both those living on earth and those living in heaven.

the angels: "This Jesus . . . will come in the same way as you saw him go into heaven" (Acts 1:11). It will not be a different person but the same resurrected, recognizable Lord who had just been instructing them. As He was taken up suddenly and unexpectedly, so will His return be sudden and unannounced. There will be no 60-minute advance warning. It will be as the deluge which "swept them all away" too swiftly for them to change (Matt. 24:39), or like the breaking in of the thief at night (Matt. 24:42-44; 2 Pet. 3:10). True, some advance signs should be recognized by watchful believers (1 Thess. 5:2-4). Also before the actual arrival of the bridegroom at midnight there was a cry, "Behold, the bridegroom! Come out to meet him" (Matt. 25:6). But the whole action was too swift for the careless ones to get ready. It is while the world is saying, "Peace and security" that "destruction will come upon them as travail comes upon a woman with child; and there will be no escape" (1 Thess. 5:3).

2. *Visibly and Openly.*

The revelation with Christ's saints will be world news. To forestall the notion of a secret and local revelation, Jesus said, "So, if they say to you, 'Lo, he is in the wilderness,' do not go out; if they say 'Lo, he is in the inner rooms,' do not believe it. For as the lightning comes from the east and shines as far as the west, so will be the coming of the Son of man" (Matt. 24:26-27). When His "sign" appears "in heaven," then "all the tribes of the earth . . . will see the Son of man coming on the clouds of heaven with power and great glory" (v. 30; see also Matt. 26:64; Luke 17:24).[8] In this age of TV via Telestar such worldwide observance no longer seems farfetched.

All of this brings us back to the phrases indicating His coming "with power and great glory" (Matt. 24:30). Paul declares, "The Lord himself will descend from heaven with a cry of command, with the archangel's call, and with the sound of the trumpet of God" (1 Thess. 4:16).

3. *No Prediction of Immediacy.*

There is a preponderance of evidence that Jesus did not expect an immediate Second Coming, and that in many ways He endeavored to get this understanding across to His disciples. All the

---

8. The reference to clouds is in Matt. 24:30; 26:64; Acts 1:9; Rev. 1:7; 14:14 ff.; cf. Dan. 7:31-14. Probably a natural cloud is intended. Some, however, interpret the cloud as the shekinah glory—the symbol or visible manifestation of the presence of God, e.g., Meyer and Gloag; cf. 2 Chron. 5:13-14, Berk.

parables which stress growth in the Kingdom imply a substantial passage of time, as between seed-sowing and harvest (Matt. 13:24-32, 36-43; Luke 13:18-19). Christ's plan to build a Church with His disciples exercising authority as viceroys implies a period of personal absence (Matt. 16:18-19; John 20:21-23; cf. 8:21). A "delay" is hinted in His warnings about alertness (Luke 12:38, 45). Jerusalem will experience a period of desolation (Luke 13:35; cf. 21:24). He warned the disciples not to pay heed to announcements of His coming in their future days of loneliness and longing (Luke 17:22-23). The perspective of the Olivet Discourse is far into the future (Luke 21:9). Also, the five foolish virgins were deceived into inadequate preparedness by supposing a soon coming of the bridegroom (Matt. 25:1-11).

When Jesus commended Mary for her beautiful action, He said that the story would be told "wherever this gospel is preached in the whole world" (Matt. 26:13). Leon Morris says that such a statement "makes it clear that Jesus was not expecting the world to end very quickly as some have thought. These words demand a fairly prolonged period of preaching."[9]

Jesus predicted the manner of Peter's death (John 21:18-23)—so Peter at least did not live in hope of seeing his Lord's return. And John carefully corrects the misunderstanding that Jesus had predicted that John would not die before Christ's return (v. 23). Perhaps most to the point is the parable that Jesus told specifically to disabuse the minds of His disciples of the notion "that the kingdom of God was to appear immediately." The parable was about a certain nobleman who "went into a far country, to receive kingly power and then return" (Luke 19:11 ff.). In those days a journey into a "far country" did not encourage expectation of a return the next month! The enterprise could take years. Here again is a reference to the Church Age as an interlude between Christ's first coming and His second, with the Church carrying on His business in His behalf during His long absence.[10]

---

9. Leon Morris, *The Story of the Cross* (London: Marshall, Morgan, and Scott, 1948), p. 16.

10. What are we to do with the statements which have sometimes been interpreted as evidence that Christ himself expected His immediate return? Here they are.

a. To the Twelve He said, "You will not have gone through all the towns of Israel, before the Son of man comes" (Matt. 10:23). A careful reading will suggest a radical break in Jesus' thought at v. 16. His thought turns from what proved to be a successful sortie around Palestine to a distant, apocalyptic picture with world dimensions (cf.

4. Unmistakable Signs.

While dates cannot be set, signs are given which are intended as harbingers of the Second Coming. The parable of the fig tree is proof that Jesus intended His disciples to be sign-conscious and alert to developments. "So also, when you see all these things, you know that he is near, at the very gates" (Matt. 24:32-33).

What are the "these things" which are to be recognized as signs

---

Mark 13:9-12). The conjunction of the two viewpoints seems to be a perfect example of a prophetic telescopic extension transferring attention from the immediate future to a distant day when the task of evangelizing the cities of Israel should be resumed. Olshausen suggests that "the words involve by way of anticipation a wider range of vision and blend the early mission of the disciples with their subsequent one" (quoted by Biederwolf, *The Millennium Bible*, p. 315).

b. Jesus said to the disciples: "There are some standing here who will not taste death before they see the Son of man coming in his kingdom" (Matt. 16:28; Mark 9:1; Luke 9:27). All three synoptists follow this announcement immediately with the account of the Transfiguration. We assume that the "some standing here" refers to Peter, James, and John who witnessed the Transfiguration. This was a special, private preview of our Lord's future power and glory, and explains the intended meaning of the prophecy.

c. In the Olivet Discourse, having described the events culminating in His appearance, Jesus concludes: "This generation will not pass away till all these things take place" (Matt. 24:34; Mark 13:30; Luke 21:32). This passage poses a problem only if "this generation" must be restricted to the people living then. But so to compress all the events of this discourse would do violence to its obviously extensive scope. It is more likely that Jesus meant either the Jews as a race (see Biederwolf's careful discussion, *The Millennium Bible*, p. 347), or He was thinking of the generation living in the time relevant to the parable of the fig tree.

d. In this same Olivet Discourse, Matthew reports Jesus as placing the end-time events "immediately" after the tribulation which seems to be identifiable with the destruction of Jerusalem in A.D. 70 (24:29). In contrast, Luke divides the chronology of the prophecy into a near bloc of events and an indefinitely distant bloc centering in the Second Coming itself. Luke's division is indicated by the words "And Jerusalem shall be trodden down by the Gentiles, until the times of the Gentiles are fulfilled" (Luke 21:20-24). Since both writers are obviously reporting the same discourse, it is admittedly difficult to reconcile Matthew's "immediately" with Luke's long span of time between the destruction of Jerusalem and the Lord's coming.

The welter of diverse and often contradictory opinions among commentators is not encouraging. We can agree with Ladd that Jesus "spoke both of the fall of Jerusalem and of his own eschatological parousia" (*Theology of the NT*, p. 198). But it is the temporal relationship of the two that is the problem. Perhaps the comment of Dean Alford is as helpful as any: "All the difficulty which this word [immediately] has been supposed to involve has arisen from confounding the *partial* fulfillment of the prophecy with its *ultimate* one. The important insertion in Luke . . . shews us that the *tribulation* includes *wrath upon this people* . . . and the treading down of Jerusalem by the Gentiles . . . and immediately after *that tribulation* which shall happen *when the cup of Gentile iniquity is full,* and *when the Gospel shall have been preached in all the world* . . . shall the coming of the Lord Himself happen" (*The New Testament for English Readers* [London: Rivingtons, 1863], 1:167).

of His coming? They include the worldwide preaching of the gospel (v. 14); the usurpation of religious authority by the Antichrist (v. 15; 2 Thess. 2:1-12); a widespread apostasy within Christendom (Matt. 24:12; 2 Thess. 2:3); a period of intense tribulation (Matt. 24:21-22; cf. Rev. 7:14); cataclysmic events in the natural order (or political?) (Matt. 24:29; cf. Acts 2:20; Rev. 6:12). It is uncertain what is "the sign of the Son of man" that is to appear "in heaven" (Matt. 24:30).[11]

5. The Question of "Imminence."

It has been insisted by some that the New Testament presents the Second Coming as an "imminent" event. By "imminent" we mean that one can never point to intervening or preparatory events which must occur first. Thus any period in church history—including the apostolic—could rightly be viewed as possibly the last; the Church should always think of Christ's coming as possible today. It is argued that only on this basis would the many exhortations to readiness and watchfulness have any cogence.[12]

However, the doctrine of imminence is not as clearly supported in the New Testament as is generally believed. This is the import of the entire Olivet Discourse. Jesus is warning against premature expectations. "See that you are not alarmed; for this must take place, but the end is not yet" (Matt. 24:6). Only when "these things begin to take place" does the Church have clear warrant to "look up" for "your redemption is drawing near" (Luke 21:28). Clearly there is an unfolding of predictions which becomes recognizable and cumulative as the age draws to a close. The Church has often mistakenly applied the signs to its contemporary world, but this does not in the least weaken Christ's obvious intention, that the Church should recognize the true end-time.

This sequence of identifiable events is just as explicitly affirmed by Paul. He exhorts the Thessalonians to divest themselves completely of the notion that "the day of the Lord has come" (2 Thess.

---

11. Luke's account suggests that the deliverance of Jerusalem from Gentile domination, thus signalling the termination of the "times of the Gentiles," might be another sign. We say "might" because it is not clear whether the deliverance of Jerusalem is by the Jews or by the coming of Christ himself. Some would add also the time of worldwide revival; but where is the New Testament evidence? And how could this be reconciled with the predicted widespread coldness and apostasy among nominal disciples?

12. "Imminence" and "immediacy" are not the same. "Immediacy" relates to the question of whether Jesus and the apostles actually predicted an immediate apocalypse, i.e., in their generation.

634 / God, Man, and Salvation

2:2). Then he explains that this day "will not come, unless the rebellion comes first, and the man of lawlessness is revealed, the son of perdition" (v. 3).

In 1 Thess. 2:19 Paul writes: "For what is our hope or joy or crown or boasting before our Lord Jesus at His coming? Is it not you?" He is not saying that they will live until the Lord comes, but that he wants them to share in the glory of that event, whether as living or by means of the resurrection (4:13-14).

Indeed almost all passages relating to the Second Coming, whether hortatory or not, are addressed to "you"—as if only those persons were involved. But it is clear that eschatological history cannot be confined to one generation. The explanation must be that Jesus, Paul, and others, while writing to the first-century believers, were speaking to the universal and ageless Church. The "you" belongs to each generation, but more especially to the generation of the fig tree signs.[13]

The hortatory passages of Christ in Matthew 24 and 25 should be viewed therefore in a triple perspective. First, some were enunciating a timeless principle of stewardship, namely that the Christian is always living in the light of the judgment, as one who must give account. Second, even if the individual's earthly life is not suddenly and unexpectedly cut off by the Second Advent, it will be cut off by death, which just as effectively brings him to judgment. Third, the kind of stewardship that constitutes readiness comes from inner loyalty; it does not depend upon exact knowledge of the end.

II. Events Surrounding the Second Coming

A. The Tribulation

The word for tribulation *(thlipsis)* is found 54 times in the New Testament, and in KJV is translated *anguish, affliction, tribulation* (21 times), *trouble, persecution,* and *burdened.* By far the majority of instances are noneschatological, describing rather the expected lot of believers in this life. The word of Jesus is typical: "In the world you have tribulation; but be of good cheer, I have overcome the world" (John 16:33; cf. Acts 14:22, *et al.*).

---

13. When Jesus promised, "I am with you always, to the close of the age" (Matt. 28:20), He was speaking to the total Church, not just to the small group of His immediate hearers on that day.

However, there are passages which seem to denote an intense but brief period of trouble immediately prior to the Second Coming. Technically, this is referred to as the great tribulation. References to it may be detected even when the term is not used. It is a time of apostasy (2 Thess. 2:3; 1 Tim. 4:1; Jude 18) and of great distress due to unrestrained wickedness (2 Tim. 3:1-5; 2 Pet. 3:3).

As far as the New Testament is concerned, our sources for more detailed information are the Olivet Discourse and Revelation (principally from 6:12 to 19:21).[14] Both blocks of material are subject to a variety of interpretations; therefore what is said at this point is tentative and undogmatic.[15]

The discussion proceeds on the assumption that both refer to the same "great tribulation" (Matt. 24:21; Rev. 7:14), though with a keen awareness of the real problems inherent in such an assumption. It is difficult to believe, even from the purely human standpoint, that John was unacquainted with Jesus' apocalyptic teachings and that he saw no connection between his own visions and the predictions of his Lord. But the deeper premise is that the Spirit who inspired both should expect us to look for the underlying unity, in spite of sometimes puzzling disparities.[16]

At any rate, John the Revelator reports visions that dramatically portray a period of suffering, satanic deception, political uprising, divine judgments, and desperate and final showdown conflicts on a

---

14. The "great tribulation" which is threatened on the sinners in the church at Thyatira (2:18-22) does not seem to be the same as "*the* great tribulation" of 7:9-17.

15. For an introduction to the *preterist, historicist,* and *futurist* schools of interpretation, see Ralph Earle, "The Book of the Revelation," *BBC,* 10:461 ff.

16. If the Revelation was written some 25 years after the destruction of Jerusalem (c. A.D. 96; see *BBC,* 10:458 ff.), then "the great tribulation" of which John writes, which belongs to the events subsequent to his writings (1:19), could not possibly refer to the period of distress perpetrated in Judea by Titus.

If therefore Jesus referred strictly to the Jerusalem catastrophe of A.D. 70, we are compelled to concede that the New Testament presents two "great tribulations." Moreover, Jesus unequivocally declared that never again would a tribulation occur as intense as the one He was describing (Matt. 24:21). If this were the tribulation of A.D. 70, the conclusion would be inescapable that the tribulation in the Apocalypse would not equal in horror the earlier one. The "greatness" of the Johannine tribulation might therefore be more in its worldwide and all-inclusive scope, in contrast to the relatively local nature of the first. On the other hand, if there is a real hermeneutical bond between Christ's "great tribulation" and John's, the opposite inference becomes equally compelling. The Mark and Matthew versions of the Olivet Discourse may have had a symbolic and partial reference to the devastation of A.D. 70, but the deeper reference was to the world conflagration yet future. In relation to the final tribulation, the destruction of Jerusalem in the first century was a mere dress rehearsal.

global scale. These descriptions make the designation "great tribulation" awesomely appropriate (Rev. 6:12-17; 8:7—9:21; 11:13-18; 12:12-17; 13:1-18; 16:1-21).[17]

B. The Antichrist

Before examining the data for such a personage, we need to observe the distinction between Antichrist and pseudo Christs.

1. Many Impostors.

The time of the great tribulation, Jesus said, would be marked by many "false Christs and false prophets" (Matt. 24:24). The word is *pseudochristos*. These are not antichrists in the sense of opposers, but pretenders, evidently copiers of Christ's teachings and imitators of His person. Their real menace will not be in their assumption of His more attractive teachings but in the demonstration of what seems to be His power: they "will show great signs and wonders." These will be so apparently genuine that even the saved will have difficulty in discerning their true nature and origin. There is a strong warning here that the last days will be marked by the supernatural in the religious realm, but these manifestations will come from Satan rather than from God. The dupes will be the miracle seekers and sensation addicts who are gullible but not soundly indoctrinated.

2. The Spirit of Antichrist.

The word translated "antichrist" *(antichristos)* is found only in the first two Epistles of John. There it is not used in our modern popular sense, but refers to those who openly oppose Christ. The term also describes the general spirit of such denial and opposition. "Who is the liar but he who denies that Jesus is the Christ? This is the antichrist, he who denies the Father and the Son" (1 John 2:22). Such a description would include the Jew who rejects the Messiahship of Jesus of Nazareth, and also the humanist who denies the divine Sonship. The theme is extended in 4:1-3 to include docetism, which denies the reality of the Incarnation. This also is antichrist.

In these Epistles the Antichrist is seen as eschatological. His "coming" is commonly known to the believers as a sign of the "last hour" (1 John 2:18). But the writer does not present a sharply

---

17. For a fair and comprehensive survey of interpretations of the multitude in Rev. 7:9, 14, see Biederwolf, *The Millennium Bible*, pp. 587-89. Ralph Earle says: "It remains an open question, however, whether the reference here should be restricted to the saints of this brief period" (*BBC*, 10:549).

focused person. In the above passage John observes that "many anti-christs have come" (even in that day), and in v. 4 the emphasis is on an impersonal spirit of Antichrist. In 2 John the "many deceivers" seem to constitute corporately "the deceiver and the antichrist." In these Johannine letters the chief mark of Antichrist is hostility to the historic Christ as the incarnate Son of God. By contrast, the false "christs" of the Gospels are marked by professed allegiance. Perhaps it could be said that a liberal theology is *anti*christ while a fanatical and showy supernaturalism is *pseudo* Christ. Church history has always had a generous supply of both, but perhaps never as boldly as now.

3. *The Man of Lawlessness.*

That the biblical teaching does not stop with the indefinite generalities of false Christs and antichrists is the conviction of many evangelical interpreters. The age-old struggle between good and evil, God and Satan, will come to a climactic and violent head.

Satan's attempt which failed with Christ in the wilderness will be repeated at the end of the age. This time it will not be a frontal appeal as it was to Christ but a successful elevation of a counterfeit Christ, a "man of lawlessness," who will give to Satan the surrender which Jesus refused. Through this man, Satan demonstrates his power over the rulership of the world. By means of him as viceroy Satan makes one last attempt to establish himself finally and immovably as master of this planet and the race upon it.

The classic passages which, according to this view, sketch the portrait of "the man of lawlessness" are 2 Thess. 2:1-12; Rev. 13:1-18; and 17:8-18. It is believed probable that Paul and John saw in this evil world ruler Daniel's "little horn" (Dan. 7:8, 20-27).[18]

In the Thessalonian letter nothing really new is being discussed, for Paul writes, "Do you not remember that when I was still with you I told you this?" (2 Thess. 2:6). It may be uncertain whether or not these Gentile believers were familiar with Daniel, but it is at least clear that Paul in his personal ministry had given careful attention to end-time events. One of those events was the revelation of "the lawless one" (v. 8).

---

18. It is only fair to note that there are possible alternatives to the view that the Book of Revelation describes a literal world ruler who shall arise at the time of the end. However, George E. Ladd sees the beast in Revelation 13 as Paul's "man of lawlessness" (*Theology of the NT*, p. 559).

This person will be the open exponent and epitome of the "mystery of lawlessness." The lawlessness is "already at work," but cannot have its complete way until first abetted by the "apostasy" (v. 3, NASB). The forces of evil will then be unleashed by the removal of some restraining power which hitherto has obstructed Satan in the full fruition of his designs. Paul therefore sees two *parousias:* first, the "one whose coming *[parousia]* is in accord with the activity of Satan, with all power and signs and false wonders" (v. 9, NASB); and second, the coming of Christ himself, who will slay the usurper "with the breath of his mouth" and "destroy him by his appearing and his coming *[parousia]*" (vv. 8-9).[19]

C. An Evil Triumvirate

Additional details are filled in by John. For one thing, the world ruler whom we popularly call the Antichrist is one of an evil triumvirate. His sponsor and power-source is "the dragon" who is Satan himself (13:4; cf. 12:9-17). But there is yet "another beast which rose out of the earth" (v. 11) who "exercises all the authority of the first beast" and who causes "the earth and its inhabitants to worship the first beast" (v. 12). The second beast too is given power to perform amazing signs. Since he promotes the worldwide worship of the Antichrist, he is indeed the false prophet, the very personification of all the false prophets of the ages (Rev. 16:13; 19:20; 20:10).

It would appear also that the Antichrist does not act in isolation but arises out of and works in conjunction with a political organization, "a beast rising out of the sea, with ten horns and seven heads" (13:1). In fact it could be argued that the Antichrist is not a person but this world-dominating bloc of nations.

There are evidences, however, that the Antichrist is a person. Attention is directed to "one of its heads" whose fatal wound "was healed" (v. 3). Following this, reference is made to "a mouth uttering haughty and blasphemous words" (v. 5); also it is in "its presence" that the false prophet acts (v. 12). Furthermore, the image to be worshipped is said to be the "image of the beast," and it is difficult to

---

19. Both here and in Revelation it is clear that Satan will deceive the nations by manifesting a great display of the miraculous through his puppet. As long as religious people see the miraculous as the chief evidence of truth and authority, just that long will they be easy marks in the last days. There are those who love the spectacular and the demonstrative, but who are nevertheless not controlled at heart by a profound "love of the truth" (v. 10); if they were, they would be able to see through the religious show.

conceive of an image (which is even made to talk—v. 15) of an impersonal political entity. It is likely, therefore, that the power of the 10 horns and 7 heads is surrendered to one man who acts as world dictator.

The mystery deepens, however, when in c. 17 the beast is seen as the riding animal for "the great harlot" (17:1 ff.), and this harlot is identified as "the great city which has dominion over the kings of the earth" (v. 18). Could John have meant any city other than Rome? No wonder many see the beast in this chapter as a revived Roman empire—or at least something analogous—and the woman a false religion.

It is clear that Paul's "man of sin" is timed to precede immediately the second coming of Christ, and that both were yet future at the time he wrote. It therefore seems impossible to restrict John's apocalyptic picture to Nero, or to the Roman Empire of his day—unless we dissociate Revelation 13 and 17 completely from 2 Thessalonians 2. But the resemblances are too striking for that to be done easily.

D. The Rapture of the Church

The fact of a rapture is unmistakably declared by Paul when he explains the gathering to Christ at His coming of both believers who have died and those yet living: "Then we who are alive, who are left, shall be caught up together with them in the clouds to meet the Lord in the air" (1 Thess. 4:17). As George E. Ladd says: "The word 'Rapture' is derived from the Latin word *rapio* which is found in the Latin Bible in verse 17 and translated 'caught up'."[20]

However, there are problems when one begins to look for evidence of timing and an order of events. Ladd says: "There is no affirmation in the Scripture that the Rapture will take place before the Tribulation begins. Such a teaching is an inference, not the assertion of the Word of God."[21] When we teach that the rapture will occur some time before the apocalypse, and that between the rapture and the Second Coming proper the great tribulation will unfold, we have no direct evidence and only slight ground for tenuous inference.

---

20. George E. Ladd, *The Blessed Hope* (Grand Rapids, Mich.: Wm. B. Erdmans Publishing Co., 1966, reprint), p. 78.

21. *Ibid.*, p. 80. See also Ladd's *Theology of the NT*, p. 556. He quotes Walvoord as conceding that "pretribulationism" is not "explicitly taught in Scripture."

1. *No Escape for the Elect.*

In the Olivet Discourse, having compared the suddenness and finality of "the coming of the Son of man," to the flood in the days of Noah, Jesus said: "Then two men will be in the field; one is taken and one is left. Two women will be grinding at the mill; one is taken and one is left" (Matt. 24:37-41). Furthermore, in connection with the worldwide revelation of Christ, the angels will "gather his elect from the four winds, from one end of heaven to the other" (v. 31). Obviously, then, the "elect" will go through the tribulation (v. 22).

Those who advocate a pretribulation rapture miss the plain teaching here by assigning the whole of the Olivet Discourse to a Second Coming to Israel. They confine the "elect" to the Jews. This, however, is arbitrary and unwarranted. It ignores the common application of *eklektos* in both the Gospels and Epistles to "those who believe and obey." The elect in the Olivet Discourse "are believers in Christ throughout the world. They are the universal community of the end time which replaces Israel and which puts all its hope on the *parousia* of Christ."[22]

2. *Who Is the "Restrainer"?*

A careful study of Paul's discussion of the Antichrist fails to reveal any of the support for pretribulationism which is commonly claimed for it. True, the Church may expect relief from its afflictions "when the Lord Jesus is revealed [*apocalupsis*] from heaven with his mighty angels in flaming fire" (2 Thess. 1:7). But in Paul's terminology "the day of the Lord" (2:2) clearly includes both "the coming of our Lord Jesus Christ and our assembling to meet him" (v. 1).

The "apostasy" which must come before "the man of lawlessness" can be revealed (2:3) is interpreted by pretribulationists as "departure"—specifically the rapture of the Church—and this meaning is made to control vv. 6-7: "And you know what is restraining now—so that he may be revealed in his time. For the mystery of lawlessness is already at work; only he who now restrains it will do so until he is out of the way."[23]

Paul uses veiled language (including the neuter "what" in v. 6 and personal "he" in v. 7), yet he assumes that his converts will understand his meaning ("you know"). This makes more likely the interpretation of Arnold Airhart: "Paul had considerable reason to

---

22. Schrenk, in *TDNT,* 4:188.
23. See *Bibliotheca Sacra,* July, 1968, pp. 217 ff.

regard Roman law and order in his day as a restrainer of lawlessness" (cf. Rom. 13:1-7). Airhart then quotes Ockenga: "The most acceptable view is that this (the restrainer) refers to the Holy Spirit working in common grace through civil government. When civil government collapses and there is a breakdown of restraining law, the result is lawlessness."[24]

3. Who Will Be "Raptured"?

Jesus will appear the second time unto salvation only to those who look for Him with true preparation (Heb. 9:28). This preparation is defined as rightness with God. The five foolish virgins were excluded, not by the condition of their lamps at the beginning of the evening, but by their condition at the moment of the bridegroom's arrival (Matt. 25:1-13). Those "who were ready went in." Readiness is always contemporary; it is never a matter of either memory or expectation but always a state relevant to *now*. The maintenance of holiness is not simply a condition for obtaining rewards but for seeing the Lord (Heb. 12:14).

This is no detraction from dependence on Christ; on the contrary Christ made possible a moment-by-moment obedience and righteousness which because it is available may rightfully be required. Having learned obedience himself "through what he suffered . . . he became the source of eternal salvation to all those who obey him [continuous present]" (Heb. 5:9). Paul was concerned also that the Philippians hold "fast the word of life, so that in the day of Christ" he would be able to rejoice that he had not toiled "in vain" (Phil. 2:16). No minister's labor can possibly be in vain if the eternal salvation of his converts is inviolably secure.

A sinner is justified in the moment of repenting trust; as such he

---

24. *BBC*, 9:518. Some have understood Rev. 3:10 to suggest a pretribulation rapture of the Church: "Because you have kept my word of patient endurance, I will keep you from the hour of trial which is coming on the whole world, to try those who dwell upon the earth." If this is a promise particularly to the church at Philadelphia that *they* will be taken by the rapture before the final great tribulation, then we have here the seven-period theory of the messages to the seven churches, which supposes that the churches and our Lord's words to them provide a preview of successive periods in church history. But in such a case, how could Philadelphia be in danger of the final great tribulation when another church period, the Laodicean, is yet to follow?

It is better to take the position that all of the warnings and all of the promises are applicable to every church and to the *whole* Church in any age. The question of 3:10 must then be decided on other grounds. For further discussion see Biederwolf, *The Millennium Bible*, pp. 550 ff.

would be saved should the Lord come in that moment. But should he live, his justification lasts only as long as his penitent trust. This means walking in the light, including the light of Rom. 12:1-2; 1 Thess. 5:23 and all the discoveries of personal need and divine provision in them concerning entire sanctification and preservation. Entire holiness is *imputed* in justification, but is *demanded* experientally when and as the Spirit challenges the will of the believer to obtain whole holiness.

Nowhere is this contingency more dramatically portrayed than in Matthew 25 where in three astonishing passages Jesus pinpoints this concept of readiness. The parable of the virgins illustrates the necessity of an up-to-the-minute spiritual vitality in the Holy Spirit as symbolized by the adequate supply of oil. The parable of the talents solemnly witnesses to the necessity of faithfulness in stewardship (cf. 1 Cor. 4:2).[25] The symbolic picture of the final separation of the sheep from the goats discloses the necessity of service, i.e., utilizing opportunity for doing good both to the bodies and souls of men.

This is a chapter of surprises, for the subjects are not wicked people by customary standards; indeed the virgins and stewards are not outsiders but insiders who expect to "make it." They are not irreligious, but careless, selfish, and lazy. The doctrinal implication is that justifying faith is expected to issue in a Spirit-filled life clear to the end. There is to be a steadfast faithfulness in stewardship that stems from inner love and loyalty, and a love for men that is practical and sacrificial. When faith becomes impotent in these areas, it becomes presumption, and "justification" is a dead letter.

III. THE QUESTION OF A MILLENNIAL REIGN

Will Christ's second coming be followed immediately by the final Judgment? Or will He establish a temporary political rule over men in the present earthly order, called the *millennium,* as a demonstration *in history* of human life as it was meant to be, politically, ethically, and socially?

The term "millennium" is the Latin equivalent to the Greek *chillioi,* meaning "1,000." Therefore chiliasm is the more traditional term, though millennialism[26] is currently the more familiar designa-

---

25. See Wesley's sermon, "The Good Steward" (*Works,* 6:136).
26. Sometimes millenarianism.

tion. The word is found in only one passage (2 Pet. 3:8) outside of Revelation.[27] Only in Rev. 20:2-7 is it used in such a manner as to form the biblical basis of the technical term "millennium."

This passage announces a period of time, specified as 1,000 years, when Satan will be bound and the martyrs will reign with Christ over the nations of earth. At the end of this age Satan will be permitted one final sifting of men, perhaps in order to discover those who have been outward conformists only—not saved by Christ even when ruled by Him. Satan will "deceive the nations which are in the four corners of the earth, Gog and Magog, to gather them for battle; their number is like the sand of the sea" (v. 8). Prompted by their own inner disloyalty, they rally to Satan's leadership and surround the "camp of the saints," thinking to throw off the yoke of Christ once for all. But instead, "Fire came down from heaven and consumed them" (v. 9).

1. *Premillennialism.*

This viewpoint literalizes the above passage, seeing it as a prophetic outline of the Golden Age of earth's history, which follows the present Church Age, and which is to be set up personally by Christ at His second coming. The prefix "pre" identifies the view as the belief that Christ returns to earth in power *before* this 1,000-year period and for the primary purpose of establishing it.

Premillennialists see in this view the fulfillment of Rev. 11:15: "The kingdom of the world has become the kingdom of our Lord and of his Christ, and he shall reign for ever and ever." But more significantly, they believe that only such an age can be the proper fulfillment of certain Old Testament promises (Isa. 2:4; cf. 66:8-24; Mic. 4:3-5; Zech. 9:9-10; Hab. 2:14). This period also includes the literal fulfillment of promises to establish forever the Davidic dynasty (Ps. 89:35-37; cf. 110:1-2; Isa. 55:3-5; cf. Acts 2:29-31). Not only is this to be a golden age of peace, but restoration of amity is to occur in the animal world (Isa. 11:6-9), great longevity will prevail (Isa. 65:20; cf. 17-19, 21-23), Israel will be restored both to safety and power with Jerusalem as the world's capital, and Christianity will be the universal religion (Isa. 11:9; cf. Zech. 13:2; Phil. 2:10). New Testament references to this future earthly kingdom are believed to include Matt.

27. However, it is in numerous compounds, such as *dischilioi* (2,000), Mark 5:13.

6:10; 19:28-29; Mark 15:43; Luke 19:12-15; 23:42; Acts 3:20-21; Rev. 20:1-6.[28]

2. *Postmillennialism.*

This is the position which understands Christ's return as occurring at the end of the millennium, instead of at the beginning. Postmillennialists apply the same Old Testament promises of a Golden Age to this period, but see their details as symbolic and "universal righteousness" as only relative. They emphasize the parables which see the kingdom of God expanding gradually; and they see this expansion taking place not by political means but solely through the preaching of the gospel until all of society is "leavened." The Kingdom thus is wholly spiritual in nature as far as its presence within "history" is concerned. The Kingdom is always personal and voluntary, and never to be equated with a particular worldwide political rule. While not espousing this position, R. Ludwigson states it as follows:

> Postmillenarians affirm that this growth will continue until the world is practically Christianized. Evil will not be wholly eradicated from the world even at the height of this period, nor will the world under the preaching of the gospel be converted down to the very last man, but the world will become a great field of good grain, though mingled with some tares of evil.[29]

Postmillennialists accept Revelation 20 as an authentic prophecy of this period, including the restraining of Satan, and his unleashing for a final whirlwind of rebellion. The "thousand years" is symbolic of a lengthy period, not to be taken literally. The final spasm of evil is seen as the "great tribulation" portrayed elsewhere in the New Testament. At its height Christ will come, signalling the general resurrection and the Judgment, to be followed by the new heavens and new earth and the eternal order.

---

28. For a strong hermeneutical and exegetical defense of the premillennial interpretation of Revelation 20, see George E. Ladd, *Crucial Questions About the Kingdom* (Grand Rapids, Mich.: Wm. B. Eerdmans Publishing Co., 1954), pp. 135-83. He says: "The fact that the relationships of these events which will see the consummation of God's kingly rule is made explicit for the first time only in the last verses of the last book of the Bible should pose no acute problem to those who believe in progressive revelation" (p. 183). His theological defense is expressed cogently in his *Theology of the NT*, pp. 629 ff.

29. The writer is deeply indebted to Ludwigson for his succinct survey of the three millenarian positions (*Survey of Bible Prophecy*, p. 97).

3. *Amillennialism.*

A growing school of biblical scholars do not find sufficient evidence to justify a firm doctrine of a millennium in the sense of an earthly political rule of Christ over the nations of men, preceding the final judgment and renovation. The "binding" of Satan was accomplished by Christ at His first coming (Matt. 12:24-29; John 12:31; Col. 2:15; Heb. 2:14; cf. Rev. 12:10). Like the postmillennialists, these scholars understand the 1,000 years to be symbolic, but more particularly of the entire gospel age which closes in a brief period of intense satanic activity and persecution. At the peak of its fury Christ will appear, but not to establish a kingdom over the remaining nations on earth. Rather, He will destroy the Antichrist and his cohorts by the flame of His presence, precipitate the general resurrection, and immediately set up the Great Judgment. This will be accompanied by the destruction of the earth in its present form, and its reconstitution as the "new heavens and the new earth." The presence here of the New Jerusalem as the center of the eternal order will effectively display total conquest of Satan's kingdom and fulfill all predictions of a glorious age.

According to amillennialists the prophecies relating to the eternal establishment of David's throne (2 Sam. 7:17, 19; Isa. 9:6-7) find their fulfillment in the present reign of Christ at the right hand of the Father (Acts 2:29-36). The holy city is seen as spiritual Zion, the Church militant and triumphant (Gal. 4:26; Heb. 12:22-23). Promises to Israel relate to a better and heavenly country (Heb. 11:10, 14-16). The restoration of nature (Isa. 11:5-9) is the new heavens and new earth described under earthly terms. The literal reconstruction of the Temple with restored animal sacrifices is no part of a divine plan and cannot be claimed as a fulfillment of Ezekiel's prophecy. This prophecy is considered to be "a figurative representation and type of the gracious presence of the Lord in His Church . . . which will manifest itself when our Lord shall appear."[30]

Dogmatism is unwarranted, in view of the great complexity of the issues and the admitted obscurity of many key passages. But it must be conceded that the New Testament's support for premillennialism is not unquestionably clear. Jesus consistently associates His

---

30. Carl F. Keil, quoted by Ludwigson, *ibid.,* p. 107. Geerhardus Vos, Oswald T. Allis, and Archibald Hughes are among many able exponents of amillennialism.

second coming with general judgment and absolute finality (Matt. 24:2—25:46).

The Epistle to the Hebrews is incontestably transtemporal. Not the slightest hope is held out to these hesitant Jewish Christians that would reinforce their expectation of a politically triumphant Jewish nation. Every such notion seems utterly dashed, and our attention is directed forward but *upward*, to "Mount Zion and to the city of the living God, the heavenly Jerusalem, and to innumerable angels" (Heb. 12:22; cf. 4:1-11; 6:4-5, 17-20; 8:1-13; 9:27-28; 10:26-39; 11:8-16, 35-40; 12:25-29; 13:12-14).[31]

As for the Pauline writings, evidences for a chiliastic (millennial) viewpoint are not only sparse but inconclusive. At the heart of his gospel, he says, is the assurance of a "day when . . . God judges the secrets of men by Jesus Christ" (Rom. 2:16). Elsewhere that day is clearly synchronized with the Second Coming (2 Thess. 1:6-10; cf. 1 Cor. 3:13; 2 Tim. 4:8). Possible support for the millennial idea might be seen in Paul's assurance that the saints will "judge the world" (1 Cor. 6:2; cf. v. 3; 2 Tim. 2:11-12); but he says nothing about the nature, time, or place of this judging. The emphasis for Paul is sharing in the triumph of Christ.[32]

To a striking degree the whole issue turns on the interpretation of three passages, one a word of Jesus, the second a word of Peter, and the third a word of Paul. When Peter asked Jesus, "What then shall we have?" Jesus replied: "Truly, I say to you, in the new world, when the Son of man shall sit on his glorious throne, you who have followed me will also sit on twelve thrones, judging the twelve tribes

31. The common interpretation of Acts 15:16-18 as a prediction of a future, literal, Davidic dynasty is of doubtful validity. "After these things" (v. 16) does not mean after the events of the Apostolic Age, but in the day following the dispersion and regathering of the Jews (Amos 9:8-10). James specifically says that "that day" is no longer future but has come, in the fulfillment of the promise that through the rebuilt tabernacle of David (the new rule of Christ) "the rest of mankind may seek the Lord." This is being quoted as a biblical proof that ministering to the Gentiles is divinely ordained and included in the promise.

32. Millennialistic implications have also been seen in 1 Cor. 15:23-28; Phil. 3:11; 1 Thess. 4:13-18; and 2 Thess. 1:5-12. Exegetes such as Geerhardus Vos strongly refute so interpreting these passages (*The Pauline Eschatology* [Grand Rapids, Mich.: Wm. B. Eerdmans Publishing Co., 1972], p. 259 and elsewhere). On the other hand A. T. Robertson observes on Phil. 3:11—"Apparently Paul is thinking here only of the resurrection of believers out from the dead and so double *ex*" (*Word Pictures*, 4:454). For a cogent statement of the position that *ek nekron* is theologically relevant to the question of two resurrections (and hence the millennial idea), see Wiley, *Christian Theology*, 3:334-36.

of Israel" (Matt. 19:27-28). Later, after the Day of Pentecost, Peter said to his fellow Jews in Jerusalem that they should repent, "that he may send the Christ appointed for you, Jesus, whom heaven must receive until the time for establishing all that God spoke by the mouth of his holy prophets from of old" (Acts 3:20-21). In writing to the Ephesians, Paul projects a future consummation: "He has made known to us in all wisdom and insight the mystery of his will, according to his purpose which he set forth in Christ as a plan for the fulness of time, to unite all things in him, things in heaven and things on earth" (Eph. 1:9-10).

The interpreter must ask, Are these three passages one? Do they refer to a common vision? Is Paul's "dispensation of the fulness of times" (KJV) his inspired way of referring to Peter's "the time" of universal fulfillment of prophecy? Do both refer to what Jesus meant by "the new world" ("the regeneration," KJV; "the next world," Phillips)? That a hermeneutical bond exists seems a reasonable assumption.[33]

Then the crucial question arises whether the Holy Spirit intends these passages to be understood as referring to a period within history, or a state beyond history. The answer is not made easier by the fact that the Apostle Peter, who heard the Lord's words and interpreted them to his Jerusalem audience, is the apostle who describes the fulfillment in apocalyptic terms: "But the day of the Lord will come like a thief, and then the heavens will pass away with a loud noise, and the elements will be dissolved with fire, and the earth and the works that are upon it will be burned up. . . . But according to his promise we wait for new heavens and a new earth in which

---

33. The relevance of Eph. 1:10 is more sharply focused by KJV, and especially NASB: "an administration suitable to the fulness of the times." If this period of consummating all things in Christ is parallel to "redemption of God's own possession" (v. 14, NASB), then the present dispensation of the Holy Spirit (within which the "promised Holy Spirit" is a "guarantee of our inheritance"—vv. 13-14) is preliminary and preparatory of the dispensation of the fulness of times. In this case indeed we have a pointer to a climactic period of time yet to follow this Church Age. However, some interpreters see the present work of the Spirit as part of the "summing up" of v. 10, and the administration *(oikonomia)* of the fullness of times the gospel age, i.e., the age in which we now live (cf. S. D. F. Salmond, *EGT,* 3:260). The Spirit, says Oscar Cullmann, is "more than a foretaste" but "already part of the fulfillment" ("Eschatology and Missions in the New Testament," *The Theology of the Christian Mission,* Gerald H. Anderson, ed. [New York: McGraw-Hill Book Co., 1965], p. 45). Acts 2:17 is relevant here—as are other passages which identify this age as the final period. The question whether or not Eph. 1:10 supports the millennial idea remains undecided.

righteousness dwells" (2 Pet. 3:10, 13). This obviously is parallel to the new heaven and new earth of John's vision (Rev. 21:1). But both passages transport us to a transtemporal, eternal order. It is difficult to reconcile such an order with the millennial idea of a last period of human history on earth that includes growing crops, procreation, and even death as we now know it.

If indeed Jesus, Peter, and Paul were speaking of a climactic period of Christly rule on earth before the final destruction, then the millennial projection can be said to be confirmed. But in that case we must assume that Peter's passage permits an earthly reign between the "day of the Lord" and the fiery holocaust, even though his wording contains no hint of it. So to interpret him would be to invoke the "law of compression." This hermeneutical principle affirms that events which in God's prophetic calendar may be far apart in time may be predicted as occurring together. Prophecy "has no perspective," says Wiley.[34]

While there is not likely to be unanimity of opinion concerning this complex issue, there may be mutual charity. Above all there must be unity of devotion to the Christ who came once according to promise, and assured us He would come again. Such devotion will prove itself in faithful service, constant readiness, and loving expectation.[35]

---

34. *Christian Theology,* 3:305 ff. George Eldon Ladd calls this "the foreshortened view of the future" (*Theology of the NT,* p. 198). A possible example is 1 Pet. 1:11. Between the "sufferings of Christ" and the "glories to follow" have now intervened almost two millennia, but this verse contains no intimation of such a temporal separation. For the significance of Christ's answer to the disciples' question in Acts 1:6 see Biederwolf, *The Millennium Bible,* p. 401.

35. For a development of NT eschatology along premillennial lines see *End Times* (teacher's volume), by Richard S. Taylor (Marion, Ind.: Aldersgate Publications Association, 1975).

35

The Eternal Order

I. Immortality and Resurrection

The New Testament knows nothing of a redemption that saves the soul but offers no hope for the total man. The undoing of sin must be accomplished at every level. This is precisely Paul's line of reasoning in Rom. 8:18-25, with its climax: "Not only the creation, but we ourselves, who have the first fruits of the Spirit, groan inwardly as we wait for adoption as sons, the redemption of our bodies" (v. 23).

A. The Christian View of Embodiment

Man is mortal as to his physical constitution, but immortal in personal spirit identity. The ability of the self to exist in a disembodied state is everywhere assumed in the New Testament (see C. 15). The related Greek view sees both materiality and embodiment as confinements to be escaped. What is unique in the biblical view is that such disembodiment is not the goal of being, nor, in itself, desirable. Corporeality and ideal existence are not seen as incompatible. Rather, the Christian hope is not only an eternal existence but an embodied life in Christ's presence.

The biological body of earthly probation is called by Paul "our lowly body" (Phil. 3:21). As such it leaves much to be desired. However, embodiment in itself is not a handicap; in fact it is elemental to fullness of life. A human spirit must have suitable modality if the enrichment of multiplied forms of activity and expression are to become possible. This need is inherent in our finiteness.

B. The Concept of Resurrection

The weight of emphasis in the New Testament is not so much on immortality as on resurrection. The self which is disembodied at the "flesh and blood" level (1 Cor. 15:50) is reembodied at a higher level; "this mortal" puts on "immortality." It isn't the isolated self which puts on immortality but the self in its wholeness as a corporeal entity (v. 53; cf. 2 Cor. 5:4; 2 Tim. 1:9-10).

The usual word for resurrection is *anastasis,* a raising or rising up. It is used of a resurrection from physical death some 40 times.[1] A bodily resurrection is strictly implied in the words of Jesus, "The hour is coming when all who are in the tombs will hear his voice and come forth" (John 5:28-29).

Two other implications seem inescapable: (1) the resurrection is not an event to be experienced only by the redeemed but equally by the wicked (cf. Acts 24:14); and (2) Jesus himself is the source of both resurrections. By inference it may be said that without the Incarnation there would have been no resurrection. The Incarnation gives a glorious hope to the believer, but it adds to the woes of the unsaved (2 Cor. 2:14-16). The rejection of a free salvation compounds the consequences of evil.

1. *Old Testament Roots.*

While Jesus is the Source of resurrection, He is not the source of the doctrine of a resurrection. This was already deeply entrenched in Jewish thought. Paul turned to his own account the tenacity of the Pharisees in holding to this belief when before the council he cried out, "With respect to the hope and resurrection of the dead I am on trial" (Acts 23:6). Before Felix he again identified himself with this well-known faith of the Pharisees: "Believing everything laid down by the law or written in the prophets, having a hope in God which these themselves accept, that there will be a resurrection of both the just and the unjust" (Acts 24:14-15).

In thus grounding his belief in the resurrection in the Old Testament scriptures, Paul was in perfect harmony with his Lord. Jesus disposed of the pettifogging "problem" of the Sadducees by declaring: "You are wrong, because you know neither the scriptures nor the power of God" (Matt. 22:29). His reference to the Scriptures is suffi-

---

1. Once the verb form becomes a command to sinners to arise from spiritual death (Eph. 5:14).

cient answer to those who say the concept of life after death is foreign to Hebrew thought (cf. Heb. 11:35). And His reference to the "power of God" is adequate reply to modern skeptics who on naturalistic grounds cannot comprehend the possibility of a resurrection (cf. Acts 26:8).

2. *Validated in Christ.*

Although the *resurrection* of Christ is not the source of the doctrine, His resurrection became the confirmation of the belief and thereafter its hermeneutic. "Now if Christ is preached as raised from the dead, how can some of you say that there is no resurrection of the dead?" (1 Cor. 15:12). Once accept the historical fact of Christ's rising from the dead, and the validity of the resurrection idea is forever established. As a Pharisee, Paul believed in a resurrection even before his conversion. But afterward, Christ's resurrection became the anchor that held his hope, turned belief into certainty, and was henceforth the fulcrum on which his gospel of eternal life rested. The "assurance" which God furnished "to all men" that the world would be judged through Jesus was God's action in "raising him from the dead" (Acts 17:31). The Easter miracle is God's assurance of the Eschaton.

C. The Dimension of Redemption

The knowledge that Jesus' resurrection made possible a total redemption turned the prospect of a resurrection from a vague belief into a glorious hope. The goal of creation, forfeited in the Fall, was now brought again into the realm of privilege and possibility. That goal was to live forever in the presence of God, in absolute freedom from sin, disease, and death, and in ever-expanding usefulness and happiness. The terrible syndrome of sin and eternal doom was now broken; the resurrection could be into the morning instead of into the night. The value of resurrection was not just resurrection per se; its wonder was the glorious hope of resurrection into a perfect fellowship with God.

Sometimes the specific character of this resurrection of the redeemed is declared (as in Luke 14:13-14); at other times it is assumed (as in Luke 20:35-36 where the term "resurrection" is used almost as if no resurrection of any kind awaited the lost). A further example is Paul's avowal of commitment to Christ: "If possibly I may attain the resurrection from the dead" (Phil. 3:10-11). There is no inference intended here that the sinners would not be raised; the reference is solely to the resurrection unto glory now opened up as an option by Christ. The whole prospect of an afterlife has been brought into a new dimension. It now means "The entering upon a new phase of sonship characterized by the possession and exercise of unique supernatural power."[2]

II. The Nature of the Believer's Resurrection

A. Christ the Pattern

The believer's new body is to be like the Lord's own resurrected body.[3] The "power at work within us" (Eph. 3:20) is the same "working of his great might which he accomplished in Christ when he raised him from the dead and made him sit at his right hand in the heavenly places"—with death behind Him forever (Eph. 1:18-21). The immediate exercise of this power is the believer's strengthening through His Spirit "in the inner man" (Eph. 3:16). But this is a stage en route—a means to the real "hope to which he has called you," and to "the riches of his glorious inheritance in the saints" (Eph. 1:18).

The future conformity to the resurrected Christ is frequently in mind. Since Christ was the first man to experience the metamorphosis from the earthly to the heavenly by means of resurrection, and since His triumph makes ours possible, He is "the first fruits of those who have fallen asleep" (1 Cor. 15:20; cf. v. 23; Acts 26:23; Col. 1:18; Rev. 1:5). The contrast between gaining a terrestrial revivification and this larger glory is dramatically put in Hebrews: "Women received their dead by resurrection. Some were tortured, refusing to accept release, that they might rise again to a better life" (11:35).[4] John writes that the basic transformation into children of God, and into perfect love which gives confidence, may be ours now (1 John 3:2; 4:17-18); but the best is yet ahead: what we shall be "does not yet appear" *(ephanerōthē),* but we "know that when he appears we shall be like him, for we shall see him as he is" (3:2).

Paul said that the new body would not be "flesh and blood"

---

2. Geerhardus Vos, *Pauline Eschatology,* p. 156, fn.
3. The future resurrection is radically different from the revivification of Lazarus, or any of the others brought back from the dead by Jesus or the apostles (John 11:43 ff.; *et al.*). They were recalled to reinhabit their old bodies, unchanged; and were still subject to another dying in the future. But the prospect that masters Paul is the transformation of "our lowly body to be like his glorious body" (Phil. 3:21).
4. Such voluntary martyrdom would suggest a high degree of certainty even in their imperfect light.

(1 Cor. 15:50), but Jesus called attention to His "flesh and bones" as evidence of corporeality, and pointed to His hands and feet as double confirmation of identity—"that it is I myself" (Luke 24:39; cf. John 20:25-27). From Paul's statement we learn that our present biological bodies, matter- and space-imprisoned, will not be resumed; from Christ we learn that the resurrected body is not a phantom but has some kind of real substance. It is clearly not meshed with the atomic structure we now know, for neither space nor materiality (such as doors) were obstacles to Christ's visible and real presence. It was clearly also a body no longer subject to pain, disease, decay, or death.[5]

B. A Resurrection, Not a New Creation

Establishing a connection between the present body and the future celestial body is very important in New Testament thought. Christ's resurrection exemplifies this basic note of continuity. This is the eloquent message of the "linen cloths lying, and the napkin, which had been on his head . . . rolled up in a place by itself" (John 20:6-7). The exact body that had been so carefully wrapped was taken again.

This was the evidence which caused John to believe.[6] "For as yet they did not know the scripture, that he must rise from the dead" (v. 9). John was not preconditioned to read outlandish conclusions into meaningless data. On the contrary, he read the data correctly because it so overwhelmingly said one thing. There was no possible explanation other than a revivification, completely self-possessed and gloriously triumphant in nature.

Jesus refused to dissect himself into a part which died and another part which relived. He said, it was "the Christ"—the whole Person—who "would suffer and on the third day rise from the dead" (Luke 24:46). This is not a mere immortality of the soul, but a reliving of the One who died. It was the embodied Christ who died, and therefore a true resurrection must be the raising up of the embodied Christ. Otherwise it would be either a Greek continuity of spirit-

---

5. That the Jesus who is now in heaven and who will return is the same essentially as the One seen during the 40 days by the disciples, is argued by the Ascension and by Stephen's recognition (Acts 7:55-56). Yet the full glory of Jesus as the Son was not seen during those 40 days in the way it was many years later by John on the isle of Patmos (Rev. 1:12 ff.).

6. "It was not the empty tomb that aroused belief in John," writes George Eldon Ladd, "but the appearance of the grave clothes" (*Theology of the NT*, p. 325).

being or a new creation. The Christian doctrine of resurrection points to a reality distinct from either alternative.

C. Change as Well as Continuity

It is just as clear that this body Jesus retook was changed into a new kind of body. It had qualities adaptable to this order—it could be seen, recognized, and touched. Yet it was a body that could with equal facility dispense with these geophysical laws and forces. Its real nature, indeed, was nonearthly; the continuing points of contact were only accommodations.[7]

This is precisely the idea expounded by Paul respecting the transformation to be experienced by believers who are alive when the Lord returns. "Lo! I tell you a mystery. We shall not all sleep, but we shall all be changed, in a moment, in the twinkling of an eye, at the last trumpet . . ." (1 Cor. 15:51 ff.; cf. 1 Thess. 4:16-17).[8] The essence of the change is from perishableness to imperishability and from mortality to immortality (v. 53). Our nature, subject to the contingencies of probation and the law of entropy, will be exchanged for a nature that operates within a different order of being. The laws of that order are not yet known to us, but they will be as native to heaven as flesh and blood are native to earth. Whatever its principle of existence and sustenance, it will have nonforfeitable and undiminishable perfections, perhaps as the perpetual creating of the Spirit.[9]

Paul speaks of the "mystery" that those alive at Christ's return will be changed without having died, but the doctrine of resurrection *as such* presupposes death. The Corinthians, as well as the Thessalonians, feared that death before the coming of the Lord would deprive them of participation. Paul makes clear in both letters that the

---

7. In an attempt to explain the vast qualitative difference between our Lord's resurrected body and the "temple of clay" laid in the tomb, some have supposed that the physical body may have disintegrated, or perhaps vaporized, leaving the grave clothes as signs that Christ was alive in a new kind of body. All such attempts to sever the old body from the new gain nothing and lose much. It is better to say simply that it was the same body but that in its resurrection it was *changed*. Any "problems" in this view are certainly no greater than supposing a disintegration or evaporation.

8. For the way *allassō*, ("to change, alter, transform") is used elsewhere, see Acts 6:14; Rom. 1:23; Gal. 4:20; Heb. 1:12.

9. The language in Corinthians has been construed as emphasizing the change of the person instead of the body. This is in supposed disagreement with Philippians, where Paul uses *metaschamatizō*, ("to remold," "transfigure") clearly in reference to the change in the body. But as Geerhardus Vos says, this "amounts to nothing more than a verbal difference inseparable from the limitations of figurative expression" (*Pauline Eschatology*, p. 208).

exemption from death enjoyed by the believers alive at the rapture represents not the norm but the exception (cf. Heb. 11:5). Victory over death through Christ is not fundamentally escape from dying, but life out of death. Paul implies this when he writes: "What you sow does not come to life unless it dies" (15:36).[10]

D. The Action of the Spirit

As the first phase of our total inheritance, the Holy Spirit begins the redemption in the regeneration and sanctification of mind and spirit. The body is "dead because of sin" (still subject to the experience of dying), but "your spirits are alive because of righteousness" (Rom. 8:10). Then comes the announcement: "If the Spirit of him who raised Jesus from the dead dwells in you, he who raised Christ Jesus from the dead will give life to your mortal bodies also through his Spirit which dwells in you" (v. 11).[11] Whatever promise is here for the present day-by-day quickening of our bodies may have its elaboration in Rom. 8:26—"the Spirit helps us in our weakness." The primary thrust, however, is toward that future day when "the mortal puts on immortality," and when the promise "shall come to pass . . . 'death is swallowed up in victory'" (1 Cor. 15:54). Thus v. 11 of Paul's discussion in Romans 8 anticipates v. 23.

The one all-important dogma, however, is that while the body is "sown a physical body, it is raised a spiritual body" (1 Cor. 15:44). To the natural body *(sōma psuchikon)* belongs the glory of the terrestrial order; to the spiritual body *(sōma pneumatikon)* belongs the glory of the heavenly order (v. 40). This greater glory is at least partly in its imperviousness to the corruption to which the natural body is liable. Vos says that "the heavenly body is characterized by incorruptableness, glory, power."[12] The spiritual body is the natural garment given by the Spirit to believers who have already been subject to the inward preparatory fashioning of the Spirit as the "earnest" (KJV). While the term *pneumatikon* "expresses the quality of the body in the

---

10. The analogy is more particularly intended to illustrate that since we see in nature the resurrection of a "dead" seed into a form different from the seed (yet with a continued identity), we ought not to stumble over the possibility of God bringing a new form out of what is buried.

11. The word for "give life" (v. 11) is *zōopoiēsa*, future indicative active of *zōopoieō*. It means "to engender living creatures," "to quicken," "make alive," "vivify." Its metaphorical use for regeneration is seen in John 6:63; 2 Cor. 3:6; *et al.*; its spiritual use as in Rom. 8:11 is also seen in Rom. 4:17; 1 Cor. 15:36; *et al.*

12. *Pauline Eschatology,* p. 182.

eschatological state," it must be agreed with Vos that every "thought of immaterialness, or etherealness or absence of physical density ought to be kept carefully removed from the term."[13]

III. THE TIME OF THE RESURRECTION

A. In Relation to the Parousia

In the teaching of Christ the final division among men will occur at the end of the harvest (Matt. 13:24-30, 36-43). Apparently the common belief was that the resurrection was a far distant future event. When Jesus assured Martha, "Your brother will rise again," she replied, "I know that he will rise again in the resurrection at the last day." Jesus responded, "I am the resurrection and the life; he who believes in me, though he die, yet shall he live" (John 11:23-25). This assurance might be interpreted as meaning that whoever is in Christ shall experience His resurrection power immediately following death, were it not for His clear declaration otherwise. In John 6:40, 44, Jesus' words are plain: "I will raise him up at the last day." Moreover, Paul clearly associates the resurrection with the Second Coming (1 Cor. 15:20-22, 52; Phil. 3:11, 20-21). The "last trumpet" will signal both events: "The dead will be raised imperishable, and we shall be changed" (v. 52). It would be difficult not to see in this the exact event described by Jesus in Matt. 24:31.

It is sometimes asserted that while Paul attached the resurrection to the Second Coming in his earlier letters, he had changed his mind by the time he wrote 2 Corinthians. There, it is asserted, he assumed that the resurrection followed death immediately. While some things in 4:16—5:10 might suggest this interpretation, nothing compels it and much is against it. Being "at home with the Lord" (v. 8) is clearly reciprocal to being "absent from the body." But it is not clear that such at-home-ness implies the immediate realization of the ultimate yearning "to put on our heavenly dwelling" (v. 2).

It is not altogether sure that by "a building from God . . . eternal in the heavens" (vv. 1-2) Paul has in mind the resurrection body. It may be rather the total hope that there waits for the believer an enlarged and expanded order of being corresponding to Jesus' promise, "In my Father's house are many rooms . . . I go to prepare a place for you" (John 14:2-3). This larger scope of course includes the ulti-

---

13. *Ibid.*, p. 166.

mate resurrection; but there is no certainty that Paul's metaphor of being anxious "to put on our heavenly dwelling" is precisely a resurrection reference.

There are other considerations. A true evangelical would hold that Paul as a personal believer might experience progressive insight into the complete plan of God. But he would also hold that the Holy Spirit would prevent such personal growth from becoming so transcribed into Scripture as to produce an irreconcilable contradiction. However, even apart from the question of inspiration, the argument is not sound. The time between writing the first letter and the second was not so great that the apostle could have forgotten what he said in the first, or knowingly take a radically revised position without some explanatory word.

But more significant is the letter to the Philippians, a yet later Epistle. In this too, the faith is affirmed that to "depart" from the flesh is to "be with Christ" (1:23). Yet "the resurrection from the dead," which he is so eager to attain (3:11), apparently awaits the coming of the Saviour from heaven, who then "will change our lowly body to be like his glorious body" (3:20-21). If Paul changed his mind in 2 Corinthians, he must have changed it back in Philippians.

The evidence therefore indicates a conscious bliss in the presence of Christ when saints leave the body. Yet this experience falls short of the ultimate resurrection life. In view of these scripture teachings, any so-called soul sleeping in the sense of a total unconsciousness between death and the resurrection is hardly tenable. At the same time, the concept of an "intermediate state" is scarcely avoidable (cf. Rom. 14:8-9 with Matt. 22:31-32; 2 Cor. 12:1-4; 2 Tim. 2:18).

B. The Question of Two Resurrections

An even knottier problem concerns the relative timing of the resurrection of the righteous and the wicked. Are they simultaneous or chronologically separate? This question is inextricably entwined with the possibility of a millennium; indeed it could very well be decisive. As Wiley says: "Those who fail to make a distinction between the two resurrections are shut up either to post or nil millennialism." He argues on the side of two resurrections not only from Revelation 20, but more especially from the phrase *ek nekrōn*, "out of, or from the dead." He writes: "We are told that the phrase occurs forty-nine times in the New Testament, and not once is it applicable to the resurrection of the wicked, or to the resurrection when considered as embracing both the righteous and the wicked."[14]

Paul's clearest statement of chronology is 1 Cor. 15:20-25. The sequence here is (1) Christ's own resurrection, (2) the resurrection of the righteous—"at his coming those who belong to Christ"; and (3) the balance of humanity, whose resurrection must be implied by "then comes the end." Yet the word *eita*, "then," does not necessarily mean a great lapse of time as is seen in v. 5: "He appeared to Cephas, then to the twelve"—all in the same day.

The question of two resurrections as well as the question of a literal 1,000-year millennium must be left undecided.

IV. The Divine Judgment

A. The Necessity of Judgment

It is significant that the Early Church considered "the resurrection of the dead, and eternal judgment" foundation doctrines (Heb. 6:1-2). The compelling question, "For otherwise how will God judge the world?" reminds us that in New Testament thought divine judgment is a moral necessity. We are dealing with a moral order that demands not only "justice" and "self-control" but "future judgment" (Acts 24:25). Its ground is the holiness and justice of God, and its objective is to reveal and adjudicate the behavior of moral agents. The "secrets of men" will be disclosed (Rom. 2:16; cf. Mark 4:22; Luke 12:2), and character will be evaluated with perfect equity in the light of knowledge and opportunity (Rom. 2:7-11). A final separating, classifying sentence will be pronounced. The lie will be flushed out from hiding, and truth, so often trampled, will prevail.

Justice demands judgment, because justice insists that evils which either defied or eluded the courts of men shall finally be called to account and be treated as they deserve. Only an infinite God can perceive without error the interwoven lines of responsibility, the multiple vectors of influence, and the shades of motive and intention that comprise the moral fabric of human life. In the scales will be placed endowment and opportunity, deception and innocence, malice and simplicity, pretense and sincerity. All the threads must be unravelled and all the knots untied. Moreover, the spreading consequences of evil deeds that keep unfolding from generation to generation, must converge in a single point of ultimate finality. Such

---

14. *Christian Theology,* 3:334, 336.

evil must be contained in finiteness and not be permitted to expand infinitely.[15]

B. A Future Event

It is impossible therefore to reduce the New Testament doctrine of judgment to the natural consequences of evil which men suffer in this life. Paul declares that the law of sowing and reaping operates both here and hereafter (Gal. 6:8-9). Both Jesus and His writing interpreters see the necessity of an official forensic judging, with the pronouncement not only of rewards and punishments but of eternal destiny. Jesus speaks frequently of "the day of judgment" (Matt. 11:22; 12:36; sometimes simply as "that day," Matt. 7:22; Luke 10:12).

The forensic and afterlife purpose of the judgment is explained by Paul, "that each one may receive good or evil according to what he has done in the body" (2 Cor. 5:10). If conduct "in the body" is to be judged, it is obvious that such judgment cannot occur until the earthly embodiment is over. The unanimous voice of the New Testament is expressed by the writer to the Hebrews, "It is appointed for men to die once, and after that comes judgment" (9:27).

The classic picture of this awesome event is in the Apocalypse of John: "Then I saw a great white throne and him who sat upon it; from his presence earth and sky fled away, and no place was found for them. And I saw the dead, great and small, standing before the throne, and books were opened; also another book was opened, which is the book of life. And the dead were judged by what was written in the books, by what they had done" (20:11-12).

The message of this passage is twofold, universality and finality. Every member of Adam's race will be present (cf. Rom. 14:11; Phil. 2:9-11). There will be no exceptions, certainly no hideouts. And this "great white throne" judgment will signal the end of that human probation which we call history. The books will be opened, then forever closed. The abuse of free will, both by angels and by men, will be so completely conquered as to be henceforth impossible. Active hostility against God shall cease, and moral choice so confirmed as to be irreversible. Never thereafter will an act of sin mar God's universe. From the verdict of this general judgment there will

---

15. In his sermon "The Great Assize," Wesley defends the moral necessity of a thorough exposure (*Works,* 5:177 ff.).

be no appeal, because the "great white throne" is the ultimate authority. It is the final court of appeal.[16]

As Redeemer, Christ's relation to the Church is different from His relation to the world: "'Those whom I love, I reprove and chasten'" (3:19). There is a corrective judgment now in process (1 Cor. 11:28-32; Heb. 12:10-11; 1 Pet. 4:17-19); but its purpose is found only in its anticipatory relation to the final judgment. From the ultimate judgment the present disciplinary judgments derive their earnestness and gravity. For the One who has purchased by His blood the right to save has also been given the right to condemn; the One who by His overcoming "sat down" with His Father "on His throne" is He who promises a sharing of that throne only to overcomers (Rev. 3:21). If the purpose of discipline is that "we may not be condemned along with the world" (1 Cor. 11:32), the inference is inescapable that if the discipline fails, we will be condemned along with the world.[17]

C. Matters to Be Judged

The "deeds done in the body" will be the subject of inquiry. This is an all-inclusive concept that involves words (Matt. 12:36-37), attitudes (Matt. 5:22), secret sins (Matt. 5:28-30), as well as overt actions. Motives will be minutely examined (1 Cor. 4:5; cf. 3:13). If even now the Word as a sword is "discerning the thoughts and intentions of the heart" (Heb. 4:12), how much more will they be disclosed and eval-

---

16. All attempts to schematize several judgments, such as the judgment of believers, the judgment of the nations, and the General Judgment, collapse when examined carefully. As to the length of the Judgment Day, Wesley was inclined to agree with the Church Fathers in drawing the inference from 2 Pet. 3:8 that it could be 1,000 years, and perhaps even longer. "For, if we consider the number of persons who are to be judged, and of actions which are to be inquired into, it does not appear that a thousand years will suffice." Then he concludes: "But God shall reveal this also in its season" (*Works*, 5:174).

17. The Gospels and Epistles, even more clearly than Revelation, uniformly assign this judging to the Son, and include both saved and unsaved. As to the Judge, see Matt. 7:22; 8:29; 16:27; 18:30, 40-50; 25:31-46; John 5:22; 12:48; Acts 10:42; 17:31; 2 Thess. 1:7-8; 2 Tim. 4:1; 2 Pet. 3:7-12. As to the involvement of the saved, see Matt. 13:41-43; 25:31-46; Rom. 14:10-12; 1 Cor. 3:13; 4:5; 2 Cor. 5:10; *et al.*

This does not mean that when one dies one's destiny is in doubt. In rejecting the notion of a particular judgment at death to be followed by the General Judgment, John Wesley says: "And this much we may allow, the moment a soul drops from the body, and stands naked before God, it cannot but know what its portion will be to all eternity.... But the Scripture gives us no reason to believe, that God will then sit in judgment upon us" (*Works*, 6:143-44).

uated at the judgment. The all-pervasive, underlying concern will be one's total stewardship of life (Matthew 25; cf. C. 29).

D. The Basis of Decision and Destiny

The basis of judgment will be the records found in "the books" (Rev. 20:12). What these books are we can only speculate. At least it is clear that a record is being written which will stand in court as incontrovertible evidence either for or against the one whose deeds are recorded. Since "all have sinned and fall short of the glory of God" (Rom. 3:23), these books alone would guarantee universal condemnation of every responsible son of Adam's race.

Fortunately there is "another book" opened, which is "the book of life" (v. 12). This cannot, in view of universal depravity, be a list of humanistically good men, but of redeemed men, whose names have been preserved therein by their faith in Jesus (Luke 10:20). This book is the record of one's repentance and forgiveness. The sins of such men have already been judged once, at Calvary. Faith during probation appropriates this judgment, so that the book of life reports, "Judged already." Facts will be uncovered, but for each adverse disclosure there will be the verdict in the book of life: "Covered by the blood."[18]

It is evident that the final verdict rests on this book of redemption: "And if any one's name was not found written in the book of life, he was thrown into the lake of fire" (Rev. 20:14). To face the judgment therefore with confidence in the merits of one's own goodness is both delusive and futile. One's whole attention should rather be concentrated on getting into the book of life. This is what the entire Bible is about. God in Christ has provided the suitable "wedding clothes" of righteousness. They are available to all, optional with none (Matt. 22:11-13; cf. Rev. 19:7-8).

Yet in Christ God has already reconciled "the world to himself, not counting their trespasses against them, and entrusting to us the message of reconciliation" (2 Cor. 5:19; cf. Rom. 11:32). There is a sense in which all come into the world already within the sphere of saving grace. On this ground some have suggested that every name

---

18. Some object that a revelation of *forgiven* sins at the Judgment would not be compatible with the promise "And I will remember their sins no more" (Heb. 8:12; cf. Jer. 31:34; Ezek. 18:21-22). John Wesley says: "It will be abundantly sufficient for them, that all the transgressions which they had committed shall not be once mentioned unto them to their disadvantage; that their sins . . . shall be remembered no more to their condemnation" (*Works,* 5:178).

is inscribed by Christ's blood in the book of life and the determinative question at the judgment will be whether it is still there. That it is removable is declared inferentially by Christ himself: "He who conquers shall be clad thus in white garments; and I will not blot out his name out of the book of life; I will confess his name before my Father" (Rev. 3:5; cf. 1:18).[19]

V. Beyond the Judgment

A. The Concept of Eternity

The word *aionios* signifies endless duration in the great majority of its 66 instances in the New Testament.[20] It is in contrast to time only insofar as time is an element in human history that is mathematically measurable by solar movement. Whatever may be the case with God, eternity in relation to man is not incompatible with time in the sense of flow of consciousness or succession of events; finite creatures could scarcely exist in meaningful activity without these modes. The reference to "fruit every month," while an obviously accommodated expression, suggests succession and movement. The fundamental note is that "time" in eternity will not move toward a *telos* (Rev. 22:5).

B. The Second Death

The term "second death" is found only in Revelation, and there only four times: 2:11; 20:6, 14; 21:8. This second death is defined in the last two references as "the lake of fire" into which "Death and Hades" are to be thrown (20:14). Also to be cast into it are "the cowardly, the faithless, the polluted, . . . murderers, fornicators, sorcerers, idolaters, and all liars" (21:8).[21]

 The termination of Hades reminds us of certain biblical terms

---

19. We can be sure at least that "the Judge of all the earth" will "deal justly" (Gen. 18:24, Berk.). This means that He will be as impartial and fair with those who have never heard the gospel as with those who have; this in turn implies that none will be lost solely because through no fault of his own he has never heard of Christ. That God will weigh ill desert in the light of opportunity to know Christ is affirmed by Jesus himself (Matt. 11:20-23; 12:41-42). Yet alongside this reassuring note is the equal certainty that Christ is God's appointed means of salvation, and the One who alone inscribes or erases names from the book of life (Acts 4:12).

20. See Vine for a discussion of this, and also for idiomatic phrases, such as *eis ton aiona; EDNTW*, 2:43, 47.

21. Obviously those who are such in personal character cannot at the same time be "in Christ."

indicative of the intermediate state. Hades is the Greek equivalent to the Hebrew *sheol* in the Old Testament, both of which refer to the temporary abode of the dead, whether righteous or unrighteous. Neither should properly be translated *hell*. The term *tartaroō* means to consign to Tartarus ("pits of darkness," NASB), the place not of men but of fallen angels, who are there "to be kept until the judgment" (2 Pet. 2:4).

The concept therefore of the second death is that of a separation from God which is subsequent to physical death. The wicked are sentenced to this destiny at the great white throne judgment, which is final and eternal. The fiery nature of the second death links it unmistakably with Gehenna *(Geenna)*, the term Jesus used to indicate eternal punishment.[22] "'For every one will be salted with fire'" (Mark 9:49); either the *chaff* will be consumed now by the fire of the Holy Spirit (Matt. 3:12; cf. Mal. 3:1-3) or, refusing that, the persistent rebel will know "a fury of fire which will consume the adversaries" (Heb. 10:27, fr. Isa. 26:11; Heb. 10:31; 12:29; 2 Thess. 1:7; cf. Mal. 4:1). Sin must be purged or the sinner both banished and punished.[23]

C. The Nature of Hell

The nature of hell is not a pleasant subject to contemplate. Its duration is as endless as is heaven (Matt. 25:46; Mark 9:43-48; Rev. 20:11). It is called by Jesus "the outer darkness" (Matt. 8:21; 22:13; 25:30), suggesting complete banishment from the presence of God and equally from hope and opportunity. It is a place and state beyond any ray of light from the heavenly order. Since light and darkness symbolize good and evil, outer darkness is absolute evil. Hell is the

---

22. Of its 12 instances, Jesus voiced all but one (Jas. 3:6). Vincent Taylor writes: "It is the Greek representative of the Hebrew Ge-Hinnom, or Valley of Hinnom, a deep, narrow glen to the south of Jerusalem" which because of its odious history "became the common refuse-place of the city, into which the bodies of criminals, carcasses of animals, and all sorts of filth were cast. From its depth and narrowness, and its fire and ascending smoke, it became the symbol of the place of the future punishment of the wicked" (*Word Studies*, 1:40). This background gives meaning to Jesus' vivid phrase "the unquenchable fire" and His adoption of Isa. 66:24, "Where their worm does not die, and the fire is not quenched" (Mark 9:43, 48). Isa. 66:15-16 clearly identifies the destroying judgments of God, though the emphasis of Jesus is on its terrible permanence and undiminishable horror.

23. Other instances of Gehenna are Matt. 5:22, 29; 10:28; 18:9; 23:15, 32; Mark 9:43, 47; Luke 12:5. G. E. Ladd comments that finding "ultimate universal salvation" in the New Testament (referring to E. Stauffer, *NT Theology*, Chap. 57) "can be done only by overlooking these sayings about Gehenna" (*NBC*, p. 391).

final consummation and just reward of those who during their earthly sojourn "loved darkness rather than light, because their deeds were evil" (John 3:19; cf. 1:4-11; Luke 11:35; 22:53; Acts 26:18; Rom. 13:12; 1 Cor. 4:5; 2 Cor. 4:6; 6:14; Eph. 5:11; 6:12; 1 Pet. 2:9; 1 John 1:6). The inherent moral propriety of sentencing recalcitrant sinners to such banishment is implied by Jesus' scathing question, "You serpents, you brood of vipers, how are you to escape being sentenced to hell?" (Matt. 23:33; hell is *Gehenna*).[24]

In all three instances this phrase "the outer darkness" is followed by the clause "there men will weep and gnash their teeth." Thus the term refers to a place as well as to a condition. Furthermore, it is not a place of unconsciousness or annihilation, but of conscious remorse and suffering.

D. The Case of Dives

The story of the rich man and Lazarus (Luke 16:19-31) must be handled with great care. The key to its exegesis is that Jesus is speaking of Hades rather than *Gehenna*. Both Lazarus and Dives are in Hades. Here, in the *prejudgment* abode of the dead, Dives lifted up his eyes and saw Lazarus there too, with the difference that Dives was suffering the torments of the damned while Lazarus was in an area of Hades called by Jesus "Abraham's bosom."

The basic truths being taught by Jesus are clear: (1) The imbalances and inequities that abound in this life must await the correction of the next life. (2) True prosperity and well-being must not be defined in terms of present outward appearances but in terms of favor or disfavor with God. (3) Hades is a state of consciousness, personal identity, memory, and either suffering or bliss. (4) The destiny that is determined by one's character at death is final and irrevocable —"a great chasm has been fixed," ruling out any possibility of a "second chance." (5) Sinners who ignore the warnings and teachings of

---

24. D. K. Innes, writing in *NBC*, p. 519, says: "The fact that on the one hand, God is omnipotent and God is love, and, on the other, eternal retribution is plainly taught in the Scriptures, raises problems for our minds that in all probability we cannot fully solve. It is easy in such cases to produce a logical answer at the cost of one side of biblical truth, and this has often been done. E. Brunner, on the other hand, invokes the conception of necessary paradox in God's revelation, saying that the Word of God is not intended to teach us objective facts about the hereafter, but merely to challenge us to action (*Eternal Hope*, 1954, 177 ff.). While not holding this doctrine, we must admit that the counsels of God are past the understanding of our finite minds. The reality and eternity of suffering in Gehenna is an element of biblical truth that an honest exegesis cannot evade."

the Scriptures would not be dissuaded from their deliberately chosen evil course by multiplying miracles for their special benefit.

These truths should be strongly woven into the fabric of our doctrinal concepts. But the story should not be misused by an over-literalization of vivid language which is plainly metaphorical. Since Dives was in his disembodied state, he obviously would have no "tongue," and Lazarus would have no "finger." But to refrain from reading physical fire into this does not neutralize the terrible reality portrayed. Here is a picture of a real suffering from the fires of memory and remorse.

E. Death and Destruction

Paul never uses "the second death," "Hades," or "Gehenna." Among his terms are "death" *(thanatos)* and "destruction" *(apoleia, olethros)*. The death which is the "wages of sin" (Rom. 6:23) is the opposite of eternal life. As such it is the separation from God which sin by its very nature requires (cf. 6:16). The law of sin is also "the law of . . . death" (Rom. 8:2); one is the corollary of the other. If sin is not escaped, death cannot be evaded either. Those "who are perishing" therefore are those who are in progression from "death to death"—from spiritual deadness now to ultimate and final death (2 Cor. 2: 15-16).

Both *death* and *destruction* are qualitative terms, not temporal. The destruction expressed by *apoleia* is loss "of well-being, not of being" (Vine; Rom. 9:22; Phil. 3:19; cf. 2 Pet. 2:1; 3:16).[25] The term *olethros* is normally translated "destruction" but carries the intense sense of utter ruin. The "punishment of eternal destruction" is the destiny of "those who do not know God" and of "those who do not obey the gospel of our Lord Jesus." It is not annihilation, but "exclusion from the presence of the Lord and from the glory of His might" (2 Thess. 1:8-9; cf. 1 Thess. 5:3; 1 Tim. 6:9, combined with *apoleia*). *Apollumi*, "to destroy utterly" (middle voice, to perish) is used by Paul, James, and Peter in the sense of "the loss of well-being in the case of the unsaved hereafter" (Vine) in Rom. 2:12; 1 Cor. 15:18; 2 Cor. 2:15; 4:3; 2 Thess. 2:10; Jas. 4:12; 2 Pet. 3:9; cf. Matt. 10:28; Luke 13:3, 5; John 3:16.

---

25. "Perdition" is a translation in KJV (Matt. 7:13; John 17:12; 2 Thess. 2:3; Phil. 1:28; 3:19; 1 Tim. 6:9). The "prepared for destruction" of Rom. 9:22 is middle voice, "indicating that the vessels of wrath fitted themselves for destruction" (Vine, *EDNTW*, 1:304).

VI. THE COLLAPSE OF EVIL

A. A Cosmic Conflict

In the background of all God's direct dealings with men is the shadow of a cosmic struggle between God and Satan. In a very real sense, man himself is the prize in this struggle; in saving man, God defeats His enemy. Satan's aim has been to dishonor God by destroying men. Through his deception sin debased man as God's crowning creation and threatened his total extinction. From the Garden of Eden onward Satan has sought to neutralize every move of God by a countermove. Speaking of Paul, Vos observes:

> In the various passages dealing with this subject one gains the impression that the Apostle was conscious of a mysterious drama being enacted behind the scenes of this visible world in the world of spirits, and that not a drama bearing its significance in itself; it is something pregnant with the supreme solution of the world-drama at the close of history.[26]

B. The Source of the Conflict

The Bible does not recognize evil as an eternal counterpart of good, in the sense of metaphysical dualism. Always evil is assumed to have had a beginning and as being primarily personal, an enemy and an intruder. Satan is characterized as "a murderer from the beginning and has nothing to do with the truth, because there is no truth in him. When he lies, he speaks according to his own nature, for he is a liar and the father of lies" (John 8:44).

The names given to Satan gather up into themselves all the malice and cunning by which this evil being has goaded and enslaved man, and used him as a tool in the cosmic war against the very throne of God. These names include "the great dragon . . . that ancient serpent, who is called the Devil *[diabolus]*, and Satan *[ho Satanas]*, the deceiver of the whole world" (Rev. 12:9; cf. 20:2), accuser, slanderer, adversary, enemy. It is this hideous power aiding and abetting man's willful sinning that has made human history not only corrupt but so strangely and irrationally demonic. The war of heaven is not only with sin, the world, and the flesh, but with Satan (cf. Eph. 6:12).

While Satan's personal origin is shrouded in mystery, Jesus may have indicated that he fell from a former heavenly estate: "I saw Satan fall like lightning from heaven" (Luke 10:18; cf. Rev. 12:7 ff.).

---

26. *Pauline Eschatology*, p. 281. See pp. 279 ff. for a discussion of Paul's demonology.

That he was not a solitary offender but one of many is revealed by Peter: "God did not spare the angels when they sinned, but cast them into hell" (2 Pet. 2:4). Evidence is abundant that Satan was and is their leader. The lesser fallen angels are not properly called devils (KJV notwithstanding), but *daimōn*, "demons."

Satan and the demons constitute a kingdom of evil (Matt. 12: 26) that is highly organized, maliciously anti-God, and therefore anti-Christ (Eph. 6:12). For some reason they have been permitted to claim this planet as their special domain, and likewise have been permitted to involve themselves with evil intent in the affairs of men (Luke 4:6; 8:29; 13:16; John 12:31; 14:30; 16:11; Acts 26:18; Eph. 2:2; 1 John 5:19). Satan himself is the embodiment of evil (John 8: 44; 1 John 3:8) in a far more literal sense than merely a figurative personification. There is no doubt, either with Jesus or the inspired writers, concerning the reality of Satan as a personal being.[27]

C. The Binding of Satan

There is undoubtedly an awareness in the minds of the Gospel writers that the temptation of Christ in the wilderness is an attempt by Satan to do with the Second Adam what he so easily did with the first in the Garden. There his cunning sophistry turned the head and heart of Adam through Eve, so that all subsequent consequences are both Adamic and satanic. It is inevitable therefore that central to God's act in Christ is the binding of the "strong man" in order that "his house" might be plundered (Matt. 12:29; 1 John 3:8; Rev. 20:2). This victory was essentially won at Calvary, and since that epochal event the Spirit has been plundering with a far greater degree of power and success than was witnessed in the pre-Christian eras.[28]

D. The Inescapable Outcome

Human history must conclude in a harvest in which "they will gather out of his kingdom all causes of sin and all evildoers, and throw them

---

27. As Eric Sauer says, "The accounts of the evangelists and the behavior and words of Jesus show clearly that we are not here concerned with a mere 'principle' of evil, but with a real, factually present, speaking and active person, not 'the evil' but 'the evil one'. 'The tempter came to him and said' (Matt. 4:3). 'Then the devil taketh him . . . and he set him on the pinnacle of the temple and saith . . .' (v. 5). Then the devil leaveth him' (v. 11). 'The devil . . . departed from him' (Luke 4:13). Similarly, in reverse: 'Jesus said unto him' (Matt. 4:7). 'Jesus answered him' (Luke 4:4). 'Then saith Jesus unto him' (Matt. 4:10)" (*The King of the Earth,* p. 64).

28. The Christian is one who has elected to change sides, and become Christ's warrior instead of Satan's pawn.

into the furnace of fire." It is fitting, therefore, that "the devil" who is "the enemy who sowed" the tares shall be destroyed also in order that his depredations shall never again disturb God's universe. The initial loosening of Satan's hold on man by means of winning man through love and enabling him through grace to participate in Satan's overthrow is a strategy peculiarly to the glory of God. It is a glory far greater than if man had been sheltered from a moral arena in which he engaged a real enemy; and certainly also far greater than if Satan had arbitrarily been destroyed at man's creation.

The whole cosmic struggle has been fought and won along moral lines, involving voluntary allegiance of free agents, instead of simply a mighty display of divine power. But when God's strategy has achieved its purpose (telos), the power will take over, and the judgment that settles man's destiny will silence and inactivate the kingdom of evil forever. "And the devil who had deceived them was thrown into the lake of fire and brimstone where the beast and the false prophet were, and they will be tormented day and night for ever and ever" (Rev. 20:10).

VII. The Hope of the Saints

"The eternal fire" which is called hell was not intended for man but "for the devil and his angels" (Matt. 25:41). It is evident, therefore, that man finds his way there only by joining forces with Satan. In so doing, he forfeits his divinely intended destiny and proper home, which is heaven. Justice alone would prepare a place appropriate for Satan, the source of all evil, but divine love sent Christ to suffer in order that He might return to the Father to "prepare a place" for the redeemed. He tells us that there are "many rooms" in His Father's house, and that His departure to prepare this place is assurance that He will return to conduct them to it, "that where I am you may be also" (John 14:2-3). "The object of Christ's departure is permanent reunion and the blessedness of the Christian" writes Marcus Dods.[29] The character of the Christian is such that to be with Christ is heaven. Yet a real place is intended just as it is made possible by a real cross.

A. Paradise

Jesus' declaration that He would come again to receive the disciples,

---

29. EGT, 1:822.

to be followed later by His inference that He might not come in their lifetime (John 21:18-23), creates a dilemma. Either He had in mind the future resurrection when He said, "Take you to myself," or in some sense He "comes again" at each death. The promise is thus relevant both to the private coming for the dying saint and the climactic future coming for the living Church. The latter horn of the dilemma is to be preferred in view of our Lord's promise to Peter, "Where I am going you cannot follow me now; but you shall follow afterward" (John 13:36). C. Ryder Smith comments that "this does not mean that Peter will meet Christ at the *Parousia,* for this is not 'following,' but as soon as he is martyred."[30]

Perhaps even more direct is Christ's word to the dying thief, "'Truly, I say to you, today you will be with me in Paradise'" (Luke 23:43; "this very day," Phillips).[31] Wilbur M. Smith writes: "Nothing else can be drawn from our Lord's words to the thief . . . than that the soul upon death enters into the presence of the Lord."[32]

The corollary is that when Jesus said on the Cross, "Father, into thy hands I commit my spirit" (Luke 23:46), His spirit was immediately at home with the Father (cf. John 14:28; 16:5). This would not exclude His *descensus* (Eph. 4:19) or His preaching "to the spirits in prison" (1 Pet. 3:19). When Jesus said to Mary after the Resurrection, "I have not yet ascended to the Father" (John 20:17), He was probably speaking of His official ascension 40 days later, not implying absence from the Father between death and resurrection. This is supported by Paul's identification of Paradise as heaven in 2 Cor. 12:2-4, and John's similar identification in Rev. 2:7.[33]

B. Heaven

According to Jesus, heaven is the location of God's throne (Matt. 5:34; 23:9, 22); therefore it must not be invoked in oaths, or, by implication, referred to flippantly. In contrast to the insecurity and change of this earth, it is a place of total security and permanence; therefore it should be the disciple's constant magnet and secret trea-

---

30. *The Bible Doctrine of the Hereafter* (London: Epworth Press, 1958), p. 169.
31. *EGT,* 1:641. The desperate expedient of Adventists to avoid the implications of this promise (thus making a place for soul-sleeping) by shifting the punctuation ("Truly I say to you today") is insupportable. The "today" *(sēmeron)* is "to be connected with what follows, not with" *legō* (I say), says A. B. Bruce.
32. *The Biblical Doctrine of Heaven* (Chicago: Moody Press, 1968), p. 160.
33. According to A. T. Robertson, "Paradise" is a Persian word referring to "an enclosed park or pleasure ground" (*Word Pictures,* 2:287).

sury (Matt. 6:19-21). Heaven is also the dwelling place of the angels who in behalf of their charges have immediate access to the Father (Matt. 18:10; 22:30; Luke 1:19; cf. Acts 12:15).

The word "heaven" *(ouranos)* corresponds to the Hebrew *samayim,* both of which fundamentally mean "sky" or "air." Hence heaven may mean the sky close at hand (Matt. 3:17; 24:31; 26:56; Luke 17:24. In fact, it is often translated "sky" or "air," as in Matt. 6:26; 16:2; Heb. 11:12, *et al.*). It may also mean the physical universe as the complement to the earth (Matt. 24:35; Heb. 1:10; 2 Pet. 3:7, *et al.*). These varying uses may explain Paul's reference to the "third heaven" (2 Cor. 12:2) as his way of making it clear that it was the eternal abode of God, angels, and saints he was claiming to have seen.[34]

1. *As the Family Home.*

Heaven is not the reward of merit but the inheritance of the saints, made theirs by virtue of their adoption as joint-heirs with Christ (Rom. 8:17; Gal. 4:7). Hence it is the future home of the "family," which makes especially meaningful Jesus' tender reference to the roominess in the Father's "house" (John 14:2). Life there will not be cold, detached, or isolated, but we shall live as one happy, loving family. The indwelling Holy Spirit is now God's "guarantee" of this inheritance (Eph. 1:14; 2 Cor. 1:22). He creates in us a "bit of heaven" that becomes our spiritual sensor of invisible realities, generating a homing instinct that keeps pulling us onward. The joys of holiness in the Spirit provide a foretaste of the happiness awaiting us. We should understand that the Christ who went to prepare the place for us (Heb. 6:20; 9:8-11, 23-24) sent the Holy Spirit to prepare us for the place. This He does by acclimating us to heavenly joys and occupations (2 Thess. 2:13). If we do not claim our "place *[kleros]* among those who are sanctified" by faith in Jesus (Acts 26:18), we will disin-

---

34. Wilbur M. Smith says: "Frequently in non-Biblical literature, and especially in Jewish apocryphal literature, the idea of seven heavens is often expressed, but this is not a Biblical term. In fact, this [2 Cor. 12:2] is the only place in the Scriptures where we find the phrase 'the third heaven,' which must mean the heaven of heavens, the abode of God. As an authority on the literature of the first century has remarked, 'For a triple division of the heavens, we look in vain in contemporary Jewish thought.' Such a division appears to have been the creation of the Christian Fathers and to have been deduced from this passage of Second Corinthians" (*Doctrine of Heaven,* p. 167). Smith also agrees with Hodge, McFadyen, and others that the third heaven is synonymous with Paradise.

herit ourselves from our "inheritance" (kleronomia) in heaven (Eph. 5:5; Col. 3:23-25).

This picture of a happy family of the redeemed should answer the question, "Will we know each other in heaven?" If we who now see "in a mirror dimly" will then see "face to face" (1 Cor. 13:12), it is certain that this will include highly clarified interpersonal relationships. With nothing to hide, nothing will be hidden. All barriers of prejudice and misunderstanding, whether based on race, language, or culture, will be dissolved. We shall not only recognize past friends but perceive one another unashamed and in clear truth. Fellowship will be unmarred by suspicion, and knowledge will be unimpaired by pretense. The world of facades will have been left behind.

Whether family and friendship groupings that have been precious in the Lord on earth will in any measure be resumed as preferred society, we do not know. The issue raised by the Sadducees, "Whose wife . . . shall she be?" (Matt. 22:28, KJV) has secretly agitated thousands of second mates. When Jesus declared that we would be "like angels in heaven" (v. 30), He was not just denying resumption of sexual relationships, but affirming such a metamorphosis as to completely transcend even the awareness of sex distinctions.

It is not necessary to suppose the destruction of the rich bond of companionship that has been built over the years, but its sexual nuances will be shed with the body. The family feeling based upon this bisexual order will necessarily be replaced by a larger family feeling—the family of God. Just as we can no longer know Christ "according to the human point of view" (2 Cor. 5:16), so then we will know no one simply according to flesh-and-blood relationships. Rather, we will say with Jesus, "Whoever does the will of my Father in heaven is my brother, and sister, and mother" (Matt. 12:50).

Admittedly, much of this is inferential and perhaps somewhat speculative, for the biblical data is scant. We must fall back on the assurance that the change in us will perfectly match the change around us, so that there will be no sense of strangeness, dislocation, or loss. Only in this way could the promise be fully meaningful: "He will wipe away every tear from their eyes: . . . neither shall there be mourning nor crying nor pain any more, for the former things have passed away" (Rev. 21:4). Whatever the details of heaven turn out to be, they will not only be right, but will seem right to everyone who reaches that wonderful place. They will seem right chiefly because our concern will not be so much with earthly loved ones as with the ineffable glory of "the throne of God and of the Lamb" (Rev. 22: 1, 3).[35]

2. *As the Throne of God.*

Perhaps the most graphic close-up of heaven in its awesome glory and theocratic structure is given by John in Revelation 4—5. Here the focal point is God and His throne, the center of universal sovereignty and power. But He is not alone. Surrounding Him are the 24 auxiliary thrones of the "elders" who represent delegated but subordinate powers.

Also present are four living creatures, similar but not identical to those seen by Ezekiel. Alford and also H. B. Swete interpret these beings as representative of redeemed nature. Wilbur Smith quotes Swete: "Nature, including Man, is represented before the throne taking its part in the fulfillment of the divine will and the worship of the Divine Majesty."[36]

A third group is the vast number of angels who contribute their exultant paeans of praise, directed especially to the Redeemer who stands before the throne (5:6): "Worthy is the Lamb who was slain, to receive power and wealth and wisdom and might and honor and glory and blessing" (5:11-12). The prominence given to the angels in this picture accurately reflects their importance throughout the Bible story as emissaries, warriors, protectors, guides, and agents of revelation in the affairs of men.

C. The New Heavens and the New Earth

The final act in the drama of earthly history will be the fulfillment of Isaiah's prophecy, "For, behold, I create new heavens and a new earth; and the former things shall not be remembered, nor come into mind" (Isa. 65:17, KJV; cf. 66:22). Of the last two clauses, F. Delitzsch comments: "Jehovah creates a new heaven and new earth which so fascinate by their splendor, so satisfy every wish, that all remembrance of the first, of wishing them back again, is utterly out of the question."[37] The "heavens" are not the heaven which is the abode of God, because that needs no renewal. The trans-

---

35. For further guidance see article by Kenneth Grider, "Heaven," *Baker's Dictionary of Theology,* p. 264.

36. *Doctrine of Heaven,* p. 208.

37. Franz Delitzsch, *Biblical Commentary on the Prophecies of Isaiah,* 3rd ed. (London: Charles Scribner's Sons, 1890-92). Vol. 2, *in loc.*

formation probably is limited to this earth, which has been the seat of Satan's depredations and the scene of sin's ravages. The "heavens" may include the earth's enveloping atmosphere, since it too has become contaminated with man's pollution. That this renovation and reconstitution occurs after the final judgment is implied by a comparison of Revelation 21 with 20.

D. The New Jerusalem

The glory of the new earth will be "the holy city, new Jerusalem," which John saw "coming down out of heaven from God, prepared as a bride adorned for her husband" (Rev. 21:2). It is debatable whether this is to be understood as a literal city or perhaps the Church—the redeemed of all ages—descending to dwell as a perfect community on earth. If a literal city is being described, its dimensions are staggering: 1,500 miles wide, long, and high, a perfect cube. F. W. Boreham reports the computations of an Australian engineer to the effect that such an area (2.25 million square miles) could accommodate 100 billion people.[38] While intriguing, such attempts to apply earthly mathematics to this new entity are sheer speculation. We cannot determine by our yardsticks what will be either possible or probable in the world to come.

The word "new" *(kainos)* is used for new heavens, new earth, and the New Jerusalem. It does not mean newness with respect to time *(neos)* but "as to form or quality, of different nature from what is contrasted as old" (Vine). The earthly Jerusalem of sacred history is the *old,* both literally and symbolically, and must not be the object of the Christian's affections, excepting as it recalls the Christ.[39]

The Epistle to the Hebrews constitutes, among other things, an earnest endeavor to wean Jewish Christians from the earthly city and all that it stood for. It seeks to incite them to be the true followers of their father Abraham who "looked forward to the city which has foundations, whose builder and maker is God" (Heb. 11:10; cf. 12:22). Abraham, with Sarah and all the patriarchs, saw beyond the promised land of Canaan on earth to "a better country, that is, a heavenly one" (v. 16). Above all, these Christians are to be true followers of Jesus who "suffered outside the gate." Abandoning

---

38. *Wisps of Wildfire* (London: 1924, pp. 202-3; quoted by Smith, p. 246).

39. For centuries Jerusalem stood for Jewish hopes and dreams. When Daniel in faraway Babylon prayed, he stood facing it. But in its carnal wickedness it came to typify not Sarah but Hagar—"for she is in slavery with her children" (Gal. 4:24).

the city abandoned by God, they must "go forth to him outside the camp, bearing abuse for him" (Heb. 13:12-13). To become thus spiritually and heavenly minded pleases God so much that He "is not ashamed to be called their God, for he has prepared for them a city" (11:16). This is the city described by John the Revelator.

VIII. Mission Accomplished

Wilbur M. Smith says: "In Revelation 21:1—22:5 we have the most extensive revelation of the eternal home of the redeemed to be found anywhere in the Scriptures and most suitably it forms the conclusion of all the revelation of the ages recorded in our Bible."[40] In this climax the heaven of God's throne and the habitation of redeemed men become one. The Second Person of the Godhead invaded a derelict earth as a man, in order to recapture it for the Father. Now the Father accepts the Kingdom and in "a great voice" announces "from the throne saying, 'Behold, the dwelling of God is with men. He will dwell with them, and they shall be his people, and God himself will be with them'" (Rev. 21:3; cf. 1 Cor. 15:24-28).

In this eternal city is no temple, "for its temple is the Lord God the Almighty and the Lamb." Its source of light will no longer be either the moon or the sun, for "its lamp is the Lamb" (21:22-23). The "tree of life" that man forfeited in the Garden of Eden will now be "on either side of the river," for the curse pronounced on man and his environment will be no more. But let John speak:

> And he showed me a river of the water of life, clear as crystal, coming from the throne of God and of the Lamb, in the middle of its street. And on either side of the river was the tree of life, bearing twelve kinds of fruit, yielding its fruit every month; and the leaves of the tree were for the healing of the nations. And there shall no longer be any curse; and the throne of God and of the Lamb shall be in it, and His bond-servants shall serve Him; and they shall see His face, and His name shall be on their foreheads. And there shall no longer be any night, and they shall not have need of the light of a lamp nor the light of the sun, because the Lord God shall illumine them; and they shall reign forever and ever (Rev. 22:1-5, NASB).

A cosmic rebellion will have ended, a maverick world will be reconquered, and a sinful race will be redeemed. God's salvation provided for men at Calvary will be triumphantly and irreversibly consummated. Meanwhile, as we wait for eternity to break in upon us,

---

40. *Doctrine of Heaven*, p. 239.

"The Spirit and the bride say, 'Come.' And let him who hears say, 'Come.' And let him who is thirsty come; let him who desires take the water of life without price" (Rev. 22:17).

SUBJECT INDEX

(including Hebrew and Greek terms)

Social ethics, justice 114 ff., 182
Sōma 257
Sōmatikōs 349
Sōma tou Theou 570
Son of David 325-28, 336
   of God 312-17
   of Man 306-12
Sons of God (OT) 134-35
Sōtēria 368-69
Soteriology 371
Soul 71 ff., 257 ff.
Sovereignty, divine 116-19, 154, 233, 432-38, 465
Spirit (see Holy Spirit) 169, 258 ff.
   of God, of the Lord 59, 166-70
Splagchnon 260
Stewardship 530
Stubbornness 124, 127 ff.
Substitution 401-3
Substitutionary
   atonement 386 ff.
Suffering, problem of 128-32
Suffering Servant 184, 189-93, 618
Supernaturalism 205
Symbols 41, 197
Synagogue 177, 600

Taah 123
Tame' 125
Teachers 604-6
Te Deum Laudamus 353
Telos 480, 613, 662
Temptation 82 ff.
Tetragrammaton 60
Theology, biblical 9, 13-27
   definition of 13-17
   of hope 613-14
   NT 203 ff.
   OT 31 ff.
   and science 14
   systematic 9, 18, 20, 22

Theophany 39 ff., 92, 131
Theos 330-31, 342
Throne of God 672
Thusia 391-92
To'ebah 125
Tongues 590-91
Torah 48-49, 97, 203, 221, 317, 333
Transformation 440-41
Transgression 124
Tribulation, the 634-36
Trinity 239 ff.
Trouble 124
Truthfulness 112
Tselem 77

Unbelief 51
Unclean 125

Vicarious atonement 385-91
Violence 124
Virgin birth 341, 353-56
Vision 196
Visions 39

War 105-6
Wisdom 107 ff., 125
   divine 152-53, 332-33
Witness of the Spirit 459-60
Witnessing 576-78
Word 333-35, 492, 520-22
Works 413-17, 540-41
Worship 578-83
Wrath of God 161-63, 279 ff., 383-84

Yada 43, 45
Yahweh 27, 60 ff., 330, 342, 567
   Mekaddishkem 62
   Sabaoth 62-63
Yasha' 172
Yeshua 161
Yetser 85 ff.
Yom 58

Zoroastrianism 151

INDEX OF AUTHORS

SCRIPTURE INDEX

(Citations of whole chapters and references in footnotes not included)

Bibliography

BOOKS

Adolfs, Robert. *The Church Is Different.* New York: Harper and Row, Inc., 1966.

Alford, Henry. *The New Testament for English Readers.* 2 vols. London: Rivingtons, 1863.

Allis, Oswald T. *Prophecy and the Church.* Philadelphia: The Presbyterian and Reformed Publishing Co., 1945.

Anderson, Charles C. *Critical Quests of Jesus.* Grand Rapids, Mich.: Wm. B. Eerdmans Publishing Co., 1969.

———. *The Historical Jesus: A Continuing Quest.* Grand Rapids, Mich.: Wm. B. Eerdmans Publishing Co., 1972.

Anderson, Gerald H., ed. *The Theology of the Christian Mission.* New York: McGraw-Hill Book Co., Inc., 1961.

Anderson, Hugh. *Jesus and Christian Origins.* New York: Oxford Press, 1964.

Arndt, W. F., and Gingrich, F. W. *A Greek-English Lexicon of the New Testament and Other Early Christian Literature.* Chicago: University of Chicago Press, 1957.

Aulen, Gustav. *The Faith of the Christian Church.* Philadelphia: Muhlenberg Press, 1948.

Baab, Otto J. *Theology of the Old Testament.* New York: Abingdon-Cokesbury, 1949.

Baillie, Donald. *God Was in Christ.* New York: Charles Scribner's Sons, 1948.

Barclay, William. *Jesus as They Saw Him.* New York: Harper and Row, 1962.

———. *The New Testament: A New Translation.* 2 vols. London: Collins, 1969.

Barmby, J. "Romans," *The Pulpit Commentary,* Spence, H. D. M., and Excell, Joseph S., eds. Grand Rapids, Mich.: Wm. B. Eerdmans Publishing Co., 1950 edition.

Barnes, Albert. *Notes on the New Testament.* Grand Rapids, Mich.: Baker Book House, 1949.

Barnett, Albert E. *Paul Becomes a Literary Influence.* Chicago: University of Chicago Press, 1941.

Baron, David. *Rays of Messiah's Glory: Christ in the Old Testament.* Grand Rapids, Mich.: Zondervan Publishing House, 1955 reprint.

Barr, James. *The Semantics of Biblical Language.* Oxford: University Press, 1961.

Barrett, C. K. *The Epistle to the Romans.* "Black's New Testament Commentaries," London: Adam and Charles Black, 1957.

———. *The First Epistle to the Corinthians.* "Harper's New Testament Commentaries." New York: Harper and Row, 1968.

————. *From First Adam to Last.* New York: Charles Scribner's Sons, 1962.

Barth, Karl. *Church Dogmatics.* Edited by G. W. Bromiley and T. F. Torrance. Edinburgh: T. and T. Clark, 1958.

————. *Epistle to the Philippians.* Translated by James W. Leitch. Richmond, Va.: John Knox Press, 1947.

————. *Christ and Adam,* trans. Small, T. A. New York: Harper and Brothers, 1957.

————. *The Preaching of the Gospel.* Translated by B. E. Hooke. Philadelphia: The Westminster Press, 1963.

————. *The Teaching of the Church Regarding Baptism.* London: SCM Press, 1958.

Barth, Markus. *Was Christ's Death a Sacrifice?* Edinburgh: Oliver and Boyd, 1961.

Beacon Bible Commentary, Harper, A. F., ed. 10 vols. Kansas City: Beacon Hill Press of Kansas City, 1964-69.

Bengel, J. A. *Gnomon of the New Testament.* Translated by James Bryce. 7th ed. Edinburgh: T. and T. Clark, 1895.

Berkhof, L. *Systematic Theology.* London: The Banner of Truth Trust, 1963.

Berkouwer, G. C. *Man: The Image of God.* Grand Rapids, Mich.: Wm. B. Eerdmans Publishing Co., 1962.

————. *The Work of Christ.* Grand Rapids, Mich.: Wm. B. Eerdmans Publishing Co., 1965.

Bernard, J. H. *A Critical and Exegetical Commentary on the Gospel According to St. John.* New York: Charles Scribner's Sons, 1929.

Biederwolf, William Edward. *The Millennium Bible.* Grand Rapids, Mich.: Baker Book House, 1964.

Black, M. *An Aramaic Approach to the Gospels and Acts.* 3rd ed. Oxford: Clarendon Press, 1967.

Blaiklock, E. M. *The Acts of the Apostles.* "Tyndale New Testament Commentaries." London: The Tyndale Press, 1963.

Bonhoeffer, Dietrich. *Christ the Center.* Translated by John Bowden. New York: Harper and Row, 1966.

Bornkamm, G. *Jesus of Nazareth.* Translated by Irene and Fraser McLuskey with James M. Robinson. New York: Harper and Row, 1960.

Bousset, Wilhelm. *Kyrios Christos.* Translated by John E. Steely. New York: Abingdon Press, 1970.

Bowman, John Wick. *Prophetic Realism and the Gospel.* Philadelphia: The Westminster Press, 1955.

Boyd, Myron F., and Harris, Merne A., compilers. *Projecting Our Heritage.* Kansas City: Beacon Hill Press of Kansas City, 1969.

Bright, John. *The Kingdom of God: The Biblical Concept and Its Meaning for the Church.* New York: Abingdon Press, 1953.

Brown, Harold O. J. *The Protest of a Troubled Protestant.* New Rochelle, N.Y.: Arlington House, 1969.

Brown, Raymond E. *Jesus, God-Man.* Milwaukee, Wis.: Bruce, 1967.

———. "The Gospel According to John." *The Anchor Bible.* Garden City, N.Y.: Doubleday and Co., 1970.

Bruce, F. F. *The Epistle to the Ephesians.* New York: Fleming H. Revell Co., 1969.

———. "1 and 2 Corinthians." *New Century Bible.* London: Marshall, Morgan, and Scott, 1971.

———. "The Epistle of Paul to the Romans," *The Tyndale New Testament Commentaries.* Wm. B. Eerdmans Publishing Co., 1963.

———. "The Epistle to the Colossians," *New International Commentary on the New Testament.* Grand Rapids, Mich.: Wm. B. Eerdmans Publishing Co., 1957.

———. "Commentary on the Book of Acts," *New International Commentary on the New Testament.* Grand Rapids, Mich.: Wm. B. Eerdmans Publishing Co., 1956.

———. *The Message of the New Testament.* Grand Rapids, Mich.: Wm. B. Eerdmans Publishing Co., 1972.

———. *The New Testament Development of Old Testament Themes.* Grand Rapids, Mich.: Wm. B. Eerdmans Publishing Co., 1968.

Bruner, Frederick D. *A Theology of the Holy Spirit.* Grand Rapids, Mich.: Wm. B. Eerdmans Publishing Co., 1970.

Brunner, H. Emil. *The Christian Doctrine of God.* Translated by Olive Wyon. Dogmatics, Vol. 1. Philadelphia: The Westminster Press, 1950.

———. *The Mediator.* Translated by Olive Wyon. Philadelphia: The Westminster Press, 1947.

———. *The Misunderstanding of the Church.* Translated by Harold Knight. Philadelphia: The Westminster Press, 1953.

Buber, Martin. *Moses: The Revelation and the Covenant.* New York: Harper and Brothers, 1958.

Bultmann, Rudolph. *Theology of the New Testament.* New York: Charles Scribner's Sons, 1970.

Burney, C. F. *Outlines of Old Testament Theology.* New York: Edwin S. Gorham, 1902.

Burrows, Millar. *An Outline of Biblical Theology.* Philadelphia: The Westminster Press, 1946.

Burton, E. DeWitt. "The Epistle to the Galatians," *International Critical Commentary.* Edinburgh: T. and T. Clark, 1921.

Cannon, W. R. *The Redeemer.* New York: Abingdon Press, 1951.

Carter, Charles W. *The Person and Ministry of the Holy Spirit*. Grand Rapids, Mich.: Baker Book House, 1974.

Carver, Frank G. *Peter, the Rock-Man*. Kansas City, Mo.: Beacon Hill Press of Kansas City, 1973.

———. "The Second Epistle of Paul to the Corinthians," *Beacon Bible Commentary*. Kansas City: Beacon Hill Press of Kansas City, 1968.

Chadwick, Samuel. *Pentecost*. Salem, Ohio: Convention Book Store, 1973 reprint.

Chamberlain, William Douglass. *An Exegetical Grammar of the Greek New Testament*. New York: The Macmillan Co., 1960.

Chambers, Oswald. *Biblical Psychology*. London: Simpkin Marshall, Ltd., 1948 reprint.

———. *He Shall Glorify Me: Talks on the Holy Spirit and Other Themes*. London: Simpkin Marshall, Ltd., 1949 reprint.

Cherbonnier, E. L. *Hardness of Heart: A Contemporary Interpretation of the Doctrine of Sin*. "Christian Faith Series," Reinhold Niebuhr, consulting editor, Garden City, N.Y.: Doubleday and Company, Inc., 1955.

Childers, Charles L. "The Gospel According to St. Luke," *Beacon Bible Commentary*. Kansas City: Beacon Hill Press of Kansas City, 1964.

Childs, Brevard S. *Biblical Theology in Crisis*. Philadelphia: The Westminster Press, 1970.

Clark, Theodore R. *Saved by His Life: A Study of the New Testament Doctrine of Reconciliation and Salvation*. New York: The Macmillan Co., 1959.

Clarke, Adam. *The Holy Bible with a Commentary and Critical Notes*. Six volumes. New York: Abingdon Press, n.d.

Clowney, Edmund. *Preaching and Biblical Theology*. Grand Rapids, Mich.: Wm. B. Eerdmans Publishing Co., 1961.

Cole, Alan. *The Body of Christ*. Philadelphia: The Westminster Press, 1965.

Conzelmann, Hans. *An Outline of the Theology of the New Testament*. Trans. by John Bowden. London: SCM Press, Ltd., 1969.

Coulson, C. A. *Science and Christian Belief*. Chapel Hill, N.C.: The University of North Carolina Press, 1955.

Cullmann, Oscar. *Baptism in the New Testament*. Translated by J. K. S. Reid. London: SCM Press, 1950.

———. *The Christology of the New Testament*. Translated by Shirley C. Guthrie and Charles A. M. Hall. Philadelphia: The Westminster Press, rev. ed., 1963.

———. *The Earliest Christian Confession*. Reid, J. K. S., trans. London: Lutterworth Press, 1949.

———. *Early Christian Worship*. Translated by A. Stewart Todd and James B. Torrance. London: SCM Press, 1953.

————. *Peter: Disciple—Apostle—Martyr.* Translated by Floyd V. Filson. Philadelphia: The Westminster Press, 1953.

Culpepper, Robert H. *Interpreting the Atonement.* Grand Rapids, Mich.: Wm. B. Eerdmans Publishing Co., 1966.

Cumming, James Elder. *Through the Eternal Spirit.* Minneapolis, Minn.: Bethany Fellowship, Inc., 1965 reprint.

Curtis, Olin A. *The Christian Faith.* New York: Methodist Book Concern, 1903.

Dale, R. W. *Christian Doctrine.* London: Hodder and Stoughton, 1896.

Dana, H. E., and Mantey, Julius R. *A Manual Grammar of the Greek New Testament.* New York: Macmillan Co., 1927.

Davidson, A. B. *The Theology of the Old Testament.* Edinburgh: T. and T. Clark, 1904.

Davies, W. D. *Paul and Rabbinic Judaism.* London: SPCK, 1948.

Davison, W. T. *The Wisdom Literature of the Old Testament.* London: Charles H. Kelly, 1894.

Dayton, Wilber. "Romans and Galatians," *Wesleyan Bible Commentary.* Carter, Charles W., ed. Grand Rapids, Mich.: Wm. B. Eerdmans Publishing Co., 1965.

de Dietrich, Suzanne. *The Witnessing Community.* Philadelphia: The Westminster Press, 1958.

Delitzsch, Franz. *Biblical Commentary on the Prophecies of Isaiah.* 3rd ed. London: Charles Scribner's Sons, Ltd., 1890-92.

Denney, James. *The Christian Doctrine of Reconciliation.* London: James Clarke and Co., n.d.

————. *The Death of Christ.* New York: A. C. Armstrong and Son, 1903.

————. "The Epistle to the Romans." *The Expositor's Greek Testament.* Grand Rapids, Mich.: Wm. B. Eerdmans Publishing Co., 1967 reprint.

Dentan, Robert. *Preface to Old Testament Theology.* New York: The Seabury Press, 1963 rev. ed.

Deschner, John. *Wesley's Christology.* Dallas: Southern Methodist University Press, 1960.

DeWolf, L. Harold. *Responsible Freedom.* New York: Harper and Row, Publishers, 1971.

Dix, Dom Gregory. *Jew and Greek.* New York: Harper and Bros., 1953.

Dod, Marcus. "The Epistle to the Hebrews." *The Expositor's Greek Testament.* Grand Rapids, Mich.: Wm. B. Eerdmans Publishing Co., 1967.

Dodd, C. H. *The Apostolic Preaching and Its Developments.* New York: Harper and Bros., 1936.

————. *The Bible and the Greeks.* London: Hodder and Stoughton, 1935.

————. *The Epistle of Paul to the Romans.* New York: Harper and Bros., 1932.

————. *The Interpretation of the Fourth Gospel.* Cambridge: University Press, 1953.

————. *The Parables of the Kingdom.* London: SCM Press, Ltd., 1954.

Douglas, J. D., ed. *New Bible Dictionary.* Grand Rapids, Mich.: Wm. B. Eerdmans Publishing Co., 1962.

Douglass, Truman B. *Preaching and the New Reformation.* New York: Harper and Bros., 1956.

Duncan, George S. "The Epistle of Paul to the Galatians," *Moffatt New Testament Commentary,* London: Hodder and Stoughton, 1934.

Earle, Ralph, *et al. Exploring the New Testament.* Kansas City: Beacon Hill Press, 1955.

————. "The Book of the Revelation," *Beacon Bible Commentary.* Kansas City: Beacon Hill Press of Kansas City, 1967.

Edersheim, Alfred. *Bible History: Old Testament.* Grand Rapids, Mich.: Wm. B. Eerdmans Publishing Co., 1949 reprint.

————. *Jesus the Messiah.* Grand Rapids, Mich.: Wm. B. Eerdmans Publishing Co., 1967 reprint.

Edman, V. Raymond. *They Found the Secret.* Grand Rapids, Mich.: Zondervan Publishing House, 1968.

Eichrodt, Walther. *Man in the Old Testament.* Chicago: Henry Regnery Co., 1951.

————. *Theology of the Old Testament.* Translated by J. A. Baker. Philadelphia: The Westminster Press, 1961.

Ellison, H. L. "I and II Chronicles," *The New Bible Commentary.* Guthrie, Donald, ed. Grand Rapids, Mich.: Wm. B. Eerdmans Publishing Co., 1970 rev. ed.

Ellyson, E. P. *Bible Holiness.* Kansas City: Beacon Hill Press, rev. 1952.

Expositor's Bible, The. Edited by W. Robertson Nicoll. New York: A. C. Armstrong and Son, 1905.

Expositor's Greek Testament. Grand Rapids, Mich.: Wm. B. Eerdmans Publishing Co., reprinted 1967.

Filson, Floyd V. *Jesus Christ the Risen Lord.* New York: Abingdon Press, 1956.

Flew, R. Newton. *Jesus and His Church.* 2nd ed. London: Epworth Press, 1943.

Forsyth, Peter T. *The Cure of Souls: An Anthology of P. T. Forsyth's Practical Writings.* Edited by Harry Escott, Grand Rapids, Mich.: Wm. B. Eerdmans Publishing Co., 1971.

————. *The Person and Place of Jesus Christ.* Boston: The Pilgrim Press, 1909.

————. *The Work of Christ.* London: Hodder and Stoughton, 1910.

Frost, Stanley Brice. *Old Testament Apocalyptic: Its Origin and Growth.* London: The Epworth Press, 1952.

Fuller, Daniel P. *Easter Faith and History.* Grand Rapids, Mich.: Wm. B. Eerdmans Publishing Co., 1964.

Fuller, R. H. *The Foundations of New Testament Christology.* New York: Charles
Scribner's Sons, 1965.

———. *The Mission and Achievement of Jesus.* Naperville, Ill.: Allenson, 1954.

———. *The New Testament in Current Study.* New York: Charles Scribner's Sons,
1962.

Gartner, B. *The Areopagus Speech and Natural Revelation.* Uppsala: C. W. K.
Gleerup, 1955.

Gelin, Albert. *The Key Concepts of the Old Testament.* Translated by George Lamb.
New York: Sheed and Ward, 1955.

Gilkey, Langdon. *Naming the Whirlwind: The Renewal of God-Language.* Indianapolis: Bobbs-Merrill Co., 1969.

Girdlestone, Robert Baker. *Synonyms of the Old Testament.* Grand Rapids, Mich.:
Wm. B. Eerdmans Publishing Co., 1956 reprint.

Godet, Frederick. *St. Paul's Epistle to the Romans.* Translated by A. Cusin.
Edinburgh: T. and T. Clark, 1884.

Goguel, Maurice. *The Primitive Church.* Translated by H. C. Snape. London:
George Allen and Unwin, 1964.

Grant, Frederick C. *An Introduction to New Testament Thought.* New York:
Abingdon Press, 1950.

Greathouse, William M. *The Fullness of the Spirit.* Kansas City: Beacon Hill
Press, 1958.

———. "The Epistle to the Romans," *Beacon Bible Commentary.* Kansas City:
Beacon Hill Press of Kansas City, 1968.

Green, Michael. "The Second Epistle of Peter," *The Tyndale New Testament
Commentaries.* Grand Rapids, Mich.: Wm. B. Eerdmans Publishing Co.,
1968.

Harrison, Everett F. *A Short Life of Christ.* Grand Rapids, Mich.: Wm. B.
Eerdmans Publishing Co., 1968.

Hasel, Gerhard F. *Old Testament Theology: Basic Issues in the Current Debate.*
Grand Rapids, Mich.: Wm. B. Eerdmans Publishing Co., 1972.

———. *The Remnant: The History and Theology of the Remnant Idea from Gensis to
Isaiah.* Berrien Springs, Mich.: Andrews University Press, 1972.

Hastings, James, ed. *The Great Texts of the Bible.* Grand Rapids, Mich.: Wm. B.
Eerdmans Publishing Co., n.d.

Hebert, Gabriel. *When Israel Came out of Egypt.* Naperville, Ill.: SCM Book
Club, 1961.

Heinisch, Paul. *Theology of the Old Testament.* Collegeville, Minn.: The Liturgical
Press, 1950.

Hendriksen, William. *New Testament Commentary: Exposition of the Pastoral Epistles.* Grand Rapids, Mich.: Baker Book House, 1957.

Hendry, George S. *The Gospel of the Incarnation.* Philadelphia: The Westminster Press, 1948.

Henry, Matthew. *Commentary on the Whole Bible.* Wilmington, Del.: Sovereign Grace Publishers, 1972.

Heschel, Abraham. *God in Search of Man.* New York: Farrar, Strauss, 1955.

Hiebert, D. Edmond. *The Thessalonian Epistles.* Chicago: Moody Press, 1971.

Higgins, A. J. B. *Jesus and the Son of Man.* London: Lutterworth Press, 1964.

―――. *The Lord's Supper in the New Testament.* Chicago: Alec R. Allenson, Inc., 1952.

Hill, David. *Greek Words and Hebrew Meanings: Studies in the Semantics of Soteriological Terms.* Cambridge: University Press, 1967.

Hooke, S. H. *The Resurrection of Christ as History and Experience.* London: Darton, Longman, and Todd, 1967.

Hordern, William. *New Directions in Theology Today.* Philadelphia: The Westminster Press, 1966.

Hort, F. J. A. *The Christian Ecclesia.* London: Macmillan and Co., 1897.

Howard, Richard E. *Newness of Life.* Kansas City: Beacon Hill Press of Kansas City, 1975.

Hunter, Archibald M. *Introducing New Testament Theology.* Philadelphia: The Westminster Press, 1957.

―――. *The Message of the New Testament.* London: SCM Press, 1943.

Huxtable, John. *The Bible Says.* Naperville, Ill.: SCM Book Club, 1962.

Jacob, Edmond. *Theology of the Old Testament.* New York: Harper and Brothers, 1958.

Jamieson, Robert; Fausset, A. R.; and Brown, David. *A Commentary on the Old and New Testaments.* Hartford, Conn.: S. S. Scranton and Co., n.d.

Jay, E. G. *Son of Man, Son of God.* London: SPCK, 1965.

Jeremias, Joachim. *The Central Message of the New Testament.* New York: Charles Scribner's Sons, 1965.

―――. *The Eucharistic Words of Jesus.* Translated by Norman Perrin. 3rd ed. New York: Charles Scribner's Sons, 1966.

―――. *Infant Baptism in the First Four Centuries.* Translated by David Cairns. London: SCM Press, 1960.

―――. *New Testament Theology: The Proclamation of Jesus.* Translated by John Bowman. New York: Charles Scribner's Sons, 1971.

Johnston, G. *The Doctrine of the Church in the New Testament.* Cambridge: University Press, 1943.

Johnstone, George, ed. "Ephesians, Philippians, Colossians and Philemon." *The Century Bible.* Greenwood, S.C.: Attic Press, 1967.

Jones, Edgar. "Proverbs and Ecclesiastes," *Torch Bible Commentary.* New York: The Macmillan Co., 1961.

Kay, David M. *Glory at the Right Hand: Psalm 110 in Early Christianity.* New York: Abingdon Press, 1973.

Kelly, J. N. D. "A Commentary on the Epistles of Peter and of Jude." *Harper's New Testament Commentaries.* New York: Harper and Row, 1969.

Kevan, E. F. "Genesis." *The New Bible Commentary.* Edited by F. Davidson. Grand Rapids, Mich.: Wm. B. Eerdmans Publishing Co., 1956.

Knight, George A. F. *A Christian Theology of the Old Testament.* Richmond, Va.: John Knox Press, 1959.

Knox, John. *The Church and the Reality of Christ.* New York: Harper and Row, 1962.

Knudson, Albert C. *The Religious Teaching of the Old Testament.* New York: Abingdon-Cokesbury Press, 1918.

Kohler, Ludwig. *Old Testament Theology.* Translated by A. S. Todd. Philadelphia: The Westminster Press, 1957.

Kramer, W. *Christ, Lord, Son of God.* Translated by B. Hardy. London: SCM Press, 1966.

Kuen, Alfred F. *I Will Build My Church.* Translated by Ruby Lindblad. Chicago: Moody Press, 1971.

Kümmel, Werner G. *Theology of the New Testament.* New York: Abingdon Press, 1973.

Küng, Hans. *The Church.* Translated by Ray and Rosaleen Ockenden. New York: Sheed and Ward, 1967.

Ladd, George E. *The Blessed Hope.* Grand Rapids, Mich.: Wm. B. Eerdmans Publishing Co., 1966 reprint.

———. *Crucial Questions About the Kingdom.* Grand Rapids, Mich.: Wm. B. Eerdmans Publishing Co., 1954.

———. *Jesus and the Kingdom.* New York: Harper and Row, 1964.

———. *The Pattern of New Testament Truth.* Grand Rapids, Mich.: Wm. B. Eerdmans Publishing Co., 1968.

———. *A Theology of the New Testament.* Grand Rapids, Mich.: Wm. B. Eerdmans Publishing Co., 1974.

Lambert, J. C. *Dictionary of the Apostolic Church.* Edited by James Hastings. Grand Rapids, Mich.: Baker Book House, 1973 reprint.

Lampe, W. H. *The Seal of the Spirit.* 2nd ed. Naperville, Ill.: Alec R. Allenson, 1967.

Lehman, Chester K. *Biblical Theology.* Scottdale, Pa.: Herald Press, 1971.

Leitch, Addison H. *Interpreting Basic Theology.* New York: Channel Press, 1961.

Lewis, Edwin. *The Ministry of the Holy Spirit.* Nashville, Tenn.: Tidings, 1944.

Lietzmann, Hans. *Messe und Herrenmahl, eine Studies zur Geschichte der Liturgie.* Berlin: Walter de Gruyter, 1955.

Lightfoot, J. B. *Saint Paul's Epistles to the Colossians and to Philemon.* Grand Rapids, Mich.: Zondervan Publishing House, 1961 rev. reprint.

————. *Paul's Epistle to the Philippians.* Rev. ed. London: Macmillan and Co., 1913.

Link, Henry C. *The Return to Religion.* New York: The Macmillan Co., 1937.

Loisy, Alfred. *The Gospel and the Church.* Translated by Christopher Home. New York: Charles Scribner's Sons, 1904.

Longenecker, Richard N. *The Christology of Early Jewish Christianity.* Naperville, Ill.: Alec R. Allenson, Inc., 1970.

Ludwigson, R. *A Survey of Bible Prophecy.* Grand Rapids, Mich.: Zondervan Publishing House, 1973.

Lundstrom, G. *The Kingdom of God in the Teaching of Jesus.* Philadelphia: The Westminster Press, 1963.

Machen, J. Gresham. *The Virgin Birth of Christ.* New York: Harper and Bros., 1930.

Mackintosh, H. R. *The Christian Experience of Forgiveness.* London: Nisbet and Co., 1927.

————. *The Person of Jesus Christ.* London: SCM Press, 1918.

Major, J. D. A.; Manson, T. W.; and Wright, C. J. *The Mission and Message of Jesus.* New York: E. P. Dutton, 1938.

Manson, T. W. *The Church's Ministry.* Philadelphia: The Westminster Press, 1948.

————. *Studies in the Gospels and Epistles.* Edited by Matthew Black. Manchester: The University Press, 1962.

————. *The Teaching of Jesus.* 2nd ed. Cambridge: Cambridge University Press, 1935.

Marshall, I. Howard. *Luke: Historian and Theologian.* Grand Rapids, Mich.: Wm. B. Eerdmans Publishing Co., 1971.

Martin, Hugh. *The Claims of Christ.* London: SCM Press, 1955.

Martin, R. P. *Carmen Christi: Philippians ii.5-11 in Recent Interpretation and in the Setting of Early Christian Worship.* Cambridge: University Press, 1967.

————. *Colossians.* Grand Rapids, Mich.: Zondervan Publishing House, 1972.

Marty, Martin E., and Peerman, Dean G., eds. *New Theology No. 5.* London: Macmillan Co., 1968.

McDonald, H. D. *Jesus, Human and Divine.* Grand Rapids, Mich.: Zondervan Publishing House, 1968.

McKeating, Henry. *God and the Future.* Naperville, Ill.: SCM Book Club, 1974.

McKenzie, John L. *Theology of the Old Testament.* New York: Doubleday, 1974.

McMillen, S. I. *None of These Diseases.* Westwood, N.J.: Fleming H. Revell Co., 1963.

McNight, Edgar V. *What Is Form Criticism?* Philadelphia: Fortress Press, 1969.

Metz, Donald S. *Studies in Biblical Holiness.* Kansas City: Beacon Hill Press of Kansas City, 1971.

Metzger, Bruce M. *A Textual Commentary on the Greek New Testament.* London and New York: United Bible Societies, 1971.

Miller, Donald G. *The People of God.* Naperville, Ill.: SCM Book Club, 1959.

Minear, Paul S. *Images of the Church in the New Testament.* Philadelphia: The Westminster Press, 1960.

Moltmann, Jurgen. *The Theology of Hope.* New York: Harper and Row, 1967.

Morris, Leon. *Apocalyptic.* Grand Rapids, Mich.: Wm. B. Eerdmans Publishing Co., 1972.

———. *The Apostolic Preaching of the Cross.* Grand Rapids, Mich.: Wm. B. Eerdmans Publishing Co., 1955.

———. *The Cross in the New Testament.* Grand Rapids, Mich.: Wm. B. Eerdmans Publishing Co., 1965.

———. "The First and Second Epistles to the Thessalonians," *The New International Commentary on the New Testament.* Grand Rapids, Mich.: Wm. B. Eerdmans Publishing Co., 1959.

———. "First Corinthians," *Tyndale New Testament Commentaries.* London: The Tyndale Press, 1966.

———. "The Gospel According to John," *The New International Commentary on the New Testament.* Grand Rapids, Mich.: Wm. B. Eerdmans Publishing Co., 1971.

———. *The Story of the Cross.* London: Marshall, Morgan, and Scott, 1948.

Moule, C. F. D. *The Sacrifice of Christ.* Philadelphia: Fortress Press, 1964.

———. *Worship in the New Testament.* Richmond, Va.: John Knox Press, 1961.

Moule, H. C. G. "The Epistle of St. Paul to the Romans," *The Expositor's Bible.* Nicoll, W. Robertson, ed. New York: A. C. Armstrong and Son, 1905.

Mounce, R. H. *The Essential Nature of New Testament Proclamation.* Grand Rapids, Mich.: Wm. B. Eerdmans Publishing Co., 1960.

Neill, Stephen, ed. *Twentieth Century Christianity.* Garden City, N.Y.: Doubleday and Co., Inc., 1963.

———. *The Interpretation of the New Testament, 1861-1961.* New York: Oxford University Press, 1964.

———. *Who Is Jesus Christ?* London: United Society for Christian Literature, 1956.

———. *Christian Holiness.* New York: Harper and Brothers, Publishers, 1960.

Nelson, J. Robert. *The Realm of Redemption*. Greenwich, Conn.: Seabury Press, 1951.

Newbigin, Leslie. *The Household of God*. New York: Friendship Press, 1954.

Nicholls, William, ed. *Conflicting Images of Man*. New York: The Seabury Press, 1966.

Niebuhr, H. Richard, and Williams, Daniel D., eds. *The Ministry in Historical Perspective*, New York: Harper and Bros., 1956.

Niles, Daniel T. *The Preacher's Task and the Stone of Stumbling*. New York: Harper and Bros., 1958.

Nygren, Anders. *Commentary on Romans*. Translated by C. C. Rasmussen. Philadelphia: Fortress Press, 1949.

———, ed. *This Is the Church*. Translated by Carl C. Rasmussen, Philadelphia: Muhlenberg Press, 1952.

Oehler, Gustave F. *Theology of the Old Testament*. Translated by George E. Day. Grand Rapids, Mich.: Zondervan Publishing House, reprint of 1889 edition.

Oesterley, W. O. E. *The Psalms*. London: SPCK, 1953.

Olshausen, Hermann. *Biblical Commentary on the New Testament*. New York: Sheldon, Blakeman, and Co., 1858.

One Volume New Testament Commentary. Grand Rapids, Mich.: Baker Book House, 1957.

Orr, J. Edwin. *One Hundred Questions About God*. Glendale, Calif.: Regal Books, 1966.

Orr, James. *The Virgin Birth of Christ*. New York: Charles Scribner's Sons, 1907.

Pannenberg, Wolfhart. *Jesus—God and Man*. Translated by Lewis L. Wilkins and Duane A. Priebe. Philadelphia: Westminster Press, 1968.

Paterson, John. *The Wisdom of Israel: Job and Proverbs*. Nashville: Abingdon Press, 1961.

Payne, J. Barton. *The Theology of the Older Testament*. Grand Rapids, Mich.: Zondervan Publishing House, 1962.

Pelikan, Jaroslav. *The Christian Intellectual*. "Religious Perspectives, Vol. 14." New York: Harper and Row, 1965.

Perrin, Norman. *What Is Redaction Criticism?* Philadelphia: Fortress Press, 1969.

Pfeiffer, Charles F., and Harrison, Everett F., eds. *Wycliffe Bible Commentary*. Chicago: Moody Press, 1952.

Pierce, C. A. *Conscience in the New Testament*. London: SCM Press, 1955.

Pinson, William M., Jr., and Fant, Clyde E., Jr., eds. *Contemporary Christian Trends*. Waco, Tex.: Word, Inc., 1972.

Plummer, Alfred. *A Critical and Exegetical Commentary on the Gospel According to St. Luke*. "The International Critical Commentary." New York: Charles Scribner's Sons.

Pollard, William G. *Science and Faith: Twin Mysteries.* New York: Thomas Nelson, Inc., 1970.

Purkiser, W. T., *et al. Exploring Our Christian Faith,* Kansas City, Mo.: Beacon Hill Press, 1960.

———. *The Gifts of the Spirit.* Kansas City: Beacon Hill Press of Kansas City, 1975.

———. *Sanctification and Its Synonyms.* Kansas City: Beacon Hill Press, 1961.

Rainsford, Marcus. *Our Lord Prays for His Own.* Chicago: Moody Press, 1950.

Ralston, Henry. *Elements of Divinity.* Nashville: Publishing House of the M.E. Church, South, 1919.

Ramm, Bernard. *The Christian View of Science and Scripture.* Grand Rapids, Mich.: Wm. B. Eerdmans Publishing Co., 1954.

Ramsey, Michael. *The Resurrection of Christ.* London: Geoffrey Bles, 1946.

Rawlinson, A. E. J. *New Testament Doctrine of the Christ.* London: Longmans, Green, and Co., 1926.

Reicke, Bo. *Glaube und Leben der Urgemeinde.* Zurich: Zwingli-Verlag, 1957.

Reid, J. K. S. *The Authority of Scripture: A Study of the Reformation and Post-Reformation Understanding of the Bible.* London: Methuen and Co., Ltd., 1957.

Richardson, Alan. *An Introduction to the Theology of the New Testament.* New York: Harper and Brothers, Publishers, 1958.

———, ed. *A Theological Word Book of the Bible.* London: SCM Press, 1950.

Richardson, Alan, and Schweitzer, W., eds. *Biblical Authority for Today,* Philadelphia: The Westminster Press, 1951.

Ridderbos, H. N. *The Coming of the Kingdom.* Translated by H. de Jongste. Philadelphia: Presbyterian and Reformed Publishing Co., 1972.

Ringenberg, L. R. *The Word of God in History.* Butler, Ind.: The Higley Press, 1953.

Ringgren, Helmer. *The Faith of the Psalmists.* Philadelphia: Fortress Press, 1963.

Robertson, A. T. *A Grammar of the Greek New Testament in the Light of Historical Research,* 2nd ed. New York: George H. Doran Co., 1915.

———. *Word Pictures in the New Testament.* 6 vols. New York: Harper and Brothers Publishers, 1933.

Robinson, H. Wheeler. *The Cross in the Old Testament.* Philadelphia: Westminster Press, 1955.

———. *Redemption and Revelation.* New York: Harper and Bros., 1942.

Robinson, J. A. T. *The Body: A Study in Pauline Theology.* Chicago: Henry Regnery Co., 1951.

Robinson, T. H. *Job and His Friends.* London: SCM Press, Ltd., 1954.

Robinson, William. *The Biblical Doctrine of the Church.* St. Louis: Bethany Press, 1948.

Roth, Leon. *God and Man in the Old Testament.* New York: Macmillan Co., 1955.

Rowley, H. H. *The Faith of Israel: Aspects of Old Testament Thought.* Philadelphia: The Westminster Press, 1956.

———. *The Relevance of Apocalyptic.* 2nd ed. London: Lutterworth Press, 1946. New and rev. ed. New York: Association Press, 1963.

———. *The Unity of the Bible.* Philadelphia: The Westminster Press, 1953.

Rylaarsdam, J. C. *Revelation in Jewish Wisdom Literature.* Chicago: The University of Chicago Press, 1946.

Ryrie, Charles C. *Biblical Theology of the New Testament.* Chicago: Moody Press, 1959.

Sanday, William, and Headlam, A. C. *A Critical and Exegetical Commentary on the Epistle to the Romans.* "International Critical Commentary." New York: Charles Scribner's Sons, 1923.

Sauer, Eric. *The Dawn of World Redemption.* Translated by G. H. Lang, with a foreword by F. F. Bruce. Grand Rapids, Mich.: Wm. B. Eerdmans Publishing Co., 1952.

———. *The King of the Earth.* Grand Rapids, Mich.: Wm. B. Eerdmans Publishing Co., 1962.

Saunders, E. W. *Jesus in the Gospels.* Englewood Cliffs, N.J.: Prentice-Hall, Inc., 1967.

Sayers, Dorothy L. *A Matter of Eternity.* Edited by Rosamond Kent Sprague. Grand Rapids, Mich.: Wm. B. Eerdmans Publishing Co., 1973.

Schaeffer, Francis A. *Back to Freedom and Dignity.* Downers Grove, Ill.: Inter-Varsity Press, 1972.

———. *Genesis in Space and Time.* Downers Grove, Ill.: Inter-Varsity Press, 1972.

Schep, J. A. *The Nature of the Resurrection Body.* Grand Rapids, Mich.: Wm. B. Eerdmans Publishing Co., 1964.

Schmidt, Karl L. *The Church.* Translated by J. R. Coates. London: Adam and Charles Black, 1950.

Schmithals, Walter. *The Office of Apostle in the Early Church.* Translated by John E. Steely. Nashville: Abingdon Press, 1969.

Schoeps, H. J. *Paul.* Translated by Harold Knight. Philadelphia: The Westminster Press, 1961.

Schofield, J. N. *Introducing Old Testament Theology.* Naperville, Ill.: SCM Book Club, 1964.

Schultz, Hermann. *Old Testament Theology.* 2 vols. Translated by J. A. Paterson. Edinburgh: T. and T. Clark, 1909.

Schweitzer, Albert. *The Mystery of the Kingdom of God*. London: Adam and Charles Black, 1950.

———. *The Quest of the Historical Jesus*. New York: The Macmillan Co., 1961. First German edition, 1906.

Schweizer, Eduard. *Das Leben Des Herren in der Gemeinde und Ihre Dienste*. Zurich: 1946.

———. *The Lord's Supper According to the New Testament*. Translated by John M. Davis. Philadelphia: Fortress Press, 1967.

Smeaton, George. *The Doctrine of the Holy Spirit*. London: The Banner of Truth Trust, 1961 reprint.

Smith, C. Ryder. *The Bible Doctrine of Grace*. London: The Epworth Press, 1956.

———. *The Bible Doctrine of the Hereafter*. London: Epworth Press, 1958.

———. *The Bible Doctrine of Man*. London: The Epworth Press, 1951.

———. *The Bible Doctrine of Salvation*. London: The Epworth Press, 1941.

———. *The Bible Doctrine of Sin*. London: The Epworth Press, 1953.

Smith, Wilbur M. *The Biblical Doctrine of Heaven*. Chicago: Moody Press, 1968.

Snaith, Norman H. *The Distinctive Ideas of the Old Testament*. Philadelphia: The Westminster Press, 1946.

Spence, H. D. M., and Exell, Joseph S., eds. *The Pulpit Commentary*. Grand Rapids, Mich.: Wm. B. Eerdmans Publishing Co., 1950 reprint.

Stagg, Frank. *The Book of Acts*. Nashville: Broadman Press, 1955.

———. *New Testament Theology*. Nashville: Broadman Press, 1962.

Stauffer, Ethelbert. *Jesus and His Story*. Translated by Richard and Clara Winston. New York: Alfred A. Knopf, 1960.

———. *New Testament Theology*. Translated by John Marsh. New York: The Macmillan Co., 1955.

Stevens, George B. *The Theology of the New Testament*. New York: Charles Scribner's Sons, 1957.

Strachan, R. H. *The Fourth Gospel*. 3rd rev. ed. London: SCM Press, Ltd., 1941.

———. "The Second Epistle General of Peter," *The Expositor's Greek Testament*. Grand Rapids, Mich.: Wm. B. Eerdmans Publishing Co., 1967 reprint.

Streeter, B. H. *The Primitive Church*. New York: The Macmillan Co., 1929.

Taylor, Richard S. *End Times*. "The Aldersgate Doctrinal Series." Marion, Ind.: The Wesleyan Press, 1975.

———. *Tongues: Their Purpose and Meaning*. Kansas City: Beacon Hill Press of Kansas City, 1973.

Taylor, Vincent. *The Atonement in New Testament Teaching*. 3rd ed. London: The Epworth Press, 1958.

———. *The Cross of Christ*. London: Macmillan and Co., 1956.

———. *Forgiveness and Reconciliation*. London: Macmillan and Co., 1956.

————. *The Gospel According to St. Mark*. New York: St. Martin's Press, 1966.

————. *Jesus and His Sacrifice*. New York: Macmillan and Co., 1937.

————. *The Names of Jesus*. London: Macmillan and Co., 1954.

Temple, William. *Nature, Man, and God*. London: Macmillan, Ltd., first edition, 1934.

Thayer, J. H. *A Greek-English Lexicon of the New Testament*. Grand Rapids, Mich.: Zondervan Publishing House, 1963 reprint.

Thomas, W. H. Griffith. *Through the Pentateuch Chapter by Chapter*. Grand Rapids, Mich.: Wm. B. Eerdmans Publishing Co., 1957.

Thompson, R. Duane. "James," *The Wesleyan Bible Commentary*. Carter, Charles W., ed. Grand Rapids, Mich.: Wm. B. Eerdmans Publishing Co., 1966.

Thomson, James G. S. S. *The Old Testament View of Revelation*. Grand Rapids, Mich.: Wm. B. Eerdmans Publishing Co., 1960.

Thornton, L. S. *The Common Life in the Body of Christ*. London: Dacre Press, 1950.

Tödt, H. E. *The Son of Man in the Synoptic Tradition*. Translated by D. M. Barton. London: SCM Press, 1965.

Toombs, Lawrence. *The Old Testament in Christian Preaching*. Philadelphia: The Westminster Press, 1961.

Tozer, A. W. *That Incredible Christian*. Harrisburg, Pa.: Christian Publications, Inc., 1964.

Turner, George Allen. *The Vision Which Transforms: Is Christian Perfection Scriptural?* Kansas City: Beacon Hill Press, 1964.

Vincent, Marvin R. *Word Studies in the New Testament*. Grand Rapids, Mich.: Wm. B. Eerdmans Publishing Co., 1965 reprint.

Vine, W. E. *Expository Dictionary of New Testament Words*. London: Oliphants, 1939.

Von Campenhausen, Hans. *The Virgin Birth in the Theology of the Ancient Church*. Naperville, Ill.: Alec R. Allerson, Inc., 1962.

Von Rad, Gerhard. *Old Testament Theology*. Translated by D. M. G. Stalker. New York: Harper and Brothers, 1962.

Vos, Geerhardus. *The Pauline Eschatology*. Grand Rapids, Mich.: Wm. B. Eerdmans Publishing Co., 1972.

Vriezen, Th. C. *An Outline of Old Testament Theology*. Boston: Charles T. Branford Co., 1958.

Walker, Thomas. *The Acts of the Apostles*. Chicago: Moody Press, 1965.

Walker, Williston. *A History of the Christian Church*. Rev. ed. New York: Charles Scribner's Sons, 1959.

Walvoord, John F. *The Church in Prophecy*. Grand Rapids, Mich.: Zondervan Publishing House, 1964.

Ward, William B. *Out of the Whirlwind*. Richmond, Va.: John Knox Press, 1958.

Weiss, J. *Earliest Christianity.* Translated by F. C. Grant. New York: Harper and Brothers, 1959.

Wesley, John. *Explanatory Notes upon the New Testament.* Naperville, Ill.: Alec R. Allenson, Inc., 1950 reprint.

―――. *Works.* 14 vols. Kansas City, Mo.: Nazarene Publishing House, n.d.

Wesleyan Bible Commentary. Carter, Charles W., ed. 7 vols. Grand Rapids, Mich.: Wm. B. Eerdmans Publishing Co., 1965-66.

Westcott, B. F. *The Gospel According to St. John.* London: James Clarke and Co., Ltd., 1880.

Westermann, Claus, ed. *Essays on Old Testament Hermeneutics.* Richmond, Va.: John Knox Press, 1964.

Whale, J. S. *Christian Doctrine.* New York: The Macmillan Co., 1942.

―――. *Victor and Victim.* Cambridge: University Press, 1960.

Whitely, D. E. H. *The Theology of St. Paul.* Philadelphia: Fortress Press, 1966.

Wilder, Amos N. *Otherworldliness and the New Testament.* New York: Harper and Brothers, 1954.

Wiley, H. Orton. *Christian Theology.* 3 vols. Kansas City: Beacon Hill Press, 1940.

―――. *The Epistle to the Hebrews.* Kansas City: Beacon Hill Press, 1959.

Williams, Colin. *The Church: New Directions in Theology Today,* Vol. 4. London: Lutterworth Press, 1969.

Williams, C. S. *A Commentary on the Acts of the Apostles.* "Black's New Testament Commentaries." London: Adam and Charles Black, 1957.

Wrede, W. *Das Messiasgeheimnis in den Evangelien.* Gottingen: Vanderhoeck and Ruprecht, 1901.

Wright, G. Ernest. *Biblical Archaeology.* Abridged edition. Philadelphia: The Westminster Press, 1960.

―――. *God Who Acts: Biblical Theology as Recital.* "Studies in Biblical Theology." London: SCM Press, 1952.

―――. *The Old Testament and Theology.* New York: Harper and Row, Publishers, 1969.

Wright, G. Ernest, and Fuller, Reginald H. *The Book of the Acts of God.* New York: Doubleday and Co., Inc., 1957.

Wynkoop, Mildred Bangs. *Foundations of Wesleyan-Arminian Theology.* Kansas City, Mo.: Beacon Hill Press of Kansas City, 1967.

―――. *A Theology of Love.* Kansas City: Beacon Hill Press of Kansas City, 1972.

Young, Edward J. *The Study of Old Testament Theology Today.* New York: Fleming H. Revell Co., 1959.

Zorn, R. O. *Church and Kingdom.* Philadelphia: Presbyterian and Reformed Publishing Co., 1962.

ARTICLES

Albright, William Foxwell. "The Old Testament and Archaeology." *Old Testament Commentary.* Edited by Herbert C. Alleman and Elmer E. Flack. Philadelphia: Muhlenberg Press, 1948.

———. "Recent Discoveries in Bible Lands." *Young's Analytical Concordance to the Bible.* New York: Funk and Wagnalls Co., 1955.

Augsburger, Myron S. "Introduction." Chester K. Lehman, *Biblical Theology, Old Testament.* Scottdale, Pa.: Herald Press, 1971.

Barclay, William. "Comparison of Paul's Missionary Preaching and Preaching to the Church." *Apostolic History and the Gospel.* Edited by W. Ward Gasque and Ralph P. Martin. Grand Rapids, Mich.: Wm. B. Eerdmans Publishing Co., 1970.

Bartlett, Gene. "Worship: Ordered Proclamation of the Gospel." *Review and Expositor,* LXII, No. 3 (summer, 1965).

Bradley, William L. "Revelation." *The Hartford Quarterly,* vol. 3 (winter, 1962), pp. 41-54.

Bromiley, Geoffrey W. "Biblical Theology." Everett F. Harrison, editor in chief. *Baker's Dictionary of Theology.* Grand Rapids, Mich.: Baker Book House, 1960.

Bruce, F. F. "The Person of Christ: Incarnation and Virgin Birth." *Basic Christian Doctrines.* Edited by Carl F. H. Henry. New York: Holt, Rinehart, and Winston, 1962.

Bruce, F. F., and Davidson, Francis. "The Wisdom Literature of the Old Testament." *The New Bible Commentary.* Edited by F. Davidson. Grand Rapids, Mich.: Wm. B. Eerdmans Publishing Co., 1956.

Brunner, H. Emil. "The Christian Understanding of Man." *The Christian Understanding of Man.* Vol. II of the Report of the Oxford Conference on Church, Community, and State. London: George Allen and Unwin, Ltd., 1938.

Campbell, J. Y. "*Koinonia* and Its Cognates in the New Testament." *Journal of Biblical Literature,* LI (1932), p. 353.

Filson, Floyd V. "Synagogue, Temple, and Church." *The Biblical Archaeologist Reader.* Edited by G. Ernest Wright and David Noel Freedman. New York: Doubleday and Co., 1961.

Gilmore, A. "The Date and Significance of the Last Supper." *Scottish Journal of Theology.* September, 1961.

Gordon, Cyrus H. "Higher Critics and Forbidden Fruit." Frank E. Gaebelein, editor. *Christianity Today Reader.* New York: Meredith Press, 1966.

Harrison, Everett F. "*Some Patterns of the Testament Didache.*" *Bibliotheca Sacra,* vol. 119, no. 474 (April, 1962).

Henry, Carl F. H. "Man." *Baker's Dictionary of Theology.* Everett F. Harrison, editor in chief. Grand Rapids, Mich.: Baker Book House, 1960.

Hull, William. "Baptism in the New Testament: A Critique." *Review and Expositor,* vol. LXV (winter, 1968).

Hunter, A. M. "Crux Criticorum—Matt. XI: 25-30—a Reappraisal." *New Testament Studies.* VIII (1962), pp. 241-49.

Hutchison, Harry. "Who Does He Think He Is?" *Scottish Journal of Theology,* XIV (September, 1961).

Jewett, Paul King. "Emil Brunner's Doctrine of Inspiration." John F. Walvoord, ed. *Inspiration and Interpretation.* Grand Rapids, Mich.: Wm. B. Eerdmans Publishing Co., 1957.

Kantzer, Kenneth. "Revelation and Inspiration in Neo-Orthodox Theology," Parts I-III. *Bibliotheca Sacra,* vol. 115, no. 459 (July, 1958), pp. 120-27; 218-28; 302-12.

Kümmel, Werner G. "The Main Types of NT Proclamation." *Encounter,* XXI (1960).

Ladd, George E. "Interim Ethics." *Baker's Dictionary of Christian Ethics.* Edited by Carl F. H. Henry. Grand Rapids, Mich.: Baker Book House, 1973.

———. "The Kingdom of God—Reign or Realm?" *Journal of Biblical Literature,* Vol. 31 (1962), pp. 230-38.

Marshall, I. H. "The Synoptic Son of Man Sayings in Recent Discussion." *New Testament Studies.* XII (1966), pp. 327-51.

Metzger, Bruce M. "The Development of Institutional Organization in the Early Church." *Ashland Theological Bulletin,* VI (spring, 1973).

Morris, Leon. "The Meaning of *Hilasterion* in Rom. 3:25." *New Testament Studies.* II (1955-56).

Munck, J. "Paul, the Apostles, and the Twelve." *Studia Theologica,* 3 (1949).

Reicke, Bo. "A Synopsis of Early Christian Preaching." *The Root of the Vine.* London: Dacre Press, 1953.

Rhodes, Arnold B. "The Message of the Bible." *Introduction to the Bible.* "The Layman's Bible Commentary," Vol. I. Balmer H. Kelly, editor. Richmond, Va.: John Knox Press, 1959.

Riesenfeld, Harold. "The Ministry in the New Testament." *The Root of the Vine.* London: Dacre Press, 1953.

Robinson, William Childs. "The Virgin Birth—A Broader Base." *Christianity Today,* XVII (Dec. 8, 1972), pp. 6-8.

Rose, Delbert R. "Distinguishing Things That Differ." *Wesleyan Theological Journal,* vol. 9, 1974.

Rust, Eric. "The Atoning Act of God in Christ." *Review and Expositor,* LIX (January, 1962), pp. 68-70.

Staples, Rob L. "Sanctification and Selfhood: A Phenomenological Analysis of the Wesleyan Message." *Wesleyan Theological Journal,* vol. 7, spring, 1972.

Taylor, Vincent. "Does the New Testament Call Jesus God?" *The Expository Times,* LXIII (January, 1962).

――――. "A Great Text Reconsidered." *New Testament Essays.* London: Epworth Press, 1970.

Tenney, Merril C. "The Historicity of the Resurrection." *Jesus of Nazareth, Saviour, and Lord.* Edited by Carl F. H. Henry. Grand Rapids, Mich.: Wm. B. Eerdmans Publishing Co., 1966.

Turner, George Allen. "Infant Baptism in Biblical and Historical Context." *Wesleyan Theological Journal,* vol. 5, 1970.

Witwer, John A. "Did Jesus Claim to Be God?" *Bibliotheca Sacra,* vol. 125 (April, 1968).

Worley, Robert C. "Preaching and Teaching in the Primitive Church." *McCormick Quarterly,* Vol. XX (November, 1966).